Business Policy and Strategic Management

(For Undergraduate and Postgraduate Students of Management and Commerce of All Leading Indian Universities)

AF512907

Dr. S. SENTHILKUMAR
MBA, M.Phil., M.Com., MS, Ph.D.
Professor

M. MARUTHA DURAI
MBA
Assistant Professor

A. SHARMILA
MBA
Assistant Professor

J. POORNIMA
MBA, M.Phil.
Assistant Professor

Sri Ganesh School of Business Management, Salem (Tamil Nadu)

S. CHAND
PUBLISHING

S Chand And Company Limited

(ISO 9001 Certified Company)

S.CHAND
PUBLISHING

S Chand And Company Limited

(ISO 9001 Certified Company)

Head Office: D-92, Sector–2, Noida – 201301, U.P. (India), Ph. 91-120-4682700

Registered Office: A-27, 2nd Floor, Mohan Co-operative Industrial Estate,
New Delhi – 110 044, Phone: 011-49731800

www.**schandpublishing.com**; e-mail: **info@schandpublishing.com**

Marketing Offices:

Chennai	:	Ph: 23632120; chennai@schandpublishing.com
Guwahati	:	Ph: 2738811, 2735640; guwahati@schandpublishing.com
Hyderabad	:	Ph: 40186018; hyderabad@schandpublishing.com
Jalandhar	:	Ph: 4645630; jalandhar@schandpublishing.com
Kolkata	:	Ph: 23357458, 23353914; kolkata@schandpublishing.com
Lucknow	:	Ph: 4003633; lucknow@schandpublishing.com
Mumbai	:	Ph: 25000297; mumbai@schandpublishing.com
Patna	:	Ph: 2260011; patna@schandpublishing.com

© S Chand And Company Limited, 2014

All rights reserved. No part of this publication may be reproduced or copied in any material form (including photocopying or storing it in any medium in form of graphics, electronic or mechanical means and whether or not transient or incidental to some other use of this publication) without written permission of the copyright owner. Any breach of this will entail legal action and prosecution without further notice.

Jurisdiction: *All disputes with respect to this publication shall be subject to the jurisdiction of the Courts, Tribunals and Forums of New Delhi, India only.*

First Edition 2014
Reprint 2022
Reprint 2024

ISBN: 978-81-219-4334-5 **Product Code:** H8STM60BMGT10ENAA14O

PRINTED IN INDIA

By Vikas Publishing House Private Limited, Plot 20/4, Site-IV, Industrial Area Sahibabad, Ghaziabad – 201 010 and Published by S Chand And Company Limited, A-27, 2nd Floor, Mohan Co-operative Industrial Estate, New Delhi – 110 044.

Preface

The standout features of the book *Business Policy and Strategic Management* are its concisely written and robust coverage of strategic management concepts and its compelling collection of business cases. Strategy is the broad concept that covers a multitude of different issues, concepts and methodology. Many topics are considered in the formulation and implementation of strategy, including Industry Analysis, Competitor Analysis, Ethics, Strength / Weakness, Value Creation, Technology, Innovation, Product Development, Diversification, Balancing the Needs of Various Stakeholders, Strategic Alliances, Organizational Design, Virtual Organizations, Reward Systems, Corporate Cultures and Corporate Governance. Strategy requires a significant amount of work to understand, and even the experts often find themselves searching for new ways to research and think about the topic. For practising managers and leaders, strategy is at the centre of the effort to create value for customers, to respond to competitive challenges, and to build strong organizations.

The text responds to growing requests by business faculty for a concise, conceptually strong treatment of strategic management principles and analytic approaches that features straight-to-the-point discussions, timely examples, and a writing style that captures the interest of students. This book is crafted with four objectives in mind:

1. To fully engage students in the task of learning what every aspiring manager needs to know about the theory and practice of strategic management.
2. To provide an attractive set of contemporary cases that involve headline strategic issues and that give students ample opportunities to apply what they read in the chapters.
3. To complement the use of a business strategy simulation.
4. To simplify the task of demonstrating student learning through course-embedded assessment.

What makes it so different? Stated plainly, it is a book on strategic management rather than a book about strategic management. The difference is subtle but important and reflects a basic question that every teacher of this material should ask — specifically, why do students take this course and what must they take away from it in order to have a successful experience? It is my belief that students expect to leave this course as better strategic thinkers and managers. They want to be able to do the things, to make the decisions, and to deliver the results that will enable their success. In essence, they come to this course wanting to become successful or to become more successful. So this text is organized and oriented in such a way as to help. Rather than try to convey all that theory has to say on a subject, the book seeks to translate what theory has to say into principles and practices that students need to know in order to accomplish what that they want to accomplish.

As mentioned, it is a subtle difference but it is an important one. It reflects an approach that is grounded firmly in theory and research but that is ever so practical in application. It reflects 18 years of experience teaching strategic management to executives, MBAs, and undergraduates. And it reflects a desire to communicate, in a straightforward and plain-spoken way, a model that has too often seemed overly esoteric and academic to students and executives alike. In essence, the approach is to render strategic management practical by making it accessible and to leverage its utility by leveraging its generalizability. Everything in the book, then, from its coverage to its organization, reflects this philosophy. The entire ten chapters conclude by noting that the Business Policy and Strategic Management process as a continual process to the modern business environment. Finally, we recognize that professors want to minimize their switching costs when adopting a new book. Although every textbook is a little unique, our table of contents offers a structure and topic coverage that parallels what market leading books provide.

Dr. S. SENTHILKUMAR
M. MARUTHA DURAI
A. SHARMILA
J. POORNIMA

Disclaimer : While the authors of this book have made every effort to avoid any mistakes or omissions and have used their skill, expertise and knowledge to the best of their capacity to provide accurate and updated information, the authors and S. Chand do not give any representation or warranty with respect to the accuracy or completeness of the contents of this publication and are selling this publication on the condition and understanding that they shall not be made liable in any manner whatsoever. S.Chand and the authors expressly disclaim all and any liability/responsibility to any person, whether a purchaser or reader of this publication or not, in respect of anything and everything forming part of the contents of this publication. S. Chand shall not be responsible for any errors, omissions or damages arising out of the use of the information contained in this publication. Further, the appearance of the personal name, location, place and incidence, if any; in the illustrations used herein is purely coincidental and work of imagination. Thus the same should in no manner be termed as defamatory to any individual.

Contents

1. Business Policy **1 – 15**

1.1.	Introduction of Business Policy	1
1.2.	Meaning of Business Policy	1
1.3.	Definition of Business Policy	1
1.4.	Features and Essentials of Business Policy	2
1.5.	Difference Between Policy and Strategy	2
1.6.	Evolution of Business Policy as Discipline	3
1.7.	Nature and Characteristics of Business Policy	4
1.8.	Types and Methods of Business Policies	4
1.9.	Application of Business Policy in Functional Areas of Management	5
1.10.	Top Ten Core Business Policies and Procedures	6
1.11.	Objectives of Business Policy	9
1.12.	Vision	9
1.13.	Mission	12

2. Strategy and Strategic Management **16 – 42**

2.1.	Introduction to Strategy	16
2.2.	Meaning and Definition of Strategy	16
2.3.	Essentials of Strategy	17
2.4.	Strategy as Action and Nature of Strategy	17
2.5.	Dimensions of Strategy	17
2.6.	Criteria for Effective Strategy	18
2.7.	Models of Strategy	18
2.8.	Characteristics and Features of Strategy	19
2.9.	Mintzberg's 5 P's of Strategy	20
2.10.	Need and Purpose of Strategy	21
2.11.	Introduction and Conceptual Framework of Strategic Management	22
2.12.	Meaning and Definition of Strategic Management	23
2.13.	Scope and Future of Strategic Management	24
2.14.	Benefits of Strategic Management	24
2.15.	Limitations of Strategic Management	26
2.16.	Importance of Strategic Management	27
2.17.	Five Facets of Strategic Management	27
2.18.	Evolution of Strategic Management in India	28
2.19.	Nature and Characteristics of Strategic Management	30
2.20.	Strategic Management Process	31
2.21.	Strategic Management Practice in India (or) Strategies of Leading Indian Companies	33

2.22. Strategic Issues in Managing Technology and Innovation 35
2.23. Strategies for Internet Economy 36
2.24. Strategic Issues in Non-Profit Organizations 38
2.25. Strategies of Indian Companies 39

3. Competitive Advantage and Strategies **43 – 70**

3.1. Competitive Advantage - Introduction 43
3.2. Meaning and Definition of Competitive Advantage 44
3.3. Competitive Advantage of Nations and its Implication on Indian Business 45
3.4. Michael Porter's 5 Forces Model 48
3.5. Pest Analysis 52
3.6. Strategic Groups Competitive Changes 53
3.7. Stages of Industry Life Cycle Analysis 55
3.8. Globalization and Industry Structure or Globalization of Production and Markets 56
3.9. National Context and Competitive Advantage Resources 57
3.10. Capabilities and Competencies of Core Competencies 58
3.11. Competitor Analysis 59
3.12. Self-Analysis of Organization 60
3.13. Low Cost and Differentiation Generic Building Blocks of Competitive Advantage 61
3.14. Strategy in the Global Environment 63
3.15. Resources and Capabilities Durability of Competitive Advantage 65
3.16. Strategy and Technology 66
3.17. Distinctive Competencies and Competitive Advantage 68
3.18. Management of Technology 68
3.19. Diversification 69
3.20. Avoiding Failure and Sustaining Competitive Advantage 70

4. Business Environment **71 – 101**

4.1. Introduction and Management of Business Environment 71
4.2. Features of Environment 71
4.3. Environmental Analysis 72
4.4. Components of External Environment 73
4.5. Components of Internal Environment 84
4.6. Environmental Scanning 86
4.7. Scenario Building 92
4.8. Organisational Responses to the Environment 93
4.9. Competitive Positioning 94
4.10. Developing Strategy through Internal Analysis 94
4.11. Value Chain 96
4.12. VRIO Analysis 97
4.13. Core Competencies Analysis 100

5. Strategic Planning **102 – 120**

5.1. Introduction - Strategic Planning 102

5.2.	Meaning and Definition of Strategic Planning	102
5.3.	Strategic, Operational and Tactical Planning	103
5.4.	Process or Steps of Strategic Planning	105
5.5.	Evolution of Strategic Planning	107
5.6.	Dimension of Strategic Decisions	109
5.7.	Challenges or Key Issues in Strategic Planning	109
5.8.	Features of a Strategic Plan	111
5.9.	Benefits of Strategic Planning	111
5.10.	Hierarchical Levels of Planning	111
5.11.	Strategies in Mature Industries	112
5.12.	Business Strategies in Emerging Industries	113
5.13.	Reasons for Failure of Strategic Plans	114
5.14.	Strategic Management for Small, Large Multiproduct and Multiple Market Organizations	114
5.15.	Business Ethics and Strategic Management	117
5.16.	Strategic Funds Programming	118
5.17.	Assessment of Economic Contribution of Strategy	119
6.	**The Strategy Hierarchy or Level of Strategy**	**121 – 235**
6.1.	Hierarchical Level of Strategy	121
6.2.	Strategies in Fragmented Industries	149
6.3.	Chaining	150
6.4.	Strategies in Embryonic and Growth Industries	152
6.5.	Application Competitive Advantage in Industry	162
6.6.	Market Entry Strategies	175
6.7.	Environmental Threat and Opportunities Profile (ETOP)	176
6.8.	Comprehensive Analysis	177
6.9.	Structuring Organisational Appraisal	180
6.10.	Corporate Portfolio Analysis	182
6.11.	Matching Structure and Strategy	182
6.12.	Meaning and Definition of Organizational Culture	185
6.13.	Competitive Cost Dynamics	186
6.14.	International Portfolio Analysis	187
6.15.	Corporate Parenting Analysis	187
6.16.	SWOT Analysis	188
6.17.	TOWS Matrix	190
6.18.	Experience Curve Analysis	192
6.19.	Life Cycle Analysis	193
6.20.	Gap Analysis	194
6.21.	Mc Kinsey 7-S Framework	195
6.22.	BCG Growth-Share Matrix	195
6.23.	GE Nine-Cell Matrix	196
6.24.	GE Multifactor Portfolio Matrix	198
6.25.	Infrastructure and Efficiency	200

6.26. Developing Superior Attributes 204
6.27. Achieving Superior Innovation 205
6.28. Achieving Superior Responsiveness to Customers 210
6.29. Building and Restructuring the Corporation 212
6.30. Mergers and Acquisition 221
6.31. Retrenchment/Defensive Strategies 226
6.32. Combination Strategy 235

7. Stakeholder, Corporate Governance and CSR, Leader 236 – 270

7.1. Stakeholders-Introduction 236
7.2. Stakeholders versus Shareholders 238
7.3. Stakeholders Expectations 240
7.4. Scenario Planning for Stakeholders 240
7.5. Industry Analysis for Stakeholders 241
7.6. Steps in Identifying Stakeholders 242
7.7. Social Responsibility 243
7.8. Ethics 243
7.9. Corporate Social Responsibility 244
7.10. Corporate Responsibility Drivers 244
7.11. Three Dimensions of Corporate Performance 244
7.12. Areas of Social Responsibility 245
7.13. Diversity and Human Rights in CSR 245
7.14. Corporate Governance 248
7.15. Models of Corporate Governance 250
7.16. Mechanisms and Controls of Corporate Governance 252
7.17. Codes/Guidelines/Choice of Governance Models 253
7.18. Governance Issues and National Culture 254
7.19. Investor Protection 254
7.20. Recent Theoretical Development of Corporate Governance 255
7.21. Globalization and Corporate Governance 256
7.22. Global Landmarks in the Emergence of Corporate Governance 258
7.23. Structure of Corporate Governance 259
7.24. 4 P's of Corporate Governance 260
7.25. Principles of Corporate Governance 260
7.26. Reasons for the Growing Demand for Corporate Governance 261
7.27. Importance of Corporate Governance 262
7.28. Prerequisites of Corporate Governance 263
7.29. Corporate Governance Committees 263
7.30. Corporate Governance: History in India 264
7.31. Recommendations of the Various Committees 264
7.32. Mandatory Recommendations 266
7.33. Leader 268
7.34. 3- Dimensions of Leadership Tasks 269
7.35. Requisites/Traits/Characteristics to be a Good Leader 269

8. Strategic Change, Decision Making and Formulation **271 – 315**

8.1. Introduction 271
8.2. Meaning and Definition of Strategic Change 273
8.3. Nature of Strategic Change 274
8.4. Creative Problem Analysis 274
8.5. Strategic Decision Making Process 275
8.6. Barriers to Change 283
8.7. Change Requirements 286
8.8. Implementation of Strategic Change 288
8.9. Types of Changes in Organization 292
8.10. Managing Strategic Change 296
8.11. A General Framework for Managing Change 299
8.12. Input Stage, Matching Stage (Selection of Matrix) and Decision Stage 301
8.13. Strategy Formulation 315

9. Strategic Control and Evaluation **316 – 343**

9.1. Introduction and Meaning of Strategic Control System 316
9.2. Types of Control 317
9.3. Characteristics of an Effective Strategic Control System 319
9.4. Guidelines for Effective Strategic Control System 320
9.5. Organization Structure and Strategic Control 320
9.6. Process of Strategic Evaluation and Control 321
9.7. Strategy Evaluation and Control 323
9.8. Strategic Control Systems Types 324
9.9. The Control Process-Feedback Model 325
9.10. Designing Strategic Control Systems 327
9.11. Objectives of Strategy Evaluation and Control 328
9.12. Strategies and Tactics to Acquire Power 329
9.13. Managing Conflict 330
9.14. Techniques of Strategic Evaluation and Control 331
9.15. Strategic Analysis 332
9.16. Product Diversification 336
9.17. Product Classification 338
9.18. Market Penetration 339
9.19. New Product Development 341

10. Strategy Implementation **344 – 406**

10.1. Introduction 344
10.2. A Strategy is Usually Successful When the Other S's in the 7-S Framework Fit into or Supports the Strategy 344
10.3. A General Framework of Strategic Implementation 345
10.4. Approaches of Strategic Implementation 346
10.5. Issues in Strategy Implementation 349
10.6. Regulatory Framework Governing Business Activity 350

10.7.	Corporate Parenting	350
10.8.	Cost of Equity Capital	351
10.9.	Capital Budgeting	352
10.10.	Business Valuation in Reference with Profitability	352
10.11.	Divestiture Decision	354
10.12.	Strategic Implementation of All Functional Areas	355
10.13.	Resource Allocation	358
10.14.	Organizational Structure	364
10.15.	Organisational Design	366
10.16.	Building the Organisation Structure	375
10.17.	External Environment and Internal Organisation Contribution	377
10.18.	Implementation of Strategy Designing Organisational Structure	378
10.19.	Checklist for Determining Appropriateness of Organisational Structure	384
10.20.	Behavioural Issues	392
10.21.	Strategic Leadership	393
10.22.	Guidelines to Create Cultured Organisation Strategy	400
10.23.	Organizational Culture–Meaning and Definition	402
10.24.	Strategy and Staffing Decisions	403

Chapter 1

BUSINESS POLICY

Business Policy - Introduction - Meaning and Definition - Features and Essentials - Differences between Strategy and Policy - Evolution of Business Policy as Discipline - Nature and Characteristics of Business Policy - Types and Methods of Business Policies - Application of Business Policy in Functional Areas of Management - Top Ten Core Business Policies and Procedures - Objectives of Business Policy, Vision, Mission, Objectives of Mission Statement.

1.1. INTRODUCTION OF BUSINESS POLICY

Why are some businesses successful, while so many others fail? Why do some businesses enhance and sustain their performance over time, while others experience erosion in their competitive position? These questions are at the heart of business policy and strategic management. Their answers require a firm to act, activate and move fast to attain and sustain competitive advantage. Competitive advantage is attained when a firm generates supernormal returns on its investment, by offering services of value, and using a cost-effective technological base. Competitive advantage is sustained when the firm appropriately exploits and develops its technological base, thereby avoiding erosion of its competitive position from competitive attacks and changes in the market preferences. The nomenclature of Business Policy is assigned to a compulsory course included in a typical management studies curriculum. Almost all the management education programs offered by universities, management institutes or business schools in India include the business policy course, by whatever nomenclature it might e addressed, normally in the later part of the degree or diploma programme. The content of the business policy course is drawn from the field of strategic management.

1.2. MEANING OF BUSINESS POLICY

Business policy refers to a set of management decisions oriented towards enhancing and sustaining the firm's competitive advantage based on a system of extrinsic and intrinsic values. Extrinsic values refer to the added values that a firm delivers or expects to deliver to the network of its stakeholders, such as the workforce, investor, customers, vendors, collaborators and the community. Intrinsic values refer to the core values, such as ethics and credibility that a firm has or should have to survive and succeed.

1.3. DEFINITION OF BUSINESS POLICY

Christensen, "The study of the function and responsibilities of senior management, the crucial problems that affect success in the total enterprise and the decisions that determine the direction of the organization and shape its future".

This comprehensive definition by Christensen and others covers many aspects of business policy.

- First, it is considered as the study of functions and responsibilities of the senior management related to those organizational problems which affect the success of the enterprise as a whole.
- Secondly, it deals with the determination of the future course of action by the organization.
- Thirdly, it involves a choice of purpose and defining what needs to be done in order to mould the character and identity of the organization.
- Lastly, it is also concerned with the mobilization of resources by the help of which the organization can achieve its goals.

In other words Business Policy is define as

"The scope or spheres within which decisions can be taken by the subordinates in an organization. It permits the lower level management to deal with the problems and issues without consulting top level management every time for decisions. Business policies are the guidelines developed by an organization to govern its actions. They define the limits within which decisions must be made. Business policy also deals with acquisition of resources with which organizational goals can be achieved. Business policy is the study of the roles and responsibilities of top level management, the significant issues affecting organizational success and the decisions affecting organization in long-run"

1.4. FEATURES AND ESSENTIALS OF BUSINESS POLICY

1. **Specific:** Policy should be specific/definite. If it is uncertain, then the implementation will become difficult.
2. **Clear:** Policy must be unambiguous. It should avoid use of jargons and connotations. There should be no misunderstandings in following the policy.
3. **Reliable/Uniform:** Policy must be uniform enough so that it can be efficiently followed by the subordinates.
4. **Appropriate:** Policy should be appropriate to the present organizational goal.
5. **Simple:** A policy should be simple and easily understood by all in the organization. Inclusive/Comprehensive- In order to have a wide scope, a policy must be comprehensive.
6. **Flexible:** Policy should be flexible in operation/application. This does not imply that a policy should be altered always, but it should be wide in scope so as to ensure that the line managers use them in repetitive/routine scenarios.
7. **Stable:** Policy should be stable else it will lead to indecisiveness and uncertainty in minds of those who look into it for guidance.

1.5. DIFFERENCE BETWEEN POLICY AND STRATEGY

The term "Policy" should not be considered as synonymous to the term "Strategy". The difference between policy and strategy can be summarized as follows-

1. Policy is a **blueprint of the organizational activities** which are repetitive/routine in nature. While strategy is concerned with those organizational decisions which have not been dealt/ faced before in same form.
2. Policy formulation is responsibility of **top level management**. While strategy formulation is basically done by **middle level management.**
3. Policy deals with **routine/daily activities** essential for effective and efficient running of an organization. While strategy deals with strategic decisions.

4. Policy is concerned with both **thought and actions.** While strategy is concerned mostly with action.
5. A policy is what is, or what is not done. While a strategy is the methodology used to **achieve a target** as prescribed by a policy.

1.6. EVOLUTION OF BUSINESS POLICY AS DISCIPLINE

1. **Origin:**1911- Harvard Business School – Integrated Course in Management aimed at providing general management capability.
2. **Hofer: Strategic Management** – A Casebook in Policy and Planning: The Business Policy evolution has undergone four Paradigm Shifts. This transition is of overlapping nature.
3. **Development of subject of Business Policy has always followed the demands of real life business.**
4. **1930 – 1960: Environment change: New Products: Continuously changing market:** Ford Foundation recommended report, by Gordon and Howell, suggested a "Capstone" course of Business Policy which would give the students an opportunity to pull together what they have learned in the separate business fields and utilise this knowledge in the analysis of complex business problems.
5. **1969:** The course was made mandatory by American Assembly of Collegiate School of Business (AACSB).
6. **1990:** The course has become an integral part of management education curriculum.
7. **Evolution of Business Policy has undergone four paradigms.**

7.1. Paradigm One: Ad-hoc Policy making.

1900–1930: Era of Mass Production – Maximising output, Normally a Single Product, Standardised and low cost product, catering to unique set of customers servicing limited geographical area – Informal control and co-ordination. The Strategic planning was centred on maximising output.

7.2 Paradigm Two – Integrated Policy Formulation.

1930–1940: Changes in Technology, Turbulence in Political environment, Emergence of new industries, Demand for novelty products even at higher costs, Product Differentiation, Market segmentation in increasingly competitive and changing markets. These all made investment decisions increasingly difficult. This was era of integrating all functional areas and framing policies to guide managerial actions.

7.3 Paradigm Three—The Concept of Strategy.

1940–1960: Planned policy became irrelevant due to increasingly complex and accelerating changes. Firms had to anticipate environmental changes. A strategy needed to be formed with critical look at basic concept of Business and its relationship to the existing environment then.

7.4 Paradigm Four —The Strategic Management.

1980 & onwards: The focus of Strategic Management is on the strategic process of business firms and responsibilities of general management.

Everything outside the four walls is changing rapidly and this phenomenon is called as "Discontinuity" by Mr. Peter Drucker. Past experiences are no guarantee for future, as science and technology is moving faster. The future is no more extension of the past or the present.

The world is substantially compressed and managing the External & Internal environment becomes crucial function.

What to produce, where to market, which new business to enter, which one to quit and how to get internally stronger and resourceful are the new stakes.

Strategic Planning is required to be done to endow the enterprise with certain fundamental competencies/distinctive strengths which could take care of eventualities resulting from unexpected environmental changes.

1.7. NATURE AND CHARACTERISTICS OF BUSINESS POLICY

1. **Policies are always in writing:** The policies in general are written procedures which specify limits or guidelines for perfection of work to be undertaken in future.
2. **Directions towards goal achievements:** A policy is formulated in context of organisational objectives. Therefore, the policy tries to contribute towards the achievements of organizational achievements by specifying limits.
3. **Persuasive function:** Formulation of policy is a function of all managers whether manager of marketing, personnel, finance department etc.
4. **Policy differs from strategy:** A layman may think, there is no difference between policy and strategy, so at times people use these words interchangeably. Policies are identified as guides to thinking in decision making while strategies devote a general program of action and a commitment of emphasis and resources towards the attainment of comprehensive objectives.
5. **Expressed in qualitative and general way:** Policies are generally expressed in a qualitative, conditional and general way. The verbs most often used in setting up policies are to maintain to continue, to follow, to adhere, to provide, to assist, to assure, to employ etc.
6. **It involves choice of purpose:** Policies involves a choice of purpose and defining what needs to be done in order to mould the character and identify of organization.
7. **Policies must be long range:** In general a policy is a written decision by top management for achieving certain results.
8. **Clarity of thought:** A policy should be clear and self explanatory thus there will be no change for wrongdoing.
9. **Policies are reflection of management philosophy:** A policy is a written and effective expression of management thought and action.

1.8. TYPES AND METHODS OF BUSINESS POLICIES

1. External Policies

Policies framed to give effect to the decisions of the Government, judiciary, trade associations and such other external forces are what are called external policies. For example, under the Income-Tax Act, every employer is bound to deduct tax from the salary payable to the employees every month. Similarly, the Government requires certain number of jobs to be reserved for the backward sections of the society. To give effect to such orders, policies may be formulated at the enterprise level.

2. Internal Policies

Policies formulated to give effect to certain decisions taken by the owners of a business establishment are what are called internal policies. For example, it may be the policy of a certain private sector organization to appoint certain categories of workers purely on contract basis. Similarly, a business organization may adopt a policy to produce only for the foreign market.

3. Appealed Policies

Such policies are formulated to give effect to the suggestions of the staff of an organization. For example, the employees may make an appeal to the top management to give employment to an eligible member of an employee's family after the latter's retirement. If such a proposal is acceptable to the management, the same may be announced as a policy.

4. Explicit Policies

Those policies of an organization that are stated outwardly are called explicit policies. Such policies form part of the organization manual. Most of the policies of an organization are explicit in nature. The sales policy, credit policy, etc., may be cited as examples.

5. Implicit Policies

These policies are not stated outwardly. For example, every organization follows certain policy for the recruitment of employees. Such a policy is not usually stated explicitly. Even the existing employees may not be aware of it.

6. Distributive Policies

Distributive policies extend goods and services to members of an organization, as well as distributing the costs of the goods/services amongst the members of the organization. Examples include government policies that impact spending for welfare, public education, highways, and public safety, or a professional organization's benefits plan.

7. Regulatory Policies

Regulatory policies, or mandates, limit the discretion of individuals and agencies, or otherwise compel certain types of behavior. These policies are generally thought to be best applied when good behavior can be easily defined and bad behavior can be easily regulated and punished through fines or sanctions. An example of a fairly successful public regulatory policy is that of a speed limit.

8. Constituent Policies

Constituent policies create executive power entities, or deal with laws. Constituent policies also deal with Fiscal Policy in some circumstances.

9. Miscellaneous Policies

Policies are dynamic; they are not just static lists of goals or laws. Policy blueprints have to be implemented, often with unexpected results. Social policies are what happens 'on the ground' when they are implemented, as well as what happens at the decision making or legislative stage.

1.9. APPLICATION OF BUSINESS POLICY IN FUNCTIONAL AREAS OF MANAGEMENT

1. **Human Resources**—Ensures the business has the best staff for the job and that they are able to work effectively in a safe environment.
2. **Finance**— Keep a record of all money coming in and going out of the business. They have responsibility for securing finances for future expansion and paying staff and suppliers.
3. **Administration**—Ensure the smooth running of the business on a day-to-day basis. They have responsibility for clerical duties, cleaning, computer and software support, security and health and safety.
4. **Operations**— The task of producing the goods or service in the most efficient way. This is done by making best use of the business's staff, machinery, building and raw materials;

5. **Marketing and Sales**—Try and maximize the level of sales by carrying out market research and promoting the goods or service through a motivated sales team.
6. **Customer Service**—It help's the customer before and after a sale has been made by providing information, giving advice, providing credit facilities, delivering goods and providing after-sales support.
7. **Research and Development**—It help's the business remain competitive by developing new goods and services and updating the existing ones.
8. **Basic Management Function**—Planning, Organizing, Staffing, Leading/Directing, Controlling/Monitoring, Motivation, etc.
9. **Basic roles**
    - **Interpersonal:** Roles that involve coordination and interaction with employees.
    - **Informational:** Roles that involve handling, sharing, and analyzing information.
    - **Decisional:** Roles that require decision-making.
10. **Management Skills**
    - **Political:** Used to build a power base and establish connections.
    - **Conceptual:** Used to analyze complex situations.
    - **Interpersonal:** Used to communicate, motivate, mentor and delegate.
    - **Diagnostic:** Ability to visualize most appropriate response to a situation.
    - **Technical:** Expertise in one's particular functional area
11. **Levels of Management**—Most organizations have three management levels: first-level, middle-level, and top-level managers. These managers are classified in a hierarchy of authority, and perform different tasks. In many organizations, the number of managers in every level resembles a pyramid. Each level is explained below in specifications of their different responsibilities and likely job titles.
12. **Top-level Managers**—Consists of board of directors, president, vice-president, CEOs, etc. They are responsible for controlling and overseeing the entire organization. They develop goals, strategic plans, company policies, and make decisions on the direction of the business. In addition, top-level managers play a significant role in the mobilization of outside resources and are accountable to the shareholders and general public.
13. **Middle-level Managers**—Consist of general managers, branch managers and department managers. They are accountable to the top management for their department's function. They devote more time to organizational and directional functions. Their roles can be emphasized as executing organizational plans in conformance with the company's policies and the objectives of the top management, they define and discuss information and policies from top management to lower management, and most importantly they inspire and provide guidance to lower level managers towards better performance.
14. **Bottom-level Managers**—Consist of supervisors, section leads, foremen, etc. They focus on controlling and directing. They usually have the responsibility of assigning employees tasks, guiding and supervising employees on day-to-day activities, ensuring quality and quantity production, making recommendations, suggestions, and up channeling employee problems, etc.

1.10. TOP TEN CORE BUSINESS POLICIES AND PROCEDURES

The Bizmanualz CEO Company Policies Procedures Manuals are designed with your core business processes in mind. The nine business procedures manuals in the series provide your entire company with examples of the primary procedures used in writing your company procedure manuals. How do the nine procedure manuals address the core business processes?

Core Business Policies and Procedures

1. **Customer Strategy & Relationships** (Marketing) is a good place to start. Most businesses talk about the customer being the most important part of any business. Well, if your customer is so critical, have you mapped out a clear customer strategy and customer relationship process? Do you have customer strategy procedures for developing awareness and education of your business in the marketplace? The Bizmanualz Sales and Marketing Policies and Procedures Manual provides sample policies and procedures to help you set marketing strategy, marketing tactics, and marketing planning to cover the first part of your marketing sales funnel—awareness and education.
2. **Employee Development & Satisfaction** is essential to your business because your employees are the ones that talk to and develop your customers. The Bizmanualz Human Resources Procedures Manual provides example procedures for hiring, administration (e.g., personnel records, compliance), compensation, and — the most important part – developing your employees. The HR manual also includes a sample Employee Handbook and an HR Manager's manual to provide a complete discussion of human resources. Keeping employees and facilities safe is the focus of the Bizmanualz Security Procedures Manual, which includes coverage of guard force management, employee conduct, emergency operations, protection, and safety.
3. **Quality, Process Improvement & Change Management** is driven by competition, your desire to excel at what you do and make your customers happy. The Bizmanualz ISO 9001 QMS Procedures Manual provides a sample quality manual, the six quality procedures required by ISO 9001, and additional supporting procedures to provide a foundation for your process improvement and change management initiatives.
4. **Financial Analysis, Reporting & Capital Management** is critical to fast growth companies. Cash is the lifeblood of your company and a fast growth company consumes cash quickly. The Bizmanualz Financial Procedures Manual has example procedures for financial administration, raising capital, managing capital, financial statement reporting, and the internal controls necessary in a fast growth company. A controller's manual is included to provide the direction and organization for controlling your company cash.
5. **Management Responsibility** addresses all of your core business processes and is integral to every area of your company. Every manual in the "CEO Company Policies Procedures Manuals" covers the management of that departmental area. Each manual provides a departmental (functional) manager's manual that describes the departmental organization structure, major responsibilities, departmental guidelines, ethics, policies, and – of course – the primary business processes for that department. The Bizmanualz Business Procedures Manual provides a simple, fast, and easy way to provide immediate oversight for all of your operations.
6. **Customer Acquisition** (Sales) is about engaging the customer and closing the sale. The Bizmanualz Sales and Marketing Procedure Manual contains procedures for the entire sales funnel, sales process, sales administration and sales management common to organizations that have to oversee a sales force. The Bizmanualz Accounting Procedures Manual contains procedures for controlling cash and the revenue cycle, which is a parallel and supporting activity to the sales process.
7. **Product Development** must obtain requirements from sales and develop products that satisfy the customer. Therefore, product development procedures are found in both the Bizmanualz Sales and Marketing Procedure Manual and the Bizmanualz ISO 9001 QMS

Procedures Manual, which contains procedures for customer requirements, as well as the design and development of new products.

8. **Product/Service Delivery** The Bizmanualz Accounting Procedures Manual contains procedures for shipping, receiving, and inventory control. But since delivery is part of ISO and quality, the Bizmanualz ISO 9001 QMS Procedures Manual also provides coverage of this critical customer facing area.
9. **Accounting Management** is about accounting transaction management, as opposed to finance which is focused more on raising, managing, and using cash effectively. The Bizmanualz Accounting Procedures Manual focus is on controlling operating cash receipts, cash disbursements, inventory and assets, the revenue cycle, and general accounting administration.
10. **Technology Management** is about all of the technology in your company. The Bizmanualz Computer, Network and IT Procedures Manual contains procedures for IT administration, IT asset management, IT training, technical support, IT security, IT disaster recovery, and software development. More in-depth continuity planning coverage is provided with the Bizmanualz Disaster Recovery Procedures Manual.

Top Ten Core Business Processes

	Top Ten Core Business Processes	Accounting Procedures	Finance Procedures	Computer & Network Procedures	Human Resources Procedures	Sales & Marketing Procedures	ISO 9001 OMS Procedures	Security Management Procedures	Disaster Recovery Procedures	Business Sampler Procedures
1	Customer Strategy & Relationship (Marketing)					X				X
2	Employee Development & Satisfaction				X			X		X
3	Quality, Process Improvement &Change Management						X			X
4	Final Analysis, Reporting, &Capital Management	X	X							X
5	Management Responsibility	X	X	X	X	X	X	X	X	X
6	Customer Acquisition (Sales)									X
7	Product Development									X
8	Product/Service Delivery									X
9	Accounting Management	X			X					X
10	Technology Management			X					X	X

Figure 1.1.

Business Process Policies and Procedures

The Bizmanualz CEO Company Policies Procedures Manuals collection is the best overall deal — you save 45% when you buy the set, compared with purchasing all nine manuals individually. The series covers all of the core business processes in one simple bundle. It includes manuals for:

- Financial Policies and Procedures
- Accounting Policies and Procedures
- Computer & IT Policies and Procedures
- Human Resources Policies and Procedures
- Sales & Marketing Policies and Procedures
- ISO 9001 Quality Policies and Procedures

- Security & Disaster Policies and Procedures
- Business Policies and Procedures Sampler

Every critical area of your company is now covered with the Bizmanualz CEO Company Policies Procedures Manuals set. Coverage is easily at hand for Accounting, Administration, Customer Service, Disaster Management, Engineering, Environmental Management, Finance & Credit, Information Technology, Manufacturing, Personnel, Sales & Marketing, Security Operations, Shipping, Purchasing, Inventory, and ISO 9001 conformance.

1.11. OBJECTIVES OF BUSINESS POLICY

The objectives of business policy have been stated by various authors in terms of knowledge, skill and attitudes. These objectives could be derived from purpose of business policy:-

1. **Knowledge**
   - Knowledge of external and internal environment is vital to understanding of business policy.
   - The information about environment helps in determination of the mission, objectives and strategies of a firm.
   - The implementation of strategy is a complex issue and is invariably the most difficult part of strategic management
   - To survey the literature and learn about the research taking place in the field of business policy is also an important knowledge objective.
2. **Skills**
   - The study of business policy should enable a student to develop analytical ability and use it to understand the situation in a given case or incident.
   - The study of business policy should lead to the skill of identifying the factors relevant in decision making. The analysis of strengths and weakness of an organisation, the threats and opportunities present in the environment.
   - The above objectives in terms of skill increase the mental ability of the lerners and enable them to link theory with practice.
   - As a part of business policy study case analysis leads to the development of oral as well as written communication skills.
3. **Attitudes**
   - The attainment of the knowledge and skill objectives should lead to the inculcation of an appropriate attitude among the learners.
   - By acting in a comprehensive manner, a generalist is able to function under conditions of partial ignorance by using his or her judgment and intuition.
   - For a general manager information and suggestions are important to pose a liberal attitude and be receptive to new ideas.
   - It is important to have the attitudes to go beyond and think when faced with a problematic situation. Developing a creative attitude is the hallmark of general manager who refuses to be board by precedents and stereo typed decision.

1.12. VISION

It refers to the category of intention, that are broad, all inclusive and forward thinking –it is what the firm ultimately like to become – aspiration of future without specifying the means to achieve those desire ends – Mangers, they usually refers to mental image of some desired future.

In other words, vision refers to the goals that are broadest, most general and all inclusive. A vision describes aspirations for the future, without specifying the means necessary to achieve those desired ends. The most effective visions are those that inspire, and this inspiration often takes the form of asking for the best, the most or greatest. It may be the best service, the most rugged product, or the greatest sense of achievement, but it must be inspirational. The vision statement of Birla 3M is: "To be the most innovative enterprise and the preferred supplier"

PURPOSE OF FIRM BUSINESS VISION MODELS [OR] THE BUSINESS VISION AND COMPANY MISSION STATEMENT

While a business must continually adapt to its competitive environment, there are certain core ideals that remain relatively steady and provide guidance in the process of strategic decision-making. These unchanging ideals form the business vision and are expressed in the company mission statement. In their 1996 article entitled Building Your Company's Vision, James Collins and Jerry Porras provided a framework for understanding business vision and articulating it in a mission statement. The mission statement communicates the firm's core ideology and visionary goals, generally consisting of the following three components:-

1. **Core values** to which the firm is committed
2. **Core purpose** of the firm
3. **Visionary goals** the firm will pursue to fulfill its mission.

The firm's core values and purpose constitute its core ideology and remain relatively constant. They are independent of industry structure and the product life cycle. The core ideology is not created in a mission statement; rather, the mission statement is simply an expression of what already exists. The specific phrasing of the ideology may change with the times, but the underlying ideology remains constant. The three components of the business vision can be portrayed as follows:-

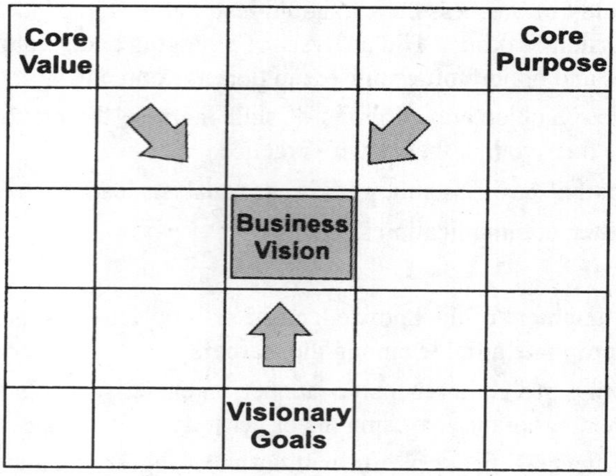

Figure 1.2. Components of Business Vision.

1. Core Values

The core values are a few values (no more than five or so) that are central to the firm. Core values reflect the deeply held values of the organization and are independent of the current industry environment and management fads. One way to determine whether a value is a core value to ask whether it would continue to be supported if circumstances changed and caused it to be seen as a liability. If the answer is that it would be kept, then it is core value. Another way to determine which values are core is to imagine the firm moving into a totally different industry. The values that would be carried with it into the new industry are the core values of the firm. Core values will not change even if the industry in which the company operates changes. If the industry changes such that the core values are not appreciated, then the firm should seek new markets where its core values are viewed as an asset. For example, if innovation is a core value but then 10 years down the road innovation is no longer valued by the current customers, rather than change its values the firm should seek new markets where innovation is advantageous. The following are a few examples of values that some firms have chosen to be in their core:-

- Excellent customer service
- Pioneering technology
- Creativity
- Integrity
- Social responsibility

2. Core Purpose

The core purpose is the reason that the firm exists. This core purpose is expressed in a carefully formulated mission statement. Like the core values, the core purpose is relatively unchanging and for many firms endures for decades or even centuries. This purpose sets the firm apart from other firms in its industry and sets the direction in which the firm will proceed. The core purpose is an idealistic reason for being. While firms exist to earn a profit, the profit motive should not be highlighted in the mission statement since it provides little direction to the firm's employees. What is more important is how the firm will earn its profit since the "how" is what defines the firm. Initial attempts at stating a core purpose often result in too specific of a statement that focuses on a product or service. To isolate the core purpose, it is useful to ask "why" in response to first-pass, product-oriented mission statements. For example, if a market research firm initially states that its purpose is to provide market research data to its customers, asking "why" leads to the fact that the data is to help customers better understand their markets. Continuing to ask "why" may lead to the revelation that the firm's core purpose is to assist its clients in reaching their objectives by helping them to better understand their markets. The core purpose and values of the firm are not selected - they are discovered. The stated ideology should not be a goal or aspiration but rather, it should portray the firm as it really is. Any attempt to state a value that is not already held by the firm's employees is likely to not be taken seriously.

3. Visionary Goals

The visionary goals are the lofty objectives that the firm's management decides to pursue. This vision describes some milestone that the firm will reach in the future and may require a decade or more to achieve. In contrast to the core ideology that the firm discovers, visionary goals are selected. These visionary goals are longer term and more challenging than strategic or tactical goals. There may be only a 50% chance of realizing the vision, but the firm must believe that it can do so. Collins and Porras describe these lofty objectives as "Big, Hairy, Audacious Goals." These goals should be challenging enough so that people nearly gasp when they learn of them and realize the effort that will be required to reach them. Most visionary goals fall into one of the following categories:-

- **Target**—quantitative or qualitative goals such as a sales target or Ford's goal to "democratize the automobile."
- **Common enemy**—centered on overtaking a specific firm such as the 1950's goal of Philip-Morris to displace RJR.

- **Role mode**—to become like another firm in a different industry or market. For example, a cycling accessories firm might strive to become "the Nike of the cycling industry."
- **Internal transformation**—especially appropriate for very large corporations. For example, GE set the goal of becoming number one or number two in every market it serves. While visionary goals may require significant stretching to achieve, many visionary companies have succeeded in reaching them. Once such a goal is reached, it needs to be replaced; otherwise, it is unlikely that the organization will continue to be successful. For example, Ford succeeded in placing the automobile within the reach of everyday people, but did not replace this goal with a better one and General Motors overtook Ford in the 1930's.

1.13. MISSION

A vision becomes tangible as a mission statement. Writing such a statement specifies a leader's belief about an organization and the direction in which it should move. It can also identify what is unique about the character of the organization. The mission statement of Ford Motor Company is a typical illustration of the mission. Ford's mission statement reads thus:

"Ford Motor Company is a world leader in automotive and automotive- related products and services as well as in newer industries, such as aerospace, communication and financial services. Our mission is to improve continually our products and services to meet our customers' needs, allowing us to prosper as a business and to provide a reasonable return for our stockholders, the owners of our business"

Many organizations develop both a vision statement as well as a mission statement. Where as the vision statement answer the question "What do we want to become?", the mission statement answer "What is our business?". Though mission statement are the hallmarks of successful organization, not all Indian firms do have then as shown in the following table-

Table 1.1

Written Mission Statements		Present	Absent	Under preparation
	Manufacturing sector	80%	17%	3%
	Service Sector	69%	19%	12%
	Infrastructure	50%	33%	17%
	Overall	72%	18%	10%

(Source: Business Today, Feb 22-Mrach 6, 1998)

1.13.1 Objectives of Mission Statement

1. Profit

Profit is the primary goal of any business enterprise. Profit is the excess of income over expenses. Profit is the main incentive, motivator, strong sustainer, and judicious allocator of resources, objective indicator of productivity and a solid basis for growth, expansion and survival. Profit enables a businessman to realize his other objectives too.

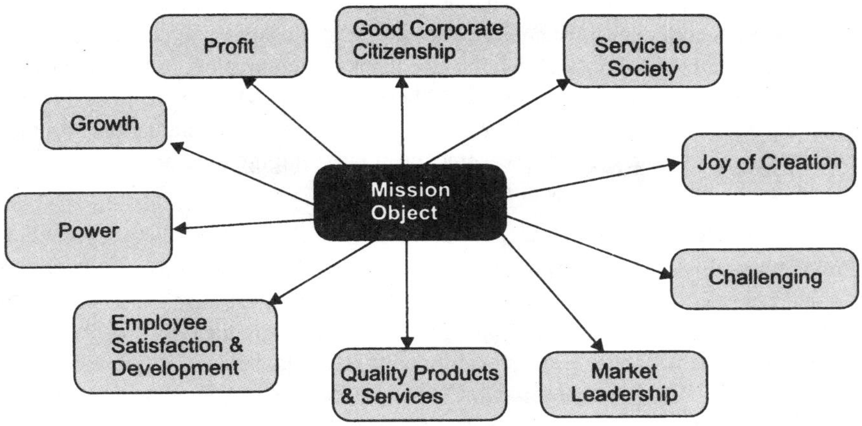

Figure 1.3. Objective of Mission Statement.

2. **Growth**

   It is another primary objective of business. Business should grow in all directions over a period of time. An enterprise which remains stagnant for long is presumed to suffer from an organic defect. The strategies adopted to achieve growth are-

   - Add more products / markets
   - Diversity into new areas
   - Integration – forward or backward
   - Increase market share
   - Expand markets
   - Cut down costs and increase productivity

3. **Power**

   Business have vast resources (in the form of money, materials, men and know how) at it's commend. These resources confer enormous economic and political power on owners and managers of business ventures. Next to the Prime Minister and Chief Ministers, perhaps, it is the business people who enjoy considerable clout in our country. Some businessmen mince no words in expressing the desire that they want more power. The late Aditya Birla used to assert that he built his empire to get more power. Several enlightened businessmen have used their power for the good of society. One such illustration in our country was J.N.Tata, who passed away in 1904. He was a pioneer in industry research, health care, art, literature and in many other areas. His name inspires awe and respect. It is hard to imagine what would have happened to the industrial map of our country if J.N.Tata had not been born in 1839 in a family of Parsi priests in Gujarat. "He was above all a patriot", wrote The Times of India (April 13, 1912) "who made no public speeches. To his mind, wealth and the industry which led to wealth were not ends in themselves, but means to an end, the stimulation of the latent resources of the country and its elevation in the scale of nations."

4. **Employee Satisfaction and Development**

   "If you want to plan for a year, plant corn. If you want to plan for 30 years, plant a tree. But if you want to plan for 100 years, plant men"-so goes a Chinese proverb. Business is people, said we, in the beginning of this chapter. Caring for employee satisfaction and providing for their development has been one of the objectives of enlightened business enterprises. Concern for employees continues to be an important aspect of management; contrary to the expectation that human element will lose its significance thanks to automation. In fact, quality of personnel is considered to be one of the hallmarks of best managed and highly respected companies. The Tatas are a legend in pursuing this objective. Either in implementing labour welfare measures, constituting safety and security measures, or in providing training and development facilities, the name of Tatas should be mentioned first.

5. **Quality Products and Services**

   Providing quality products and services is yet another objective of business. Those who insisted on and persisted in quality survived competition and stayed ahead of others in the market. Persistent quality of products earns brand loyalty a vital ingredient of success. Hindustan Lever is flourishing mainly because of the quality of its products. Some of its products like Liril, Vim, Lifebuoy, Surf; Rin, Sunlight, Signal, Close-up, Lux, Rexona, Pears and others have become household names throughout the country. These products are accepted by buyers as safe, of high quality and reasonably priced. Behind its quality products, Hindustan Lever has an excellent Research and Development (R&D) set-up and a high degree of professional management. The company is sitting pretty and is almost invincible. There are other business people who believe in quick money. Quick money comes through short-cuts. These are the people who give us razor blades which fail to give us one smooth and neat shave, bulbs that do not give at least 100 light hours of service, leaky taps and adulterated goods. Such enterprises will not survive for long.

6. **Market Leadership**

   To earn market leadership is yet another objective of business. To earn a niche for oneself in the market, innovation is the key factor. Innovation may be in product, advertising, distribution, finance or in any other field. Blow Plast retains its market leadership. by introducing soft luggage bags and totes. Hindustan Lever earned leadership in tooth paste by introducing mouth-washer in its 'Close-up.' Asian Paints adopted unconventional channels for the sale of its paints, which has pushed them ahead of their competitors. Ambani of Reliance Textiles introduced convertible debentures which have become attractive. This and other financial wizardies enabled Reliance to receive unprecedented response from investing public to any of its issues of securities.

7. **Challenging**

   Business offers vast scope and poses formidable challenges. Success in a business venture smacks of the abilities of individuals who own and failure betrays their inability and incompetence. The worth of an individual is tested more in business than in any other profession. For Ratan Tata running business has been a challenge. Confessed Tata is an interview thus: "I have asked myself this quite often. I don't have monetary ownership in the company in which I work and I am not given to propagating the position I am in. I ask myself why I am doing this and I think it is perhaps the challenge. If I had an ideological choice, I would probably want to do something more for the uplift of the people of India. I have a strong desire not to make money but 'to see happiness created in a place where there isn't".

8. **Joy of Creation**

   It is through business strategies new ideas and innovations are given a shape and are converted into useful products and services for the benefit of customers. Although it may be too difficult to list all the products and services that business houses have provided us till now, it is interesting to mention that in the coming two or three decades, the following will receive considerable attention from researchers and business people-

- Readily available artificial human organs, except the brain.
- A means of transportation without an automobile, perhaps an individual flying machine.
- Drugs to cure or prevent cancer and the common cold.
- A personal telephone, no larger than a cigarette pack, that can be used from any location.
- A pocket sized personal/business computer i.e., a laptop or palm computers.
- Clothing that can be cleaned by placing it in a 'cleaning chamber' for one minute.
- A synthetic material to replace wood.
- A simple injection to determine the sex of an unborn child.

9. Service to Society

Business is a part of society and has several obligations towards it. Some of them are-

- Providing safe and quality goods at reasonable prices
- Providing employment
- Patronising cultural and religious activities
- Maintaining and protecting ecology and
- Supporting less privileged sections of people in society like scheduled castes and scheduled tribes, the physically handicapped, women and children.

10. Good Corporate Citizenship

Good corporate citizenship implies that the business unit complies with the rules of the land, pays taxes to the government regularly, discharges its obligations to society and cares for its employees and customers. Bending rules of the land, evading tax payments by under-invoicing exports and dubious tax- planning; cornering licenses at the cost of others; adulteration of quality products; and indulging in other unethical practices may earn money. But such practices hardly speak highly of corporate citizenship. The Tatas are a contrast to the general trend. Unethical practices are anathema to the Tatas. The best way to substantiate this claim is to quote J.R.D. Tata. *"This factor has also worked against our growth. What would have happened if our philosophy was like that of some other companies which do not stop at any means to attain their ends. I have often thought of that and I have come to the conclusion that if we were like these other groups, we would be twice as big as we are today. What we have sacrificed is a 100 per cent growth."*

Chapter 2

STRATEGY AND STRATEGIC MANAGEMENT

Introduction - Meaning and Definition of Strategy - Essentials of Strategy - Strategy as Action and Nature of Strategy - Dimensions of Strategy - Criteria for Effective Strategy - Models of Strategy - Characteristics and Features of Strategy - Mintzberg's 5P's of Strategy - Need and Purpose of Strategy - Introduction and Conceptual Framework of Strategic Management - Meaning and Definition of Strategic Management - Scope and Future of Strategic Management- Benefits, Limitations and Importance of Strategic Management - Five Facets of Strategic Management - Evolution of Strategic Management in India - Nature and Characteristics of Strategic Management - Strategic Management Process - Strategic Management Practice in India or Strategies of Leading Indian Companies - Strategic Issues in Managing Technology and Innovation - Strategies for Internet Economy, Strategies Guidelines for Internet Economy - Strategic Issues in Non-Profit Organisation - Strategies of Indian Companies.

2.1. INTRODUCTION TO STRATEGY

The word "strategy" is hopelessly mis-used. It should mean something like "The understanding that we all share about the way things are developing in our industry, where we are positioned in this, and what we are going to do about this, given both constraints and opportunities." All the rest is tactics, the "how" that answers to this "what". Tactics are hard work to install, keep up to date and track, but they are pretty easy to define once the strategy is in place.

2.2. MEANING AND DEFINITION OF STRATEGY

Generally the company's concept of Strategy consists of the competitive moves and business approaches that managers employ to attract and please customers, compete successfully, grow the business, conduct operations and achieve targeted objectives.

A strategy is defined as "a unified, comprehensive and integrated plan that relates to the strategic advantages of the firm to the challenges of the environment. It is designed to ensure that the basic objectives of the enterprise are achieved through proper execution by the organisation

Military Origins of Strategy:

Strategy is a term that comes from the Greek Strategic, meaning "Generalship". In the military, strategy often refers to manoeuvring troops into position before the enemy is actually engaged. In this sense, strategy refers to the deployment of troops. Once the enemy has been engaged, attention shifts to tactics. Here, the employment of troops is central. Substitute "resources" for troops and the transfer of the concept to the business world begins to take form.

"Examines wars and battles from the time of the ancient Greeks through World War II. He concludes that Clausewitz' definition of strategy as "the art of the employment of battles as a means to gain the object of war" is seriously flawed in that this view of strategy intrudes upon policy and makes battle the only means of achieving strategic ends" **—B.H. Liddell Hart**

"The determination of the basic long-term goals and objectives of an enterprise and the adoption of the courses of action and the allocation of resources necessary for carrying out these goals"
—**Alfred D. Chandler**

2.3. ESSENTIALS OF STRATEGY

Strategy includes the determination and evaluation of alternative paths to an already established Mission and Objectives of enterprise and choosing the alternative to be adapted. Four important aspects of Strategy are:-

1. Long Term Objectives: It emphasises on long term growth and development. These Objectives give direction for implementing Strategy.

2. Competitive Advantages: The external environment is continuously monitored & Strategy is made to have the firm a continuous Competitive Advantage.

3. Vector is a Direction with Force: Series of actions are to be taken & they should have same direction for whole organisation.

4. Synergy: Once a series of decisions are taken to accomplish the objectives in same direction, there will be synergy. Synergy can happen due to Competitive Advantages and Growth Vector. The Objectives need be measurable and could be ROI, Sales Growth Rate,

2.4. STRATEGY AS ACTION AND NATURE OF STRATEGY

Three types of actions are involved in Strategy:-

1. Determination of long term goals & objectives
2. Adoption of courses of action
3. Allocation of resources

Therefore, Strategy is "Creation of unique & valued position involving a different set of activities. The Company that is strategically positioned performs different activities from rivals or performs similar activities in different ways" – **Michael Porter.**

2.4.1 Nature of Strategy

1. Strategy is a major course of action through which organisation relates itself to its **External Environment.**

2. Strategy is blend of internal & external factors. **Face opportunities and threats** provided by External factors, Internal factors are matched with them.

3. Strategic actions are different for different situations. Strategy is combination of actions to solve a certain problem to **Achieve a Desirable End.**

4. Strategy may involve contradictory actions simultaneously or with a gap of time like closing down some **Operations and Expanding** some at same time.

5. Strategy is **Future Oriented**. New situations, which have not arisen in past will require revised Strategic Actions.

6. Strategy requires some **Systems and Norms** for its efficient adoption in any organisation.

7. Strategy provides overall **Framework for Guiding Enterprise Thinking and Action.**

2.5. DIMENSIONS OF STRATEGY

1. Effective formal strategy contains three essential elements viz.,

- Most important **objectives to be achieved**.
- The most significant **policies guiding or limiting action** and
- Major action sequences that are to accomplish the **defined goals within the limits set.**

2. Effective strategies develop around a few key concepts and thrusts, which give them cohesion, **balance and focus.**

3. Strategy deals not just with the **unpredictable** but also with the unknowable.

4. Complex business organisations have a number of hierarchically related and **mutually supporting strategies.**

2.6. CRITERIA FOR EFFECTIVE STRATEGY

Although each strategic situation is unique, there are some common criteria that tend to explain an effective strategy. Criteria for effective strategy include:

1. Clear, decisive objectives: All efforts should be directed towards clearly understood, decisive and attainable overall goals. All goals need not be written down or numerically precise but they must be understood and be decisive.

2. Maintaining the initiative: The strategy preserves freedom of action and enhances commitment. It sets the pace and determines the course of events rather than reacting to them.

3. Concentration: The strategy concentrates superior power at the place and time likely to be decisive. The strategy must define precisely what will make the enterprise superior in power, best in critical dimensions in relation to its competitors. A distinctive competency yields greater success with fewer resources.

4. Flexibility: The strategy must purposely be built in resources, buffers and dimensions for flexibility and manoeuvre. Reserved capabilities, planned manoeuvrability and repositioning allow one to use minimum resource while keeping competitors at a relative disadvantage.

5. Coordinated and committed leadership: The strategy should provide responsible, committed leadership for each of its major goals. Care should be taken in selecting the leaders in such a way that their own interest and values match with the requirements of their roles. Commitment but not acceptance is the basic requirement.

6. Surprise: The strategy should make used of speed, secrecy and intelligence to attack exposed or unprepared competitors at an unexpected time. Thus surprise and correct time are important.

7. Security: The organisation should secure or develop resources required, securely maintain all vital operating points for the enterprise, an effective intelligence system to prevent the effects of surprises by the competitors.

2.7. MODELS OF STRATEGY

"Today, "business model" and "strategy" are among the most sloppily used terms in business; they are often stretched to mean everything – and end up meaning nothing." **—Magretta**

"A business model outlines the essential details of a firm's value proposition for its various stakeholders and the activity system the firm uses to create and deliver value to its customers. If Porter [1996, 2001] is used to define strategy, a business model may be defined as an abstract representation of some aspect of a firm's strategy. However, unlike strategy, business models do not consider a firm's competitive positioning." **—Seddon**

One framework has been developed by Professor Mark Moore2 of Harvard's Kennedy School of Government, a teacher at the Australian and New Zealand School of Government (ANZSOG). It is an adaptation of a private sector business strategy model.

1. Private Sector Model

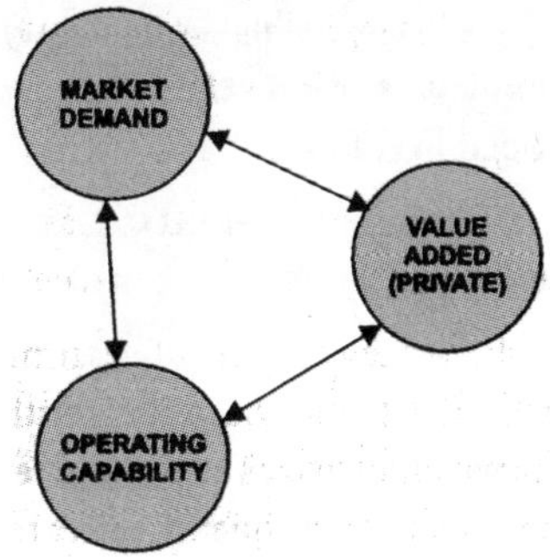

Figure 2.1. Business Policy Model.

One class of private sector model focuses on three key variables and their relationships. Essentially a business's strategy can be analyzed by reference to:-

- Its output, or value added
- Market demand
- Its operating capability and by reference to their relationships to one another.

The only variable that requires elucidation is "value added", the difference between the cost of the inputs purchased by the business and the market value of its output.
Value added can be increased either by reducing the amount of input used to produce a given output or by increasing the quantity or quality of output with a given input (or by some mixture of these two). "Value added" is either the actual or desired output of the business, depending on whether the purpose of the analysis is positive or normative.

2. Competition Policy Strategy Model

Adapting this for a competition policy strategy, the key variables are:-

- The value added to the public (public value).
- The operating capability. This includes the resources and strengths and weaknesses of the policy. (The model can also be extended to include "co-producers").
- The "authorizing environment" i.e. the political environment which gives rise to legislation, regulation and other political requirements and values which govern the work of the competition policy strategy.

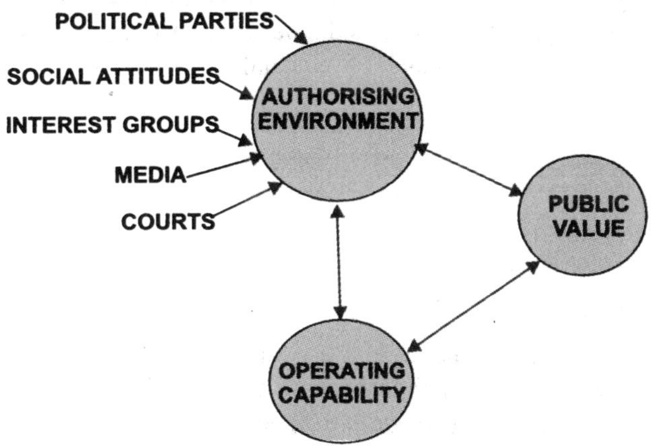

Figure 2.2. Competition Policy Strategy Model.

2.8. CHARACTERISTICS AND FEATURES OF STRATEGY

1. Strategy is significant because it is not possible to foresee the future. Without a perfect foresight, the firms must be **ready to deal with the uncertain events** which constitute the business environment.

2. Strategy deals with long term developments rather than routine operations, i.e. it deals with **probability of innovations** or new products, new methods of productions, or new markets to be developed in future.

3. Strategy is created to take into account the probable behavior of customers and competitors. Strategies dealing with employees will **predict the employee behavior.**

4. Strategy relates the firm to its environment, particularly the external environment in all actions whether objective setting, or actions and resources required for its achievement. This definition emphasizes on the **systems approach of management** and treats an organization as part of the society consequently affected by it.

5. Strategy is the right **combination of factors both external and internal.** In relating an organization to its environment, the management must also consider the internal factors too, particularly its strengths and weaknesses, to take various courses of action.

6. **Strategy is relative combination of actions.** The combination is to meet a particular condition, to solve certain problems, or to attain a desirable objective. It may take any form; for every situation varies and, therefore, requires a somewhat different approach.

7. Strategy may even **involve contradictory action.** Since strategic action depends on environmental variables, a manager may take an action today and revise or reverse his steps tomorrow depending on the situations.

8. Strategy is **forward looking.** It has orientation towards the future. Strategic action is required in a new situation. Nothing-new requiring solutions can exist in the past, and so strategy is relevant only to the future.

2.9. MINTZBERG'S 5 P's OF STRATEGY

The word "strategy" has been used implicitly in different ways even if it has traditionally been defined in only one. Explicit recognition of multiple definitions can help people to man oeuvre through this difficult field. Mintzberg provides five definitions of strategy:

1. **Plan**
2. **Ploy**
3. **Pattern**
4. **Position**
5. **Perspective**

1. **Plan:** Strategy is a plan - some sort of consciously intended course of action, a guideline (or set of guidelines) to deal with a situation. By this definition strategies have two essential characteristics: they are made in advance of the actions to which they apply, and they are developed consciously and purposefully.

2. **Ploy:** As plan, a strategy can be a ploy too, really just a specific man oeuvre intended to outwit an opponent or competitor.

3. **Pattern:** If strategies can be intended (whether as general plans or specific ploys), they can also be realized. In other words, defining strategy as plan is not sufficient; we also need a definition that encompasses the resulting behaviour: Strategy is a pattern - specifically, a pattern in a stream of actions. Strategy is consistency in behaviour, whether or not intended. The definitions of strategy as plan and pattern can be quite independent of one another: plans may go unrealized, while patterns may appear

without preconception. Plans are intended strategy, whereas patterns are realized strategy; from this we can distinguish deliberate strategies, where intentions that existed previously were realized, and emergent strategies where patterns developed in the absence of intentions, or despite them.

4. Position: Strategy is a position—specifically a means of locating an organization in an "environment". By this definition strategy becomes the mediating force, or "match", between organization and environment, that is, between the internal and the external context.

5. Perspective: Strategy is a perspective—its content consisting not just of a chosen position, but of an ingrained way of perceiving the world. Strategy in this respect is to the organization what personality is to the individual. What is of key importance is that strategy is a perspective shared by members of an organization, through their intentions and / or by their actions. In effect, when we talk of strategy in this context, we are entering the realm of the collective mind - individuals united by common thinking and / or behaviour.

2.10. NEED AND PURPOSE OF STRATEGY

1. Expanding the Company's Profit and Objectives: The success of any good enterprise is based on the measures that are laid out by the various stakeholders. In commerce, business strategy is important for the achievement of the objectives set. In a commercial setting, the main aims normally revolve around making lots and lots of profits, growing and expanding, and most importantly, diversifying. These goals must be achieved for business success in any flourishing industry.

2. Guidelines for Implementing Plans: There are very many business strategies that can be utilized by new or old ventures in order to compete healthily in the market. Most corporations that have taken the market by storm normally have a history of good and functional strategies that have been set and adhered to strictly. Therefore, it is important that once they have been drawn and enacted, the measures are implemented and put into the system.

3. Provides Impact of Daily Operations: There are various sources form which strategies can be obtained and put into use. The main route is through the educational systems. Students here are trained on the various commercial factors that are important for success. They are also exposed to various career skills and aspects such as team building, branding, and marketing etc. that impact on the daily operations of any businesses.

4. Establishing the Entrepreneurial and Managerial Skills: In addition, there is the internet and enterprising talks and conferences. Through these platforms, a lot of information exchanges have taken place to highlight the various factors encountered in the enterprise world. There are lots of issues that are discussed here. For instance, communication and entrepreneurship skills, as well as financial accountability and management skills are expounded on immensely.

5. Updating Current Strategy by Seminars and Workshops: The various governing authorities across the universe have ensured that these strategies are enacted and achieved through various support options by offering financial and moral support. They have also organized a series of seminars and workshops for the business personalities to sharpen their skills, expertise, and knowledge. All these factors are vital for any business.

6. Promoting Enterprise: Technological measures have been handy in promoting enterprising. The use of state of the art technologies in conducting business has brought about fast, cheap, and increased productivity. It is one measure that has boosted operations such as the communication and management of data. Other activities that have been enhanced by technology are financial accounting and auditing.

7. Role and Functions of Manager: Proper management techniques are also part and parcel of these strategies. Management is one of the determinants of the success of any business organization. When companies are managed poorly, no matter their potential, they are destined for success. The managers are supposed to do various roles ranging from regulating, planning, coordinating, directing and organizing the resources of the organizations.

8. Expansion and growth of industries: These business strategies have done a commendable job in ensuring the success of many organizations. Those parties that have enacted realizable objectives have achieved them through hard work and dedication. They have promoted the general growth and expansion of the industry within which they operate.

2.11. INTRODUCTION AND CONCEPTUAL FRAMEWORK OF STRATEGIC MANAGEMENT

Strategic management can also be defined as a bundle of decisions and acts which a manager undertakes and which decides the result of the firm's performance. The manager must have a thorough knowledge and analysis of the general and competitive organizational environment so as to take right decisions. They should conduct a SWOT Analysis (Strengths, Weaknesses, Opportunities, and Threats), i.e., they should make best possible utilization of strengths, minimize the organizational weaknesses, make use of arising opportunities from the business environment and shouldn't ignore the threats. Strategic Management is a way in which strategists set the objectives and proceed about attaining them. It deals with making and implementing decisions about future direction of an organization. It helps us to identify the direction in which an organization is moving. It is applicable to both small as well as large organizations as even the smallest organization face competition and, by formulating and implementing appropriate strategies, they can attain sustainable competitive advantage. Strategic Management is all about identification and description of the strategies that managers can carry so as to achieve better performance and a competitive advantage for their organization. An organization is said to have competitive advantage if its profitability is higher than the average profitability for all companies in its industry.

Strategic management is a continuous process that evaluates and controls the business and the industries in which an organization is involved; evaluates its competitors and sets goals and strategies to meet all existing and potential competitors; and then reevaluates strategies on a regular basis to determine how it has been implemented and whether it was successful or does it needs replacement.

Brinkerhoff (1991 and 1994) characterizes strategic management as looking out, looking in, and looking ahead. "Looking out" means exploring beyond the boundaries of your organization to set feasible objectives, identify key stakeholders, and build constituencies for change. "Looking in" implies critically assessing and strengthening your systems and structures for managing personnel, finances, and other essential resources. Finally, "looking ahead" entails melding your strategy with structures and resources to reach your policy goals, while monitoring your progress and adjusting your approach as needed. Strategic management comprises five key facets: goal-setting, analysis, strategy formation, strategy implementation, and strategy monitoring. These are the integral elements that, when applied together, distinguish strategic management from less comprehensive approaches, such as operational management or long-term planning. Strategic management is an iterative, continuous process that involves important interactions and feedback among the five key facets, which are explained in more detail in Figure 2.3.

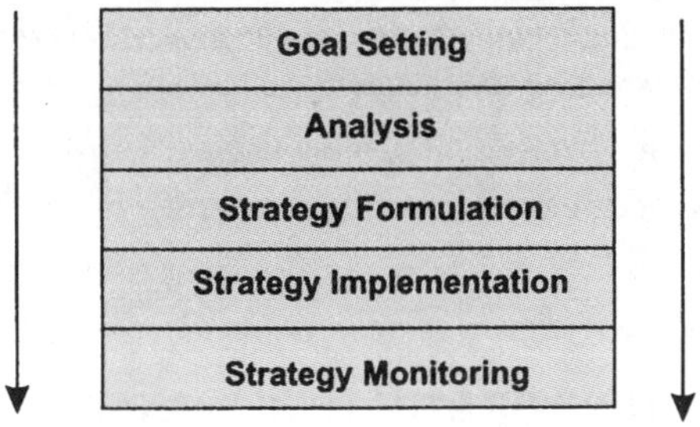

Figure 2.3. Five Facets of Strategic Management.

As mentioned, you can use strategic management to help move health sector reforms through the various stages in the policy process. The framework of the policy stages can help you determine your location in the policy process and identify tasks to be done. By applying a strategic management approach to each subsequent stage of the policy process, you can further implementation of health sector reforms. Consider each stage of the policy cycle from a strategic perspective, balancing the looking-out, looking-in, and looking-ahead issues. In so doing, you can effectively integrate a strategic management approach into the policy cycle.

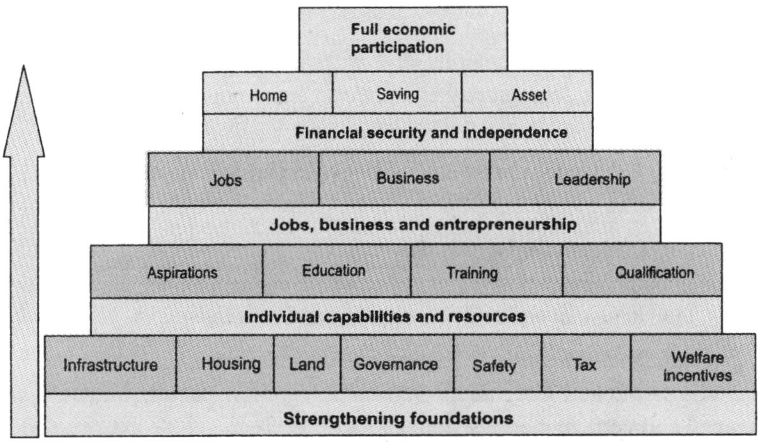

Figure 2.4. Key Areas in Developing a Strategy.

2.12. MEANING AND DEFINITION OF STRATEGIC MANAGEMENT

Strategic management consists of the analysis, decisions, and actions an organization undertakes in order to create and sustain competitive advantages. This definition captures two main elements that go to the heart of the field of strategic management.

In other words, **Strategic Management** is a field that deals with the major intended and emergent initiatives taken by general managers on behalf of owners, involving utilization of resources, to enhance the performance of firms in their external environments. It entails specifying the organization's mission, vision and objectives, developing policies and plans, often in terms of projects and programs, which are designed to achieve these objectives, and then allocating resources to implement the policies and plans, projects and programs.

In short, Strategic management can be used to determine mission, vision, values, goals, objectives, roles and responsibilities, timelines, etc.

Lloyd L. Byars - *"Strategic management is concern with making decisions about organizations future direction and implementing those decisions".*

According to Glueck - *"Strategic management is a stream of decisions and actions, which leads to the development of an effective strategy or strategies to help achieve corporate objectives".*

Pearce and Robinson - *"It is the set of decisions and actions resulting in formulation and implementation of strategies designed to achieve the objectives of an organization"*

2.13. SCOPE AND FUTURE OF STRATEGIC MANAGEMENT

1. **Subject Matter of Management**
   Strategic management includes strategy, concepts, characteristics, functions, and types of business policy.
2. **Strategy and Business Policy**
   It includes strategy, concepts characteristics, functions, and types of business policy.
3. **Strategic Management Overview**
   In includes strategic management nature and scope, characteristics, process, components, limitations.
4. **Strategic Environment**
   In includes micro, macro internal and external environment political, social, cultural, technological, legal, demography and demand and competitive environment.
5. **Types of Strategy**
   It includes grand strategy, stability strategy, expansion strategy, retrenchment, strategy, combination strategy.
6. **Value Chain Concept and Analysis**
   It includes organizational analysis, process of organizational analysis, company profile analysis, industry analysis, strategic analysis and choice.
7. **Integration, Diversification, Mergers and Acquisitions**
   It includes horizontal integration, vertical integration; factors influence diversifications, horizontal and vertical mergers strategy.
8. **Strategy Change Management**
   It includes strategy change power and conflict.
9. **Implementation and Control**
   It includes corporate culture, leadership, and culture guiding and evaluating strategy.
10. **Current Issues of Strategic Management**
    It includes strategic audit and managing technology.

2.14. BENEFITS OF STRATEGIC MANAGEMENT

1. **Strategic decisions are futuristic**

Strategies are essentially for the future. Strategic decisions are taken based on forecast are turn based on available data on trends. The managers involved in strategic planning concentrate on developing projections that would take the company to better strategic position.

2. **Strategies have multi- functional and multi- business effects**

Every company has several business units. Strategic decisions are coordinate in nature among all the business units of company.

3. Strategies are defined based on study on environment

The firms have to define their strategies position with regard to the environment and decide strategies that will take it to the desired positions. The firms are part of the system, where customers, stake holders, competitors, etc.

4. Allocation of resources and improve co-ordination

Strategic planning ensures a rational allocation of resources and improves co-ordination between various divisions of the organizations. It helps managers to think and anticipate problem before occur.

5. Clarity in direction of activities

Strategies focus on direction of activities by specifying what activities are to be undertaken for achieving organizational goal. They make the organizational objective more clear and specific.

6. Increase the organizational effectiveness

Strategies ensure organizational effectiveness in several ways. The concept of effectiveness is that the organization is able to achieve its objectives within the given resources.

7. Sets the strategic direction to the firm

Strategic management process clearly defines what is the desired level of performance (mission/goals/objectives) and it sets the direction so that everyone in the organization knows where they are heading towards. Strategic management act as a road map to everyone in the organization and it clearly defines the way to get to the final destination/desired level of performance.

8. Focus on critical factors of the organization

Strategic management identifies the critical factors that are strategically important to the organization. When critical factors are identifies company can analyze and take relevant measures to ensure satisfactory performance in those areas.

9. Understanding the changing environment

Strategic management predicts the future changes that can take place. Predicting future changes that can take place will help the organization to be proactive and take necessary steps to manage change with contingency planning and change management strategies.

10. Obtaining sustainable competitive advantage

This is the most important and the most critical benefit of strategic planning. By a successful strategic management process company should be able to build a competitive advantage over other competitors which can be sustained overtime without being imitated or outperformed by its competitors. Strategic management identifies the competitive advantages that can be generated through strengths of the organization and take necessary steps to effectively obtain it.

11. Lead to better performance

The successful strategic management should ensure that the company performs very well and generates profits for its owners. When the competitive advantage is built company can thrive on that to make profits and record good performance.

12. Ensure the long term survival in the market place

Strategic management identifies opportunities and threat that influence the organizational performance. It makes use of opportunities and minimizes threat to make sure that company can survive in the market by outperforming its rivals.

13. Simplifies complex scenarios and develop suitable strategies

Current business world is too complex, volatile and dynamic. A firm without strategic management finds it hard to interpret the complexities faced by the organization. In contrast firm with strategic management makes the business complexities simple, predict future dynamics and take proactive steps to minimize threats and make use of opportunities.

14. According to Gordon Greenley, strategic management offers the following benefits:

1. It allows for identification, prioritization and exploitation of opportunities.
2. It provides objective view of management problems
3. It provides a framework for improved coordination and control of activities.
4. It minimizes the effects of adverse conditions and changes
5. It allows decision making to support established objectives
6. It allows more effective allocation of time and resources to identified opportunities.
7. It allows fewer resources and less time to be devoted to correcting erroneous and ad hoc decisions
8. It creates a framework for internal communication among personnel.
9. It helps integrate the behavior of individuals into a total effort
10. It provides a basis for clarifying individual responsibilities.
11. It encourages forward thinking
12. It provides a cooperative, integrated enthusiastic approach to tackling problems and opportunities
13. It encourages a favourable attitude towards change
14. It gives a degree of discipline and formality to the management of a business

2.15. LIMITATIONS OF STRATEGIC MANAGEMENT

1. Lack of Accuracy

The strategic management system is based on forecasting future events which are uncertain and hazy. Plans are founded on various assumptions and parameters.

2. Danger of Rigidity

In many instances managers particularly lower-level managers regard budget estimates as the rigid dictates of policy and business operations are performed according to the original estimates.

3. Internal Resistance

Mere preparation of plans does not serve the purpose unless the management at all levels feels the responsibility for effectuating the targets set out on plan.

4. Costly Exercise

A comprehensive strategic planning exercise calls for considerable time, money and effort for special research studies and information pertaining to the economic, social, political, technological and competitive aspects of the business environment and their likely effects on the future of the enterprise.

5. Complex and Dynamic Environment

The strategic management is essential to overcome the problems posed by complex and dynamic environment. However this becomes a serious limitation on effective strategic management.

6. Limitations in Implementation

There are various problems in implementing a strategy. Through this aspect will be at a greater length, here it is sufficient to say that many organizational problems cannot be solved by strategic management alone but to require the use of other aspects of management.

2.16. IMPORTANCE OF STRATEGIC MANAGEMENT

A well-formulated strategy can bring various benefits to the organization in present as well as in future.

1. Strategic management takes into account the future and anticipates for it.

2. A strategy is made on rational and logical manner, thus its efficiency and its success are ensured.

3. Strategic management reduces frustration because it has been planned in such a way that it follows a procedure.

4. It brings growth in the organization because it seeks opportunities.

5. With strategic management organizations can avoid helter & skelter and they can work directionally.

6. Strategic management also adds to the reputation of the organization because of consistency that results from organizations success.

7. Often companies draw to a close because of lack of proper strategy to run it. With strategic management companies can foresee the events in future and that's why they can remain stable in the market.

8. Strategic management looks at the threats present in the external environment and thus companies can either work to get rid of them or else neutralizes the threats in such a way that they become an opportunity for their success.

9. Strategic management focuses on proactive approach which enables organization to grasp every opportunity that is available in the market.

2.17. FIVE FACETS OF STRATEGIC MANAGEMENT

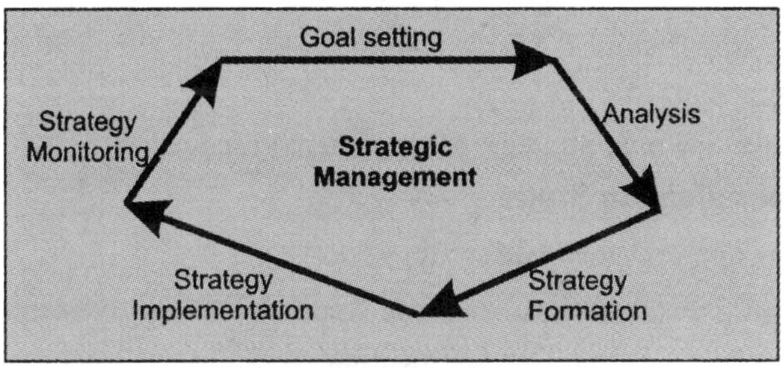

Figure 2.5. Five Facets.

1. **Goal Setting**
   - Enables you to articulate your vision.
   - Identify what are the needs to be accomplished.
   - Define short-and long- term objective and relate them to the organization goal.
2. **Analysis**
   - Guides you to collect and consider information so that the situation is understood completely.
   - Assess the external environment and internal situations in order to identify the strength and weakness of the organization and also to identify the opportunities that are faced to reach the goals.

3. Strategy Formation

- To determine a strategy that reflects, prioritize, develop option to make decisions.
- Review the results of the analysis and identify the issues that is to be addressed while implementation.
- Prioritize them in terms of urgency and magnitude.
- Use these results to design alternative strategies and plans that address the key strategy.

4. Strategy Implementation

- Assemble the necessary resources and apply them.
- Choose the plan to be practiced and marshal the resources and commitments for moving ahead
- Build new capacities or tap the capacities to reach the result.

5. Strategy Monitoring

- Check the progress towards achieving the goals and assess whether any changes in the environment necessitates alteration to the strategy.
- Modify plans and actions to adjust to the changes in the operating environment.
- Monitoring will reflect in the feedback of analysis, strategy design and implementation in the immediate term and goal-setting over longer term.

2.18. EVOLUTION OF STRATEGIC MANAGEMENT IN INDIA

Till 1980 Pre–Liberalisation Stage

- Strategic management on Government fringes.
- Entwining enterprise objectives into the national Planning framework.
- Grabbing opportunities, high diversification, non- competitive scales, and weak technology.
- Secretive & one man Strategic Management Process.

1980–2000: Liberalisation Stage

- 'Foreign Complex' governed strategy.
- Strategy of focus on rationalisation and operations improvement.
- Strategy of growth through acquisitions, internationalisation and product market expansion.
- Employing international consulting firms in Strategic Management.

2000 Onwards: Post Liberalisation Stage

- 'Global maverick' mindset & Acquire professional skills in Strategic Management and synergise entrepreneurial flair.
- Portfolio rationalisation, entry into emerging sectors.
- Mobilise resources and ensure adequate growth through existing business.
- De-merge businesses as independent companies and improve market capabilities.
- Development of Technology capabilities
- Decentralise organisations, develop institutionalised control mechanism.

Table 2.1 Other Contrary Opinions of Evolutions of Strategic Management in India.

Period	1950's	1960's	1970's	1980's	1990's	After 2000's
Dominant theme	Budgeting planning & control	Long term planning & Environment Scanning	Environment Scanning & Strategic Planning	Strategic Planning System Approach	The quest for competitive Advantage	Strategic Innovations
Main Issues	Financial Control through annual budgets	Financial control through medium term projections	Portfolio Planning	Positioning approach with focus on value chain analysis	Competitve advantage, Benchmarking & Resource based Approach	Conscept of strategic & organizational advantage
Principal Concepts & Techniques	Budgetinginvestment planning & Project proposal	Forecasting Investment Planning Models	Portfolio Planning, Experience Curves	Organizational synergy, industry structure & competitor analysis	Resource Analysis & . analysis of Core Competencies	Dynamic Source of Competitive advantage, Knowledge & learning.
Organizational Implications	Strategic planning Structures, functional designs	Strategic plannin structures, Multidivional organizations	Financial control organization, e.g. SBU portfolio Restructuring	Strategic control organizational structures. eg. Matrix Horizontal	Structures & IT controls	Virrual organization Alliances and Networks & knowledge nased firms

2.19. NATURE AND CHARACTERISTICS OF STRATEGIC MANAGEMENT

1. Basic Financial Planning (Budgeting)

James McKinsey (1889-1937), founder of the global management consultancy that bears his name, was a professor of cost accounting at the school of business at the University of Chicago. Early efforts in corporate strategy were generally limited to the development of a budget, with managers realizing that there was a need to plan the allocation of funds. Later, in the first half of the 1900s, business managers expanded the budgeting process into the future. Budgeting and strategic changes (such as entering a new market) were synthesized into the extended budgeting process, so that the budget supported the strategic objectives of the firm. With the exception of the Great Depression, the competitive environment at this time was fairly stable and predictable.

2. Long-Range Planning (Extrapolation)

Long-range Planning was simply an extension of one year financial planning into five-year budgets and detailed operating plans. It involved little or no consideration of social or political factors, assuming that markets would be relatively stable. Gradually, it developed to encompass issues of growth and diversification. In the 1960s, George Steiner did much to focus business manager's attention on strategic planning, bringing the issue of long-range planning to the forefront. He gathered information about how different companies were using long-range plans in order to allocate resources and to plan for growth and diversification. A number of other linear approaches also developed in the same time period, including "game theory". Another development was "operations research", an approach that focused upon the manipulation of models containing multiple variables. Both have made a contribution to the field of strategy.

3. The Problem with Strategic Planning (Analysis)

The fuel for the modern growth in interest in all things strategic has been analysis. While analysis has been the watchword, data has been the password. Managers have assumed that anything which could not be analyzed could not be managed. The belief in analysis is part of a search for a logical commercial regime, a system of management which will, under any circumstances, produce a successful result. Indeed, all the analysis in the world can lead to decisions which are plainly wrong. IBM had all the data about its markets, yet reached the wrong conclusions.

4. Complex Systems Strategy

Complexity-based approaches or "complex adaptive systems," were developed in response to the apparent failure of equilibrium-based approaches. Complexity-based thinkers will fall into a number of different camps. The majority believe that the environment must be understood in terms of its complexity, chaos, and ecological constructs. This group subscribes to the Darwinian hypotheses (upward evolution of a system) as a metaphor for the business environment. This kind of thinking has resulted in the idea of "self-organizing" companies. The complexity group falls into two categories. One might be called a "pure" complexity-based group, the other a "hybrid". In the case of the former, theorists generally apply the concept of emergence to every situation. According to this group predictive modeling is rendered useless by the chaotic nature of the environment. They would suggest that any attempt to plan for the future is pointless.

5. Concerned with scope of the organization

Strategic management is concerned with the scope of an organization's activities. For example, should an organization concentrate on one area of activity or should it have many. This includes important decisions about product range or geographical coverage and is concerned with the organization's boundaries.

6. "Matching" Resources with the environment

Strategic management is concerned with matching the resources and activities of an organization to the environment in which it operates. This is often referred to as "strategic fit". The notion of strategic fit is developing strategy by identifying opportunities in the business environment and adapting resources and competencies to take advantage of those opportunities. Such a strategic fit is important to achieve the correct positioning of the firm to meet clearly identified market needs.

7. Influenced by Stakeholders

The strategic decisions of an organization are not only influenced by environmental forces and resource availability, but also by the values and expectations of the stakeholders of the organization.

8. Affect Operational Decisions

Strategic management affects operational decisions because it is at the operational level that real strategic advantage can be achieved. If the operational aspects of the organization are not in line with the strategy, then, no matter how well conceived the strategy is, it will not succeed.

9. Integrating Intuition and Analysis

In a sense, strategic management process integrates intuition and analysis. Intuition means inner voice or a gut feeling. Intuition is essential for making decisions in situations of great uncertainty or little precedents. But in most situations, an objective, logical, systematic approach for making major decisions in an organization is required, which is provided by "strategic analysis". Analytical thinking and intuitive thinking complement each other in strategic management.

2.20. STRATEGIC MANAGEMENT PROCESS

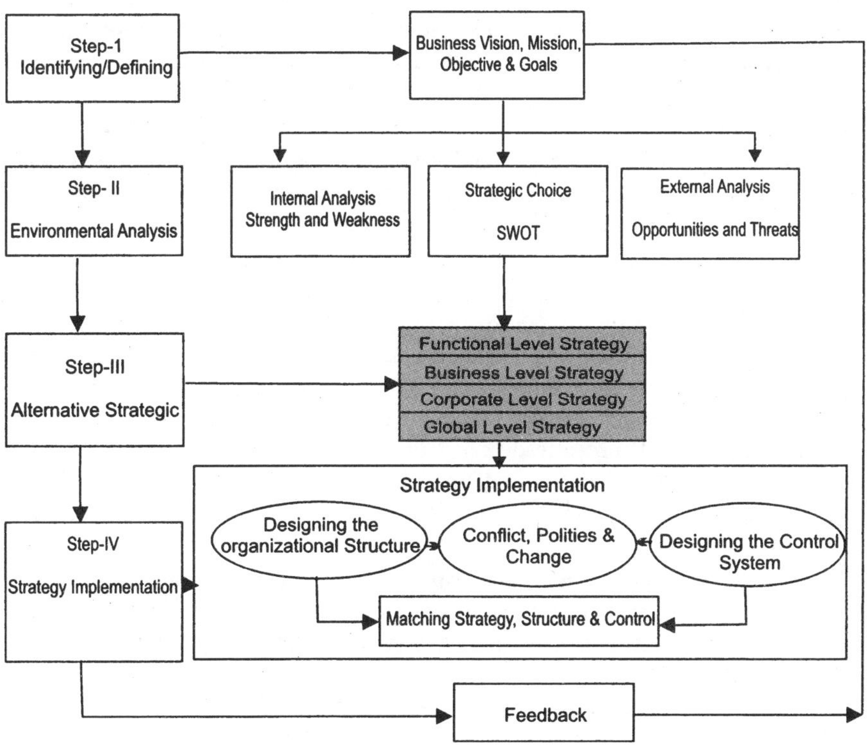

Figure 2.6. Strategic Management Process.

Dynamic in nature, the strategic management process is the full set of commitments, decisions and actions needed for a firm to achieve strategic competitiveness and earn above average returns. The process of strategic management is depicted through a model which consists of different phases; each phase having a number of elements.

Step 1 : Identifying/Defining Business Mission, Purpose and Objectives: It is the logical starting point as they lay foundation for strategic management. Every organization has a mission, purpose and objectives, even if these elements are not consciously designed, written and communicated. These elements relate the organization with the society and states that it has to achieve for itself and to the society.

Mission and Goals: Defining the mission and goals of the organization is the first step in strategy management process. The mission tells clearly why the organization exists and what it would be doing. Organizations set goals, which they hope to achieve in the medium to long-term basis. Normally organizations work with a hierarchy of goals such as sizeable market share, maximizing shareholders wealth, profit and so on.

Step 2: Environmental Analysis: Environmental factors – both internal environment and external environment – are analyzed to

- Identify changes in the environment
- Identify the present and future threats and opportunities and
- Assess critically its own strengths and weaknesses.

Organizational environment encompasses all factors both inside and outside the organization that can influence the organization positively and negatively. Environment factors may help in building a sustainable competitive advantage.

External Analysis: It aims to understand the opportunities and threats in the environment. In this stage examination of three environments normally takes place, the Industry Environment in which the organization operates, the National Environment and the Macro Environment forces such as social, economical, government and legal, International and technological factors, which affect the organization. The competitive structure of the industry, competing firms and the competitive position are analyzed during this phase.

Internal Analysis: Identifying strengths and weakness of the organization involves identification of quantity and quality of resources and distinctive competencies that help in building competitive advantage to achieve superior efficiency, quality, innovation and customer loyalty.

Step 3: Strategic Alternatives and Choice: Strategic choice involves generating a series of alternatives in the light of internal strengths and weaknesses and external opportunities and threats, which is known as SWOT analysis. The purpose of strategic choice is to build organization's strength, to exploit the opportunities and set right weaknesses and to minimize threat. Finally, strategies are evolved at functional level, business level, corporate level and global level. Functional Strategies are directed to improve the effectiveness of functional operations of the firm such as manufacturing, finance, R&D, marketing and human resources. Corporate level strategies enable organizations to maximize the long run profitability of the organization. Vertical integration (Backward and forward integration), Diversification, Strategic alliances, Acquisitions and Joint ventures are examples of corporate level strategies.

Step 4: Strategy Implementation: The fifth step of strategic management process is the implementation of strategy. The logically developed strategy is to be put into action. The organization cannot reap the benefits of strategic management, unless the strategy is effectively implemented. It consists of four steps are as follows.

- Designing the appropriate organizational structure.
- Designing the control systems.
- Matching strategy, structure and controls and
- Managing conflicts, politics and change.

Structure: Structure involves allocation of duties, responsibilities and decision making authority and integration among the ranks and files of organization. It is widely believed that structure follows strategy. Some of the options available in this regard are tall structure, flat structure centralized decision making authority, decentralized decision making authority, autonomous units and semi autonomous units and different mechanisms for integration of sub units.

Control: The purpose of strategic control is to determine whether the given strategy is effective in achieving organizational objective and moving on the right track. The organizational control may be classified as market control, output control and bureaucratic control. The control system requires development of perceptible organizational culture. Besides, the type of reward and incentive systems also needs to be decided and established towards this end.

Matching Strategy, Structure and Control: In successful organizations a fit among strategy, structure and controls is observed. Different strategies and environments call for different structures and control systems. Cost leadership strategy warrants a simple organization, which lays emphasis on efficiency whereas differentiation strategy revolves around R&D and technical creativity. A fit among strategy, structure and control is essential to ensure success of organizations.

Matching Conflicts, Politics and Change: Conflict is common in organizations. The reasons for conflicts are resource sharing and different agendas of different subgroups within the organizations. Power struggles and coalition building are consequences of such conflicts. The organizational politics plays a key role in strategy implementation. The power and conflict will cause organizational inertia and prevent organizational change. Power, Politics, Conflict and inertia should be analyzed and managed effectively so that mission could be fulfilled and change could be introduced smoothly.

Feedback: Strategic Management is an ongoing process. Periodic feedback reveals whether objectives are attainable or implementation is poor or not. The feedback is fed into next round of strategic formulation and implementation. It may reaffirm objectives or suggest changes in goals and objectives.

2.21. STRATEGIC MANAGEMENT PRACTICE IN INDIA (OR) STRATEGIES OF LEADING INDIAN COMPANIES

1. Going Global Crompton Greaves Way (B): International Expansion Strategy

In 2005, Crompton Greaves exported to at least 60 countries. More than half the company's exports were derived from the developed world, including G7 countries. Its power transformer package accounted for more than half of India's exports. In this segment, the company became a preferred supplier in many countries. The company's ceiling fans were uniquely the only Indian ceiling fans sold in West Europe, Australia and North America. For a number of years, Crompton Greaves viewed itself as a domestic company, which understandably translated to a predominant commitment of its resources to the Indian market. With changing priorities over the last few years, the company had progressively positioned itself as an international company with a greater allocation of its corporate attention to the global markets. This change was not only advisable for the sake of visibility, but absolutely necessary for long-term sustainability, considering the marginal and even flat growth within certain market segments within India. In today's environment, the customer looked for a 'Solutions Company,' not just a 'Products Company,' which could offer products and services. To enhance all the products and services in its portfolio, could Crompton Greaves leverage on the Pauwels facilities and network and emerge as a 'Solutions Company'? The 'Pauwels' brand, which enjoyed an enviable reputation worldwide, would certainly be a competitive advantage.

2. Coca Cola India

On August 5, 2003, The Center for Science and Environment, an NGO in India, attacked the safety of Coca-Cola India's products in a press release titled "Twelve Major Drink Brands sold in and around Delhi Contain a Deadly Cocktail of Pesticide Residues." Though Coke was well within the Indian government's legal limits for pesticide residue in beverages, the country's standards were weak and full of loopholes, making them meaningless. Coke India CEO Sanjiv Gupta had to decide on the most effective communication strategy to restore public trust and had to weigh a larger policy decision at the same time: Should Coke take on a leadership role and help create higher standards for food and beverage safety?

3. Southwest Airlines

Southwest Airlines has consistently been successful in terms of profitability, good employee and union relations, and customer satisfaction at a time when most airline carriers are struggling in all these areas. Central to the company's success is a culture of flexibility, family-orientation, and fun. (This case is one of seven that are examined in the article, "Rebuilding the Social Contract at Work: Lessons from Leading Cases," by Thomas Kochan (1999). The article can be found in References on this site. The article contains footnotes and references not included in this version of the case.) While 90% of its employees are unionized, labor relations have been remarkably positive, especially by industry standards. There are no formal structures for labor or union participation in management decision making, but the company led by top managers who actively solicit and respond to employee views has taken the lead on developing and maintaining this culture. One critical cornerstone of the company's success in a fairly unstable industry (since deregulation in the 1980s) is the fact that the unions are not interested in pushing their roles beyond the traditional collective bargaining and grievance functions they perform. In this regard, Southwest differs from some other well-known cases of Human Resource-based and customer-oriented success stories.

4. Toyota Recalls

In the fall of 2009, Toyota Motor Corporation, once revered for its commitment to quality and reliability, faced a highly publicized series of recalls in the United States representing approximately a year's worth of sales in one of its most important markets. While the first Toyota recall was met with widespread disbelief but continuing support for the brand, subsequent revelations and recalls tested the brand's resilience in the U.S. The firm's initial public response to the problems - a mixture of silence from top executives and vague, misleading public statements - frustrated U.S. government officials and the public. Not until weeks after the news first broke did Toyota organize a clear message around its commitment to return to quality. In late February 2010 Toyota President Akio Toyoda reluctantly accepts an invitation to testify to the U.S. Congress, 148 days after the first recall announcement. He has to decide what to say.

5. Foxconn Technology Group

The case describes the challenges that Foxconn faced after a series of suicides took place at its plants. The response of Foxconn's management is presented and the associated implications for Foxconn's stock price are discussed. The case objective is to discuss the relationships between human capital morale and engagement, firm profitability, capital market pressures, and supply chain responsibility.

6. Delhi Metro Rail Corporation

In 2009, the Delhi Metro Rail Corporation, the organization tasked with building a Mass Transit System for India's capital city Delhi, witnessed the biggest crisis in its history. A bridge under construction collapsed killing six people and injuring 15 more. Despite its history of meeting deadlines and working with allocated costs, the Corporation came under a lot of public censure. There was immense pressure on the Corporation to suspend its engineers and fire the construction contractor. On the other hand, it had to meet the deadline of operationalizing the second phase of the Metro Network by October 2010 in time for the the XIXth Commonwealth Games. The case focuses on the challenges that the Managing Director Dr. E. Sreedharan faced as the crisis unfolded. It examines the Corporation's unique structure and management ethic that had so far enabled it to function within timeline and costs.

7. The Promise and Perils of Globalization: The Case of Nike

This case study of Nike Inc. traces the evolution of Nike's policies and practices vis-à-vis labor and environmental standards. The case illustrates the company's evolving definition and commitment to good corporate citizenship and the continuing controversy surrounding the company's practices in this arena. The issues raised by Nike's practices, and the dilemmas it faces, are by no means unique to this company. The issues are common to all companies engaging in international business. As a result, this case concludes by examining the more general questions that globalization poses for companies seeking to balance both corporate citizenship and corporate performance in today's highly volatile market.

2.22. STRATEGIC ISSUES IN MANAGING TECHNOLOGY AND INNOVATION

1. The Role of Management: Due to increased competition and accelerated product development cycles, innovation and the management of technology is becoming crucial to corporate success. The importance of technology and innovation must be emphasized by people at the very top and reinforced by people throughout the corporation. Management has an obligation to not only encourage new product development, but also to develop a system to ensure that technology is being used most effectively with the consumer in mind.

2. External Scanning: Corporations need to continually scan their external societal and task environments for new developments in technology that may have some application to their current or potential products, Stakeholders, especially customers, can be important participant in the new product development process.

a. **Technological Developments:** Focusing one's scanning efforts too closely on one's own industry is dangerous. Most new developments that threaten existing business practices and technologies do not come from existing competitors or even from within traditional industries. A new technology that can substitute for an existing technology at a lower cost and provide higher quality can change the very basis for competition in an industry.

b. **Impact of Stakeholders on Innovation:** A company should look to its stakeholders, especially its customers, suppliers, and distributors, for sources product and service improvements. These groups of people have the most to gain from innovative new products or services. Under certain circumstances, they may propose new directions for product development. Some of the methods of gathering information from key stakeholders are using lead users, market research, and new product experimentation.

c. **Lead Users:** Companies should look to lead users for help in product development, especially in high technology industries where things move so quickly that a product is becoming obsolete by the time it arrives on the market. These lead users are "companies, organizations, or individuals that are well ahead of market trends and have needs that go far beyond those of the average user. They are the first to adopt a product because they benefit significantly from its use-even if it is not fully developed.

d. **Market Research:** A more traditional method of obtaining new product ideas is to use market research to survey current users regarding what they would like in a new product. This method has been successfully used by companies such as Procter & Gamble to identify consumer preferences. It is especially useful in directing incremental improvements to existing products.

e. **New Product Experimentation:** Instead of using lead users or market research to test the potential of innovative products, by "probing" potential markets with early versions of the products, learning from the probes, and probing again.

3. Internal Scanning: In addition to scanning the external environment, strategists should also assess their company's ability to innovate effectively by asking the following questions:-

- Has the company developed the resources needed to try new ideas?
- Do the managers allow experimentation with new products or services?
- Does the corporation encourage risk taking and tolerate mistakes?
- Are people more concerned with new ideas or with defending their turf?
- Is it easy to form autonomous project teams?

4. Strategy Formulation: Research and development strategy deals not only with the decision to be a leader or a follower in terms of technology and market entry but also with the source of the technology. Should a company develop its own technology or purchase it from others? The strategy also takes into account a company's particular mix of basic versus applied and product versus process R&D. The particular mix should suit the level of industry development and the firm's particular corporate and business strategies. In addition, R&D strategy in a large corporation deals with the proper balance of its product portfolio based on the life cycle of the products.

5. Organizing for Innovation-Corporate Entrepreneurship: Corporate entrepreneurship (also called entrepreneurship) is defined by Guth and Ginsburg as "the birth of new business within existing organizations, that is, internal innovation or venturing; and the transformation of organizations through renewal of the key ideas on which they are built, that is, strategic renewal. A large corporation that wants to encourage innovation and creativity within its firm must choose a structure that will give the new business unit an appropriate amount of freedom while maintaining some degree of control at headquarters.

Operational Relatedness	Very Important	Uncertain	Not Important
Unrelated	3 Special Business Units	6 Independent Business Units	9 Complete Spin-off
Party Related	2 New Product Business Department	5 New Venue Division	8 Contracting
Strongly Related	1 Direct Integration	4 Micro Ventures Department	7 Nurturing and Contracting

Figure 2.7. Designs for Corporate Entrepreneurship.

2.23. STRATEGIES FOR INTERNET ECONOMY

Introduction

The internet economy refers to conducting business through markets whose infrastructure is based on the internet and world-wide web. An internet economy differs frcm a traditional economy in a number of ways, including: communication, market segmentation, distribution costs and price. The internet is changing the nature and competition in every industry.

Definition

According to David yoffie: "competing in the internet age is more than just a matter of having to do everything faster".

1. Impact of the Internet and E-Commerce

- Impact on external industry environment
- Changes character of the market and competitive environment
- Creates new driving forces and key success factors

- Breeds formation of new strategic groups

2. **Impact on Internal Company Environment**
   - Having, or not having, e-commerce capabilities tilts the scales toward valuable resource strengths or threatening weaknesses
   - Creatively reconfiguring the value chain will affect a firm's competitiveness vis-à-vis rivals

2.23.1 Characteristics of Internet Market Structure

1. **Internet is composed of**
   - Integrated network of users' connected computers
   - Banks of servers and high-speed computers
   - Digital switches and routers
   - Telecommunications equipment and lines
2. **Supply Side of the Internet Economy**

   Major groups of Internet and e-commerce firms comprising the supply side include-
   - Makers of specialized communications components and equipment
   - Providers of communications services
   - Suppliers of computer components and hardware
   - Developers of specialized software
   - E-commerce enterprises
   - Business-to-business merchants
   - Business-to-consumer merchants
   - Media companies
   - Content providers
3. **Strategy-Shaping Characteristics of the E-Commerce Environment**
   - Internet makes it feasible for companies everywhere to compete in global markets Competition in an industry is greatly intensified by new e-commerce strategic initiatives of existing rivals and by entry of new, enterprising e-commerce rivals Entry barriers into e-commerce world are relatively low On-line buyers gain bargaining power.
   - Internet makes it feasible for firms to reach beyond their borders to find the best suppliers and, further, to collaborate closely with them to achieve efficiency gains and cost-savings.
   - Internet and PC technologies are advancing rapidly, often in uncertain and unexpected directions.
   - Internet results in much faster diffusion of new technology and new ideas across the world
   - E-commerce environment demands that firms move swiftly - "at Internet speed"
   - Internet and e-commerce technology open up a host of opportunities for reconfiguring industry and company value chains.
   - Internet can be an economical means of delivering customer service.
   - Capital for funding potentially profitable e-commerce businesses is readily available
   - Needed e-commerce resource in short supply is human talent, in the form of both technological expertise and managerial know-how

4. Effects of the Internet and E-Commerce

- Can produce important shifts in an industry's competitive forces
- Alters industry value chains, spawning substantial opportunities for increasing efficiency and reducing costs
- Affects a company's resource strengths and weaknesses
- Rapid pace of technological change with an often uncertain direction

2.23.2 Strategies Guidelines for Internet Economy

1. Develop an E- Business Strategy

The first step to competing in the digital economy is to develop an e-business strategy. The strategy that is developed must define how an organization will use the internet to create and maintain competitive advantage over its competition. Th strategy development process includes all stakeholders. The information that is used to develop the strategy must be of ig quality and represent the operational, functional and behavioral side of organization.

2. Hire and Develop Capable Staff

Hiring and developing capable staff will require that organizational redefine and expand the knowledge requirements of the staff and redefine the power structure and decisions making process within organization.

3. Build the Knowledge Management System

Knowledge Management has been around for sometime. In the digital economy it is more important because it can represent the difference between being a market-leader. Knowledge management system must consider, monitor. Aggregate and analyze only that information that is critical success of enterprise.

4. Focus on Being a Market Leader in Process Innovation

Innovation does not have to be a new product. It can be a new way of performing a task or interfacing with customers. The effort of focusing on process innovation is important because it targets resources on internal optimization.

2.24. STRATEGIC ISSUES IN NON-PROFIT ORGANIZATIONS

1. Non-Profit Oraganization: An organization that provides some service or good with no intention of earning a profit. It includes private nonprofit corporations (such as hospitals, institutes, private colleges, and organized charities) as well as public governmental units/agencies (such as welfare departments, prisons and state universities)

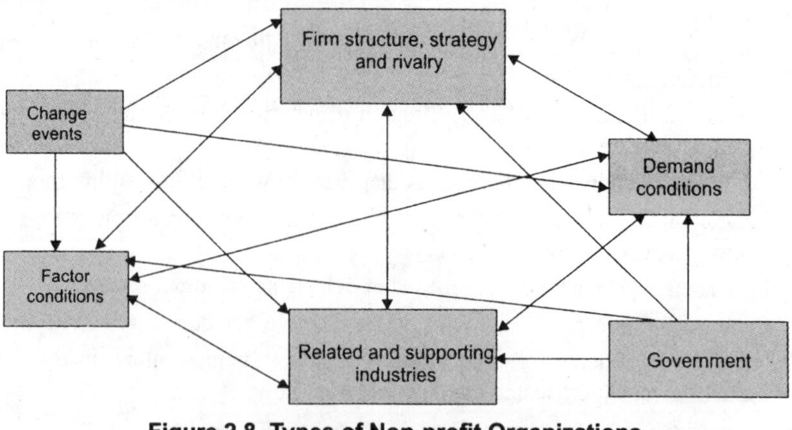

Figure 2.8. Types of Non-profit Organizations.

2. Importance of Revenue Source: NFPs are dependent on dues, assessments or donations for their revenue sources. In NFP organizations there is likely to be a very different sort of relationship between the organizations providing and the person receiving the service. Because the recipient of the service typically does not pay the entire cost of the service, outside sponsors are required.

3. Pattern of Influence on Strategic Decision Making: Pattern of influence is derived from its source of revenues. Those who fund the NFP are likely to have significant influence on its operations

4. Usefulness of Strategic Management and Techniques: Some Strategic Management concepts can be equally applied to business and not for profit organizations whereas others cannot. The concept of competitive advantage is less useful to the typical not-for-profit organizations than the related concept of Institutional advantage. A NFP organization is said to have institutional advantage when it performs its tasks more effectively than other comparable organizations. Portfolio analysis may be more difficult to apply to NFPs. Situation (SWOT) analysis; mission statements, stakeholder analysis, and corporate governance are all relevant to the strategic assessment of NFPs as they are to a profit making organizations. Strategic management is difficult to apply where the output of an NFP is difficult to measure. Thus it is very likely that most of the NFPs have not used strategic management because its concepts, techniques and prescription does not lend themselves to situations where sponsors, rather than the market place determine the value. However the situation is changing nowadays.

5. Impact of Constraints on Strategic Management: Several characteristics peculiar to the not for profit organization constrain its behavior and affects it strategic management. The constraints are as follows:

- Service is often intangible/hard to measure
- Client influence may be weak
- Strong employee commitments to professions
- Resource contributors intrude on internal management
- Restraints on use of rewards and punishments

2.25. STRATEGIES OF INDIAN COMPANIES

1. Samsung—The Making of a Global Brand

In 1998, South Korea's leading consumer electronics major, Samsung Electronics Corporation (Samsung), entered into an agreement with the International Olympic Association to sponsor the 1998 Seoul Olympics. According to company sources, Samsung wanted to sponsor Olympics to establish itself as a global brand. Analysts felt that by associating itself with the Olympics, Samsung would increase its brand visibility and brand recall among its consumers worldwide. They also pointed out that to become the next Sony of the consumer electronics market, Samsung would have to invest heavily in marketing In the late 1990s, Samsung entered into various marketing alliances with companies worldwide and sponsored events to enhance its brand awareness. Due to its marketing efforts, its brand value appreciated by 200% from \$3.1 billion in 1999 to \$8.3 billion in 2002. Consequently, in 2002, Samsung emerged as the only non-Japanese brand from Asia to be listed in the global top 100 brands valued by Inter brand Inc. The company was ranked 34th in Inter brand's list of the world's top 100 brands.

2. BMW's Marketing Strategy in India

In January 2011, the BMW5 Series won the coveted 'Premium Automobile of the Year' award given by CNBC TV-18-Overdrive. This was just one of several awards that the BMW 5 series won in India. On the success of the BMW 5 Series, Dr. Andreas Schaaf, President, BMW India, said, "The new BMW 5 Series has contributed tremendously to the success story of BMW in India and is the largest selling luxury sedan in its segment. The new BMW 5 Series has received extremely positive feedback from the market and has positioned itself as the best business limousine in India". BMW India, a 100% subsidiary of Munich, Germany-based BMW, entered India in 2006 The company established a state-of-the-art assembly plant in Chennai, South India, in January 2007, and its first vehicle in the country, the BMW 5 was launched in June 2007. The company followed an aggressive marketing strategy for the Indian market. It brought in several new products, launched premium dealerships across the country, even in Tier-II and Tier-III cities, and positioned itself as a strong and aspiration brand. BMW went on to become one of the top selling luxury automobiles in India, and in 2009, it surpassed the then market leader Mercedes Benz, selling 3,619 units as against Benz's 3,247. For the second consecutive year, it maintained its position and sold 6,246 units in 2010. In the process, BMW achieved the 'highest sales by a manufacturer in the luxury car segment in a year' in the Indian market.

3. Pricing Strategies of Nestle India Ltd

At what price profitability? This may well be the question that Nestle India Ltd's investors ask the management. In 2012, the company's strategy of focusing on long-term profitable growth has led to slower sales growth, although the profit margins have improved.But nobody would have expected that its sales in the domestic market would rise by a mere 7.6% year-on-year (y-o-y) in the September quarter, a little over half of the 13.7% growth it had achieved in the June quarter.In the first half, Nestle's volumes had risen by 1.1% while sales had risen by 14.2%. In the last quarter, it appears that volumes may well have declined on a y-o-y basis—the company does not give volume growth figures. It did say that net sales growth was affected by portfolio and channel optimization, and by pricing for value. The company has been hiking product prices, and has stopped selling products that do not meet its internal criterion for profitability. While one affects demand, at a time when the economy is slowing, the other creates a high base effect of sales from discontinued products. An improvement in profitability is no doubt desirable, but a steady trend of declining sales growth rates is disconcerting. Its gross profit (sales less input costs) rose by 12.4% during the September quarter; but a sharp increase in employee costs, and other expenses, meant that its operating profit rose by only 8.3%. Otherwise, Nestle may have reported a decline in its profit, instead of the 2.3% growth in net profit that it reported. The firm knows it is treading a tricky path, but is sticking to it. Eventually, the base effect will wane and the reported sales growth and that of continuing products will converge. Till then, the reported numbers are likely to disappoint. On the profitability front, too, there was a surprise. While the company's operating profit margin widened by 9 basis points (bps) to 20.9%, on a sequential basis it declined by 92 bps. That may indicate volatile food inflation will continue to affect performance. One basis point is one-hundredth of a percentage point. Nestle is in the process of turning back the clock from a time when it focused on volume-led sales growth, to one where it is focusing on profitable growth. Its earnings statement mentions that it stands by the "strategy of long term sustainable profitable growth". How this will affect the company's near- to medium-term performance is a question they would like an answer to. Data from Thomson Reuters shows the stock trades at 34 times its 2013 forecasted earnings per share.

4. Lenovo's Persistent PC Strategy in India

For Lenovo (992:HK), the global narrative is close to "Mission Accomplished." The company used to trail far behind market leaders Hewlett-Packard (HPQ) and Dell (DELL), but is now on track to achieve its goal of becoming the world's largest PC vendor. According to Gartner (IT), the Chinese company is already there, having passed HP in the third quarter with a 15.7 percent share of global PC shipments. Rival research firm IDC says there's still a little way to go, with Lenovo and HP neck-and-neck. Once Lenovo does get to the top, what next? Being No.1 in the PC business right now is a bit of a tarnished prize because the PC industry is struggling to withstand the transformation of the electronics industry wrought by Apple's (AAPL) iPad and other tablets, as well as Apple's iPhone and other smartphones. What's a PC company to do? One answer: Look to India and other emerging markets. PCs may seem a slow-growth business in developed markets, but Amar Babu, managing director of Lenovo's India business, says he still sees opportunities in developing countries such as India, whose PC penetration is low. Indians still want to buy computers, says Mumbai-based Babu. Only 8 percent or 9 percent of Indians own PCs, a tiny figure when you consider that the penetration rate in developed countries is about 10 times larger. You might think this would create an opportunity for tablets, with Indian consumers leapfrogging to a more advanced technology and skipping the one in the middle. That's what happened in telecom, with millions of Indians who never had land lines finally getting connected via cell phones. But Babu says that is not going to happen with computers. "The PC is still the choice for first device, not a tablet," he says. That's because a tablet can't match a PC when it comes to creating content, with its larger screen size; a lot of these applications are still used for education, he says. "People still feel comfortable having the PC as their first device." Lenovo is already the top PC vendor in India, with 17.1 percent of the market in the second quarter, according to IDC statistics. HP was well behind, at 13.7 percent. Babu has plans to keep Lenovo on top, despite the growth slowdown in the Indian economy. The PC market in India last year grew at about an 8 percent clip, he says—not bad when compared to the West, but Lenovo and other PC vendors had become accustomed to growth rates between 15 and 25 percent. "There has been an impact of the slowdown," says Babu, "in all segments of the market."

5. Business Strategies for the Indian Cement Industry

Cement is the single most important and profitable product in the building material sector and with the consumption of cement in India to touch 600 million tonnes by the year 2020.-this is truly the California Gold Rush of the new century. With an 8% GDP growth rate, governmental infrastructure augmentation and population expansion, the Indian cement industry is a market of opportunities waiting to be tapped. A direct implication of this sectoral growth is the influx of multinationals like Holcim and Lafarge, which will drive Indian cement companies in the building industry to adapt new business strategies to complement the higher demand and competition. A cogent analytical research on governmental reports, industry data and cement MNC annual reports has been performed. On analysis and scrutiny of the distinct variables involved in this market, this paper investigates the current and future trends in the Indian cement industry and enumerates key business strategies that cement conglomerates will have to adapt to compete in the Indian building materials market.

6. Lupin Limited—India's Leading Pharma Company

The case presents the strategies adopted by Lupin Limited to emerge as one of the leading pharmaceutical companies in India. For the fiscal 2004-05, Lupin reported revenues of Rs. 12.12 billion, placing it among the top six companies in the Indian pharma industry. The company aims at achieving the revenues of US$ 1 billion by 2009. To achieve this target, Lupin has made heavy investments in R&D, manufacturing processes and is focusing on exports. Notwithstanding Lupin's success till date and its plans for future growth, the company faces significant threat in the form of product patents, high debts and rising competition from both local and foreign pharma companies. The case highlights the challenges facing Lupin and its plans to overcome these challenges.

Issues:

- Recent trends in the Indian Pharmaceutical Industry
- Lupin's journey from a drug manufacturer to a national level pharma company
- Growth Strategies of Lupin Limited
- Importance of patents (product and process) in the pharma industry
- Product patent regime in India

7. Vodafone Essar Marketing Strategy

Vodafone Essar plans to sell the low price handsets from its 4 lakhs distribution outlets. The company will buy the low cost cell phones from the firm ZTE that is located in China. The Company ZTE will ship more than 10 million low cost cell phones to India that will then be sold by the company Vodafone Essar. Vodafone Essar Company also has plans to expand in the near future and for this it is planning to take a loan overseas of around US$ 500 million. The company Vodafone Essar Limited will use the money to expand the company's network, better its technology, and open more distribution centers. All these measures will help to increase the customer base of the company Vodafone Essar. Vodafone Essar is one of the topmost companies in the telecom sector in India and is well known for the best quality of products and services offered to its customers. And this is the reason that the customer base of the company Vodafone Essar Limited has been increasing at a very rapid pace. The company is planning to launch low price cell phones in the country and also expand its operations. This is sure to help the company Vodafone Essar to grow and prosper even more in the future.

8. Steel Authority of India Limited (SAIL)

The Steel Authority of India Limited (SAIL) has always been the forerunner in the steel sector and tops the list of steel-making companies in India. They are fully integrated iron and steel maker – where they produce both basic and special steels. These are used for domestic construction, engineering, power, railway, automotive and defence purposes. The main agenda is however to export. SAIL has been ranked amongst the top ten public sector Indian companies in terms of turnover. SAIL has its forte in manufacturing and selling a wide range of steel products. SAIL's wide range of long and flat steel products have high demand in the domestic as well as international market. SAIL carries on its business through the wide network of 37 Branch Sales Offices which are spread across four regions, 25 Departmental Warehouses, 42 Consignment Agents and 27 Customer Contact Offices. There are in all more than 2000 dealers and thus the marketing division of Steel Authority of India Limited is quite strong. This ensures that virtually every district of the country gets quality steel. There is a well-equipped Research and Development Centre for Iron and Steel (RDCIS) at Ranchi of Steel Authority of India Limited. It helps in producing quality steel and also for developing new technologies for the steel industry.

Chapter 3

COMPETITIVE ADVANTAGE AND STRATEGIES

Introduction - Concept, Meaning and Definition of Competitive Advantage - Competetive Advantage of Nation's and its Implication on Indian Business - Determinants of Nation's Competitive Advantage - Porter's Five Forces Model - PEST Analysis - Strategic Groups Competitive Changes - Stages of Industry Life Cycle Analysis - Globalization and Industry Structure - National Context and Competitive Advantage Resources - Capabilities and Competencies of Core Competencies - Competitor Analysis - Self-Analysis of Organization - Usage Patterns of Self-Analysis of Organization - Low Cost and Differentiation Generic Building Blocks of Competitive Advantage - Focus on the Building Blocks of Competitive Advantage - Institute Continuous Improvement and Learning - Track Best Industrial Practice and Use Benchmarking - Strategy in the Global Environment - Nature of Competitive Advantage in Global Industries - Resources and Capabilities Durability of Competitive Advantage - Strategy and Technology - Distinctive Competencies and Competitive Advantage - Management of Technology - The Role of Diversification - Limits - Forms and Means - Avoiding Failures and Sustaining Competitive Advantage.

3.1. COMPETITIVE ADVANTAGE - INTRODUCTION

Competitive advantage is essentially a position of superiority on the part of the firm in relation to its competition in any of the multitude of functions/activities performed by the firm. It means that a firm can gain a competitive advantage in several ways. For example, some firms may be superior in production, some in R&D and some others in marketing. And within given function, the superiority may be rooted in different aspects of the function. For example, superiority in production may emanate from different aspects; the firm may be a more efficient producer compared to its competitors, or, it may have more flexible production system, or else, it may have the strength of variety. Superiority can also mean that the firm performs a given function differently distinct from the way other firms perform it. In either case, the firm gains a competitive advantage.

It will be clear from the above explanation that in developing a competitive advantage, a firm basically figures out how it can perform a particular function or group of functions, either, in a superior way, or in a distinctive way, relative to competition. The only other criterion is that the superiority/distinction has to be of value to the customer and should be perceived by him as such. Without this condition being fulfilled, no competitive advantage accrues to the firm, from the superiority/distinction. In other words, there are two questions;

1. Do I perform some function in a superior /distinctive way, compared to competition?

2. Does the superiority/distinction mean something in terms of customer value?

Competitive advantage is thus superior or distinctive competence of the firm relative to competition in some area. The superior or distinctive competence must mean something in terms of customer value. The areas may include practically all functions/activities, which business firms normally carry out, such as marketing, R&D, production, finance, new product launch, brand management etc. The superiority or distinction may also cover the resource and capability dimension and factors like technology. Outstanding leaders in any industry possess superiority/distinction in several functions/areas.

3.2. MEANING AND DEFINITION OF COMPETITIVE ADVANTAGE

A competitive advantage is an advantage over competitors gained by offering consumers greater value, either by means of lower prices or by providing greater benefits and service that justifies higher prices. Porter suggested four "generic" business strategies that could be adopted in order to gain competitive advantage. The strategies relate to the extent to which the scope of a business' activities are narrow versus broad and the extent to which a business seeks to differentiate its products.

"There are two basic types of competitive advantage: cost advantage and differentiation advantage. While this two-fold division comprehends most of the competitive advantage cases, a deeper analysis could be made, breaking down the factors that enable a company to achieve either a cost or a differentiation advantage."

- Cost advantage
- Differentiation advantage

Differentiation, for instance, can be achieved through innovative products, through a better customer service and so on. Cost leadership, similarly, can be achieved through economies of scale, better relationship with suppliers and the like.

A competitive advantage exists when the firm is able to deliver the same benefits as competitors but at a lower cost (cost advantage), or deliver benefits that exceed those of competing products (differentiation advantage). Thus, a competitive advantage enables the firm to create superior value for its customers and superior profits for itself. Cost and differentiation advantages are known as positional advantages since they describe the firm's position in the industry as a leader in either cost or differentiation.

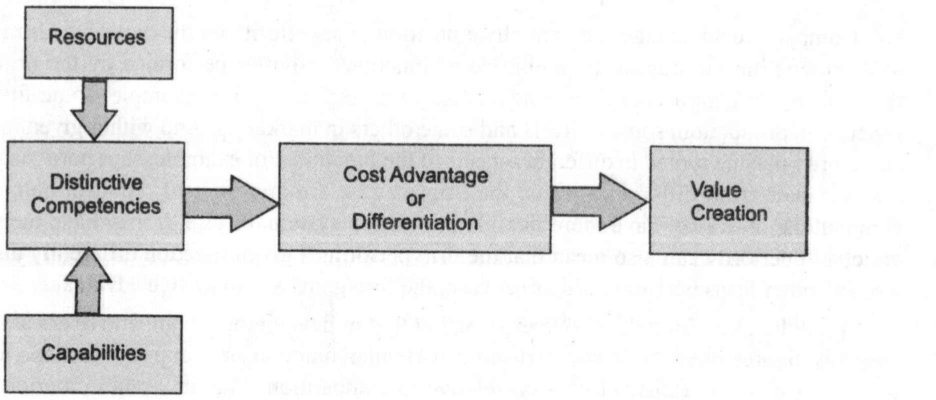

Figure 3.1. Porter's Model of Competitive Advantage.

(i) Resources and Capabilities

According to the resource-based view, in order to develop a competitive advantage the firm must have resources and capabilities that are superior to those of its competitors. Without this superiority, the competitors simply could replicate what the firm was doing and any advantage quickly would disappear. Resources are the firm-specific assets useful for creating a cost or differentiation advantage and that few competitors can acquire easily. The following are some examples of such resources:-

- Patents and trademarks

- Proprietary know-how
- Installed customer base
- Reputation of the firm
- Brand equity

(ii) Capabilities refer to the firm's ability to utilize its resources effectively. An example of a capability is the ability to bring a product to market faster than competitors. Such capabilities are embedded in the routines of the organization and are not easily documented as procedures and thus are difficult for competitors to replicate. The firm's resources and capabilities together form its distinctive competencies. These competencies enable innovation, efficiency, quality, and customer responsiveness, all of which can be leveraged to create a cost advantage or a differentiation advantage.

3.3. COMPETITIVE ADVANTAGE OF NATIONS AND ITS IMPLICATION ON INDIAN BUSINESS

Introduction

Competitive advantage of nations is not a vague idea. Nations do demonstrate in concrete terms their superiority in select industries. As in the case of enterprises, nations too build competitive advantage through a planned effort over time. Different countries have competitive advantage in different industries. National competitive advantage often occurs in a cluster of industries rather than in an economy per se. For example, Germany is always spotted for high-performance autos, Japan for consumer electronics, Switzerland for banking, Italy for footwear and the US for commercial aircraft. Their competitive advantage in the respective industries is transparent; they are better than their best worldwide competitors. In other words, no single nation can be competitive in every industry. When a particular industry in a country operates on a higher plane of performance the country acquires a competitive advantage in that field. This position is normally acquired through the capacity of all the players in the given industry for innovation and technology up-gradation. Again, in several cases, nations acquire competitive advantage in particular industries because it is in those industries that their home environment is strong in terms of industry competitiveness and innovation.

The competitive advantage of nations by Michael Porter

The central question in economics is why a nation becomes a home base for successful international competitors in an industry? Hence why are firms in a particular nation able to create and sustain competitive advantage against the best competitors? The answers to these questions are of central concern to firms that must compete in the international markets. These answers have implication to all firms in a country. A nation's standard of living in the long term depends on its ability to attain a high level of productivity in the industries in which its firms compete. This rests on the firm's capacity to achieve improved quality or greater efficiency. Changes in the nature of competition internationally have weakened the traditional explanations of dominance of international trade. Some see national competitiveness as a macroeconomic phenomenon while others see it as function of cheap and abundant labor. Plenty of natural resources have also been expounded as one reason for competitiveness, while some have looked it as an influence of government policy. Management practices have also been put forward to explain competitiveness. These conflicting explanations merit the asking of the question" what is competitiveness"? Is a competitive nation-

- One competitive in all industries
- Who has favorable exchange rate
- Ability of a nations industry to command high prices in markets
- Large positive balance of trade
- Rising share of world exports

- One that creates jobs
- Low labor costs

The principal economic goal of a nation is to produce a high and rising standard of living for its citizens. This ability depends on the productivity with which nations resources are employed. Productivity is the value of output produced by a unit of factor input. This depends on the quality and features of products and the efficiency with which they are produced. National productivity determines the competitiveness of a nation. Sustained productivity requires continuous up gradation of the economy. Thus nations firms must relentlessly improve productivity in existing industries by raising product quality, adding desirable features, improving production technology and boosting production efficiency. It must also develop the capabilities required to compete in more and more sophisticated industry segments, where productivity is generally higher. An upgrading economy is thus one which has the capability of competing successfully in new and sophisticated industries. The aim is to support high wages and command premium prices. International trade and foreign investment provide opportunities to do so.

- A nation can specialize in those industries in which its firms are relatively more productive
- No nation can be competitive in everything
- International competition necessitates meeting of higher standards both in features and in productivity.
- A rising share of exports in increasingly sophisticated industries can support productivity growth

Hence the core question is why nations are able to compete in sophisticated industries and activities involving high productivity. To understand this, need is to concentrate on specific industries and industry segments. Concentration on macroeconomic aggregates does not explain why and how meaningful and commercially valuable skills and technology are created. This can be understood only at the level of particular industries.

Methodology

- Competing internationally means exports and/or locating activities abroad. This study is concerned with determinants of international success in relatively sophisticated industries and segments of industries involving complex technology or human skills.
- To be successful, firms must possess competitive advantage. This competitive advantage must be sustained over time. This can be achieved through lower costs or differentiation of products which enable higher prices.
- International advantage is often concentrated in narrowly defined industries or segments of a particular industry.
- Increased trade has led to increased specialization and in narrow segments of industries.
- In many industries and in many distinct segments of industries, true international competitive advantage is based only in few nations. Hence the influence of nations applies to industries and segments.
- Hence the unit of analysis has been taken as the industries or segments of industries.

3.3.1 Determinants of Nation's Competitive Advantage

A nation achieves international success in a particular industry based on four attributes:-

A : Factor conditions: consist of factors of production

B : Demand conditions: the nature of home demand for a product

C : Related and supporting industries

D : Firm strategy, structure and rivalry

The determinants, individually and as a system create the context in which a nations firms are born and compete. It also determines the availability of resources, skills necessary for competitive advantage. It also determines the information that shapes the perception and the direction in which resources and skills are deployed, the goals of the persona in the acts, and the pressures on firms to invest and innovate.

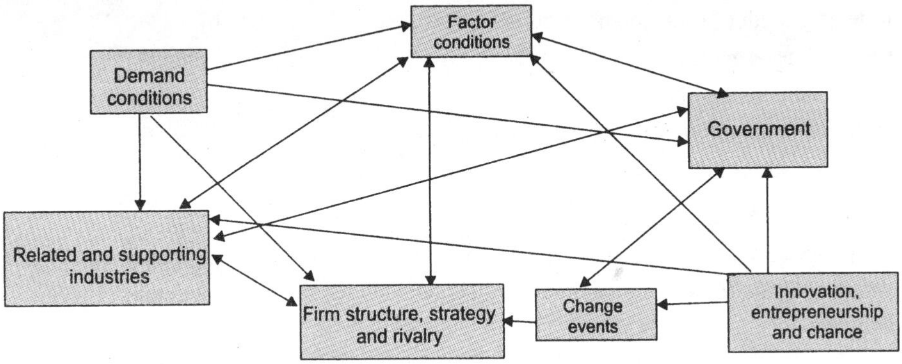

Figure 3.2. Determinants of Nation's Competitive Advantage.

(a) Factor Conditions

1. Are inputs necessary to compete in any industry? A nation's endowments of factors play a major role in gaining competitive advantage.

2. Important are the rate at which they are created, upgraded and made more specialized to industries.

3. They include—human resources, physical resources, knowledge resources—these reside in universities, research labs, trade associations etc, capital resources, and infrastructure.

4. A nations firms gain competitive advantage if they possess low cost or uniquely high quality factors of the particulars that are significant to competition in a particular industry.

5. Competitive advantage depends on how efficiently and effectively they are deployed. These factors are mobile and mere possession of these does not confirm advantage for a long time.

6. Advanced factors like research institutes, highly educated personnel etc, are more significant for competitive advantage. However these are built on the basic factors. Specialized factors are more important for competitive advantage. These require more focused investments.

7. Significant and sustained competitive advantage is seen when both specialized and generalized factors for a particular industry are present. The ability to continuously generate these factors and upgrade them.

8. Innovations are the key to offset certain disadvantages due to non possession of factors. Innovations are stimulated if a nations firm faces trends in factor costs early.

(b) Demand Conditions

Three factors are important: composition, size and pattern of growth and mechanisms by which nations domestic preferences are transmitted to foreign markets. Home demand composition is influenced by-

1. Mix and character of home buyer needs
2. Pressure from local customers to innovate
3. Size, necessity and visibility of home demand
4. Range of segments

5. Sophisticated and demanding buyers

6. Anticipatory buyers needs- if domestic needs foreshadow international buyers needs defined by social and cultural factors

7. Number of independent buyers

8. Rate of growth of home demand

9. Early home demand

10. Early saturation of home demand

11. Internationalization of domestic demand

12. Presence of mobile buyers

(c) Related and Supporting Industries

Is the presence of internationally competitive supplier and related industries. This gives competitive advantage through:

1. Efficient access to inputs

2. Provide ongoing coordination

3. Help in the process of innovation and upgrading based on exchange of research and development, information and ideas.

4. Leads to new competitive industries

5. Pulls demand for complimentary products

6. Reinforce competitive advantage of other related industries

(d) Firm Strategy, Structure and Rivalry

1. Management practices and modes of organization which are favored to suit the industries which a nation is competitive in. These include training, orientation of leaders, management styles, individual initiative, tools for decision making, ability to coordinate etc.

2. Attitudes towards authority, competition, norms of interpersonal communication—Language skills, inclination to learn

3. Goals, ownership structures national prestige, sustained commitment

4. Domestic rivalry—in price, research and development, innovation, technology, emotional and personal

5. New business formation

(e) Role of Chance Events: Chance events create the discontinuities that allow shifts in competitive position. National attributes play an important role in taking advantage of the shifts created by chance events.

(f) Innovation, Entrepreneurship and Chance: Innovation and entrepreneurship are at the heart of national advantage. The determinants play a large role in locating where invention and entrepreneurship are most likely to occur in a particular industry. National factor conditions mechanisms affect the pool of knowledge and talent.

(g) Role of Government: The role of government is to influence the four determinants positively so as to facilitate generation of competitive advantage in industries.

3.4. MICHAEL PORTER'S 5 FORCES MODEL

Introduction

Michael Porter, an authority on competitive strategy, contends that a corporation is most concerned with the intensity of competition within its industry. Basic competitive forces, which determine the industry level. "The collective strength of these forces," determines the ultimate profit potential in the industry, where profit potential is measured in terms of long-run return on invested capital. "The stronger each of these forces is, the more companies are limited in their ability to raise prices and earn greater profits. In carefully scanning its industry, the corporation must assess the importance to its success of each six forces: threat of new entrants, rivalry among existing firms, threat of substitute products, bargaining power of buyers, bargaining power of suppliers, and relative power of other stakeholders.

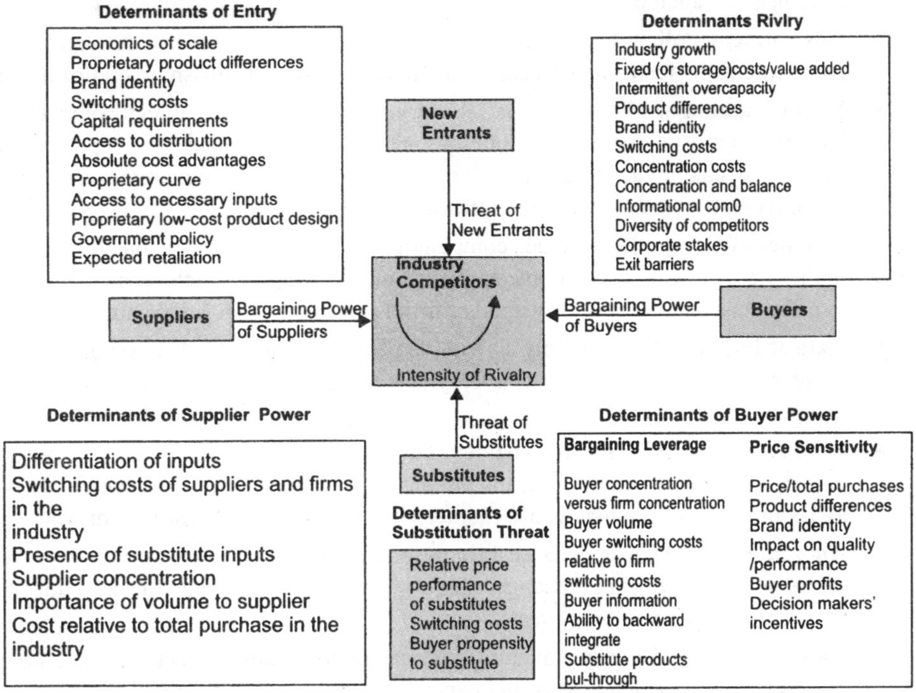

Figure 3.3. M. Porter's 5 Forces Model.

1. New Entrants and its Determinants are newcomers to an existing industry. They typically bring new capacity a desire to gain market share, and substantial resources. Therefore they are threat to an established corporation. The threat of entry depends on the presence of entry barriers and the reaction that can be expected from existing competitors. An entry barrier is an obstruction that makes it difficult for a company to enter an industry. Some of the possible barriers are as following:

- **Economics of Scale:** Scale economies in the production and scale of microprocessors for example, gave Intel a significant cost advantage over any new rival.
- **Product Differentiation:** A company which shows differentiation in its product line. For example corporation like Procter & Gamble, General Mills, which manufacture products Tide and Cheerios among many others, create high entry barriers through their high levels of advertising and promotion.
- **Capital Requirement:** The need to invest huge financial resources in manufacturing facilities in order to produce large commercial air planes creates significant barriers to entry to new competitors for Being and Airbus.
- **Switching Costs:** Once a software program such as Excel or Word becomes established in an office, office managers are reluctant to switch to new program because of high training cost.
- **Access to Distribution Channel:** Small entrepreneurs often have difficulty obtaining supermarket shelf space for their goods because large retailers charge for space on

their shelves and give priority to the established firms who can pay for the advertising needed to create high customer demand.

- **Cost Disadvantages Independent of Size:** Microsoft`s development of the first widely adopted operating system (MS-DOS) for the IBM-type personal computer gave it a significant advantage over potential competitors. Its introduction of Windows helped to cement advantage.
- **Government Policy:** Governments can limit entry into an industry through licensing requirements by restricting access to raw materials, such as off-shore oil drilling sites.
- **Rivalry among Existing Firms:** Rivalry is the amount of direct competition in industry. In most industries, corporations are mutually dependent. A competitive move by one firm can be expected to have a noticeable effect on its competitors and thus may cause retaliation or countervailing efforts.
- **Number of Competitors:** When competitors are few and roughly equal in size, such as in the U.S. Auto and major home appliance industries, they watch each other carefully to make sure that any move by another firm is matched by an equal counter move.
- **Rate of Industry Growth:** any slowing in passenger traffic tends to set off price wars in the airline industry because the only part too growth is to take sales away from a competitor.
- **Product or Service Characteristics:** Many people choose a video rental store based on location, variety of selection, and pricing because they view videos (taps and DVDs) as a commodity- a product whose characteristics are the same regardless of who sells it.
- **Amount of Fixed Cost:** Because airlines must fly their planes on a schedule regardless of the number of paying passengers for any one flight, they offer cheap standby fares whenever a plane has empty seats.
- **Capacity:** If the only way a manufacturer can increase capacity is in a large increment by building a new plant (as in the paper industry), it will run that new plant at full capacity to keep its unit costs as low as possible. Producing so many units' results in the selling price falling throughout the industry.
- **Height of Exit Barriers:** Exit barriers keep a company from leaving an industry. The brewing industry, for example, has a low percentage of companies that leave the industry because breweries are specialized assets with few uses expect for making beer.
- **Diversity of Rivals:** Rivals with different ideas of how to compete are likely to cross paths often and unknowingly challenge each other`s position. This situation happens often in retailing.

2. Threat of Substitute Products or Services: Substitute products are those products that appear to be different but can satisfy the same need as another product. According to Porter, "Substitutes limit the potential returns of an industry by placing a ceiling on the prices firms in the industry can profitably charge." To the extent that switching costs are low, substitutes may have a strong effect on an industry. Tea can be considered a substitute for coffee. If the price of coffee goes up high enough, coffee drinkers will slowly begin switching to tea. The price of tea thus puts a price ceiling on the price of coffee. Sometimes a difficult task, the identification of possible substitute products or services means searching for products or services that can perform the same function, even though they may not appear to be easily substitutable.

3. Bargaining Power of Buyers: Buyers affect an industry through their ability to force down prices, bargain for higher quality or more services, and play competitors against each other. A buyer or distributor is powerful if some of the following factors hold true-

1. A buyer purchases a large proportion of the seller's product or service (e.g., oil filters purchased b a major automaker).

2. A buyer has the potential to integrate backward by producing the product itself (e.g., a newspaper chain could make its own paper).

3. Alternative suppliers are plentiful because the product is standard or undifferentiated (e.g., motorists can choose among many gas stations.)

4. Changing suppliers cost little (e.g., office supplies are sold by many vendors).

5. The purchased product represents a high percentage of a buyer's costs, thus providing an incentive to shop around for a lower price (e.g., gasoline purchased for resale by convenience stores makes up half their costs but only a small portion of their profits).

6. A buyer earns low profits and its thus sensitive to costs and service differences (e.g., grocery stores have small margin).

7. The purchased product is unimportant to the final quality or price of a buyer`s products or services and thus can be easily substituted without adversely affecting the final product (e.g., electric wire bought for use in lamps).

4. Bargaining Power of Suppliers: Suppliers can affect an industry through their ability to raise prices or reduce the quality of purchased goods and services. A supplier or supplier group is powerful if some of the following factors apply:

1. The suppliers industry is dominated by few companies, but it sells to many (e.g., the petroleum industry).
2. Its products and services is unique or it has built up switching costs (e.g., word processing software).
3. Substitutes are not only readily available (e.g., electricity).
4. Suppliers are able to integrate forward and compete directly with their present customers (e.g., a microprocessor producer like Intel could easily make the complete PC).
5. A purchasing industry buys only a small portion of the supplier group`s goods and services and is thus important to the suppliers (e.g., sales of lawn mower tires are less important to the tire industry than are sales of auto tires).

5. Complementors (Sixth Force)

Andrew Grove, the former CEO of Intel, has argued that Porter`s five force model ignores a sixth force: the power, vigor and competence of Complementors. Complementors are companies that sell products that add value to (complement) the products of the companies in an industry because when used together, the product better satisfy the customer demand. For example the Complementors to the personal computer industry are the companies that make software applications to run on those machines. Grove's argument has a strong foundation in economic theory, which has long argued that both substitutes and complements influence demand in an industry. Moreover, recent research has emphasized the importance of complementary products in determining demand and profitability in many high-technology industries such as computer industry. When the number of Complementors is increasing and they produce attractive complementary products, this boosts demand and profits in the industry and can open up many opportunities for creating values.The systematic analysis of forces in the industry environment using the Porter framework is a powerful tool helps managers to think strategically. It is important to recognize that one competitive force often affects the others, so that all need to be considered and thought about when performing industry analysis leads managers to think systematically about the way their strategic choices will both be affected by the forces and change conditions in the industry competition and how their choices will affect the five forces and change conditions in the industry.

3.5. PEST ANALYSIS

A PEST analysis is an analysis of the external macro-environment that affects all firms. P.E.S.T. is an acronym for the Political, Economic, Social, and Technological factors of the external macro-environment. Such external factors usually are beyond the firm's control and sometimes present themselves as threats. For this reason, some say that "pest" is an appropriate term for these factors. However, changes in the external environment also create new opportunities and the letters sometimes are rearranged to construct the more optimistic term of STEP analysis. Many macro-environmental factors are country-specific and a PEST analysis will need to be performed for all countries of interest. The following are examples of some of the factors that might be considered in a PEST analysis.

1. **Political Analysis**
   - Political stability
   - Risk of military invasion
   - Legal framework for contract enforcement
   - Intellectual property protection
   - Trade regulations & tariffs
   - Favored trading partners
   - Anti-trust laws
   - Pricing regulations
   - Taxation - tax rates and incentives
   - Wage legislation - minimum wage and overtime
   - Work week
   - Mandatory employee benefits
   - Industrial safety regulations
   - Product labeling requirements
2. **Economic Analysis**
   - Type of economic system in countries of operation
   - Government intervention in the free market
   - Comparative advantages of host country
   - Exchange rates & stability of host country currency
   - Efficiency of financial markets
   - Infrastructure quality
   - Skill level of workforce
   - Labor costs
   - Business cycle stage (e.g. prosperity, recession, recovery)
   - Economic growth rate
   - Discretionary income
   - Unemployment rate
   - Inflation rate and Interest rates
3. **Social Analysis**
   - Demographics
   - Class structure

- Education
- Culture (gender roles, etc.)
- Entrepreneurial spirit
- Attitudes (health, environmental consciousness, etc.)
- Leisure interests

4. **Technological Analysis**
   - Recent technological developments
   - Technology's impact on product offering
   - Impact on cost structure
   - Impact on value chain structure
   - Rate of technological diffusion

The number of macro-environmental factors is virtually unlimited. In practice, the firm must prioritize and monitor those factors that influence its industry. Even so, it may be difficult to forecast future trends with an acceptable level of accuracy. In this regard, the firm may turn to scenario planning techniques to deal with high levels of uncertainty in important macro-environmental variables.

3.6. STRATEGIC GROUPS COMPETITIVE CHANGES

Strategic groups are sets of firms within an industry that share the same or highly similar competitive attributes. These attributes include pricing practices, level of technology investment and leadership, product scope and scale capabilities, and product quality. By identifying strategic groups, analysts and managers are better able to understand the different types of strategies that multiple firms are adopting within the same industry. Strategic Group Maps a useful way to analyze strategic groups is through the creation of strategic group maps. Strategic group maps present the various competitive positions that similar firms occupy within an industry. Strategic group maps are not difficult to create; however, there are a few simple guidelines managers want to use when developing them.

a) Identify Key Competitive Attributes. As mentioned previously, many firms share similar competitive attributes such as pricing practices and product scope. The first step in developing a strategic group map is to identify key competitive attributes that logically differentiate firms in a competitive set. This is not always known in advance of creating the map so it is important to be ready to create multiple maps using different variables.

b) Create Map Based Upon Two Key Attribute Variables. For the variables selected, assign each variable to the X and Y axis, respectively. Also, select a logical gradation value for each axis so that differences will be readily observable. When complete, plot each firm's location on the map for the industry being analyzed. As each firm is plotted use a third variable—such as revenue—to represent the actual plot size of each firm. Using a variable like revenue helps the reader understand the relative performance of each firm in terms of the third variable.

c) Identify Strategic Groups. Once all of the firms have been plotted, enclose each group of firms that emerges in a shape that reflects the positioning on the strategic group. At this point, assess whether or not the differences between each group are meaningful or whether other variables must be selected from which another set of strategic groups can be drawn.

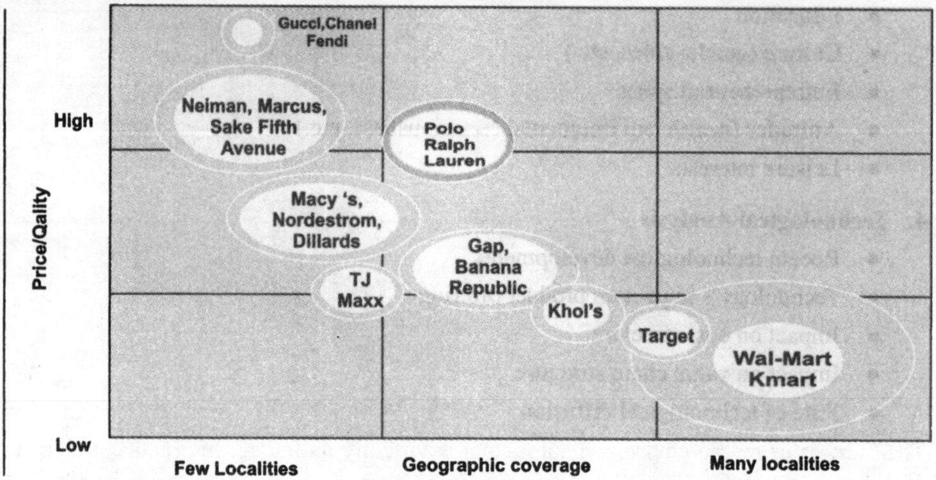

Figure 3.4. Examples of Strategic Group's in Retail Industry.

The above is an example of a strategic group map for the retail Industry. Strategic group creation and analysis provides an effective way to develop a clearer understanding of how firms within an industry compete. Since each strategic group depicts firms with similar—if not identical—competitive attributes within the industry, the map helps managers identify important differences among competitive positions. These differences can be subject to further analysis to helps explain more subtle differences in performance.

d) Strategic Group's Competitive Changes During Industry Evolution

Companies in an industry often differ significantly from each other with respect to the way they strategically position their products in the market in terms of such factors as the distribution channels they use, the market segments they serve, the quality of their products, technological leadership, customer service, pricing policy, advertising policy, and promotions. As a result of these differences, within most industries, it is possible to observe groups of companies in which each company follows the same basic product positioning strategy as the other companies in the group, but a strategy that is different from that followed by companies are known as strategic groups. Normally, the basic differences between the positioning strategies that companies in different strategic group use can be captured by a relatively small number of strategic factors. For example, in the pharmaceutical industry, two main strategic groups stand out. One group, which includes such companies as Merck, Eli Lilly, and Pfizer, is characterized on competitive position based on heavy R&D spending and a focus on developing new, proprietary, blockbuster drugs. The companies in this proprietary strategic group are pursuing a high – risk, high return strategy. It is a high-risk strategy because basic drug research is difficult and expensive. The risks are high because the failure rate in new drug development is very high. This lets these proprietary companies charge a high price for the patented drug allowing them to earn millions, if not billions, of dollars over the lifetime of the patent.

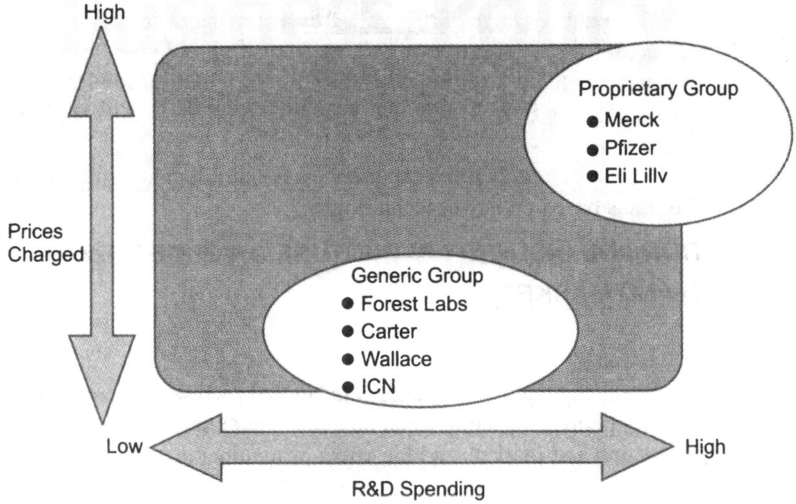

Figure 3.5. Strategic Groups in the Pharmaceutical Industries.

e) The Second Strategic Group Might be Characterized as the Generic Drug Strategic Group. This group of companies which includes Forest Labs, ICN, and Carter Wallace, focuses on the manufacture of generic drugs: low cost copies of drugs that were developed by companies in the proprietary group whose patents have now expired. Low R&D spending and an emphasis on low prices characterize the competitive positing of companies in this strategic group. They are pursuing a low-risk, low return strategy. It is low risk because they are not investing millions of dollars in R&D. It is low return because they cannot charge high prices

3.7. STAGES OF INDUSTRY LIFE CYCLE ANALYSIS

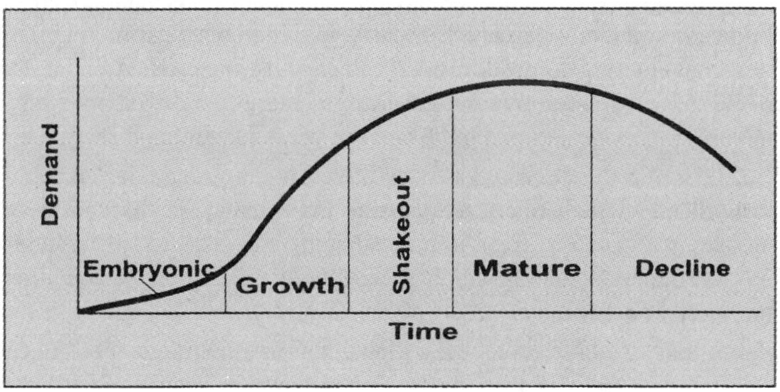

Figure 3.6. Industry Life Cycle Stages.

1. Introduction stage: The introduction stage of the industry lifecycle is characterized by slow growth in sales and high costs as a result of limited production. Organizations invest in research and development to produce new product. During this stage profit will be negative and sales are insufficient to cover the capital outlay on research and development. An advantage of being first mover is that an organization may set the industry standard even in the face of superior technology.

2. Growth stage: In the growth stage sales increase rapidly as the market grows allowing firms to collect the benefits of economics of scale. The increase in products sales brings greater profits which in turn attracts new entrance to the markets.

3. Maturity stage: The maturity stage of lifecycle sees a slowing in sales growth and profits as the market become saturated. Firms will begin to exit the industry and low cost competition based on effective production and technically proficient processes become more important. During the maturity stage of the lifecycle it is conceivable that a product may be benefit from innovation or finding new consumer benefits.

4. Decline stage: In the decline stage firms experience a fall in sales and profitability. Consumer loyalty shifts to new products based on newer technologies.

3.8. GLOBALIZATION AND INDUSTRY STRUCTURE OR GLOBALIZATION OF PRODUCTION AND MARKETS

Introduction

Many important processes operating at the level of the global and national environments directly and indirectly affect the competitive structure of an industry. There are two things to be considered the globalization of production and markets and the effect of national or country-specific factors on home industries` competitive advantage. The forces of globalization are -

1. Tremendous growth in international trade and commerce
2. Innovation in information technology and transportation
3. Creation of a global labor force
4. Absorbent borders between countries
5. Falling barriers to trade and investment
6. Growing Consumer pressures
7. Expanded Cross national co-operation

i. Regulations prohibiting foreign companies from entering domestic market: The past fifty years have been a dramatic lowering of barriers to cross-border trade and investment. For example, the average tariff rate on manufactured goods traded between advanced nations has fallen from around 40 percent to under 4 percent. Similarly, in nation after nation, regulations prohibiting foreign companies from entering domestic market and establishing production facilities, or acquiring domestic companies, have been removed. As a result of these two developments, there has been a surge in both the volume of international trade and the value of foreign direct investment.

ii. The globalization of production has been increasing as companies take advantage of lower barriers to cross-border and investment to disperse important parts of their production process around the globe. Doing so enables them to take advantage of national differences in the cost and quality of factors of production such as labor, energy, land and capital, which allow them to lower their cost structures and boost energy.

iii. Huge global marketplace: As for the globalization of markets, it has been argued that the world's economic system is moving from one which national markets are distinct entities, isolated from trade barriers and barriers of distance, time, and culture, toward a system in which national markets are merging into one huge global marketplace. Increasingly customers around the world demand and use the same basic product offering.

iv. Potential competitors exist both in home and other national market: The trend towards the globalization of production and markets has several important implications for competition within an industry. First, industry boundaries do not stop national borders. Because many industries are becoming global in scope, actual and potential competitors exist not only in a company's home market but also in other national market. Managers who analyze only their home market can be caught unprepared by the entry of efficient foreign competitors. The globalization of markets and production implies that companies around the globe are finding their home markets under attack from foreign.

v. Maximize efficiency, quality, customer responsiveness and innovative ability: The shift from national to global markets during the past twenty years has intensified competitive rivalry in industry after industry. National markets that once were consolidated oligopolies, dominated by three or four companies and subjected to relatively little foreign competition, have been transformed into segments of fragmented global industries, where a large number of companies battle each other for market share in country after country. This rivalry has driven down profit rates and made it all the more critical for companies to maximize their efficiency, quality, customer responsiveness and innovative ability.

vi. Ruling edge of technology: As the competitive intensity has increased companies strive to gain an advantage over their competitors by pioneering new products, processes, and ways of doing business. The result has been to compress product life cycles and make it vital for companies to stay on the leading edge of technology.

vii. Investment open for all: Finally, although globalization has increased both the threat of entry and the intensity of rivalry within many formerly protected national markets, it has also created enormous opportunities for companies based in those markets. The steady decline in barriers to cross-border trade and investment has opened up many once protected markets to companies based outside them.

3.9. NATIONAL CONTEXT AND COMPETITIVE ADVANTAGE RESOURCES

Introduction

The competitive advantage of nations as transformed thinking about the basis of national competitiveness, and has a massive impact on public policies toward regional and national development. In spite of globalization of markets and production successful companies in certain industries are found in specific countries-

- Japan has most successful consumer electronic companies in the world.
- Germany has many successful chemical engineering companies in the world.
- United States has many of the world's successful companies in computers and biotechnology.
- It shows that national context has an important bearing on the competitive position of the companies in the global markets.

Determinants of competitive advantage: According to porter, a nation's competitiveness depends on the capacity of its industry to innovate and upgrade.

Figure 3.7. National Competitive Advantage.

1. Factor Conditions: Factor endowments—the cost and quality of factors of production - are a prime determinant of the certain countries might have in certain industries. Factor of production include basic factors, such as land, labor, capital, raw materials, and advanced factors, advanced factors, such as technological know-how, managerial sophistication, and physical infrastructure. For example, technological know-how- in combination with some basic factors, which might be a pool of relatively low-cost venture capital that can be used to fund risky start-ups in industries such as biotechnology.

2. Demand Conditions: Home demand plays an important role in providing the impetus for "upgrading" competitive advantage. Companies are typically most sensitive to the needs of their closest customers. Thus the characteristic of home demand are particularly important in shaping the attributes of domestically made products and creating pressures for innovation and quality. A nation's companies gain competitive advantage if their domestic customers are sophisticated and demanding and pressure local companies to meet high standards of product quality and produce innovative products.

3. Related and Supporting Industries: The benefit of investments in advanced factors of production by related and supporting industries can spill over into an industry, thereby helping it achieve a strong competitive position internationally. Swedish strength in fabricated steel products (such as ball bearing and cutting tools) has drawn on strengths in Sweden's specialty steel industry. One consequence of this process is that successful industries within a country tend to be grouped into clusters of related industries.

4. Firm Strategy, Structure and Rivalry: The conditions in home-nation that either hinder in the firm's creation or sustaining of international competitiveness. Porter notes that no one managerial, ownership or operational strategy is universally appropriate. It depends on the fit and flexibility of what works for that industry in that country at that time. Rivalry includes companies to look for the ways to improve efficiency, which makes them better international competitors. Domestic rivalry creates pressure to innovate, improve quality, reduce costs, and invest in upgrading advanced factors. For example, the dominance of engineers on the top management teams of German and Japanese companies can be attributed to emphasis in these countries on improving the manufacturing process and product design.

3.10. CAPABILITIES AND COMPETENCIES OF CORE COMPETENCIES

1. Recognizing the competition: Core competencies are those capabilities that are critical to a business achieving competitive advantage. The starting point for analyzing core competencies is recognizing that competition between businesses is as much a race for competence mastery as it is for market position and market power. Senior management cannot focus on all activities of a business and the competencies required undertaking them. So the goal is for management to focus attention on competencies that really affect competitive advantage.

2. The work of Hamel and Prahalad: The main ideas about Core Competencies where developed by C K Prahalad and G Hamel through a series of articles in the Harvard Business Review followed by a best-selling book -Competing for the Future. Their central idea is that over time companies may develop key areas of expertise which are distinctive to that company and critical to the company's long term growth. 'In the 1990s managers will be judged on their ability to identify, cultivate, and exploit the core competencies that make growth possible - indeed, they'll have to rethink the concept of the corporation it self.' C K Prahalad and G Hamel 1990. These areas of expertise may be in any area but are most likely to develop in the critical, central areas of the company where the most value is added to its products. For example, for a manufacturer of electronic equipment, key areas of expertise could be in the design of the electronic components and circuits. For a ceramics manufacturer, they could be the routines and processes at the heart of the production process. For a software company the key skills may be in the overall simplicity and utility of the program for users or alternatively in the high quality of software code writing they have achieved.

3. Core competencies are not seen as being fixed: Core Competencies should change in response to changes in the company's environment. They are flexible and evolve over time. As a business evolves and adapts to new circumstances and opportunities, so its Core Competencies will have to adapt and change.

4. Identifying Core Competencies: Provides potential access to a wide variety of markets. Clear distinctive brand proposition that focuses solely on a closely-defined customer group

5. Makes a significant contribution to the perceived customer benefits of the end product: Core competencies are the skills that enable a business to deliver a fundamental customer benefit - in other words: what is it that causes customers to choose one product over another? To identify core competencies in a particular market, ask questions such as "why is the customer willing to pay more or less for one product or service than another?" "What is a customer actually paying for?

6. Difficult for competitors to imitate: A core competence should be "competitively unique": In many industries, most skills can be considered a prerequisite for participation and do not provide any significant competitor differentiation. To qualify as "core", a competence should be something that other competitors wish they had within their own business. Example: Why does Dell have such a strong position in the personal computer market?

1. Online customer "bespoken" of each computer built
2. Minimization of working capital in the production process
3. High manufacturing and distribution quality—reliable products at competitive prices

7. Generate a differentiated advantage over rival businesses: A competence which is central to the business's operations but which is not exceptional in some way should not be considered as a core competence, as it will not differentiate the business from any other similar businesses. For example, a process which uses common computer components and is staffed by people with only basic training cannot be regarded as a core competence. Such a process is highly unlikely to generate a differentiated advantage over rival businesses. However it is possible to develop such a process into a core competence with suitable investment in equipment and training.

3.11. COMPETITOR ANALYSIS

Competitor analysis begins with identifying present as well as potential competitors. It portrays an essential appendage to conduct an industry analysis. An industry analysis gives information regarding probable sources of competition (including all the possible strategic actions and reactions and effects on profitability for all the organizations competing in the industry). However, a well-thought competitor analysis permits an organization to concentrate on those organizations with which it will be in direct competition, and it is especially important when an organization faces a few potential competitors

Organizations must operate within a competitive industry environment. They do not exist in vacuum. Analyzing organization's competitors helps an organization to discover its weaknesses, to identify opportunities for and threats to the organization from the industrial environment. While formulating an organization's strategy, managers must consider the strategies of organization's competitors. Competitor analysis is a driver of an organization's strategy and effects on how firms act or react in their sectors. The organization does a competitor analysis to measure / assess its standing amongst the competitors

Michael Porter in Porter's Five Forces Model has assumed that the competitive environment within an industry depends on five forces- Threat of new potential entrants, Threat of substitute product/services, bargaining power of suppliers, bargaining power of buyers, Rivalry among current competitors. These five forces should be used as a conceptual background for identifying an organization's competitive strengths and weaknesses and threats to and opportunities for the organization from it's competitive environment.The main objectives of doing competitor analysis can be summarized as follows:

- To study the market;
- To predict and forecast organization's demand and supply;
- To formulate strategy;
- To increase the market share;
- To study the market trend and pattern;
- To develop strategy for organizational growth;
- When the organization is planning for the diversification and expansion plan;
- To study forthcoming trends in the industry;
- Understanding the current strategy strengths and weaknesses of a competitor can suggest opportunities and threats that will merit a response;
- Insight into future competitor strategies may help in predicting upcoming threats and opportunities.

Competitors should be analyzed along various dimensions such as their size, growth and profitability, reputation, objectives, culture, cost structure, strengths and weaknesses, business strategies, exit barriers, etc.

3.12. SELF-ANALYSIS OF ORGANIZATION

An organizational self-assessment strengthens any organization that is implementing this process: it includes working on the organization's identity by analyzing its internal strengths and weaknesses and by identifying opportunities and constraints linked to the environment. The results help to establish a realistic picture of existing capacities, and the organization is able to learn and to adapt more easily to a changing environment. At the same time, this assessment facilitates the planning and implementation of any project or activity. Representatives who know about and can agree on a corporate identity are able to act more coherently and efficiently in any field, including that of the disability sector.

In the field of development and cooperation, joint projects are usually implemented by two or more organizations working both together and independently of each other. Sometimes a shared identity may result from this cooperation, which can create ambivalence and insecurity within and outside the organizations concerned. Knowing one's own identity and being aware of one's capacities and deficiencies facilitates any cooperation and the planning of a joint project, as the mutual expectations are more realistic. A synthesis of an organizational self-assessment and a stakeholder analysis gives the persons and organizations concerned a realistic impression of their potential as a disability movement. On this basis, they will be able to develop a strategy for joint activities that is adapted to their specific national context.

3.12.1 Usage Patterns of Self Analysis of Organization

Who should use this?

- For larger organizations, regular distribution of this evaluation to key staff, board and volunteers is a springboard for internal communication, about problem areas or identify places where you're doing a good job.
- For organizations with limited staffing, this assessment provides a good way to identify the skills needed as you focus on board development and recruitment.
- For newer organizations, this tool can help forecast future staffing, technology or development needs.

- For organizations in leadership or other transition, this evaluation tool may help clarify areas of needed growth and attention before a search begins.

How should we use it?

- **Complete the assessment as a group.** Whether at an annual board retreat or a weekly staff meeting, completing this form as a group--and coming to consensus on how you rate each item--can open up avenues of discussion in a timely and immediate way.
- **Hand out the assessment to be completed (and analyzed) before a meeting.** This way, you can ask individuals to rank items based on personal opinions. Tallying the responses and presenting the results when the group convenes creates ánticipation for the meeting. It also fosters healthy discussion about "snapshot" evaluation and gives a roadmap to future evaluations.
- **Assign sections of the assessment to staff members with direct responsibility.** By allowing program staff to evaluate programming, or IT staff to evaluate information systems, you will get a more clear picture whether you and your colleagues (or subordinates) see eye-to-eye about their department's performance

How will your organization benefit?

- Identify successes and opportunities for improvement
- Jump-start a change initiative or energize current initiatives
- Energize the workforce
- Focus the organization on common goals
- Assess your organization's performance against the competition
- Align your resources with your strategic objectives
- Deliver world-class results

3.13. LOW COST AND DIFFERENTIATION GENERIC BUILDING BLOCKS OF COMPETITIVE ADVANTAGE

The four factors that build and sustain competitive advantage-superior efficiency, quality, innovation, and customer responsiveness are the product of the company's distinctive competencies. In turn, they allow a company to (1) differentiate its product offering, and hence create greater perceived customer value, and (2) lower its cost structure. These factors are generic building blocks of competitive advantage: any company, regardless of its industry or the products or services it produces, can pursue them. Although they are discussed sequentially below, they are highly interrelated, and the important ways they affect each other should be noted. For example, superior quality can lead to superior efficiency, and innovation can enhance efficiency, quality, and responsiveness to customers.

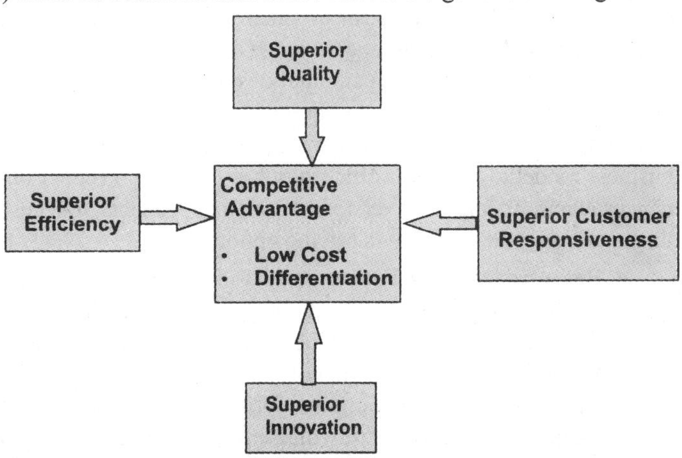

Figure 3.8. Generic Building Blocks of Competitive Advantage.

1. Efficiency: A business is simply a device for transforming inputs into outputs. Inputs are basic factors of production such as labor, land, capital, management, and technological know-how. Outputs are the goods and services that the business produces. The simplest measure of efficiency is the quantity of inputs that it takes to produce a given output, that is, efficiency = outputs/inputs. The more efficient a company is, the fewer the inputs required to produce a given output. For example, if it takes General Motors thirty hours of employee time to assemble a car and it takes Ford twenty-five hours, we can say that ford is more efficient than GM. And as long as other things are equal, such as wage rates, we can assume from this information that Ford will have a longer cost structure than GM. Thus, efficiency helps a company attain a competitive advantage through a lower cost structure. There are two most important components of efficiency for many companies are employee productivity and capital productivity. Employee productivity is usually measured by output per employee and capital productivity by output per unit of invested capital. Holding all else constant, the company with typically have the lowest cost structure and therefore a cost-based competitive advantage. The concept of productivity is not limited to employee and capital productivity.

2. Quality, Reliability and other Attributes: A product can be thought of as a bundle of attributes. For example, the attributes of many physical products include the form, features, performance, durability, reliability, style, and design of the product. A product is said to have superior quality when customers perceive there to be greater value in the attributes of a specific product, compared to the same attributes in rival products. For example, a Rolex watch has attributes-such as design, styling, performance, and reliability-that customers perceive as being superior to the same attributes in many other watches. Thus, we can refer to Rolex as a high-quality product: Rolex has differentiated its watches by these attributes. Among the various attributes of products, one in particular has taken on special significance in the last two decades: reliability. A product can be said to be reliable when it consistently does it well, and rarely, if ever, breaks down. Increasing product reliability has been the central goal of an influential management that is commonly referred to as total quality management.

3. Innovation: Innovation refers to the act of creating new products or processes. There are two main types of innovation: product innovation and process innovation. Product innovation is the development of products that are new to the world or have superior attributes to existing products. Example are Intel's invention of the micro-processor in the early 1970s Cisco`s development of the router for routing data over the Internet in the mid-1980s, and Palm's development of the Palm Pilot, the commercially successful hand-held computer, in the mid-1990s. Process innovation is the development of new process for producing products and delivering them to customers. Examples include Toyota, which developed a range of new techniques collectively known as the Toyota lean production system for making automobiles: just-in-time inventory system, self-managing teams and reduced setup times for complex equipment. Wal-Mart pioneered efforts to use information systems to manage its logistics, product mix, and product pricing, and Staples applied the supermarket business model to the retail office supplies business. Product innovation creates value by creating new products, or enhanced versions of existing products, that customers perceive as more desirable, thus increasing the company's pricing options.

4. Responsiveness to Customers: To achieve superior responsiveness to customers, a company must be able to do a better job than competitors of identifying and satisfying its customers' needs. Customers will then place more value on its products, creating a differentiation based on competitive advantage. Improving the quality of a company's product offering is consistent with achieving responsiveness, as is developing new products with features that existing products lack. In other words, achieving superior quality and innovation is integral to achieving superior responsiveness to customers. Another factor that stands out in any discussion of responsiveness to customers is the need to customize goods and services to the unique demands of individual customers or customer groups. Another factor that stands out of the responsiveness of customers is the need to customize goods and services to the unique demands of individual customers or customer groups. For example the proliferation of soft drinks and beer can be viewed partly as a response to this trend. Automobile companies have become more adept at customizing cars to the demands of individual customers. For instance, following the lead of Toyota, the Saturn division of General Motors builds care to order for individual customers letting them choose from a wide range of colors and options.

3.13.1 Focus on the Building Blocks of Competitive Advantage

1. Maintaining a competitive advantage requires a company to continue focusing on all four generic building blocks of competitive **advantage-efficiency, quality, innovation and responsiveness to customers-** and develop distinctive competencies that contribute to superior performance in these areas.
2. Many companies become unbalanced in their pursuit of distinctive competencies.
3. For example, focused on engineering quality at the expense of almost everything else including, most important, responsiveness to customers. Other companies fail to focus on any distinctive competency to all.

3.13.2 Institute Continuous Improvement and Learning

1. The only constant thing in the world id change. Today's source of competitive advantage may soon be rapidly imitated by capable competitors or made obsolete by innovation of a rival.
2. In such a dynamic and fast-placed environment, the only way that a company can maintain a competitive advantage over time is to continuously improve its efficiency, quality, innovation, and responsiveness to customers.
3. For instant, companies like General Electric and Toyota have a reputation for being learning organizations. This means that they are continually analyzing the process that underlies the efficiency, quality, innovation, and responsiveness to customers.

3.13.3 Track Best Industrial Practice and Use Benchmarking

1. One of the best ways to develop distinctive competencies that contributes to superior efficiency, quality, innovation, and responsiveness to customers is to identify and adopt best industrial practice.
2. It requires tracking the practice of other companies, and perhaps the best way to do so is through benchmarking the process of measuring the company against the products, practices, and services of some of the most efficient global competitors.
3. For example, Xerox was in trouble in its early 1980's,Xerox benchmarked L.L Bean for distribution procedures, Deere & Company for central computer operation, Procter & Gamble for marketing, and Florida Power & Light for total quality management process.
4. Overcoming the internal forces that are a barrier to change within an organization is one of the key requirements for maintaining a competitive advantage.
5. Once all the steps have been taken, implementing change requires good leadership, the judicious use of power, and appropriate changes in organizational structure and control system.

3.14. STRATEGY IN THE GLOBAL ENVIRONMENT

During the last half of the twentieth century, many barriers to international trade fell and a wave of firms began pursuing global strategies to gain a competitive advantage. However, some industries benefit more from globalization than do others, and some nations have a comparative advantage over other nations in certain industries. To create a successful global strategy, managers first must understand the nature of global industries and the dynamics of global competition.

Sources of Competitive Advantage from a Global Strategy

A well-designed global strategy can help a firm to gain a competitive advantage. This advantage can arise from the following sources:

1. **Efficiency**
   - Economies of scale from access to more customers and markets
   - Exploit another country's resources —labor, raw materials
   - Extend the product life cycle —older products can be sold in lesser developed countries
   - Operational flexibility—shift production as costs, exchange rates, etc. change over time
2. **Strategic**
   - First mover advantage and only provider of a product to a market
   - Cross subsidization between countries
   - Transfer price
3. **Risk**
   - Diversify macroeconomic risks
   - Diversify operational risks (labor problems, earthquakes, wars)
4. **Learning:** Broaden learning opportunities due to diversity of operating environments
5. **Reputation:** Crossover customers between markets - reputation and brand identification

Sumantra Ghoshal of INSEAD proposed a framework comprising three categories of strategic objectives and three sources of advantage that can be used to achieve them. Assembling these into a matrix results in the following framework.

Table 3.1.

Strategic Objectives	Sources of Competitive Advantage		
Efficiency in Operations	National Differences	Scale Economies	Scope Economies
	Exploit factor cost differences	Scale in each activity	Sharing investments and costs
Flexibility	Market or policy-induced changes	Balancing scale with strategic & operational risks	Portfolio diversification
Innovation and Learning	Societal differences in management and organization	Experience - cost reduction and innovation	Shared learning across activities

3.14.1 Nature of Competitive Advantage in Global Industries

A global industry can be defined as-

- An industry in which firms must compete in all world markets of that product in order to survive.
- An industry in which a firm's competitive advantage depends on economies of scale and economies of scope gained across markets.

- Some industries are more suited for globalization than are others. The following drivers determine an industry's globalization potential.

1. Cost Drivers: Location of strategic resources, Differences in country costs, Potential for economies of scale (production, R&D, etc.) Flat experience curves in an industry inhibit globalization. One reason that the facsimile industry had more global potential than the furniture industry is that for fax machines, the production costs drop 30%-40% with each doubling of volume; the curve is much flatter for the furniture industry and many service industries. Industries for which the larger expenses are in R&D, such as the aircraft industry, exhibit more economies of scale than those industries for which the larger expenses are rent and labor, such as the dry cleaning industry.

2. Customer Drivers: Common customer needs favor globalization. For example, the facsimile industry's customers have more homogeneous needs than those of the furniture industry, whose needs are defined by local tastes, culture, etc.

3. Global Customers: If a firm's customers are other global businesses, globalization may be required to reach these customers in all their markets. Furthermore, global customers often require globally standardized products. Global channels require a globally coordinated marketing program. Strong established local distribution channels inhibit globalization.

4. Transferable Marketing: Whether marketing elements such as brand names and advertising require little local adaptation. World Brands with non-dictionary names may be developed in order to benefit from a single global advertising campaign.

5. Competitive Drivers: The existence of many global competitors indicates that an industry is ripe for globalization. Global competitors will have a cost advantage over local competitors. When competitors begin leveraging their global positions through cross-subsidization, an industry is ripe for globalization.

6. Government Drivers: Trade policies, Technical standards, Regulations- The furniture industry is an example of an industry that did not lend itself to globalization before the 1960's. Because furniture has a high bulk compared to its value, and because furniture is easily damaged in shipping, transport costs traditionally were high. Government trade barriers also were unfavorable. The Swedish furniture company IKEA pioneered a move towards globalization in the furniture industry. IKEA's furniture was unassembled and therefore could be shipped more economically. IKEA also lowered costs by involving the customer in the value chain; the customer carried the furniture home and assembled it himself. IKEA also had a frugal culture that gave it cost advantages. IKEA successfully expanded in Europe since customers in different countries were willing to purchase similar designs.

3.15. RESOURCES AND CAPABILITIES DURABILITY OF COMPETITIVE ADVANTAGE

1. Resources are the capital or financial, physical, social or human, technological, and organizational factor endowments that allow company to create value for its customers. Company resources are divided into two types: Tangible resources are something physical, such as land, building, plants, equipments, inventory and money. Intangible resources are non-physical entities that are the creation of company and its employees, such as brand names, the reputation of the company, the knowledge that employees have gained through experience, and the intellectual property of the company, including patents, copyrights and trademarks. For example, Polaroid`s distinctive competency in instant photography was based on a firm- specific and valuable intangible resources. Another important quality of a resource that lead to a distinctive competency is that it is valuable in some way creating strong demand for the company's product. Polaroid's technological know-how was valuable while it created strong demand for its photographic products; it became far less valuable when superior digital technology came along.

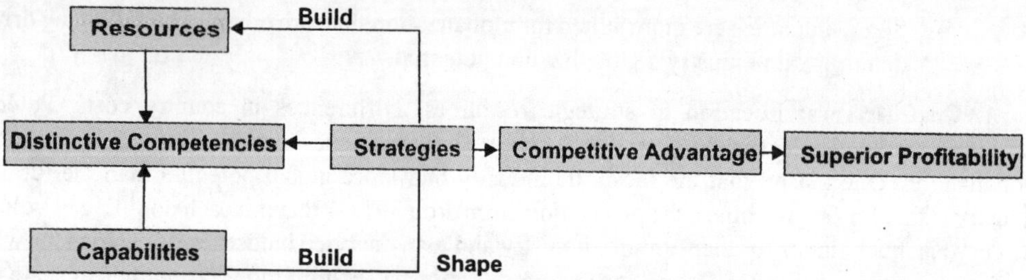

Figure 3.9. Resource of Competitive Advantage.

2. Capabilities refers to a company's skills at coordinating its resources and putting them to productive use. These skills reside in an organization's rules, routine and procedures, that is, the style or manner through which it makes decisions and manages its internal processes to achieve organizational objectives. More generally, a company's capabilities are the product of its organizational structure, processes, and control systems. They specify how and where decisions are made within a company, the kind of behaviors the company rewards, and the company's cultural norms and values. Capabilities are intangible. They reside not so much in individuals as in the way individuals interact cooperate, and make decisions within the context of an organization.

3. A Critical Distinction: The Distinction between resources and capabilities is critical to understand what generates a distinctive competency. A company may have firm-specific and valuable resources, but unless it has the capability to use those resources effectively, it may not be able to create a distinctive competency. It is also important to recognize that a company may not need firm-specific and valuable resources to establish a distinctive competency so long as it does have capabilities that no competitor processes. For example, the steel mini-mill operator Nucor is widely acknowledged to be the most cost-efficient steel maker in the United States. Its distinctive competency in low-cost steel making does not come from any firm-specific and valuable resources. Nucor has the same resources (plant, equipment, skilled, employees, know-how) as many other mini-mill operators. What distinguishes Nucor is it's unique to manager its resources in a highly productive way. Specifically, Nucor's structure, control system, and culture promote efficiency at all levels within the company.

4. In sum, for a company to have a distinctive competency it must at a minimum have either : A firm-specific and valuable resource and the capabilities (skills) necessary to take advantage of that resource.

- A firm-specific capability to manage resources- A company's distinctive competency is strongest when it possesses both firm-specific and valuable resources and firm-specific capabilities to manage those resources
- The relationship of company's strategies, distinctive competencies, and competitive advantage. Distinctive competencies shape the strategies that the company pursues, which lead to competitive advantage and superior profitability. However, it is also very important to realize that the strategies a company adopts can build new resources and capabilities or strengthen the existing resources and capabilities of the company, thereby enhancing the distinctive competencies and strategies is not a liner one; rather, it is a reciprocal one in which distinctive competencies shape strategies and strategies help to build and create distinctive

3.16. STRATEGY AND TECHNOLOGY

Technology means as follows

- The body of scientific knowledge use in the production of goods or services

- Accounting for an even larger share of economic activity
- Revolutionizing aspects of the product or production system in industries not thought of as high-tech

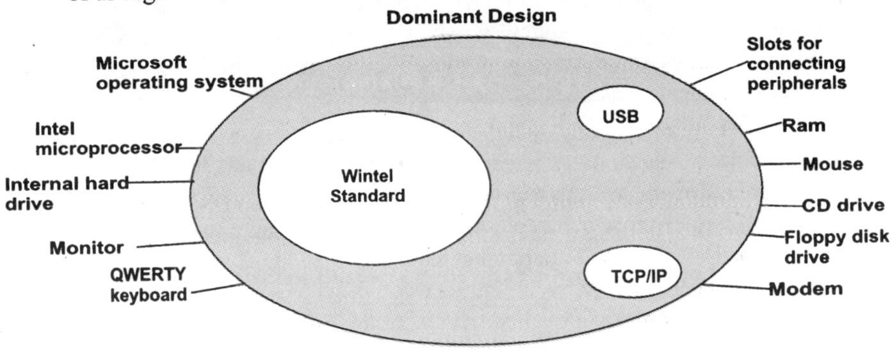

Figure 3.10. Technical Standard for Personal Computers.

Benefits of Standards

1. **Standards help**
   - Guarantee compatibility between products and their compliments
   - Reduce confusion in the minds of consumers
   - Reduce production costs through mass-production
   - Reduce the risks associated with supplying complementary products and help
2. **Three ways standards emerge**
   - Companies may lobby the government to mandate an industry standard c.
   - Standards are often set by cooperation among businesses or industry forums.
   - Standards are often selected competitively by market demand.
   - Network effects
   - Positive feedback loop
3. **Successful strategies for competitors**
   - Ensure a supply of complements
   - Leverage killer applications
   - Aggressively price and market
   - Cooperate with competitors
   - License the format
   - Capturing First-Mover Advantages
4. **Sources of first-mover advantages**
   - Exploit network effects and positive feedback loops Locking customers into its technology
   - Establish significant brand loyalty.
   - Enable economies of scale and learning effects
   - Create switching costs for customers
   - Accumulate valuable knowledge

3.17. DISTINCTIVE COMPETENCIES AND COMPETITIVE ADVANTAGE

A company has a competitive advantage over its rivals when its profitability is greater than the average profitability for all companies in its industry. It has a sustained competitive advantage when it is able to maintain above-average profitability over a number of years. The primary objective of strategy is to achieve a competitive advantage because then superior profitability will follow. Thus strategy is the driver of competitive advantage and profitability.

Distinctive Competencies are firm-specific strengths that allow a company to differentiate its products and/or achieve substantially lower costs than its rivals and thus gain a competitive advantage. For example, Toyota has distinctive competencies in the development and operation of manufacturing processes. Toyota pioneered a whole range of manufacturing techniques, such as just-in-time inventory system, self managing teams, and reduced setup times for complex equipment. These competencies, collectively known as the Toyota lean production system, helped it attain superior efficiency and product quality, which are the basis of its competitive advantage in the global automobile industry. Distinctive competencies arise from two complementary sources; resources and capabilities.

3.18. MANAGEMENT OF TECHNOLOGY

1. Global standards in quality: With the rapid growth in global trade, companies must now implement changes quickly. Technology provides a means to accomplish this. Firms must bring new products to market quickly while meeting customer's quality demands. To succeed in the international marketplace, firms must also drive out unnecessary development and administrative steps to reduce costs and product development times. The growth of global standards in quality and business processes has also increased the need for companies to use technology to implement the changes needed to meet new requirements.

2. Operations: Technology assists companies with managing changes to operations. Companies have successfully reduced costs by examining business processes and eliminating actions that customers do not perceive as valuable. A key challenge for both company leaders and technology staff, however, is shifting focus from projects centered on cost reductions to projects that develop innovative products and drive revenue. Both companies and consumers have benefited from technology-driven improvements such as online orders, ticketless travel and just-in-time inventory management.

3. Support: Examining how a firm's departments use internal support services results in identification of functions that multiple departments can share. Automation allows companies to eliminate duplication and even outsource some administrative functions, such as accounting or mortgage processing. Organizations must also consider the return on investment when deploying new technology, however. For example, companies should carefully evaluate decisions to implement an expensive new technology if it only benefits a few staff members.

4. Centralization: Advances in technology provide companies with the opportunity to place decision-making authority at the optimum level. Firms can use technology to centralize purchasing and logistics to take advantage of cost savings. Decentralizing responses to customer needs provides the opportunity for firms to tailor marketing decisions to fit local or fast-changing markets. Companies can also take advantage of advances in communications technology to integrate their computer systems with their customers and suppliers.

5. Challenges: Organizations must not only look at present opportunities to benefit from technology, but also must anticipate future changes. A company that focuses only on current profits may miss chances to implement changes that could affect its future profitability or survival. Organizations that relied on strategic five-year plans in the past now find they must re-examine these plans every 12 to 18 months. Organizations must also determine the appropriate scope of changes and manage internal culture changes needed to successfully integrate new technology.

3.19. DIVERSIFICATION

Meaning of Diversification

A portfolio strategy designed to reduce exposure to risk by combining a variety of investments, such as stocks, bonds, and real estate, which are unlikely to all move in the same direction. The goal of diversification is to reduce the risk in a portfolio. Volatility is limited by the fact that not all asset classes or industries or individual companies move up and down in value at the same time or at the same rate. Diversification reduces both the upside and downside potential and allows for more consistent performance under a wide range of economic conditions.

3.19.1 Necessity, Role and Importance of Diversification

Often companies diversify for a host of good reasons. In other cases, it becomes a survival strategy when single product or service strategy reaches the limits of revenue generation. To achieve genuine success from planned diversification firms must reinforce internal development; pursue value-chain acquisitions, form strategic alliances and joint ventures. However, diversification must be driven by

- Opportunities afforded in the business environment
- In possession of right resources and
- Own the right skills sets to make structural adjustments to extend the range of goods or Services to your existing customers or new markets.
- By extending your portfolio of products or services, you can ensure new regular revenue streams to boost growth prospects.
- To improve core process execution and
- Enhance a business unit's structural position by creating additional value through synergetic integration of new businesses into the existing ones.
- Improve its competitive advantage and thereby, increasing the value for owners.

3.19.2 Limitations of Diversification

1. Huge funds are required for diversification.
2. The internal savings of the business may not be sufficient to finance growth.
3. The functions and responsibilities of top executives increase because of need to handle new product, technology and markets.
4. They may find problems in coordination, which may lead to inefficient operations.
5. Diversification may involve new technology
6. New markets and the present staff may face problems in adjusting to this growth pattern.
7. Diversification may lead to unknown products and markets leading to more risk.

3.19.3 Forms and Means of Diversification

1. **Vertical Integration**—integrating business along the value chain, both upstream and downstream, so that one efficiently feeds the other,
2. **Horizontal Diversification**—moving into more than one industry or new industry relates to the existing ones or pursue a strategy of unrelated diversification,
3. **Geographical Diversification**—open up new markets, moving into new geographical area to overcome limited growth opportunities in the local market.
4. **Means** of achieving diversification include **internal development, acquisitions, strategic alliances,** and **joint ventures.** As each route has its own set of issues, benefits,

and limitations, various forms and means of diversification can be mixed and matched to create a range of options.

3.20. AVOIDING FAILURE AND SUSTAINING COMPETITIVE ADVANTAGE

When a company loses its competitive advantage, its profitability falls. The company does not necessarily fail, it may just have average or below-average profitability and can remain in this mode for a considerable time, although its resources & capital base is shrinking. Reasons for failure:

a) Inertia: The Inertia argument says that companies find it difficult to change their strategies & structures in order to adapt to changing competitive conditions.

b) Prior strategic commitments: A company's prior strategic commitment not only limits its ability to imitate rivals but may also cause competitive disadvantage.

c) The Icarus Paradox: According to Miler, many companies become so dazzled by their early success that they believe more of the same type of effort is the way to future success. As a result, they can become so specialized and inner directed that they lose sight of market realities and the fundamental requirements for achieving a competitive advantage. Sooner or later, this leads to failure.

Steps to Avoid Failure:

a) Focus on the building blocks of competitive advantage: Maintaining a competitive advantage requires a company to continue focusing on all four generic building blocks of competitive advantage – efficiency, quality, innovation, and responsiveness to customers and to develop distinctive competencies that contribute to superior performance in these areas.

b) Institute continuous improvement and learning: In such a dynamic fast to paced environment, the only way that a company can maintain competitive advantage overtime is to continually improve it's efficiently, quality innovation and responsiveness to customer. The way to do this is to recognize the importance of learning within the organization.

c) Track best industrial practice and use benchmarking: Benchmarking is the process of measuring the company against the products, practices and services of some of its most efficient global competitors.

d) Overcome inertia: Overcoming the internal forces that are a barrier to change within an organization is one of the key requirements for maintaining a competitive advantage. Once this step has been taken, implementing change requires good leadership, the judicious use of power and appropriate changes in organizational structure and control systems.

Chapter 4

BUSINESS ENVIRONMENT

Introduction and Meaning of Business Environment - Features - Environmental Analysis - Components of External Environment - Economic Environment - Important Quotes - Social and Cultural Environment - Political Environment - Legal Environment - Technological Environment - Natural Environment - International Environment - Tax Operating/Competitive Environment - Components of Internal Environment - Human Resources - Other Organisational Resources - The Organisation Mission - Culture - Environmental Scanning - Scenario Building - Organisational Responses to the Environment - Competitive Positioning - Developing Strategy through Internal Analysis - Value Chain - VRIO Analysis - Core Competence.

4.1. INTRODUCTION AND MANAGEMENT OF BUSINESS ENVIRONMENT

Managers must have a deep understanding and appreciation of the environment in which they and their organisations function. To illustrate the importance of environment to an organisation, consider the analogy of a swimmer crossing a wide stream. The swimmer must assess the current, obstacles and distance before setting out. If these elements are not properly understood, the swimmer might end up too far upstream or downstream. The organisation is like a swimmer and the environment is like the stream. Just as the swimmer needs to understand conditions in the water, the organisation must understand the basic ingredients of its environment to properly maneuver (or change direction) among them.

The environment of business is the conditions, events and influences that surround and affect it (Davis). Since the organisation is part of a broader social system, it has to work within the framework provided by the society and its innumerable constituents. For the sake of simplicity, the environmental forces could be classified into two categories: Internal Environment and External Environment. The internal environment consists of conditions and forces within an organisation that affect its management. The internal environment includes the organisation mission, corporate culture, owners and the board of directors, employees, other units of the organisation and unions. The external environment consists of those factors that affect a firm from outside its organisational boundaries. Of course, the boundary that separates the organization from its external environment is not always clear and precise. For example, shareholders are part of the organisation, but in another sense, they are a part of its environment.

4.2. FEATURES OF ENVIRONMENT

1. **Complex:** The environment comprises of multifarious events, factors, conditions and influences arising from various sources. They interact with each other constantly and often produce an entirely new set of influences. It is not easy to state clearly as to what kind of forces constitutes a given environment.
2. **Dynamic:** The environment of an organisation is dynamic and constantly changing. Changes in technology, government regulations, competitive forces etc. compel organisations to

shift gears and change direction quite often. At times, there could be too many changes in too little time, leading to shocks and surprises in the market place.

3. **Challenging:** All firms are impacted by political, legal, economic, technological and social systems and trends. Together, these elements comprise the macro-environment of business firms. Because these forces are so dynamic, their constant change presents myriad opportunities and threats or constraints to strategic managers. In this chapter, we will look into the external environmental forces and their pivotal role in strategy formulation.
4. **External and Internal Environment**: While analysing the total (macro) environment, it is more effective to deal, with the external forces first and then the internal, although some opine that the reverse order is better. For example, analysis of the internal environment might reveal a cash surplus and the top management might then decide to search the external environment for an investment opportunity, such as an acquisition. Even here, examining the external environment is essential to find whether the timing is right for an acquisition or any other use of cash. While deciding the internal-external order of analysis, one should not lose sight of aspects that work well in one set of conditions and change colour in another set of circumstances.

For Example, Arvind Mills was struggling earlier because it took huge loans for the installation of what has turned out to be excess capacity. Due to flourishing markets in the early 90s, the management overestimated future sales and increased plant capacity. When demand subsided, fashion changes occurred and new entrants came with a bang, Arvind Mills market share fell drastically. Also, denim (its main product) is not regularly used by an average person, as it is a fashion item. The company is now exploring overseas markets seriously in order to pay off its debts and survive. Thus, a large production capacity may be an internal strength in an expanding economy but it could be a tremendous burden and an internal weakness in a recessionary period. Here, it would be better to first evaluate the external environment, then the internal.

In actual practice, since both external and internal forces interact and impact organisational survival and growth, managers would do well to examine both sets of factors at the same time. The external environment reveals opportunities and threats and the internal environment uncovers strengths and weaknesses. An opportunity is a favourable condition in the organisation environment that enables it to consolidate and strengthen its position. A threat is an unfavorable condition that creates a risk and causes damage to an organisation. For example, the slowdown in the US market is a real threat to Indian software exporters while outsourcing is perceived as an opportunity to be exploited. A Strength is an in-built capability which an organisation can use to gain strategic advantage over its competitors. (Say superior R&D skills of Ranbaxy Laboratories Ltd). A weakness is an inherent Limitation that creates a strategic disadvantage (say Colgate single product image). Managers often use SWOT (acronym for strengths, weaknesses, opportunities and threats) analysis to match the strengths and weaknesses existing within the organisation with the threats and opportunities operating in the environment before formulating an effective strategy

4.3. ENVIRONMENTAL ANALYSIS

In order to survive and flourish in a highly competitive and turbulent environment, every organisation must strike a happy balance between environment, values and resources (Thompson). Because organisations are open systems, environmental factors inevitably influence them and it is up to managers to ensure that this influence is harnessed in a positive way, leading to organizational success (P S Thomas). Environmental Analysis is the process of monitoring the organizational environment to identify both present and future threats and opportunities that may influence the firm ability to reach its goals.

If properly used, environmental analysis can help ensure organizational success in many ways:

- It helps firms to adjust to environmental change at the right time, that is, encashing opportunities as they arise and eliminating the negative impacts of environmental threats through proactive planning. It also helps the organisation to come out with an early warning system to ward off threats from competitive forces and develop suitable strategies to turn problems into opportunities.
- It tries to improve organisational performance by making managers and divisional managers aware of issues that arise in the firm environment by having a direct impact on planning and by linking corporate and. divisional planning (Certo and Peter).
- It helps strategists to focus on alternatives that help achieve predetermined goals and eliminate those options that are not in line with anticipated opportunities or threats.

4.4. COMPONENTS OF EXTERNAL ENVIRONMENT

Most managers readily agree that an organisation external environment is more difficult to understand and manage than the internal environment. The reasons are fairly obvious. The external forces are frustratingly large in number, difficult to assess and predict and are not easily amenable to advance planning and policy making. Writers like Schilit have, therefore, suggested that in the external environment are very significant; managers must be able to recognise opportunities and threats from outside and respond to these properly Essentially, organisations have to deal with economic, social, political, technological, regulatory, market and supplier related effects which offer opportunities and pose threats at regular intervals. To remain competitive, organisations must visualise these trends and deploy their resources judiciously. We will now examine each one of the external environmental forces to understand better how they affect strategic management.

4.4.1 Economic Environment

Economic factors throw light on the nature and direction of the economy in which a firm operates. Consumption patterns are usually governed by the relative affluence of market segments. Therefore, while carrying out strategic planning exercises, the firm must focus attention on economic trends in the segments that affect its industry. Low interest rates on personal savings, for example, could compel individuals to move towards equity and bond markets, leading to a boom for the capital market activity and mutual fund industry. At the national and international level, the firm must look into the general availability of credit, the level of disposable income and the propensity of people to spend. Interest rates, inflation rates, unemployment rates and trends in the gross national product, governmental policies, sectoral growth rates of agriculture, industry infrastructure, etc. are other economic influences it must consider.

Table 4.1.

Macro Indictor	1999-2000	2000-01	200-02	2000-03 (BE)
1. Fiscal deficit (%of GDP)	5.4	5.7	5.7	5.3
2. Fiscal deficit (Rs.crore)	104.717	1.18.818	131,721	1,35,524
3. Defense outlay (revenue + capital) (Rs. crore)	47,071	49,632	57.000	65.000
4. Major Subsides (Rs, crore)	24,481	26,842	30,523	39,801

5. Interest payments (% 04 revenue expenditure)	36.23	35.74	35.25	34.48
6. Estimated staff strength (nos.)	37,76,666	32,67.344	33,21,503	33,42,645
7. Income tax (Rs. Crore)	25,654	31764	34,438	42,524
8. Corporation tax (Rs. crore)	30,392	35,696	39,059	48,616
9. Excise duty (Rs. crore)	61,902	68,526	74,520	91.433
10. Customs duty (Rs. crore)	48,420	47,542	43.170	45,190
11. Service tax (Rs. crore)	2,126	2,613	3,600	6,026
12. Food stocks (million tones)	31 4	457	58	46*
13. Disinvestment target (As crore)	10,000	10,000	12,000	12,000
14. Disinvestment proceeds (As crore)	1,829	1,870	5,632	4,777
As on 1 March 2002				As on December 2002

Common Indicators:

Table 4.2.

National Income	GNP Personal Disposal Income, Retail Sales
Savings	Personal Savings, Corporate Savings
Investment	Industry Investment, FDI Flows
Price, Wages, Productivity	Inflation Rate, Raw Material Price Index Changes, Labour Productivity
Capital Market	Equity Market, Bond Market
Policy Initiatives	Fiscal Policy, Monetary Policy, Labour and Employment Policy
International Transaction	Exchange Rates, Exports Imports, Balance of Payments
Sectoral Growth	Agriculture, Industry, Infrastructure, Services

The potential impact of, international economic forces was largely discounted till the early 90s. Thanks to liberalization, opening up of the economy and the dismantling of quantitative restrictions, every move on the international arena needs a careful look. The fall of NASDAQ, the interest rate cut by Federal Reserve, the collapse of Korean electronics and automobile makers, the entry of Chinese goods into Indian markets and a host of other relevant economic forces significantly impact Indian manufacturers. Corporate planners will have to closely monitor other economic indicators also for various reasons. Pattern of income distributions in the country impacts the type of products demanded by people belonging to various income groups. Figures relating to savings and investment habits of people in South India speak volume about why the fixed deposit market is booming there. During the last 12 months or so, the industrial growth rate has fallen to 5.5 per cent, GDP growth projections have come down to 5.8 per cent, agriculture is having a bad run, capital goods production has shown a negative trend, car sales have come down from 37 per cent to just 2 per cent; cement sales have not picked up significantly, the investment climate has suffered badly due to falling stock indices and their is the systemic failure of stock exchanges in Calcutta and Bombay. (India Today, March 12, 2001; Nov 20, 2000; August 21, 2000). Despite these negative trends, the quality of growth during the past 5 years or so has changed dramatically. The services sector now accounts for nearly 50 per cent of national incomes; family incomes are rising faster than individual incomes; job opportunities are more diverse; productivity of capital and labour has increased; industry is more competitive today than it was a decade back. India exports are on a roll now. The Government's target of achieving a 1 per cent share of global trade seems achievable. The low interest rates should give a boost to consumer spending in the days ahead.

Important Quotes:

GDP: It is the value of a nation annual total production of goods and services and serves as a major indicator of economic growth. A decline in GDP signals reduced consumer expenditure and lower demand for business outputs. (GDP rates have fallen from 7.5 per cent in 1996-97 to 5.8 per cent in 2000-2001).

Interest Rates: It encourage consumer spending. Retailers, construction companies, automobile manufacturers benefit because lower rates trigger demand for durable goods. Lower rates are conducive to capital expenditures and to mergers and acquisitions. In contrast, high rates dampen business plans to raise funds so expand or to replace outdated facilities.

Inflation Rates: High rates boost costs of doing business and result in constraints on business operations. It may even compel governments to take action that slows the growth of the economy.

Unemployment Rate: When unemployment is high, the company is able to be very selective about whom it hires but consumer buying may decline because fewer people are working. The slowdown in the US market and the subsequent exodus of HIB visa holders is currently proving to be advantageous to Indian software majors in terms of hiring experienced personnel, low attrition rates, better bargaining power in terms of billing rates with overseas players etc.

Fiscal Deficit: It is the difference between what a government earns and what it spends. This is estimated to be 5,6 per cent of GDP in 2003-04 (incidentally this is the second highest consolidated fiscal deficit in the world after Turkey see Business Thday, p.44, 16-03-2003). Source. P Wright et al. Strategic Management.

4.4.2 Social and Cultural Environment

The social factors that affect a firm include the values, attitudes, beliefs, opinions and lifestyles of persons in the firm external environment, as developed from demographic, cultural, religious, educational and ethnic conditioning. Like other forces in the external environment, social factors change continually. As social attitudes, beliefs and values change, so does the demand for various types of dresses, books, leisure activities, etc. Let examine these factors in greater detail.

- **Demographic Factors**

Demographic characteristics such as population, age distribution, religious composition, literacy levels, inter-state migration, rural-urban mobility, income distribution, etc. influence a firm's strategic plans significantly. The entry of women into the labour market has, in recent times, affected the hiring and compensation policies of their employers. This has also expanded the market for a wide range of products and services necessitated by their absence from their homes (such as convenience foods, microwave ovens, day-care centres etc.,). The shifts in age distribution caused by improved birth control methods have literally compelled producers to go after youth oriented goods (beauty products, hair and slain care preparations, fitness equipment etc). The growing number of senior citizens has made many a government to pay more attention to tax exemptions, social security benefits etc. Another important concern is the desire for a better quality of work life. Employees expect more from organisations than simply a pay cheque. They want cleaner air and water as well as more leisure time to enjoy life more fully.

Labour mobility across different occupations and regions, in recent times, has cut down wage differentials greatly. If labour is heterogeneous, as is the case in India, managing people becomes a tough and demanding task. The explosive population growth during the last decade has serious implications for the Indian government which is wanting to go after sophisticated technologies and discarding traditional, labour intensive methods. The presence of a large number of English speaking engineers, at the same time, has encouraged many software giants to set up shop in India. Cheap labour, rise in income levels and favourable governmental initiatives have made the Indian market more attractive to multinationals in recent times.

- **Cultural Factors**

Social attitudes, values, customs, beliefs, rituals and practices also influence business practices in a major way. Christmas offers great financial opportunities for card companies, toy retailers, tree growers, mail order catalogue firms and other related businesses. Social values refer to abstract thinking about what is good, right and desirable. Beliefs, on the other hand, reflect the characteristics of physical and social phenomena. We may believe, for example, that a high- fat diet causes cancer or that chocolate causes acne. Beliefs are important (whether right or wrong) in that they affect how we may behave and what we buy. For example, Mc Donald does not serve the beef burgers in India because Indians consider the cow as a sacred animal (Hindu traditions prohibit the consumption of beef in any form). Values and beliefs vary from culture to culture and before going ahead in a big way, companies must study the socio-cultural environment of a country thoroughly to avoid costly mistakes. To market soup in Japan, the manager/marketer must realize that soup is regarded as a breakfast drink in Japan rather than as a dish served with lunch or dinner. The loyalty shown by Japanese workers towards their employees, to take another example, is far greater than that shown by Indian workers for their employers. The distinction obviously can be traced back to their respective socio-cultural roots.

Most Indians still believe in work, in getting married, in offering prayers to God daily, in giving to charity and in being honest. These core values are passed on from parents to children and are reinforced by major social institutions such as schools, temples, churches, governments etc. Increasing pressure from social activists has forced the government to ban cow slaughter in India (a modern meat processing plant set up in Punjab, near Chandigarh, Punjab metals Ltd, employing a large number of people had to be closed down because of stiff resistance to animal slaughter). Rural women, likewise, joined hands in getting certain evil habits (drinking, gutka, drugs) rooted out of villages and educational institutions. Marketers, should respect the core values of a society and respond in an appropriate manner.

- **Religious, Ethical and Moral Factors**

India is a country where people belonging to almost all religious faiths live Hindus, Muslims, Sikhs, Christians, Buddhists and Jams. They speak different languages. With a population of over I billion and 65 per cent literacy level, the country offers exciting opportunities to marketers. The country specific risks like corruption, political instability, vast cultural differences, poor infrastructure etc are equally threatening. The ethical and moral roots of society are, however, very strong. People believe in joint family system (especially in North India), daily, believe in destiny, respect elders and senior citizens, perform rituals scrupulously and are generally god-fearing. The spread of consumerism, the rise of a middle-class with high disposable incomes, the flashy lifestyles of people working in software, telecom, media and multinational companies and stock market addicts seems to have changed the socio-cultural scenario in recent times. After the 90s, people have started rationalising the philosophy ends justify the means. Such lower ethical standards have now become a real threat to business organisations which have, traditionally, been carrying out their operations in a fair way.

4.4.3 Political Environment

Many political factors influence how managers formulate and implement strategic direction. Due to the socialist leanings of some of the ministers, Coca Cola and IBM had to move out of India in the late 70s. A deep-seated fear of multinationals made the political leaders to shut the door on giant multinational companies for a painfully long time. Entry barriers, protectionist policies, high tariffs, anti-nationalist slogans, bad publicity have had a cumulative effect in creating a closed economic model where people had to wait for years to buy a Bajaj scooter or a Fiat car in India. When things turned from bad to worse, the situation was sought to be remedied through a bold liberalization programme in the early 90s. Apart from a willingness to bend the rules and get along with the times, political stability is also essential for economic growth. After the Babri Masjid demolition in 1992, economic reforms again took a back seat and the then Prime Minister, P V NarasimaRao, could not carry on the bold liberalization programme further. The subsequent securities scam derailed the economy further. Subsidies were never cut as planned at that time, public sector units could not be put on sale, Industrial Disputes Act remained intact, Urban Land Ceiling Act could not be amended (it happened finally in 1999), a National Renewal Fund could not be set up and the insurance sector reforms remained in the basket. Now small donations (imagine how cheaply India most / powerful are willing to sell their souls!) to political parties a mere $2,127 in the case of the BharatiyaJanata Party Bangaru Laxman and $4,255 by the Samata Party Jaya Jaitly for introducing arms dealers to higher ups have again come in the way of the bold economic steps proposed by the NDA government led by Vajpayee. The Tehelka expose, covering the whole lot of shady deals on videotapes in the recent past, has put a big question mark on crucial economic issues such as disinvestment, downsizing, dereservation, labour reforms, power sector reforms, etc.

4.4.4 Legal Environment

The legal framework/regulatory environment is decided by the political party in power. The government, therefore, may legislate on matters like wage fixation, managerial remuneration, safety and health at work, location of plants, entry of multinationals, price control, import- export policy, licensing policy etc. in a centrally planned and controlled economy like India, it is the government that lays down the rules of the game and industry has to scrupulously adhere to the rule book. Lobbying, political donations, public awareness campaigns still help in bending the policy stipulations a bit but, by and large, the levers of control are held by the ministers and bureaucrats only. During the license-permit-raj that prevailed till the late 80s, CEOs of most companies in India were expected to know the domestic market (only), know the government, make short-term plans, be able to handle diversified companies and also implement the vision of the Babu, the owner (Team. C.D). The family owned businesses that existed wantel fixers, yes-men, collaborators and people with right connections with government officials. Licensing policies, quota restrictions, import duties, forex regulations, restrictions on FDI flows, controls on distribution and pricing of commodities, regulations on all aspects of corporate functioning have really put the captains of industry in a spot and pushed them to the wall. A sort of love-hate relationship between corporate heads and bureaucrats prevailed for a frustratingly long time. The liberalization measures, macroeconomic reforms and structural adjustments brought about in the early 90s have altered the economic scenario quite dramatically.

Capital Market Reforms

1991-92

Financial Institutions free to decide on debt-equity swaps. Harshad Mehta boom begins.

1992-93

SEBI announces guidelines on equity market disclosure and transparency; Foreign Institutional Investors (FIIs) allowed to hold upto 24 per cent of local companies. Individual FIIs can hold maximum five per cent of total equity in a single company. Sensex records 4,367, the highest- ever level at that time. Harshad Mehta led boom run comes to an end in April 92.

1993-94

Comptroller of Capital Issues (CCI) abolished, issue pricing to be market determined; Securities and Exchanges Board of India (SEBI) empowered as market regulator; Indian firms allowed to access European markets via Euro equities. Private mutual funds allowed; OTCEI set up; Screen based NSE in the process of being set up.

1994-95

SEBI (Substantial Acquisition of Shares and Takeovers) Regulations, 1994 India takeover code passed; State owned mutual fund, Unit Trust of India (UTI), brought under SEBI jurisdiction

1996-97

IPO norms tightened to boost quality of issues; P0 issuers need to have three year dividend paying record; public sector banks allowed to access markets and price issues at premium; stock exchanges asked to set up clearing houses; stock lending scheme announced; a committee, headed by P N Bhagwati, modifies the takeover code to make management changes less difficult.

1997-98

Entry barriers for unlisted companies lowered; SEBI rules changed to create walls between issuer and registrars of issues; disclosure norms made more stringent; Multiple categories of merchant bankers merged into one category; merchant bankers banned from non-capital market transactions.

1998-99

Rolling settlements for dematerialized shares; infrastructure companies get easier public issue norms; IPOs to go through depositories.

1999-00

Securities Laws Amendment Bill, 1999, passed in Parliament, incorporating derivatives and units of investment schemes as securities; as defined by the Securities Contract and Regulation Act, 1956. Rolling settlement allowed in 10 scripts; companies free to determine par value of new issues; Rediff and Satyam Infoway come out with ADR issues. Software companies like Infosys start overtaking the likes of Hindustan Lever and Reliance in market capitalization.

2000-01

Dematerialized trading made compulsory; rolling settlements introduced; Internet trading permitted. Volumes start to pick up; Dotcom boom turns to bust on US bourses as doubts surface about the future of e-commerce bellwethers like Amazon. The depressed sentiments spread to the Indian market resulting in Indian software scripts being hammered even though the Indian bourses have no listed dotcoms; after bear hammering to the tune of over Rs. 20,000 crore after the 2001 budget, SEBI jumps into corporatize stock-exchanges fully; major stocks covering over 75 per cent of daily turnover pushed to rolling settlement from July 2001.

Banking and Finance Reforms

1992-93

Narasimhan Committee on bank reforms submits report; SLR, CRR cut to reduce state preemption of loan funds; number of lending rates cut from six to four; capital adequacy norms laid down for the first time; 364-day treasuries introduced with market related rates; other securities rates raised to bring them close to market rates; guidelines for entry of new private banks issued; deposit rates freed, subject to ceiling.

1993-94

SBI Act amended to allow the banks to access equity market; The number of interest rates cut from 4 to 3. Floor lending and deposit rates brought down; budget provides As. 5,700 crore to capitalise banks to meet new provisioning norms; prudential norms laying down maximum Non- performing Assets laid out; Debt recovery tribunals set up; Malhotra committee report recommends private sector entry into the insurance sector.

1994-95

Banks free to determine PLRs.; no minimum lending rate for loans above Rs. 2 lakh; ad hoc treasury bills limited by agreement between government and the RBI, to limit monetization of government debt.

1995-96

IDBI Act amended. IDBI raises As. 1,200 crore through its initial public offering; SBI becomes first Indian bank to be listed overseas, following a GDR issue; RBI allows setting up of primary dealership firms to deal in government securities; six primary dealership firms, promoted by banks and financial institutions, granted license to operate.

1996-97

CRR cut from 13 per cent to 10 per cent; Prime Lending Rates cut. Government decides to allow setting up of private sector Local Area Banks, which will operate in three contiguous non-metro districts.

1997-98

Interest on foreign currency deposits deregulated to not more than Libor Fixed interest rate: regime relaxed; Banks freed to assess working capital needs of borrowers; RBI Act amended after CAB scam. RBI gets sweeping powers to register and regulate NBFCs.

1998-99

Banks get tougher provisioning norms for government securities, state guaranteed loans; risk weights assigned to government securities, state government guaranteed loans, torex open positions; NBFC regulations tightened; Insurance Regulation and Development (IRD) Bill introduced in Parliament.

1999-00

IRDA Act passed in Parliament, allows private equity in insurance, caps foreign equity at 26 per cent of total, sets up Insurance Regulation Development Authority (IRDA); banks allowed to operate different PLRs. for different maturities; Times Bank merged with HDFC Bank; ICICI and ICICI Bank get listed in NYSE after their respective ADA issues.

2000-01

Amendments to Banking Companies Acquisition and Transfer of Undertakings Act allow banks to enter insurance sector; government says it will cut its stake in public sector banks to 33 per cent, but will retain the public sector character of these banks; state owned banks announced voluntary retirement schemes (VRS) to shed staff. About 10 to 15 per cent of bank staff apply; ABI allows NBFCs to convert themselves into banks. However, big industrial groups such as the Tatas, Birlas and Reliance not allowed to start banks. Large industrial houses not allowed to hold more than 10 per cent; IRDA issues licenses to private insurers - initially, 11 joint ventures get licensees; Bank of Madura merged with ICICI Bank; RBI announces Cut in bank rate to combat slowdown. Announces cut in CAR; IDBI Act amended to make film financing an eligible activity of the financial institution.

Tax Reforms

1991-92

Sharp 15 per cent cut in fiscal deficit targeted; export subsidy phase-out to cut costs; fertilizer price hike to cut farm sops.

1992-93

Lower income tax rates, fewer slabs, higher exemption limits. Deductions rationalized; presumptive tax on small traders, capital gains tax modified to take inflation into account; wealth tax on productive assets abolished; Chelliah Committee on Tax Reforms suggests moderate rates, wider tax base, improved compliance. Excise changed from specific to ad valorem rates in many cases.

1993-94

Excise duty simplified by merging special and basic excise Duty rates; Capital gains on FIIs cut to a concessional rate of 30 per cent.

1996-97

Tax holiday for companies in road, bridge, port building as also maintenance and other core sectors. Also for water supply, sanitation, and sewerage. MAT slapped on corporate MAT excludes companies in power and infrastructure sectors; corporate surcharge cut from 15 to 7.5 per cent; import duties cut on crude, petroleum intermediates, chemicals, plastics, rubber, electronic components; Modvat extended to textiles.

1997-98

Maximum income tax rate cut to 30 per cent from 40 per cent; lowest to 10 per cent from 15 per cent; standard deduction hiked; Corporate tax cut to 35 and 48 per cent from 40 and 55 per cent, respectively; corporate surcharge abolished; Exporters exempt from MAT; dividend taxation for individuals abolished; Interest tax at source on income from government securities abolished; Five year tax holiday for telecom, power, industrial parks; seven year holiday for oil exploration; VDIS 97, a tax amnesty scheme, nets Rs. 10,000 crore.

1998-99

10 year tax holiday on FTZs and STPs; also on waterways, ports, paging, data networks, satellite services; gifts exempt from gift tax; simpler tax administration scheme - Saral - introduced; Import duties on IT equipment cut; Previously exempted items to attract 5 per cent excise duty; service tax net widened to cover 12 more services; downsizing government spoken about for the first time.

1999-00

Excise rate slabs cut from 11 to 3: making them 8, 16 and 24 per cent; Modvat credit ceiling lifted from 95 per cent of the admissible amount to 100 per cent; peak custom duties cut from 45 to 40 per cent; custom duty slabs cut from seven to five; M&As (mergers and acquisitions) made easier by relaxing carry forward and setoff of accumulated losses and depreciation. Demergers made tax neutral; tax holidays for cold storage facilities; entertainment exports given sops similar to merchandise exporters; domestic trade tax reforms: all states to implement uniform floor sales tax from January and VAT by April, Sales tax sops to go by January 1, downsizing cut from the agenda, staff spending and recruitment increase.

2000-01

Cenvat scheme ramps up effective duty rates, number of slabs cut from five to four; peak duty on consumer goods hiked to 38.5 per cent, from 35 per cent; tax exemptions on export income to be removed in phases; Dividend distribution taxes hiked; excise on diesel cut from 16 per cent to 12 per cent; gasoline from 32 per cent to 16 per cent, as government bulks at passing on global price hike to consumers: defence spending upped by a record As. 13,000 crore.

Structural Adjustments

Phasing out subsidies; dismantling price controls and entry barriers; public sector disinvestment (apart from Modern Food Industries and BALCO, government is going to divest its stake in 27 PSUs including Air India, MarutiUdyog and VSNL to raise Rs. 12,000 crore in 2001-2002); exit policy (introduced in the form of voluntary separation scheme in PSUs and public sector banks; companies employing 1000 or more workers allowed to lay off surplus workers; VRS scheme in PSBs is a grand success in laying off nearly one lakh employees); downsizing bureaucracy (3 million strong bureaucracy to be cut down to size in a phased manner; 30 per cent overstaffing at present to be reduced at 2 per cent a year); right sizing is the new mantra; dereservation of the small scale sector.

Liberalization Measures

De-licensing; Do control; De regulation; FERA &. MRTP liberalization; Open exim policy; Full convertibility of rupee: Encouraging exports, FDI flows, etc.

(Source: ET. 2212/2001; Business World 2/4/2001, 12/3/2001/: India Today, The Babu Burden, 5/2/2001).

Obviously companies that want tu do business globally must pay attention to the above developments closely and learn to adapt the. mselves to the laws of the land. The rules of competition, trademark rights, price controls, product quality laws and a number of other legal issues in individual countries may be of special importance to global companies such as Coca-Cola, Unilever, IBM, and McDonald's.

4.4.5 Technological Environment

Technological factors represent major opportunities and threats that must be taken into account while formulating strategies. Technological breakthroughs can dramatically influence the organisation products, services markets, suppliers, distributors, competitors, customers, manufacturing processes, marketing practices and competitive position. Technological advancements can open up new markets, result in a proliferation of new and improved products, change the relative cost position in an industry and render existing products and services obsolete. Technological changes can reduce or eliminate cost barriers between businesses, create shorter production runs, create shortages in technical skills and result in changing values and expectations of customers and employees (F R David).

Table 4.3. Characteristics of Technological Changes

Key Characteristics	Effects
Technology is changing fast	Customers will expect and accept new ideas
Technology is getting cheaper	Competition will come from unexpected quarters
Technology is becoming easily available	Product life cycles will be shorter
Technology is touching lives in more and more areas.	New things will make old products, skills, knowledge obsolete necessitating continuous change.

Technological advancements can create new competitive advantages that are more powerful than existing ones. Recent technological advances, as we well know, in computers, lasers, robotics, satellite networks, fibre optics, biometrics, cloning and other related areas have paved the way for significant operational improvements. Manufacturers, banks and retailers, for example, have used advances in computer technology to carry out their traditional tasks at lower costs and higher levels of customer satisfaction. Consider the case of an old economy giant, Ford Motor company, which is morphing into a new economy animal using web-based technologies to the best advantage (Anand). Thanks to the internet, the old days of being able to concentrate only on the nuts and bolts of the business seem to be over. The winners are going to be companies that move closer and connect well with customers. Take the stunningly successful case of MP3, a freely-available standard for the compression and transmission of digital audio. The big guns of the music business Sony, RCA and the rest were so confident about their control over the music industry that they couldn't see the threat posed by a tiny player like MP3.com, which quietly spun its own B-web. The company didn't try doing everything: the B-web had a combination of content companies (like MP3); manufacturers such as S3 (maker of the Rio MP3 player); distribution technologies (like Napster); and, of course, hundreds of thousands of teenagers who swore by the music, but couldn't pay for it.

Technological change, thus, can create or even decimate existing businesses or even entire industries since it shifts demand from one product to another. Examples of such change include the shifts from vacuum tubes to transistors, from steam locomotives to diesel and electric engines, from fountain pens to ball points, from propeller aero planes to jets and from typewriters to computer-based word processors (Wright).

Table 4.4. Effect of Technological Change on Enterprises

	Technological Changes Affecting the Functions	Effect of the Changes
Marketing	Television, Fax	The way in which customers are targeted, approached, convinced
R&D	CAD, Solid modeling, Advanced materials	Wider possibilities, faster development times

Manufacturing	CNC, Microelectronics, Micro-hydraulics, Robotics	Shrinking of the factories, Manpower reduction, Lower cycle times
Materials management	ERP systems, Communications technology	Comprehensive planning systems, systemic rigidity, Global sourcing changes in motivating to employees
HRD	Communications technology	Changes in motivating offerings to employees
Systems	Faster computers, Smarter applications	Extremely fast obsolescence
Finance	Communication technology	Global financing, Rapidly fluctuating markets.

4.4.6 Natural Environment

The natural environment comprises of ecological, geographical and topographical factors (such as natural resources, weather, climate, location etc) that are relevant to business. Industries were set up historically, in places where natural resources were available in abundance. This has created pockets of affluence, congestion and pollution all at the same time. The natural endowments began to be used recklessly leading to air, water and land pollution and ozone depletion gradually. Air pollution is created by dust particles and gaseous discharges that contaminate the air and cause global warming. Over the years, the growing number of coal- burning factories, thermal plants, automobiles, etc. has precipitated the problem further. Water pollution occurs mainly when industrial toxic wastes are thrown into the nature waterways. Land pollution is caused by the disposal of hazardous industrial toxic wastes in underground dumps.

The situation has become quite alarming in recent years when pollution levels have risen to unmanageable proportions causing serious damage to the ozone layer heating up the soil, water and air. Thanks to environmental activists, many companies are now seriously trying to come out with (a) eco-friendly products (b) modify processes (c) redesign production equipment and (d) recycle by-products. Steel companies have been forced to spend heavily in cleaner burning fuels and pollution control equipment. The automobile industry has been asked to redesign engines that conform to strict emission control norms. The gasoline industry has been compelled to formulate new low-lead or no-lead products. And thousands of companies have und it necessary to direct their R&D efforts towards finding ecologically superior products such as Sear phosphate-free laundry detergent, Pepsi cola biodegradable plastic soft drink bottle (Pearce and Robinson).

4.4.7 International Environment

International developments can greatly impact the ability of an organisation to do business abroad. For example, fluctuations of the rupee against foreign currencies influence the ability of an Indian company to compete in global markets. When the price of the rupee is high against foreign currencies, Indian companies find it difficult to compete in the international market. Conversely, when the rupee falls against foreign currencies, new business opportunities open up. International factors influence domestic companies in another way, i.e., by producing new global competitors. For example, a number of technological advances pioneered in the United States have led to successful products. Yet, in regard to such items as phonographs, colour televisions, audio and video tape recorders, telephones, semi conductors and computers, US producers have gradually lost a major share of the domestic market to foreign competitors who took the basic technology and successfully built upon it. International factors assume greater importance when domestic companies directly depend on imports or exports to certain countries. For example, the slowdown in US economy is impacting the fortunes of software exporters in India, who derive more than 60 per cent of their revenues from the Silicon Valley. The dismantling of quantitative restrictions, to take another example from 1.4.2001, is going to affect the fortunes of domestic companies manufacturing goods, such as dry cell batteries, toys, stereos, telephone equipment, shoes, wrist watches, drinks and juices, chandeliers, colour televisions etc (especially cheap imports from China). Thanks to the advances in transportation and communication technology in the past century, almost no part of the world is cut off from the rest. The world is a big global village now and virtually every organization it offers and from which place it operates, is affected by international or the other.

4.4.8 Task/Operating/Competitive Environment

The task environment is that part of the external environment which consists of specific outside forces with which an organisation interfaces in the course of carrying out its operations. It consists of the actors in the organisation immediate environment (micro-environment). Usually a single organisation has difficulty in exerting a direct influence on the external environment but it may be more successful in affecting its own task or market environments. The various elements of the micro-environment need not necessarily affect all the firms in a particular industry in the same way. Important elements in the task environment of an organisation typically include: clients, competitors, suppliers, labour supply and government agencies (regulators).

(a) Clients: Include the customers, owners and partners of an organisation. The purpose of a business is to create and sustain customers. In an open market, the organisation turns into a lifeless machine without customers. We cannot think of hospitals without patients, universities without students, departmental stores without shoppers. Organisations that stay close to the customer survive and flourish in a competitive environment. Owners, shareholders and partners, too, have a stake in the continued success of an organisation. They get appropriate economic returns on their investments. Additionally, they can exert greater influence on the way the firm deals with environmental pollution, worker safety, product liability, etc.

(b) Competitors: Competitor's actions and responses to them are a key in determining whether a firm will prosper. Important data about competitors that should be examined from time to time include a number of product lines, product differentiation, prices, quality, market share, advertising location, productivity, service, competitive advantages etc. Competition may be local, regional, national or international in scope, and this is constantly changing. In higher-technology fields, competition can be fierce and turbulent. For example, computer companies have undergone dramatic changes and extremely tough product and price competition within a rapidly expanding market. In recent years, deregulation has changed the face of competition in several industries such as banking, airlines, media, telecommunications, passenger car industry, etc.

(c) Suppliers: Suppliers of raw materials, equipment, parts and money are a very important part of any organisation external environment. Without a continuous flow of supplies, the organisation profitability will suffer. The energy crisis in the early 70s affected the fortunes of many companies which depended heavily on petroleum for running their show. Generally speaking, organisations must have sources of supply that are dependable in terms of quantity, quality, delivery and service and that offer suitable prices and terms of purchase. Over dependence on a single source of supply should also be avoided. The organisation should also be able to get credit on easy terms for its operations.

(d) Labour: The environment labour supply represents those individuals that may be employed to work for the organisation. All organisations need qualified, trained hands to take care of assigned duties. This, in turn, is influenced by the economy, employment, sociocultural factors, technological growth, unions, etc. The influence of unions for regulating supply of labour when required is diminishing in recent years due to recessionary trends, global competition, deregulation, disenchantment of members over limited successes achieved by unions, etc.

(e) Regulators: (Government Agencies) The task environment contains a number of government agencies that provide services and monitor compliance with laws and regulations at local, state or regional and national levels, these regulatory bodies have the potential to control, legislate and influence an organisations policies and practices. They also exercise considerable influence on the cost of doing business, when doing business globally, the firm must also take into account the procedures to be adopted in line with the stipulations laid down by institutions such as IFC, World Bank, IMF, Environmental Protection Agency, etc.

4.5. COMPONENTS OF INTERNAL ENVIRONMENT

Organisations also have an internal environment which includes all the elements within the organisation boundaries such as human resources, other resources, mission, culture, etc. An outline of these factors is given below (Wright).

Table 4.5. Important Aspects of an Organisation Internal Environment

Turnover and absenteeism	**Personnel Aspects**
Structure	Labour relations
Communication Network	Recruitment practices
Record of success	Training programmes
Hierarchy of objectives	Performance appraisal system
Policies, procedures and rules	Incentive systems
Ability of management team	Turnover and absenteeism
Marketing Aspects	**Production Aspects**
Product strategy	Plant facility layout
Market segmentation	Research and development
Pricing strategy	Use of technology
Promotion strategy	Purchasing of raw materials
Distribution strategy	Inventory control
Financial Aspects	**Managerial Aspects**
Liquidity Profitability Activity Investment opportunity	Management style Management competence Managerial values and norms

(Source: Certo and Peter, Strategic Management)

4.5.1 Human Resources

A firm's real assets are its human resources consisting of board of directors, top management, middle management, supervisors and employees. The board vision, commitment, knowledge, experience, political connections all help in taking the firm to commanding heights. Same is the case with the top management which provides direction and middle management which translates rhetoric into action plans. Managers with vision, drive and enthusiasm always help the firm steer out of troubles and stay ahead of competition. Organisation employees are also a key element of its internal environment. When managers and employees embrace the same values and have the same goals, everyone wins. When they work at cross purposes, however, or when conflict and hostility pervade the organisation, everybody loses.

4.5.2 Other Organisational Resources

Other organisational resources (capital, land, equipment, plant, structure, technology processes, etc) should always be properly aligned with the firm strengths and combined in an appropriate manner to produce results. Factors such as proper location, up-to-date technology, adequate capacity, efficient distribution network, reliable and cost-effective sources of supply etc help the firm in realizing its professed goals.

4.5.3 The Organisation Mission

Organisations are set up for a purpose. Although the purpose may change over time, it is essential that stakeholders understand the reason for the organisation existence, that is, the organisation mission. An organisation mission is a statement of its unique purpose that sets a business apart from other firms of its type and identifies the scope of the business operations in product and market terms (Pearce and David). The mission at the corporate level is stated in fairly broad terms but is sufficiently precise to provide direction to the organisation. At the business unit level, the mission is narrower in scope and more clearly defined. It is necessary that an organisation carefully understand its mission because a clear sense of purpose is essential to set proper goals. C K Prahalad argued that organisations should spend a considerable amount of time in understanding what proficiencies they possess. For instance, Sony has used its skills in miniaturising audio, video and electronics products as its particular strategic competence. Likewise, AT&T diversification into the credit card field was an application of its strategic competence in transaction processing, based on its extensive billing experience in the telephone industry (Stalk, Evans). Companies that have lost sight of their goals, in India too, have slipped badly and lost their sheen and value in the market place (NEPC Group, Arvind Mills, UB Group, Damania Group, Modi Group, to name a few). They failed because they were not able to determine clearly which activities fitted into their strategic direction and capabilities and which ones did not.

4.5.4 Culture

In a similar vein, culture is important to organisations because as individuals act on shared values and other aspects of organizational culture, their behaviours can have a major impact on organisational effectiveness. Organisational cultures, of course, develop from a variety of sources. Strong founders may leave a major influence on the culture that develops within an organisation. For example, Ray Kroc, the founder of McDonald espoused service, cleanliness and value still the corporate creed. As reward systems, policies and procedures are established, they impact culture by further specifying notions of appropriate behaviour. Further, critical incidents such as an employee being rewarded or fired for pushing a major innovation, may add to individual's perceptions of internal norms over time. For example, a consistent and shared emphasis on innovation has helped 3M produce a steady stream of new products as well as make continual improvements in existing ones.

One way that managers can try to fit the sensitivity of their organisation to various environmental factors is to design and implement an internal system that gathers and analyses targeted feedback from key employees. Other important sources of information, such as customers, suppliers, consultants, etc could also be contacted likewise. Some of the key questions that could be posed to employees while carrying out such an analysis would include those given below.

Sample Questions for an Internal Environmental Analysis

Organisational Aspects

Does the company delegate authority appropriately?

Is the organisational structure of the company appropriate?

Are jobs and performance goals clearly understood by workers?

Marketing Aspects

Is market research used to the best advantage?

Is advertising used efficiently and effectively?

Can the product distribution system of the company be improved?

Financial Aspects

Does an analysis of the income statement for the company pinpoint improvements that can be made?

Does an analysis of the balance sheet for the company pinpoint improvements that can be made?

Can break even analysis be used to better align costs in relation to profits?

Personnel Aspects

Are training programmes adequate?

Can procedures for recruitment and selection of employees be improved?

Is our performance appraisal system fair and accurate?

Production Aspects

Can the organisation improve its level of technology?

Can the flow of work within the plant be made more efficient?

Can the organisation lower its reject rate?

(Source: Certo and Peter)

4.6. ENVIRONMENTAL SCANNING

Sources

Environmental analysis or scanning, as stated earlier, is a process by which organisations monitor their internal and external environment to spot opportunities and threats affecting their business. The basic purpose is to help management determine the future direction of the organisation. Scanning simply involves reviewing and evaluating whatever information about internal and external environments can be gleaned from several distinct sources. Important sources of Formation for environmental scanning include the following:

International Source

- World Development Report
- World Economic Survey
- Statistical Year Book
- Year book of International Trade Statistics

Government Sources

- Census of India
- Five Year Plan Reports
- India Year Book
- Economic Survey
- Annual Survey of Industries
- Centre for Monitoring Indian Economy Reports
- Monthly Bulletins of RBI
- Yojana
- Indian Trade Journal
- Reports of Tariff Commission, NCAER, CII, FICCI, ASSOCHAM

Other Sources

- The Bombay Stock Exchange Directory
- Kothari Industrial Directory
- Economic Times
- Financial Express
- Business Line
- Business Standard
- Commerce/Capital
- Southern Economist! Eastern Economist
- Business Today
- Business India
- Business World
- ICICI Portfolio Studies; CRISIL Research Reports
- MC Kinsey Quarterly
- Harvard Business Review
- Fortune
- Economic and Political Weekly

General Environment Scanning

Environmental scanning is one component of the global environmental analysis. Environmental monitoring, environmental forecasting and environmental assessment complete the global environmental analysis. Environmental scanning refers to the macro environment. The global environment refers to the macro environment which comprises industries, markets, companies, clients and competitors. Consequently, there exist corresponding analyses on the micro-level. Suppliers, customers and competitors representing the micro environment of a company are analyzed within the industry analysis.

Environmental scanning can be defined as 'the study and interpretation of the political, economic, social and technological events and trends which influence a business, an industry or even a total market'. The factors which need to be considered for environmental scanning are events, trends, issues and expectations of the different interest groups. Issues are often forerunners of trend breaks. A trend break could be a value shift in society, a technological innovation that might be permanent or a paradigm change. Issues are less deep-seated and can be 'a temporary short-lived reaction to a social phenomenon'. A trend can be defined as an 'environmental phenomenon that has adopted a structural character'.

- SWOT Analysis
- TOWS Matrix Analysis
- Other Techniques

4.6.1 Introduction–Swot Analysis

SWOT stands for strengths, weaknesses, opportunities and threats. SWOT analysis is a widely used framework to summaries a company situation or current position. Any company undertaking strategic planning will have to carry out SWOT analysis: establishing its current position in the light of its strengths, weaknesses, opportunities and threats. Environmental and industry analyses provide information needed to identify opportunities and threats, while internal analysis provides information needed to identify strengths and weaknesses. These are the fundamental areas of focus in SWOT analysis.

SWOT analysis stands at the core of strategic management. It is important to note that strengths and weaknesses are intrinsic (potential) value creating skills or assets or the lack thereof, relative to competitive forces. Opportunities and threats, however, are external factors that are not created by the company, but emerge as a result of the competitive dynamics caused by or in the market.

Opportunities: An opportunity is a major favourable situation in a firm environment. Examples include market growth, favourable changes in competitive or regulatory framework, technological developments or demographic changes, increase in demand, opportunity to introduce products in new markets, turning R&D into cash by licensing or selling patents etc The level of detail and perceived degree of realism determine the extent of opportunity analysis,.

Threats: A threat is a major unfavorable situation in a firm environment. Examples include increase in competition, slow market growth, increased power of buyers or suppliers, changes in regulations, etc. These forces pose serious threats to a company because they may cause lower sales, higher cost of operations, higher cost of capital, inability to make break-even, shrinking margins or profitability etc. Your competitor opportunity may well be a threat to you.

Strengths: Strength is something a company possesses or is good at doing Examples include a skill, valuable assets, alliances or cooperative ventures, experienced sales force, easy access to raw materials, brand reputation, etc. Strengths are not a growing market, new products, etc.

Weaknesses: A weakness is something a company lacks or does poorly. Examples include lack of skills or expertise, deficiencies in assets, inferior capabilities in functional areas etc,, Though weaknesses are often seen as the logical of the company threats, the company lack of strength in a particular area or market is not necessarily a relative weakness because competitors may also lack this particular strength.

Carrying out SWOT Analysis

The first thing that a SWOT analysis does is to evaluate the strengths and weaknesses in terms of skills, resources and competencies. The analyst then should see whether the mnternal capabilities match with the demands of the key success factors. The job of a strategist is to capitalize on the organization strengths while minimizing the effects of its weaknesses in order to take advantage of opportunities and overcome threats in the environment. SWOT analysis for a typical firm is given below

Strengths

- Rolled-Up Competitions
- Established customer base
- Annual Subscription Model
- High customer switching costs
- Expertise is SIS integration
- Evolved Grade Center and enrolment manager
- Long term customer relationship
- Centrality of CMS as campus application
- Expertise with authentication and directory integration

Weaknesses

- Customer dissatisfaction with design
- Siloed course structure
- Faculty centric design paradigm
- Inability to open courses and content to larger learning community
- High costs vs. emerging inexpensive web 2.0 collaboration tools
- Lack of integration with web 2.0 cloud tools
- Dependence on central IT

Opportunities

- Engage customer base in roadmap development
- Move to transparent model
- Strategic partnership with SIS providers
- Invest in interoperability with web 2.0 collaboration tools
- Re-design to conform to emerging active learning consensus
- Integration with cloud storage and publishing tools
- Grow SaaS model of delivery

Threats

- Open and community source CMS traction
- Encroachment on middleware space from SIS providers (authentication, grade center enrolment etc.)
- Consumer web 2.0
- collaboration tools (Ning, Netvibes etc.)
- Community dissatisfaction with design philosophy
- Mismatch of higher education and BB corporate culture

Figure 4.1. SWOT Analysis

Steps in Swot Analysis

The three important steps in SWOT analysis are:

1. Identification
2. Conclusion
3. Translation

1. Identification

- Identify company resource strengths and competitive capabilities
- Identify company resource weaknesses and competitive deficiencies
- Identify company opportunities
- Identify external threats

2. Conclusion

- Draw conclusions about the company overall situation.

3. Translation

Translate the conclusions into strategic actions by acting on them:

- Match the company strategy to its strengths and opportunities
- Correct important weaknesses
- Defend against external threats

In devising a SWOT analysis, there are several factors that will enhance the quality of the material:

- Keep it brief, pages of analysis are usually not required.
- Relate strengths and weaknesses, wherever possible, to industry key factors for success.
- Strengths and weaknesses should also be stated in competitive terms, that is, in comparison with competitors.
- Statements should be specific and avoid blandness.
- Analysis should reflect the gap, that is, where the company wishes to be and where it is now.
- It is important to be realistic about the strengths and weaknesses of one own and competitive organizations.

Probably the biggest mistake that is commonly made in SWOT analysis is to provide a long list of points but little logic, argument and evidence. A short list with each point well argued is more likely to be convincing.

4.6.2 TOWS Matrix

TOWS matrix is just an extension of SWOT matrix. TOWS stand for threats, opportunities, weaknesses and strengths. This matrix was proposed by Heinz Weihrich as a strategy formulation matching tool.

TOWS analysis poses a number of questions:

What actions should a company take? Should it focus on using company strengths to capitalize on opportunities, or acquire strengths in order to be able to capture opportunities ? Or should it actively try to minimize weaknesses and avoid threats?

TOWS matrix illustrates how internal strengths and weaknesses can be matched with external opportunities and threats to generate four sets of possible alternative strategies. This matrix can be used to generate corporate as well as business strategies. An example of TOWS matrix is shown below:

To generate a TOWS matrix, the following steps are to be followed:

1. List external opportunities available in the company current and future environment, in the block on the left side of the matrix.

2. List external threats facing the company now and in future in the block on the left side of the matrix.

3. List the specific areas of current and future strengths for the company, in the strengths blockacross the top of the matrix.

Table 4.6

Internal factors/External factors	Strengths (S)	Weaknesses (W)
Opportunities(O)	**SO** strategies: strategies that use strengths to take advantage of opportunities,	**WO** strategies: strategies that take advantage of opportunities by over -coming weaknesses
Threats(T)	**ST** strategies: strategies that use strengths to avoid threats.	**WT** strategies: strategies that minimize weaknesses and avoid threats.

4. List the specific areas of current and future weaknesses for the company in the weaknessesbox across the top of the matrix.

5. Generate a series of possible alternative strategies for the company based on particular combinations of the four sets of factors. The four sets of strategies that emerge are:

- **SO Strategies:** SO strategies are generated by thinking of ways in which a company can use its strengths to take advantage of opportunities. This is the most desirable and advantageous strategy as it seeks to mass up the firm strengths to exploit opportunities. For example, Hindustan Lever has been augmenting its strengths by taking over businesses in the food industry, to exploit the growing potential of the food business.
- **ST Strategies:** ST strategies use a company strengths as a way to avoid threats. A company may use its technological, financial and marketing strengths to combat a new competition. Pot example, Hindustan Lever has been employing this strategy to fight the increasing competition from companies like Nirma, Procter & Gamble etc.,
- **WO Strategies:** WO Strategies attempt to take advantage of opportunities by overcoming its weaknesses. For example, for textile machinery manufacturers in India the main weakness was dependence on foreign firms for technology and the long time taken to execute an order. The strategy followed was the thrust given to R&D to develop indigenous technology so as to be in a better position to exploit the opportunity of growing demand for textile machinery.
- **WT Strategies:** WT Strategies are basically defensive strategies and primarily aimed at minimizing weaknesses and avoiding threats. For example, managerial weakness may be solved by change of managerial personnel, training and development etc. Weakness due to excess manpower may be addressed by restructuring, downsizing, delayering and voluntary retirement schemes. External threats maybe met by joint ventures and other types of strategic alliances. In some cases, an unprofitable business that cannot be revived may be divested.

Strategies which utilize a strength to take advantage of an opportunity ate generally referred to as exploitative or developmental strategies.Strategies which use a strength to eliminate a weakness may be referred to as blockingstrategies which overcome a weakness to take advantage of an opportunity or eliminate a threat may be referred to as remedial strategies

The TOWS matrix is a very useful tool for generating a series of alternative strategies that the decision-makers of the firm might not otherwise have considered. It can be used for the company as a whole or it can be used for a specific business unit within a company. However, it may be noted that the TOWS matrix is only one of many ways to generate alternative strategies.

Critical Assessment of Swot Analysis

SWOT analysis is one of the most basic techniques for analyzing firm and industry conditions. It provides the material for analyzing internal conditions as well as external conditions of a firm. SWOT analysis can be used in many ways to aid strategic analysis. For example, it can be used for a systematic discussion of a firm resources and basic alternatives that emerge from such an analysis. Such a discussion is necessary because a strength to one firm may be a weakness for another firm, and vice-versa. For example, increased health consciousness of people is a threat to some firms (e.g. tobacco) while it is an opportunity to others (e.g. health clubs).

According to Johnson and Sholes (2OO2), a SWOT analysis summarizes the key issues from the business environment and the strategic capability of an organization that impacts strategy development. This can also be useful as a basis for judging future courses of action. The aim is to identify the extent to which the current strengths and weaknesses are relevant to, and capable of, dealing with the changes taking place in the business environment. It can also be used to assess whether there are opportunities to exploit further the unique resources or core competencies of the organization. Overall, SWOT analysis helps focus discussion on future choices and the extent to which the company is capable of supporting its strategies.

Advantages and Limitations

Advantages

1. It is simple.
2. It portrays the essence of strategy formulation: matching a firm internal strengths and weaknesses with its external opportunities and threats.
3. Together with other techniques like Value Chain Analysis and RBV, SWOT analysis improves the quality of internal analysis.

Limitations:

1. It gives a static perspective, and does not reveal the dynamics of competitive environment.
2. SWOT emphasizes a single dimension of strategy (i.e. strength or weakness) and ignores other factors needed for competitive success.
3. A firm strengthdo not necessarily help the firm create value or competitive advantage.
4. SWOTs focus on the external environment is too narrow
5. Hill and Westbrook criticize SWOT analysis by saying that it is not a panacea. According to them, some of the criticisms against SWOT analysis are:
   a. It generates lengthy lists
   b. It uses no weights to reflect priorities
   c. It uses ambiguous words and phrases
   d. The same factor can be placed in two categories (e.g. an opportunity may also be a threat).
6. There is no obligation to verify opinions with data or analysis.
7. It is only a simple level of analysis. There is no logical link to strategy implementation.
8. SWOT helps only as a starting point. By itself, SWOT analysis rarely helps a firm develop competitive advantage that it can sustain over time.

4.6.3 Other Techniques

Some of the more popular ones in this category include (Bright and Milton) the following.

Expert Opinion: Knowledgeable people are selected and asked to assign importance and probability ratings to various possible future developments. The most refined version, the Delphi method, puts experts through several rounds of event assessment where they keep refining their assumptions and judgment's.

Dynamic Modeling: Researchers build sets of equations that attempt to describe the underlying system. The coefficients in the equations are fitted through statistical means. Econometric models of more than three hundred equations, for example, are used to forecast changes in the US economy.

Cross-impact Analysis: Researchers identity a set of key trends (those high in importance and/ or probability). The question is then put: event A occurs, what will be the impact on all other trends? The results are then used to build sets of chains, with one event triggering others.

Demand/Hazard Forecasting: Researchers identity major events that would greatly affect the firm. Each event is rated for its convergence with several major trends taking place in society and for its appeal to each major public group in the society The higher the event convergence and appeal, the higher its probability of occurring. The highest-scoring events are then researched further.

After implementing the environmental analysis process, management should continually evaluate and strive to improve it. The process, as pointed out by Certo and Peter, be linked to current planning operations, responsive to the information needs of top management, supported by key managers and performed by people who understand the difference between being an analyst and being a strategist.

4.7. SCENARIO BUILDING

The environments surrounding most firms are varied, complex and challenging. It is not easy to present the collected data in a simple, easy-to-understand format. Scenario building is a useful way of solving this complexity. Scenarios are stories about what the future environment might hold an how a firm might respond to this future. Scenario help strategists in focusing attention on the emerging picture after thoroughly analysing the pros and cons of a particular situation by integrating objective and subjective parts of various factors. Scenarios help managers to predict how things will turn out, explain what forces will shape the future and have a feel for the situations that are likely to unfold. Scenarios can be developed thus (Pearce & Robinson).

- Prepare the background by assessing the overall social environment under investigation (such as social legislation).
- Select critical indicators and search for future events that may affect the key trends (e.g., growing distrust of business).
- Analyse reasons for past behaviour for each trend (e.g., perceived disregard for air and water quality).
- Forecast each indicator in at least three scenarios, showing the least favourable environment, the likely environment and the most favourable environment.
- Write the scenario from the viewpoint oi someone in the future and describe conditions then and how they developed.
- Condense the scenario for each trend to a few paragraphs.

There are several guidelines for developing useful scenarios.

(1) Avoid focusing exclusively on controllable issues. Scenarios generally present alternative views of uncontrollable developments not simply lay out the plans and outcomes of internally controlled decisions.

(2) Actively seek out contrarian views. Scenario building compels managers to bring in outsiders with fresh perspectives who will invariably raise questions regarding things insiders may take for granted

(3) Do reality check as scenarios begin to form. Are the scenarios relevant for the line managers who will decide the firm future success? Scenarios should address worries that keep line managers up at night. If they do not, they remain pious, academic intentions with little tangible rewards

(4) Don't get bogged down in too many scenarios or too many details. A scenario is not supposed to capture everything and present a complex picture to the management. The purpose of scenarios, it is worth reiterating again, is to describe different worlds, not to detail all the outcomes possible in the same world.

4.8. ORGANISATIONAL RESPONSES TO THE ENVIRONMENT

Given the myriad issues, problems and opportunities in an organisation environments, how should the organisation adapt? Each organisation must assess its own unique situation and adapt according to the wisdom of its top management. It is not easy to come out with clear cut answers because the relationships between the organisation and its many environments are multifarious and difficult to predict. Even more difficult is the task of stating exactly what an organisation should do in response to a particular situation in the environment. For example, the removal of quantitative restrictions on consumer items, agricultural products, import of second hand vehicles is going to impact a number of domestic organisations in the days ahead. In such a scenario, the number of possible organisational responses are too numerous to be catalogued in a specific way. However, certain commonly used organisational responses could be stated thus:

- **Boundary-spanning Response:** In every organisation there are certain positions called boundary roles that link the organisation with its various external constituencies. These roles are filled by public relations representatives, sales people, purchasing agents etc. These boundary spanners spend a great amount of time with external groups and help present the organisation interest in dealings with the environment. They also convey the information about the environment to the organisation management. They, thus, help the firm to scan the environmental forces closely and take steps proactively in order to survive and progress in a complex and dynamic environment.
- **Strategic Responses:** Another way that an organisation adapts to its environment is through a strategic response. The options here include maintaining the status quo (even after removal of quantitative restrictions Bajaj Auto, for example, may not curtail production of scooters because management may feel that it is doing very well currently), altering strategy a bit (cut the prices a bit and advertise aggressively highlighting quality, service and reliability aspects more prominently) or adopting an entirely new strategy (reduced emphasis on scooters and expand the motor cycle market in line with global trends, or even venture into an alliance with an international car manufacturer). If the market that a company currently serves is growing rapidly (as is the case with motor cycle segment), the firm might decide to invest even more heavily in products and services for that market. The firm may like to pursue new markets for old products, introduce new products to old markets, or introduce new products to new markets. Alternatively, if a market is shrinking or does not offer reasonable possibilities for growth (say, the moped market), the company may decide to cut back, or to get out of competition altogether. Firms also indulge in domain shifts (changes in the mix of products and service offered so that the firm will interface with more favourable environmental elements) to regain the lost glory. Moving out of current products or services or locations into a more favourable domain, diversifications, expansion of product/service portfolio are all part of this strategy

- **Flexible Structural Designs:** An organization may also respond to environmental changes by altering its structural form. A firm that operates in an environment with relatively low levels of uncertainty might use a bureaucratic design putting emphasis on rules, order and conformance. Alternatively, a firm that operates in a turbulent environment might favour an organic structure, emphasizing informality, team structure, risk taking, initiative and creativity at various operating levels.
- **Mergers, Takeovers, Acquisitions and Alliances:** Companies may also engage in these kinds of strategies for a variety of reasons such as gaining entry into new markets, expanding its presence in a current market, enhancing its market share, consolidating its position in a particular region or segment etc.

4.9. COMPETITIVE POSITIONING

Competitive positioning is about defining how you'll "differentiate" your offering and create value for your market. It's about carving out a spot in the competitive landscape, putting your stake in the ground, and winning mindshare in the marketplace – being known for a certain "something."

A good positioning strategy is influenced by:

- **Market profile:** Size, competitors, stage of growth
- **Customer segments:** Groups of prospects with similar wants & needs
- **Competitive analysis:** Strengths, weaknesses, opportunities and threats in the landscape
- **Method for delivering value:** How you deliver value to your market at the highest level

When your market clearly sees how your offering is different from that of your competition, it's easier to influence the market and win mindshare. Without **differentiation**, it takes more time and budget to entice the market to engage with you; as a result, many companies end up competing on price – a tough position to sustain over the long term.

One of the key elements that many small to mid-size companies overlook is how they provide value at the highest level. There are three essential methods for delivering value: operational excellence, product leadership and customer intimacy.

4.10. DEVELOPING STRATEGY THROUGH INTERNAL ANALYSIS

Internal Analysis

By exploiting internal resources and capabilities and meeting the demanding standards of global competition, firms create value for customers. Value is measured by a product's performance characteristics and by its attributes for which customers are willing to pay. Those particular bundles of resources and capabilities that provide unique advantages to the firm are considered core competencies. Core competencies are resources and capabilities that serve as a source of a firm's competitive advantage over rivals. Core competencies distinguish a company competitively and reflect its personality. Core competencies emerge over time through an organizational process of accumulating and learning how to deploy different resources and capabilities. As the capacity to take action, core competencies are "crown jewels of a company," the activities the company performs especially well compared with competitors and through which the firm adds unique value to its goods or services over a long period of time.

Sometimes consistency and predictability provide value to customers, such as the type of value Walgreens drugstores provides. As a Fortune magazine writer noted, "Do you realize that from 1975 to today, Walgreens beat Intel? It beat Intel nearly two to one, GE almost five to one. It beat 3M, Coke, Boeing, Motorola. Walgreens was able to do this by using its core competencies to offer value desired by its target customer group. Instead of responding to the trends of the day, "During the Internet scare of 1998 and 1999, when slogans of 'Change or Die!' were all but graffitied on the subway, Walgreens obstinately stuck to its corporate credo of 'Crawl, walk, run.' Its refusal to act until it thoroughly understood the implications of e-commerce was deeply unfashionable, but...

Walgreens is the epitome of the inner-directed company. Thus, Walgreens creates value by focusing on the unique capabilities it has built, nurtured, and continues to improve across time.

Internal analysis tells the strategist what is inside the organization—helps answer the question, "what strengths can we leverage?"

During the past several decades, the strategic management process was concerned largely with understanding the characteristics of the industry in which the firm competed and, in light of those characteristics, determining how the firm should position it relative to competitors. This emphasis on industry characteristics and competitive strategy may have understated the role of the firm's resources and capabilities in developing competitive advantage. In the current competitive landscape, core competencies, in combination with product-market positions, are the firm's most important sources of competitive advantage. The core competencies of a firm, in addition to its analysis of its general, industry, and competitor environments, should drive its selection of strategies. As Clayton Christensen noted, "Successful strategists need to cultivate a deep understanding of the processes of competition and progress and of the factors that undergird each advantage. Only thus will they be able to see when old advantages are poised to disappear and how new advantages can be built in their stead." By drawing on internal analysis and emphasizing core competencies when formulating strategies, companies learn to compete primarily on the basis of firm-specific differences, but they must be aware of how things are changing as well.

Resources and Capabilities

Resources

Broad in scope, resources cover a spectrum of individual, social, and organizational phenomena. Typically, resources alone do not yield a competitive advantage. In fact, the core competencies that yield a competitive advantage are created through the unique bundling of several resources. For example, Amazon.com has combined service and distribution resources to develop its competitive advantages. The firm started as an online bookseller, directly shipping orders to customers. It quickly grew large and established a distribution network through which it could ship "millions of different items to millions of different customers." Compared with Amazon's use of combined resources, traditional bricks-and-mortar companies, such as Toys "R" Us and Borders, found it hard to establish an effective online presence. These difficulties led them to develop partnerships with Amazon. Through these arrangements, Amazon now handles online presence and the shipping of goods for several firms, including Toys "R" Us and Borders, which now can focus on sales in their stores. Arrangements such as these are useful to the bricks-and-mortar companies because they are not accustomed to shipping so much diverse merchandise directly to individuals.

Some of a firm's resources are tangible while others are intangible. Tangible resources are assets that can be seen and quantified. Production equipment, manufacturing plants, and formal reporting structures are examples of tangible resources. Intangible resources typically include assets that are rooted deeply in the firm's history and have accumulated over time. Because they are embedded in unique patterns of routines, intangible resources are relatively difficult for competitors to analyze and imitate. Knowledge, trust between managers and employees, ideas, the capacity for innovation, managerial capabilities, organizational routines (the unique ways people work together), scientific capabilities, and the firm's reputation for its goods or services and how it interacts with people (such as employees, customers, and suppliers) are all examples of intangible resources. The four types of tangible resources are financial, organizational, physical, and technological. The three types of intangible resources are human, innovation, and reputational.

As a manager or entrepreneur, you will be challenged to understand fully the strategic value of your firm's tangible and intangible resources. The strategic value of resources is indicated by the degree to which they can contribute to the development of core competencies, and, ultimately, competitive advantage. For example, as a tangible resource, a distribution facility is assigned a monetary value on the firm's balance sheet. The real value of the facility, however, is grounded in a variety of factors, such as its proximity to raw materials and customers, but also in intangible factors such as the manner in which workers integrate their actions internally and with other stakeholders, such as suppliers and customers.

Capabilities

Capabilities are the firm's capacity to deploy resources that have been purposely integrated to achieve a desired end state. The glue that holds an organization together, capabilities emerge over time through complex interactions among tangible and intangible resources. Capabilities can be tangible, like a business process that is automated, but most of them tend to be tacit and intangible. Critical to forming competitive advantages, capabilities are often based on developing, carrying, and exchanging information and knowledge through the firm's human capital. Because a knowledge base is grounded in organizational actions that may not be explicitly understood by all employees, repetition and practice increase the value of a firm's capabilities.

The foundation of many capabilities lies in the skills and knowledge of a firm's employees and, often, their functional expertise. Hence, the value of human capital in developing and using capabilities and, ultimately, core competencies cannot be overstated. Firms committed to continuously developing their people's capabilities seem to accept the adage that "the person who knows how will always have a job. The person who knows why will always be his boss."

Global business leaders increasingly support the view that the knowledge possessed by human capital is among the most significant of an organization's capabilities and may ultimately be at the root of all competitive advantages. But firms must also be able to use the knowledge that they have and transfer it among their operating businesses For example, researchers have suggested that "in the information age, things are ancillary, knowledge is central. A company's value derives not from things, but from knowledge, know-how, intellectual assets, competencies—all of it embedded in people." Given this reality, the firm's challenge is to create an environment that allows people to fit their individual pieces of knowledge together so that, collectively, employees possess as much organizational knowledge as possible.

To help them develop an environment in which knowledge is widely spread across all employees, some organizations have created the new upper-level managerial position of chief learning officer (CLO). Establishing a CLO position highlights a firm's belief that "future success will depend on competencies that traditionally have not been actively managed or measured—including creativity and the speed with which new ideas are learned and shared." In general, the firm should manage knowledge in ways that will support its efforts to create value for customers.

4.11. VALUE CHAIN

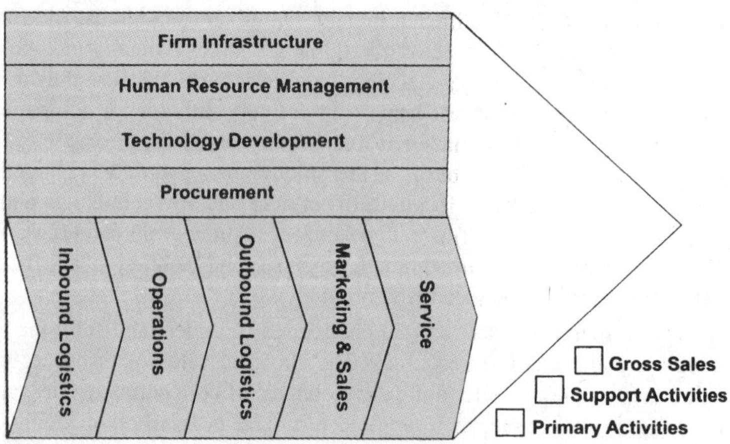

Figure 4.2. Value Chain Porte.

Capabilities are often developed in specific functional areas (such as manufacturing, R&D, and marketing) or in a part of a functional area (for example, advertising). The value chain, popularized by Michael Porter's book Competitive Advantage, is a useful tool for taking stock of organizational capabilities. A value chain is a chain of activities. In the value chain, some of the activities are deemed to be primary, in the sense that these activities add direct value. In the preceding figure, primary activities are logistics (inbound and outbound), marketing, and service. Support activities include how the firm is organized (infrastructure), human resources, technology, and procurement. Products pass through all activities of the chain in order, and at each activity, the product gains some value. A firm is effective to the extent that the chain of activities gives the products more added value than the sum of added values of all activities.

It is important not to mix the concept of the value chain with the costs occurring throughout the activities. A diamond cutter can be used as an example of the difference. The cutting activity may have a low cost, but the activity adds to much of the value of the end product, since a rough diamond is significantly less valuable than a cut, polished diamond. Research suggests a relationship between capabilities developed in particular functional areas and the firm's financial performance at both the corporate and business-unit levels, suggesting the need to develop capabilities at both levels.

4.12. VRIO ANALYSIS

Given that almost anything a firm possesses can be considered a resource or capability, how should you attempt to narrow down the ones that are core competencies, and explain why firm performance differs? To lead to a sustainable competitive advantage, a resource or capability should be valuable, rare, inimitable (including nonsubstitutable), and organized. This VRIO framework is the foundation for internal analysis. VRIO is an acronym for valuable, rare, inimitable, and organization.

If you ask managers why their firms do well while others do poorly, a common answer is likely to be "our people." But this is really not an answer. It may be the start of an answer, but you need to probe more deeply—what is it about "our people" that is especially valuable? Why don't competitors have similar people? Can't competitors hire our people away? Or is it that there something special about the organization that brings out the best in people? These kinds of questions form the basis of VRIO and get to the heart of why some resources help firms more than others.

Valuable?	Rare?	Difficult to Imitate?	Supported by Organization?	Competitive Implications	Performance
No	–	–		Competitive Disadvantage	Below Normal
Yes	No	–		Competitive Party	Normal
Yes	Yes	No		Temporary Competitive Advantage	Above Normal
Yes	Yes	Yes	Yes	Sustained Competitive Advantage	Above Normal

Figure 4.3. VRIO and Relative Firm Performance.

Moreover, your ability to identify whether an organization has VRIO resources will also likely explain their competitive position. In the figure, you can see that a firm's performance relative to industry peers is likely to vary according to the level to which resources, capabilities, and ultimately core competences satisfy VRIO criteria. The four criteria are explored next.

- **Valuable**

A resource or capability is said to be valuable if it allows the firm to exploit opportunities or negate threats in the environment. Union Pacific's extensive network of rail-line property and equipment in the Gulf Coast of the United States is valuable because it allows the company to provide a cost-effective way to transport chemicals. Because the Gulf Coast is the gateway for the majority of chemical production in the United States, the rail network allows the firm to exploit a market opportunity. Delta's control of the majority of gates at the Cincinnati / Northern Kentucky International Airport (CVG) gives it a significant advantage in many markets. Travelers worldwide have rated CVG one of the best airports for service and convenience 10 years running. The possession of this resource allows Delta to minimize the threat of competition in this city. Delta controls air travel in this desirable hub city, which means that this asset (resource) has significant value. If a resource does not allow a firm to minimize threats or exploit opportunities, it does not enhance the competitive position of the firm. In fact, some scholars suggest that owning resources that do not meet the VRIO test of value actually puts the firm at a competitive disadvantage.

- **Rare**

A resource is rare simply if it is not widely possessed by other competitors. Of the criteria this is probably the easiest to judge. For example, Coke's brand name is valuable but most of Coke's competitors (Pepsi, 7Up, RC) also have widely recognized brand names, making it not that rare. Of course, Coke's brand may be the most recognized, but that makes it more valuable, not rarer, in this case.

A firm that possesses valuable resources that are not rare is not in a position of advantage relative to competitors. Rather, valuable resources that are commonly held by many competitors simply allow firms to be at par with competitors. However, when a firm maintains possession of valuable resources that are rare in the industry they are in a position of competitive advantage over firms that do not possess the resource. They may be able to exploit opportunities or negate threats in ways that those lacking the resource will not be able to do. Delta's virtual control of air traffic through Cincinnati gives it a valuable and rare resource in that market.

How rare do the resources need to be for a firm to have a competitive advantage? In practice, this is a difficult question to answer unequivocally. At the two extremes (i.e., one firm possesses the resource or all firms possess it), the concept is intuitive. If only one firm possesses the resource, it has significant advantage over all other competitors. For instance, Monsanto had such an advantage for many years because they owned the patent to aspartame, the chemical compound in NutraSweet, they had a valuable and extremely rare resource. Because during the lifetime of the patent they were the only firm that could sell aspartame, they had an advantage in the artificial sweetener market. However, meeting the condition of rarity does not always require exclusive ownership. When only a few firms possess the resource, they will have an advantage over the remaining competitors. For instance, Toyota and Honda both have the capabilities to build cars of high quality at relatively low cost. Their products regularly beat rival firms' products in both short-term and long-term quality ratings. Thus, the criterion of rarity requires that the resource not be widely possessed in the industry. It also suggests that the more exclusive a firms access to a particularly valuable resource, the greater the benefit for having it.

- **Inimitable**

An inimitable (the opposite of imitable) resource is difficult to imitate or to create ready substitutes for. A resource is inimitable and non substitutable if it is difficult for another firm to acquire it or to substitute something else in its place. A valuable and rare resource or capability will grant a competitive advantage as long as other firms do not gain subsequently possession of the resource or a close substitute. If a resource is valuable and rare and responsible for a market leader's competitive advantage, it is likely that competitors lacking the resource or capability will do all that they can to obtain the resource or capability themselves. This leads us to the third criterion—inimitability. The concept of imitation includes any form of acquiring the lacking resource or substituting a similar resource that provides equivalent benefits. The criterion important to be addressed is whether competitors face a cost disadvantage in acquiring or substituting the resource that is lacking. There are numerous ways that firms may acquire resources or capabilities that they lack.

As strategy researcher Scott Gallagher notes

"This is probably the toughest criterion to examine because given enough time and money almost any resource can be imitated. Even patents only last 17 years and can be invented around in even less time. Therefore, one way to think about this is to compare how long you think it will take for competitors to imitate or substitute something else for that resource and compare it to the useful life of the product. Another way to help determine if a resource is inimitable is why/how it came about. Inimitable resources are often a result of historical, ambiguous, or socially complex causes. For example, the U.S. Army paid for Coke to build bottling plants around the world during World War II. This is an example of history creating an inimitable asset. Generally, intangible (also called tacit) resources or capabilities, like corporate culture or reputation, are very hard to imitate and therefore inimitable.

- **Organized**

The fourth and final VRIO criterion that determines whether a resource or capability is the source of competitive advantage recognizes that mere possession or control is necessary but not sufficient to gain an advantage. The firm must likewise have the organizational capability to exploit the resources. The question of organization is broad and encompasses many facets of a firm but essentially means that the firm is able to capture any value that the resource or capability might generate. Organization, essentially the same form as that taken in the P-O-L-C framework, spans such firm characteristics as control systems, reporting relationships, compensation policies, and management interface with both customers and value-adding functions in the firm. Although listed as the last criterion in the VRIO tool, the question of organization is a necessary condition to be satisfied if a firm is to reap the benefits of any of the three preceding conditions. Thus, a valuable but widely held resource only leads to competitive parity for a firm if they also possess the capabilities to exploit the resource. Likewise, a firm that possesses a valuable and rare resource will not gain a competitive advantage unless it can actually put that resource to effective use.

Many firms have valuable and rare resources that they fail to exploit (the question of imitation is not relevant until the firm exploits valuable and rare resources). For instance, for many years Novell had a significant competitive advantage in computer networking based on its core NetWare product. In high-technology industries, remaining at the top requires continuous innovation. Novell's decline during the mid- to late 1990s led many to speculate that Novell was unable to innovate in the face of changing markets and technology. However, shortly after new CEO Eric Schmidt arrived from Sun Microsystems to attempt to turnaround the firm, he arrived at a different conclusion. Schmidt commented: "I walk down Novell hallways and marvel at the incredible potential of innovation here. But, Novell has had a difficult time in the past turning innovation into products in the marketplace."

He later commented to a few key executives that it appeared the company was suffering from "organizational constipation." Novell appeared to still have innovative resources and capabilities, but they lacked the organizational capability (e.g., product development and marketing) to get those new products to market in a timely manner.

Likewise, Xerox proved unable to exploit its innovative resources. Xerox created a successful research team housed in a dedicated facility in Palo Alto, California, known as Xerox PARC. Scientists in this group invented an impressive list of innovative products, including laser printers, Ethernet, graphical interface software, computers, and the computer mouse. History has demonstrated that these technologies were commercially successful. Unfortunately, for Xerox shareholders, these commercially successful innovations were exploited by other firms. Xerox's organization was not structured in a way that information about these innovations flowed to the right people in a timely fashion. Bureaucracy was also suffocating ideas once they were disseminated. Compensation policies did not reward managers for adopting these new innovations but rather rewarded current profits over long-term success. Thus, Xerox was never able exploit the innovative resources and capabilities embodied in their off-site Xerox PARC research center.

SWOT and VRIO

As you already know, many scholars refer to core competencies. A core competency is simply a resource, capability, or bundle of resources and capabilities that is VRIO. While VRIO resources are the best, they are quite rare, and it is not uncommon for successful firms to simply be combinations of a large number of VR _ O or even V _ _ O resources and capabilities. Recall that even a VRIO resource can be considered a strength under a traditional SWOT analysis.

4.13. CORE COMPETENCIES ANALYSIS

Industry structure analysis is well suited to describing the what of competitiveness, i.e., what makes one firm or one industry more profitable than another. But understanding the particulars of such advantages as low cost, quality, customer service and time to market may still leave the question of why largely unanswered.

For example, why do some companies seem able to continually create new forms of competitive advantage while others seem able only to observe and follow? Why are some firms net advantage creators and others net advantage imitators? For assessing competitive advantage it is necessary not only to keep score of existing advantages—what they are and who has them—but also to discover what it is that drives the process of advantage creation. Industry structure analysis is much better suited to the first task than to the second. Thus, industry structure analysis must be supplemented by an equally explicit core competence focus. Organizations need to be viewed not only as a portfolio of products or services, but also as a portfolio of core competencies. Core competencies are created by superior integration of technological, physical and human resources. They represent distinctive skills as well as intangible, invisible, intellectual assets and cultural capabilities. Cultural capabilities refer to the ability to manage change, the ability to learn and team working. Organizations should be viewed as a bundle of a few core competencies, each supported by several individual skills.

Core competencies are the connective tissue that holds together a portfolio of seemingly diverse businesses. They are the lingua franca that allows managers to translate insights and experience from one business setting into another. Core competence-based diversification reduces risk and investment and increases the opportunities for transferring learning and best practice across business units. For instance, the New York Times stated that Microsoft's only factory asset is the human imagination. This company has excelled in inventing new ways of using information technology for a wide variety of end users. In contrast, using its core competence in information processing, Xerox developed icons, pull-down menus and the computer mouse, but failed to exploit the marketplace. A core competence is identified by the following tests.

- Can it be leveraged?—does it provide potential access to a wide variety of markets?
- Does it enhance customer value?—does it make a significant contribution to the perceived customer benefits of the end product?
- Can it be imitated?—does it reduce the threat of imitation by competitors?

Applying the value chain approach to core competencies for competitive advantage includes the following steps:

- validate core competencies in current businesses;
- export or leverage core competencies to the value chains of other existing businesses;
- use core competencies to reconfigure the value chains of existing businesses; and
- use core competencies to create new value chains.

Chapter 5

STRATEGIC PLANNING

Introduction - Meaning and Definition of Strategic Planning - Strategic, Operational and Tactical Planning - Differences and Description - Process or Steps of Strategic Planning - Evolution of Strategic Planning - Dimension of Strategic Decisions - Challenges - Features of a Strategic Plan – Benefits - Hierarchical Levels of Planning - Strategies in Mature Industries- Business Strategies in Emerging Industries - Reasons for Failure of Strategic Plans - Strategic Management for Small, Large, Multiproduct and Multiple Market Organizations - Business Ethics and Strategic Management-Strategic Funds Programming - Assessment of Economic Contribution of Strategy.

5.1. INTRODUCTION - STRATEGIC PLANNING

The necessity of planning arises because of the fact that business organizations have to operate, survive and progress in a highly dynamic environment where change is the rule, not the exception. The change may be sudden and extensive, or it may be slow and almost imperceptible. The rapid advances in technology, global competition, changing preferences of customers, changing policies of government, have multiplied the problems of managers all over the globe. Most of these changes are thrust on managers and they are forced to adjust their activities (customer service, teamwork, speed, product/service quality, productivity improvement have become the new corporate mantras) in order to take full advantage of favorable developments or to minimize the adverse effects of unfavorable ones. Successful managers try to visualize the problems before they turn into emergencies. Successful managers deal with foreseen problems, and unsuccessful managers' struggle with unforeseen problems. The difference lies in planning (Terry). Managers charged with the responsibility of achieving definite targets do not wait for the future. They make the future (Drucker). They introduce original initiatives by removing present difficulties; anticipating future problems; changing the goals to meet internal and external challenges; experimenting with creative ideas; attempting to shape the future and creating a more desirable environment.

Planning is the process of deciding in advance what should be accomplished and how it should be realized. It involves selecting objectives and how to achieve them. Strategic planning is a type of planning. But unlike short-term planning, strategic planning involves an extended time-frame, the deployment of a large percentage of the resources of an organization, a wide spectrum of activities and a major eventual impact.

5.2. MEANING AND DEFINITION OF STRATEGIC PLANNING

It is an organization's process of defining its strategy, or direction, and making decisions on allocating its resources to pursue this strategy. In order to determine the direction of the organization, it is necessary to understand its current position and the possible avenues through which it can pursue a particular course of action. Generally, strategic planning deals with at least one of three key questions-

- "What do we do?"
- "For whom do we do it?"
- "How do we excel?

The key components of 'strategic planning' include an understanding of the firm's vision, mission, values and strategies. (Often a "Vision Statement" and a "Mission Statement" may encapsulate the vision and mission)

1. "*Strategic Planning is the process of deciding on the objectives of the organization, on changes in these objectives, on the resources used to attain these objectives, and on the policies that are to govern the acquisition, use, and disposition of these resources*".

—Robert Anthony

2. "*Strategic Planning is the continuous process of making present entrepreneurial (risk-Taking) decisions systematically and with the greatest knowledge of their futurity organizing systematically the efforts needed to carry out these decisions; measuring the results of these decisions against expectations through organized, systematic feedback*"

—Peter Drucker

3. "*Strategic Planning is a planning for the fulfillment of the Organization's fundamental purposes. It includes the process of establishing and clarifying purposes, and determining the major means and "Pathways" (Strategies) through which these objectives will be pursued*".

—Peter B Vaill

5.3. STRATEGIC, OPERATIONAL AND TACTICAL PLANNING

Strategic planning, thus, is long-term in nature. It tends to be a top management responsibility. It requires looking outside the organization for threats and opportunities. It also requires looking inside the organization for finding out weaknesses and strengths. It affects many parts of the organization as its decisions have enduring effects that are difficult to reverse. It tries to equip the organization with capabilities needed to confront future uncertainties by taking a holistic view of the entire organization. Its focus is clearly on the 'jungle, not the trees'. The main objective is to position the firm in an advantageous relation to the environment, keeping its own internal capabilities in mind. In simple terms, strategic planning is the process of determining the major objectives of an organization and the policies and strategies that will govern the acquisition, use and disposition of resources to achieve those objectives.

The strategic plans are designed to meet the broad objectives of an organization. They are long-range plans. Tactical plans are concerned with implementing strategic plans by coordinating the work of various departments in an organization. They are known as intermediate plans. Operational plans are short-range plans. They offer details as to how the strategic plans will be accomplished. Table 5.1 draws the distinction of these terms with clarity.

Figure 5.1.

Table 5.1. Comparison Between Strategic Planning and Operational Planning

Strategic (long-range) Plans	Intermediate (Tactical) Plans	Operational (Short-range) Plans
• Long-range plan • Time-frame: 3 or more years • Top management responsibility • Concerned with broad objectives • Focus on planning and forecasting	• Intermediate plan • Time-frame: 2-3 years • Performed by managers at middle level • Concerned with integrating of the organization departments in the organization • Focus on coordination	• Short-range plan • Time frame: one year • Done usually at lower levels • Covers day-to-day the work of various operations; implements internal goals • Focus on control primarily.

5.3.1 More Detailed Description on Strategic, Operational and Tactical Planning

Strategic Plans

To best understand the relationship between the different types of plans, let's start at the top. Strategic plans are designed with the entire organization in mind and begin with an organization's mission. Top-level managers, such as CEOs or presidents, will design and execute strategic plans to paint a picture of the desired future and long-term goals of the organization. Essentially, strategic plans look ahead to where the organization wants to be in three, five, even ten years. Strategic plans, provided by top-level managers, serve as the framework for lower-level planning.

Tommy is a top-level manager for Nino's Pizzeria. As a top-level manager, Tommy must use strategic planning to ensure the long-term goals of the organization are reached. For Tommy, that means developing long-term strategies for achieving growth, improving productivity and profitability, boosting return on investments, improving customer service and finding ways to give back to the community in which it operates.

For example, Tommy's strategic plans for achieving growth, improving productivity and profitability and boosting return on investments are all part of the desired future of the pizzeria. Strategic plans also tend to require multilevel involvement so that each level of the organization plays a significant role in achieving the goals being strategically planned for. Top-level managers, such as Tommy, develop the organizational objectives so that middle- and lower-level managers can create compatible plans aligned with those objectives.

Tactical Plans

Now that you have a general idea for how organizational planning evolves, let's look at the next level of planning, known as tactical planning. Tactical plans support strategic plans by translating them into specific plans relevant to a distinct area of the organization. Tactical plans are concerned with the responsibility and functionality of lower-level departments to fulfill their parts of the strategic plan.

For example, when Martha, the middle-level manager at Nino's, learns about Tommy's strategic plan for increasing productivity, Martha immediately begins to think about possible tactical plans to ensure that happens. Tactical planning for Martha might include things like testing a new process in making pizzas that has been proven to shorten the amount of time it takes for prepping the pizza to be cooked or perhaps looking into purchasing a better oven that can speed up the amount of time it takes to cook a pizza or even considering ways to better map out delivery routes and drivers. As a tactical planner, Martha needs to create a set of calculated actions that take a shorter amount of time and are narrower in scope than the strategic plan is but still help to bring the organization closer to the long-term goal.

Operational Plans

Operational plans sit at the bottom of the totem pole; they are the plans that are made by frontline, or low-level, managers. All operational plans are focused on the specific procedures and processes that occur within the lowest levels of the organization. Managers must plan the routine tasks of the department using a high level of detail. Frank, the frontline manager at Nino's Pizzeria, is responsible for operational planning. Operational planning activities for Frank would include things like scheduling employees each week; assessing, ordering and stocking inventory; creating a monthly budget; developing a promotional advertisement for the quarter to increase the sales of a certain product (such as the Hawaiian pizza) or outlining an employee's performance goals for the year.

Operational plans can be either single-use or ongoing plans. Single-use plans are those plans that are intended to be used only once. They include activities that would not be repeated and often have an expiration. Creating a monthly budget and developing a promotional advertisement for the quarter to increase the sales of a certain product are examples of how Frank would utilize single-use planning. Ongoing plans are those plans that are built to withstand the test of time. They are created with the intent to be used several times and undergo changes when necessary. Outlining an employee's performance goals for the year would be considered an ongoing plan that Frank must develop, assess and update, if necessary. Ongoing plans are typically a policy, procedure or rule. Policies are general statements, or guidelines, that aid a manager in understanding routine responsibilities of his or her role as a manager. Examples of policies include things such as hiring, training, outlining and assessing performance appraisals and disciplining and terminating subordinates. A procedure details the step-by-step process of carrying out a certain task, such as assessing, ordering and stocking inventory. A rule provides managers and employees with specific and explicit guidelines of behavior that is what they should and should not do as a member of the organization.

5.4. PROCESS OR STEPS OF STRATEGIC PLANNING

1. **Farm business strategy is not a race, it's a process:** Organizations need strategy to guide them in achieving objectives that fulfill their vision and mission. For producers, the purpose of strategizing is to determine how the farm business will reach its performance targets, outperform rivals, find and maintain competitive advantages and build a long-term competitive position.
2. **The basic steps of the process are as follows:**
   - Develop a clear understanding of what should be accomplished in the business and why.
   - Look outside the farm at the environment in which the business operates in order to identify potential opportunities and threats.
   - Evaluate the farm business to identify its strengths and weaknesses in terms of being able to compete in its business environment now and in the future.
   - Review current strategies and evaluate new strategies that appear to fit the situation.
   - Develop a plan of action for implementing selected strategies.
   - Identify the factors that are critical to the successful implementation of strategies and methods for frequent monitoring.

- Recognize the assumptions underlying the selection of strategies.

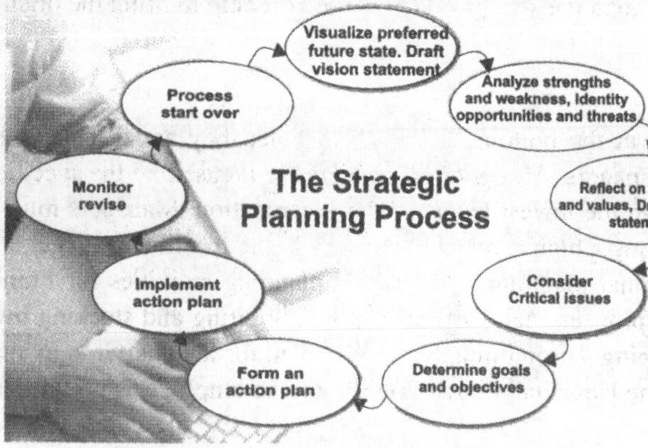

Figure 5.2. The Strategic Planning Process.

3. **Parts of a whole**. Each step in strategic planning involves information gathering, reflective thinking and communication."Obviously, most farmers gather information, think and communicate with others on a continuing basis," Dobbins notes. "An advantage of systematic strategic planning, as opposed to a more piecemeal approach, is the balance struck among the different steps. Systematic strategic planning emphasizes the connection of the steps in the process."
4. **SWOT works.** SWOT is an acronym for Strengths, Weaknesses, Opportunities and Threats. Using SWOT, the farm business manager can develop strategies that will allow the farm business to use its strengths to capitalize on opportunities and deflect threats while minimizing the weaknesses of the business.
5. **To begin this internal scanning:** The business needs to be broken down into comprehensible chunks. It is useful to group similar parts of the business together into units. A strategic business unit is based on important strategic elements common to each of the parts being grouped. Essentially, the farm business manager assesses what the business offers to its customers.
6. **Marketing based on available resources:** The manager can answer this in a number of different ways. One way is to answer in terms of available resources. Another way is to answer in terms of what markets the business serves or what products the business produces. For instance, the manager of a crop farm might want to think of its commodity crops as one unit and its crops produced on contract as another unit. The same manager might think of corn as one unit and soybeans as another. The first half of SWOT concerns the business itself, its internal strengths and weaknesses. These are things that the business can control, such as employees or machinery.
7. **Identifying the internal strengths and weaknesses:** The business is a two-stage process. The first part is to identify what the business does better than the competition. The second part is to consider how the business does it better.An internal analysis also lists the resources and capabilities that lie behind the strengths and weaknesses. Resources are the physical assets used in the business. While they are important, they are seldom the source of a competitive advantage.

5.5. EVOLUTION OF STRATEGIC PLANNING

1. Drucker: Peter Drucker set a "classic" definition of strategic planning in his seminal 1973 book Management. In Management, Drucker indicated that planning was nothing new – it was simply the organized performance of an old task. Drucker's definition was simple – planning was the continuos process of making entrepreneurial decisions systematically and with the best possible sense of "futurity", systematically organizing the efforts required to carry out the decisions and then measuring the results of those decisions against expectations (systematic feedback). Drucker's basic thesis was that organizations needed to treat management (and therefore planning) as a disciplined science. With discipline came the opportunity to learn from previous experience and to share those experiences throughout an organization

2. Porter: In the 1980's, Porter put forth the proposition that strategy should better reflect the nature of competition and resources within a given business market or environment. Porter spearheaded the push to planning based on the nature of external, competitive forces in an industry or business sector. In Competitive Strategy and Competitive Advantage, Porter defined a planning model and process that was based on gaining an understanding of the competitive forces that define an industry and it's attractiveness from a business perspective.

3. Emerging Issues – Planning Under Attack: Theory is one thing – implementation and reality another. In concert with the theoretical concepts of planning developed by academics and corporations came the more practical issue of implementing strategic planning exercises and turning plans into 'action". Even more important was the concept of linking plans to reality and results. Companies began reporting "problems" with strategic planning – or at least problems with the way their companies were doing it. Throughout the Eighties, the recession, increasing globalization of economies and increased competitive pressures, combined to challenge traditional business notions and processes. Many corporate "strategic plans" were failing. As a result, much blame was placed on the concept of strategic planning. Headquarters staff almost always preferred to "plan" while "customer" facing personnel were always left to implement. In viewing the evolution of planning from a historical perspective, there appear to be several explanations for the failure of planning to deliver on expectations. As most early (or traditional) planning methodologies used similar approaches to strategy development and plan implementation the issues were common to all:

4. A "Top Down" View of Organizations: These were for the most part centralized, 'top down" exercises, characterized by teams of corporate planners sequestered at headquarters, occasionally calling for information or data, finally presenting their plan (very often a financial forecast or budget spreadsheet) to Senior Management. The plan (once blessed) was then presented to "operations" managers charged with execution. The "plan" descended from above. Implementation was a tactical consideration. As a result, the plans were far removed from the actual corporate "reality" existing beyond headquarters staff. One of the most frequent complaints by academics and practitioners was that strategic planning as practiced by many organizations was too inwardly focused and did not involve those who knew the most about markets, external environment and the actual strengths and capabilities of an organization related to its objectives.

5. Planning Definitions and Expectations: As researchers began looking at "planning failures" other observations were made. In many organizations there were significant stereotypes, and misperceptions regarding the planning process. Many of these were affecting the planning process and most importantly the quality of the plans themselves.

6. Strategy is based on Inspiration and Individual Brilliance: In many organizations, strategies were historically believed to be the "brainchild" of individuals, inspired to great leaps of insight and creativity. The common planning structure placed a limited number of individuals in planning roles and expected performance to follow. With the emergence of complex markets and organizations, it became increasingly obvious that many more minds (reflecting increasing prevalence of "team" structures) needed to be involved in the planning process. Not only would this approach enhance sharing of knowledge and information but also increased the level of creative input and idea generation to the planning process. In addition, multiple individuals would balance individual operating styles and analytical strengths and weaknesses across the organization.

7. Complexity of Organizations: Another factor influencing the planning and implementation process was the continual evolution of the organization into highly complex structures, frequently with geographic and/or business function groups. These complex structures place a tremendous burden on the planning and implementation process. In some cases, organizational planning has devolved to the point that

business units engage in strategic planning and have strategic plans while the organization as a whole no longer has a cohesive vision or plan for the future.

8. As complex organizations begin to develop internal differences and silos (based on values, social structures, geographic cultural foundations), successful planning, as a shared, ongoing exercise involving a broad cross-section of an organization, becomes an even greater burden.

9. Technology and Pace of Change: The pace of change in almost all aspects of civilization has never been faster. The Internet economy, technological innovation, changing political and economic landscapes places another burden on the strategic planning process. Planning on "Internet Time" has become a common phrase and means planning for 6-month timeframes rather than traditional 1 to 5 year planning horizons. Predicting the future (a critical component of strategic planning) is an increasingly difficult task, despite the fact more and more "data" can be exchanged, analyzed and shared. Today's technologies allow organizations to gather vol umes of data previously unavailable at any cost. As Knowledge Management (KM) and KM systems evolve, the planning process will need to adapt and integrate this flood of information.

10. Planning Evolution: As a result of the influences discussed above, planning models and methodologies have been evolving. Although these planning methodologies or frameworks have certainly evolved from original approaches, the basic tenets of Ansoff, Drucker, et al still hold. Regardless of methodology, the building blocks of effective planning still consist of assessing current position / status, setting direction (i.e., strategy), implementing and assessing results. In many cases it's the framework, tools and methodologies that have changed.

11. The following section outlines some useful planning methodologies, beginning with the balanced scorecard approach to planning.

(a) Balanced Scorecard

The Balanced Scorecard approach ties or translates the strategic objectives of an organization to clearly defined performance measures. The approach, developed by Kaplan and Norton, was born of the belief that in order to improve strategic planning and ultimately the effectiveness of those plans, there needed to be a tighter link between objectives and day-to-day operational realities. The Balanced Scorecard identifies four key perspectives related to ultimate organizational success. The basic premise of the framework is that all four measures are ultimately critical for long term success. These perspectives of performance include:-

- Financial
- Customer or Stakeholder
- Internal Organizational Processes

(b) Innovation and Learning

The balanced scorecard identifies the knowledge; skills and systems that your employees and staff will need (their learning and growth) to help them to innovate, solve problems and build the right strategic capabilities. These capabilities will lead to the delivery of specific value to stakeholders or the marketplace which in the end provides the highest possible value to shareholders – or in the case of public sector or government organizations – the taxpayer or ultimate shareholder.

5.6. DIMENSION OF STRATEGIC DECISIONS

1. **Strategic issues require top-management decisions:** Strategic issues involve thinking in totality of the organization's objectives in which a considerable amount of risk is involved. Hence, problems calling for strategic decisions require to be considered by the top management.
2. **Strategic issues involve the allocation of large amounts of company resources:** It may require either a huge financial investment to venture into a new area of business or the organization may require a huge amount of manpower with new skill sets.
3. **Strategic issues are likely to have a significant impact on the long term prosperity of the firm:** Generally the results of strategic implementation are seen on a long term basis and not on immediate terms.
4. **Strategic issues are future oriented:** Strategic thinking involves predicting the future environmental conditions and how to orient for the changed conditions.
5. **Strategic issues usually have major multifunctional or multi business consequences:** As they involve organization in totality they affect different sections of the organization with varying degree.
6. **Strategic issues necessitate consideration of factors in the firm's external environment:** Strategic focus in an organization involves orienting its internal environment to the changes of external environment.

5.7. CHALLENGES OR KEY ISSUES IN STRATEGIC PLANNING

1. Planning differ depending on attitude and culture of the company: Every year at about this time or a little earlier, we start the process of 'strategic' planning. The annual planning process, for all its focus on analysis, or template completion, can easily fall into the apparently comfortable tactic of merely updating the activity from last year's plans. Often, however, what is really needed is a fresh approach which can pay dividends. Approaches to planning differ, depending upon the attitude and culture of the company involved, which in turn affect the relative importance given to different elements of the process and the output. Some companies are heavily financially oriented, making the desired output more focused on numbers than the thinking behind those numbers.

2. Forecast based on time period differ: Not all companies perform truly strategic (long -term) market-centered planning, but all companies generally aim to produce a set of financial forecasts. The major differences are in the way they get there and as a consequence the basis on which those forecasts are derived. First and foremost, the organization needs to be clear about what issues can get in the way of developing a sound strategic plan before deciding on an appropriate approach. Clearly all planning is driven to an extent by profit and financial forecasts but there is a need to be clear what else the plan has to deliver for the organization, the individual, and the brand – the planning 'need' – otherwise the process used may be sub-optimal. Why does the organization need a plan? What is it meant to deliver over and above the financial projections?

3. Many companies are often unaware of the issues and constraints: It will affect the planning process and output , for example the local operating company situation. Are the right resources, the right experience and the right information available at a local level to develop and complete the plan? Can the local markets get the right quality of information they need to drive good quality thinking? If not, then how can this be provided to ensure the right level of thinking is achieved? It could also be that the chosen approach is too sophisticated or inappropriate to deliver the required answers. For example, the process may have all the 'standard' elements of analysis but there is no thought given to what each element is telling them.

4. Maximization of return: All companies do have a structured process but if the process does not drive the necessary thinking then the resulting plans can be limited. If the process does not challenge the planners to consider different ways of doing things but is merely a set of agreed templates and a time line for deliverables, the resultant forecast simply becomes a straight line projection from historical sales data, and activity remains the same as last year no matter whether or not things are changing in the market. This is the apparently 'safe' option but it rarely maximizes return on investment and is often not safe at all.

5. Different approaches to strategic planning in our experience: The data-driven approach is based on hard data collected from a variety of sources, both primary panels and syndicated data, from which a market model is then built by brand from the bottom up. Issues are then identified but there seems to be no real focus on what drives success in local markets, or on what competitors will do and the impact of their actions. This approach can simply lead to 'more of the same', making a projection based on the previous year and no real change in approach, with the whole focus being on next year's revenue. While many companies may not use such an apparently numbers-focused approach they still act in the same way, with the forecast being the key, rather than the rationale behind it.

6. Overcome the inevitable local variances: This consists of a pre-defined plan with key headings that can be amplified or contracted, but with certain key elements which must be completed. This option works well as it provides a structured process for analysis, with check questions at each stage. However in some cases we have seen that such an approach can still be very financially focused. Sometimes it does not analyze the brand and company strengths and weaknesses in a meaningful market-centered manner, to enable a market -led SWOT analysis and often there is still not enough competitive focus.

7. Marketing excellence' approach: The next level is often seen in the 'marketing excellence' approach, where the organization provides an integrated planning tool comprising standard marketing planning software. In a sophisticated example this allows local working but is linked into a central supporting database, with aspects that can be adapted and others that are fixed. The beauty of such a process is that it is transparent, allowing a clear overview of who is performing well and enabling experience and successes to be shared. However when this is a relatively new process people tend to take time to get to grips with the process resulting in 'doing the process' rather than really thinking about what each step is telling them. Moreover for this approach to be used effectively, senior management must understand the process very well so that they can interrogate the people who are developing the plan.

8. Summary of key issues: In summary the key issues in strategic planning are-

- Not being clear about the planning 'need'
- Not being aware of the issues and constraints that will affect the planning process and output
- Approach too sophisticated or not appropriate to deliver the required answers
- The financial forecast is all that matters, with the thinking behind those forecasts being ignored or not challenged/considered
- Process not challenging people to think or act differently
- Insufficient external focus: environment and/or competitors
- Lack of real focus on (new) opportunities for growth
- Poor expertise at local level
- More tactical/operational than strategic focus

5.8. FEATURES OF A STRATEGIC PLAN

1. It is high-level
2. It is general
3. Its time-span is long-range
4. It affects the whole organization
5. It is usually developed from the ground upwards
6. It covers a wide range of activities
7. It exploits a particular concept

5.9. BENEFITS OF STRATEGIC PLANNING

1. It provides the roadmap for the firm; it shows the way for achieving targets.
2. It helps the firm utilize its resources in the best possible manner. It allows more effective allocation of time and resources for identifying opportunities.
3. The firm can respond to environmental changes in a better way-by exploiting opportunities to its advantage and avoiding costly mistakes in investment decisions.
4. It minimizes the chances of mistakes and unpleasant surprises. It seeks to prepare the firms to confront future challenges through certain proactive steps and even shape the future to its advantage.
5. It creates a framework for internal communication among personnel. It helps to integrate the behavior of individuals into a total effort. It provides a basis for the clarification of individual responsibilities.
6. It gives encouragement to forward thinking.
7. It encourages a favourable attitude towards change.
8. It provides a cooperative, integrated and enthusiastic approach for tackling problems and realizing opportunities.

5.10. HIERARCHICAL LEVELS OF PLANNING

Levels of Strategic Planning

Three Different Levels: Corporate, Business and Functional.

1. Corporate Level Strategic Planning: It is the process of defining the overall character and purpose of the organization, the business it will enter and leave and how resources will be distributed among those businesses. Strategy at this level is typically developed by top management (The Board of Directors, CEO, etc.,). The decisions are broad-based, carry greater risk and affect most parts of the organization (e.g. The type of business that the organization should enter, changes required in growth strategy, acquisition and diversification decisions, etc.

2. Business Level Strategic Planning: It is the planning process concerned primarily with how to manage the interests and operations of a particular unit within the organization, commonly known as a strategic business unit (SBU). A strategic business unit is a distinct business with its own set of competitors that can be managed reasonably independently of other businesses within the organization. Generally, the heads of the respective business units develop business strategies, with the approval of top management. Strategies at this level are aimed at deciding the competitive advantage to build, determining responses to changing market situations, allocating resources within the business unit and coordinating functional-level strategies developed by functional managers.

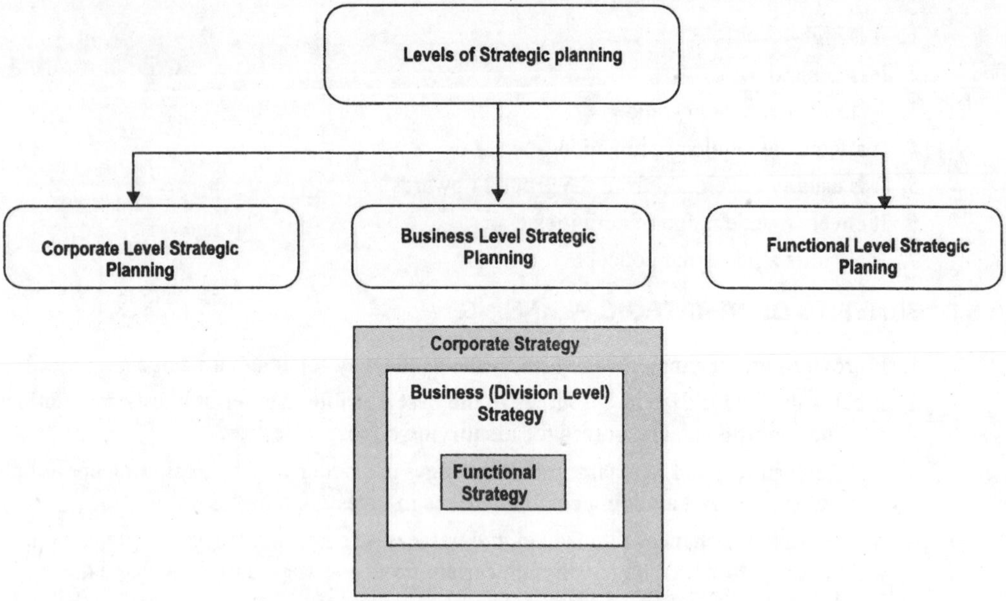

Figure 5.3. Levels of Strategic Planning.

3. Functional Level Strategic Planning: It is the process of determining policies and procedures for (relatively narrow levels of activity) different functions of an enterprise like marketing, finance, personnel, etc., These are developed by functional managers and are typically reviewed by business unit heads. Coordinating strategies across the three levels is crucial in maximizing strategic impact. The strength of the business level strategy is enhanced when functional level strategies support its basic thrust. Similarly, the corporate level is likely to have greater impact when business level strategies support one another in bolstering the corporate level strategy.

5.11. STRATEGIES IN MATURE INDUSTRIES

1. **Often with excess production capacity:** Strategies will ultimately depend on a specific analysis of the industry, but here are some general strategies based on game theory, resource-based strategy and competitive industry analysis:
2. **Consider buying rival companies and closing down capacity:** This may sound harsh but it has been successfully attempted in steel, textiles and food industries in the past. The survivors are more sound.
3. **Decrease the cost base:** This is a key decision but the survivors are much more likely to be those that have lower costs. It follows that, if this is really not an option at this stage, then some other fundamental change is required. There are risks in such an approach but some individual companies will have to take the decision to invest to reduce industry costs.
4. **Link through to customers and End-users:** It may be possible to reduce the risk by securing part of the market by negotiating a contractual link of some kind. Some car industry suppliers have secured their future in this way.
5. **Introduce a stronger service element into the Product Portfolio:** By providing a much higher service element, some companies have found the means of survival. This has the great strategic merit that it takes the company away from simple global competition for two reasons: first, because service has to be regional or even local in some cases; second,

because service by its nature has to be tailored to the individual customer and therefore is no longer subject to simple cost comparison with rivals. Smaller companies have used this strategy successfully.

6. **Beware industries that are supported by funds from their governments:** This has probably been the most single important factor in some countries for the survival of inefficient or even efficient companies. Unless it can be tackled at government to government level, it is best to avoid the country.
7. **Competing in mature industries:** About 80% of all U.S. industries are now competing in "mature" industries that are characterized by:-
   - Demand that is saturated and slow-growing if not declining;
   - Excess supply of competition too willing to discount;
   - Eroding margins, profits, and returns;
   - Emphasis on cost-cutting to stay ahead of margin erosion;
   - And consolidation of competitors.
8. **Be the low cost producer :** The firms that are obsessed with cutting costs and discounting prices reason that: whoever can get their production costs for goods and/or services down the fastest can-cut prices faster; win market share; achieve growing economies of scale to lower costs further to support another round of discounting; etc. Wal-Mart has succeeded in part due to this strategy.
9. **Lead, Niche, or Harvest/Sell:** Conventional wisdom is that in mature to declining industries each firm should pick one of several pathways to boldly pursue. To "lead" implies cost-volume-price leadership as well as to buy, merge, or bluff out competitors to rationalize excess capacity. Be the last blacksmith or airline in business and then you will make money.
10. **Strategies for maintaining competitive advantage:** Both analyzer and defender strategies may be appropriate for units with a leading, or at least a profitable, share of one or more major segments in a mature industry. Appropriate for developed industries that are still experiencing some technological change and may have opportunities for continued growth. Works where the basic technology is not very complex or is unlikely to change dramatically.
11. **Marketing strategies for mature markets**
    - Strategies for extending volume growth
    - Increased penetration strategy
    - Discovering why nonusers are uninterested.
    - Developing and selling integrated systems that help improve the basic product's performance or ease of use.
    - Offering services that improve its performance or ease of use for the potential customer.
    - Expanding distribution or developing more convenient and accessible channels.

5.12. BUSINESS STRATEGIES IN EMERGING INDUSTRIES

1. Technologies that are most proprietary to the pioneering firms and technological uncertainty will unfold
2. Competitor uncertainty because of inadequate information about competitors, buyers, and the timing of demand
3. High initial costs but steep cost declines

4. Few entry barriers
5. First-time buyers requiring initial inducement to purchase
6. Inability to obtain raw materials and components until suppliers gear up to meet the industry's needs
7. Need for high-risk capital because of the industry's uncertain prospects
8. For success in this industry setting, business strategies require one or more of these features:
9. The ability to shape the industry's structure
10. The ability to rapidly improve product quality and performance features
11. Advantageous relationships with key suppliers and promising distribution channels
12. The ability to establish the firm's technology as the dominant one
13. The early acquisition of a core group of loyal customers and then the expansion of that customer base
14. The ability to forecast future competitors

5.13. REASONS FOR FAILURE OF STRATEGIC PLANS

In general, strategic plans can fail for two types of reasons: Inappropriate strategy and poor implementation.

(a) Inappropriate strategies may arise due to:-

1. Inaccurate intelligence gathering,
2. Failure to understand the true nature of the problem
3. Strategies incapable of obtaining the desired objective,
4. Poor fit between the external environment and organizational resources, infeasibility

(b) Poor implementation of a strategy can happen due to:

- Over-estimation of resources and abilities
- Failure to co-ordinate, ineffective attempts to gain the support of others or resistance
- Under-estimation of time, personnel, or financial requirements, failure to follow the plan

5.14. STRATEGIC MANAGEMENT FOR SMALL, LARGE MULTIPRODUCT AND MULTIPLE MARKET ORGANIZATIONS

1. Strategic Management for Small Organization

(i) Strategically myopic: The majority of small firms are led by owner-managers who are strategically myopic. While this may seem a harsh comment, it reflects their lack of long-term vision as to where their company is headed, and their stronger orientation toward operational rather than strategic issues. Such strategic myopia may be attributed to the managerial environment in which many small business owners find themselves; too often they are busy dealing with the daily challenges associated with running their firm to find sufficient time to consider their future strategic directions.

(ii) Small firms lack formal business plans: In comparison to the Fortune 500 companies, the majority of small firms lack formal business plans and a coherent approach to strategy formulation (Unni, 1984). A survey of 500 small businesses in the United States during the mid-1990s found that fewer than 42 per cent possessed a formal business plan (Managing Office Technology, 1994). It has been argued that small business owner-managers do not plan because they lack the knowledge, confidence or skills to do so (Posner, 1985). Research into the impact formal business planning has on small firm performance remains equivocal due in part to the general absence of such planning within the majority of companies.

Entrepreneur		Owner-Manager
HI	RISK ORIENTATION	LO
HI	INNOVATION ORIENTAION	LO
HI	GROWTH ORIENTATION	LO
HI	PROFIT MAXIMISATION ORIENTAION	LO
HI	STRATEGIC ORIENTATION	LO
LO	LIFESTYLE ORIENTATION	HI
LO	FUNCTIONAL TASK ORIENTATION	HI

(iii) Owner-managers the absence of formal business planning

- lack of time to devote to such activities
- Lack of knowledge about how to plan
- Inadequate planning skills
- Unwillingness to share strategies with others or commit ideas to paper

(iv) Strategy and the growth cycle of small firms

Research into the growth of small firms has indicated a series of stage-models in which the business moves through a number of defined stages as it grows (Churchill & Lewis, 1983). While various models identify different numbers of stages, these models generally suggest that the business is initially conceived in the mind or minds of its founders (pre start-up), is then established (start-up) and passes through several additional stages as it grows into a mature large firm.

(v) The entrepreneurial process

A potential starting point to understand the strategic management process within the small entrepreneurial firm is the three-stage entrepreneurial process. This process starts with the capacity of entrepreneurial individuals to recognize new opportunities and become passionate about exploiting them. This ability to recognize a commercial opportunity has been considered by some academic writers to be more important than strategy, planning, venture financing, team building or networks.

(vi) Multiple product management professionals

When a company expands to multiple products and product families, firms must integrate a broad set of skills among multiple product management professionals. Read how to address the challenges of multiple products and product managers.

2. Strategic Management for Large Multiproduct and Multiple Market Organizations

1. Additional strategic duties executives like market analysis, writing business requirements and defining positioning: Product management covers a wide array of activities from market analysis to on-going sales support. In a small company, product managers often act as a product release expediter, ensuring that all the scheduled work has been done and that nothing has fallen through the cracks. As a company gets larger, product management takes on additional strategic duties previously performed by the senior executives such as market analysis, writing business requirements, and defining positioning. When a company expands to multiple products and product families, firms must integrate a broad set of skills among multiple product management professionals.

2. Product management is all about scalability: As products and companies grow, so do the time demands; one person cannot do everything. So one product manager becomes two or three, each attempting to do whatever is necessary for product success. The more people we add, the more we find two people doing some things and no one doing others. Communications problems are the result of unclear spheres of responsibility. Let's explore some techniques for ensuring clear communications when there are multiple products and multiple product managers.

3. Requirements reviews: Many companies are now running requirement review meetings, achieving the same benefits as developers? Design review meetings. Requirement reviews can be implemented instantly without impact on the current company organization. Bringing together product managers from across the company puts an incredibly diverse set of skills in one room. Are the requirements well-written? Have they clearly articulated the problem? Can they be verified? Are there cross-product opportunities? Requirements reviews provide a forum for integrating products and features by leveraging the skills of all product managers.

4. Product management triad: For large products or product lines, the span of activities quickly become more than one person can realistically perform. Requests for product management attention exceeds the time available for one person. But when there is more demand than supply, product managers usually spend their time in their personal comfort zone. A sales-oriented product manager will support the sales channel with better presentations and sales tools, while a development-oriented product manager will spend time with the product features.

5. Multiple product managers: In this scenario, companies frequently assign multiple product managers to a single product. An ideal organization is one that separates the roles of product management and product marketing. Often called inbound and outbound marketing, product management focuses on market requirements and working closely with development, while product marketing defines a go-to-market strategy and works closely with Marcom and Sales. These two categories of activities usually involve vastly different skills, so it's logical to split the job in two. Many companies go further to define a third, business-oriented, strategic role staffed by a senior person. Called the product management triad, this triumvirate works as a team to meet the product needs in the areas of business, technology, and marketing.

6. Multiple product managers in a product suite: Large product families have many products and features that require product management attention, particularly in identifying the links and cross-product opportunities. To manage a large product line, product managers are assigned to each major product in the family with an additional product manager ensuring consistency between the various products.

7. Coordinating components into coherent release plan: Imagine an enterprise implementation with a server-based architecture, various client components, and implementation services. Coordinating these components into a coherent release plan is incredibly challenging. For example, an enterprise network fault management system has server-side monitoring and response mechanism running on a third-party database. There are various clients including an error-correlation display, various map views of the network, and an operator console showing outstanding faults pending correction. Installation and implementation services are a critical aspect of the offering. Each of these must be defined, built, and launched. Releasing these as a single coordinated offering can be a nightmare.

8. Multiple Product Managers Approaching Microsoft Office: A suite most of us are familiar with. Assign a product manager for the Office family architecture including APIs, common look-and-feel, shared features such as dictionaries and themes, and various cross-product opportunities. Then add a product manager each for Word, Excel, PowerPoint, Access, Outlook, SharePoint, and any other products in the suite. Each individual product manager focuses only on the needs of his product while the suite product manager reviews the requirements for each of the products. PowerPoint needs to have tables; so does FrontPage--the suite product manager realize that she already has tables in Excel. So she requires a grid-tool API from the Excel team and mandates that any team requiring tables in their product shall invoke the Excel API. This ensures consistency across products, is better for clients, and is better for the Development teams, allowing them to focus their energies on new functionality. There is no need to reinvent a feature that already exists.

9. Create architectural services and implementation: Frequently, companies attempt to create architectural services and also implement those services in the client in the same release. This is terribly difficult and beyond what most companies can realistically achieve. A more reliable technique is to employ frequent, staggered releases. Architecture features in release 1 are implemented in client components in release 1.1. In other words, complete the basement before you build a house on top of it.

5.15. BUSINESS ETHICS AND STRATEGIC MANAGEMENT

In this chapter we will explore the question of ethics in managerial decision making. From a management perspective, an ethical decision is one that reasonable or typical stake holders would find acceptable. Ethics is defined as the discipline dealing with the good or bad with moral duty and obligations. Business ethics is concerned with truth, justice and a variety of aspects such as the expectations of the society, fair competition, advertising, public relations, social responsibilities, consumer autonomy and corporate behavior at home country and host country. Managers and Top Management have responsibility to institutionalize ethics by framing a code of ethics for the organization.

The purpose of ethics is not to change the basic values of an employee, or to educate them on moral standards. As a adult, most people have already developed a value system based on their culture and upbringing. The goal of business ethics is more to help people think through the moral and social implications of business decisions. Every Strategic /decision has a moral consequence. The Main aim of business ethics is to provide people with the means for dealing with moral complications. Ethical decisions in a business have implications such as satisfied work force, high sales, low regulation cost, more customers and high goodwill. Some of ethical issues for business are relation of employees and employers, interaction between organization and customers, interaction between organization and shareholders, work environment, environmental issues, bribes, employees rights protection, product safety, etc. Below is a list of some significant ethical principles to be followed for a successful business:

1. Protect the basic rights of the employees/workers.
2. Follow health, safety and environmental standards.
3. Continuously improvise the products, operations and production facilities to optimize the resource consumption
4. Do not replicate the packaging style so as to mislead the consumers.
5. Indulge in truthful and reliable advertising.
6. Strictly adhere to the product safety standards.
7. Accept new ideas. Encourage feedback from both employees as well as customers.
8. Present factual information. Maintain accurate and true business records.

9. Treat everyone (employees, partners and customers) with respect and integrity.
10. The mission and vision of the company should be very clear to it.
11. Do not get engaged in business relationships that lead to conflicts of interest. Discourage black marketing, corruption and hoarding.
12. Meet all the commitments and obligations timely.
13. Encourage free and open competition. Do not ruin competitors' image by fraudulent practices.
14. The policies and procedures of the Company should be updated regularly.
15. Maintain confidentiality of personal data and proprietary records held by the company.
16. Do not accept child labour, forced labour or any other human right abuses.

A classic example is the Bhopal gas tragedy where in 1984 over 3000 people died overnight when there is a leak of methyl isocyanides from the Union Carbide plant. While there is some controversy over the responsibility for the accident, the facts are that this plant was not profitable, and a strategic decision had recently been made to sell the plant. Under this circumstances, as purely economic consideration might dictate, various cost cutting measures were in place. These measures included decreased maintenance expenses, and substantial reduction of quality workers. Instead of the original twelve operators per shift, there were six. In addition, there was suggestion of sabotage from a disgruntled employee. (Trotter, Day and Love 1989). All the cost reduction measures made sense from an economic standpoint, and certainly the managers in union carbide (both the India and US) did not want the Bhopal accident to occur. However what stands out is a failure to look beyond the economic standpoint and consider whether the cost savings were being obtained at too high risk to the community. Although the Bhopal gas disaster has the dubious distinction of being the world's worst industrial disaster, such cases frequently come up worldwide.

5.16. STRATEGIC FUNDS PROGRAMMING

The Strategic Programme Fund was established in 2003 to support the Government's international goals. Strategic Funds Programming is designed to help Managers Bridge the gap between strategy and action. The process has been implemented successfully in companies in the United States and Europe, and has the potential to help corporations deal with the frustrations of getting a formulated strategy moving. Diplomacy is about making a difference to the world around us. Britain's diplomats excel in the traditional skills of negotiation and lobbying. But in today's interconnected world, where civil society has more influence than ever before, it is essential that we engage with an extraordinary range of actors to promote British interests and support our strategic objectives. The Strategic Programme Fund (SPF) helps to deliver the four foreign policy objectives:

- To counter terrorism and weapons proliferation and their causes;
- To prevent and resolve conflict;
- To promote a low carbon, high growth, global economy;
- To develop effective international institutions above all the UN and EU.

Having funds available to help the diplomats achieve these objectives is crucial to their work. It allows them access to the people and groups that matter around the world, not just the governments who are the traditional contacts of diplomats. It makes it possible to sow the seeds of change, or to experiment with new ways of engaging people on the issues that matter to us and the rest of the global community. And it shows that the UK is actively engaged in making a difference, not just talking about it.

The High Commission through the Foreign and Commonwealth Office is currently receiving bids for some projects from the following mandatory fields. Priority areas in the 2013/2014 Strategic Program Fund are:

- Violence against women
- Business
- Human Rights

Given the ever-expanding number of investment options and the growing complexity of the financial markets in today's global economy, the ability to maximize investment potential can be challenging and time-consuming for even the most sophisticated individual investors. Strategic Fund Programming is an asset allocation program designed to meet the specific investment objectives. It combines the personal service and experience of investment managers to create a custom portfolio specifically for the customers. The goal of Strategic Fund Programming is

- To deliver a diversified portfolio using mutual funds and ETFs
- To reduce portfolio risk and the potential for increased returns.
- Diversification does not assure a profit or protect against loss

Tailored to Fit Your Needs

Strategic Fund Programming is based on a process-driven methodology to fit the individual investing needs. Whether your goal is portfolio growth, maintaining a balance of growth and income, or preserving capital we have a solution that is right for you. Our process begins with an eight-question risk tolerance questionnaire. A solution is tailored based upon your responses.

Determine the risk tolerance, time horizon and incestment goals

↓

Build an asset allocation model that fits the objectives

↓

Research and due diligence: construct the protfolio with appropriate mutual funds and/or ETfs

↓

Rebalance your portfolio to stay on track

↓

Ongoing portfolio monitoring

5.17. ASSESSMENT OF ECONOMIC CONTRIBUTION OF STRATEGY

The operations can provide a strong base for the economic growth of communities, regions and countries. It focuses on ensuring the presence that brings sustainable socio-economic benefits to the places where they work. The direct economic contribution is made up of the value which would add by paying wages, employee benefits, taxes and royalties and our returns to capital (dividend and interest payments and the money we retained for future investment) along with the payments that make to the suppliers. However, the true economic contribution is far greater once the multiplier effects of their presence in an area are considered. These include the indirect effects of people spending their wages, governments distributing tax and royalty revenues, and neighboring communities using the infrastructure developed for their operations. The economic contributions can be done in three major ways. They are:

1. **Direct economic contribution**
   - The wage and employee benefit payments
   - The spending with local suppliers
   - The investments in local infrastructure
   - The housing facilities
   - The support provided for health, education and other services
   - The payments into benefits receiving trusts
   - The company, payroll, export and sales taxes, royalty and rent payments
2. **Indirect economic contribution**
   - The employees and our suppliers' employees spending their wages locally
   - Economic activity triggered by local communities using infrastructure developed for their operations (eg roads, airports, water supplies, sanitation systems, electric power, freight services)
   - Government expenditure on local goods and services, funded by the taxes made
3. **Community contributions**
   - Rice purchasing plan
   - Diversifying the local market by improving regional transport
   - Awarding catering contracts to local community gardens
   - Building a boarding house and temporary camp to alleviate rental inflation.

Chapter 6

THE STRATEGY HIERARCHY OR LEVEL OF STRATEGY

Hierarchical Level of Strategy - Introduction and Meaning of Corporate Level Stategry - Business Level Strategy - Customer Needs and Product Differentiation - Customer Groups and Market Segmentation - Distinctive Competencies - Dynamics of Business Level Strategy - Choosing a Generic Business Level Strategy - Cost-Leadership Strategy - Cost-Leadership Differentiation Strategy - Stuck in the Middle - Competitive Positioning and Business Level Strategy - Strategic Group Analysis - Choosing an Investment Strategy at the Business Level - Business Level Strategy and Game Theory - Functional Level Strategies - Nature and Strategies in Fragmented Industries - Chaining - Strategies in Embryonic and Growth Industries - Strategic Implications: Crossing the Chasm - Strategic Implications of Differences in Growth Rates - Porter's Five Forces Model of Competition in an Industry - Expansion or Growth Strategies - Mergers - Takeover - Joint Venture - Strategic Alliances - Stability Strategies - Retrenchment Strategies - Combination (Mixed Strategy) - Market Entry Strategies - Environmental Threat and Opportunity Profile (ETOP) - Comprehensive Analysis - Business Intelligence Systems - Balance Scorecard - Structuring Organizational Appraisal - Corporate Portfolio Analysis - Matching Structure and Strategy - Maintaining the Structure - Changing the Structure to Strategy - Difficulties in Matching Structure to Strategy - Mechanism for Matching Structure to Strategy - Meaning and Definition of Organizational Culture-Competitive Cost Dynamics - International Portfolio Analysis - Corporate Parenting Analysis - SWOT Analysis - Carrying Out SWOT Analysis - TOWS Matrix - Experience Curve Analysis - Life Cycle Analysis - GAP Analysis - McKinsey7-s Framework - BCG Growth - Share Matrix - GE Nine Cell Matrix - GE Multifactor Portfolio Martix - Infrastructure and Efficiency - Achieving Superior Quality - Attaining Superior Reliability - Developing Superior Attributes - Achieving Superior Innovation - Achieving Superior Responsivensess to Customers - Building and Restructuring the Corporation - Mergers and Acquisitions - Reasons for Mergers and Acquisitions - Types of Mergers - The Merger Process - Retrenchment / Defensive Strategies - Combination Strategy.

6.1. HIERARCHICAL LEVEL OF STRATEGY

Strategy may operate at different levels of an organization -corporate level, business level, and functional level. While strategy may be about competing and surviving as a firm, one can argue that products, not corporations compete, and products are developed by business units. The role of the corporation then is to manage its business units and products so that each is competitive and so that each contributes to corporate purposes. Strategy can be formulated on three different levels:

- Corporate level
- Business level
- Functional or Departmental level

Consider Textron, Inc., a successful conglomerate corporation that pursues profits through a range of businesses in unrelated industries. Textron has four core business segments:-

- Aircraft—32% of revenues
- Automotive—25% of revenues
- Industrial—39% of revenues
- Finance—4% of revenues.

While the corporation must manage its portfolio of businesses to grow and survive, the success of a diversified firm depends upon its ability to manage each of its product lines. While there is no single competitor to Textron, we can talk about the competitors and strategy of each of its business units. In the finance business segment, for example, the chief rivals are major banks providing commercial financing. Many managers consider the business level to be the proper focus for strategic planning.

6.1.1 Corporate Level Strategy

Corporate strategy refers to the overall strategy for a diversified company. It is concerned with the mix of businesses the company should compete in, and the ways in which strategies of individual units should be coordinated and integrated.

Corporate level strategies are basically about the choice of direction that a firm adopts in order to achieve its objectives. They are basically about decisions related to allocating resources among the different businesses of a firm, transferring resources from one set of businesses to others, and managing and nurturing a portfolio of businesses in such a way that the overall corporate objectives are achieved. Corporate level strategy covers the strategic scope of the organization as a whole. For most organizations the corporate strategic plan is the only strategic plan required. Often strategy at the corporate level is simply referred to as corporate strategy, or in unified companies the corporate business strategy. The process that produces it is called corporate strategic planning, or sometimes simply corporate planning. In a few situations however, it may be justified to speak of corporate level strategy to distinguish it from other kinds of planning.

"From Competitive Advantage to Corporate Strategy"

On Competition, Michael E. Porter Corporate strategy is what makes the corporate whole add up to more than the sum of its business parts. The track record of corporate strategies had been dismal. A study of the diversification records of 33 large U.S. companies from 1950 to 1986 shows that diversification--whether through acquisition, joint venture, or start-up--generally has not brought the competitive advantages or profitability expected. Portfolio management, restructuring, transferring skills, and sharing activities are four concepts of corporate strategy that companies most commonly use. Portfolio management no longer works very well in the United States because of its highly developed capital market. Restructuring is merely a stopgap measure that will not build shareholder value over the long term because it usually produces an unwieldy conglomerate. Companies have the best chance of being successful at diversification if they capitalize on the existing relationships between business units by having them transfer skills and share activities. Corporate level strategy fundamentally is concerned with the selection of businesses in which the company should compete and with the development and coordination of that portfolio of businesses.

Corporate level strategy is concerned with

1. **Reach**—defining the issues that are corporate responsibilities; these might include identifying the overall goals of the corporation, the types of businesses in which the corporation should be involved, and the way in which businesses will be integrated and managed.

2. **Competitive Contact**—defining where in the corporation competition is to be localized. Take the case of insurance: In the mid-1990's, Aetna as a corporation was clearly identified with

its commercial and property casualty insurance products. The conglomerate Textron was not. For Textron, competition in the insurance markets took place specifically at the business unit level, through its subsidiary, Paul Revere. (Textron divested itself of The Paul Revere Corporation in 1997.)

3. Managing Activities and Business Interrelationships—Corporate strategy seeks to develop synergies by sharing and coordinating staff and other resources across business units, investing financial resources across business units, and using business units to complement other corporate business activities.

4. Management Practices—Corporations decide how business units are to be governed: through direct corporate intervention (centralization) or through more or less autonomous government (decentralization) that relies on persuasion and rewards.

5. Corporations are responsible for creating value through their businesses. They do so by managing their portfolio of businesses, ensuring that the businesses are successful over the long-term, developing business units, and sometimes ensuring that each business is compatible with others in the portfolio.

Table 6.1

Level of Strategy	Corporate, Business, and Functional Strategy	Example
Corporals strategy	Market definition	Diversification into new productor graphic markets
Business strategy	Market Navigation	Attempts to secure competitive advantage in existing product or graphic markets
Functional strategy	Support of corporate strategy and business strategy	Information systems, human resources practices and production processess that faciinto achivement of corporate and business strategy

6.1.2 Business Level Strategy

What is Business Level Strategy?

At the heart of business-level strategy is the objective of developing a firm-specific business model that will allow a company to gain a competitive advantage over its Business-Level rivals in a market or industry. According to Abell, the process of business definition entails decisions about (1) customers needs, or what is to be satisfied, (2) customer groups, or who is to be satisfied, and (3) distinctive competencies, or how customer needs are to be satisfied.' These three decisions are the basis of the choice of a business-level strategy because they determine where and how a company seeks to compete in a business or industry essentially, how a company proposes to create value for customers. Consequently, the ways in which a company makes these three decisions to gain a competitive advantage over its rivals need to be considered.

1. Customer Needs and Product Differentiation

Customer Needs Customer needs are desires, wants, or cravings that can be satisfied by means of the attributes or characteristics of a product—a good or service. For example, a person's craving for something sweet can be satisfied by a box of Godiva chocolates, a carton of Ben & Jerry's ice cream, a Snickers bar, or a spoonful of sugar. Two factors determine which product a customer chooses to satisfy these needs: (1) the price of the product and (2) the way a product is differentiated from other products of its type.

Product differentiation is the process of designing products to satisfy customers' needs. A company obtains a competitive advantage when it creates, designs, and supplies a product in a way that better satisfies customer needs than its rivals do and chooses the correct pricing option—the one that results in the level of demand that optimizes profitability. Consider the luxury segment of the car market, where customers pay more than $35,000 to satisfy their needs for personal transportation. In this segment, Cadillac, Mercedes-Benz, Infiniti, BMW, Jaguar, Lexus, Lincoln, Audi, Volvo, Acura, and others are engaged in a continuing battle to design the "perfect" luxury car—the one that best meets the needs of those who have decided to purchase a personal luxury vehicle. Over time, the companies that attract the most luxury car buyers—because they have the distinctive competencies that allow them to produce the cars that possess the features or qualities these customers desire the most—are the ones that achieve a sustained competitive advantage over rivals.

There are many different luxury carmakers because even within this car market segment, customers have widely different kinds of needs. As a result, luxury carmakers can differentiate their product in a number of ways to satisfy a particular group of customers, just as Toyota did in the Opening Case in the sports utility segment. For example, some customers highly value a sporty ride and performance handling; Mercedes-Benz and BMW are on the cutting edge of technical design, which allows them to be able to offer this driving experience that no other maker has been able to match.

2. Customer Groups and Market Segmentation

Market segmentation is the way a company decides to group customers, based on Groups and important differences in their needs or preferences, in order to gain a competitive Market advantage. One principal way of grouping customers and segmenting the market is Segmentation by what customers areable and willing to pay for a particular product. Once price has been taken into consideration, the other principal method of segmenting customers is according to the specific kinds of need that is being satisfied by a particular product. Managers, such as designers and engineers, have to think strategically about which segments they are going to compete in and then how they will differentiate their products for each segment. The result of this choice process determines a particular company's product range.

Market segmentation is an evolving, ongoing process that presents considerable opportunities for strategic managers. For example, in the car industry, savvy strategists often recognize opportunities to create a product for a new market segment that will attract a specific group of car buyers who before had to "satisfies' and buy a model that did not meet their needs exactly but was a reasonable compromise. This was the origin of the sports utility market segment. Many people wanted a more rugged and powerful vehicle capable of holding many people or towing heavy loads. They liked the comfort of a car but also the qualities of a pickup; by combining these two, carmakers created the SUV market segment. This process continues in the sports utility and other segments. Obviously, differentiation increases as new models are introduced and costs increase. However, if the right products are being made, the extra demand the new products generate results in sales revenues that more than make up for increasing costs and profitability increases. If managers make mistakes, however, and design products that have little appeal or price them too high, then the opposite occurs, and profitability will fall. In 2002, for example, Ford announced that it was ending production of its $52,000 luxury Lincoln truck after announcing that sales had been only in the hundreds, and not the 10,000 a year it had projected.

In general, a company can adopt three alternative strategies toward market segmentation. First, it can choose not to recognize that different groups of customers have different needs and instead adopt the approach of serving the average customer. Second, it can choose to segment its market into different constituencies and develop a product to suit the needs of each. For example, Sony offers twenty-four different nineteen-inch color television sets, each targeted at a different market segment.

Third, a company can choose to recognize that the market is segmented but concentrate on serving only one of a few market segments or niches, such as the luxury car segment pursued by BMW.

The decision to provide many products for many market niches allows a company to satisfy a wider range of customer needs better. As a result, when it prices the product correctly, customer demand for the company's products rises and generates more revenue than would be the case if the company offered just one product for the whole market.

Sometimes the nature of the product or the nature of the industry does not allow much differentiation, which is the case, for example, with bulk chemicals and cement. In these industries, there may be little opportunity for obtaining a competitive advantage through product differentiation and market segmentation because there is little opportunity for serving customers' needs and customer groups in different ways. Instead, price is the main criterion that customers use to evaluate the product, and the competitive advantage lies with the company that has superior efficiency and the lowest cost structure, which allows it to charge the lowest prices.

3. Distinctive Competencies

The third issue in Business-Level Strategy is to decide which distinctive competencies to create and build to achieve competitive advantage in satisfying particular customers' needs and customer groups. There are four main ways companies can pursue a competitive advantage: superior efficiency, quality innovation, and responsiveness to customers. In choosing a business-level strategy, strategic managers must decide which business model to follow that will best allow them to organize and combine their company's distinctive competencies to gain a competitive advantage.

6.1.2.1 The Dynamics of Business-Level Strategy

Companies pursue a business-level strategy to gain a competitive advantage that allows them to outperform rivals and achieve above-average profitability. In determining how to achieve a competitive advantage, strategic managers have to make a consistent or compatible set of choices concerning (1) how to differentiate and price their product, (2) when and how much to segment their market to maximize demand, (3) and where and how to invest their capital to develop distinctive competencies that will create the most value while keeping their cost structures viable (because of the need to be price competitive). These three decisions determine which business-level strategy a company is pursuing. They also set in motion the specific set of functional-level strategies needed to create the differentiation and value and cost structure positions needed to pursue such a strategy. Business-level strategy is therefore the main determinant of a company's business model.

Figure 6.2 presents a way of thinking about the relationships of these variables in a company's business mode. The decision to differentiate a product increases the perceived value to the customer, so that market demand for the product increases. In turn, increased demand leads to economies of scale, which lowers the cost structure and unit costs. Thus, from this point of view, differentiation can lower unit costs. Differentiation also requires additional expenditures on resources, for example, to improve product quality or support a higher level of service so that an increase in differentiation will also raise a company's cost structure and result in a higher unit cost.

To maximize profitability, managers must choose the pricing option that compensates for the extra costs of product differentiation but does not choke off an increase in expected demand. They must also search for other ways to reduce costs and therefore lower the company's cost structure but will not harm its level of differentiation. There are many specific functional strategies a company can adopt to achieve this. For example, Nordstrom, the luxury department store retailer, differentiates itself in the retail clothing industry by providing a high-quality shopping experience with elegant store operations and a high level of customer service, all of which raise Nordstrom's cost structure. However, Nordstrom can still lower its cost structure by, for example, managing its inventories efficiently and increasing inventory turnover. Also, its strategy of being highly responsive to customers results in more customers and higher demand, which means that sales per square foot increase, and this enables it to make more intensive use of its facilities and salespeople, which leads to scale economies and lower costs. Thus, no matter what the level of differentiation is that a company chooses to pursue in its business model, it always has to recognize the way its cost structure will vary as a result of its choice of differentiation and the other specific strategies it adopts to lower its cost structure; differentiation and cost structure decisions affect one another.

The last main dynamic shown in Figure 6.1 concerns the impact of the industry's competitive structure on a company's differentiation, cost structure, and pricing choices. Recall that strategic thinking takes place in an environment where watchful and agile competitors and potential competitors exist; so one company's choices are always made with reference to those of its major competitors. Often, therefore, a company may be forced to increase its level of differentiation because its competitors start to offer products with new or improved features. If competitors also decide to develop products for new market segments, this will also force it to follow suit.

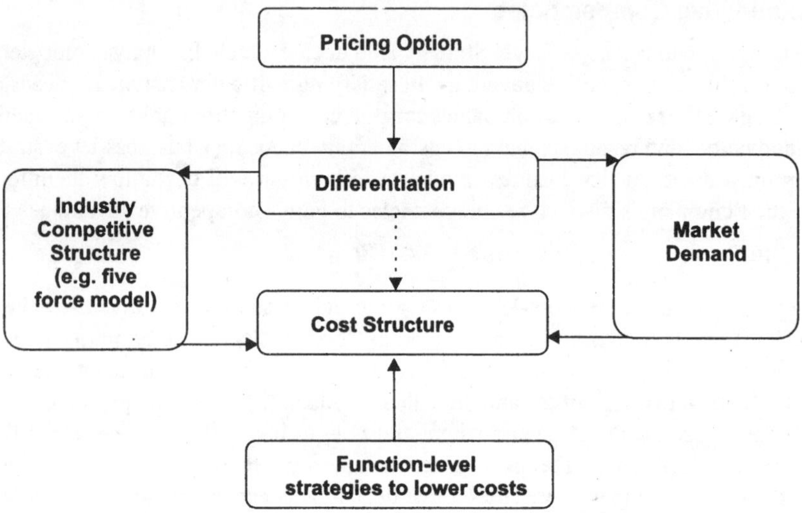

Figure 6.1. The Dynamics of Business Level Strategy.

On the cost side of the equation, industry competition drives a company's cost structure because differentiation increases costs and competitors' pricing decisions affect a company's pricing options. For example, a company's ability to charge a high premium price depends on the other choices customers have and its competitors' pricing choices. Companies need to consider carefully whether they can recoup the extra costs of differentiation given the pricing choices of the other companies in the industry. For example, Dell's decision not to choose a high-price option for its state- of-the-art computers led to problems for its competitors because they lacked Dell's low cost structure. Because they were forced to match Dell's low prices to compete effectively, many started to see losses because they had higher costs and this helped Dell gain more market share.

In sum, the task facing strategic managers at the business level is to position a company with respect to both differentiation and cost structure. That is, the choice of business-level strategy revolves around (1) how to differentiate products to create more value for customers, which permits a broader range of pricing options and (2) how to invest in functional activities to achieve a cost structure that also gives it a broader range of pricing choices. Maximizing profitability is about making the right choices with regard to value creation through differentiation, costs, and pricing given both the demand conditions in the company's market and the competitive conditions in the company's industry.

6.1.2.2 Choosing a Generic Business Level Strategy

In developing a business-level strategy and business model, usually strategic managers emphasize one of five generic competitive strategies: cost leadership, differentiation, cost leadership and differentiation, focus differentiation, and focus cost leadership. These strategies are called generic because all companies or businesses Strategy can pursue them regardless of whether they are manufacturing, service, or nonprofit enterprises. These strategies are also generic because they can be pursued in different kinds of industry environments. Each of the generic strategies results from a company consistent choice on product, market, and distinctive competencies—choices that reinforce each other and result in a competitive business model (see Table 6.2).

Table 6.2 Product/Market/Distinctive Competency Choices and Generic Competitive Strategies

	Cost Leadership	Differentiation	Focus
Product Differentiation	Low (Principally by price)	High (Principally by uniqueness)	Low to high (price or uniqueness)
Market Segmentation	Low (mass market)	High (many market segments)	Low (one or a few segments)
Distinctive Competency	Manufacturing and materials management	Research and development, sales and marketing	Any kind of distinctive competency

6.1.2.3 Cost-Leadership Strategy

A company's business model in pursuing a cost-leadership strategy is based on the intent to outperform competitors by doing everything it can to establish a cost structure that allows it to produce or provide goods or services at a lower unit cost than they can. It is also about finding ways to lower the cost structure given its choice of differentiation because differentiation typically raises costs. In essence, a company pursuing a cost-leadership strategy seeks to achieve a competitive advantage and above-average profitability by developing a business model primarily aimed at lowering its cost structure.

Two advantages accrue from a cost-leadership strategy. First, if its closest rivals in an industry, for example, those that compete in the same price range or market segment, charge similar prices for their products, the cost leader achieves superior profitability than its competitors because of its lower costs. Second, and more common, because of its lower cost structure, the cost leader is able to charge a lower price than its competitors, and this gives it a competitive advantage.

Strategic Choices: The cost leader chooses a low to moderate level of product differentiation relative to its competitors. Differentiation is expensive; the more a company expends resources to make its products distinct, the more its costs rise. The cost leader aims for a level of differentiation not markedly inferior to that of the differentiator (a company that competes by spending resources on product development), but a level obtainable at low cost. The cost leader does not try to be the industry leader in differentiation; it waits until customers want a feature or service before providing it. For example, a cost leader does not introduce a theater-quality sound system in DVD sets; instead, it adds such sound quality only when it is obvious that customers want it. Wal-Mart, for example, does not spend hundreds of millions of dollars on store design to create an attractive shopping experience as chains like Macy's, Dillard's, or Saks Fifth Avenue have done. Nor does it follow Kmart's strategy and pay celebrities like Martha Stewart millions to promote the distinctness or quality of its products. As Wal-Mart puts it in its mission statement, "We think of ourselves as buyers for our customers and we apply our considerable strengths to get the best value for you."

The cost leader also frequently ignores the many different market segments in an industry and positions its products to appeal to the "Average" customer. The reason the cost leader makes this choice is that developing or selling many different products tailored to the needs of different market segments is an expensive proposition. A cost leader normally engages in only a limited amount of market segmentation. In targeting the average customer, strategic managers try to produce or provide the least or smallest number of products that will be desired by the highest number of customers, something at the heart of Wal-Mart's and BJ's approach. Thus, although a customer may not get exactly the product he or she wants, paying a lower price than at the cost leader's competitors attracts more customers to its products.

In developing distinctive competencies, the overriding goal of the cost leader must be to increase its efficiency and lower its cost structure compared with its rivals. The development of distinctive competencies in manufacturing, materials management, and information technology is central to achieving this goal. For example, manufacturing companies pursuing a low-cost strategy concentrate on doing all they can to ride down the experience curve so that they can keep lowering their costs. Achieving a low-cost position requires that the company develop skills in flexible manufacturing, adopt efficient materials management techniques, and do all it can to increase inventory turnover

Consequently, the manufacturing and materials management functions are the center of attention for a company pursuing a cost-leadership strategy, and the other functions shape their distinctive competencies to meet the needs of manufacturing and materials management. The sales function, for example, may develop the competency of capturing large, stable sets of customers' orders. In turn, this allows manufacturing to make longer production runs and so achieve economies of scale and reduce costs. At Dell, for example, online customers are provided with a limited set of choices so that Dell can customize PCs to a customer's need at low cost. Finding ways to customize its products at low cost is an important task facing managers pursuing a cost-leadership strategy. The human resource function may focus on instituting training programs and compensation systems that lower costs by improving employees' productivity, and the research and development function may specialize in process improvements to lower the manufacturing costs. Wal-Mart has taken advantage of advances in information technology to lower the costs associated with getting goods from manufacturers to customers just as Dell, the cost leader in the personal computer industry, uses the Internet to lower the cost of selling its computers. Strategy implementation, another source of cost savings in pursuing cost leadership, is the design of the organizational structure to match this strategy, since structure is a major source of a company's costs. Thus, a low-cost strategy usually implies tight production or sales controls and rigorous use of budgets to control the production process.

Advantages and Disadvantages

The advantages of each generic strategy are best discussed in terms of Porter's five forces model. The five forces are threats from competitors, powerful suppliers, powerful buyers, substitute products, and new entrants. The cost leader is protected from industry competitors by its cost advantage. Its lower costs also mean that it will be less affected than its competitors by increases in the price of inputs if there are powerful suppliers and less affected by a fall in the price it can charge for its products if there are powerful buyers. Moreover, since cost leadership usually requires a big market share, the cost leader purchases in relatively large quantities, increasing its bargaining power over suppliers. If substitute products start to come onto the market, the cost leader can reduce its price to compete with them and retain its market share. Finally, the leader's cost advantage constitutes a barrier to entry, since other companies are unable to enter the industry and match the leader's costs or prices. The cost leader is therefore relatively safe as long as it can maintain its cost advantage, and price is the key for a significant number of buyers

The principal dangers of the cost-leadership approach lurk in competitors' ability to find ways to lower their cost structures and beat the cost leader at its own game. For instance, if technological change makes experience curve economies obsolete, new companies may apply lower-cost technologies that give them a cost advantage over the cost leader. Competitors may also draw a cost advantage from labor-cost savings. Foreign competitors in the Third World have very low labor costs; for example, wage costs in the United States are roughly 600 percent more than they are in Malaysia, China, or Mexico. Most U.S. companies now assemble their products abroad as part of their low-cost strategy; many are forced to do so simply to compete and stay in business.

Competitors' ability to imitate the cost leader's methods easily is another threat to the cost-leadership strategy. For example, companies in China routinely take apart the electronic products of Japanese companies like Sony and Panasonic to see how they are designed and assembled. Then, using Chinese-made components and a huge pool of inexpensive domestic labor, they manufacture clones of these products and flood the U.S. market with inexpensive tape players, radios, phones, and DVD players.

Finally, the cost-leadership strategy carries a risk that strategic managers in their single-minded desire to reduce costs might make decisions that decrease costs but then drastically affect demand for the product. This happened to Gateway Computer in 2001, when, to reduce the costs of customer service, customer support people were instructed not to help customers who were experiencing problems with their new Gateway computers if they had installed their own new software on the machines. New buyers, most of whom install, and Gateway's sales began to fall as word spread. Within six months, managers had reversed their decision, and once again Gateway began offering full customer support.

Implications: To pursue a full-blown cost-leadership strategy, strategic managers need to devote enormous efforts to incorporate all the latest information, materials management, and manufacturing technology into their operations to find new ways to reduce costs. By using new technology will also raise quality and increase responsiveness to customers as well. Pursuing a business model based on a low-cost approach is an ongoing endeavor that requires ongoing strategic thinking to make sure the business model is aligned to changing environmental opportunities and threats.

Strategic managers in companies throughout the industry are watching the cost leader and will move quickly to imitate its innovations because they also want to reduce their costs. A differentiator cannot let a cost leader get too great a cost advantage because the leader might then be able to use its high profits to invest more in product differentiation and beat the differentiator at its own competitive game! For example, Toyota and Honda began as cost leaders, manufacturing simple low-priced cars. Their cars sold well, and they then invested their profits to design and make new models of cars that became increasingly differentiated in features and quality. Today, Toyota and Honda, with cars in every market segment, are essentially pursuing a differentiation strategy, although Toyota remains the global cost leader as well. Its managers' ability to sustain both a low cost and a differentiation strategy has made it the most profitable car company in the world by far.

A cost leader must also respond to the strategic moves of its differentiated competitors and increase the quality and features of its products if it is to prosper in the long run. Even low-priced products, such as Timex watches and Bic razors, cannot be too inferior to the more expensive Seiko watches or Gillette razors if the low-cost, low- price policy is to succeed. All business-level strategy plays out with all rivals closely watching each other's strategic moves. If Seiko brings out a novel kind of liquid-crystal-illuminated watch dial or Gillette a three-bladed razor, managers at Timex and Bic will respond within months by incorporating these innovations in their low-priced products. This situation is very common in the high-priced women's fashion industry as well. As soon as the famous designers like Gucci and Dior have shown their spring and fall collections, their designs are copied and the plans transmitted to factories in Malaysia, where workers are ready to manufacture low-priced imitations that within months will reach low-price clothing retail stores around the world.

A generic strategy like cost leadership should be thought of as a specific plan of action that helps strategic managers keep focused on how to compete most effectively over time. It is all too easy for strategic managers, flush with the success of their cost- leadership strategy, to become less vigilant and lose sight of changes in the five forces of competition, and in the macro environment, that change the rules of the competitive game. McDonald's, long the cost leader in the fast food industry, was surprised when rivals like Taco Bell began to offer 99-cent daily specials. McDonald's had to learn how to make fast food more cheaply to compete, and the need to do so drove its managers to adopt new cooking techniques and food management practices that have ratcheted it down the experience curve. Today, 99-cent meals are a permanent fixture on most fast food menus.

Differentiation Strategy: The objective of the generic differentiation strategy is to achieve a competitive advantage by creating a product (good or service) that customers perceive as different or distinct in some important way. The differentiated company's ability to satisfy customers' needs in a way that its competitors cannot means that it can charge a premium price (one higher than that charged by its closest rivals). The ability to increase revenues by charging premium prices (rather than by reducing costs, as the cost leader does) allows the differentiator to outperform its competitors and achieve superior profitability. The customers pay a premium price when they believe the product's differentiated qualities are worth the extra money. Consequently, differentiated products are often priced on the basis of what the market will bear.

Thus, Mercedes-Benz cars are more expensive than the cars of its closest rivals because customers believe they offer more features and confer more status on their owners. Similarly, a BMW is not a lot more expensive to produce than a Honda, but customers who perceive that the distinct sporty ride and prestige of owning a BMW is something worth paying a lot more for determine its high price. (In fact, in Japan, BMW prices its entry cars quite modestly to attract young, well-heeled Japanese customers from Honda.) Similarly, Rolex watches do not cost much to produce, their design has not changed very much for years, and their gold content represents only a small fraction of the price. Customers, however, buy a Rolex because of the distinct qualities they perceive in it: its look and its ability to confer status on its wearer.

Strategic Choices: A differentiator chooses a high level of product differentiation to gain a competitive advantage. Product differentiation can be achieved in three principal ways quality, innovation, and responsiveness to customer needs. For example, Procter & Gamble claims that its product quality is high and that Ivory soap is 99.44 percent pure. Maytag stresses reliability and the best repair record of any other washer on the market. IBM promotes the quality service provided by its well-trained sales force. Innovation is commonly the source of differentiation for technologically complex products, and many people pay a premium price for new and innovative products, such as a state-of-the-art computer, DVD player or car.

When differentiation is based on responsiveness to customers, a company offers comprehensive after-sales service and product repair. This is an especially important consideration for complex products such as cars and domestic appliances, which are likely to break down periodically. Maytag, Dell Computer, and BMW all excel in responsiveness to customers. In service organizations, quality-of-service attributes are also very important. Neiman Marcus, Nordstrom, and FedEx can charge premium prices because they offer an exceptionally high level of service. Firms of lawyers, accountants, and consultants stress the service aspects of their operations to clients: their knowledge, professionalism, and reputation.

Finally, a product's appeal to customers' psychological desires is a source of differentiation. The appeal can be to prestige or status, as it is with BMWs and Rolex watches; to safety of home and family, as with Aetna or Prudential Insurance; or simply providing a superior shopping experience, as with Target and Macy's. Differentiation can also be tailored to age groups and to socioeconomic groups. Indeed, the bases of differentiation are endless. A company that pursues a differentiation strategy strives to differentiate itself along as many dimensions as possible. The less it resembles its rivals, the more it is protected from competition and the wider is its market appeal. Thus, BMWs offer more than prestige; they also offer technological sophistication, luxury, reliability, and good, although very expensive, repair service. All these bases of differentiation help increase sales. Generally, a differentiator chooses to segment its market into many segments and niches, just as Toyota did. Strategic managers recognize the revenue-enhancing ability of being able to attract more customers willing to pay a premium price in each market segment. Now and then, a company offers a product designed for most market segments and decides to be a broad differentiator, but a company might choose to serve just those segments in which it has a specific differentiation advantage. I example, Sony produces twenty-four models of television sets, filling all the niches from mid-priced to high-priced sets. However, its lowest-priced model is always priced about $60 above that of its competitors, bringing into play the premium price factor. Consumers have to pay extra for a Sony. Similarly, although Mercedes-Benz has filled niches below its high-priced models with its S and C series, recently it has produced a car for the low-priced market segment. It sells this car only in Europe because it fears introducing it in the United States would dilute its exclusive image and affect its differentiated appeal.

Finally, in choosing wh:ch distinctive competency to pursue, a differentiate company concentrates on the organizational functions that provide the source of it differentiation advantage. Differentiation on the basis of innovation and technological competency depends on the R&D function. Efforts to improve service to customers depend on the quality of the sales function. Because developing the distinctive competency needed to provide a differentiation advantage is often expensive, a differentiator normally has a higher cost structure than the cot leader does.

Building new competencies in the functions that sustain its differentiated appeal does not mean neglecting cost control. The differentiator studies how the cost leader operates and attempts to copy cost-saving innovations that will reduce its costs while preserving the source of its competitive advantage. The differentiator must control all costs that do not contribute to its differentiation advantage so that the price of the product does not exceed what customers are willing to pay. Otherwise, it risks letting the cost leader go upmarket and steal its customers. Also, since superior profitability is the result of controlling costs as well as maximizing value and revenues, it pays to watch costs closely. The issue is not to minimize them to the point of losing the source of differentiation. The owners of the famous Savoy Hotel in London, England, face just this problem. The Savoy's reputation has always been based on the incredibly high level of service it offers its customers. Three hotel employees serve the needs of each guest, and in every room, a guest can summon a waiter, maid, or valet by pressing a button at bedside. The cost of offering this level of service has been so high that the hotel makes less than 1 percent net profit every year. Its owners try to find ways to reduce costs to increase profits, but if they reduce the number of hotel staff (the main source of the Savoy's high costs), they may destroy the main source of its differentiated appeal.

Advantages and Disadvantages

The advantages of the differentiation strategy can also be discussed in the context of the five forces model. Differentiation safeguards a company against competitors to the degree that customers develop brand loyalty for its products, a valuable asset that protects the company on all front Powerful suppliers are rarely a problem because the differentiated company's strategy is geared more toward the price it can charge than toward costs. Also, differentiator can often pass on price increases to customers because they are willing to pay the premium price. Thus, a differentiator can tolerate moderate increases in the prices of its inputs better than the cost leader can. Differentiators are unlikely to experience problems with powerful buyers because the differentiator offers a distinct product. Only it can supply the product, and it commands brand loyalty. Differentiation and brand loyalty also create a barrier to entry for other companies seeking to enter the industry. New companies are forced to develop their own distinctive competency to be able to compete, an expensive undertaking.

Finally, the threat of substitute products depends on the ability of competitors' products to meet the same customers' needs as the differentiator's products and to break customers' brand loyalty. This can happen; phone companies are suffering as alternative ways of making phone calls through digital fiber-optic cable, satellite, and the Internet are becoming increasingly available. The issue is how much of a premium price a company can charge for distinctness before customers switch products. In the phone industry, the answer is "not much"; the large carriers were forced to reduce prices drastically so that 7 cents a minute is a common rate, down from 37 cents just a decade ago.

The main problems with a differentiation strategy center on strategic managers' long-term ability to maintain a product's perceived difference or distinctness in customers' eyes. What has become increasingly apparent is how quickly agile competitors move to imitate and copy successful differentiators. This has happened across many industries, such as retailing, computers, autos, home electronics, telecommunications, and pharmaceuticals. Patents and first-mover advantages (the advantages of being the first to market a product or service) last only so long, and as the overall quality of products produced by all companies goes up, brand loyalty declines. The story of the way American Express lost its competitive advantage.

A strategy of differentiation, then, requires a company to develop a competitive advantage by making choices about its product, market, and distinctive competencies that reinforce each other and together increase the value of a good or service in the eyes of customers. When a product has distinctness in customers' eyes, differentiators can charge a premium price. The disadvantages of a differentiation strategy are the ease -with which competitors can imitate a differentiator's product and the difficulty of maintaining a premium price. When differentiation stems from the design or physical features of the product, differentiators are at great risk because imitation is easy. The risk is that over time, products such as VCRs or stereos become commodity-like products, for which the importance of differentiation diminishes as customers become more price sensitive. When differentiation stems from quality o service or reliability or from any intangible source, such as FedEx's guarantee or the prestige of a Rolex, a company is much more secure. It is difficult to imitate intangibles, and the differentiator can reap the benefits of this strategy for a long time. Nevertheless, all differentiators must watch out for imitators and be careful that they do not charge a price higher than the market will bear.

6.1.2.4 Cost-Leadership Differentiation Strategy

Changes in technology—in particular, the development of flexible manufacturing and technologies and new digital, electronic, and information technologies have made the choice between cost- leadership and differentiation strategies less clear-cut.

New technologies provide many ways for companies pursuing a cost-leadership strategy to differentiate their goods and services increasingly while maintaining a low cost structure. Conversely, technological developments often provide many ways for a company that has traditionally pursued a differentiation strategy to find ways to do it at a significantly lower cost so that it can choose a lower pricing option and build demand. The result has been that companies pursuing the different strategies have been drawn into closer competition for customers; rivalry among competitors has increased as they jockey for position, and competitive advantage has become more fragile and short lived than ever before.

Companies like Dell, BMW, and Toyota are continuously experimenting with new ways to reduce costs and segment their markets. The use of robots and flexible manufacturing cells reduces the costs of retooling the production line, and the costs associated with small production runs make it much easier to produce a wide variety of vehicle models and maintain an efficient cost structure. Today, flexible manufacturing enables a company pursuing differentiation to manufacture a range of products at a cost comparable to that of the cost leader. BMW, for example, has taken advantage of flexible manufacturing technologies to reduce its costs, but it also chose to charge only a modest premium price to boost its sales revenues and obtain its profits that way. Its new strategy worked: its market share and profitability have increased in recent years. Indeed, a factor promoting the trend toward market fragmentation and niche marketing in many customer goods industries, such as mobile phones, computers, and appliances, is the substantial reduction of the costs of differentiation by flexible manufacturing.

Another way that a differentiated producer may be able to realize significant economies of scale is by standardizing many of the component parts used in its end products. Toyota's various models of sports utility vehicles are built on only three different car platforms. As a result, Toyota is able to realize significant economies of scale in the manufacture and bulk purchase of standardized component parts despite its high level of market segmentation. Indeed, Toyota is driving the simultaneous cost- leadership and differentiation strategy business model in the car industry, and companies like Ford and DaimlerChrysler are struggling to keep up.

A company can also reduce both production and marketing costs if it limits the number of options it allows customers to choose from for a particular model of car. Increasingly, carmakers, for example, offer a model with an economy, luxury, or sports package that appeal to the principal market segments. Package offerings substantially lower manufacturing costs because long production runs of the various packages are possible. Once again, the company is getting gains from differentiation and from low cost at the same time. Just-in-time inventory systems can also help reduce costs and improve the quality and reliability of a company's products. This benefit is important to differentiated companies, for which quality and reliability areessential ingredients of the product's appeal. Rolls Royces, for example, are never supposed to break down. Improved quality control enhances a company's reputation and thus allows it to charge a premium price.

The Internet and e-commerce also provide an inexpensive way of informing millions of potential customers about the nature and quality of a company's products. Similarly, when customers do their own work on the Internet, such as managing their own finances, stock trades, bill paying, travel booking, and purchasing, the company is no longer bearing these costs because they have been shifted to customers. Direct selling to the customer also avoids the need to use wholesalers and other intermediaries, which results in great cost savings. It has been estimated that 40 percent of the profit in a new car goes to the dealership that sells the car and for costs associated with marketing the car.

Finally, the costs of making low-cost and differentiated products are often not very different because both are produced in countries with low labor costs. For example, the work of sewing an inexpensive cotton shirt for Sears does not cost less than sewing an expensive silk designer shirt for Nordstrom. The raw materials may cost more, but here too companies in countries like Malaysia, India, and China are constantly experimenting with ways to reduce the costs of weaving and dying silk and linen and assembling the final product. Differentiators try to charge what the market will bear (the highest price they can get) so that the profits to be obtained from selling foreign-made differentiated products can be enormous. For example, a $100 pair of Nike shoes may cost less than $1 in labor costs.

Taking advantage of the many ways new technology allows them to manage their value chains more efficiently; many companies are reaping the gains that follow from positioning themselves competitively to obtain the benefits from both low-cost and differentiation strategies. Like Nike, these companies can charge a premium price for their products compared with the price charged by the cost leader—the sneaker sold in Wal-Mart, for example—and their attention to reducing costs probably means they have lower costs than the pure differentiator, which is still focused solely on providing distinct products with high perceived quality. As a result, they achieve at least an equal, and probably a higher, level of profitability than companies pursuing only one of the generic strategies. Hence, the combined strategy is the most profitable to pursue, which is why companies have moved rapidly to take advantage of the new manufacturing and information technologies.

Focus Strategies: Low Cost Differentiation The last generic competitive strategies, the focus low-cost and focus differentiation and strategies, are directed toward serving the needs of a particular or specific market segment or niche. In general, focus strategies position a company to compete for customers in a particular market segment, which can be defined geographically, by type of customer, or by segment of the product line. For example, a geographic niche can be defined by region or even by locality. Selecting a niche by type of customer might mean serving only the very rich, the very young, or the very adventurous. Concentrating on only a segment of the product line means focusing only on vegetarian foods or very fast automobiles or designer clothes or sunglasses. In following a focus strategy, a company is specializing in some way. Once it has chosen its market segment, a focused company positions itself using either a differentiation or a low-cost approach. Figure 6.2 compares these with a pure cost-leadership or differentiation strategy.

In essence, a focused company is a specialized differentiator or a cost leader. If a company uses a focused low-cost approach, it competes against the cost leader in the market segments in which it has no cost disadvantage. For example, in local lumber, cement, bookkeeping, or pizza delivery markets, the focuser may have lower materials or transportation costs than the low-cost national company. The focuser may also have a cost advantage because it is producing complex or custom-built products that do not lend themselves easily to economies of scale in production and therefore offer few experience curve advantages. With a focus strategy, a company concentrates on small-volume custom products, for which it has a cost advantage, and leaves the large-volume standardized market to the cost leader—low-priced Mexican food specials versus Big Macs, for example.

	Offers products to only one group of customers	Offers products to many kinds of customers
Offers low-priced products to customers	Focused Cost-Leadership strategy	Cost-Leadership strategy
Offers unique or distinctive products to customers	Focused differentiation Strategy	Differentiation Strategy

Figure 6.2. Why Focus Strategies are Different.

If a company uses a focused differentiation approach, then all the means of differentiation that are open to the differentiator are available to the focused company. The point is that the focused company positions itself to compete with the differentiator in just one or a few segments. For example, Porsche, a focused company, competes against GM only in the sports car segment of the car market. Focused companies are likely to develop differentiated product qualities successfully because of their knowledge of a small customer set (such as sports car buyers), knowledge of a region, or expertise in a particular field (such as corporate law, management consulting, or web site management for retail customers or restaurants).

Concentration on a small range of products sometimes allows a focuser to develop innovations faster than a large differentiator can. However, the focuser does not attempt to serve all market segments because that would bring it into direct competition with the differentiator. Instead, it concentrates on building market share in one market segment; if it is successful, it may begin to serve more and more market segments and chip away at the differentiator's competitive advantage.

The way in which many small software companies have emerged to take advantage of specialized niches in the outsourcing market.

The many avenues a focused company can take to develop a competitive advantage explain why there are so many small companies in relation to large ones. A focused company has enormous opportunity to develop its own niche and compete against companies pursuing low-cost and differentiated strategies. A focus strategy provides an opportunity for an entrepreneur to find and then exploit a gap in the market by developing an innovative product that customers cannot do without. The steel mini-mills are a good example of how focused companies specializing in one market can grow so efficient that they become the cost leaders. Many large companies started with a focus strategy, and, of course, one means by which companies can expand is to take over other focused companies. For example, Cisco Systems, the largest Internet router maker, grew by buying over fifty small specialist software and hardware companies. Its managers believed these companies possessed the products and knowledge that would allow it to become the leading differentiator in the industry, and despite the downturn in e-commerce Cisco remains the dominant industry competitor.

Advantages and Disadvantages

A focused company's competitive advantages stem from the source of its distinctive competency: efficiency, quality, innovation, or responsiveness to customers. The company is protected from rivals to the extent that it can provide a product or service they cannot. This ability also gives the focuser power over its buyers because they cannot get the same thing from anyone else. With regard to powerful suppliers, however,.a focused company is at a disadvantage, because it buys in small volume and thus is in the suppliers' power. However, as long as it can pass on price increases to loyal customers, this disadvantage may not be a significant problem. Potential entrants have to overcome the loyalty from customers the focuser has generated, and the development of customer loyalty also lessens the threat from substitute products. This protection from the five forces allows the focuser to earn above-average returns on its investment. Another advantage of the focus strategy is that it permits a company to stay close to its customers and respond to their changing needs. The difficulty a large differentiator sometimes experiences in managing a large number of market segments is not an issue for a focuser.

Because a focuser produces a small volume, its cost structure may be higher than that of a low-cost company. Higher costs can reduce profitability if a focuser is forced to invest heavily in developing a distinctive competency, such as expensive product innovation, in order to compete with a differentiated company. However, once again, flexible manufacturing systems are opening up new opportunities for focused companies because small production runs become possible at a lower cost. Increasingly, small, specialized companies are competing with large companies in specific market segments in which their cost disadvantage is much reduced. A second problem is that the focuser's niche can suddenly disappear because of technological change or changes in customers' tastes. Unlike the more generalist differentiator, a focuser cannot move easily to new niches, given its concentration of resources and competency in one or a few niches. For example, clothing store chain Brooks Brothers, whose focus was on providing formal business attire, ran into great difficulty in the 1990s when business casual became the clothing norm at most companies. It found it hard to adapt to the changing market and was bought out in 2001. Diners have become almost a thing of the past as they have become unable to compete with the low prices and speed of fast food chains like McDonald's and the upscale atmosphere of Starbuck's. The disappearance of niches is one reason that so many small companies fail.

Finally, there is the very real prospect that differentiators will compete for a focuser's niche by offering a product that can satisfy the demands of the focuser's customers; for example, GM's new midsize Cadillac and Ford's new midsized Jaguar are aimed at Lexus, BMW, and Mercedes-Benz buyers. A focuser is vulnerable and has to defend its niche constantly.

6.1.2.5 Stuck in the Middle

Successful competitive positioning requires that a company make consistent product, market, and distinctive competency choices. In other words, a company must achieve a fit among the three components of business-level strategy to create a business model that gives it a competitive advantage. Thus, a low-cost company cannot strive for a high level of market segmentation, as a differentiator does, and provide a wide range of products because those choices would raise its cost structure too much and the company would lose its low-cost advantage. Similarly, a differentiator with a competency in innovation that tries to reduce its expenditures on research and development or one with a competency in responsiveness to customers through after-sales service that seeks to economize on iales force to decrease costs is asking for trouble because it will lose its competitive advantage as its distinctive competency disappears.

6.1.2.6 Competitive Positioning and Business Level Strategy

Business-level strategy determines how a company will compete for customers in a particular market segment or industry. In every market segment or industry, typically and several companies are competing for the same set of customers. This means that the actions of one company will have an impact on the others, and over time, companies competing for the same customers become rivals locked in a competitive struggle to be the ones that obtain a competitive advantage and achieve above-average profitability. How many companies might be expected to achieve above-average profitability in a particular market or industry? And how can managers increase their chances of being one of the fortunate few? Several tools are useful in helping managers to position their companies competitively with regard to both the customer and their competitors. Here, we examine three of these tools: strategic group analysis, investment analysis, and game theory.

6.1.2.7 Strategic Group Analysis

Strategic group analysis helps a company identify the strategies that its industry rivals are pursuing. Within most industries, strategic groups emerge, each composed of companies pursuing a similar generic strategy. All the companies inside an industry pursuing a low-cost strategy form one strategic group, all those seeking to pursue a broad differentiation strategy constitute another strategic group, and all those pursuing a focus differentiation or low-cost strategy form yet other strategic groups.

The concept of strategic groups has a number of implications for business-level strategy. First, strategic managers can map their competitors according to their choice of generic strategy. They can identify the different ways rivals have decided what customers' needs to satisfy, which customer groups to serve, and which distinctive competencies to develop. They can then use this knowledge to position themselves closer to customers and differentiate themselves from their competitors. In other words, careful strategic group analysis allows managers to uncover the most important basis of competition in an industry and identify products and market segments where they can compete most successfully for customers. Such analysis also helps to reveal what competencies are likely to be most valuable in the future so that companies can make the right investment decision. For example, the need to develop new models of cars that can be sold across the world and are assembled reliably by low-cost labor has dominated competitive positioning in the global car industry. U.S. car companies have bought or formed alliances with almost every other foreign car manufacturer to obtain marketing, design, or manufacturing knowledge.

Second, a company's nearest competitors are those companies pursuing a similar strategy in its strategic group. Customers tend to view the products of such enterprises as being direct substitutes for each other. Thus, a major threat to a company's profitability may arise primarily from within its own strategic group, not necessarily from the other companies in the industry pursuing different generic business-level strategies. For example, the competition for Toyota comes from Honda, Ford, and Volkswagen, not from Hyundai or Rolls Royce. Third, different strategic groups can have a different standing with respect to each of Porter's five competitive forces because these forces affect companies in different ways. In other words, the risk of new entry by potential competitors, the degree of rivalry among companies within a group, the bargaining power of buyers, the bargaining power of suppliers, and the competitive force of substitute products can all vary in intensity among different strategic groups within the same industry. In the global car industry, for example, the smaller, more focused companies pursuing both low-cost and differentiated luxury strategies were in big trouble in the 1990s. Their input costs were rising, and they could not afford billions of dollars to design new models and build new flexible manufacturing plants needed to produce them. Indeed, some European, Korean, and even Japanese companies started to lose billions of dollars, while the big differentiators such as Toyota, Volkswagen, and Ford were making record profits. the mobility barriers are factors that inhibit the movement of companies between groups in an industry. The relative height of mobility barriers determines how successfully companies in one group can compete with companies in another group. For example, can a company in the differentiation strategic group also pursue a low-cost strategy and thus achieve the low cost-differentiation strategy? To the degree that one or more companies in one group can develop or obtain the functional and financial resources they need to lower their costs or embark on a major R&D expansion, they may be able to compete successfully with companies in another strategic group. In effect, they have created yet another strategic group: a combined low-cost and differentiation strategic group, which has the strongest competitive advantage and the greatest ability to earn above-average profits. In fact, the need to pursue a simultaneous global low-cost and differentiation strategy has been the major driving force behind the wave of merger activities among the large car companies that has left just a handful of global giants to compete in the 2000s. For example, Daimler Benz took over Chrysler, GM took control of Isuzu, and Ford merged with Mazda to pursue a global low-cost/differentiation strategy. Thus, the strategic group map in the global car industry has changed dramatically as companies fight to survive in the rapidly consolidating global car industry. A few companies like BMW and Porsche still pursue a focus differentiated strategy. However, some analysts believe it is only a matter of time before they will be forced to join with one of the low-cost/differentiators.

6.1.2.8 Choosing an Investment Strategy at the Business Level

A second major choice to be made at the business level is which type of investment to pursue in support of the competitive strategy. An investment strategy sets Strategy the amount and type of resources—human, functional, and financial—that must be invested to maximize a company's profitability over time. A company's return on invested capital is a major indicator of its competitive advantage in an industry. Generic competitive strategies provide competitive advantages but they are expensive to develop and maintain. For example, a simultaneous differentiation/cost-leadership strategy is the most expensive, because it requires that a company invest resources not only in functions such as R&D, sales, and marketing to develop distinctive competencies but also in functions such as manufacturing and materials management to find ways to reduce costs. A focus strategy is probably the least expensive because fewer resources are needed to serve one market segment than the whole market.

In deciding on an investment strategy, a company must evaluate the potential return (on invested capital) from investing in a generic competitive strategy against the cost. In this way, it can determine whether pursuing a certain strategy is likely to be profitable and how profitability will change as competition within the industry changes. Two factors are crucial in choosing an investment strategy: the strength of a company's position in an industry relative to its competitors and the stage of the industry's life cycle in which the company is competing.

In determining the strength of a company's relative competitive position, market share and distinctive competencies become important. A large market share signals greater potential returns from future investment because it suggests a company has brand loyalty and is in a strong competitive position. Similarly, the more difficult it is to imitate a company's distinctive competencies, such as those in R&D or manufacturing and marketing, the stronger a company's relative competitive position becomes. These two attributes also reinforce one another; for example, a large market share may help a company to create and develop distinctive competencies because high demand allows it to ride down the experience curve and lower its cost structure. Also, a large market share can create a large cash flow, which may allow for more investment to develop competencies in R&D or elsewhere. In general, companies with the largest market share and the strongest distinctive competencies are in the best position to build and sustain their competitive advantage. Companies with a small market share and little potential for developing a distinctive competency are in a much weaker competitive position.

The second main factor influencing the investment attractiveness of a generic strategy is the stage of the industry life cycle. A particular industry environment, presenting different opportunities and threats, accompanies each life cycle stage. Each stage therefore has different implications for the investment of resources needed to obtain a competitive advantage. Competition is strongest in the shakeout stage of the life cycle and least important in the embryonic stage, for example. The risks of pursuing a strategy change over time. The difference in risk explains why the potential returns from investing in a competitive strategy depend on the life cycle stage. Table 6.3 summarizes the relationship among the stage of the life cycle, the competitive position, and the investment strategy at the business level.

Table 6.3

	Strong Competitive Position	**Weak Competitive Position**
Embryonic	Share building	Share building
Growth	Growth	Market concentration
Shakeout	Share increasing	Market concentration or harvest/ liquidation
Maturity	Hold-and-maintain or profit	Harvest or liquidation/divestiture
Decline	Market concentration or harvest (asset reduction)	Turnaround, liquidation, or divestitur

Embryonic Strategy: In the embryonic stage, all companies, weak and strong, emphasize the development of a distinctive competency and an associated business model. During this stage, investment needs are great because a company has to establish a competitive advantage. Many fledgling companies in the industry are seeking resources to develop a distinctive competency. Thus, the appropriate business-level investment strategy is a share-building strategy. The aim is to build market share by developing a stable and distinct competitive advantage to attract customers who have no knowledge of the company's products. Companies require large amounts of capital to build research and development competencies or sales and service competencies. They cannot generate much of this capital internally. Thus, a company's success depends on its ability to demonstrate a distinct competency to attract outside investors, or venture capitalists. If a company gains the resources to develop a distinctive competency, it will be in a relatively stronger competitive position. If it fails, its only option may be to exit the industry. In fact, companies in weak competitive positions at all stages in the life cycle may choose to exit the industry to cut their losses.

Growth Strategies: At the growth stage, the task facing a company is to consolidate its position and provide the base it needs to survive the coming shakeout. Thus, the appropriate investment strategy is the growth strategy. The goal is to maintain its relative competitive position in a rapidly expanding market and, if possible, to increase it—in other words, to grow with the expanding market.

However, other companies are entering the market and catching up with the industry's innovators. As a result, first movers—companies first into the market with a particular kind of good or service—often require successive waves of capital infusion to maintain the momentum generated by their success in the embryonic stage. For example, differentiators need to engage in extensive research and development to maintain their technological lead, and cost leaders need to invest in state-of-the-art machinery and computers to obtain new experience curve economies. All this investment is very expensive.

The growth stage is also the time when companies attempt to consolidate existing market niches and enter new ones so that they can increase their market share. Increasing the level of market segmentation to become a broad differentiator is expensive as well. A company has to invest resources to develop a new sales and marketing competency. Consequently, at the growth stage, companies fine-tune their competitive strategy and make business- level investment decisions about the relative advantages of a differentiation, low-cost, or focus strategy, given financial needs and relative competitive position. If one company has emerged as the cost leader, for example, some others may decide to compete head-to-head with it and enter this strategic group, but others will not and instead will pursue a growth strategy using a differentiation or focus approach and invest resources in developing other competencies. As a result, strategic groups start to develop in an industry as each company seeks the best way to invest its scarce resources to maximize its competitive advantage.

Companies must spend a lot of money just to keep up with growth in the market, and finding additional resources to develop new skills and competencies is a difficult task for strategic managers. Consequently, companies in a weak competitive position at this stage engage in a market concentration strategy to consolidate their position. They seek to specialize in some way and may adopt a focus strategy and move to a focused strategic group to reduce their investment needs. If they are very weak, they may also choose to exit the industry and sell out to a stronger competitor.

Shakeout Strategies: By the shakeout stage, demand is increasing slowly, and competition by price or product characteristics becomes intense. Companies in strong competitive positions need resources to invest in a share-increasing strategy to attract customers from weak companies exiting the market. In other words, companies attempt to maintain and increase market share despite fierce competition. The way companies invest their resources depends on their generic strategy.

For cost leaders, because of the price wars that can occur, investment in cost control is crucial if they are to survive the shakeout stage; they must do all they can to reduce costs. Differentiators in a strong competitive position choose to forge ahead and become broad differentiators. Their investment is likely to be oriented toward marketing, and they are likely to develop a sophisticated after-sales service network They also widen the product range to match the range of customers' needs. Differentiators in a weak position reduce their investment burden by withdrawing to a focused strategy—the market concentration strategy—to specialize in a particular niche or product. Weak companies exiting the industry engage in a harvest or liquidation strategy, both of which are discussed later in this chapter.

Maturity Strategies: By the maturity stage, a relatively stable strategic group structure has emerged in the industry, and companies have learned how their competitors will probably react to their competitive moves. At this point, companies want to reap the rewards of their previous investments in developing a generic strategy. Until now, profits have been reinvested in the business, and dividends have been small. Investors in strong companies have obtained their rewards through the appreciation of the value of their stock, because the company has reinvested most of its capital to maintain and increase market share. As market growth slows in the maturity stage, a company's investment strategy depends on the level of competition in the industry and the source of the company's competitive advantage.

In environments in which competition is high because of technological change or low barriers to entry; companies need to defend their competitive position. Strategic managers need to continue to invest heavily in maintaining the company's competitive advantage. Both low-cost companies and differentiators adopt a hold-and-maintain strategy to support their generic strategies. They expend resources to develop their distinctive competency so as to remain the market leaders. For example, differentiated companies may invest in improved after-sales service, and low-cost companies may invest in the latest production technologies.

It is at this point, however, that companies realize they must begin to pursue both a low-cost and a differentiation strategy if they are to protect themselves from aggressive competitors (both at home and abroad) that are watching for any opportunity or perceived weakness to take the lead in the industry. Differentiators take advantage of their strong position to develop flexible manufacturing systems to reduce their production costs. Cost leaders move to start differentiating their products to expand their market share by serving more market segments. For example, Gallo moved from the bulk wine segment and began marketing premium wines and wine coolers to take advantage of its low production costs. Soon, Gallo's new premium brands, like Falling Leaf chardonnay, became the best-selling wines in the United States.

Historically, however, many companies have felt protected from competition within the industry in the maturity stage and decide to exploit their competitive advantage to the fullest by engaging in a profit strategy: they attempt to maximize their present returns, not their future profitability, from previous investments. Typically, they reinvest proportionally less in improving their functional resources and increased returns to shareholders. The profit strategy works well only as long as competitive forces remain relatively constant, so that a company can maintain the profit margins developed by its competitive strategy. However, it must be alert to threats from the environment and take care not to become complacent and unresponsive to changes. All too often, market leaders fail to exercise vigilance in managing the environment, imagining that they are impervious to competition. Kodak, which had profited for so long from its strengths in film processing, was slow to respond to the threat of electronic imaging techniques. Sears and Kmart woke up too late to the threat posed by Wal-Mart. Paradoxically, very successful companies often fail to sense changes in the market.

Decline Strategies: The decline stage of an industry's life cycle begins when demand for its product starts to fall. Among the many possible reasons for decline are foreign competition and the loss of a company's distinctive competency as its rivals enter with new or more efficient technologies. A company must now decide what investment strategy to adopt in order to deal with new circumstances within its industry. The initial strategies that companies can adopt are market concentration and asset reduction.

With a **market concentration strategy**, a company attempts to consolidate its product and market choices. It narrows its product range and exits marginal niches in an attempt to redeploy its resources more effectively and improve its competitive position. Reducing customer groups served may also allow it to pursue a focus strategy in order to survive the decline stage. An asset reduction strategy requires a company to limit or decrease its investment in a business and to extract, or milk, the investment as much as it can. This approach is sometimes called a harvest strategy because a company will exit the industry once it has "harvested" all the returns it can. It reduces to a minimum the assets it employs in the business and forgoes investment for the sake of immediate profits.3° A market concentration strategy generally indicates that a company is trying to turn around its business so that it can survive in the long run. Low-cost companies are more likely to pursue a harvest strategy because a smaller market share means higher costs and they are unable to move to a focus strategy. Differentiators, in contrast, have a competitive advantage in this stage if they can move to a focus strategy.

At any stage of the life cycle, companies that are in weak competitive positions may apply turnaround strategies. The questions that a company has to answer are whether it has the resources available to develop a viable business-level strategy to compete in the industry and how much it will cost. A company stuck in the middle, for example, must assess the investment costs of developing a low-cost or differentiation strategy. Perhaps a company pursuing a low-cost strategy has not made the right product or market choices, or perhaps a differentiation has been missing niche opportunities. In such cases, the company can redeploy resources and change its strategy.

If a company decides that turnaround is not possible for competitive or life cycle reasons, then the two remaining investment alternatives are liquidation and divestiture: exit the industry by liquidating assets or selling the whole business. Both are radical forms of harvesting strategy, because the company is seeking to get back as much as it can from its investment in the business. Often, however, it can exit only at a loss and take a tax write-off. Timing is important; the earlier a company senses that divestiture is necessary, the more it can get for its assets. There are many stories about companies that buy weak or declining companies, thinking they can turn them around, and as the new acquisitions become a drain on their resources they then realize their mistake.

Strategic managers must always consider the costs of pursuing a generic strategy when developing or refining their business models. The issue is how to invest a company's capital in resources that will result in the greatest potential future returns, Achieving superior performance and profitability requires constant attention to the bottom line—to understanding how to increase a company's return on invested capital through the investment strategy in its business model.

6.1.2.9 Business Level Strategy and Game Theory

Companies are in a constant competitive struggle with rivals in their industry and strategic group to gain more business from customers. A useful way of viewing this struggle is as a competitive game between companies, where companies are continually using competitive moves and tactics to compete effectively in an industry. Companies that understand the nature of the competitive game they are playing can often make better strategic moves that increase the profitability of their business-level strategies. For example, they can find a better way to pursue a cost leadership or a differentiation strategy. A branch of work in the social sciences known as game theory can be used to model competition between a company and its rivals and help managers improve their business models and strategies.

From a game theory perspective, companies in an industry can be viewed as players that are all simultaneously making choices about which generic strategies to pursue to maximize their profitability. The problem strategic managers face is that the potential profitability of each strategy is not some fixed amount; it varies depending on the strategy one company selects and also the strategies that its rivals select. There are two basic types of game: sequential move games and simultaneous move games. In a sequential move game, such as chess, players move in turn, and one player can select a strategy to pursue after considering its rival's choice of strategies. In a *simultaneous move game,* the players act at the same time, in ignorance of their rival's current actions. The classic game of rock-paper-scissors is a simultaneous move game.

In the business world, both sequential and simultaneous move games are commonplace as strategic managers jockey for competitive position in the industry Indeed, game theory is particularly useful in analyzing situations where a company is competing against a limited number of rivals, and there is a considerable level of interdependence in the industry, as occurs in a consolidated industry. In such a setting, the profitability of a strategy depends critically on the strategy pursued by rival companies. Several of the basic principles that underlie game theory are examined below; these principles can be useful in determining which business-level strategies managers should pursue.

Look Forward and Reason Back: One of the most basic messages of game theory is that managers need to think strategically in two related ways: (1) look forward, think ahead, and anticipate how rivals will respond to whatever strategic moves they make, and (2) reason backward to determine which strategic moves to pursue today given their assessment of how the company's rivals will respond to various future strategic moves. Managers who do both of these things should be able to discover the specific competitive strategy that will lead to the greatest potential returns. This cardinal principle of game theory is known as look forward and reason back, to understand its importance consider this scenario.

Two large companies, UPS and FedEx, which specialize in next-day delivery of packages, dominate the U.S. air express industry. They have a very high fixed cost structure because they need to invest in a capital-intensive nationwide network of aircraft, trucks, and package sorting facilities. The key to their profitability is to increase volume sufficiently so that these fixed costs can be spread out over a large number of packages, reducing the unit cost of transporting each package.

Imagine that a bright young manager at UPS calculates that if UPS cuts prices for next-day delivery service by 15 percent, the volume of packages the company ships will grow by over 30 percent, and so will UPS's total revenues and profitability. Is this a smart move? The answer depends on whether the bright young manager has remembered to look forward and reason back and think through how FedEx would respond to UPS's price cuts. Because UPS and FedEx are competing directly against each other, their strategies are interdependent. If UPS cuts prices, FedEx will lose market share, its volume of shipments will decline, and its profitability will suffer. Because FedEx is unlikely to accept this result, if UPS cuts prices by 15 percent, FedEx is likely to follow and cut its prices by 15 percent in order to hold onto market share. The net result is that the average level of prices in the industry will fall by 15 percent, as will revenues, and both players will see their profitability decline—a lose-lose situation. By looking forward and reasoning back, the new manager discovers that the strategy of cutting prices is not a good one.

Know Thy Rival: At this juncture, the question of whether this example is rather contrived might arise. After all, could UPS managers really anticipate how FedEx's profits could be affected if UPS cut its prices by 15 percent? And could UPS really assign a probability to FedEx's likely response? The answer is that although UPS's managers cannot calculate exactly what the profit impact and probabilities would be, they can make an informed decision by collecting competitive information and thinking strategically. For example, they could estimate FedEx's cost structure by looking at FedEx's published financial accounts. And because they are in the same business as FedEx and use the same basic business model, they can assess the effect of falling demand on FedEx's cost structure and bottom line. Moreover, by looking at the history of FedEx's competitive behavior, they can assess how FedEx will respond to a price cut. This illustrates a second basic principle of game theory: know thy rivals. In other words, in thinking strategically, managers put themselves in the position of a rival to answer the question of how that rival is likely to act in a particular situation. If a company's managers are to be effective at looking forward and reasoning back, they must have a good understanding of what their rival is likely to do under different scenarios, and they need to be able to extrapolate their rival's future behavior based on this understanding.

Find the Most Profitable Dominant Strategy: A dominant strategy is one that makes you better off than you would be if you played any other strategy, no matter what strategy your opponent uses. To grasp this concept, consider a simultaneous move game based on a situation that developed in the U.S. car industry in the early 1990s (so far we have been considering a sequential move game). Two car companies, Ford and GM, both differentiators, have to decide whether to introduce cash-back rebate programs in November to move unsold inventory that is building up on the lots of car dealers nationwide. Each company can make one of two moves: offer rebates or do not offer rebates. Because the advanced planning associated with launching such a strategy is fairly extensive, both companies must make a decision about what to do by mid-October, which is before they have had a chance to see what their rival is doing. In each of the previous four years, both companies have introduced just such programs on November 1 and kept them in place until December 31. Customers have become conditioned to expect these programs and increasingly have held back their new car purchases in anticipation of the cash rebate programs beginning in November. This learned behavior by customers has increased the strategic importance of the rebate programs and made the rebate programs themselves increasingly expensive for the automobile companies.

Strategy Shapes the Payoff Structure of the Game: An important lesson of game theory is that through its choice of strategy, a company can alter the payoff structure of the competitive game being played in the industry. To understand this, consider once more the cash rebate game played by Ford and GM where both companies are compelled to choose a dominant strategy that depresses total payoff. How can they extricate themselves from this predicament? By changing the behavior of customers. Recall that rebates were necessary only because customers had come to expect them and held off purchasing a car until the rebates were introduced. In a self-fulfilling prophecy, this depresses demand and forces the companies to introduce rebates to move unsold inventory on the lots of car dealers. If these expectations could be changed, customers would not hold off their purchases in anticipation of the rebates being introduced in November of each year. Companies would no longer have to introduce rebates to move unsold inventory on the lots of car dealers. So how can a company change customer behavior? Through its choice of strategy. This is what GM actually did. After several years of rebate wars, GM decided to issue a new credit card that allowed cardholders to apply 5 percent of their charges toward buying or leasing a new GM car, up to $500 a year with a maximum of $3,500.

6.1.3 Functional Level Strategy

The functional level of the organization is the level of the operating divisions and departments. The strategic issues at the functional level are related to business processes and the value chain. Functional level strategies in marketing, finance, operations, human resources, and R&D involve the development and coordination of resources through which business unit level strategies can be executed efficiently and effectively.

Functional units of an organization are involved in higher level strategies by providing input into the business unit level and corporate level strategy, such as providing information on resources and capabilities on which the higher level strategies can be based. Once the higher-level strategy is developed, the functional units translate it into discrete action-plans that each department or division must accomplish for the strategy to succeed. Yarns, fibers, and a variety of petrochemical products. For each product group, the nature of market in terms of customers, competition, and marketing channel differs.

Therefore, it requires different strategies for its different product groups. Thus, where SBU concept is applied, each SBU sets its own strategies to make the best use of its resources (its strategic advantages) given the environment it faces. At such a level, strategy is a comprehensive plan providing objectives for SBUs, allocation of re-sources among functional areas and coordination between them for making optimal contribution to the achievement of corporate-level objectives. Such strategies operate within the overall strategies of the organization. The corporate strategy sets the long-term objectives of the firm and the broad constraints and policies within which a SBU operates. The corporate level will help the SBU define its scope of operations and also limit or enhance the SBUs operations by the resources the corporate level assigns to it. There is a difference between corporate-level and business-level strategies.

For example, Andrews says that in an organization of any size or diversity, corporate strategy usually applies to the whole enterprise, while business strategy, less comprehensive, defines the choice of product or service and market of individual business within the firm. In other words, business strategy relates to the 'how' and corporate strategy to the 'what'. Corporate strategy defines the business in which a company will compete preferably in a way that focuses resources to convert distinctive competence into competitive advantage.' Corporate strategy is not the sum total of business strategies of the corporation but it deals with different subject matter. While the corporation is concerned with and has impact on business strategy, the former is concerned with the shape and balancing of growth and renewal rather than in market execution.

In short functional strategy is the approach taken by a functional area to achieve corporate and business unit objectives and strategies by maximizing resource productivity. It is concerned with developing and nurturing a distinctive competence to provide a company or business unit with a competitive advantage. Just as a multi-divisional corporation has several business units, each with its own business strategy, each business unit has its own set of departments, each with its own functional strategy.

6.1.3.1 Nature and Characteristics of Functional Strategy

1. Long term direction

Functional strategies are essential to implement business strategy. In fact, the effectiveness of a corporate or business strategy execution depends critically on the manner in which strategies are implemented at the functional level. The corporate strategy provides the long-term direction and scope of a firm. The business strategy outlines the competitive posture of its operations in an industry.

2. Functional success

The functional strategy clarifies the business strategy, giving specific, short-term guidance to operating managers in the areas of operations. Marketing, finance, HR, R&D, etc., and increase the likelihood of their success.

3. Quality assurance and mass production

Orientation of the functional strategy, therefore, depends on the business strategy. For example, if a business unit follows a differentiation strategy through high quality products, its production strategy emphasized expensive quality assurance processes over cheaper, high-volume production, a human resource functional strategy that emphasizes hiring and training of a highly skilled, but costly, workforce, and a marketing functional strategy that emphasizes extensive advertising to increase demand rather than using marketing incentives to retailers.

4. Low-cost competitive strategy

Similarly, if the business unit follows a low-cost competitive strategy, a different set of functional strategies emphasizing cost-cutting measures would be needed to support the business strategy.

5. Glueck and Jauch's approach on functional strategy

The strategic decisions are implemented by all the parts of an organization.

- There is a basis available for controlling activities in different functional areas of a business.
- The time spent by functional managers on decision making may be reduced.
- Similar situations occurring in different functional areas are handled by the functional managers in a consistent manner.
- Coordination across different functions takes place where necessary.

6. Functional strategies focusing

- Specify more precisely how corporate and business strategies are to be implemented.
- Establish a mechanism to make sure that strategies are implemented.
- Lead to new strengths which can be used for strategy in the future.

7. Development of functional strategies

The process of developing functional strategies is quite similar to that of strategy formulation, with the difference that functional heads are responsible for their formulation and implementation.

Environmental factors relevant to each functional area will have an impact on the choice of strategies. Finally, the actual process of choice involves a negotiation between functional managers and business unit managers. Thus, functional strategies are generally formulated in all key functional areas. For each of the functional strategies, a set of policies will have to establish for appropriate areas of the business. The policies will ensure that the strategies are carried out as intended and that the different functional areas are working towards the same ends.

Table 6.4 Difference Between Functional Strategy and Business Strategy.

Particulars	Functional Strategy	Business Strategy
1. Time Horizon	Functional strategies focus on short-term goals short time horizon of functional strategies is critical to the successful implementation of a business strategy for two reasons: It focuses the attention of functional managers on what needs to be done now. It allows functional managers to adjust to changing current conditions.	Business strategies focus on the firm's long-term competitive posture (3 to 5 years)
2. Specificity	Functional strategies provide more specific direction to functional managers by helping them to know what needs to be done and focus on results. Clarifying for to management how they intend to accomplish the business strategy. This increases top management's confidence and sense of control.	Business strategies provide general direction
3. Participants	Functional strategy is the responsibility of the operating managers of the functional area. Functional strategies are approved through negotiation between business unit managers and operating managers of the functional area.	Business strategy is the responsibility of the head of the business unit. Business strategies are approved through negotiation between corporate managers and business unit managers.

6.1.3.2 Key Functional Areas of the Functional Strategies

1. Financial Strategy

In the financial management area, the major concern of the strategy relates to the acquisition and utilization of funds. Major issues involved are the sources from where the funds will come, from equity or by borrowing. How much of the borrowing will be short term and how much long term. In terms of usage of funds, the policy decisions would relate to whether and to what extent funds have to be deployed in fixed assets and current assets. The long term or capital investment decisions relate to buying or leasing the fixed assets.

2. Cash Flow

Apart from capital budgeting, another consideration in financial strategy which influences other functional areas is the cash flow. A company may frame and dividend policies based on availability on cash. In case a company proposes expansion through internally generated funds, it may reduce bonus and dividend. This is particularly so when it has formulated ambitious growth strategies which require large cash. Similarly, if the firm has high risk business, it should have a conservative debt/

equity ratio to guard against heavy interest burden. The funds positions and optimization orientation of top management also determines the accounts receivable and payable policies. Financial strategies and policies may even determine the accounting policies as these affect the profitability, balance-sheet and hence cash flow through taxes, dividend, bonus, etc.

3. Marketing Strategy

Functional strategies in marketing area are required for marketing – mix decisions, i.e., the four P's of marketing, viz., Product design, Product distribution, Pricing and Promotion aspects of marketing. In terms of specifics, the product decisions relate to such issues as the variety of product (shape, size, model, etc.,) quality requirements, introduction/withdrawal of products, nature of customers, etc., Specific policies are also required regarding distribution channels i.e., through retailers or direct selling? What would be the spread of distribution network? Whether new dealers will be established or old ones developed? The promotion strategies will relate to mode of promotion, coverage and nature (corporate, product or brand promotion). Again, very clear and specific strategies will have to be made about pricing, etc., full cost or standard cost based pricing. Offensive vs. defensive postures also influence pricing policies.

4. HR Strategy

HR strategy deals with matters like HR planning, recruitment and selection, training and development, compensation management, performance management, rewards and incentives etc., what compensation / reward system will be able to attract people of the desired type to join the organization so as to meet the task requirements demanded by the strategy? What strategies are necessary to groom internal people for new positions? The problem becomes acute in the context of turnaround strategies. On the one hand, the most competent people leave and the firm finds it difficult to attract suitable replacements. On the other hand, it faces the problem of surplus staff. HR strategies for retrenchment, though painful, are quite necessary but difficult to develop.

5. Production Strategy

The functions relating to production need strategies relating to quality assurance, machine utilization, location of facilities, balancing the line, scheduling of production and materials management. The strategy for entering into export market will dictate a different policy regarding quality of products and maintenance. Location of facilities may be determined by closeness to market or input supply points. Decisions must be made to determine whether and how much to make or buy, on the basis of cost differential, availability, criticality of the item, capacity if expansion becomes necessary. In case of bought out items, policies regarding number of suppliers and the criteria for selecting them are necessary.

6. R&D Strategy

In the area of research and development, functional strategies regarding the nature of research are necessary. In case of expansion through new product development, heavy emphasis has to be laid on basic and applied research. On the contrary, for expansion in the same line, research emphasis has to be on product/process improvement to cut cost and to add value. It may be noted that in case of basic research the firm should be prepared to commit resources and wait for outcome for several years. It cannot have basic research unless it is prepare to commit resources on long-term basis.

7. Overview

The functional-level strategies which aims at improving the effectiveness of a company's operations and thus its ability to attain superior efficiency, quality, innovation and customer responsiveness. It is important to keep in mind the relationships of functional strategies, distinctive competencies; differentiation, low cost, value creation and profitability (fig.6.3). Note that distinctive competencies shape the functional-level strategies that a company can pursue and that through their choices with regard to functional-level strategies, managers can build resources and capabilities that enhance a company's distinctive competencies.

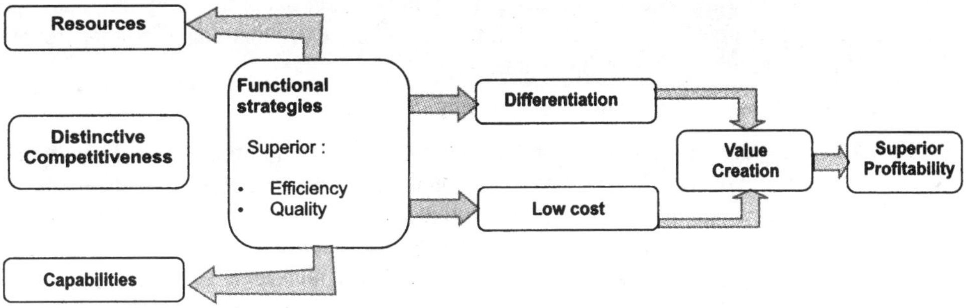

Figure 6.3. The Roots of Competitive Advantage.

Note also that the ability of a company to attain superior efficiency, quality, innovation and customer responsiveness will determine if its product offering is differentiated from that of rivals and if it has a low cost structure. Recall that companies that increase value through differentiation, while simultaneously lowering their cost structure, create more value than their rivals and this leads to a competitive advantage and superior profitability.

8. Achieving Superior Efficiency

A company is a device for transforming inputs (labor, land, capital, management and technological know-how) into outputs (the goods and services produced). The simplest measure of efficiency is the quantity of inputs that it takes to produce a given output; that is,

$$\text{Efficiency} = \frac{\text{Outputs}}{\text{Inputs}}$$

The more efficient a company is, the fewer the inputs required to produce a given output and therefore the lower its cost structure will be. Put another way, an efficient company has higher productivity and therefore lower costs than its rivals. Here we review the steps that companies can take at the functional level to increase their efficiency and thereby lower their cost structure.

9. Marketing and Efficiency

The marketing strategy that a company adopts can have a major impact on efficiency and cost structure. Marketing strategy refers to the position that a company takes with regard to pricing, promotion, advertising, product design and distribution. Some of the steps leading to greater efficiency are fairly obvious. For example, riding down the experience curve to achieve a lower cost structure can be facilitated by aggressive pricing, promotions, and advertising, all of which are the task of the marketing function. Other aspects of marketing strategy have a less obvious but no less important impact on efficiency. One important aspect is the relationship of customer defection rates, cost structure, and unit costs.

10. R&D Strategy and Efficiency

The role of superior research and development (R&D) in helping a company achieve and greater efficiency and a lower cost structure is twofold. First, the R&D function can boost efficiency by designing products that are easy to manufacture. By cutting down on the number of parts that make up a product, R&D can dramatically decrease the required assembly time, which translates into higher employee productivity, lower costs, and higher profitability. For example, after Texas Instruments redesigned an infrared sighting mechanism that it supplies to the Pentagon, it found that it had reduced the number of parts from 47 to 12, the number of assembly steps from 56 to 13, the time spent fabricating metal from 757 minutes per unit to 219 minutes per unit, and unit assembly time from 129 minutes to 20 minutes. The result was a substantial decline in production costs. Design for manufacturing requires close coordination between the production and R&D functions of the company, of course. Cross-functional teams that contain production and R&D personnel who work jointly on the problem best achieve this.

11. Human Resource Strategy and Efficiency

Employee productivity is one of the key determinants of an enterprise's efficiency, Strategy and cost structure, and profitability. Productive manufacturing employees can lower the cost of goods sold as a percentage of revenues, a productive sales force can increase sales revenues for a given level of expenses, and productive employees in the company's R&D function can boost the percentage of revenues generated from new products for a given level of R&D expenses. Thus, productive employees lower the costs of generating revenues, increase the return on sales, and by extension boost the company's return on invested capital. The challenge for a company's human resource function is to devise ways to increase employee productivity. Among the choices it has are hiring strategies, training employees, organizing the work force into self-managing teams, and linking pay to performance.

12. Self-Managing Teams

The use of self-managing teams, whose members coordinate their own activities, including making their own hiring, training, work, and reward decisions, has been spreading rapidly. The typical team comprises five to fifteen employees who produce an entire product or undertake an entire task. Team members learn all team tasks and rotate from job to job. Because a more flexible work force is one result, team members can fill in for absent coworkers and take over managerial duties such as work and vacation scheduling, ordering materials, and hiring new members. The greater responsibility thrust on team members and the empowerment it implies are seen as motivators.

13. Information Systems, the Internet and Efficiency

With the rapid spread of computers, the explosive growth of the Internet and corporate intranets (internal corporate computer networks based on Internet standards), and the spread of high-bandwidth fiber optics and digital wireless technology, the information systems function is moving to center stage in the quest for operating efficiencies and a lower cost structure. The impact of information systems on productivity is wide ranging and potentially affects all other activities of a company. The company has just 300 service agents handling all of its customer accounts, compared to the 900 it would need if sales were not handled online. The difference represents an annual saving of $20 million a year. Moreover, without automated customer service functions, Cisco calculates that it would need at least 1,000 additional service engineers, which would cost around $75 million.

14. Infrastructure and Efficiency

A company's infrastructure—that is, its structure, culture, style of strategic leadership, and control system—determines the context within which all other value creation activities take place. ft follows that improving infrastructure can help a company increase efficiency and lower its cost structure. Above all, an appropriate infrastructure can help foster a companywide commitment to efficiency aid promote cooperation among different functions in pursuit of efficiency goals. These issues are addressed at length in later chapters.

15. TQM

The quality can be thought of in terms of two dimensions: product reliability and other product attributes. High-quality products are both reliable, in the sense that they do the job they were designed for and do it well, and are also perceived by consumers to have superior attributes. We also noted that superior quality gives a company two advantages. First, a strong reputation for quality allows a company to differentiate itself from rivals by creating more value in the eyes of customers, and this gives it the option of charging a premium price for its products. Second, eliminating defects or errors from the production process reduces waste, increases efficiency, and lowers the cost structure of the company and increases its profitability. For example, reducing the number of defects in a company's manufacturing process will lower the cost of goods sold as a percentage of revenues, thereby raising the company's return on sales and return on invested capital.

16. Focus on the Customer

TQM practitioners see a focus on the customer as the starting point, and indeed, whole quality philosophy. The marketing function, because it provides the primary point of contact with the customer, should play a major role here. It needs to identify what customers want from the good or service that the company provides, what the company actually provides to customers, and the gap between what customers want and what they get, which could be called the quality gap. Then, together with the other functions of the company, it needs to formulate a plan for closing the quality gap.

17. Supplier Relations

A major source of poor quality finished goods is poor quality component parts. To decrease product defects, a company has to work with its suppliers to improve the quality of the parts they supply. The primary responsibility in this area falls on the materials management function, which interacts with suppliers. To implement JIT systems with suppliers and to get suppliers to adopt their own TQM programs, two steps are necessary. First, the number of suppliers has to be reduced to manageable proportions. Second, the company must commit to building a cooperative long-term relationship with the suppliers that remain. Asking suppliers to invest in JIT and TQM systems is asking them to make major investments that tie them to the company. For example, in order to implement a JIT system fully, the company may ask a supplier to relocate its manufacturing plant so that it is next door to the company's assembly plant. Suppliers are likely to be hesitant about making such investments unless they feel that the company is committed to an enduring, long-term relationship with them.

6.2. STRATEGIES IN FRAGMENTED INDUSTRIES

A fragmented industry is one composed of a large number of small and medium-sized companies—for example, the dry cleaning, restaurant, health club, and the legal services industries. There are several reasons that an industry may consist of many small companies rather than a few large ones.

First, fragmented industries are characterized by low barriers to entry because of the lack of economies of scale. Many home buyers, for example, have a preference for dealing with local real estate agents, whom they perceive as having better local knowledge than national chains. Second, in some industries, there may even be diseconomies of scale. In the restaurant business, for example, customers often prefer the unique food and style of a popular local restaurant rather than the standardized offerings of some national chain. Third, low entry barriers that permit constant entry by new companies also serve to keep an industry fragmented. The restaurant industry exemplifies this situation. The costs of opening a restaurant are moderate and can be borne by a single entrepreneur. High transportation costs, too, can keep an industry fragmented, and local or regional production may be the only efficient way to satisfy customers' needs, as in the cement business. Finally, an industry may be fragmented because customers' needs are so specialized that only small job lots of products are required, and thus there is no room for a large mass-production operation to satisfy the market.

For some fragmented industries, these factors dictate the competitive strategy to pursue, and the focus strategy stands out as a principal choice. Companies may specialize by customer group, customer need, or geographic region, so that many small specialty companies operate in local or regional market segments. All kinds of custom-made products—furniture, clothing, hats, boots, and so on—fall into this category, as do all small service operations that cater to particular customers' needs, such as laundries, restaurants, health clubs, and furniture rental stores. Indeed, service companies make up a large proportion of the enterprises in fragmented industries because they provide personalized service to clients and therefore need to be responsive to their needs. Strategic managers are eager to gain the cost advantages of pursuing a low-cost strategy or the sales-revenue-enhancing advantages of differentiation by circumventing the problems of a fragmented industry and finding a way to consolidate it. Consolidated industries offer much higher potential returns, and during the past thirty years, many companies have developed competitive strategies to consolidate fragmented industries and obtain these returns. These companies include large retailers such as Wal-Mart and Target, fast food chains such as McDonald's and Burger King, video rental chains such as Blockbuster Video and Hollywood Video, chains of health clubs such as Bally's and President and First Lady, repair shops like Midas Muffler, and even lawyers, consultants, and tax preparers. To grow, consolidate their industries, and become the industry leaders, these companies have pioneered new business models and used several specific strategies such as chaining, franchising, horizontal merger, and also using the Internet and IT.

Many of these pioneered a new business model in an industry that lowers costs or confers a differentiation advantage (or both). The way that a company can do this is by competing in a very different way from established rivals. Managers in a fragmented industry must seek out cost or differentiation advantages that others have not recognized. Once a company has a cost or differential advantage, it can increase its revenues at the expense of competitors and consolidate the industry in the process. Moreover, as the company pioneering the new business model grows larger, it may be able to capture additional scale economies and so increase its competitive advantage. The pioneering company can then use its growing cost-based advantage to choose a low-price option, price aggressively, generate high demand, and drive its established rivals out of the industry.

6.3. CHAINING

Companies such as Wal-Mart and Midas International pursue a chaining strategy to obtain the advantages of cost leadership. They establish networks of linked merchandising outlets that are so interconnected that they function as one large business entity. The consolidated buying power that these companies possess through their nationwide store chains allows them to negotiate large price reductions with their suppliers, which promotes their competitive advantage. They overcome the barrier of high transportation costs by establishing sophisticated regional distribution centers, which can economize on inventory costs and maximize responsiveness to the needs of stores and customers. (This is Wal-Mart's specialty.) They also realize economies of scale from sharing managerial skills across the chain and from placing nationwide, rather than local, advertising.

The U.S. food retail business during the 1950s, when supermarkets revolutionized the business model behind the selling of food products, is a good example of the advantages of the chaining business model. Prior to the development of supermarkets, the food retail industry was fragmented with many small mom-and-pop retailers selling a limited range of products and providing full service to customers, including home delivery. Mostly regionally based at first, with fewer than a hundred stores, the first supermarkets differentiated themselves by offering a much larger selection of items in a big store layout. At the same time, they lowered their costs by moving from a full-service to a self-service model (they needed far fewer employees to run a store), and they passed on those cost savings to customers in the form of lower prices. In other words, the supermarkets competed in a very different way from established food retailers: they adopted a new business model.

As the supermarkets started to grow, opening hundreds of more stores, they were able to capture scale economies that were not available to smaller retailers. For example, by clustering their stores around central distribution warehouses in different cities and eventually regions, they were able to gain distribution efficiencies and reduce the amount of inventory they had to hold in a store. Also, by buying from vendors in large quantities, they were able to demand deep price discounts that they passed on to customers in the form of lower prices, enabling them to gain even more market share from smaller retailers. In the 1970s and 1980s, the supermarkets were also the first to introduce information systems based on point-of-sale terminals that tracked the sale of individual items. The information provided enabled the supermarkets to optimize their stocking of items, quickly cutting back on items that were not selling and devoting more shelf space to items that were selling faster. This reducing the need to hold inventory took even more costs out of the systems and ensured a good match between customer demands and items in the supermarket, which further differentiated the supermarkets from smaller retailers. Although these information systems were expensive to implement, the supermarkets could spread the costs over a large volume of sales. The small mom-and-pop retailers could not afford such systems because their sales base was too small. As a consequence of these developments, the food retail industry was becoming consolidated by the 1980s, a trend that is accelerating today. The small mom-and-pop food retailer is now almost extinct.

The new supermarket business model that provided a cost and differentiation advantage over the old established mom-and-pop model has been applied to a wide range of retail industries, consolidating one after the other. Barnes & Noble and Borders applied the supermarket business model to book retailing; Staples applied it to office supplies, Best Buy to electronic retailing, Home Depot to building supplies, and so on. In each case, the company that introduced the new business model helped to change the underlying competitive structure of the industry to its advantage, consolidating the industry and weakening the five forces of competition in the process.

Franchising: For differentiated companies in fragmented industries, such as McDonald's or Century 21 Real Estate, the competitive advantage comes from a business model that employs franchise agreements. In franchising, the franchisor (parent) grants to its franchisees the right to use the parent's name, reputation, and business skills at a particular location or area. When franchisees also manage the business, they are strongly motivated to make the business model work effectively and make sure that quality and standards are consistently high so that customers' needs are always satisfied. Such motivation is particularly critical in a strategy of differentiation, where it is important for a company to maintain its distinctive edge. One reason that industries are fragmented is the difficulty of maintaining control over the many small outlets that must be operated while at the same time retaining their differentiated appeal. The franchising model solves this problem. In addition, franchising lessens the financial burden of swift expansion and so permits rapid growth of the company. Finally, a nationwide franchised company can reap the advantages of large-scale advertising, as well as economies in purchasing, management, and distribution, as McDonald's does very efficiently. Indeed, McDonald's is able to pursue cost leadership and differentiation simultaneously only because franchising allows costs to be controlled locally and differentiation to be achieved by marketing on a national level.

Horizontal Merger: Companies such as Anheuser-Busch, Dillard's Department Stores, and Blockbuster Entertainment have been choosing a strategy of horizontal merger to consolidate their respective industries. For example, Dillard's arranged the merger of regional store chains in order to form a national company. By pursuing horizontal merger, companies are able to obtain economies of scale or secure a national market for their product. As a result, they are able to pursue a cost-leadership or a differentiation strategy or both.

Using IT and the Internet: The arrival of new technology often gives a company the opportunity to develop new business models that can consolidate a fragmented industry. eBay and Amazon.com, for example, used the Internet to develop a new business model—auctions and book- selling—that is consolidating a fragmented industry. Before eBay, the auction business was extremely fragmented, with local auctions in cities being the principal way in which people could dispose of their antiques and collectibles. By harnessing the Internet, eBay can now assure sellers that they are getting wide visibility for their collectibles and are likely to receive a higher price for their product. Similarly, Amazon.com's success in the book market has accelerated the consolidation of the book retail industry, with many small bookstores closing because they cannot compete by price or selection.

The challenge in a fragmented industry is to figure out the best strategy to overcome a fragmented market so that the competitive advantages associated with different generic business-level strategies can be realized. It is difficult to think of any major service activities—from consulting and accounting firms to businesses satisfying the smallest customer need, such as beauty parlors and car repair shops—that have not been consolidated by companies that developed new business models or used franchising and horizontal mergers.

6.4. STRATEGIES IN EMBRYONIC AND GROWTH INDUSTRIES

An embryonic industry is one that is just beginning to develop, and a growth industry is one in which first-time demand is expanding rapidly as many new customers enter the market. Embryonic and growth industries pose special challenges in choosing and pursuing a business-level strategy because the attributes of customers change as market demand expands and new groups of customers who have new and evolving needs emerge. Also, other factors affect the rate at which a market grows and expands. Strategic managers have to be aware of the way competitive dynamics in embryonic and growth industries change over time because they commonly have to build and develop new kinds of competencies and refine their business models to compete effectively over time.

Most embryonic industries emerge when a technological innovation creates new product or market opportunities that companies start to take advantage of. For example, a century ago, the car industry was born following the development of a new technology, the internal combustion engine, which gave rise to many new products, including the motorcar and motorbus. In 1975, the PC industry was born after new microprocessor technology was developed to build the world's first commercially available PC, the Altair 8800, sold by MITS. Shortly afterward, the PC software industry was born when a Harvard dropout, Bill Gates, and his old school friend, Paul Allen, wrote a version of a popular computer language, BASIC, that would run on the Altair 8800. In 1986, the Internet protocol (IP) network equipment industry was born following the development of the router, an IP switch, by an obscure California start-up, Cisco Systems.

Customer demand for the products of an embryonic industry is frequently limited at first for a variety of reasons. Strategic managers who understand how markets develop are in a much better position to build a business model and strategy that will lead to a sustained competitive advantage. Reasons for slow growth in market demand include (1) the limited performance and poor quality of the first products, (2) customer unfamiliarity with what the new product can do for them, (3) poorly developed distribution channels to get the product to customers, (4) a lack of complementary products to increase the value of the product for customer, and (5) high production costs because of small volumes of production. For example, demand for the first cars was limited by their poor performance (they were no faster than a horse, far noisier, and frequently broke down), a lack of important complementary products such as a network of paved roads and gas stations, and high production costs, which made them a luxury item. Similarly, demand for the first PCs was limited because buyers had to be able to program a computer to use it, and there were no software application programs that could be purchased to run on the PCs. Because of such problems, early demand for the products of embryonic industries comes from a small set of technologically sophisticated customers who are willing to put up with, and may even enjoy, imperfections in the product.

Computer hobbyists, who got great joy out of tinkering with their imperfect machines and finding ways to make them work, bought the first PCs. An industry moves from an embryonic to a growth stage when a mass market starts to develop for the industry's product (a mass market is one in which large numbers of customers enter the market). Mass markets typically start to develop when three things occur: (1) ongoing technological progress makes a product easier to use and increases the value of the product to the average customer, (2) key complementary products are developed that do the same, and (3) companies in the industry strive to find ways to reduce production costs so they can lower their cost structure and choose a low price option, and this stimulates high demand. For example, a mass market for cars emerged when (1) technological progress increased the performance of cars, (2) a network of paved roads and gas stations was established (which meant a car could go more places and thus had more value), and (3) Henry Ford began to mass-produce cars, which dramatically lowered production costs and allowed him to reduce prices, causing the demand for cars to surge. Similarly, the mass market for PCs started to emerge when technological advances made them easier to use, a supply of complementary software such as spreadsheets and word processing programs was developed that increased the value of owning a PC, and companies in the industry started to use mass production to build PCs at low cost. Strategic managers with knowledge about changing market demand can focus on how they must change their business models to build competencies in low-cost manufacturing and product development. For example, they need to share their knowledge with companies that can supply complementary products so that customers will be convinced the new product is worth buying. Another important factor they must understand is how customer groups and needs change over time.

The Changing Nature of Market Demand The development of most markets follows an S-shaped growth curve similar to that illustrated in Figure 6.4. As the stage of market development moves from embryonic to growth, customer demand first accelerates and then decelerates as market approaches saturation. In a saturated market, most customers have already bought the product, and demand is limited to replacement demand; the market is mature. Figure 6.4 shows that different groups of customers who have different needs enter the market over time.

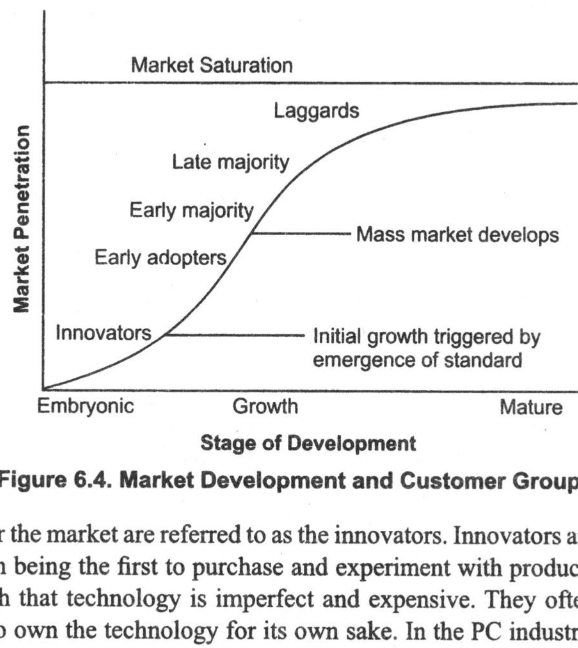

Figure 6.4. Market Development and Customer Groups.

The first groups of customers to enter the market are referred to as the innovators. Innovators are "technocrats" who get great delight from being the first to purchase and experiment with products based on a new technology, even though that technology is imperfect and expensive. They often have an engineering mindset and want to own the technology for its own sake. In the PC industry, the first customers were software engineers and computer hobbyists who wanted to write computer code at home.

The early adopters are the second group of customers to enter the market. Early adopters understand that the technology might have important future applications and are willing to experiment with it to see if they can pioneer uses for it, often by finding new ways to satisfy customer needs. Early adopters are often visionaries appreciate how the technology may be used in the future and try to be the first the 'internet and web-based technology, who saw in X994 that the Internet could be used in innovative ways to sell books. He saw this possibility before anyone else and was one of the first dot-com pioneers to purchase web servers and related so and use it to sell products over the Internet. Amazon was thus an early adopter.

Both innovators and early adopters enter the market while the industry is in its embryonic stage. The next group of customers, the early majority, represents thing wave or edge of the mass market; their entry signifies the beginning of the g stage. Customers in the early majority are comfortable with the new technology products. However, they are pragmatists: they weigh the benefits of adoption products against their costs and wait to enter the market until they are confident that products will offer them tangible benefits. Once they start to enter the market ever, they do so in large numbers. This is what happened in the PC market after introduction of the PC in 1981. For the early majority, IBM's entry into the r legitimized the technology and signaled that the benefits of adoption would be the costs of purchasing and learning to use the product. The growth of the PC market was then given further impetus by the development of important applications that added value to it, such as new spreadsheet and word processing programs. These applications transformed the PC from a hobbyist's toy into a business productivity tool.

Once the mass market attains a critical mass, with something like 30 percent of the potential market penetrated, the next wave of customers enters the market. This wave is characterized as the late majority: the customers who purchase a new technology or product only when it is clear it will be around for a long time. A typical late majority customer group is the customers who started to enter the PC market in the mid 1990s who were older and somewhat intimidated by computers. However, watching others similar to themselves buying PCs to send email and browse the Web, they overcame their hesitancy and started to purchase PCs. By 2002, some 65 percent of homes in the United States had at least one PC, suggesting that the product was well into the late majority group and thus the market was approaching saturation. Indeed, the entry of the late majority signals the end of the growth stage.

Laggards, the last group of customers to enter the market, are inherently conservative and technophobic. They often refuse to adopt a new technology even if its benefits are obvious or unless they are forced by circumstances—to reply to a colleague's email, for example—to do so. People who stick to using typewriters rather than computers to write letters and books could be considered laggards today.

Figure 6.5 looks at the differences among these groups of consumers in a somewhat different way. The bell-shaped curve represents the total market, and the divisions in the curve show the percentage of customers who on average fall into each customer group. The early adopters are a very small percentage of the total customers who will ultimately buy the product. Thus, it illustrates a vital competitive fact: Most market demand and industry profits arise when the early and late majority enters the market. And research has found that although many of the early pioneering companies do well in attracting innovators and early adopters, many of these companies often fail to attract a significant share of early and late majority customers and ultimately go out of business.

6.4.1 Strategic Implications : Crossing the Chasm

Why are pioneering companies often unable to develop a business model that allows them to become the market leaders? Once again, the issue revolves around understanding the basic issues in business-level strategy: identifying customer needs, identifying customer groups, and choosing distinctive competencies. Innovators and early adopters have very different customer needs from the early majority. In an influential book, Geoffrey Moore argued that as a consequence of the differences in customer needs between these groups, the distinctive competencies required for companies to succeed in the emerging mass market are quite different from the distinctive competencies required to succeed in the embryonic market. Therefore, different strategies and business models are often required as a market develops over time for these reasons:

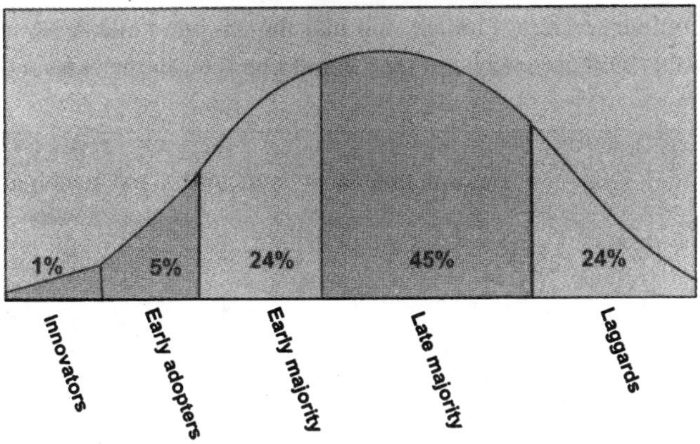

Figure 6.5. Market Share of Different Customer Groups.

- Innovators and early adopters are technologically sophisticated individuals who are willing to tolerate engineering imperfections in the product. The early majority, however, value ease of use and reliability. Companies competing in an embryonic market typically pay more attention to increasing the performance of a product than to its ease of use and reliability. Those competing in a mass market need to make sure that the product is reliable and easy to use. Thus, the product development capabilities required for success are different as a market develops over time.
- Innovators and early adopters are typically reached through specialized distribution channels, and the products are often sold by word of mouth or focused promotion campaigns. Reaching the early majority requires mass-market distribution channels and mass media advertising campaigns, which require a different set of marketing and sales capabilities.
- Because innovators and the early majority are relatively few in number and are not particularly price sensitive, companies serving them do not need capabilities in mass production. To serve a rapidly growing mass markct, large-scale manufacturing capabilities may be critical to ensure that a high-quality product can be produced reliably at a low price point.
- In sum, the competencies (resources and capabilities) required to compete in an embryonic market populated by early adopters and innovators are very different from those required to compete in a high-growth mass market populated by the early majority. As a consequence, the transition between the embryonic market and the mass market is not a smooth, seamless one. Rather, it represents a competitive chasm, or gulf, that companies must cross. According to Moore, many companies do not or cannot develop the right business model; they fall into the chasm and go out of business. This insight is consistent with the observation that although embryonic markets are frequently populated by large numbers of small companies, once the mass market begins to develop, the number of companies in the marketplace drops off sharply.
- Figure 6.6 illustrates Moore's thesis by showing that a wide chasm exists between innovators and early majority that is, between the embryonic market and the rapidly growing mass market. Note also that other smaller chasms exist between other sets of customers, and that these too represent important, although less dramatic, breaks in the nature of the market that require changes in business-level strategy (for example, a different approach to market segmentation). The implication of Moore's thesis is that a company must often build new competencies if it is to cross the chasm: it must accumulate new resources and capabilities to build and sustain a competitive advantage. Strategy in Action 6.2 describes how the early

leader in online services, Prodigy, fell into the chasm, while AOL successfully crossed it because AOL built competencies that were to be vital in the mass market and Prodigy did not.

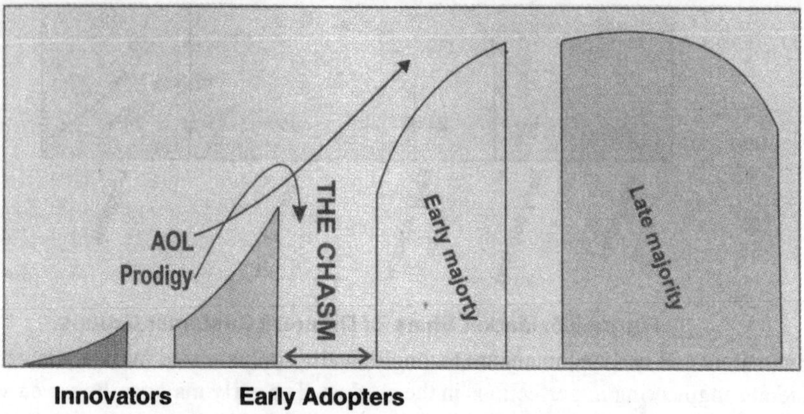

Figure 6.6. The Chasm: AOL and Prodigy.

To cross this chasm successfully, Moore argues, companies need to find a beachhead, a strategic opportunity, to compete for the mass market. By this, he means that managers must correctly identify the customer needs of the first wave of early majority users who are the leading edge of the mass market. Even in a market where the majority of customers are still innovators and early adopters, some members of the early majority will start to enter. Once companies have identified these customers' needs, they must alter their business model in response by developing new competencies and redesigning products. Strategic managers must also look to their company's value chains and develop distribution channels and marketing strategies for reaching the early majority. They must also design the product so that it matches the needs of the early majority, can be modified easily, and can be produced or provided at low cost. In this way, they will have ready a suitable product, at a reasonable price that they can sell to the early majority as they start to enter the market in large numbers.

Equally important, industry pioneers must not become too focused on the needs of their early or initial customers because this may lead them to ignore the needs of the early majority, which can lead them to competitive disaster. In fact, anticipating the moves of their competitors by drawing on game theory principles is another useful tool they can use to help them choose the right business model, as the early history of Apple Computer illustrates. Apple stumbled across the leading edge of the early majority in 1979 when it noticed that business customers were beginning to purchase the Apple II in order to run VisiCalc, the first business spreadsheet program made for PCs. It soon became a best-seller and helped to drive sales of the Apple II. However, Apple failed to appreciate the real importance of this event—that it revealed the needs of business customers—and instead continued to focus its sales and marketing efforts on computer hobbyists and higher educational institutions, where many of its early adopters were to be found. In fact, Apple had a direct sales force that visited universities but no sales force visiting businesses! Although VisiCalc was helping to sell Apple computers, Apple made no effort to develop its own business applications or get other companies to do so. Apple had found a beachhead—the developing needs of business customers—but squandered that advantage. It was left to IBM to recognize the importance of the business customer group and develop a business model to meet the needs of the early majority. It entered the market with its IBM PC in 1981, which was an instant success and the beginning of Apple's problems. IBM offered a version of VisiCalc for the IBM PC, along with an early word processing program, Easy Writer. This, together with IBM's established business-focused sales force, soon propelled IBM into a leadership position among the early majority of business and home office users.

Strategic Implications of Market Growth Rates: A final important issue that strategic managers must understand in embryonic and growth industries is that different markets develop at different rates. The rate at which a market develops can be assessed by its growth rate, which measures the rate at which the industry's product spreads in the marketplace. Figure 6.4 charts the growth rates of a number of important products in the United States from their initial introduction to the present time. Although many of these products display the classic S-shaped growth curve, their markets have grown at different rates. For example, demand for TVs has grown more rapidly than demand for cars. The market growth rates for new kinds of products seem to have accelerated over time, probably because the increasing use of the mass media and low-cost mass production help to accelerate the demand for new products. However, there are also differences in the growth rate for new products introduced at around the same time.

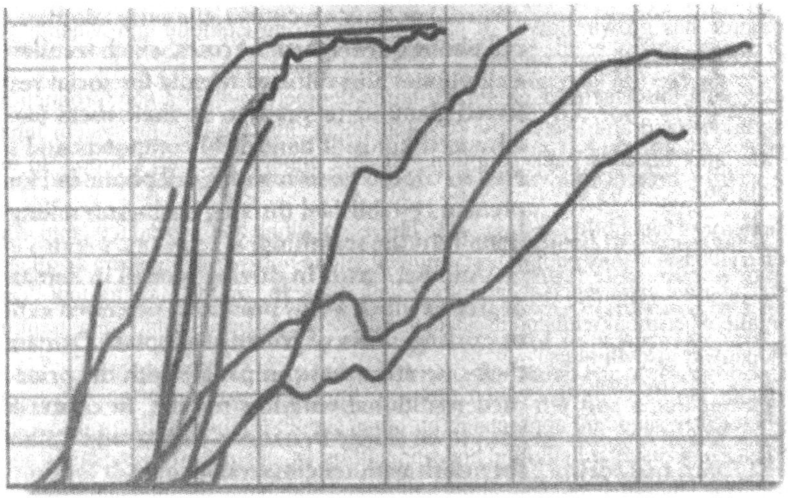

Figure 6.7. Differences in Diffusion Rates.

Source: Peter Brimelow, "The Silent Boom," Forbes, July 7, 1997, pp. 170—171. Reprinted by permission of Forbes Magazine © 2002 Forbes, Inc.

For example, the cell phone was introduced somewhat later than the PC, and yet market demand of Automobile (1886), Cellphone (1983), Electricity (1873), Microwave (1953), PC (1975), Radio (1905), Telephone (1876), Television (1926), VCR (1952) has grown more rapidly. Similarly, following the introduction of the PaimPilot in 1996, demand for hand-held computers has grown even more rapidly than demand for cell phones did.

Factors Affecting Market Growth Rates

A number of factors explain the variation in market growth rates for different products and thus the speed with which a particular industry develops. It is important for strategic managers to understand the source of these differences, for by their choice of strategy and business model, they can accelerate or retard the rate at which a particular market grows.1° In other words, business-level strategy is a major determinant of industry profitability.

The first factor that accelerates customer demand 'is a new product's relative advantage, that is, the degree to which a new product is perceived as better at satisfying customer needs than the product it supersedes. The degree of relative advantage can be measured by the extra value it provides for customers, which can be economic or social in nature. For example, the early growth in demand for cell phones was partly driven by their economic benefits. Early studies showed that because business customers could always be reached by cell phone, they made better use of their time—for example, by not showing up at a meeting that had been canceled at the last minute—and saved two hours per week in time that would otherwise have been wasted.

For busy executives, the early adopters, the productivity benefits of own cell phone outweighed the costs, which translated into a relative economic advantage Cell phones also diffused rapidly for social reasons, in particular, because they transferred glamour or prestige on their users (something that also drives demand advanced kinds of hand-held computers and smart phones). Indeed, it was covered so cool to be seen with a cell phone in Hong Kong in the 1980s that some entrepreneurs established thriving businesses selling fake cell phones to people who c not afford the real thing.

Another factor in driving growth in demand is compatibility, which refers t degree to which a new product is perceived as being consistent with the current n or existing values of potential adopters. Demand for cell phones grew rapidly because their operation was compatible with the prior experience of potential adopters used traditional wire-line phones. In contrast, demand for contraceptive proc has grown slowly in nations with strong Catholic and Muslim communities because they clash with religious values.

Complexity is a third factor. Complexity is the degree to which a new production perceived as difficult to understand and use. Early PCs with their clunky operating system interfaces were complex to use, and this held back adoption. The firs phones were very simple to use, and this accelerated adoption.

A fourth factor is trial ability, which is the degree to which a new product c experimented with on a hands-on trial basis. Many people first used cell phone borrowing one from a colleague to make a call, and this positive experience accelerate growth rates. In contrast, the original PCs were more difficult to obtain experiment with and use because they were expensive and some training involved, and this led to slower growth rates.

A fifth factor is observability, which refers to the degree to which the rest adopting a new product can be clearly seen and appreciated by other people PaimPilot diffused rapidly because it was easy to observe its users scheduling, entering addresses, documenting expenses, and so on. The utility of was clear. The same was true of the cell phone and hence its rapid adoption. It is less easy to observe the benefits that many people got from using PCs because were often used behind closed doors in a business setting.

A final factor that is very important in the growth of many new products availability of complementary products. Cell phone use grew rapidly because important complement—a nationwide telecommunications network to route was already in place; cell phone operators merely had to build out cell sites are next them to that network.

6.4.2 Strategic Implications of Differences in Growth Rates

Strategic perspective, companies can increase the demand for a new technological product if they develop a business model that clearly shows its relative ad make it as compatible as possible with customers' prior needs and expectations reduce its complexity, make it possible for customers to try and observe other the technology or product, and make sure that the necessary complement products are in place. These considerations must drive product development company's business-level strategy. Many companies that have paid attention factors have invested in developing the right kinds of distinctive competency gained a competitive advantage and market share as a result.

The early success of Apple was based on the fact that the less complex its Apple II PC made it easier to use than competing designs. The relative economic advantage because some key complements (particularly VisiCaic, the first business spreadsheet) soon became available for the machine. As we noted earlier, however, Apple largely squandered its early advantage by not paying attention to the way customer needs were evolving. Similarly, the first Sony PlayStation was very popular because Sony pioneered the marketing strategy of setting up displays in retail stores where potential customers could try a PlayStation and others could observe them trying it.

Another important issue is that new products often spread in a way that is analogous to a viral model of infection. Lead adopters (the first customers who buy a product) in a community become "infected" with the product (enthused by it). Subsequently, they infect other people by telling them about its advantages, and after having observed the benefits of the product, these others also adopt it. A good example of this model of diffusion occurred with Hotmail, the free email service now owned by Microsoft. When it was established, its developers decided to add a tag line on the bottom of the email that read "get your free e-mail at Hotmail.com' This tag line proved remarkably efficient in recruiting new members. Someone would sign on at one institution, say the University of Washington, and send email via Hotmail to friends. Some of the recipients would also sign on. Within a few days, there would be ten members at the University of Washington, then one hundred, and within a month a thousand—all "infected" from the original user.

Companies promoting new products can take advantage of this viral diffusion phenomenon by identifying and aggressively courting potential opinion leaders— customers whose views command respect—in a community. For example, when the manufacturers of new high-tech medical equipment, such as an MRI scanner, start to sell a new product, they first try to get well-known doctors at major research and teaching hospitals to adopt the technology. They may give these opinion leaders free machines for their research purposes and work closely with them in developing the technology. Once these opinion leaders commit to the technology, and particularly if they give it their stamp of approval by using it for research and teaching purposes, doctors at many other hospitals often follow.

In sum, understanding competitive dynamics in embryonic and growth industries is an important strategic issue. The way in which different kinds of customer groups emerge and customer needs change are important determinants of business- level strategy. Similarly, understanding the factors that affect a market's growth rate allow managers to tailor their business model to a changing industry environment.

As a result of fierce competition in the shakeout stage, an industry becomes consolidated, and so a mature industry is often dominated by a small number of large companies. Although it may also contain many medium-sized companies and a host of small, specialized ones, the large companies determine the nature of competition in the industry because they can influence the five competitive forces. Indeed, these large companies owe their leading positions to the fact that they developed the most successful generic business-level strategies in the industry. By the end of the shakeout stage, strategic groups of companies pursuing similar generic competitive strategies have normally emerged in an industry composing one strategic group, all those pursuing differentiation constitute another, and other companies focusing on particular kinds of market niches form still other strategic groups. Finally, companies whose business models are responding to changing customer needs may be developing both low-cost and differentiation competencies, which will change strategic group structure and promote competition.

The companies in an industry constantly analyze each other's business-level strategies, and they know that if they move to change their strategies, their actions are likely to stimulate a competitive response from rivals in their strategic group and other groups that may be threatened by the change in strategy Industry companies are, in other words, playing a competitive game, and such games can be analyzed using game theory. For example, a differentiator that starts to lower its prices because it has adopted a more cost-efficient technology not only threatens other differentiators in its group, it also threatens low-cost companies, which see their competitive edge being eroded. These other companies may now change their strategies in response, most likely by reducing their prices, as is currently occurring in the PC industry.

Thus, the way one company changes its strategy and fine-tunes its business model over time affects the way the other companies in the industry pursue theirs. Hence, the high level of strategic interdependence that exists in mature, consolidated industries makes it very important for managers to look forward and reason back before launching a strategic initiative. They must think through how their rivals will respond to their actions and pursue a strategy that makes the most sense given this reasoning. In fact, the main issue facing a company in a mature industry is to adopt a competitive strategy that simultaneously enables it to maximize its profitability given the strategies that all other companies in the industry are likely to pursue. No generic strategy will generate above-average profits if competitive forces in an industry are so strong that companies are at the mercy of each other, potential entrants, powerful suppliers, powerful customers, and others. As a result, in mature industries, competitive strategy revolves around understanding how large companies collectively try to reduce the strength of industry competition to preserve both company and industry profitability. Interdependent companies can help protect their competitive advantage and profitability by adopting competitive moves and tactics to reduce the threat of each competitive force. In the next sections, we examine the various price and non-price competitive moves and tactics that companies use—first, to deter entry into an industry, and second, to reduce the level of rivalry within an industry. Many of these competitive moves and tactics were first understood by applying the principles of game theory to analyzing competitive interactions in a consolidated industry. We then discuss methods that companies can employ to gain more control over suppliers and buyers.

Product Proliferation: Companies most commonly produce a range of products aimed at different market segments so that they have broad product lines. Sometimes, to reduce the threat of entry, they expand the range of products they make to fill a wide variety of niches. This creates a barrier to entry because potential competitors now find it harder to break into an industry in which all the niches are filled.' This strategy of pursuing a broad product line to deter entry is known as product proliferation.

Because the large U.S. carmakers were so slow to fill the small-car niches (they did not pursue a product proliferation strategy), they were vulnerable to the entry of the Japanese into these market segments in the United States in the 1980s. Ford and GM really had no excuse for this situation, for in their European operations, they had a long history of small-car manufacturing. Managers should have seen the opening and filled it ten years earlier, but the (mistaken) view was that "small cars mean small profits" Better small profits than no profits! In the soap and detergent industry, on the other hand, competition is based on the production of new kinds of soaps and detergents to satisfy or create new desires by customers. Thus, the number of soaps and detergents, and especially the way they are packaged (powder, liquid, or tablets), proliferates, making it very difficult for prospective entrants to attack a new market segment. Figure 6.8 indicates how product proliferation can deter entry. It depicts product space in the restaurant industry along two dimensions: atmosphere, which ranges from fast food to candlelight dining, and quality of food, which ranges from average to gourmet. The circles represent product spaces filled by restaurants located along the two dimensions. Thus, McDonald's is situated in the average quality/fast food area. A gap in the product space gives a potential entrant or an existing rival an opportunity to enter the market and make inroads. The shaded unoccupied product space represents areas where new restaurants can enter the market. When all the product spaces are filled, this barrier to entry makes it much more difficult for a new company to gain a foothold in the market and differentiate itself.

Pricing Games: In some situations, pricing strategies can be used to deter entry by other companies, thus protecting the profit margins of companies already in an industry. One entry-deterring strategy is to cut prices every time a new company enters the industry or, even better, every time a potential entrant is contemplating entry, and then raise prices once the new or potential entrant has withdrawn. The goal here is to send a signal to potential entrants that new entry will be met with price cuts. If incumbent companies in an industry consistently pursue such a strategy, potential entrants will come to understand that their entry will spark off a price war, the threat of new entry will be reduced, average prices will be higher, and industry profitability will increase.

The pricing signal sent must be clear and credible. Put differently, it is important that established companies in the industry develop a reputation for responding to new entry by aggressively cutting prices. If they lack this reputation and do not always cut prices when a new firm enters their industry, the signal will lack credibility, and potential entrants will be more likely to try their luck and risk entry.

Large airlines have been known to pursue such a selective price-cutting strategy to deter budget airlines from entering their most profitable markets. For example, if a budget airline were to try to enter a profitable market, say, flights from New York to Chicago, the response of the established airlines might be to increase the number of daily flights they run between those two cities. Increasing capacity in this manner has the effect of driving down prices and making the market less attractive for the new entrant, which subsequently withdraws from the market. Once the new entrant has gone, the airlines might reduce the number of flights they run per day, thereby raising prices. Companies must be very careful when they pursue such a pricing strategy however, for it could be perceived as predatory pricing that is, pricing to drive out competitors, which is illegal under U.S. antitrust law. Predatory pricing involve using revenue generated in one product market to support pricing below the company's costs of production in another to drive rivals out of the market.

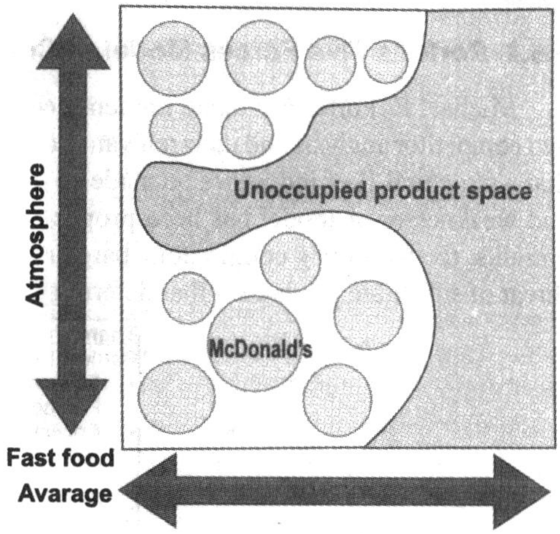

Figure 6.8. Product Proliferation in the Restaurant Industry.

A second entry deterring pricing strategy is known as limit pricing. Limited pricing is a strategy that can be used when the established companies in an industry enjoy small scale economies, but those scale economies are not sufficient to deter entry. The justification is that initially, new entrants will have a lower sales volume that established companies and will not enjoy the same scale economies. However, imagine that for established companies in the industry, the profit-maximizing output Q1 and the prevailing price for their product is P1. This price is above the average.

The structure of potential new entrants, so although they will not be as profitable as established companies, the potential competitors still have an incentive to enter the market. Established companies can eliminate this incentive by charging a price that is below the average cost structure of new entrants, but still above their own average cost structure. By adopting such a price, established companies can effectively deter entry and still be profitable. In fact, a limit-pricing strategy may well be consistent with maximizing the long-run profitability of an industry precisely because it reduces the incentive that potential entrants have to enter the market. However, a limit-pricing strategy will not keep out an entrant that plans to adopt a new technology that will give it a cost advantage over established companies or that has pioneered a new business model that its managers expect will also give it a competitive advantage. In fact, many of the most successful entrants into mature industries are companies that have done just this. For example, the Japanese car companies were able to enter the U.S. market because they had pioneered new lean manufacturing technologies that gave them a cost and quality advantage over established U.S. companies. Today, Japanese car companies' share of the U.S. market is limited only by an informal trade agreement; it could easily double if they were allowed to import all the cars they wished and sell them at whatever price they chose, which might drive one or more U.S. car companies out of the market.

It is also important to note that selective price-cutting and limit-pricing strategies may not deter a strong potential competitor—for example, a leading company in another industry that is trying to find profitable investment opportunities in other industries. It is difficult, for example, to imagine 3M's being afraid to enter an industry because companies there threaten to drive down prices. 3M has the resources to withstand any short-term losses. Hewlett-Packard also had few worries about entering the highly competitive PC industry because of its powerful set of distinctive competencies. Hence, when faced with such a scenario, it may be in the interests of incumbent companies to accept new entry gracefully, giving up market share gradually to the new entrants to prevent price wars from developing and thus save their profits, if this is feasible.

6.5. APPLICATION COMPETITIVE ADVANTAGE IN INDUSTRY

An industry is defined as a group of companies offering products or services that are close substitutes of each other. Close substitutes are those products or services that satisfy the same basic customer needs, example, tea is a close substitute of coffee as it is considered a healthier alternative with lower caffeine content and antioxidant properties that help develop body resistance to cancer and heart disease. Any analysis of the tea or coffee industry would have to consider the other stimulant as a close substitute.

6.5.1 Porter's Five Forces Model of Competition in an Industry

Michael E. Porter has made immense contribution in the development of the ideas of industry and competitor analysis and their relevance to the formulation of competitive strategies. He advocates that a structural II of industries be made so that a firm is in a better position to identify its strengths and weaknesses. A model has been proposed consisting of five competitive forces—threat of new entrants, rivalry among competitors, bargaining power of suppliers, bargaining power of buyers and threat of substitute products—that determine the intensity of industry competition and profitability.

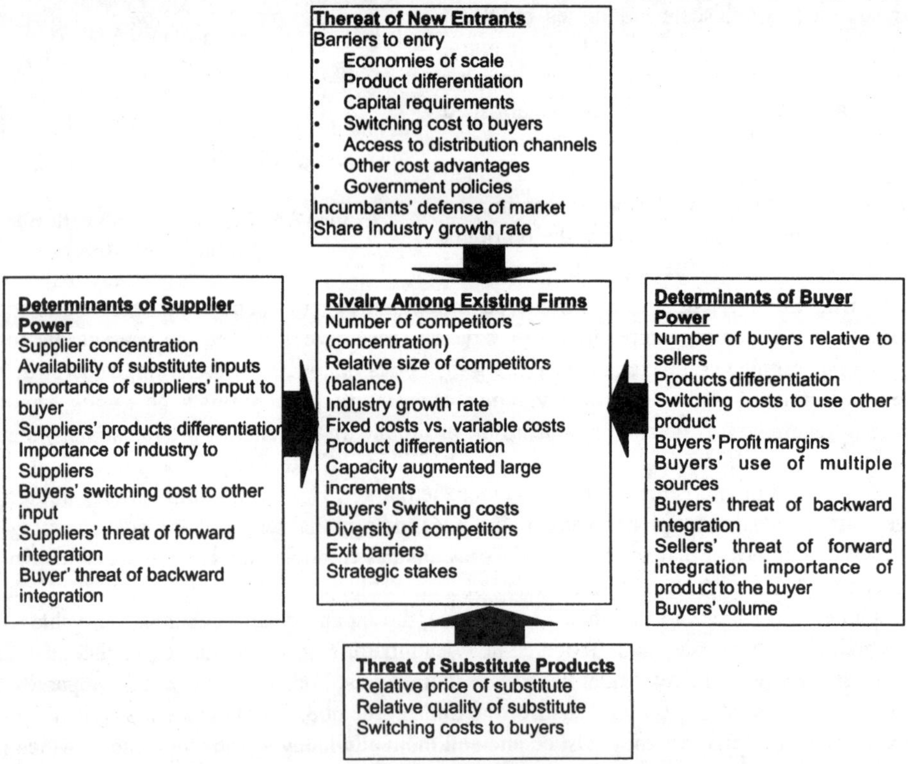

Figure 6.9. Porter's Five Force Model of Competition.

Threat of New Entrants

Any industry that is perceived as being profitable tends to attract new entrants. These new entrants are firms that are interested in investing in the industry to share the growth prospects. Such new entrants augment the existing production capacity and often possess a desire to make large a investments and secure substantial market share. The existing firms have either to share a growing market pie with a larger number of competitors or part with some of their own market share to the new entrants. Either may, new entrants may cause comparatively lesser sales volume and revenue and lower the returns for all the firms in the industry.

The chance that new entrants will enter into an industry depends on two factors: the entry barriers to an industry and the expected retaliation from existing firms. Of these, entry barriers are significant de-motivators fornew entrants. The concept of entry barriers implies that there are substantial costs involved in entering into a new industry. The higher the entry barriers in an industry, the less likely are the new entrants to enter hat industry. So, higher entry barriers serve to keep out potential entrants into an industry.

The entry barriers may arise as a consequence of several factors such as those given below:

- *Economies of* scale in production and sale of products leading to lower costs for existing firms Capital requirements being very high may prevent new entrants from making investments.
- *Switching costs* from the existing products or services to a new one may discourage customers from making new commitments owing to the costs incurred in buying new ancillary equipments, retraining employees or establishing a new network of relationship.
- *Product differentiation* by existing firms based on perceived distinctiveness by the customers based effective advertising, reputation as a service provider, brand loyalty of customers towards existing firms or some such other factor.
- *Access to distribution channel* can be monopolized by the existing firms on the basis of their long-term relationship with the distributors
- Cost disadvantages independent of scale may arise from proprietary products technology, exclusive access to raw materials, favourable location and benefit of governmental subsidies.
- *Government policies* through licensing and other means can prevent the entry of new firms to an industry. Besides the entry barriers, the expected retaliation to the new entrants from the existing firms may be a potential threat to entry. Any potential entrant to an industry would have to predict the likely moves that the existing firms could make. For instance, an existing firm with a large stake in the industry may lower its price to create a difficult situation for the new entrant. Or an existing firm with substantial resources may attempt to alter the basis of competition so that the new entrant is discouraged from making a foray. Despite the formidable hurdles posed by existing firms, new firms do enter industries if they find them to be promising. The popular strategy for doing so is finding market niches not served by existing firms and to gradually build up a presence in the industry.

Rivalry among Competitors

Competition is a game in which normally, one player loses at the expense of the other. A move on the part of a player may cause other players to make countermoves or initiate efforts to protect themselves from the danger posed by the initial move, in this manner, firms within an industry are mutually dependent. The situation in an industry keeps changing with the actions and reactions of the constituent firms. The desire to be the market leader or to corner a larger market share leads to rivalry among competitors. The extent of the rivalry among competitors in an industry affects the competition within that industry. When the rivalry is weak, there is likely to be lesser competition; when such rivalry is high, the level of competition is higher. This has implications for existing firms as well as those firms contemplating entry into the industry. The dimensions of rivalry among competitors are several. Some of the major ones are described below: -

- *Competitive structure refers* to the number of competitors, their size and their diversity. Different types of competitive structures have different implications for the existing firms and for the new entrants; structures could either be fragmented or consolidated.
- *A fragmented* structure means that there area large number of small or medium-sized companies, none of them in a position to dominate the industry, This structure is characterised by low entry barriers and less or no differentiation, leading to product becoming commodities. Competition is intense and the industry faces booms and busts, leading to frequent changing of the structure.
- *A consolidated* structure consists of a few large companies (an oligopolistic market) or of just one large firm (a monopoly). Such a structure has a closely knit group of companies whose actions and reactions are matched: the actions of one lead to reactions from others. Competitive actions of the competitors are under close watch by the others as they affect the distribution of market share. The intensity of competition may range from benign tolerance to fierce rivalry. In some industries, the competitors may adopt a policy of 'live and let live', while in others, there might be cutthroat competition leading to under pricing or severely fought competitive battles on the basis of other factors such as delivery, advertising or after-sale service. Diversity among competitors means that different firms in an industry have different ideas on the basis of which to compete, different set of goals to achieve, or different organizational cultures. An industry with greater diversity poses a higher potential challenge to existing firms or new entrants for devising competitive strategies.
- *Demand conditions* refer to the nature of the customer demand existing in an industry. A high demand or a growing demand tends to moderate competition as each firm has enough for it and need not grab it from others. Stagnant demand may lead to competitive strategies designed to snatch market share from others. Declining demand may cause companies to maintain their market shares. Existing firms or new entrants need to take the demand conditions in the industry into account for the purpose of formulating business strategies.
- *Exit barriers* restrict the firms in an industry and prevent them from leaving, even though the returns might be low or might even be sometimes negative. The exit barriers are economic, strategic or emotional factors preventing companies from moving out after divestment of their businesses. Economic factors could be the high investments committed to plant and equipment that have no alternative usage and high fixed costs of exit, such as, high retrenchment costs or high severance pay owing to labour agreements. Strategic factors could be inter linkages between the different businesses of a company such as a firm being its own supplier or buyer or different businesses sharing a common pool of resources. Emotional factors could be a sentimental attachment to a business, it being an ancestral business or one founded by the entrepreneur on his own, or unwillingness to part with a business owing to loyalty to employees or distributors. Collectively, the three factors of competitive structure demand conditions and exit barriers determine the business strategies that a firm is likely to adopt.

As we described these three factors constituting the force of competitive rivalry within an industry, you must have noticed that business strategies are critically dependent on the industry environment. The nature of industry environment varies across industries and also with time. There might be embryonic or introductory industries, growth or sunrise industries, mature or stable industries and declining or sunset industries. Each of these industries would require a different approach to the formulation of business strategies. It is also important to note that industries respond to time and follow a life cycle. An industry in the mature stage today might be a declining industry tomorrow. Here again, it is important for firms to align their business strategies to the changing conditions in the industry environment. The competitive equations change, so do the demand conditions. Entry barriers erected today may fall by the wayside as soon as some new development takes place. Such is the dynamic nature of strategic management where anything that a firm might do today does not guarantee success tomorrow, unless there is a willingness to respond to environmental conditions as they arise in between.

Bargaining Power of Buyers

The bargaining power of buyers constitutes the ability of the buyers, individually or collectively, to force a reduction in prices of products or services, demand a higher quality or better service or to seek more value for their purchases in any way. A high buyer bargaining power constitutes a negative feature for existing firms or new entrants of an industry. A low buyer bargaining power enables a firm to pass on the cost escalation to buyers or to make the buyers accept a lower quality of product and service at a higher price.

The bargaining power of buyers is high under these conditions:

- When the buyers are few in number.
- When the few buyers place large orders individually.
- When alternative suppliers are present, willing to supply at a lower price or on favourable selling conditions.
- When the switching costs of buyers from one supplier to the other is low.
- When the buyer itself charges a low price for its products and is sensitive to price increases .
- When the purchased product constitutes a high percentage of a buyer's costs, making it look around for lower-priced supplies.
- When the buyer itself has the ability to integrate backwards and create its own captive supply source.

Bargaining Power of Suppliers: Like the bargaining power of buyers, suppliers to have a level of bargaining power. The bargaining power of suppliers constitutes their ability, individually or collectively, to forces increase in the price of the products or services or makes the buyers accept a lower quality of product or level of service. A high supplier bargaining power constitutes a positive feature for the existing firms or new entrants of an industry. A low supplier bargaining power prevents a firm from passing on its cost increases to the buyers or to make the buyers accept a lower quality of product and service at a higher price.

The bargaining power of suppliers is high under these conditions:

- When the suppliers are few and the buyers are many.
- When the products or services are unique and are not commonly available.
- When the substitutes of the products or services supplied are not freely available.
- When the switching costs of a supplier from one buyer to the other is low.
- When the supplier is not critically dependent on the products or services supplied.
- When the buyer buys in small quantities and, therefore, is not important to the supplier.
- When the suppliers have the ability to integrate forward and use their own supplies for production of the end product or service.

Threat of Substitute Products: Substitute products or services are those that apparently are different, but satisfy the same set of customer needs. We referred to the example of tea and coffee as substitutable products in the beginning of this section. We could also include aerated drinks as another form of substitute in the category of products serving the customer needs for drinks. Other examples of substitute products and services could be alternative modes of transportation, postal, fax and courier services and electrical gadgets like bulbs and tubelights. The platform for substitutability in every case is the serving of the customer need.

The availability of close substitutes constitutes a negative competitive force in an industry. In other words, those industries which have no close substitutes are more attractive than those that have one or more of such substitutes. Obviously, firms in an industry having no close substitutes can charge a higher price and earn higher returns. For industries where close substitutes are available, the level of price of products chargeable is restricted by the price of the substitute available. Thus, firms have to formulate their business strategies keeping in view the intensity of the competitive force arising out of the presence or absence of the threat of substitutes.

The purpose of an industry analysis, in the context of strategic choice, is to determine the industry attractiveness and to understand the structure and dynamics of the industry with a view to finding out the continued relevance to strategic alternatives that are there before a firm. It follows that, for instance, if the industry is not, or is no longer sufficiently attractive (i.e., it does not offer long-term growth opportunities) then the strategic alternatives that lie within the industry should not be considered, It also means that alternatives may have to be sought outside the industry, calling for diversification moves. Using the five forces model of industry competition, a firm can analyze its critical strengths and weaknesses, its position within the industry, the areas where strategic changes may yield the maximum profits and the significant opportunities and threats.

6.5.2 Expansion or Growth Strategies

Growth is a way of life. Almost all organizations plan to expand. This strategy is followed when an organization aims at higher growth by broadening its one or more of its business in terms of their respective customer groups, customers functions, and alternative technologies singly or jointly – in order to improve its overall performance. E.g. A chocolate manufacturer expands its customer groups to include middle aged and old persons among its existing customers comprising of children and adolescents.

There are four types of Expansion (Growth) strategies

i. Expansion through concentration
ii. Expansion through integration
iii. Expansion through diversification
iv. Expansion through cooperation

i. Expansion through concentration

It involves converging resources in one or more of firms businesses in terms of their respective customer needs, customer functions, or alternative technologies either singly or jointly, in such a manner that it results in expansions. A firm that is familiar with an industry would naturally like to invest more in known business rather than unknown business. Concentration can be done through

a. Market Penetration: It involves selling more products to the same market by focusing intensely on existing markets with its present products, increasing usage by existing customers and increasing market share and restructures a mature market by driving out competitors E.g. Low pricing strategies

b. Market Development: It involves selling the same products to new markets by attracting new users to its existing products. Market development can be geographic wise and demographic wise. E.g. XEROX Company educated small business entrepreneurs to create new markets.

c. Product Development: It involves selling new products to the same markets by introducing newer products in existing markets. E.g. the tourism industry in India has not been able to attract new customers in significant numbers. New products such as selling India as a golfing or ayuerveda-based medical treatment destination are some of the product development efforts in the tourism industry to attract more tourists.

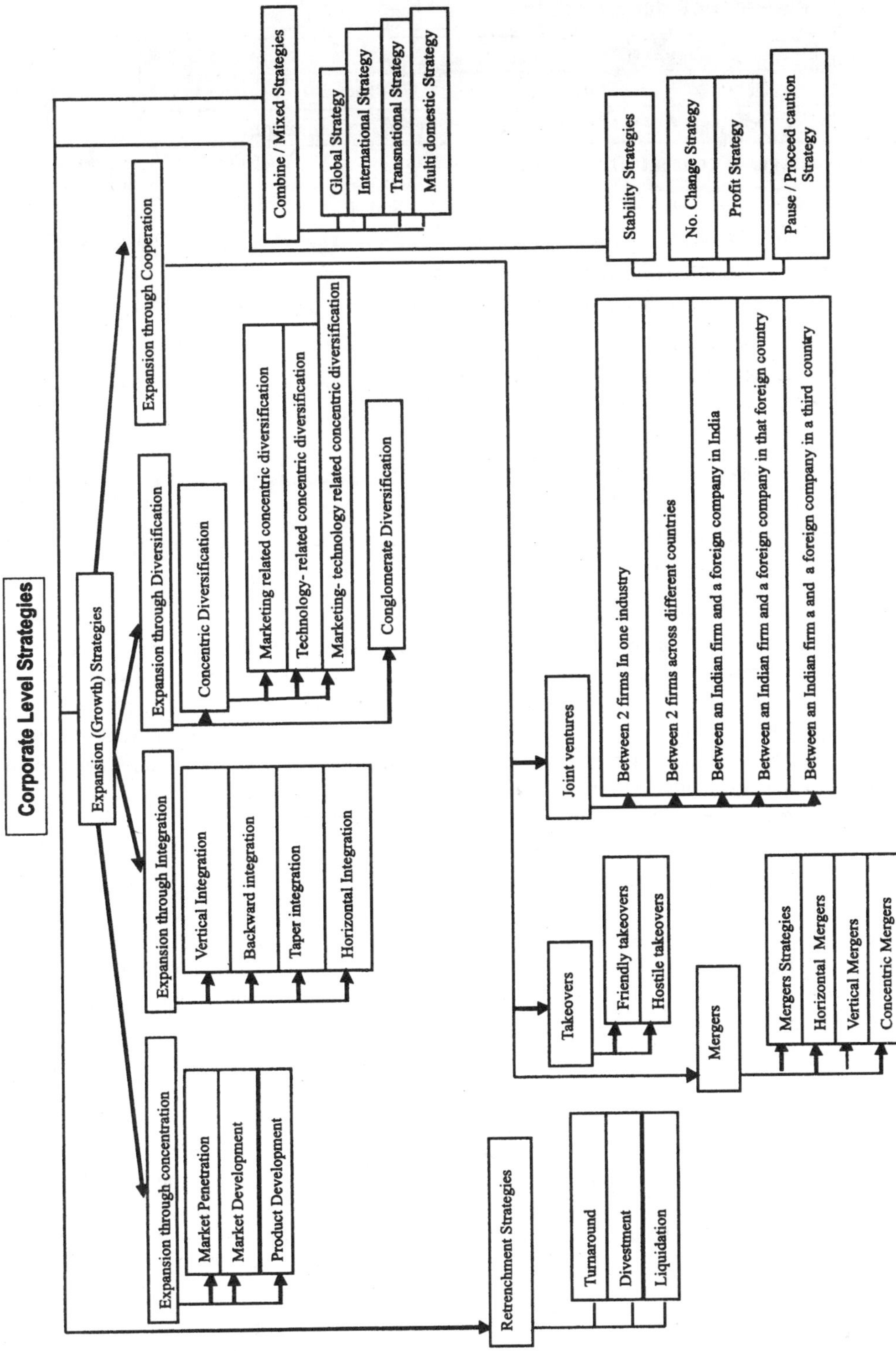
Corporate Level Strategies
Expansion (Growth) Strategies
Expansion through concentration
Market Penetration
Market Development
Product Development
Expansion through Integration
Vertical Integration
Backward integration
Taper integration
Horizontal Integration
Expansion through Diversification
Concentric Diversification
Marketing related concentric diversification
Technology- related concentric diversification
Marketing- technology related concentric diversification
Conglomerate Diversification
Expansion through Cooperation
Combine / Mixed Strategies
Global Strategy
International Strategy
Transnational Strategy
Multi domestic Strategy
Stability Strategies
No. Change Strategy
Profit Strategy
Pause / Proceed caution Strategy
Joint ventures
Between 2 firms In one industry
Between 2 firms across different countries
Between an Indian firm and a foreign company in India
Between an Indian firm and a foreign company in that foreign country
Between an Indian firm a and a foreign company in a third country
Takeovers
Friendly takeovers
Hostile takeovers
Mergers
Mergers Strategies
Horizontal Mergers
Vertical Mergers
Concentric Mergers
Retrenchment Strategies
Turnaround
Divestment
Liquidation

Figure 6.10.

Ansoff"s Product-Market Matrix

Nature of market	Present	New
Present	Market Penetration	Product Development
New	Market Development	Diversification

Advantages of concentration strategies

1. Involves minimal organizational changes and is less threatening.
2. Enables the firm to specialize by gaining the in-depth knowledge of the businesses.
3. Enables the firm to develop competitive advantage.
4. Decision-making can be made easily as there is a high level of productivity.
5. Systems and processes within the firm become familiar to the people in the organization.

Disadvantages of concentration strategies

1. It is dependent on one industry if there is any worse condition in the industry the firm will be affected.
2. Factors such as product obsolescence, fickleness of market, emergence of newer technologies are threat to concentrated firm.
3. Mangers may not be able to sustain interest and find the work less challenging.
4. It may lead to cash flow problems.

ii. Expansion through Integration

It is done where the company attempts to widen the scope of its business definition in such a manner that it results in serving the same set of customers. The alternative technology of the business undergoes a change. It is combing activities related to the present activity of a firm. Such a combination may be done through value chain. A value chain is a set of interrelated activity performed by an organization right from the procurement of basic raw materials down to the marketing of finished products to the ultimate customers. E.g. Several process based industry such as petro chemicals, steel, textiles of hydrocarbons have integrate firm

A make or buy decision is then made when firms wish to negotiate with the suppliers or buyers. The cost of making the items used in the manufacture of ones owns products are to be evaluated against the cost of procuring them from suppliers. If the cost of making is less that the cost of procurement then the firm moves up the value chain to make the item itself. Like wise if the cost of selling the finished products is lesser than the price paid to the sellers to do the same thing then the firm would go for direct selling. Among the integration strategies are of two type's vertical and horizontal integration.

a. Vertical integration: When an organization starts making new products that serve its own needs vertical integration takes place. Vertical integration could be of two types Back ward and forward integration.

b. Backward integration means moving back to the source of raw materials while forward integration moves the organization nearer to the ultimate customer. Generally when firms vertically integrate they do so in a complete manner that is they move backward or forward decisively resulting in a full integration but when a firm does not commit it fully it is possible to have partial vertical integration strategies too. Two such partial vertical integration strategies are 'taper' integration and 'quasi' integration.

c. Taper integration requires firms to make a part of their own requirements and to buy the rest from outsiders. Through quasi integration strategies firm purchase most of their requirements from other firms in which they have an ownership stake. Ancillary industrial units and outsourcing through sub contracting are adapted forms of quasi integration.

d. Horizontal Integration: When an organization takes up the same type of products at the same level of production or marketing process, it is said to follow a strategy of horizontal integration. When a luggage company takes over its rival luggage company, it is horizontal integration. Horizontal integration strategy may be frequently adopted with a view to expand geographically by buying a competitors business, to increase the market share or to benefit from economics of scale.

iii. Expansion through diversification

Diversification is a much used and much talked about set of strategies. It involves a substantial change in the business definition—singly or jointly—in terms of customer groups or alternative technologies of one or more of a firm's businesses. There are two categories, concentric and conglomerate diversification.

Different Types of Diversification Strategies

Nature	Related Technology	Unrelated Technology
Similar Type of Product	Marketing technology related concentric diversification	Marketing related concentric diversification
New Type of Product	Technology related concentric diversification	Conglomerate diversification

a. Concentric Diversification: When an organization takes up an activity in such a manner that is related to the existing business definition of one or more of firms businesses, either in terms of customer groups, customer's functions or alternative technologies, it is called concentric diversification. Concentric diversification may be of three types -

- Marketing related concentric diversification
- Technology related concentric diversification
- Marketing technology related concentric diversification

a1. Marketing Related Concentric Diversification: When a similar type of product is offered with a help of unrelated technology for e.g., a company in the sewing machine business diversifies in to kitchen ware and household appliances, which are sold to house wives through a chain of retails stores.

a2. Technology Related Concentric Diversification: When a new type of product or service is provided with the help of related technology, for e.g., a leasing firm offering hire- purchase services to institutional customers also starts consumer financing for the purchase of durable sot individual customers.

a3. Marketing Technology Related Concentric Diversification: When a similar type of product is provided with the help of related technology, for e.g., a rain coat manufacturer makes other rubber based items, such as water proof shoes and rubber gloves sold through the same retail outlets

b. Conglomerate Diversification: When an organization adopts a strategy which requires taking of those activities which are unrelated to the existing businesses definition of one or more of its businesses either in terms of their respective customer groups, customer functions or alternative technologies. Example of Indian company which have adopted apart of growth and expansion through conglomerate diversification the classic examples is of ITC, a cigarette company diversifying into the hotel industry

iv. Expansion Through Cooperation: The term cooperation expresses the idea of simultaneous competition and cooperation among rival firms for mutual benefits.

Cooperative strategies could be of the following types and it has been discussed in detail in next segment.

- Merger
- Takeover
- Joint Venture
- Strategic Alliances
- Stability Strategies

MERGERS:

- A merger is a combination of two or more organizations in which one acquires the assets and liabilities of the other in exchange for shares or cash or both the organization are dissolved and the assets and liabilities are combined and new stock is issued. For the organization, which acquires another, it is an acquisition. For the organization, which is acquired, it is a merger. If both the organization dissolves their identity to create a new organization, it is consolidation. There are different types of mergers they are horizontal merger, vertical merger, concentric merger and conglomerate merger.
- **Horizontal Mergers:** It takes place when there is a combination of two or more organizations in the same business. E.g A company making footwear combines with another footwear company, or a retailer of pharmaceutical combines with another retailer in the same businesses.
- **Vertical Merger:** It takes place when there is a combination of two or more organizations, not necessarily in the same business, which create complementarities either in terms of supply of raw materials (input) or marketing of goods and services (outputs). E.g A footwear company combines with a leather tannery or with a chain shoe retail stores
- **Concentric Mergers:** It takes place when there is a combination of two or more organizations related to each other either in terms of customer functions, customer groups, or the alternative technologies used. E.g. A footwear company combining with a hosiery firm making socks or another specialty footwear company, or with a leather goods company making purse, hand bags and so on.
- **Conglomerate Mergers:** It takes place when there is a combination of two or more organizations unrelated to each other, either in terms of customer functions, customer groups, or alternative technologies used. E.g A footwear company combining with a pharmaceutical firm.

Reasons for mergers or Why the buyer wishes to Merge

1. To increase the value of the organization's stock
2. To increase the growth rate and make a good investment
3. To improve stability of earning and sales
4. To balance, complete, or diversify product line
5. To reduce competition
6. To acquire needed resources quickly
7. To avail tax concessions and benefits
8. To take advantages of synergy

Why the seller wishes to merge

1. To increase the value of the owner's stock and investment
2. To increase the growth rate
3. To acquire resources to stabilize operations

4. To benefit from tax legislation
5. To deal with top management succession problem

TAKEOVER : Takeover or acquisition is a popular strategic alternative adopted by Indian companies. Acquisitions usually are based on the strong motivation of the buyer firm to acquire. Takeovers are frequently classified as hostile takeovers (which are against the wishes of the acquired firm) and friendly takeovers (by mutual consent)

- **Friendly takeovers** are where a takeover is not resisted or opposed, by the existing management or professionals. E.g: Tata Tea's takeover of Consolidated Coffee (a grower of coffee beans) and Asian Coffee (a processor) is an example of a friendly takeover.
- **Hostile takeovers** is where a takeover is resisted, or expected to be opposed, by the existing management or professionals

Advantages of Takeovers

1. Ensure management accountability
2. Offer easy growth opportunities
3. Create mobility of resources
4. Avoid gestation periods and hurdles involved in new projects
5. Offer a chance to sick units to survive
6. Open up alternatives for selective divestment.

JOINT VENTURE : Joint ventures are a special case of consolidation where two or more companies from a temporary form a temporary partnership (also called a consortium) for a specified purpose. They occur when an independent firm is created by at least two other firms. Joint ventures may be useful to gain access to a new business mainly under these conditions

- When an activity is uneconomical for an organization to do alone
- When the risk of business has to be shared
- When the distinctive competence of two or more organization can be brought together.
- When the organization has to overcome the hurdles, such as import quotas, tariffs, nationalistic – political interests, and cultural roadblocks

Types of joint ventures

1. Between two firms in one industry
2. Between two firms across different countries
3. Between an Indian firm and a foreign company in India
4. Between an Indian firm and a foreign company in that foreign country
5. Between an Indian firma and a foreign company in a third country

STRATEGIC ALLIANCES : They are partnership between firms whereby their resources, capabilities and core competencies are combined to pursue mutual interest to develop, manufacture, or distribute goods or services.

There are various advantages-

- Two or more firms unite to pursue a set of agreed upon goals but remain independent subsequent to the formation of the alliances. A pooling of resources, investment and risks occurs for mutual gain
- The partner firms contribute on a continuing basis in one or more key strategic areas, for example, technology, product and so forth.
- Strategic alliances offer a growth route in which merging one's entity, acquiring or being acquired, or creating a joint venture may not be required

- Global partners can help local firms by developing global quality consciousness, creating adherence to international quality standards, providing access to state of the art technology, gaining entry to world wide mass markets, and making funds available for expansions.

E.g: Ranbaxy Company went into strategic alliance with Elilly of the US to realize its mission of becoming a research based international pharmaceutical company.

E.g: Synergistic benefits arising out of strategic alliance is that of Taj Hotels and British Airways, where both create advantages for each other through complementarities of airlines and hotel services

STABILITY STRATEGIES : The stability grand strategy is adopted by an organization when it attempts at an incremental improvement of its functional performance by marginally changing one or more of its businesses in terms of their respective customer groups, customer functions, and alternative technologies – either singly or collectively. E.g: A copier machine company provides better after sales service to its existing customer to improve its company product image, and increase the sale of accessories and consumables. This strategy may be relevant for a firm operating in a reasonably certain and predictable environment. Stability strategy can be of three types –No Change Strategy, Profit Strategy, Pause/ Proceed – with – caution Strategy.

- **No-Change Strategy:** It is a conscious decision to do nothing new. The firm will continue with its present business definition. When a firm has a stable internal and external environment the firm will continue with its present strategy. The firm has no new strengths and weaknesses within the organization and there are no opportunities or threats in the external environment. Taking into account this situation the firm decides to maintain its strategy. Several small and medium sized firm operating in a familiar market- more often a niche market that is limited in scope – and offering products or services through a time tested technology rely on the No – Change Strategy.
- **Profit Strategy:** No firm can continue with the No – Change Strategy. Sometimes things do change and the firm is faced with the situation where it has to do something. A firm may assess the situation and assume that its problem are short lived and will go away with time. Till then a firm tries to sustain its profitability by adopting a profit strategy For instance in a situation when the profit is becoming lower firm takes measures to reduce investments, cut costs, raise prices, increase productivity and adopt other measures to solve the temporary difficulties. The problem arises due to unfavorable situation like economic recession, government attitude, and industry down turn, competitive pressures and like. During this kind of situation that the firm assumes to be temporary it would adopt profit strategies. Some firms to overcome these difficulties would sell off assets such as prime land in a commercial area and move to suburbs. Others have removed some of its non-core business to raise money, while others have decided to provide outsourcing service to other organizations.
- **Pause/ Proceed With Caution Strategy:** It is employed by the firm that wish to test the ground before moving ahead with a full fledged grand strategy, or by firms that have an intense pace of expansion and wish to rest for a while before moving ahead. The purpose is to allow all the people in the organization to adapt to the changes. It is a deliberate and conscious attempt to postpone strategic changes to a more opportune time. E.g: In the India shoe market dominated by Bata and Liberty, Hindustan Levers better known for soaps and detergents, produces substantial quantity of shoes and shoe uppers for the export market. In late 2000, it started selling a few thousand pairs in the cities to find out the market reaction. This is a pause proceed with caution strategy before it goes full steam into another FMCG sector that has a lot of potential.

RETRENCHMENT STRATEGIES : A retrenchment grand strategy is followed when an organization aims at a contraction of its activities through substantial reduction or the elimination of the scope of one or more of its businesses in terms of their respective customer groups, customer functions, or alternative technologies either singly or jointly in order to improve its overall performance. E.g: A corporate hospital decides to focus only on special treatment and realize higher revenues by reducing its commitment to general case which is less profitable. The growth of industries and markets are threatened by various external and internal developments (External developments - government policies, demand saturation, emergence of substitute products, or changing customer needs. Internal Developments – poor management, wrong strategies, poor quality of functional management and so on.) In these situations the industries and markets and consequently the companies face the danger of decline and will go for adopting retrenchment strategies. E.g: fountain pens, manual type writers, tele printers, steam engines, jute and jute products, slide rules, calculators and wooden toys are some products that have either disappeared or face decline. There are three types of retrenchment strategies - Turnaround Strategies, Divestment Strategies and Liquidation strategies.

i. Turnaround Strategies: Turn around strategies derives their name from the action involved that is reversing a negative trend. There are certain conditions or indicators which point out that a turnaround is needed for an organization to survive. They are

- Persistent Negative cash flows
- Negative Profits
- Declining market share
- Deterioration in Physical facilities
- Over manning, high turnover of employees, and low morale
- Uncompetitive products or services
- Mis management

An organization which faces one or more of these issues is referred to as a 'sick' company

There are three ways in which turnarounds can be managed

- The existing chief executive and management team handles the entire turnaround strategy with the advisory support of a external consultant.
- In another case the existing team withdraws temporarily and an executive consultant or turnaround specialist is employed to do the job.
- The last method involves the replacement of the existing team specially the chief executive, or merging the sick organization with a healthy one.

ii. Divestment Strategies - A divestment strategy involves the sale or liquidation of a portion of business, or a major division. Profit centre or SBU. Divestment is usually a part of rehabilitation or restructuring plan and is adopted when a turnaround has been attempted but has proved to be unsuccessful. Harvesting strategies a variant of the divestment strategies, involve a process of gradually letting a company business wither away in a carefully controlled manner

Reasons for Divestment

- The business that has been acquired proves to be a mismatch and cannot be integrated within the company. Similarly a project that proves to be in viable in the long term is divested
- Persistent negative cash flows from a particular business create financial problems for the whole company, creating a need for the divestment of that business.
- Severity of competition and the inability of a firm to cope with it may cause it to divest.
- Technological up gradation is required if the business is to survive but where it is not possible for the firm to invest in it. A preferable option would be to divest
- Divestment may be done because by selling off a part of a business the company may be in a position to survive

- A better alternative may be available for investment, causing a firm to divest a part of its unprofitable business.
- Divestment by one firm may be a part of merger plan executed with another firm, where mutual exchange of unprofitable divisions may take place.
- Lastly a firm may divest in order to attract the provisions of the MRTP Act or owing to oversize and the resultant inability to manage a large business. E.g: TATA group is a highly diversified entity with a range of businesses under its fold. They identified their non – core businesses for divestment. TOMCO was divested and sold to Hindustan Levers as soaps and a detergent was not considered a core business for the Tatas. Similarly, the pharmaceuticals companies of the Tatas- Merind and Tata pharma – were divested to Wockhardt. The cosmetics company Lakme was divested and sold to Hindustan Levers, as besides being a non core business, it was found to be a non- competitive and would have required substantial investment to be sustained.

iii. Liquidation Strategies: A retrenchment strategy which is considered the most extreme and unattractive is the liquidation strategy, which involves closing down a firm and selling its assets. It is considered as the last resort because it leads to serious consequences such as loss of employment for workers and other employees, termination of opportunities where a firm could pursue any future activities and the stigma of failure.

The psychological implications

- The prospects of liquidation create a bad impact on the company's reputation.
- For many executives who are closely associated firms, liquidation may be a traumatic experience.

Legal aspects of liquidation

Under the Companies Act 1956, liquidation is termed as winding up. The Act defines winding up of a company as the process whereby its life is ended and its property administered for the benefit of its creditors and members. The Act provides for a liquidator who takes control of the company, collect its assets, pay it debts, and finally distributes any surplus among the members according to their rights.

COMBINATION (MIXED STRATEGIES) : The combination grand strategy is followed when an organization adopts a mixture of stability, expansion and retrenchment either at the same time in its different business or at different times in the same business with the aim of improving its performance. Complicated situations generally require complex solutions. Combination strategies are the complex solutions that strategists have to offer when faced with the difficulties of real life businesses. E.g A paint company augments its offering of decorative paints to provide a wider variety to its customers (stability) and expands its product range to include industrial and automotive paints (expansion). Simultaneously, it decides to close down the division which undertakes large scale painting contract jobs (retrenchment). It would be difficult to find an organization that has survived and grown by adopting a single pure strategy. The complexity of doing business demands that different strategies be adopted to suit the situational demands made upon the organization. An organization which has followed a stability strategy for quite some time has to think of expansion. Any organization which has been on an expansion path for long has to pause to consolidate its businesses.

i. Global Strategies: Developing strategies on a global scale is not an easy task. Managers have to learn other languages, understand host country laws, deal with volatile currencies, face political uncertainties, and redesign products to suit different customer needs and expectations.

ii. Global Expansion Strategies: A firm can choose four types of strategies— Global Strategy, International Strategy, Transnational Strategy and Multidomestic Strategy two sets of factors affect firm's decision to adopt international strategies: extent of cost pressures and the extent of pressures for local responsiveness. Cost pressures denote the demand on a firm to minimize its unit costs. Pressures for local responsiveness makes a firm tailor its strategies to respond to national-level differences in terms of variables like customer preferences and tastes, government policies, or business practices

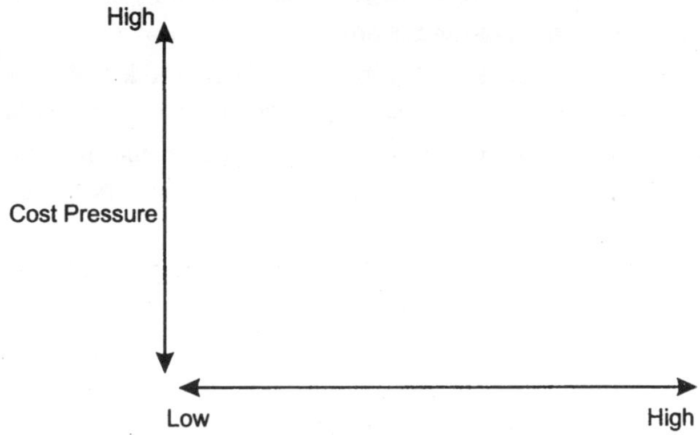

Figure 6.11. Pressure for Local Responsiveness.

Firms adopt an international strategy when they create value by transferring products and services to foreign markets where these products and services are not available. This is a simple strategy in the sense that an international firm, by maintaining a tight control over its overseas operations, offers standardized products and services in different countries with little or no differentiation. Most international companies, such as, Coca Cola, McDonald, IBM, Kellogg, Proctor and Gamble, Microsoft, and several others adopt this strategy for the different countries they operate in.

iii. Multi domestic strategy when they try to achieve a high level of local responsiveness by matching their products and services offerings to the national conditions operating in the countries they operate in. In this case, the multi domestic firm attempts to extensively customize their products and services according to the local conditions operating in the different countries. Obviously, this leads to a high-cost structure as functions, such as, research and development, production, and marketing have to be duplicated.

iv. Global strategy when they rely on a low-cost approach based on reaping the benefits of experience-curve effects and location economies and offering standardized products and services across different countries. The global firm tries to focus intensively on a low-cost structure by leveraging their expertise in providing certain products and services, and concentrating the production of these standardized products and services at a few favorable locations around the world. These products and services are offered in an undifferentiated manner in all countries the global firm operates in, usually at competitive prices.

v. Firms adopt a **transnational strategy** when they adopt a combined approach of low-cost and high local responsiveness simultaneously for their products and services.

6.6. MARKET ENTRY STRATEGIES

Once the MNC decides to target a particular country, it has to decide the best mode of entry. Mode of entry means the manner in which the firm would commence its international operations. There are several entry modes, each with their own sets of advantages and disadvantages. A firm would have to decide which mode suits its circumstances best before it could be adopted. The different entry modes are:

(1) Export entry modes: Under these modes, the firm produces in the home country and markets in the overseas markets.

- Direct exports do not involve home-country intermediaries and marketing is done either through direct agent/distributor or through direct branch/subsidiary in the overseas markets.

- Indirect exports involving intermediaries in the home country and who are responsible for exporting the firm's products.

(2) **Contractual entry modes:** These modes involve non-equity associations between an international company and a company or any other legal entity in the overseas markets.

- Licensing is an arrangement where the international company transfers knowledge, technology, patent, and so on for a limited period of time to an overseas entity in return for some form of payment, usually a royalty payment.
- Franchising: Franchising involves the right to use a business format, usually a brand name, in the overseas market in return for the franchise receiving some form of payment.
- Other forms of contractual arrangements, such as, technical agreements (for technology transfers), service contracts (for technical support or expertise provision), contract manufacturing, production sharing, turnkey operations, build-operate-transfer (BOT) arrangements, etc.

(3) **Investment entry modes:** These modes involve ownership of production units in the overseas market based on some form of equity investment of direct foreign investment.

- Joint venture and strategic alliances involve a cooperative partnership between two or more firms with financial interests as the basis of cooperation, (These entry options have been discussed earlier under the heading of cooperative strategies.)
- Independent ventures or wholly-owned subsidiaries are modes in which the parent international company holds 100 percent equity and is in full control. Such facilities may be created either through a new venture known as a Greenfield venture or acquired through takeover strategies.

6.7. ENVIRONMENTAL THREAT AND OPPORTUNITIES PROFILE (ETOP)

Environmental diagnosis is concerned with assessment of Environmental factors in term of these being opportunity or threat and their impact. It is related with identifying opportunities and threats based on Environmental monitoring. Environmental threat and opportunities profile (ETOP) is an important technique which is widely needed in Environmental diagnosis.

Techniques for Preparing (ETOP)

It can be prepared in following way

1. Identify the different components of relevant environment: The economic environment may be divided into rate of economic growth, rate of inflation, monetary policy, fiscal policy and so on or competitive environment may be divided into threats of entry and exit, competitive position of competitors etc

2. Assessing importance of environmental factors: The degree of importance can be in qualitative terms like high, medium, low, or it can be quantified like 3,2,1. it may be mentioned that all the environmental variables.

3. Assessing impact factors: An environmental factor which is relevant may either present threats or provide opportunities depending upon the nature of Environmental factors and their behavior. Positive impact of a factor is opportunities and negative impact is threat.

4. Combining importance and impact factor: Combination of importance and impact factor give a clear picture of industry sector. If both variables have been quantified, these can be combined by multiplication.

Benefits of ETOP

1. Help to determine the key factors of threats and opportunities.

2. Good tool to qualify the factors related to company's strategy.
3. Can consider many factors for each special case.

Limitations of ETOP

1. It does not shows the interactions between the factors.
2. It can reflect the dynamic environment.
3. It's a subjective analysis tool.

6.8. COMPREHENSIVE ANALYSIS

While it would be useful to use a range of analytical methods to evaluate the strengths and weaknesses of a firm and to determine its capability, a better way is to use a combination of techniques. as each one of these have a different purpose and limitations. A comprehensive analysis helps to deal with these limitations. We describe below three popular methods and techniques of key factor rating, business intelligence systems and balanced scorecard for performing a comprehensive analysis.

A. KEY FACTOR RATING

A comprehensive method, which can be used in association with a financial analysis, is that of key factor rating. Many systems have been evolved by consultants to assess organizational strengths and weaknesses. Essentially, these systems are based on rating, depending on a number of key factors, each of which is analyzed on the basis of a series of thoughtful and penetrating questions. A detailed study of the areas covered by these questions leads to a reliable appraisal of an organization. If we consider the different factors that have been mentioned in Section 4.2 under various headings of functional capabilities, we can suggest the following illustrative questions that can be asked with regard to the different functional areas. The sequence of questions roughly corresponds to factors included under different sub-sections dealing with functional capability.

I. For financial capability factors

1. *Questions related to sources of funds:* Is the organization's capital structure satisfactory? Can the organization raise capital in the market? Where does the effective controllership rest? Is the debt-equity ratio satisfactory as compared to other competitive organizations? Does the financing pattern cause the organization to be dependent on outsiders? Is the reserves and surplus position healthy? Is relationship with banks and financial institutions cordial?

2. *Question related to usage of funds:* Are adequate investment opportunities available? How does the organization compare with others so far as the dividend record is concerned? What type of relationship exists with its shareholders?

3. *Questions related to management of funds:* How effective and efficient are the financial, accounting and budgetary systems? Does the management control system satisfy the organizational needs? What trends do the various financial ratios indicate? Have they been satisfactory over the last few years? What strengths and weaknesses does the ratio analysis indicate? Has inflation been taken into account? What is the status of the ongoing projects? Have there been time-and cost-overruns? How far have the tax advantages accrued to the organization?

II. For marketing capability factors

1. *Questions related to products or services:* Does the organization offer the requisite variety of products or services? What is the level of product differentiation? Does the product-mix satisfy market requirements? Are there products which do not contribute to profitability? What steps have been taken to phase out such products? How do the products compare with others in the industry in terms of quality, packaging. etc?

2. *Questions related to price:* What pricing objectives are pursued? Are they oriented towards profit maximization or sales revenue maximization? Do the pricing policies conform to market requirements? Does the organization avail of price protection and other advantages available to it?

3. *Questions related to promotion:* Does the organization use relevant promotional tools? Are the different forms of promotion used effectively in generating sales? What does market research indicate with regard to promotion and public relations? Are the funds allocated to promotion being used effectively?

4. *Questions related to integrative and systemic factors*: How does the organization compare with others of its kind in terms of market standing and image? What strengths and weaknesses are there in the marketing organization? How effective is the marketing management information system?

III. For operations capability factors

1. *Questions related to the production system:* Does the plant location offer any unique advantages or disadvantages? Is the layout appropriate? Is the plant capacity of the requisite level? Do work systems support efficiency and productivity? What is the extent of vertical integration? Does it offer certain unique advantages to the organization?

2. *Questions related to operations and control* is aggregate planning able to absorb short-term demand fluctuations? Is there an adequate supply of the factors of production? Does the organization have any unique advantages with respect to its factors of production? Is the material supply system reliable? Does the organization have access to sources of material supply not available to its competitors? What is the efficiency and effectiveness of the inventory control system? How effective are the cost, quality and maintenance systems?

3. *Questions related to the R & D system* Does the organization possess certain distinct advantages with respect to its R & D personnel, facilities and technology? Does it possess patent rights? Does it have access to the latest technology? How far do technology collaborations benefit the organization?

IV. For personnel capability factors

1. *Questions related to the personnel system:* How effective are the various personnel systems like manpower planning, selection, development etc? What importance does the personnel function enjoy within the organization?

2. *Questions related to organizational and employee characteristics:* How does the organization compare with others of its kind in terms of corporate image? Does the organization possess unique advantages with regard to the quality of its managers, staff and workers? How is the organization perceived as an employer? What special benefits does the organization offer to its employees that others do not offer?

3. *Questions related to industrial relations:* what is the organization's record with regard to industrial relations? Is the union-management relationship amicable? Have the outstanding issues been resolved? How effectively does the system of collective bargaining work? Does the organization offer safety, welfare and security measures over and above the statutory requirements? What is the general level of employee satisfaction and morale? Does it benefit the organisation in terms of competitive advantage through increased productivity and low cost?

V. For information management capability factors

1. *Questions related to acquisition and retention of information:* Where does the organization stand with respect to the sources, quantity, quality and timeliness of information for decision making? What is the level of its retention capacity for information? How secure are its information systems?

2. *Questions related to processing and synthesis of information*: How well does the database management work in the organization? What is the state-of-the art with respect to computer systems and software capability of the organization? What is the level of its ability to synthesized information?

3. ***Questions related to retrieval and usage of information***: Is the availability and appropriateness of the information format adequate? What is the capacity of the organization to assimilate and use information?

4. ***Questions related to transmission and dissemination***: What are the speed, scope, width and depth of coverage of information in the organization? What is the level of willingness on the part of managers to accept information?

5. ***Questions related to integrative systemic and supportive factors***: What is the situation regarding the availability of the IT infrastructure within the organization? Is it relevant and compatible with the organizational needs? Does the organization carry out regular and periodical up gradation of its IT facilities? Is there willingness on the part of the top management to invest in the latest IT systems? Are competent IT professionals available within the organization? Does the top management support IT application within organization?

VI. For general management capability factors

1. ***Questions related to general management system***: Does the organization use strategic management systems and what is the level of their effectiveness? Have the mission, purposes and objectives been identified clearly? What is the effectiveness level of the strategy formulation, implementation and evaluation processes? Is the management information system reliable? Does the organization possess distinctive advantages with respect to its corporate planning system? Are the rewards and incentives systems for top managers consistent with the achievement of objectives?

2. ***Questions related to general managers***: Does the top management possess the required orientation to implement strategies? As compared to similar organizations, what are the qualities and capabilities of the general managers? Do these qualities and capabilities offer any unique advantages to the organization?

3. ***Questions related to external relationships***: What is the level of influence that the organization has on governmental regulatory institutions and financial institutions? Is the organization able to manage its public relations well? Does the organization discharge its social responsibilities well? How does the organization compare with regard to its public image with respect to its competitors?

4. ***Questions related to organizational climate***: Does the organizational culture support the achievement of objectives? Is the use of power, political equations and the balance of vested interests conducive to the achievement of its objectives? Do these factors offer any unique advantages? How effectively does the organization imbibe strategic changes? Is the nature of organizational structure and controls consistent with strategy implementation? Key factors rating is quite a comprehensive method as you can observe from the range of issues covered. Yet, it has some limitations. First, its comprehensiveness may make it an unwieldy method to use. It will require a variety of information from different parts of an organization, making it a slow and inefficient method. Secondly, this method is basically a subjective method as managers have to assign the rating on the basis of their judgments. Subjectivity has its limits and would require improvement based on reference to objective factors as one set of factors after the other are considered. Lastly, the key factor rating method needs to be dovetailed with the audit processes that are ongoing in organizations. Otherwise there is a possibility of evaluation efforts being duplicated. Having answered the questions for each of the functional areas detailed above, the strategists are in a position to pinpoint the strengths and weaknesses in each of the functional areas. Based on this, the organizational capability can be judged.

B. BUSINESS INTELLIGENCE SYSTEMS

Information technology has made a huge impact on the way organization's use their information systems for organizational appraisal. Methods like key factors rating and balanced scorecard are implemented by the means of sophisticated IT tools to make them feasible for the purpose of decision-making. Business intelligence is one of th concepts used for discovering knowledge from various internal and external data repositories available to an organization to support effective decision-making. Business intelligence (BI), a term coined by Howard J. Dresner of the Gartner Group in 1989, became popular in the late 1990s. BI is defined by the Gartner Group as 'a broad category of applications and technologies for gathering, storing, analyzing, and providing access to data to help enterprise users make better business decisions. The applications of BI include the activities of decision support systems, query and reporting, online analytical processing (OLAP). Statistical analysis, forecasting, and data mining. BI can help an organization in strategic and operational decision-making. A Gartner survey ranked the strategic use of B! in the following order.

- Corporate performance management
- Optimizing customer relations, monitoring business activity and traditional decision support
- Packaged stand-alone BI applications for specific operations or strategies
- Management reporting of business intelligence

Among these, the issue of corporate performance management is of interest to us here. This application can be used to uncover the strengths and weaknesses of the organization and can help in determining the organizational capability. Among several techniques in corporate performance management. is the immensely popular one of the balanced scorecard.

C. BALANCED SCORECARD

Here we need to focus again on the balanced scorecard as a means of assessment of strengths and weaknesses of an organization. Proposed by Robert S. Kaplan and David P. Norton. Balanced scorecard attempts to do away with the bias in performance measures towards financial indices and tries to build a holistic system of measurement. Balanced scorecard is considered as 'a set of measures that gives top managers a fast hut comprehensive view of the business (It) includes financial measures that tell the results of actions already taken. And it complements the financial measures no customer satisfaction, internal processes, and the organization's innovation and improvement activities— operational measures that arc the drivers of future financial performance. The balanced scorecard identifies four key performance measures as follows:

- Customer perspective: 'How do customers see its'?'
- Internal business perspective: 'What must we excel at?'
- Innovation and learning perspective: 'Can we continue to improve and create value?'
- Financial perspective: 'How do we look at shareholders?'

Each of these perspectives could be used individually, but using them in combination provides deeper insights and a balanced approach to strategy formulation. One perspective is not allowed to outweigh others when the strengths and weaknesses of an organization are assessed. The balanced scorecard is per se a comprehensive strategic management system,'9 but for our limited purpose here, it could as well be used as a means to identify the strengths and weaknesses in an organization, Keeping score of the strengths and weaknesses in critical areas of performance enables, a quantitative as well as qualitative analysis of the organization.

6.9. STRUCTURING ORGANISATIONAL APPRAISAL

Just as environmental appraisal is structured through an environmental threat and opportunity profile, organizational appraisal can also be structured through various techniques. For instance, Glueck proposes a preparation of the strategic advantage profile (SAP) where the results of organizational appraisal are presented in a summarized form. Another approach, suggested by Rowe et al, is to prepare a company capability profile as a means for assessing a company's strengths and weakness in dealing with the opportunities and threats in the external environment. We propose a similar approach here of making an organizational capability profile, which can be summarized in the form of a strategic advantage profile. The SAP is then matched with the environmental threats and opportunity profile, prepared while structuring the environmental appraisal, in order to look for strategic alternatives and exercise a strategic choice.

Preparing the Organizational Capability Profile

The organizational capability profile (OCP) is drawn in the form of a chart as depicted in which shows a summarized OCP. The strategists are required to systematically assess the various functional areas and subjectively assign values to the different functional capability factors and sub-factors, along a scale ranging from values of —5 to +5. A detailed OCP may run into several pages where each of the sub-factors constituting the different functional capability factors can be assessed. In this manner, a summarized OCP, as shown in table 6.5, may be prepared.

Table 6.5 Summarized form of Organizational Capability Profile.

S. No	Capability factors	Weakness-5	Normal-0	Strength+5
1.	Financial capability factors a. Sources of funds b. Usage of funds c. Management of funds			
2.	Marketing Related factors a. Product-related b. Price-related c. Promotion-related d. Integrative and systematic			
3.	Operations capability factors a. Production system b. Operations and control system c. R & D system			
4.	Personnel capability factors a. Personnel system b. Organizational and employee characteristics c. Industrial relations			
5.	Information management capability factors a. Acquisition and retention of information b. Retrieval and usage of Information c. Processing and usage of information d. Transmission and dissemination of information e. Integrative, systemic and supportive			
6.	General management capability factors a. General management system b. External relations c. Organizational climate			

After completion of the chart, the strategists are in a position to assess the relative strengths and weaknesses of an organization in each of the six functional areas and identify the gaps that need to be corrected or opportunities that could be used. The preparation of an OCP provides a convenient method to determine the relative priorities of an organization is a vis that of its competitors, its vulnerability to outside influences, the factors that support or oppose, threats to its existence and its overall capability to compete in a given industry.

6.10. CORPORATE PORTFOLIO ANALYSIS

Cooperate portfolio analysis (or simply, portfolio analysis) could be defined as a set of techniques that help strategists in taking strategic decisions with regard to individual products or businesses in a firm's portfolio. It is primarily used for competitive analysis and strategic planning in multi-product and multi business firms. If may also be used in less diversified firms, if these consist of a main business and other minor complementary interests. The main advantages in adopting a portfolio approach in a multi-product, multi business firm is that resources could be targeted at the corporate level to those businesses that possess the greatest potential for creating competitive advantage. For instance, a diversified company may decide to divert resources from its cash-rich businesses to more prospective ones that hold promise of a faster growth, so that the company achieves its corporate level objectives in an optimal manner.

Corporate portfolio techniques evolved during the mid-1960s and several of these soon became quite popular. During the 1970s, there arose a tendency to discredit the techniques when it was realized that the assumptions underlying them did not always hold good. Currently, however, it is accepted that these techniques are useful, not as being purely prescriptive, but as an important and decisive part of a set of criteria—normative as well as descriptive—that assist strategists in exercising a strategic choice.

There are a number of techniques that could be considered as corporate portfolio analysis techniques. Among them we have the Boston Consulting Group (BCG) or product portfolio, General Electric's nine cells, Hofer's Product-Market Evolution, Directional Policy and the Strategic Position and Action Evaluation juices. Not all of these techniques have retained their popularity and importance though. We will describe General Electric's Nine-cell matrix as an illustration of the corporate portfolio matrices.

6.11. MATCHING STRUCTURE AND STRATEGY

There is close relationship between an organization's strategy and its structure. The understanding of this relationship is important so that in implementing the strategy, the organization structure is designed according to the needs of the strategy. The relationship between strategy and structure can be thought in terms of utilizing structure for strategy implementation because structure is a means to an end and not an end in itself. The master appropriate end is the objectives for which the organization exists in the first place, as revealed by its strategy. Without coordination between strategy and structure, the most likely outcomes are confusion, misdirection, and splintered efforts within the organization.

According to Chandler, "Changes in organizations strategy bring about new administration problems which, in turn, require a new refashioned structure if the new strategy is to be successfully implemented". Structure tends to follow the growth strategy of the organization but not until inefficiency and internal operating problems provoke a structural adjustment. Thus organizational actions proceed in a particular sequence; new strategy creation, emergence of new administrative problems, a decline in portability and performance, a shift to a more appropriate organization structure, then recovery to improved strategy execution and more profit and performance.

However, this sequence can be broken if suitable organization structure is conceived at the starting point of strategy implementation. The relationship between strategy and structure, however, should not be viewed merely as one-way traffic; rather it should be viewed as two-way traffic. On the one hand, the structure should be according to the need the strategy so that it is implemented effectively. On the other hand, structure of the organization may plays critical role in influencing its choice of strategy. Recognition of this two-way interaction between strategy and structure is crucial for a complete understanding of the criteria, which underlie structural design. It becomes obvious that a top management perspective in structural design is necessary when one understands that such a design is a result of overall strategy, and the success of the strategy is also dependent on that design.

Strategic managers should strive to keep their structures (and processes) as simple as possible and trim every vestige of unnecessary bureaucracy — e.g., extra layers of management. Fundamentally, the structural decision is one of prioritizing standardization versus flexibility and selecting the basic structure that best achieves the required priority. Therefore, strategic managers must evaluate the advantages and disadvantages of each of the structural building-blocks and match them with the requirements of the strategy. For example, a different structure may be required to carry-out a defender/cost leadership competitive strategy than that for a prospector) differentiation strategy. Defender strategies require a high degree of structural standardization to create cost efficiencies while prospector strategies require a great deal of structural flexibility to develop new technologies and innovative products and services.

6.11.1 Maintaining the Structure

If there is a good match between the characteristics of the current organizational structure and the requirements of the strategy, then the present basic structure should be maintained. However, additional coordinating mechanisms may be required. It is not often that organizational structure alone will create long-term competitive advantage. However, structure is a key implementation area (especially when coupled with an effective culture). When it is viewed as an organizational strength, efforts should be made to keep it effective — whether it is or is not rare among competitors. In maintaining the present structure management should:-

1. Evaluate the present level of communication and coordination and discuss needed additional communication channels and coordinating mechanisms;
2. Evaluate the present structure to ensure that there are opportunities for innovation where appropriate;
3. Evaluate the management team to ensure that the leadership skills match their positions; and
4. Inventory the present skills to ensure that they are matched to the structure and strategy.

6.11.2 Changing the Structure

If the comparison of the present structure and requirements of the strategy suggest a need to change the basic organizational structure, then management must develop a plan and move very carefully. Ineffective or inappropriate organizational structure can debilitate the organization's strategy — such as might be the case with too many organizational layers, thus delaying decision-making — but by itself structure is not generally seen as a significant long-term competitive disadvantage. However, where the organizational structure is viewed as a weakness, action must be taken. Re-organization represents a significant change for employees and is often viewed as threatening. To help managers think though re-organization, a re-engineering approach may be taken. Re-engineering reconsiders and changes how tasks connect to each other to produce more efficient overall systems of work. Therefore, when changing the structure, management should:

1. Develop a flowchart of the total process, including its interfaces with other value chain activities;

2. Simplify first, eliminating tasks and steps where possible and analyzing how to streamline the performance of what remains;
3. Determine which parts can be automated (usually those that are repetitive, time- consuming, and require little thought or decision);
4. Consider introducing advanced technologies that can be upgraded to achieve next- generation capability and provide a basis for further productivity gains in the future;
5. Evaluate each activity to determine whether it is strategy critical (strategy-critical activities are candidates for benchmarking to achieve best-in-industry performance status);
6. Weigh the pros and cons of outsourcing activities that are non-critical or that contribute little to the organizational capabilities and core competencies;
7. Compare the advantages and disadvantages of the organizational building-blocks regarding standardization and flexibility; and
8. Design a structure for performing the activities that remain, and then re-organize the personnel and groups who perform these activities into the new structure.

Changing the organizational structure can be a difficult task and may require some new thinking and new approaches to old problems. Re-engineering efforts that have been undertaken by health care organizations indicate that the use of integrating mechanisms, such as codifying the process, and the use of internal teams and committees during implementation appear to be most effective. In addition, as they undertake re-structuring, strategic managers need to evaluate what competitive benefits are actually accruing to ensure that managers are not just re-organizing to be like everyone else, but for improved outcomes — they must understand how reengineering affects their competitive position.

6.11.3 Difficulties in Matching Structure to Strategy

In evaluating whether the structure is designed properly to meet the needs of the strategy, two questions can be posed:

1) What functions and activities should be performed for the success of the strategy?

2) Is structure adaptable to the pressure of the external environment?

The answer of these two questions should point squarely at the functions essential to strategic success. However, in applying the test of consistence of strategy and structure, the strategist frequently meets three difficulties:

1) Strategy Unclear: He attempts to relate structure to strategy; he may find the strategy unclear, emerging. The basic question that should be put for answer before diagnosing the structural adequacy is: how definite is the strategy? If the answer to this question is uncertain, how does a manager test the adequacy of his organization structure? Therefore, if the strategy is precise, clear and definite, the adequacy of organization structure can be tested easily.

2) Implicit: The symptoms of organizational malfunctions are nc always explicit unlike the physical object. Things are to be interpreted on the basis of various qualitative factors, which may become subjective. It is a common human tendency to cover up unpleasant things and organizational situations fall in this category. Therefore, the strategist has to build up his information system in such a way that he is able to monitor organizational adequacy.

3) Multiple Causes: In applying the test of adequacy is that malfunctioning symptoms have multiple causes. Many of external factors may cause malfunctioning in the organization and not the structure itself. For example, if the profit is down because of increased competition and consequence lower price realization, the correction will be required in strategic posture and the organization should be analyzed in the context of both internal as well as external factors to pinpoint the exact nature of problem and consequently the remedial action. These problems must be kept in mind while relating structure to strategy.

6.11.4 Mechanism for Matching Structure to Strategy

The first aspect of structure-strategy fit relates to the **type of functions that the organization structure should facilitate to perform.** There are tests, which any good organization structure should satisfy. First implement the strategy properly, certain functions must be performed. Therefore, the structure should ensure that all the necessary activities are performed and there is no duplication in the performance of the activities. Second, an activity's contribution to strategy should determine its rank and placement in the organizational hierarchy. Thus key activities should never be subordinated to non-key activities. Revenue earning or result-producing activities should never subordinate to support activities. By making success causing for the major building blocks for the structure, the chances are greatly improved that strategy will be effectively implemented.

The second aspect of structure-strategy fit relates to the adaptive character of the environmental pressure on the organization. Organization has to interact continuously with its environment and this interaction some sort of changes are brought continuously in the organization. If the change is a minor one and comes within the purview of established programs of action, the change will be absorbed within the system; major or rapid changes throw the organization out of equilibrium seriously affecting its functioning. New equilibrium is reached by taking new programs. Therefore, the organization structure should be able absorb these changes.

In relating structure to strategy, following strategic principles organizing may be helpful. These principles are not strictly in **accordance with traditional principles of organizing**. These principles are considered the especially pertinent for a firm with multiple products and multiple industry-market opportunities. These should also suit the smaller but growing firms in a dynamic volatile environment.

1) It is better to delegate authority and decentralize strategic planning and operations for businesses, which are relatively, mature, predictable, and stable. This frees top management for strategic planning in the relatively unknown areas of opportunities.

2) Strategic planning for the unknown areas should be centralized, as this requires close supervision of top management. The critical early choices in unknown fields can pose major unpredictable risks on resource allocations and technological commitments, which are among the most important decision areas for the management.

3) In centralization-decentralization continuum, there should be centralized measurements. This implies after-the-fact measurement and not the control which is affected by the divisional heads.

4) Emphasis should be on result-centered rather than profit centered decentralization. It is not necessary to effect total profit and loss divisionalization in order to delegate decision making authority to lower echelon managers. Decentralization can be confined to those key operating and support areas that have within their make-up tradeoff issues, which a subordinate manager can resolve to, affect timely and market knowledgeable strategic decisions. In other words, neither centralization nor decentralization are cut and dried propositions. Many graduations are available to resourceful management, and entrepreneurial type of responsibilities can be assigned with significant leverage for achieving results without handing over complete profit responsibility. Various forms of organization structure and their suitability to strategies suggest that no one form is suitable for all situations. Therefore, many companies opt for combination of more than one form.

6.12. MEANING AND DEFINITION OF ORGANIZATIONAL CULTURE

Organizational culture is another element which affects strategy implementation as it provides a framework within, which the behavior of the members takes place. Though there are differing views on what constitute an organizational culture, generally, it is defined as a set of assumptions the members of an organization share in common. Organizational culture is the invisible power which is accumulated through the constant efforts of its people. It is belief, common perception and understanding of an organization. This unique feature of the organization makes it distinctive from other organizations. The experiences and manner of performing are instrumental in forming the organizational culture. It is the environment under which an employee deals with its organization and an organization deals with its employees.

According to **Reilly**, "Organizational culture is the set of assumptions, beliefs, values, and norms that are shared by an organization's members".

Table 6.6. Formal Components of Corporate Culture.

	Component	Description	Effect on Organizational Culture
1)	Mission/Vision	The milestones to be reached.	Could be unrealistic.
2)	Policies	Statements designed to be guidelines to behavioral decision,	Policies, if not drafted properly can provide leeway.
3)	Procedures	Methods of providing specific guidelines,	Can facilitate or create obstacles in smooth functioning.
4)	Rules	Specific instructions for performing a task.	Rules could be a means or an end in them.
5)	State of Organizational Development	Organization at young, growing, maturing, or mature stage of development,	Stage of organizational development has direct impact on work culture.

6.13. COMPETITIVE COST DYNAMICS

Cost Dynamics is a term used by Porter to indicate that in addition to Analyzing Cost behavior at a point in time (Cost Drivers), a firm must also consider how the absolute and relative cost of Value Activities will change over time independent of its strategy. A firm with insight into cost dynamics may be able to position itself to gain a Cost Advantage by anticipating these changes and moving quickly to respond to them.

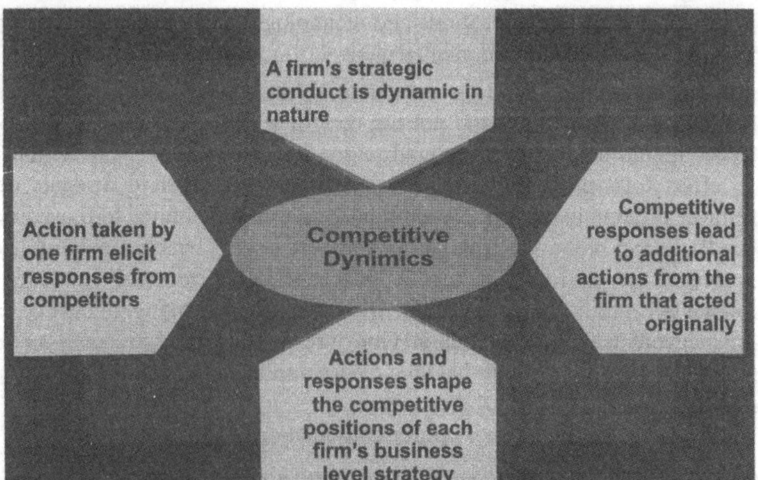

Figure 6.12. Process of Competitive Cost Dynamics.

Sources of Cost Dynamics

The most important sources of Competitive cost dynamics are:

- **Industry Real Growth.** For example, growth of an entire industry may open up possibilities to achieve Economies of Scale.
- **Differential Scale Sensitivity.** As market or sales volumes grow or decrease, this may affect some firms more than others.
- **Different Learning Rates.**
- **Differential Technological Change.**
- **Relative Inflation of Costs.** For example if oil prices go up, this may shift the relative cost of certain activities compared to others.
- **Aging.** Older machines require more maintenance costs. An older employee typically receives a higher salary.
- **Market Adjustment.** When competitors are increasingly adopting similar value activities, this may increase the cost level for these activities

6.14. INTERNATIONAL PORTFOLIO ANALYSIS

International Portfolio Analysis provides a good snapshot of collective SBU's pursuing global ventures. Country attractiveness is measured against competitive strength. A country's attractiveness is composed of its market size, the market rate of growth, the extent and type of government regulation, and economic and political factors. A product's competitive strength is composed of its market share, product fit, contribution margin, and market support. Depending on where a product fits on the matrix, it should either receive more funding or be harvested for cash. Portfolio analysis might not be useful, however, to corporations operating in a global industry rather than a multi-domestic one. In discussing the importance of global industries, Porter argues against the use of portfolio analysis on a country-by-country basis.

Portfolio Matrix for Plotting Products by Country

Competitive Strenghts

	High		Low
High	Invest/Grow		Dominate/Divest Joint venture
		Selective Strategies	
Low			Harvest/Divest Combine/License

6.15. CORPORATE PARENTING ANALYSIS

Campbell, Goold and Alexander suggest that two issues must be addressed by the diversified corporation: (a) What businesses should a diversified corporation own and why and (b) What organizational structure, management processes and philosophy will foster superior performance from the corporation's individual business units? They proposed the concept of corporate parenting to consider the role of the corporate headquarters in managing a set of businesses in a portfolio. A diversified corporation or a multi-business company is often viewed as consisting of a corporate headquarter or center with SBUs acting as satellites. The manner in which the center manages and nurtures the individual businesses is termed as corporate parenting. The total corporation is viewed in terms of resources and capabilities that can be used to build individual businesses as well as create synergies across these businesses. In this manner, corporate parenting attempts to do away with one major drawback of the corporate portfolio techniques. While portfolio techniques consider the industry attractiveness of various industries and focuses on the cash contributions that each business could make to the overall portfolio of businesses, corporate parenting views the organization in its totality as a diversified corporation and focuses on the value created from the relationship between the parent and its businesses.

6.16. SWOT ANALYSIS

Every organization is a part of an industry. Almost all organizations face competition, either directly or indirectly. Thus, the industry and competition are vital considerations in making a strategic choice. The industry provides the context in which an organization operates, while competitors *vie* for the same set of the customers by offering more or less identical products. It is quite obvious that any strategic choice made by an organization cannot be made unless the industry and competition have been analyzed. Apart from the external forces that are present in the industry and in the competitor analyses, it is useful to look inward and perform a SWOT analysis. SWOT stands for strengths, weaknesses, opportunities and threats. SWOT analysis is a widely used framework to summaries a company situation or current position. Any company undertaking strategic planning will have to carry out SWOT analysis: establishing its current position in the light of its strengths, weaknesses, opportunities and threats. Environmental and industry analysis provide information needed to identify opportunities and threats, while internal analysis provides information needed to identify strengths and weaknesses. These are the fundamental areas of focus in SWOT analysis.

SWOT analysis stands at the core of strategic management. It is important to note that strengths and weaknesses are intrinsic (potential) value creating skills or assets or the lack thereof, relative to competitive forces. Opportunities and threats, however, are external factors that are not created by the company, but emerge as a result of the competitive dynamics caused by or in the market.

Opportunities: An opportunity is a major favourable situation in a firm environment. Examples include market growth, favourable changes in competitive or regulatory framework, technological developments or demographic changes, increase in demand, opportunity to introduce products in new markets, turning R&D into cash by licensing or selling patents etc The level of detail and perceived degree of realism determine the extent of opportunity analysis

Threats: A threat is a major unfavorable situation in a firm environment. Examples include increase in competition, slow market growth, increased power of buyers or suppliers, changes in regulations etc. These forces pose serious threats to a company because they may cause lower sales, higher cost of operations, higher cost of capital, inability to make break-even, shrinking margins or profitability etc. Your competitor opportunity may well be a threat to you.

Strengths: Strength is something a company possesses or is good at doing Examples include a skill, valuable assets, alliances or cooperative ventures, experienced sales force, easy access to raw materials, brand reputation etc. Strengths are not a growing market, new products, etc.

Weaknesses: A weakness is something a company lacks or does poorly. Examples include lack of skills or expertise, deficiencies in assets, inferior capabilities in functional areas etc., Though weaknesses are often seen as the logical of the company threats, the company lack of strength in a particular area or market is not necessarily a relative weakness because competitors may also lack this particular strength.

Carrying Out SWOT Analysis

The first thing that a SWOT analysis does is to evaluate the strengths and weaknesses in terms of skills, resources and competencies. The analyst then should see whether the internal capabilities match with the demands of the key success factors. The job of a strategist is to capitalize on the organization strengths while minimizing the effects of its weaknesses in order to take advantage of opportunities and overcome threats in the environment. SWOT analysis for a typical firm is given below

STRENGTHS
- Rollled-Up Competitors
- Established customer base
- Annual Subscriprion Model
- High customer switching costs
- Expertise is SIS integration
- Evolved Grade Center and enrolment manager
- Long-term customer relationships
- Centrality of CMS as campus application and directory integration

WEAKNESSES
- Customer dissatisfaction with design
- Siloed course structure
- Faculti centric design paradigm
- Inability to open courses and content to larger learning comunity
- High costs VS. emerging inexpensive Web 2.0 collaboration tools
- Lack of integration with Web 2.0 cloud tools
- Dependence on central IT

OPPORTUNITIES
- Engage customer base in roadmap development
- Move to transparent model
- Strategic partnership with SIS providers
- Invest in introperability with Web 2.0 collaboration tools
- Re-design to conform to emerging active learning consensus
- Integration with cloud storage and publishing tools
- Grow SaaS model of devilery

THREATS
- Open and community Source CMS traction
- Encroachment on middleware space from SIS providers (authentication, grade centre, enrolment etc.)
- Consumer Web 2.0 collaboration tools (Ning, netvibes etc.)
- A Google App CMS
- Community dissatisfaction with design philosophy
- Mismatch of higher education and BB corporate culture

Steps in SWOT Analysis

The three important steps in SWOT analysis are:

1 Identification

2. Conclusion

3. Translation

1. Identification.
- Identify company resource strengths and competitive capabilities
- Identify company resource weaknesses and competitive deficiencies
- Identify company opportunities
- Identify external threats

2. Conclusion
- Draw conclusions about the company overall situation.

3. Translation

Translate the conclusions into strategic actions by acting on them:
- Match the company strategy to its strengths and opportunities
- Correct important weaknesses
- Defend against external threats

In devising a SWOT analysis, there are several factors that will enhance the quality of the material:

- Keep it brief, pages of analysis are usually not required.
- Relate strengths and weaknesses, wherever possible, to industry key factors for success.
- Strengths and weaknesses should also be stated in competitive terms, that is, in comparison with competitors.
- Statements should be specific and avoid blandness.
- Analysis should reflect the gap, that is, where the company wishes to be and where it is now.
- It is important to be realistic about the strengths and weaknesses of one own and competitive organizations.

Probably the biggest mistake that is commonly made in SWOT analysis is to provide a long list of points but little logic, argument and evidence. A short list with each point well argued is more likely to be convincing.

6.17. TOWS MATRIX

TOWS matrix is just an extension of SWOT matrix. TOWS stand for Threats, Opportunities, Weaknesses and Strengths. This matrix was proposed by Heinz Weihrich as a strategy formulation matching tool.

TOWS analysis poses a number of questions

What actions should a company take? Should it focus on using company strengths to capitalize on opportunities, or acquire strengths in order to be able to capture opportunities ? Or should it actively try to minimize weaknesses and avoid threats? TOWS matrix illustrates how internal strengths and weaknesses can be matched with external opportunities and threats to generate four sets of possible alternative strategies. This matrix can be used to generate corporate as well as business strategies. An example of TOWS matrix is shown below:

To generate a TOWS matrix, the following steps are to be followed

1. List external opportunities available in the company current and future environment, in the block on the left side of the matrix.
2. List external threats facing the company now and in future in the block on the left side of the matrix.
3. List the specific areas of current and future strengths for the company, in the strengths block across the top of the matrix.
4. List the specific areas of current and future weaknesses for the company in the weaknesses box across the top of the matrix.
5. Generate a series of possible alternative strategies for the company based on particular combinations of the four sets of factors. The four sets of strategies that emerge are:

Table 6.7.

Internal factors/ External factors	Strengths (S)	Weaknesses (W)
Opportunities(O)	**SO** strategies: strategies that use strengths to take advantage of opportunities,	**WO** strategies: strategies that take advantage of opportunities by over -coming weaknesses
Threats(T)	**ST** strategies: strategies that use strengths to avoid threats.	**WT** strategies: strategies that minimize weaknesses and avoid threats.

SO Strategies

SO strategies are generated by thinking of ways in which a company can use its strengths to take advantage of opportunities. This is the most desirable and advantageous strategy as it seeks to mass up the firm strengths to exploit opportunities. For example, Hindustan Lever has been augmenting its strengths by taking over businesses in the food industry, to exploit the growing potential of the food business.

ST Strategies

ST strategies use company strengths as a way to avoid threats. A company may use its technological, financial and marketing strengths to combat a new competition. For example, Hindustan Lever has been employing this strategy to fight the increasing competition from companies like Nirma, Procter & Gamble etc.,

WO Strategies

WO Strategies attempt to take advantage of opportunities by overcoming its weaknesses. For example, for textile machinery manufacturers in India the main weakness was dependence on foreign firms for technology and the long time taken to execute an order. The strategy followed was the thrust given to R&D to develop indigenous technology so as to be in a better position to exploit the opportunity of growing demand for textile machinery.

WT Strategies

WT Strategies are basically defensive strategies and primarily aimed at minimizing weaknesses and avoiding threats. For example, managerial weakness may be solved by change of managerial personnel, training and development etc. Weakness due to excess manpower may be addressed by restructuring, downsizing, and delayering and voluntary retirement schemes. External threats maybe met by joint ventures and other types of strategic alliances. In some cases, an unprofitable business that cannot be revived may be divested. Strategies which utilize strength to take advantage of an opportunity ate generally referred to as exploitative or developmental strategies. Strategies which use a strength to eliminate a weakness may be referred to as blocking strategies which overcome a weakness to take advantage of an opportunity or eliminate a threat may be referred to as remedial strategies. The TOWS matrix is a very useful tool for generating a series of alternative strategies that the decision-makers of the firm might not otherwise have considered. It can be used for the company as a whole or it can be used for a specific business unit within a company. However, it may be noted that the TOWS matrix is only one of many ways to generate alternative strategies.

Critical Assessment of SWOT Analysis

SWOT analysis is one of the most basic techniques for analyzing firm and industry conditions. It provides the material for analyzing internal conditions as well as external conditions of a firm. SWOT analysis can be used in many ways to aid strategic analysis. For example, it can be used for a systematic discussion of a firm resources and basic alternatives that emerge from such an analysis. Such a discussion is necessary because a strength to one firm may be a weakness for another firm, and vice-versa. For example, increased health consciousness of people is a threat to some firms (e.g. tobacco) while it is an opportunity to others (E.g. health clubs).

According to Johnson and Sholes (2OO2), a SWOT analysis summarizes the key issues from the business environment and the strategic capability of an organization that impacts strategy development. This can also be useful as a basis for judging future courses of action. The aim is to identify the extent to which the current strengths and weaknesses are relevant to, and capable of, dealing with the changes taking place in the business environment. It can also be used to assess whether there are opportunities to exploit further the unique resources or core competencies of the organization. Overall, SWOT analysis helps focus discussion on future choices and the extent to which the company is capable of supporting its strategies.

Advantages and Limitations

Advantages

1. It is simple.
2. It portrays the essence of strategy formulation: matching a firm internal strengths and weaknesses with its external opportunities and threats.
3. Together with other techniques like Value Chain Analysis and RBV, SWOT analysis improves the quality of internal analysis.

Limitations

1. It gives a static perspective, and does not reveal the dynamics of competitive environment.
2. SWOT emphasizes a single dimension of strategy (i.e. strength or weakness) and ignores other factors needed for competitive success.
3. Firm strengths do not necessarily help the firm create value or competitive advantage.
4. SWOTs focus on the external environment is too narrow
5. Hill and Westbrook criticize SWOT analysis by saying that it is not a panacea. According to them, some of the criticisms against SWOT analysis are:
   a. It generates lengthy lists
   b. It uses no weights to reflect priorities
   c. It uses ambiguous words and phrases
   d. The same factor can be placed in two categories (e.g. an opportunity may also be a threat).
6. There is no obligation to verify opinions with data or analysis.
7. It is only a simple level of analysis. There is no logical link to strategy implementation.
8. SWOT helps only as a starting point. By itself, SWOT analysis rarely helps a firm develop competitive advantage that it can sustain over time.

In spite of the above criticism and its limitations, SWOT analysis is still a popular analytical tool used by most organizations. It is definitely a useful aid in generating alternative strategies, through what is called TOWS matrix.

6.18. EXPERIENCE CURVE ANALYSIS

Meaning

The concept of the experience curve is akin to a learning curve, which explains that efficiency increases as learning is gained by workers through repetitive productive work. The experience curve is based on the commonly observed phenomenon that unit cost declines as a firm accumulates experience in terms of the cumulative volume of production. In simple terms, the more a company produces the more experience it accumulates. The implication is that larger firms in an industry would tend to have lower unit costs as compared to smaller companies, thereby gaining a competitive cost advantage. An experience curve results flow a variety of factors such as learning effects, economies of scale, product redesign and technological improvements in production.

According to the experience effects theory, if a business produces and sells more units than its competitors, it should also be honing its ability to produce them better than its competitors. By producing better means that the products are of a better quality and are also produced at a lower comparative cost. With lower costs, the pricing can be competitively, thus attracting greater volumes of sale, which in turn, would further lower costs. In this manner, a beneficial, self-perpetuating cycle results that brings in more sales to the experienced producer. Obviously, the logic of the experience curve dictates that lower costs lie in focusing on mass markets. Thus, firms that employ the business strategies of being the first-movers in an industry and capitalizing on their experience to lower costs and garner higher market share than their competitors are destined to gain higher competitive advantage. These firms adopt the business strategy of cost leadership in the industry. However, an experience curve has a limited appeal since specialization offers an alternative route to lower costs. Firms employing the differentiation business strategies rely on a narrow range of products and markets, specializing in catering to a niche market which is not found viable by the larger, layers in the industry. Such firms are often second-movers or late-movers to an industry. The larger players in the industry would prefer the cost leadership route to reap the advantages of the experience curve.

The concept of experience curve is relevant for a number of areas in strategic management. For instance, **the experience curve is considered to be a barrier for new firms contemplating entry** in an industry. It is also used to build market share and discourage competition. For quite some time, till the 1990s, in the two- wheeler industry in India, the experience curve phenomenon seemed to have worked in favour of Bajaj which for the past several years had been the market leader. Serious competition faced by Bajaj Auto I from LML Ltd. and Kinetic Engineering, has altered the competitive situation in the two-wheeler in India. The primary strategic advantage that Bajaj Auto has had is in terms of costs. Other competitors including some like Gujarat Narmada, found it extremely difficult to compete due to the cost differentials that existed. Thus, experience curve yields competitive advantage to a firm if it is a first-mover in an industry successful in cornering a large market share.

6.19. LIFE CYCLE ANALYSIS

Students of management and allied areas are quite familiar with the concept of the product life cycle. Likewise, life cycles are found in markets, businesses and industries. Life cycle is a conceptual model that suggests that products, markets, businesses and industries evolve through sequential stages of introduction, growth, maturity and decline. From the viewpoint of strategic analysis, it is important to note that as cycles move from one stage to the next, the strategic considerations too change.

Let us take the case of the **Familiar Product Life Cycle (PLC).** Almost all marketing textbooks deal' PLC. Essentially, PLC is an S-shaped curve which exhibits relationship of sales with respect to time for a product that passes through the four successive stages introduction (slow sales growth), growth (rapid market acceptance), maturity (slowdown in growth rate) decline (sharp downward drift). If markets, businesses or industries are substituted for product, the concept of PLC could work just as well.

The main advantage of the life cycle concept is that it can be used to diagnose a portfolio of products (or markets, businesses or industries) in order to establish the stage at which each of them exists. Particular attention is to be paid on the businesses that are in the declining stage. Depending on the diagnosis, appropriate strategic choice could be made. For instance, expansion may be feasible alternative for businesses in the introductory and growth stages. Mature businesses may be used as sources of cash for investment in other businesses which need resources. A combination of strategies like selective harvesting, retrenchment, etc. may be adopted for declining businesses. In this way, a balanced portfolio of businesses may be built up by exercising a strategic choice based on the life cycle concept.

The life cycle concept provides a useful framework for analysis for the formulation of strategies, as demonstrated in the previous paragraph. Section 8.5 also discussed the business under different conditions in the embryonic, growth, maturity and decline stages of an industry. Its the benefit of the life cycle concept lies in its ability to provide strategists a convenient method of broad approach to business strategy formulation on the basis of the understanding of the stage of a business is in at a particular point of time. Here, it is significant to note that the life cycle concept is not be used as a guide to when a change occurs in the life cycle. Rather, it is a useful guide to what changes occur over a period of time with regard to the market or industry conditions. Further, it is also remember that the life cycle can sometimes be reversible, as seen in the case of products that are a declining trend. Products, markets, businesses and industries sometimes experience reverse trends happens often in the case of fashion when discarded dress fashions again come in vogue. Strategists be aware of the possibility of such reverse trends in the life cycle.

6.20. GAP ANALYSIS

Focusing on alternatives could be done by visualizing a future state and working backwards from it. This is done through gap analysis. Companies set objectives for a future period of time say 3 to 5 years, and then works backward to find out where it can reach through the present level of efforts. By analyzing the difference between the projected and desire performance, a gap could be found.

Gap analysis is formal study of what a business is doing currently and where it wants to go in the future. It can be conducted in different perspectives, as follows

1. Organization (E.g. Human Resources)
2. Business Direction
3. Business Processes
4. Information Technology

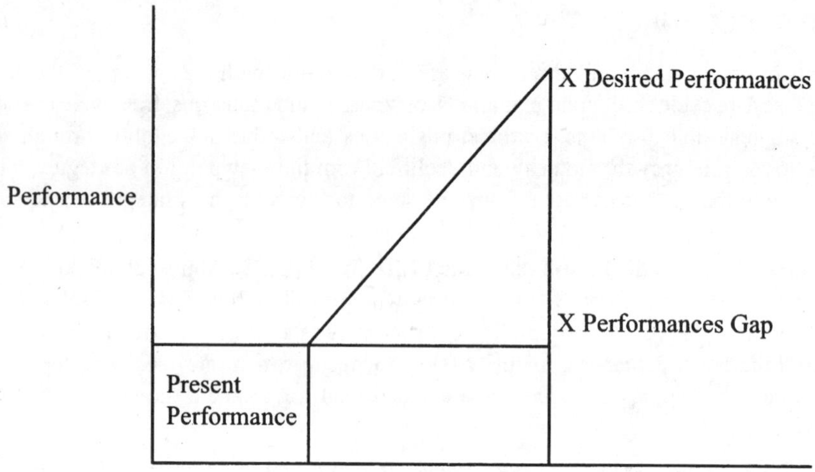

Figure 6.13. Gap Analysis.

Advantages of Gap Analysis

1. It provides an analysis of skill gaps in an organization, department or role.
2. Analysis helps companies to prioritize their training resources.
3. Analysis can help with recruitment and training and its gives management a basis for deciding which staff should be retained and which are expendable.

Disadvantages of Gap Analysis

1. Conducting a skill gap analysis can be costly in terms of the required investment in paper-based assessments or software, as well as the time required from staff to participate and for management to evaluate the results.
2. It may be simpler and more cost-effective to ask line managers to identify skill gaps in their departments, or simply to ask staff in which areas they need additional training.

3. The assessment can be subjective and open to distortion if staff does not answers questions correctly.

6.21. MC KINSEY 7-S FRAMEWORK

MC KINSEY 7-S Framework is one of the most important models which provide help in identifying the issues involved in strategy implementation besides the formulation of strategy itself. Consultants at Mckinsey & company a consulting firm in USA have related 7 factors strategy, Structure, Style, Staff, Skills, System and Shared values for organizational success as presented.

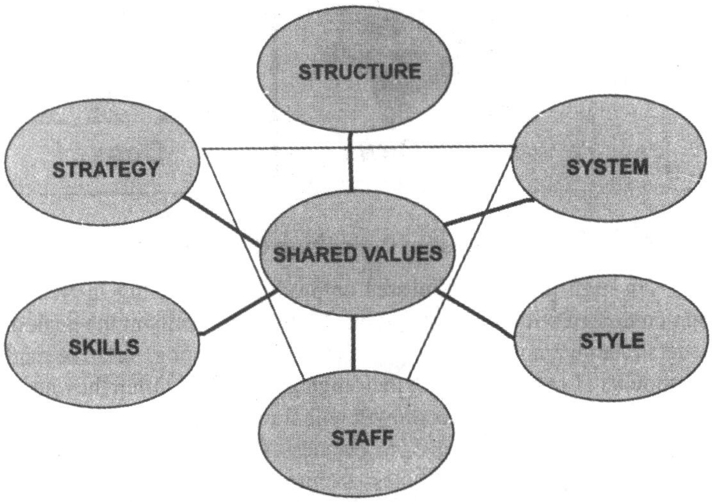

Figure 6.14. Mc Kinsey Framework.

The various components of Mckinseys frame work are as follows:

1. Strategy means to achieve organizational purpose.
2. Structure basic framework to designate responsibilities and functions.
3. System Management tools planning, decision, making, communication and control.
4. Staff: human resources of the organization
5. Skills: organizational and individual capabilities
6. Style: how managers lead and motivate
7. Share values: values, objectives, goals which organizational pursues.

6.22. BCG GROWTH-SHARE MATRIX

It is based on the observation that a company's business units can be classified into four categories based on combinations of market growth and market share relative to the largest competitor, hence the name "growth-share". The growth-share matrix thus maps the business unit positions within these two important determinants of profitability.

The relative market share serves as a measure of SBU strength in the market. The market growth rate provides a measure of market attractiveness. Each of the corporation's product lines or business units is plotted on the matrix according to both the growth rate of the industry in which it competes and its relative market share.

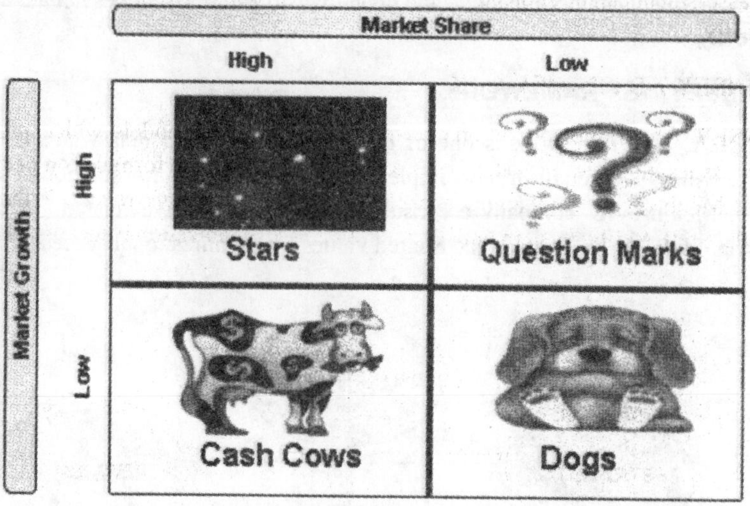

Figure 6.15. The Boston Consulting Group Box ("BCG Box").

Stars: Stars are high growth businesses or products competing in markets where they are relatively strong compared with the competition. They are typically at the peak of their product life cycle. Stars generate large amounts of cash because of their strong relative market share, but also consume large amounts of cash because of their high growth rate. Often they need heavy investment to sustain their growth. Eventually their growth will slow and will become cash cows.

Cash Cows: Cash cows are low-growth businesses or products with a relatively high market share. These are mature, successful businesses with relatively little need for investment. They typically bring in far more money than is needed to maintain their market share. In this decline stage of their life cycle, these products are "milked" for cash that will be invested in new question marks.

Question Marks: Question Marks are businesses or products with low market share but which operate in higher growth markets. Question marks are growing rapidly and thus consume large amounts of cash, but because they have low market shares they do not generate much cash. A question mark (also known as a "problem child") has the potential to gain market share and become a star, and eventually a cash cow when the market growth slows. If the question mark does not succeed in becoming the market leader, then after years of cash consumption it will degenerate into a dog when the market growth declines. Management have to think hard about "question marks" - which ones should they invest in? Which ones should they allow to fail or shrink?

Dogs: Dogs have low market share and a low growth rate and thus neither generate nor consume a large amount of cash. However, dogs are cash traps because of the money tied up in a business that has little potential. Such businesses are candidates for divestiture. The Boston Consulting Group Portfolio Matrix simplicity is its strength - the relative positions of the firm's entire business portfolio can be displayed in a single diagram. Its limitation is market growth rate is only one factor in industry attractiveness, and relative market share is only one factor in competitive advantage. The growth-share matrix overlooks many other factors in these two important determinants of profitability.

6.23. GE NINE-CELL MATRIX

IA-BS MATRIX: (INDUSTRY ATTRACTIVENESS AND BUSINESS STRENGTH MATRIX)

This corporate portfolio analysis technique is based on the pioneering efforts of the general Electric (GE) Company of the United States, supported by the consulting firm of McKinsey &company. The following Exhibit shows a typical GE nine-cell matrix.

The vertical axis represents industry attractiveness, which is a weighted composite rating based on eight different factors. These factors are: market size and growth rate, industry profit margin, competitive intensity, seasonality, cyclicality, economies of scale, technology and social, environmental, legal and human impacts. The horizontal axis represents business strength competitive position which is again a weighted composite rating based on seven factors. These factors are: relative market share, profit margins, ability to compete on price and quality, knowledge of customer and market, competitive strengths and weaknesses, technological capability and calibre of management. As can be seen from the list of the factors, good use can be made of the industry, competitor and SWOT analyses information for determining the weightage and rating to assign to each factor. The industry attractiveness and business unit strength are calculated by first identifying the criteria for each, determining the value of each parameter in the criteria and multiplying that value by a weighting factor. The result is a quantitative measure of industry attractiveness and the business unit's relative performance in that industry. The two composite values for industry attractiveness and business strength / competitive position are plotted for each business in a company's portfolio. The pie charts (or circles) not shown in the exhibit denote the proportional size of the industry and the dark segments represent the company's market share.

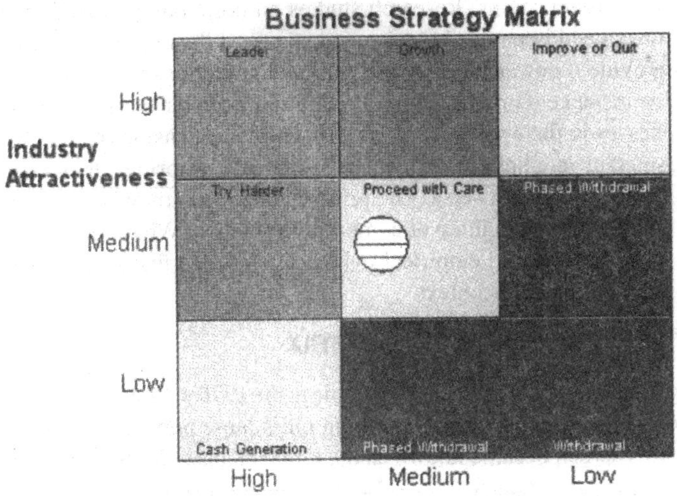

Fig. 6.16. Exhibit General Electric Nine-cell Matrix.

The nine cells of the GE matrix are grouped on the basis of low to high industry attractiveness and weak to strong business strength. Three zones, of three cells each, are made, denoting different combinations represented by green, yellow and red colours. For this reason, the GE matrix is also known as the stoplight strategy matrix. go ahead', to grow and build, indicating expansion strategies. Businesses in the green zone attract major investment. For the yellow zone, the signals is 'wait and see', indicating hold-and-maintain type of strategies, aimed at stability and consolidation. For the red zone, the signals is 'stop', indicating retrenchment strategies of divestment and liquidation or a rebuilding approach for adopting turnaround strategies.

The GE nine-cell matrix offers some distinct advantages. It incorporates a large variety of strategic variables like the market share and industry size. The GE matrix is also a powerful analytical tool to channel corporate resources to businesses that combine medium to high industry attractiveness with average to strong business strength/competitive position. On the other hand, the major drawback of the GE matrix is that it only provides broad strategic prescriptions rather than the specifics of business strategy. Overall, corporate portfolio analysis can help companies that are running diverse businesses, to develop feasible strategic alternatives and to allocate resources among them. Other benefits include a more perceptive understanding of the businesses, leading to better strategic decisions and availability of an interesting vocabulary and graphic aids for communication.

Like all analytical techniques, portfolio analysis has its drawbacks. Problems arise in measuring parameters like the actual growth rate of a business. There are also organizational and motivational problems arising due to the adoption of the recommendations emerging out of portfolio analysis. There are four major flaws of the portfolio techniques. First, an assessment of businesses in terms of just two dimensions of market share and industry growth can be misleading as a number of other factors need to be taken into account. Secondly, the relation between relative market share and cost savings is not directly proportional; companies with low market share and focused on a market niche could have low operations cost. Third, a high market share in a low-growth industry does not necessarily result in a large cash flow. Lastly, none of the portfolio techniques treat the source of value creation from diversification strategies. SBUs cannot be just treated as independent units as they are linked to the corporate headquarters and share skills and competencies. Real value may be derived from managing successfully, a diversified portfolio of businesses, rather than just putting together the 'right' portfolio of businesses.

No organized evidence is available regarding the use and application of portfolio analysis techniques by Indian organizations. Research studies on corporate planning in Indian companies, though dealing with several issues, fail to take cognizance of the use of portfolio models. However, these models do provide a powerful analytical tool and could be appropriately adapted to suit the Indian context. For instance, companies could take into account the governmental priorities and rate different businesses in their portfolio along the priority dimension (e.g. high, medium, or low). Whenever the businesses rate high in terms of governmental priorities, they may be considered as high potential businesses and vice versa. The priority dimension may be used along with the other dimensions of product/market evolution or competitive position. What is being suggested, however, lies in the realm of conjecture and empirical evidence is needed first to establish the suitability of the portfolio models in the Indian context.

6.24. GE MULTIFACTOR PORTFOLIO MATRIX

In consulting engagements with General Electric in the 1970's, McKinsey & Company developed a nine-cell portfolio matrix as a tool for screening GE's large portfolio of strategic business units (SBU). This business screen became known as the GE/McKinsey Matrix and is shown below:

The GE / McKinsey matrix is similar to the BCG growth-share matrix in that it maps strategic business units on a grid of the industry and the SBU's position in the industry. The GE matrix however, attempts to improve upon the BCG matrix in the following two ways:

		Business Unit Strength		
		High	Medium	Low
Industry Attractiveness	High			
	Medium			
	Low			

GE / McKinsey Matrix

- The GE matrix generalizes the axes as "Industry Attractiveness" and "Business Unit Strength" whereas the BCG matrix uses the market growth rate as a proxy for industry attractiveness and relative market share as a proxy for the strength of the business unit.
- The GE matrix has nine cells vs. four cells in the BCG matrix.
- Industry attractiveness and business unit strength are calculated by first identifying criteria for each, determining the value of each parameter in the criteria, and multiplying that value

by a weighting factor. The result is a quantitative measure of industry attractiveness and the business unit's relative performance in that industry.

Industry Attractiveness

The vertical axis of the GE / McKinsey matrix is industry attractiveness, which is determined by factors such as the following:

- Market growth rate
- Market size
- Demand variability
- Industry profitability
- Industry rivalry
- Global opportunities
- Macro environmental factors (PEST)

Each factor is assigned a weighting that is appropriate for the industry

Business Unit Strength

The horizontal axis of the GE / McKinsey Matrix is the strength of the business unit. Some factors that can be used to determine business unit strength include:

- Market share
- Growth in market share
- Brand equity
- Distribution channel access
- Production capacity
- Profit margins relative to competitors

The business unit strength index can be calculated by multiplying the estimated value of each factor by the factor's weighting, as done for industry attractiveness.

Plotting the Information

Each business unit can be portrayed as a circle plotted on the matrix, with the information conveyed as follows:

- Market size is represented by the size of the circle.
- Market share is shown by using the circle as a pie chart.
- The expected future position of the circle is portrayed by means of an arrow.

The following is an example of such a representation:

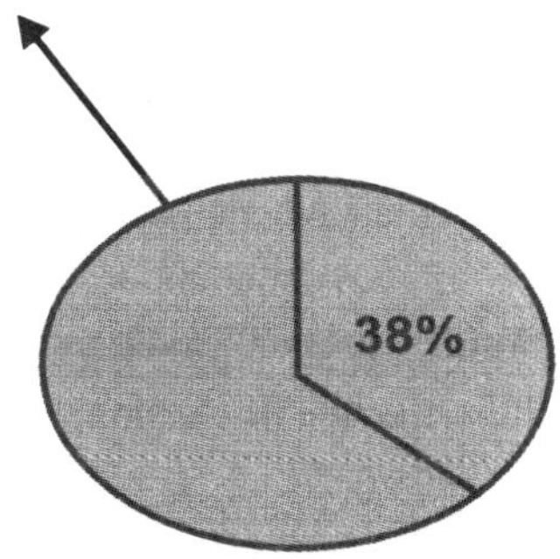

Figure 6.17.

The shading of the above circle indicates a 38% market share for the strategic business unit. The arrow in the upward left direction indicates that the business unit is projected to gain strength relative to competitors, and that the business unit is in an industry that is projected to become more attractive. The tip of the arrow indicates the future position of the center point of the circle.

Strategic Implications

Resource allocation recommendations can be made to grow, hold, or harvest a strategic business unit based on its position on the matrix as follows:

- Grow strong business units in attractive industries, average business units in attractive industries, and strong business units in average industries.
- Hold average businesses in average industries, strong businesses in weak industries, and weak business in attractive industries.

- Harvest weak business units in unattractive industries, average business units in unattractive industries, and weak business units in average industries.

There are strategy variations within these three groups. For example, within the harvest group the firm would be inclined to quickly divest itself of a weak business in an unattractive industry, whereas it might perform a phased harvest of an average business unit in the same industry.

6.25. INFRASTRUCTURE AND EFFICIENCY

A company's infrastructure—that is, its structure, culture, style of strategic leader- ship, and control system—determines the context within which all other value creation activities take place. It follows that improving infrastructure can help a company increase efficiency and lower its cost structure. Above all, an appropriate infrastructure can help foster a companywide commitment to efficiency aid promote cooperation among different functions in pursuit of efficiency goals. For now, it is important to note that strategic leadership is especially important in building a companywide commitment to efficiency. The leadership task is to articulate a vision that recognizes the need for all functions of a company to focus on improving efficiency. It is not enough to improve the efficiency of production, or of marketing, or of R&D in a piecemeal fashion. Achieving superior efficiency requires a companywide commitment to this goal that must be articulated by general and functional managers. A further leadership task is to facilitate cross-functional cooperation needed to achieve superior efficiency.

For example, designing products that are easy to manufacture requires that production and R&D personnel communicate; integrating JIT systems with production scheduling requires close communication between material management and production; designing self-managing teams to perform production tasks requires close cooperation between human resources and production; and so on. Table 6.8 summarizes the primary roles that various functions must take in order to achieve superior efficiency. Bear in mind that achieving superior efficiency is not something that can be tackled on a function-by-function basis.

Table 6.8.

Value Creation Function	Primary Roles
Infrastructure (leadership)	Provide companywide commitment to efficiency Facilitate cooperation among functions
Production	Where appropriate, pursue economies of scale & learning economics Implement flexible manufacturing systems
Marketing	Where appropriate, adopt aggressive marketing to ride down the experience curve. Limit customer defection rates by building brand loyalty
	Secondary Roles
Materials Management	Implement JIT systems
R&D	Design products for ease of manufacture Seek process innovations
Information systems	Use information systems to automate processes. Use information systems to reduce costs of production
Human resources	Institute training programs to build skills Implement self-managing teams Implement pay for performance

1. Achieving Superior Quality

The quality can be thought of in terms of two dimensions: product reliability and other product attributes. High-quality products are both reliable, in the sense that they do the job they were designed for and do it well, and are also perceived by consumers to have superior attributes. We also noted that superior quality gives a company two advantages. First, a strong reputation for quality allows a company to differentiate itself from rivals by creating more value in the eyes of customers, and this gives it the option of charging a premium price for its products. Second, eliminating defects or errors from the production process reduces waste, increases efficiency, and lowers the cost structure of the company and increases its profitability. For example, reducing the number of defects in a company's manufacturing process will lower the cost of goods sold as a percentage of revenues, thereby raising the company's return on sales and return on invested capital. In this section, we look in more depth at what managers can do to enhance the reliability and other attributes of the company's product offering.

2. Attaining Superior Reliabilty

The principal tool that managers use to increase the reliability of their product offering is Total Quality Management, or some variation of that tool, such as the Six Sigma Reliability quality improvement methodology made famous by General Electric. Total Quality Management (TQM) stresses that all company operations should be oriented toward improving the reliability of a company's product offerings. The TQM concept was developed by a number of American consultants, including W. Edwards Deming, Joseph Juran, and A. V. Feigenbaum. Originally, these consultants won few converts in the United States. However, managers in Japan embraced their ideas enthusiastically and even named their premier annual prize for manufacturing excellence after Deming. The philosophy underlying TQM, as articulated by Deming, is based on the following five-step chain reaction:

1. Improved quality means that costs decrease because of less rework, fewer mistakes, fewer delays, and better use of time and materials.
2. As a result, productivity improves.
3. Better quality leads to higher market share and allows the company to raise prices.
4. This increases the company's profitability and allows it to stay in business.
5. Thus the company creates more jobs.

- Deming identified a number of steps that should be part of any TQM program: A company should have a clear business model to specify where it is going and how it is going to get there.
- Management should embrace the philosophy that mistakes, defects, and poor-quality materials are not acceptable and should be eliminated.
- Quality of supervision should be improved by allowing more time for supervisors to work with employees and giving them appropriate skills for the job.
- Management should create an environment in which employees will not fear reporting problems or recommending improvements.
- Work standards should be defined not only as numbers or quotas but should also include some notion of quality to promote the production of defect-free output.

Management is responsible for training employees in new skills to keep pace with changes in the workplace.

- Achieving better quality requires the commitment of everyone in the company.

3. Implementing Reliability Improvement Methodologies

Among companies that have successfully adopted quality improvement methodologies, certain imperatives stand out. These are discussed below in the order in which they are usually tackled in companies implementing quality improvement programs. What needs to be stressed first, however, is that TQM is a cross-functional process. Its implementation requires close cooperation among all functions in the pursuit of the common goal of improving quality; it is a process that cuts across functions. The role played by the different functions in implementing TQM is summarized in Table 6.9.

Table 6.9. The Role Played by Different Functions in Implementing TQM

Value Creation Function	Primary Roles
Infrastructure (leadership)	Provide leadership and commitment to quality Find ways to measure quality Set goals and create incentives Solicit input from employees Encourage cooperation among functions
Production	Shorten production runs Trace defects back to source
Marketing	Focus on the customer Provide customers feedback on quality
	Secondary Roles
Materials Management	Rationalize suppliers Help suppliers implement TQM Trace defects back to suppliers
R&D	Design products that are easy to manufacture
Information systems	Use information systems to monitor defect rates
Human resources	Institute TQM training programs Organize employees into quality teams

4. Build Organization Commitment to Quality

There is evidence that TQM will do little to improve the performance of a company unless everyone in the organization embraces it. When Xerox launched its quality program, its first step was to educate the entire work force, from top management to down, in the importance and operation of the TQM concepts. It did so by forming groups, beginning with a group at the top of the organization that included the CEO. The top group was the first to receive basic TQM training. Each member of this group was then given the task of training a group at the next level in the hierarchy and so on down throughout the organization until all 100,000 employees had received basic TQM training. Both top management and the human resource function of the company can play a major role in this process. Top management has the responsibility of exercising the leadership required to make a commitment to quality an organization-wide goal. The human resource function must take on responsibility for companywide training in TQM techniques.

5. Focus on the Customer. TQM practitioners see a focus on the customer as the starting point, and indeed, of the whole quality philosophy. The marketing function, because it provides the primary point of contact with the customer, should play a major role here. It needs to identify what customers want from the good or service that the company provides, what the company actually provides to customers, and the gap between what customers want and what they get, which could be called the quality gap. Then, together with the other functions of the company, it needs to formulate a plan for closing the quality gap.

6. Find Ways to Measure Quality. Another imperative of any TQM program is to create a metric that can be used to measure quality. This is relatively easy in manufacturing companies, where quality can be measured by criteria such as defects per million parts. It tends to be more difficult in service companies, but with a little creativity, suitable metrics can be devised. For example, one of the metrics Florida Power & Light uses to measure quality is meter-reading errors per month. Another is the frequency and duration of power outages. L. L. Bean, the Freeport, Maine, mail-order retailer of outdoor gear, uses the percentage of orders that are correctly filled as one of its quality measures. For some banks, the key measures are the number of customer defections per year and the number of statement errors per thousand customers. The common theme that runs through all these examples is identifying what quality means from a customer's perspective and devising a method to gauge this. Top management should take primary responsibility for formulating metrics to measure quality, but to succeed in this effort, it must receive input from the various functions of the company.

7. Set Goals and Create Incentives. Once a metric has been devised, the next step is to set a challenging quality goal and create incentives for reaching it. Xerox again provides an example. When it introduced its TQM program, its initial goal was to reduce defective parts from 25,000 per million to 1,000 per million. One way of creating incentives to attain such a goal is to link rewards, like bonus pay and promotional opportunities, to the goal. Thus, within many companies that have adopted self-managing teams, the bonus pay of team members is determined in part by their ability to attain quality goals. The task of setting goals and creating incentives is one of the key tasks of top management.

8. Solicit Input from Employees. Employees can be a vital source of information regarding the sources of poor quality. Therefore, a framework must be established for soliciting employee suggestions for improvements. Quality circles, which are meetings of groups of employees, have often been used to achieve this goal. Other companies have used self-managing teams as forums for discussing quality improvement ideas. Whatever forum is used, soliciting input from lower-level employees requires that management be open to receiving, and acting on, bad news and criticism from employees. According to Deming, one problem with U.S. management is that it has grown used to "killing the bearer of bad tidings." But, he argues, managers who are committed to the quality concept must recognize that bad news is a gold mine of information.

9. Identify Defects and Trace Them to Source. TQM preaches the need to identify defects during the work process, trace them to their source, find out what caused them, and make corrections so that they do not recur. Production and materials management typically have primary responsibility for this task. To uncover defects, Deming advocates the use of statistical procedures to pinpoint variations in the quality of goods or services. Deming views variation as the enemy of quality. Once variations have been identified, they must be traced to their source and eliminated. One technique that helps greatly in tracing defects to their source is reducing lot sizes for manufactured products. With short production runs, defects show up immediately. Consequently, they can be quickly traced to the source, and the problem can be addressed. Reducing lot sizes also means that when defective products are produced, their number will not be large, thus decreasing waste. Flexible manufacturing techniques, discussed earlier, can be used to reduce lot sizes without raising costs. Consequently, adopting flexible manufacturing techniques is an important aspect of a TQM program.

10. JIT inventory systems also play a part. Under a JIT system, defective parts enter the manufacturing process immediately; they are not warehoused for several months before use. Hence, defective inputs can be quickly spotted. The problem can then be traced to the supply source and corrected before more defective parts are produced. Under a more traditional system, the practice of warehousing parts for months before they are used may mean that large numbers of defects are produced by a supplier before they enter the production process.

11. Supplier Relations. A major source of poor-quality finished goods is poor- quality component parts. To decrease product defects, a company has to work with its suppliers to improve the quality of the parts they supply. The primary responsibility in this area falls on the materials management function, which interacts with suppliers.

To implement JIT systems with suppliers and to get suppliers to adopt their own TQM programs, two steps are necessary. First, the number of suppliers has to be reduced to manageable proportions. Second, the company must commit to building a cooperative long-term relationship with the suppliers that remain. Asking suppliers to invest in JIT and TQM systems is asking them to make major investments that tie them to the company. For example, in order to implement a JIT system fully, the company may ask a supplier to relocate its manufacturing plant so that it is next door to the company's assembly plant. Suppliers are likely to be hesitant about making such investments unless they feel that the company is committed to an enduring, long-term relationship with them.

12. Design for Ease of Manufacture. The more assembly steps a product requires, the more opportunities there are for making mistakes. Designing products with fewer parts should make assembly easier and result in fewer defects. Both R&D and manufacturing need to be involved in designing products that are easy to manufacture.

13. Break Down Barriers Among Functions. Implementing TQM requires organization-wide commitment and substantial cooperation among functions. R&D has to cooperate with production to design products that are easy to manufacture, marketing has to cooperate with production and R&D so that customer problems identified by marketing can be acted on, human resource management has to cooperate with all the other functions of the company in order to devise suitable quality-training programs, and so on.

6.26. DEVELOPING SUPERIOR ATTRIBUTES

A product is a bundle of different attributes, and reliability is just one of them, albeit an important one. Products can also be differentiated by attributes such as their form, features, performance, durability, and styling. In addition, a company can differentiate itself by emphasizing attributes of the service associated with the product, such as ordering ease, prompt delivery, easy installation, the availability of customer training and consulting, and maintenance services. Dell Computer, for example, differentiates itself on ease of ordering (via the Web), prompt delivery, easy installation, and the ready availability of customer support and maintenance services. Differentiation can also be based on the attributes of the people in the company whom customers interact with when making a product purchase, such as their competence, courtesy, credibility, responsiveness, and communication. Singapore Airlines, for example, enjoys an excellent reputation for quality service, largely because passengers perceive their flight attendants as competent, courteous, and responsive to their needs. Thus, we can talk about the product attributes, service attributes, and personnel attributes associated with a company's product offering (see Table 6.10).

For a product to be regarded as high quality, a company's product offering must be seen as superior to that of rivals. Achieving a perception of high quality on any of these attributes requires specific actions by managers. First, it is important for managers to collect marketing intelligence indicating which of these attributes are most important to customers. For example, consumers of personal computers may place a low weight on durability because they expect their PC to be made obsolete by technological advances within three years, but they may place a high weight on features and performance. Similarly, ease of ordering and timely delivery may be very important attributes for customers of online booksellers (as they indeed are for customers of Amazon.com), whereas customer training and consulting may be very important attributes for customers who purchase complex business-to-business software to manage their relationships with suppliers.

Second, once the company has identified the attributes that are important to customers, it needs to design its products, and the associated services, so that those attributes are embodied in the product, and it needs to make sure that personnel in the company are appropriately trained so that the correct attributes are emphasized, This requires close coordination between marketing and product development (the topic of the next section), and the involvement of the human resource management function in employee selection and training.

Third, the company must decide which of the significant attributes to promote and how best to position those attributes in the minds of consumers, that is, how to tailor the marketing message so that it creates a consistent image in the minds of customers. At this point, it is important to recognize that although a product might be differentiated on the basis of six attributes, covering all of those attributes in the company's communication messages may lead to an unfocused message. Many marketing experts advocate promoting only one or two central attributes to customers. For example, Volvo consistently emphasizes the safety and durability of its vehicles in all marketing messages, creating the perception in the minds of consumers (backed by product design) that Volvo cars are safe and durable. Volvo cars are also very reliable and have high performance, but the company does not emphasize these attributes in its marketing messages. In contrast, Porsche emphasizes performance and styling in all of its marketing messages; thus, a Porsche is positioned differently in the minds of consumers than a Volvo is. Both are regarded as high-quality products because both have superior attributes, but the attributes that the two companies have chosen to emphasize are very different. They are differentiated from the average car in different ways.

Table 6.10. Attributes Associated with a Product Offering

Product Attributes	Service Attributes	Associated Personnel attributes
Form	Ordering ease	Competence
Features	Delivery	Courtesy
Performance	Installation	Credibility
Durability	Customer training	Reliability
Reliability	Customer consulting	Responsiveness
Style	Maintenance and repair	Communication

Finally, it must be recognized that competition does not stand still, but instead produces continual improvement in product attributes and often the development of new product attributes. This is obvious in fast-moving high-tech industries where product features that were considered leading edge just a few years ago are now obsolete, but the same process is also at work in more stable industries. For example, the rapid diffusion of microwave ovens during the 1980s required food companies to build new attributes into their frozen food products: they had to maintain their texture and consistency while being microwaved. A product could not be considered high quality unless it could do that. This speaks to the importance of having a strong R&D function in the company that can work with marketing and manufacturing to continually upgrade the quality of the attributes that are designed into the company's product offerings.

6.27. ACHIEVING SUPERIOR INNOVATION

In many ways, building distinctive competencies that result in innovation is the most important source of competitive advantage. This is because innovation can result in new products that better satisfy customer needs, can improve the quality (attributes) of existing products, or can reduce the costs of making products that customers want. Thus, the ability to develop innovative new products or processes gives a company a major competitive advantage that allows it to (1) differentiate its products and charge a premium price and/or (2) lower its cost structure below that of its rivals.

Competitors, however, attempt to imitate successful innovations and often succeed. Therefore, maintaining a competitive advantage requires a continuing commitment to innovation.

1. Robert Cooper found that successful new product launches are major drivers of superior profitability. Cooper looked at more than 200 new product introductions and found that of those classified as successes, some 50 percent achieve a return on investment in excess of 33 percent, half have a payback period of two years or less, and half achieve a market share in excess of 35 percent. Many companies have established a track record for successful innovation. Among them are Du Pont, which has produced a steady stream of successful innovations,\such s cellophane, Nylon, Freon, and Teflon; Sony, whose successes include the Walkman, the Compact Disc, and the PlayStation; Nokia, which has been a leader in the development of wireless phones; Pfizer, a drug company that during the 1990s and early 2000s produced eight blockbuster new drugs; 3M, which has applied its core competency in tapes and adhesives to developing a wide range of. New products; Intel, which has consistently managed to lead in the development of innovative new microprocessors to run personal computers; and Cisco Systems, whose innovations helped to pave the for the rapid growth of the Internet.

2. The High Failure Rate of Innovation

Although promoting innovation can be a source of competitive advantage, the failure rate of innovative new products is high. One study of product development in the chemical, drug, petroleum, and electronics industries suggested that only about 20 percent of R&D projects ultimately result in a commercially successful products or process. An in-depth case study of product development in three companies (one in chemicals and two in drugs) reported that about 60 percent of R&D projects reached technical completion, 30 percent were commercialized, and only 12 percent earned a profit that exceeded the company's cost of capital.38 A famous study by the consulting division of Booz, Allen & Hamilton found that over one-third of 13,000 new customer and industrial products failed to meet company-specific financial and strategic performance criteria.39 Another study found that 45 percent of new products introduced into the marketplace did not meet their profitability goals.This evidence suggests that many R&D projects do not result in a commercial product and that between 33 percent and 60 percent of all new products that do reach the marketplace fail to generate an adequate economic return. Two well-publicized product failures are Apple Computer's Newton, a personal digital assistant, and Sony's Betamax format in the video player and recorder market. While many reasons have been advanced to explain why so many new products fail to generate an economic return, five explanations for failure appear on most lists: uncertainty, poor commercialization, poor positioning strategy, technological myopia, and being slow to market.

3. Uncertainty: New-product development is an inherently risky process. It requires testing a hypothesis whose answer is impossible to know prior to market introduction: Have we tapped an unmet customer need? Is there sufficient market demand for this new technology? Although good market research can reduce the uncertainty about likely future demand for a new technology, uncertainty cannot be eradicated, so a certain failure rate is to be expected. The failure rate is higher for quantum product innovations than for incremental innovations. A **quantum innovation** represents a radical departure from existing technology—the introduction of something that is new to the world. The development of the World Wide Web can be considered a quantum innovation in communications technology. Other quantum innovations include the development of the first photocopier by Xerox, the first videocassette recorder by AMPEX, and the first contact lenses by Bausch and Lomb. Incremental innovation refers to an extension of existing technology. For example, Intel's Pentium Pro microprocessor is an incremental product innovation because it builds on the existing microprocessor architecture of Intel's X86 series. The uncertainty of future demand for a new product much greater if that product represents a quantum innovation that is new to the world than if it is an incremental innovation designed to replace an established product whose demand profile is already well known. Consequently, the failure rate tends to be higher for quantum innovations.

4. Poor Commercialization. A second reason frequently cited to explain the high failure rate of new product introductions is poor commercialization—something that occurs when there is definite customer demand for a new product, but the product is not well adapted to customer needs because of factors such as poor design and poor quality. For instance, many of the early personal computers failed to sell because customers needed to understand computer programming to use them. Steve Jobs at Apple Computer understood that if the technology could be made user friendly (if it could be commercialized), there would be an enormous market for it. Hence, the original personal computers that Apple marketed incorporated little in the way of radically new technology but they made existing technology accessible to the average person. Paradoxically, the failure of Apple Computer to establish a market for the Newton, the hand-held personal digital system that Apple introduced in the summer of 1993, can be traced to poor commercialization of a potentially attractive technology. Apple predicted a $1 billion market for the Newton, but sales failed to materialize when it became clear that the Newton's handwriting software, an attribute that Apple chose to emphasize in its marketing promotions, could not adequately recognize messages written on the Newton's message pad.

5. Poor Positioning Strategy. Poor positioning strategy arises when a company introduces a potentially attractive new product, but sales fail to materialize because it is poorly positioned in the marketplace. Positioning strategy is the specific set of options a company adopts for a product on four main dimensions of marketing: price, distribution, promotion and advertising, and product features. Apart from poor product quality, another reason for the failure of the Apple Newton was poor positioning strategy. The Newton was introduced at such a high initial price (close to $1,000) that there would probably have been few buyers even if the technology had been adequately commercialized.

6. Technological Myopia. Another reason that many new product introductions fail is that companies often make the mistake of marketing a technology for which there is not enough customer demand. Technological myopia occurs when a company gets blinded by the wizardry of a new technology and fails to examine whether there is customer demand for the product. This problem may have been a factor in the failure of the desktop computer introduced by NeXT in the late 1980s (NeXT was founded by Steve Jobs, the founder of Apple Computer). Technologically, the NeXT machines were clearly ahead of their time with advanced software and hardware features that would not be incorporated into most PCs for another decade. However, customer acceptance was very slow, primarily because of the complete lack of applications software such as spreadsheet and word processing programs to run on the machines. Management at NeXT was so enthused by the technology incorporated in their new computer that they ignored this basic market reality. After several years of slow sales, NeXT eventually withdrew the machines from the marketplace.

7. Slow to Market. Finally, companies fail when they are slow to get their products to market. The more time that elapses between initial development and final marketing—that is, the slower the "cycle time"—the more likely it is that someone else will beat the company to market and gain a first-mover advantage. By and large, slow innovators update their products less frequently than fast innovators do. Consequently, they can be perceived as technical laggards relative to the fast innovators. In the car industry, General Motors has suffered from being a slow innovator. Its product development cycle has been about five years, compared with two to three years at Honda, Toyota, and Mazda and three to four years at Ford. Because they are based on five-year-old technology and design concepts, GM cars' are already out of date when they reach the market.

8. Building Competencies in Innovation

Companies can take a number of steps to build a competency in innovation and avoid failure. Five of the most important steps seem to be i) building skills in basic and applied scientific research, ii) developing a good process for project selection and project management, iii) cross-functional integration, iv) product development teams, and v) partly parallel development processes.

i) Building Skills in Basic and Applied Research. Building skills in basic and applied research requires the employment of research scientists and engineers and the establishment of a work environment that fosters creativity. A number of top companies try to achieve this by setting up university-style research facilities, where scientists and engineers are given time to work on their own research projects, in addition to projects that are linked directly to ongoing company research. At Hewlett- Packard, for example, company labs are open to engineers around the clock. Hewlett- Packard even encourages its corporate researchers to devote 10 percent of company time to exploring their own ideas and does not penalize them if they fail. 3M allows researchers to spend 15 percent of the workweek researching any topic that intrigues them, as long as there is the potential of a payoff for the company. The most famous outcome of this policy is the ubiquitous Post-its. The idea for them evolved from a researcher's desire to find a way to keep the bookmark from falling out of his hymnal. Post-its are now a major 3M business, with annual revenues of around $300 million.

ii) Project Selection and Management. Project management is the overall management of the innovation process, from generation of the original concept, through development, and into final production and shipping. Project management requires three important skills: the ability to generate as many good ideas as possible, the ability to select among competing projects at an early stage of development so that the most promising receive funding and potential costly failures are killed off, and the ability to minimize time to market. The concept of the development funnel, divided into three phases, summarizes what is required to build these skills.

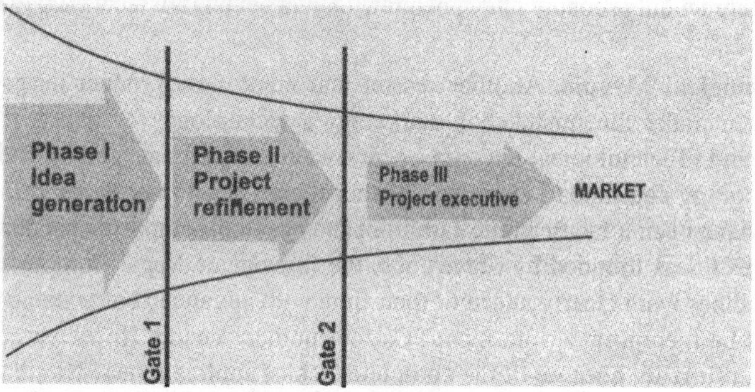

Figure 6.18. The Development Funnel.

The objective in Phase I is to widen the mouth of the tunnel to encourage as much idea generation as possible. To this end, a company should solicit input from all its functions, as well as from customers, competitors, and suppliers. At Gate 1, the funnel narrows. Here ideas are reviewed by a cross-functional team of managers who did not participate in the original concept development. Concepts that are ready to proceed then move to Phase II, where the details of the project proposal are worked out. Note that Gate I is not a go/no-go evaluation point. At this screen, ideas may be sent back for further concept development and then resubmitted for evaluation.

During Phase II, which typically lasts only one or two months, the data and information from Phase I are put into a form that will enable senior management to evaluate proposed projects against competing projects. Normally, this requires the development of a careful project plan, complete with details of the proposed target market, attainable market share, likely revenues, development costs, production costs, key milestones, and the like. The next big selection point, Gate 2, is a go/no-go evaluation point. Senior managers review the projects under consideration and select those that seem likely winners and make most sense from a strategic perspective given the long-term goals of the company. The overriding objective is to select projects whose successful completion will help to maintain or build a competitive advantage for the company. A related objective is to ensure that the company does not spread its scarce capital and human resources too thinly over too many projects and instead concentrates resources on projects where the probability of success and potential returns are most attractive. Any project selected to go forward at this stage will be funded and staffed, the expectation being that it will be carried through to market introduction. In Phase III, the project development proposal is executed by a cross- functional product development team

iii) Cross-Functional Integration. Tight cross-functional integration between R&D, production, and marketing can help a company to ensure that:

a) Product development projects are driven by customer needs.
b) New products are designed for ease of manufacture.
c) Development costs are kept in check.
d) Time to market is minimized.
e) Close integration between R&D and marketing is achieved to ensure that product development projects are driven by the needs of customers.

iv) Product Development Teams. One of the best ways to achieve cross-functional integration is to establish cross-functional product development teams, composed of representatives from R&D, marketing, and production. The objective of a team should be to take a product development project from the initial concept development to market introduction. A number of attributes seem to be important in order for a product development team to function effectively and meet all its development milestones.

v) Partly Parallel Development Processes. One way in which a product development team can compress the time it takes to develop a product and bring to market is to use a partly parallel development process. Traditionally, product development processes have been organized on a sequential basis. A problem with this kind of process is that product development proceeds without manufacturing issues in mind. Most significant, because the basic design of a product is completed prior to the design of a manufacturing process and full-scale commercial production, there is no early warning system to indicate manufacturability. As a consequence, the company may find that it cannot cost-efficiently manufacture the product and have to send it back to the design stage for redesign. The cycle time lengthens as the product bounces back and forth between stages.

To solve this problem, companies typically use a process similar to that illustrated in Figure 6.19. In the partly parallel development process, development stages overlap so that, for example, work starts on the development of the production process before the product design is finalized. By reducing the need for expensive and time- consuming product redesigns, such a process can significantly reduce the time it takes to develop a new product and bring it to market. For an example, consider what occurred after Intel Corporation introduced its 386 microprocessor in 1986. A number of companies, including IBM and Compaq, were racing to be the first to introduce a 386-based personal computer. Compaq beat IBM by six months and gained a major share of the high-power market mainly because it used a cross-functional team and a partly parallel process to develop the product. The team included engineers (R&D) and marketing, production, and finance people. Each function worked in parallel rather than sequentially. While engineers were designing the product, production people were setting up the manufacturing facilities, marketing people were working on distribution and planning marketing campaigns, and the finance people were working on project funding.

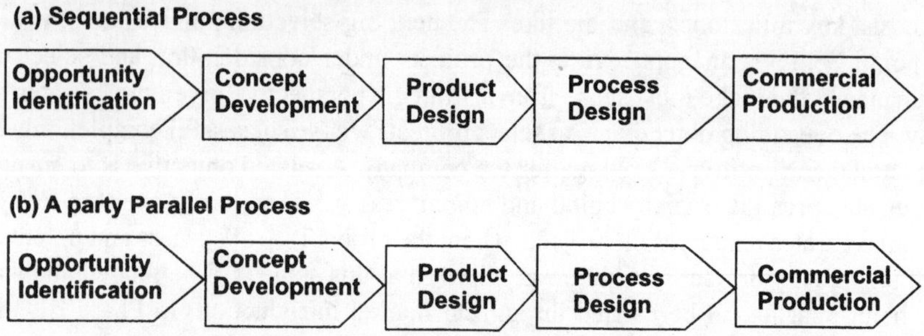

Figure 6.19. Sequential and Partly Parallel Development.

6.28. ACHIEVING SUPERIOR RESPONSIVENESS TO CUSTOMERS

To achieve superior responsiveness to customers, a company must give customers what they want, when they want it, and at a price they are willing to pay—so long as the company's long-term profitability is not compromised in the process. Customer responsiveness is an important differentiating attribute that can help to build brand loyalty. Strong product differentiation and brand loyalty give a company more pricing options; it can charge a premium price for its products or keep prices low to sell more goods and services to customers. Either way, the company that is more responsive to its customers' needs than rivals will have a competitive advantage, all else being equal.

1. Achieving superior responsiveness to customers means giving customers value for money, and steps taken to improve the efficiency of a company's production process and the quality of its products should be consistent with this aim. In addition, giving customers what they want may require the development of new products with new features. In other words, achieving superior efficiency, quality, and innovation are all part of achieving superior responsiveness to customers. There are two other prerequisites f6r attaining this goal. First, a company has to develop a competency in listening to and focusing on its customers and in investigating and identifying their needs. Second, it constantly needs to seek better ways to satisfy those needs.

2. Customer Focus: A company cannot be responsive to its customers needs unless it knows what those needs are. Thus, the first step to building superior responsiveness to customers is to motivate the whole company to focus on the customer. The means to this end are demonstrating leadership, shaping employee attitudes, and using mechanisms for bringing customers into the company.

3. Leadership: Customer focus must start at the top of the organization. A commitment to superior responsiveness to customers brings attitudinal changes throughout a company that ultimately can be built only through strong leadership. A mission statement that puts customers first is one way to send a clear message to employees about the desired focus. Another avenue is top management's own actions. For example, Tom Monaghan, the founder of Domino's Pizza, stayed close to the customer by visiting as many stores as possible every week, running some deliveries himself, insisting that other top managers do the same, and eating Domino's pizza regularly.

4. Employee Attitudes: Leadership alone is not enough to attain a superior customer focus. All employees must see the customer as the focus of their activity and be trained to focus on the customer, whether their function is marketing, manufacturing, R&D, or accounting. The objective should be to make employees think of themselves as customers—to put themselves in customers' shoes. At that point, employees will be better able to identify ways to improve the quality of a customer's experience with the company.

To reinforce this mindset, incentive systems within the company should reward employees for satisfying customers. For example, senior managers at the Four Seasons hotel chain, who pride themselves on their customer, focus, like to tell the story of Roy Dyment, a doorman in Toronto who neglected to load a departing guest's briefcase into his taxi. The doorman called the guest, a lawyer, in Washington D.C., and found that he desperately needed the briefcase for a morning meeting. Dyment hopped on a plane to Washington and returned if—without first securing approval from his boss. Far from punishing Dyment for making a mistake and for not checking with management before going to Washington, the Four Seasons responded by naming Dyment Employee of the Year. This action sent a powerful message to Four Seasons employees about the importance of satisfying customer needs.

5. Bringing Customers into the Company: "Know thy customer" is one of the keys to achieving superior responsiveness to customers. Knowing the customer not only requires that employees think like customers themselves; it also demands that they listen to what their customers have to say and, as much as possible, bring them into the company. Although this may not involve physically bringing customers into the company, it does mean bringing in customers' opinions by soliciting feedback from customers on the company's goods and services and by building information systems that communicate the feedback to the relevant people.

For an example, consider **direct selling clothing retailer Lands' End**. Through its catalog, the Internet, and customer service telephone operators, Lands' End actively solicits comments from its customers about the quality of its clothing and the kind of merchandise they want it to supply. Indeed, it was customers' insistence that initially prompted the company to move into the clothing segment. Lands' End used to supply equipment for sailboats through mail-order catalogs. However, it received so many requests from customers to include outdoor clothing in its offering that it responded by expanding the catalog to fill this need. Soon clothing became the main business, and Lands End dropped the sailboat equipment. Today, the company still pays close attention to customer requests. Every month, a computer printout of customer requests and comments is given to managers. This feedback helps the company to fine-tune the merchandise it sells. Indeed, frequently new lines of merchandise are introduced in response to customer requests.

6. Satisfying Customer Needs: Once a focus on the customer is an integral part of the company, the next requirement is to satisfy customer needs that have been identified. As already noted, efficiency, quality, and innovation are crucial competencies that help a company satisfy customer needs. Beyond that, companies can provide a higher level of satisfaction if they differentiate their products by (1) customizing them, where possible, to the requirements of individual customers and (2) reducing the time it takes to respond to or satisfy customer needs.

7. Customization is varying the features of a good or service to tailor it to the unique needs or tastes of groups of customers or, in the extreme case, individual customers. Although extensive customization can raise costs, the development of flexible manufacturing technologies has made it possible to customize products to a much greater extent than was feasible ten to fifteen years ago without experiencing a prohibitive rise in cost structure (particularly when flexible manufacturing technologies are linked with web-based information systems). For example, online retailers such as Amazon.com have used web-based technologies to develop a home page customized for each individual user. When a customer accesses Amazon.com, he or she is offered a list of recommendations for books or music to purchase based on an analysis of prior buying history, a powerful competency that gives Amazon.com a competitive advantage.

The trend toward customization has fragmented many markets, particularly customer markets, into ever smaller niches. An example of this fragmentation occurred in Japan in the early 1980s when Honda dominated the motorcycle market there. Second-place Yamaha decided to go after Honda's lead. It announced the opening of a new factory that, when operating at full capacity, would make Yamaha the world's largest manufacturer of motorcycles. Honda responded by proliferating its product line and stepping up its rate of new-product introduction. At the start of what became known as the "Motorcycle wars: Honda had 60 motorcycles in its product line. Over the next eighteen months, it rapidly increased its range to 113 models, customizing them to ever smaller niches. Honda was able to accomplish this without bearing a prohibitive cost penalty because it has a competency in flexible manufacturing. The flood of **Honda's** customized models pushed Yamaha out of much of the market, effectively stalling its bid to overtake Honda.

8. Response Time: Giving customers what they want when they want it requires speed of response to customer demands. To gain a competitive advantage, a company must often respond to customer demands very quickly, whether the transaction is a furniture manufacturer's delivery of a product once it has been ordered, a bank's processing of a loan application, an automobile manufacturer's delivery of a spare part for a car that broke down, or the wait in a supermarket checkout line. We live in a fast-paced society, where time is a valuable commodity. Companies that can satisfy customer demands for rapid response build brand loyalty, differentiate their products, and can charge higher prices for them. Increased speed often lets a company choose a premium pricing option, as the mail delivery industry illustrates. The air express niche of the mail delivery industry is based on the notion that customers are often willing to pay considerably more for overnight express mail as opposed to regular mail. Another example of the value of rapid response is Caterpillar, the manufacturer of heavy earth-moving equipment, which can get a spare part to any point in the world within twenty-four hours. Downtime for heavy construction equipment is very costly, so Caterpillar's ability to respond quickly in the event of equipment malfunction is of prime importance to its customers. As a result, many of them have remained loyal to Caterpillar despite the aggressive low-price competition from Komatsu of Japan.

6.29. BUILDING AND RESTRUCTURING THE CORPORATION

There are four types of Strategic alternatives available at corporate level. They are as follows

I. Stability Strategy (makes no change to the firm's current activities)

II. Expansion Strategy (expands the firm's activities)

III. Retrenchment Strategy (reduces the firm's level of activities)

IV. Combination Strategy (uses several strategies at the same time simultaneously or over time)

Pearce and Robinson call the above strategies "grand Strategies . A grand strategy is defined as "a comprehensive general approach that guides a firm's major action". Glueck and Jauch refer them as "generic strategies at corporate level" because all types of organization can generally pursue them.

I. Stability Strategy

Stability Strategy implies continuing the current activities of the firm without any significant change in direction. If the environment is unstable and the firm is doing well, then it may believe that it is better to make no changes. A firm is to be following a stability strategy if it is satisfied with the same consumer groups and maintaining the same market share, satisfied with incremental improvements of functional performance and management does not want to take any risks that might be associated with expansion or growth. Stability strategy is most likely to be pursued by small business or firms in mature stage of development. Stability strategy are implemented by "steady as it goes" approaches to decisions. No major functional changes are made in product line, markets or functions. However stability strategy is not a "do nothing approach not does it mean that goals such as profit growth are abandoned. The stability strategy can be designed to increase profits through such approaches as improving efficiency in current operations.

Reason to go for Stability Strategy

- The firm is doing well or perceives itself as successful.
- It is less risky
- It is easier and more comfortable
- The environment is relatively unstable
- Too much expansion can lead to ineffectiveness

Types of Stability Strategies

Some of the popular stability strategies are:

Pause/Proceed with caution strategy

Some of the organization pursues stability strategy for a temporary period of time until the particular environmental situation changes, especially if they have been growing too fast in the previous period. Stability strategy enables a company to consolidate its resources after prolonged rapid growth. Sometimes, firms that wish to test the ground before moving ahead with full-fledged grand strategy employ stability strategy first.

No change strategy

A no change strategy is a decision to do nothing new, i.e, continue the current operations and policies for the foreseeable future. If there is no significant opportunities and threats operating in the environment or if there is no major new strengths and weaknesses within the organization or if there is no new competitors or threat of substitutes, the firms may decide not to do anything new.

Profit Strategy

The profit strategy is an attempt to artificially maintain profits by reducing investments and short term expenditures. Rather than announcing the company's poor position to shareholders and other investors at large, top management may be tempted difficulty, but if continued to long, it will lead to a serious deterioration in the company's position. The profit strategy is thus usually the top management's short term and often self-servicing response to the situation. In general, stability strategies can very useful in the short run, but they can be dangerous if followed to long.

II. Growth/Expansion Strategies

Growth strategies are the most widely used pursued corporate strategies. Companies that do business in expanding industries must grow to survive. A company can grow internally by expanding its operations or it can grow externally through mergers, acquisitions, joint ventures or strategic alliances.

Reasons to go for Growth Strategies

- **To obtain the economies of scale:** Growth helps firms to achieve large-scale operations, whereby fixed cost can be scraped over a large volume of production.
- **To attract merit:** Talented people prefer to work in firms with growth.
- **To increase profits:** in the long run, growth is necessary for increasing profits of the organization, especially in the turbulent and hyper-competitive environment.
- **To become a market leader:** Growth allows a firms to reach leadership positions in the market. Companies such as Reliance Industries, TISCO etc reached commanding heights due to growth strategies.
- **To fulfill natural urge:** A healthy firm normally has a natural urge for growth. Growth opportunities provide great stimulus to such urge. Further, in a dynamic world characterized by the growth of many firms around it, a firm would have a natural urge for growth.
- **To ensure survival:** Sometimes, growth is essential for survival. In some cases, a firm may not be able to survive unless it has critical minimum level of business. Further, if a firm does not grow when competitors are growing, it may undermine its competitiveness.

Types of Growth Strategies

The growth strategy are divided into three types-

i) Intensive Strategies

ii) Integration Strategies

iii) Diversification Strategies.

i) Intensive Strategies

Without moving outside the organization's current range of product or services, it may be possible to attract customers by intensive advertising, and by realigning the product and market options available to the organization. These strategies are generally referred to as intensification or concentration strategies. By intensifying efforts, the firm will be able to increase its sales and market share of the current product-line faster. This is probably the most successful internal growth strategy for firms whose products or services are in the final stages of the product life cycle. Most of the approaches of intensive strategies deal with product market realignments. Thus there are three important intensive strategies.

a) Market Penetration

b) Market Development

c) Product Development

a. Market Penetration

Market penetration seeks to increase market share for existing products in the existing markets through greater marketing efforts. This inclues activities like increasing the sale force, increasing promotional effort, giving incentives etc. Market Penetration is generally achieved through the following three major approaches.

Increasing the sales to the current customers

- Increasing the size of the purchase.
- Advertising other uses.
- Giving price incentives for increased use.

For example, if customers of toothpaste who brush once a day are convinced to brush twice a day, the sales of the product to the current consumers might almost double.

Awaiting competitor's customers

If the firm succeeds in making the customers to switch from the competitor's brands to the firm's brands, while maintaining its existing customer intact, there will be an increase in the firm's sales. This can be done through

- Increasing the promotional offers
- Establishing sharper brand differentiation
- Offering price cuts.

Awaiting non – users to buy the product

If there are a significant number of non-users of a product who could be made users of the product, there will be an opportunity to increase market share. This can be done through

- Inducing the trial use through sampling, price incentives, etc.
- Advertising the new users.
- In India there is a very large rural market for cosmetics, which can be tapped through this approach. This strategy will be effective when
- Current markets are not saturated.
- Usage rate of present customer is low.
- Economies of scale can bring down the costs.
- Market shares of major competitors are decline while total sales are increasing.

b. Market Development

Market Development seeks to increase market share by selling the present products in new markets. This can be achieved through the following approaches.

By entering new geographic markets

A company, which has been confined to some part of a country, may expand to other parts and foreign markets. Thus, market development can be achieved through

- Regional expansion.
- National expansion
- International expansion

For example Nirma, which was confined to local markets or some parts of the country in beginning, later expanded to the regional market and then to the national market.

By entering new market segments

- This can be achieved through
- Developing product versions to appeal to other segments.
- Entering other channels of distribution
- Advertising in other media

For example, HLL entered the low price detergent segment by introducing a low-priced detergent called "wheel" to compete with "Nirma" this strategy will be effective when

- New untapped or unsaturated market exist
- New channels of distribution are available.
- The firm has excess production capacity
- The firm's industry is becoming rapidly global
- The firm has resources for expanded operations.

c. Product Development

Product Development seeks to increase the market share by developing new or improved products for present markets.

- Developing new product features
- Developing quality variations
- Developing additional models and sizes.

For example, Hindustan lever keeps on adding new product new brands or improved versions of consumer products from time to time to maintain its market share. This strategy will be effective when

- The firm's products are in maturity stage
- The firm's witness one of the rapid technological developments in the industry.
- The firm in a high growth industry
- Competitors bring out improved quality products from time to time
- The firm has strong R&D capabilities.

2. Integration Strategies

Integration basically means combining activities relating to the present activity of a firm. Such a combination can be done on the basis of the industry value chain. A company performs a number of activities to transform an input to output. These activities includes right from the procurement of raw materials to the production of finished goods and their marketing and distribution to the ultimate consumers. These activities are called Value Chain activities.

Expanding the firm's range of activities backward integration into the sources of supply and/or forward into the distribution channels is called vertical integration. Thus, if a manufacturer invests in facilities to produce raw materials or component parts that it formerly purchased from outside suppliers, it remains in the same industry, but its scope of operations extended two stages of industry value chain.

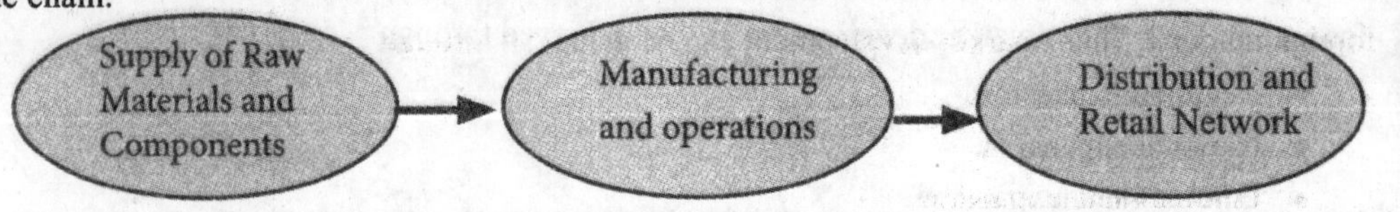

Similarly if a manufacturer opens a chain of retail outlets to market its products directly to consumers, it remains in the same industry, but its scope of operations extend from manufacturing to retailing. Viewed from a broader angle, the firm's own value chain activities are often closely linked to value chain activities of the suppliers and distributors. Supplier's value chain is important because the costs, performance features and quality of the inputs influence a firm's own costs and product differentiation capabilities. Anything the firm does to lower costs or improves quality of its inputs will enhance its own competitiveness in the market. Similarly, the costs and margins paid to distributors and retailers become a part of the price the consumers pay. Besides, the activities of distributors and retailers affect consumer's satisfaction.

a. Vertical Integration

Vertical Integration (the degree to which a firm operates vertically in multiple locations on an industry's value chain from extracting raw materials to manufacturing to retailing. More specifically, assuming a function previously provided by a supplier is called **backward integration** (going backward on an industry's value chain). The purchase of pentasia chemicals by Asian Paints Limited for the chemicals required for the manufacturing of paints is an example of backward integration. Assuming a function previously provided by a distributor is labeled **forward integration** (going toward on an industry's value chain). Arvind Mills, for example, used forward integration when it expanded out of its successful fabric manufacturing business to make and makes its own branded shirts and pants.

Vertical growth is a logical strategy for a corporative or business unit with a strong competitive position in a highly attractive industry (especially when technology is predicatable and markets are growing. To keep and even improve its competitive position, the company may use backward integration to minimize resource acquistion costs and inefficient operations as well as forward integration to gain more control over product distribution. The firm, ineffect, builds on its distinctive competence by expanding along the industry's value chain to gain grater competitive advantage.

Although backward integration is usually more profitable then forward integration, it can reduce a corporation's strategic flexibility. The resulting encumbrance of expensive assets that might be hard to sell could create an exit barrier, preventing the corporation from learing that particular industry. When sales of its aulor were declining, Hindustan Motors (the makers of Ambassdor cars), for example, resoated to offering outside parts suppliers the use of its idle factories and workers).

Vertical Integration Continuum

Full Integration	Taper Integration	Quasi Integration	Long-term Contract

Figure 6.20. Vertical Integration Continuum.

Full Integration : A firm internally makes 100% of its key supplies and completely controls its distributors. Large oil companies, such as BP Amoco and Royal Dutch Shell, are fully integrated. They own the oil rigs that pump the oil out of the ground, the ships and pipelines that transport the oil, the refineries that convert the oil to gasoline, and the trucks that delivers the gasoline to company owned and franchised gas stations. If a corporation does not want the disadvantages of full vertical integration, it may choose either taper or quasi-integration strategies.

Taper Integration: A firm internally produces less then half of its own requirements and buys the rest from outside supplies. Incase of Asian Paints Limited, its purchase of pentasia chemicals allows it to produce the basic chemicals it needs to process into interior paints. In terms of distributors, a firm sells of its goods through company owned and loies and the rest through general wholesalers. Both Xerox and IBM experimented (unsuccessfully) with selling their products through their own stories.

Quasi Integration: A company does not make any of its key supplies but purchases most of its requirements from outside supplies that are under its partial control. For example, by purchasing 20% of the common stock of a key supplier, in focus systems, Motorola guarenteed its access to 'In focus' technology and enabled Motorola to establish joint venture with 'In focus' to manufacture flat – panel video displays.

Long-term Contracts: It's an agreements between two separate firms to provide agreed-upon goods and services to each other for a specified period of time. This cannot really be considered vertical integration unless the contract specifies that the supplies or distributor cannot have a similar reletionship with a competitive firm. In this case, the supplier or distributor is really a captive company that, although officially independend, does most of its business with the contracted firm and its formally tied to the other company through a long-term contract.

Advantages of Vertical Integration

1. A secure supply of raw materials or distribution channels
2. Control over raw materials and other inputs required for production or distribution channels.
3. Access to new business opportunities and technologies.
4. Elimination of need to deal with a wide variety of suppliers and distributors.

Risks

1. Increased costs, expenses and capital requirement.
2. Loss of flexibility in investments.
3. Problems associated with unbalanced facilities or unfulfilled demand.
4. Additional administrative costs associated with managing a more complex set of activities.

Disadvantages of Vertical Integration

1. It boosts the firm's capital investments.
2. It increases the business risk.
3. It denies financial resources to more worthwhile pursuits.
4. It locks a firm into relying on its own-in-house sources of supply.
5. It poses all kinds of capacity matching problems
6. It calls for radically different skills and capabilities, which may be lacked by the manufacturer.
7. Outsourcing of component parts may be cheaper and less complicated than in house manufacturing.

Most of the world's auto makers, despite their expertise in automobile technology and manufacturing, strongly feel that purchasing many of their key parts and components from manufacturing specialist's results in:

- Higher quality
- Lower costs
- Greater design flexibility

So they feel that vertical integration option is not preferable.

b. Horizontal Integration

The degree to which a firm operates in multiple geographic locations at the same point in an industry's value chain. Horizontal integration for a firm may range from full to partial ownership to long-term contracts. For example, IBM, purchased the Indian BPO major Daksh to obtain access to American and Asian Markets. Many commutor airlines engage in long-term contracts with other airlines in order to offer a complete arrangement for travelors. For example, Jet airways provides world-class frequent flyer benefits to the customers, through their alliances with British Airways. KLM Royal Dutch Airlines and Northwest Airlines provides flight reservation directly from the destinations outside India for domestic travel.

Advantages of Horizontal Integration

1. It yields access to new markets.
2. It provides economies of scale.
3. It allows transfer of resources and capabilities.

When Horizontal Integration is Appropriate

Horizontal integration is an appropriate strategy when,

1. A firm competes in a growing industry
2. Increased economies of scale provide a major competitive advantage.
3. A firm has both the capital and human talent needed to successfully manage an expanded the firm.

It should be noted that horizontal integration might not be an appropriate strategy if competitors are doing poorly due to an overall decline in industry sales.

Some increased risks are associated with both types of integration. For horizontally integrated firms, the risk comes from increased commitment to one types of business. For vertically integrated firms, the risk comes shortage of managers with appropriate skills or expertise to manage the expanded activities. If there is much more potential profit in downstream or upstream activities, it is better to go in a vertical integration.

Strategic Outsourcing

Outsourcing has evolved beyond being viewed as a purely tactical exercise to reduce costs and increase operational efficiencies. Businesses today are using it to achieve their enterprise-wide strategic goals and focus on core competencies.

Strategic outsourcing can help companies

- Adapt flexibly to business change
- Improve quality and productivity
- Respond quickly to completion
- Penetrate new markets

Strategic outsourcing services can range from Application Development and Maintenance (ADM) to business process outsourcing to setting up turnkey IT centers on a BOT model (Build-Operate-Transfer), to business re-engineering.

A technology-enabled market

Outsourcing provides access to a highly skilled global workforce, which can supply a wide array of services. To leverage these services effectively and benefit from lower operational costs and higher service levels, there are several business models to choose from. These are:

1. Staff augmentation: This model provides specialized resources, cost flexibility and satisfies short-term time-to-market demands.

2. Out-tasking: This model is suitable for short-term business needs, to fill skill gaps. However the integration of different out-tasked outcomes may not be a seamless one.

3. Project-based outsourcing: Vendors and clients share risks and rewards through this collaborative model. This model has high client benefits as it holds the vendor accountable for an entire project, and allows the application of industry best practices in the outsourcing process.

Managed services model: This model fosters the development of long-term, multi-year, SLA-based relationships to provide integrated solutions across the enterprise. The service provider takes responsibility and accountability for agreed- upon strategic business outcomes. Projects typically have a large scope and scale and the knowledge gained by the vendor is invested back into the system so that the client's benefits increase year on year. These partnerships allow the sharing of risks and rewards, encourage innovation, embrace business change and contribute significantly to the strategic goals of both partners. Making complex decisions to obtain desired business outcomes requires a high level of sourcing maturity. It involves an understanding of factors that influence who should outsource, to whom, why, where and when.

The managed services model has become central to the **business strategy of many companies** and could be a key driver of global competitiveness.

iii) Diversification Strategies

Diversification is the process of adding new businesses to the existing businesses of the company. In other words, diversification adds new products or markets to the existing ones. A diversified company is one that has two or more distinct businesses. The diversification strategy is concerned with achieving a greater market from a greater range of products in order to maximize profits. From the risk point of view, companies attempt to spread their risk by diversifying into several products and industries. For example, an air-conditioning company may add room-heaters in its present product lines, or a company reducing cameras may branch off into the manufacturing of coping machines.

Diversification can be achieved through a variety of ways:-

- Through mergers and acquisitions
- Through joint ventures and strategic alliances
- Through starting up a new business unit.

Thus the first concern in diversifying is what new industries to get into and whether to enter by starting a new business unit or by acquiring a company already in the industry or by forming a joint venture or strategic alliance with anthor Company. A company can diversify narrowly into a few industries or broadly into many industries. The ultimate objective of diversification is to build shareholder value, i.e., increasing value of the firm's stock.

Reasons for Diversification

The important reasons for a company diversifying their business are:

- **Saturation or decline of the current business:** If the company is faced with diminishing market opportunities and stagnating sales in its principal business, it may become necessary to enter new businesses to achieve growth.
- **Better opportunities:** Even when the current business provides scope for further growth, there may be better opportunities in new lines of business. A firm in a industmay be tempted to enter a industry
- **Sharing of resources and strengths:** Diversification enables companies to leverage existing competencies and capabilities by expanding into businesses where these resources become valuable competitive assets. By sharing production facilities, technological capabilities, managerial expertise, distribution channels, sales force, financial resources etc., synergy can be obtained.
- **New avenues for reducing costs:**Diversifying into closely related businesses opens new avenues for reducing costs.
- **Technologies and products:** By expanding into industries, the company can obtain new technologies and products, which can complement its present businesses.

- **Use of brand name:** Through diversification, the company can transfer its powerful and well-known brand name to the products of other businesses.
- **Risk minimization:** The big risk of a single-business firm is having all its eggs in one industry basket. If the market is eroded by the appearance of new technologies, new products or fast consumer preferences, then a company prospects can quickly diminish. For example, digital cameras have diminished markets for film and film processing; CD and DVD technology has replaced cassette tapes and floppy disks and mobile phones are dominating landline phones. Thus, there are substantial risks to single-business companies, and diversification into other businesses minimizes this risk. But diversification itself can become risky.

Risks of Diversification

Diversification has several risks. They are:

- There is no guarantee that the firm will succeed in the new business. In fact, many diversifications have been failures.
- If the new lines of business result in huge losses, that adversely affects the main business of the company.
- Diversification may sometimes result in neglect of the old business.
- Diversification may invite retaliatory moves by competitors, which may adversely affect even the old businesses.

Types of Diversification

a. Concentric diversification

b. Conglomerate diversification

a. Concentric Diversification

Adding a new, but related business is called concentric diversification. It involves acquisition of businesses that are related to the acquiring firm in terms of technology, markets or products. The selected new business has compatibility with the firm current business. The ideal concentric diversification occurs when the combined profits increase the strengths and opportunities and decrease the weaknesses and threats. Thus, the acquiring firm searches for new businesses whose products, markets, distribution channels and technologies are similar to its own, and whose acquisition results in This is possible with related diversification because companies strive to enter product markets that share resources and capabilities with their existing business units. Diversification must create value for shareholders. But this is not always the case. Acquiring firms typically pay premiums when they acquire a target firm. Besides, the risks and uncertainties are high.

Advantages

- Increases the firm stock value.
- Increases the growth rate of the firm.
- Better use of funds than ploughing them back into internal growth.
- Improves the stability of earnings and sales.
- Balances the product line when the life cycle of the current products has peaked. Helps to acquire a needed resource quickly (e.g. technology or innovative management etc.)
- Achieves tax savings.
- Increases efficiency and profitability through synergy.
- Reduces risk.

b. Conglomerate Diversification

Adding a new, but unrelated business is called conglomerate diversification. The new business will have no, relationship to the company technology, products or markets. For example, ITC which is basically and cigarette manufacturer, has diversified into hotels, edible oils, financial services etc. Similarly, Reliance Industries, which is basically a textile manufacturer, has diversified into petro-chemicals, telecommunications, retailing etc. Unlike concentric diversification, conglomerate diversification does not result in much of synergy. The main objective is profit motive. But it has important advantages.

Advantages

1. Business risk is scattered over diverse industries.
2. Financial resources are invested in industries that offer the best profit prospects.
3. Buying distressed businesses at a low price can enhance shareholder wealth.
4. Company profitability can be more stable in economic upswings and downswings.

Disadvantages

1. It is difficult to manage different businesses effectively.
2. The new business may not provide any competitive advantage if it has no strategic- fits

Table 6.11 Differences Between Concentric and Conglomerate Diversification

Concentric Diversification	Conglomerate Diversification
The company diversifies into businesses related to the existing businesses.	The company diversifies into businesses that are unrelated to the existing business.
There is commonality in markets, products or technology.	No commonality in markets, products or technology.
The main objective is to increase shareholder value through 'synergy' which is achieved through sharing of skills, resources and capabilities.	The main objective is to increase shareholder value through profit maximization.
Less risky	More risky

Diversification into both Related and Unrelated Businesses

Some companies may diversify into both related and unrelated businesses. The actual practice varies from company to company. There are three types of enterprises in this respect

1. **Dominant business enterprises:** In such enterprises, one major business accounts for 50 to 80 per cent of total revenues and the remaining comes from small related and unrelated businesses, e.g. TISCO.
2. **Narrowly diversified enterprise:** These are enterprises that are diversified around a few (two to five) related or unrelated businesses e.g. BPL.
3. **Broadly diversified enterprises:** These enterprises are diversified around a wide-ranging collection of related and unrelated businesses e.g. ITC, Reliance Industries

6.30. MERGERS AND ACQUISITION

Introduction

Profitable growth is one of the prime objectives of any business firm. Growth can be achieved internally or externally. Internal growth in assets, sales and profits takes place when a fire-i introduces a new product or increases the capacity for the existing products. Increasing the capacities and thereby achieving growth takes time and involves a lot of risk. Alternatively, business firms can quickly increase their growth rate by Mergers and Acquisitions. A fain may use mergers and acquisitions to increase competitiveness and consolidate its position. With the opening up of Indian economy, businėss firms have now the freedom to expand, diversify and modernize the operations and set up new undertakings with lesser restrictions and government control. In such economic conditions, experienced entrepreneurs always remain in search of opportunities to take over loss-making and sick units and to expand their operations and increase their market share. So, the free economic environment plays a very important role in accelerating the merger and acquisition activities

6.30.1 Meaning of Terms

1. **Merger:** A merger occurs when two or more organizations of about equal size combine to become one through an exchange of stock or cash or both. Mergers can take place in different ways.
2. **Acquisition:** An acquisition occurs when a large organization purchases a smaller firm, or vice-versa.
3. **Consolidation:** If both firms dissolve their identity to create a new firm, it is called consolidation or amalgamation.
4. **Friendly Merger:** When both firms desire a merger or acquisition, it is termed as a friendly merger.
5. **Takeover:** A surprise attempt by one company to acquire control of another company against the will of the current management is called a takeover or hostile takeover. It is usually done through the purchase of controlling share of voting stock in a publicly traded company. In the case of a takeover, the acquiring firm retains its identity whereas the target firm loses its identify after restructuring.
6. **Demergers:** Demerger or split or division of a company is the opposite of mergers and acquisitions. This happens when a part of the undertaking is transferred to a newly formed company or to an existing company. The size of the company after demerger would reduce.

6.30.2 Reasons for Mergers and Acquisitions

There are several reasons why firms merge with or acquire other firms:

1. **To gain economies of scale:** One of the most frequent reasons given for mergers and acquisitions is to gain economies of scale. Economies of scale are generally associated with the manufacturing operations, so that the ratio of output to input improves with the volume of operations. This gives the company a competitive advantage by gaining an ability to reduce prices, to gain more market share or earn higher profits while maintaining prices.
2. **To achieve diversification of the portfolio:** Another popular reason for companies to merge or acquire is to diversify their products. When the company finds it difficult to sustain itself, mergers and acquisitions help to widen the growth opportunities for the company and smoothen the ups and downs of their life cycles.
3. **To quickly acquire valuable resources:** Sometimes, mergers and acquisitions help to quickly gain access to new product lines, new technologies, new skills and competencies, new sales force, new distribution channels, or a brand name.
4. **To reduce risks and borrowing costs:** Due to diverse portfolio, the risk of the combined operations reduces, when one segment is running deficit, the other segment is likely to be surplus with a effect Due to this inbuilt safety, the costs associated with borrowings would reduce.
5. **To achieve growth:** Growth through mergers and acquisitions takes place to acquire market power. With the additional combined market share, the company will have the power to control the price in a better manner. This will hopefully lead to better profitability.

6. **To gain additional capacity:** A company can gain additional capacity in a market already being serviced by the acquiring firm.

7. **To obtain taxation or investment incentives:** A company that has incurred losses in the past can carry such losses forward and offset them against future taxable profits and reduce tax liabilities. Such a company, when merged with a company with large taxable profits, would help to absorb some tax liability of the latter. A similar advantage exists when a company is modernizing or investing heavily in plant and machinery which entitles it to substantial investment incentives, but has not much taxable profits to offset them with. Acquiring or merging such a company with a highly profitable company would help make full use of the investment incentives for the latter.

8. **To gain managerial expertise:** Sometimes, acquisitions/mergers help to acquire unique managerial expertise available with the target company. This expertise may be embodied in the team of managers as well as the systems in operation in the target company.

9. **To acquire market supremacy:** Some of the mergers and acquisitions take place with a view to seek additional power in the market. With the additional combined market share, the company can afford to control the price in a better manner. For example, with Ceat and Dunlop, Goenka has a control on over 40 percent of market share of automotive tyres in India. Apart from the improvement of operating efficiency, the merger could also contribute to increased profitability in terms of post-merger asset stripping i.e., selling off such assets in the acquired firm that are considered to be not value adding by the acquiring firm. Such asset stripping would bring ready cash into the merged business.

10. **To bypass legal hurdles:** Some mergers and acquisitions have taken place to exploit legal loopholes or bypass legal hurdles. For example, the mergers carried out by the Chabria group and Vijay Mallaya group in the liquor business (where licensing is strictly regulated) illustrates this point.

11. **To take over sick units:** The sick unit referred to the Board for Industrial and Financial Reconstruction (BIFR) are taken over as per the norms and guidelines of banks, fmancial institutions. The merger of the loss-making New Bank of India with the profitable Punjab National Bank and the merger of Bank of Madurai with ICICI Bank are examples of such mergers.

6.30.3 Types of Mergers

The major types of mergers are:

1. Horizontal mergers
2. Vertical mergers
3. Lateral or allied mergers
4. Conglomerate mergers
5. Concentric mergers
6. Circular mergers

1. **Horizontal Mergers:** Here the companies producing the same product or doing the same business join together. The main purpose of such mergers is to obtain economies of scale in production by eliminating duplication of facilities and operations and broadening the product line, reduction in the investment of fixed assets and working capital, elimination of competition, reduction in advertising cost, increase the market power and to have better control over the market. But the horizontal mergers cannot guarantee the market for the product and regular supply of raw materials. They may also lead to monopoly and concentration of economic power in few hands.

Examples

- Union Carbide was acquired by Khaitan
- Allwyn was acquired by Voltas
- Bank of Madhura was merged with ICICI Bank.
- Damodar Cement was merged with ACC.

2. **Vertical Merger:** This is the joining of two or more companies involved in different stages of the production or distribution of the same product or service. The essential objective of such a merger is to ensure a source of supply required for the production of goods or services to ensure a ready market for the goods or services produced.

Vertical mergers are brought into existence with the following objectives in view

- To ensure economies of scale.
- To eliminate the wasteful and unnecessary expenses involved in carrying on the connected process separately.
- To avoid middlemen functioning between various units.
- To maintain control over the quality of raw materials and finished goods.

Example:

- Videocon Narmada Electronics Ltd., merged with Videocon International Ltd.
- A Borjan Tea Estate was merged with TATA Tea Ltd.
- Gujarat Godrej Innovative Chemical Ltd. was merged with Godrej Soaps Ltd.

Vertical merger may take the form of forward integration or backward integration. When a company combines with the supplier of materials, it is called backward integration. If a company combines with a customer, it is called forward integration.

3. **Lateral or allied mergers:** Lateral merger takes place when the firms producing different products which are related in some way come together.

Example:

When a company is producing ink, paper, case board, join with the printing press, it is called lateral merger. Here different firm's produce different goods but are related in some way come together.

4. **Conglomerated mergers:** It is the merger of two or more companies producing unrelated products. The companies involved in the merger may be manufacturing totally different products. Of course, there may be some common features between them such as same channel of distribution or technology. Such mergers help to utilize the financial resources optimally and increase the debt capacity of the firms. It also enables the company to diversify its objectives.
5. **Concentric mergers:** If the activities of the segments brought together are so related that there is carryover of specific management functions or complementarily in relative strengths among them.
6. **Circular mergers:** A transaction to combine companies that operate within the same general market but offer a different product mix to the same target group of customers. A company engages in circular merger to offer or greater range of products or services within their market.

6.30.4 The Merger Process

Once the top management has decided to pursue the route of mergers and acquisitions, the operational managers have to get into the action of looking out for suitable candidates. The process of screening and selecting candidates should proceed in a systematic manner, from general to the more specific. The following are the steps involved in the merger process.

1. **Identify Industries:** First, a set of industries are selected which meet the strategic objectives of the company. This may be in terms of size. For example, a company wanting to acquire a medium-sized investment will leave out the large investment industries. Similarly, if the company wants to spread its risks, it might look at other industries for merger or acquisitions. If it is already a diversified company then it may look at all possible industries in certain sectors.
2. **Select Sectors:** In this step, a broad group of acceptable sectors are identified. For each of these sectors, data relating to sales turnover and growth, return on investment, market share, competition etc. is collected for various participating companies. On the basis of this comparison, the more desirable sectors are chosen.
3. **Choose Companies:** Generally, the size of the company is characterized by the sales turnover and the asset levels, which in turn determine the cost level of the acquisition. Size of the company is important because it is quite difficult to acquire companies which are bigger in size than the acquiring firm. However, the trend among Indian companies is to acquire even firms which are larger than themselves. Tata's acquisition of Corus steel plant which is almost five times bigger than TISCO is an example. Potential companies are also looked at with respect to the competitive environment in which they operate. At this stage, the acquiring firm also starts considering what new strategies they would pursue to make the acquired firm stronger in their market segments.
4. **Evaluate Cost of Acquisition and Returns:** In this step, the financial obligations associated with the merger or acquisition is considered. All the potential candidates are listed and compared with respect to their likely return on investments. The future expected returns are also developed on the basis of different market scenarios. The risks and uncertainties are incorporated to determine the possible variations in returns. Finally, the various possible candidates are ranked on their position against each of the identified objectives.
5. **Rank the Candidates:** The ranking has to be done according to common screening criteria identified by the corporate management. In general, the acquisition or merger should result in returns far in excess of the cost of acquisition. The company must also identify its concept of fit and should take into account not only the cost of acquiring, but also the cost of integrating the acquired unit with itself and improving its performance further. Various desirable parameters are weighed to develop a composite index for ranking of the potential candidates.

   In order to ensure successful acquisitions, it is important to focus on the fit between the two firms. There are three types of fits to be considered:- Strategic fit, Financial fit, Organizational/cultural fit.

   a. **Strategic Fit:** The concept of strategic fit is basically concerned with matching the strategic rationale for specific merger and acquisition opportunity with the organizations strategic capabilities and market situation.

   b. **Financial Fit:** The financial fit shows whether the cash flow profile, financing profile, investment profile and risk profile of the two companies are compatible. For example, if both the companies are in the fast growing business, they would both be cash hogs, i.e.; both would require huge amounts of cash to fund their business growth goals. In such a situation, financial fit would be low. On the other hand, if one business is maturing and is a cash cow i.e. it generates surplus cash, then the firm could use this surplus cash by acquiring a business that has substantial growth opportunity.

   c. **Organizational Cultural Fit:** This fit is required to see whether the cultures of the two firms are likely to clash. There may be a need for some cultural/organization system to achieve compatibility between the cultures of both the companies. For example, the operating procedures, leadership and communication systems need to be designed to accommodate the differences in the two cultures.

6. **Identify good candidates:** In general, the acquirer is seeking to acquire a company which will increase the overall economic value of the company. To achieve this, the acquiring company should seek target firms for acquisition which have:

- High market share
- Growing market
- Large sales volume
- Good management systems
- Diversified portfolio or its potential
- A return on investment above a benchmark specified for acquisition

But, a firm having such desirable features may not be available for sale. If it were available, then every other company in the market would like to bid for it. As a result, the price of such an acquisition may raise sky high. Thus, the strong and perpetual players of the take-over game believe that the acquisition of companies is very similar to buying shares or stock in the market. To strike a good deal and make money, one has to look for the inefficiencies and oddities in the take-over trade.

7. **Decide the Extent of Ecquisition/Retention:** Candidates for acquisition can be classified on the basis of how much of the target company can be or will be acquired, and how much of it will be retained. In principle, a company may acquire the whole or part of a company, and may retain the whole of acquisition, part of it, or none of it. If the company acquires and retains the whole of it, the acquired company must be carefully integrated into the management system of the acquiring company. This is of crucial importance; otherwise the mismatch of the two can adversely affect the performance of the whole organization. Similarly, the candidates can also be classified by other criteria such as distinctiveness or the distance from the present activities or operations of the acquiring company.
8. **Merger Implementation:** In implementation stage, the tax, regulatory and market issues dominate the merger process. In this stage, issues like registration of the merger, obtaining board and shareholder approvals, announcement to the public, notifying to stock exchanges are activities that need to be attended to.
9. **Post-Merger Integration:** This is the final stage. This stage involves actions like reorganization, which may include activities like asset stripping, improving the operating efficiency, setting up managerial systems at the acquired firm, streamlining the operations of the combined firm to ensure that the projected synergies are obtained, and initiatives in establishing the right kind of corporate culture, providing the right managerial leadership, ensuring the competitiveness of the combined firms etc.

Peter Ducker (1981) has identified five guidelines for successful acquisition.

- Acquirer must contribute something to the acquired company
- A common core of unity is required
- Acquirer must respect the business of the acquired company
- The acquiring company must be able to provide top management of the acquired company, within a year or so.

6.31. RETRENCHMENT/DEFENSIVE STRATEGIES

Strategies are also called retrenchment strategies. They are the last resortstrategies. A company may pursue retrenchment strategies when it has a weak competitive position in some or all of its product lines resulting in poor performance sales are down and profits are dwindling. In an attempt to eliminate the weaknesses that are dragging the company down, management to follow one or more of the following retrenchment strategies.

I. Turnaround Strategies
II. Diverstiture
III. Bankruptcy
IV. Liquidation

I. Turnaround Strategy

A firm said to be sick when it faces a severe cash crunch or a consistent downtrend in its operating profits. Such firms become insolvent unless appropriate internal and external actions are taken to change the financial picture of the firm. This process of recovery is called turnaround strategy

Any successful turnaround strategy consists of three inter-related phases

a. The first phase is the diagnosis of impending trouble. Many authors and research studies have indicated distinct early warning signals of corporate sickness.
b. The second phase involves analyzing the causes of sickness to restore the firm on its profit track. These measures are of both short-term and long-term nature.
c. The third and final phase involves implementation of change process and its monitoring.

When Turnaround Becomes Necessary

Do companies turn sick overnight and qualify as potential candidates for turnaround or do they become sick slowly which can be stopped by timely corrective action? Obviously, the latter is true in most of the cases. But the reality is also that companies becoming sick often do not themselves recognize this fact, and fail to take timely action to remedy the situation. Despite the fact that factors that lead to sickness may vary from company to company, there are some common signals which herald the onset of sickness. John M Harris has listed a dozen danger signals of impending sickness.

1. Decreasing market share: This is the most significant symptom of a major sickness. A company which is losing its market share to competition needs to sit up and take careful note. Regular monitoring of market share helps companies to keep a tag on their performance in the market vis-à-vis their competitors. Any indication of declining market share should trigger off immediate corrective action.

2. Decreasing constant rupee sales: Sales figures, to be meaningful, should be adjusted for inflation. If constant rupee sales figures are showing a declining trend, then this is a danger signal to watch out.

3. Decreasing profitability: Profit figures are a good indication of a company health. Care must be taken to interpret the profit figures correctly, so as to avoid any misjudgments. Decreasing profitability can show up as smaller profits in absolute terms or lower profits per rupee of sales or decreasing return on investment or smaller profit margins.

4. Increasing dependence on debt: A company overly reliant on debt soon gets into a tight corner with very few options left. A substantial rise in the amount of debt, a lopsided debt-to-equity ratio and a lowered corporate credit rating may cause banks and other financial institutions to impose restrictions and become reluctant to lend money. Once financial institutions are hesitant to lend money, the company rating on the stock market also slides down and it becomes very difficult for the company to raise funds from the public too.

5. Restricted dividend policies: Dividends frequently missed or restricted dividends signal danger. Often, such companies may have earlier paid substantially higher proportion of earnings as dividends when in fact they should have been reinvesting in the business. Current inability to pay dividends is an indication of the gravity of the situation.

6. Failure to reinvest sufficiently in the business: For a company to stay competitive and keep on the fast growth track, it is essential to reinvest adequate amounts in plant, equipment and maintenance. When a business is growing, the combination of new investments and reinvestments often warrants borrowing. Companies which fail to recognize this fact and try to finance growth with only their internal funds are applying brakes in the path of growth.

7. Diversification at the expense of the core business: It is a well-observed fact that once companies reach a particular level of maturity in the existing business, they start looking for diversification. Often this is done at the cost of the core business, which then starts to deteriorate and decline. Diversification in new ventures should be sought as a supplement and not as a substitute for the primary core business.

8. Lack of planning: In many companies, particularly those built by individual entrepreneurs the concept of planning is generally lacking. This can often result in major setbacks as limited thought or planning go into the actions and their consequences.

9. Inflexible chief executives: A chief executive who is unwilling to listen to fresh ideas from others is a signal of impending bad news. Even if the CEO recognizes the danger signals, his unwillingness to accept any proposal from his subordinates further blocks the path towards recovery.

10. Management succession problems: When nearly all the top managers are in their mid-fifties, there may be a serious vacuum at the second line of command. As these older managers retire or leave because of perception of decreasing opportunities, there is bound to be serious management crisis.

11. Unquestioning boards of directors: Directors, who have family, social or business ties with the chief executive or have served very long on the board, may no longer be objective in their judgment. Thus, these directors serve limited purpose in terms of questioning or cautioning the CEO about his actions.

12. A management team unwilling to learn from its competitors: Companies in decline often adopt a closed attitude and are not willing to learn anything from their competitors. Companies which have survived tough competitive times continuously analyses their competitors moves.

Causes of Corporate Decline

A great deal of research has been conducted into the causes of corporate decline. The major causes for corporate decline are discussed below, though some of the causes of decline overlap with the danger signals of sickness.

1. Lack of or inadequate financial controls: This is often a major cause of decline. Weak control means that management is unable to find out on which products or markets it is making or losing money. Weak financial control is often reflected in the absence of any cash-flow forecasts, and inadequate costing systems and budgetary controls.

2. Inadequate management: In analyzing the poor quality of management, there are five typical situations where this problem may occur.

a. One-man rule: The presence of a single, domineering chief executive unwilling to adapt to new ideas, characterizes many declining companies. Often, the early reasons for success become the later day causes of decline as the CEO invariably tends to repeat his past policies unmindful of the changed or changing environment.

b. Combined chairman and chief executive: In such a situation, there is no effective in the system.

c. Ineffective board of directors: A board may be ineffective for a number of reasons such as directors who are mere rubber stamps, or who have no real interest or knowledge of the business, or because they may all be drawn from one particular functional area or industry thus representing a lop-sided board.

d. Management of core business: Diversification becomes a substitute and not a supplement to the core business resulting in eventual financial losses.

e. Lack of management skills: Managers just below the CEO level often lack adequate management skills and this may be a contributory reason for the decline of a firm.

3. Competition: Competition as a reason of corporate decline occurs in the form of product and/or price competition. All products after a certain period of time become obsolete and are replaced with newer substitutes. A firm which fails to introduce new products at the right time is likely to face a declining fortune.

4. High cost structure: A company that has a higher cost structure than its competitors is likely to be at a competitive disadvantage. The high cost structure may be due to:

a. Relative cost disadvantages because of the firm inability to take advantage of scale economies.

b. Absolute cost disadvantages arising out of lack of control of strategic variables.

c. Cost disadvantages due to diversification.

d. cost disadvantages due to management style and organization structure,

e. operating inefficiencies, and

f. Unfavorable government policies.

5. Changes in market demand: This may be due to decline in demand in which case the firm either has to find a new use for its existing product or diversify into a new product line. In case the changes in market demand are due to cyclical market decline, then the firm has to find ways and means to boost up sales during the low sales period.

6. Lack of marketing effort: Firms that are going through a phase of declining profits are characterized by management and employee complacency. This is most visibly exhibited in a lack of marketing effort on the part of the firm.

7. Big projects and acquisitions: Often a cause of corporate decline is the starting of new big projects or large acquisitions. The new projects may lead to decline because of under-estimation of capital requirement, start up difficulties or high market entry costs.

8. Firm Acquisition Period: A firm acquiring new firms may end up in trouble in case the acquired firm has a weak competitive position in its market, or due to the inadequacy of the management in the post-acquisition period leading to corporate decline.

9. Financial policy: The three types of financial policies that directly lead to corporate decline are:

a. High debt-equity ratio,

b. Conservative financial policy, and

c. Use of inappropriate financing sources.

10. Overtrading: When firm sales grow faster than it is able to finance from internal sources and borrowings, it results in overtrading.

Types of Turnaround Strategies

Slater has classified the turnaround strategies into two broad categories. These are strategic turnaround and operating turnaround. Whether a sick business needs strategic or operating turnaround can be ascertained by analyzing the current strategic and operating health of the business. The operating turnarounds are easier to carry out and can be applied only when there are averages to strong strategic strengths (product-market relationship) in the business. The strategic turnaround choices may involve either a new way to compete existing business or entering an altogether new business. Entering a new business as a turnaround strategy can be approached through the process of product portfolio management. The strategic turnaround focuses either on increasing the market share in a given product-market framework or by shifting the product-market relationship in a new direction by re-positioning.

The operating turnaround strategies are of four types. These are:

- Revenue-increasing strategies
- Cost-cutting strategies
- Asset-reduction strategies
- Combination Strategies

The focus of all these choices is on short-term profit. Thus, if a sick firm is operating much below its break-even, it must take steps to reduce the levels of fixed cost and help in reducing the total costs of the firm. In real life, it is always a difficult choice to identify the assets which can be sold without affecting the productivity of the business. To identify saleable assets, the firm may have to keep in mind its strategic move in the next two to three years. The turnaround strategies appropriate under different circumstances are:

If the sick firm is operating substantially but not extremely below its break-even point, then the most appropriate turnaround strategy is the one which generates extra revenues. These may be in the form of price reduction to increase sales, stimulating product demand through promotional efforts or sometimes by introducing scaled down versions of the main products of the firm. The increased quantities of product sales not only result in higher sales but also reduce the per unit cost, thus leading to higher operating profits.

If the firm is operating closer but below break-even point then the turnaround strategy calls for application of combination strategies. Under combination strategies cost-reducing, revenue generating and asset-reduction actions are pursued simultaneously in an integrated and balanced manner. The combination strategies have a direct favorable impact on cash flows as well as on profits.

If the firm is operating around break-even point, it usually needs **cost-reduction** strategies, since cost-reduction actions are easily carried out as compared to revenue generating actions, the former is usually preferred for quick short-term profit increases.

Slater has, however, linked the choice of turnaround strategies to the causes of decline. The recommended choice of strategies includes change in management and organizational processes, improved financial controls, growth via acquisition and new financial strategies. Closely associated to the choice of turnaround strategy is the concept of turnaround process. We will focus on this aspect in the next section.

Turnaround Process

The process of turning a sick company into a profitable one is rather complex and difficult. It is complex because a successful turnaround strategy demands corrective actions in many deficient areas of the firm. It is necessary that all these actions are integrated and do not contradict each other. The turnaround process is difficult because it involves perceptual and attitudinal changes at all levels as far as employees are concerned. These human change processes tend to become very sensitive when the firm is in a crisis situation. Therefore, many a time, a change in the leadership or even an active intervention from outside is suggested for bringing about such changes in the organization.

As soon as the **parameters of corporate performance** are indicative of unsatisfactory corporate performance, it becomes necessary to immediately tighten the controls within the organization. Effective controls have a positive impact on cost-reduction, that is, profit improvement and also on the net cash-flows of the firm. But this tightening of the financial and administrative control do not guarantee a stable turnaround process. In fact, controls coupled with poor quality image of the product may hasten the process of corporate failure. So while the controls are being effected, it is necessary that the strategic posture of the company may also be overhauled. This involves major changes in the product-mix, customer-mix and the pattern of resources deployment in the company. These two stages of change further need to be complemented by changes in top management and many organizational processes. If these changes produce early results which are satisfactory, then for long-term effects it is necessary to reinforce these changes.

Prahlad and Thomas have presented ten propositions for turning around sick units.

These propositions are

a. Revival of a sick unit requires the formulation and implementation of a new strategy. Localizing problems and sequencing the corrective actions helps in the revival of the sick unit.

b. The successful implementation of the turnaround strategy requires appropriate organization structure, a participative type of decision making environment, effective administrative and budgetary controls, training, performance evaluation, career progression and rewards.

c. The turnaround strategy must focus on profit generation and profits must be regarded as a legitimate goal.

d. The acceptance and the commitment of managers and employees of the organization towards revival measures must be high if not total. Openness in management processes helps in gaining commitment and thus facilitates the implementation process.

e. Openness in the change process leads to confidence in the top management and its strategy. Understanding of technical processes and problem-solving attitude in overcoming technical snags is essential for turning around sick companies.

f. Consultants can play a vital role in objective analysis of problems as well as in implementing innovative changes.

g. The active support given to the chief executive by the appointing authorities is critical for the implementation of turnaround strategy.

h. Leadership provides the focus for action in sick units.

i. Thus, from these propositions, it is evident that in any turnaround process, the important issues are strategy, the management process, the technical competence and the leadership.

Turnaround Management in Public Sector Undertakings

Public Sector Enterprises (PSEs) in India represent the 'commanding heights' in terms of investment and turnover. However, a sizeable number of PSEs are still in the red and there is great pressure on them to stage a turnaround. Different PSEs have adopted different strategies for managing a turnaround. One commonly adopted strategy has been of diversification where the PSEs have ventured into related areas, such as airlines diversifying into hotels, milk procurement and supply organizations venturing into marketing of fruits and vegetables. Another strategy that is sought to be used for turnaround is that of re-organization and amalgamation of sick units into viable ones and changing the product-mix. For example, **Bharat Heavy Plates and Vessels Ltd. (BHPV),** a sick company, is being amalgamated into BHEL.

Hindustan Machine Tools (HMI) and Bharat Heavy Electricals Limited (BHEL) are two public sector units which have successfully used the diversification strategy to turnaround. HMT's strategy of diversification has been based on the use of surpluses from old ventures, to diversify into allied profitable products and gradually expanding. BHEL has decided to venture into telecommunications, metropolitan transportation and defense protection. The diversification plans entail a major change in management thinking and shifting from an area of monopoly to one which is highly competitive and also internal re-organization revolving around the concept of the product managers. The success of BHEL diversification plan has made BHEL one of the Navartana companies.

National Textile Corporation (NTC) embarked on a turnaround programme in 1988. The main planks of this turnaround strategy are:

- Restructuring and amalgamation of non-viable units with viable ones.
- up gradation and change in product-mix,

- shedding-off surplus labour, and
- Re-structuring of the capital structure.

NTC has clearly spelled out short and long-term objectives.

II. Diverstiture

Selling a division or part of an organization is called divestiture. This strategy is often used to raise capital for further strategic acquisitions or investments. Divestiture is generally used as a part of turnaround strategy to get rid of businesses that are unprofitable, that require too much capital or that do not fit well with the firm other activities.

Divestiture is an appropriate strategy to be pursued under the following circumstances:

1. When a business cannot be turned around
2. When a business needs more resources than the company can provide
3. When a business is responsible for a firm overall poor performance
4. When a business is a misfit with the rest of the organization
5. When a large amount of cash is required quickly
6. When government legal actions threaten the existence of a business.

Reasons for Divestitures

1. Poor fit of a division: When the parent company feels that a particular division within the company cannot be managed profitably, it may think of selling the division to another company. This does not mean the division itself is unprofitable. The other firm with greater expertise in the line of business could manage the division more profitably. This means the division can be managed better by someone else than the selling company.

2. Reverse synergy: Synergy refers to additional gains that can be derived when two firms combine. When synergy exists, the combined entity is worth more than the sum of the parts valued separately. In other words, $2 + 2 = 5$. Reverse synergy exists when the parts are worth more separately than they are within the parent company corporate structure. In other words, $2 + 2 = 3$. In such a case, an outside bidder might be able to pay more for a division than what the division is worth to the parent company.

3. Poor performance: Companies may want to divest divisions when they are not sufficiently profitable. The division may earn a rate of return, which is less than the cost of capital of the parent company. A division may turn out to be unprofitable due to various reasons such as increase in the material and labour cost, decline in the demand etc.

4. Capital market factors: A divestiture may also take place because the post divestiture firm, as well as the divested division, has greater access to capital markets. The combined capital structure may not help the company to attract the capital from the investors. Some investors are looking at steel companies and others may be looking for cement companies. These two groups of investors are not interested in investing in combined company, with cement and steel businesses due to the cyclical nature of businesses. So each group of investors are interested in stand-alone cement or steel companies. So divestitures may provide greater access to capital markets for the two firms as separate companies rather than the combined corporation.

5. Cash flow factors: Selling a division results in immediate cash inflows. The companies that are under financial distress or in insolvency may be forced to sell profitable and valuable divisions to tide over the crisis.

6. To release the managerial talent: Sometime the management may be overburdened with the management of the conglomerate leading to inefficiency. So they sell one or more divisions of the company. After the divestiture, the existing management can concentrate on the remaining businesses and can conduct the business more efficiently.

7. To correct the mistakes committed in investment decisions: Many companies in India diversified into unrelated areas during the pre-liberalization period. Afterwards they realized that such a diversification into unrelated areas was a big mistake. To correct the mistake committed earlier, they had to go for divestiture. This is because they moved into product market areas with which they had less familiarity than their existing activities.

8. To realize profit from the sale of profitable divisions: This type of divestiture occurs when a firm acquires under-performing businesses, makes it profitable and then sells it to other companies. The parent company may repeat this process to make profit out of it.

9. To reduce the debt burden: Many companies sell their assets or divisions to reduce their debt and bring the balance in the capital structure of the firm.

10. To help to finance new acquisitions: Companies may sell less profitable divisions and buy more profitable divisions in order to increase the profitability of the company as a whole.

Types of Divestitures

1. Spin-off: It is a kind of demerger when an existing parent company distributes on a pro-rata basis the shares of the new company to the shareholders of the parent company free of cost. There is no money transaction, subsidiary assets are not revalued, and transaction is treated as stock dividend. Both the companies exist and carry on their businesses independently after spin-off. During spin-off, a new company comes into existence. The shareholders of the parent company become the shareholders of the new company spun-off.

a. **Involuntary Spin-off:** When faced with an adverse regulatory ruling, a firm may be forced to spin-off to comply with the legal formalities.

b. **Defensive Spin-off:** Defensive spin-off is a takeover defense. Company may choose to spin-off divisions to make it less attractive to the bidder.

c. **Tax consequences of Spin-off:** Shares allotted to the shareholders during spin-off is not taxed as capital gain or as dividend.

2. Sell-off: It is a form of restructuring, where a firm sells a division to another company. When the business unit is sold, payment is received generally in the form of cash or securities. When the firm decides to sell a poorly performing division, this asset goes to another owner, who presumably values it more highly because he can use the asset more advantageously than the seller. The seller receives cash in the place of asset. So the firm can use this cash more efficiently than it was utilizing the asset that was sold. The firm can also get premium for the assets because the buyer can more advantageously use such assets. Sell-off generally has positive impact on the market price of shares of both the buyer and seller companies. So sell-offs are beneficial for the shareholders of both the companies.

3. Voluntary corporate liquidation or Bust-ups: It is also known as "complete sell-off". The companies normally go for voluntary liquidation because they create value to the shareholders. The firm may have a higher value in liquidation than the current market value. Here the firm sells its assets/divisions to multiple parties which may result in a higher value being realized than if they had to be sold as a whole. Through a series of spin-offs or sell-offs a company may go ultimately for liquidation.

4. Equity carves outs: It is a different type of divestiture and different form of spin-off and sell-off. It resembles Initial Public Offering (IPO) of some portion of equity stock of a wholly owned subsidiary by the parent company. The parent company may sell a 100% interest in subsidiary company or it may choose to remain in the subsidiary line of business by selling only a partial interest (shares) and keeping the remaining percentage of ownership. After the sale of shares to the public, the subsidiary company shares will be listed and traded separately in the capital market. The parent company receives cash from the sale of shares of the subsidiary company. The parent company may still control the company by holding controlling interest in the subsidiary. Many firms look to equity carve outs as a means of reducing their exposure to a riskier line of business. They also help to raise funds for the parent company.

Spin-offs vs Equity carve outs

The following are the differences between the spin-offs and equity carve outs:

- In case of spin-off, there is no new set of shareholders. The same shareholders in the parent company become shareholders in the spun-off company.
- In case of equity carve outs, there will be new shareholders as shares are sold to the public.
- In case of spin-off, there is no cash inflow to the parent company. The shareholders of the parent company are allotted free shares in the new company. In case of equity carve outs, as the shares of the subsidiary company are sold to the public, this results in cash inflow to the parent company.
- In case of spin-off, there is a formation of a new company.
- In case of equity carve outs, there is no new company that comes into existence. Here the shares of a subsidiary company are now offered to the public for sale.

5. Leveraged buyouts (LBO's): A leveraged buyout is an acquisition of a company in which the acquisition is substantially financed through debt. Debt typically forms 70-90% of the purchase price. Much of the debt may be secured by the assets of the company (asset based lending). Firms with assets that have a high collateral value can more easily obtain such loans. So LBOs are generally found in capital intensive industries. Debt is obtained on the basis of company future earnings potential. In LBOs, a buyer generally looks for a company with high growth rate and good market share. The company should, be profitable and the demand for the product should be known and stable, so that the earnings can be forecasted. The company should have low debt and its liquidity position should be very good. Low operating risk of such companies allows the acquisition with high degree of financial leverage and risk. The lender is prepared to lend even if the company is highly leveraged because he has full confidence in the abilities of buyer to fully utilize the potential of the business and convert it into an enormous value. He also charges high rate of interest for the loan as it involves high risk.

III. Bankruptcy

This is a form of defensive strategy. It allows organizations to file a petition in the court for legal protection to the firm, in case the firm is not in a position to pay its debts. The court decides the claims on the company and settles the corporation obligations.

IV. Liquidation

Liquidation occurs when an entire company is dissolved and its assets are sold. It is a strategy of the last resort. When there are no buyers for a business which wants to be sold, the company may be wound up and its assets may be sold to satisfy debt obligations.

Liquidation becomes the inevitable strategy under the following circumstances:

1. When an organization has pursued both turnaround strategy and divestiture strategy, but failed.
2. When an organization only alternative is bankruptcy. A company can legally declare bankruptcy first and then wind up the company to raise needed funds to pay debts.
3. When the shareholders of a company can minimize their losses by selling the assets of a business.

6.32. COMBINATION STRATEGY

A company can pursue a combination of two or more corporate strategies simultaneously. But a combination strategy can be exceptionally risky if carried too far. No organization can afford to pursue all the strategies that might benefit the firm. Difficult decisions must be made. Priorities must be established. Organizations like individuals have limited resources, so organizations must choose among alternative strategies. In large diversified companies, a combination strategy is commonly employed when different divisions pursue different strategies. Also, organizations struggling to survive may employ a combination of several defensive strategies.

Chapter 7

STAKEHOLDER, CORPORATE GOVERNANCE AND CSR, LEADER

Introduction and Meaning of Stakeholder - Participants of Stakeholders - The Organization of Stakeholder Relationship - Stakeholders versus Shareholders - Stakeholders Expectations - Scenario Planning for Stakeholders - Industry Analysis for Stakeholders - Steps in Identifying Stakeholders - Social Responsibility - Ethics - Introduction and Meaning of Corporate Social Responsibility - CSR Drivers - Three Dimensions of Corporate Performance - Areas of Social Responsibility - Diversity and Human Right in CSR - Introduction and Meaning of CG - Governance Highlights the Variation in the Points of View - Corporate Governance (CG) - Models of Corporate Governance - Mechanisms and Controls of CG - Codes/Guidelines Choice of Governance Models - Governance Issues and National Culture - Investor Protection - Recent Theoretical Development of CG - Globalization and CG - Global Landmarks in the Emergence of CG - Structure of Corporate Governance - 4 P's of CG - Principles of CG - Reasons for the Growing Demand for CG - Importance of CG - Prerequisites of CG - CG Committees - CG History in India - Mandatory Recommendations - Leader - Meaning and Definition - 3-Dimensions of Leadership Tasks - Requisites/Traits/Characteristics to be a Good Leader.

7.1. STAKEHOLDERS- Introduction

A stakeholder is any individual or organization that is affected by the activities of a business. They may have a direct or indirect interest in the business, and may be in contact with the business on a daily basis, or may just occasionally. Stakeholders are the individuals and groups who can affect and are affected by, the strategic outcomes achieved and who have enforceable claims on a firm's performance. Stakeholders can support the effective strategic management of an organization. They could also withhold participation essential for effective strategic management of an organization. At the extreme, they could oppose the top management of an organization in strategy formulation and implementation. Organization that can effectively manage stakeholders relationships generally outperform those that do not. Managing stakeholder's relationships, therefore, is critical for the strategic management of an organization. Stakeholders can be divided into internal and external stakeholders.

- Internal stakeholders include shareholders/ owners, managers and employees.
- External Stakeholders include customers, suppliers and the government.

The main participants of stakeholders are

1. **Shareholders** (not for a sole trader or partnership though)—they will be interested in their dividends and capital growth of their shares.
2. **Management and employees** they may also be shareholders—they will be interested in their job security, prospects and pay.

3. **Customers and suppliers.**
4. **Banks and other financial organizations lending money to the business.**
5. **Government**—especially the Inland Revenue and the Customs and Excise who will be collecting tax from them.
6. **Trade Unions**—who will represent the interests of the workers.
7. **Pressure Groups**—who are interested in whether the business is acting appropriately towards their area of interest.

Meaning of Stakeholders

Business and other organizations must consider stakeholders' interests. The term "stakeholder" is one most often encountered in corporate literature, although the term can be applied to government and social activist activities as well. A stakeholder can be broadly defined as any person or organization affected by an organization's activities. However, this term is usually applied to identify specific interest groups.

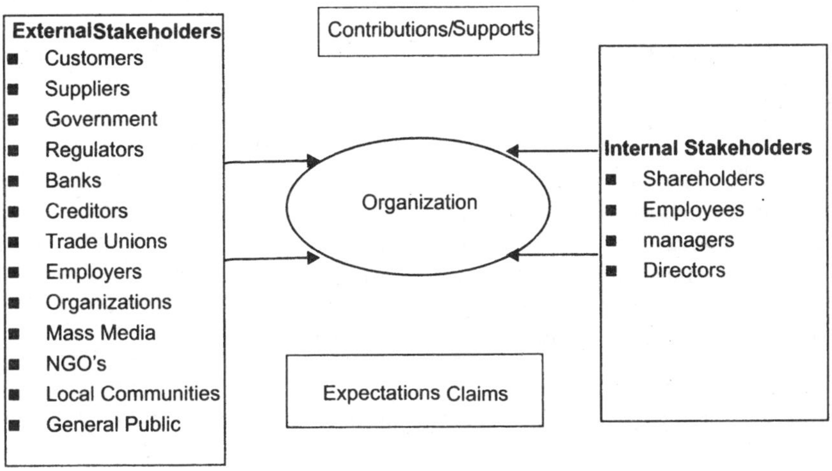

Figure 7.1. The Organization-Stakeholder Relationship.

The stake holders association with the organization is a two-way relationship. Stakeholders provide support to the organization and contribute in many different ways. In return, the organization tries to satisfy the expectations of the stakeholders and honour their legitimate claims. External stakeholders such as customers pay the price for the products and services, supplies supply materials, creditors provide finance and the government provides support through legislation and regulation and so on. Internal stakeholders such as shareholders buy shares, employees provide skills and labour, managers undertake decision-making and directors offer guidance and supervision to the organization's managers. In return, the stakeholders have expectations and claim. An external stakeholder like customer will expect good quality and fair dealing and claim value for her money. The government will expect that the organization pays taxes and follows the rules and regulations. An internal stakeholder like the shareholders will expect effective performance of the organization and claim high returns on their investments. Employees will expect fair dealing from their employing organization and claim compensation in terms of salary and wages.

As you might have noticed while reading the above matter, the nature of expectations and claims of the different types of stakeholders are diverse. Some stakeholders desire to receive monetary compensation while others expect non-monetary returns such as quality of the product or compliance. Customers expect value for their money while employees expect a good salary. The government expects corporate taxes while the directors expect compliance with their directions. Besides the diversity of stakeholder's expectations and claims, organizations also realize that all stakeholders are not equally important to them. Further managers need to understand that different stakeholders not only have diverse expectations and claims, but these may also vary over a period of time under different conditions. For instance, customers expect better quality when they are getting that level of quality at the same price from competitors. Different industries also have different configurations of stakeholders vying for an organizations attention. For example polluting industries such as oil, and gas or chemical processing may have to take special care of the environmental protections agencies and activists, while advertising agencies or banks need not bother about them such as much. Even within an industry, as conditions change, the demands of customers on organizations too may alter. With the growing importance of environmental issues, for instance, all organizations need to give greater importance to stakeholders dealing with environmental protection. All this complexity in the relationships between the organizations and their stakeholders creates the need for analyzing the relative importance of stakeholders so that the organization can effectively manage its relationship with them. In other words, organizations need to know how important a stakeholder is relative to the other stakeholders, so that it can pay commensurate attention to its expectations and claims.

7.2. STAKEHOLDERS VERSUS SHAREHOLDERS

1. Meaning

Shareholders hold shares in the company—**that is they own part of it. Stakeholders** have an interest in the company **but do not own it** (unless they are shareholders). Often the aims and objectives of the stakeholders are not the same as shareholders and they come into conflict. The conflict often arises because while shareholders want short-term profits, the other stakeholders' desires tend to cost money and reduce profits. The owners often have to balance their own wishes against those of the other stakeholders or risk losing their ability to generate future profits (e.g. the workers may go on strike or the customers refuse to buy the company's products).

2. Power

Stakeholder power is an important factor to consider whenever you are asked to write about the relationship between a business and its stakeholders. In the context of strategy, what is important is the **power and influence that a stakeholder has over the business objectives.** For stakeholders to have power and influence, **their desire to exert influence must be combined with their ability to exert** influence on the business. The power a stakeholder can exert will reflect the extent to which:-

- The stakeholder can disrupt the business' plans
- The stakeholder causes uncertainty in the plans
- The business needs and relies on the stakeholder

3. Role in Business

In business, a stakeholder is usually an investor in your company whose actions determine the outcome of your business decisions. Stakeholders don't have to be equity shareholders. They can also be your employees, who have a stake in your company's success and incentive for your products to succeed. They can be business partners, who rely on your success to keep the supply chain going. Every business takes a different approach to stakeholders. The roles of stakeholders differ between businesses, dependent on the rules and responsibilities laid out at the founding of your company or as your business evolved over the years. The most common definition of a stakeholder, however, is a large investor that has the clout to hold a viable "stake" in your company.

4. Decision Making

The most common gathering of stakeholders in a publicly traded company is the board of directors, comprised of high-ranking executives and occasional outsiders who hold large amounts of equity in the company. Any one of these stakeholders has the power to disrupt decisions or introduce new ideas to the company. The board of directors has the power to appoint all levels of senior management—including the CEO—and remove them if necessary. Members of the board dictate the future of the company and are involved in all major business decisions.

5. Direct Management

While the board of directors is a more "hands off" approach to controlling a company, some stakeholders prefer the "hands on" approach by directly assuming management positions. Stakeholders can take over certain departments – such as human resources or research and development – to micromanage the business and insure success. In privately owned and publicly traded companies, large investors often directly participate in business decisions on the management level.

6. Investors

Stakeholders are regarded as large investors, who will either increase or decrease their stakes in your company according to your financial performance. Ideally, they act as guardian angels for everyday investors, poring over financial reports and pressuring management to change tactics if necessary. Certain stakeholders, known as activist investors, will make wildly unpredictable investments and divestitures in order to move the share price and attract media attention to a certain issue. Carl Icahn is well known for this high pressure tactic, which is used to mold companies more to his liking.

7. Corporate Conscience

Large stakeholders are generally high profile investors, and would like to steer clear of companies that trample human rights and environmental laws. They monitor your company's outsourcing activities and globalization initiatives, and may vote against your business decisions if they are deemed harmful to the company's long-term goals.

8. Other Responsibilities

Of course, this is only a broad description of stakeholder responsibilities. Ideally, you'll have stakeholders who care about these four issues, but more often than not, short-term profits take precedence over long-term sustainability. While stakeholders may own your company, it's easier to control your investors when your company is privately held than publicly traded. Often times, the large influx of cash from a successful IPO turns out to be a deal with the devil when your company is suddenly taken over by a board of directors that ousts you. On the flip side, however, stakeholders can keep your company grounded and focused on its most profitable products and sustain your company's earnings growth. The reality is that stakeholders do not have equality in terms of their power and influence. For example:

- Senior managers have more influence than environmental activists
- A venture capitalist with 40% of the company's share capital will have a greater influence that a small shareholder
- Banks have a considerable impact on firms facing cash flow problems but can be ignored by a cash rich firm
- A customer that provides 50% of a business' revenues exerts significantly more influence than several smaller customer accounts
- Businesses that operate from many locations across the country will be less relevant to the local community than a business which is the dominant employer in a town or village
- Governments exercise relatively little influence on many well-established and competitive business-to-business markets. However their power is much stronger over businesses in

markets which are regulated (e.g. water, gas & electricity) or where the public sector has a direct stake (e.g. retail banking).

- Employees have traditionally sought to increase their power as stakeholders by grouping together in trade unions and exercising that power through industrial action. However, in the last two decades the level of union membership has declined significantly as has the total time lost to industrial action.

7.3. STAKEHOLDERS EXPECTATIONS

The importance of stakeholder management is to support an organization in achieving its strategic objectives by interpreting and influencing both the external and internal environments and by creating positive relationships with stakeholders through the appropriate management of their expectations and agreed objectives. Stakeholder Management is a process and control that must be planned and guided by underlying Principles. Stakeholder management, within business or projects, prepares a strategy utilizing information (or intelligence) gathered during the following common processes:

1. **Stakeholder identification:** Interested parties either internal or external to organization/ project. A stakeholder map is helpful for identifying the stakeholders.
2. **Stakeholder analysis:** Recognize and acknowledge stakeholder's needs, concerns, wants, authority, common relationships, interfaces and align this information within the Stakeholder Matrix.
3. **Stakeholder matrix:** Positioning stakeholders according to the level of influence, impact or enhancement they may provide to the business or its projects.
4. **Stakeholder engagement:** Different to Stakeholder Management in that the engagement does not seek to develop the project/business requirements, solution or problem creation, or establishing roles and responsibilities. It is primarily focused at getting to know and understand each other, at the Executive level. Engagement is the opportunity to discuss and agree expectations of communication and, primarily, agree a set of Values and Principles that all stakeholders will abide by.
5. **Communicating information**: Expectations are established and agreed for the manner in which communications are managed between stakeholder who receives communications, when, how and to what level of detail. Protocols may be established including security and confidentiality classifications.

   A stakeholder agreement is a collection of agreed decisions between stakeholders. This may be the lexicon of an organization or project, or the Values of an initiative, the objectives, or the model of the organization, etc. These should be signed by key stakeholder representatives. Contemporary or modern business and project practice favors transparent, honest and open stakeholder management processes.

7.4. SCENARIO PLANNING FOR STAKEHOLDERS

Overview

Scenarios are possible and plausible pictures of the future. They are created through a series of conversations, through which a group of people invent and consider several varied stories about how the world may turn out. Ideally, these stories should be carefully researched and full of detail, able to expose new understandings and some surprises. Scenarios are powerful tools for challenging assumptions about the world, and in so doing; they lift the barriers of our own creativity and understanding about the future. The term "scenario planning" was originally coined by the

RAND Corporation during and after World War II, as part of their corporate strategy. When Herman Kahn left the RAND Corporation, he set up the Hudson Institute and further developed the process, and went on to write a book called "The Year 2000" which was published in 1967. Since the late 60's, the process has taken off as a tool and has evolved considerably from its origins.

Scenario planning as a process started with a paradigm of "predict and control", where probabilistic scenarios were sketched out about the future. This paradigm as a basis for the process has changed significantly over the years, mainly due to the work of Pierre Wack at Shell in the 1970's. Wack separated issues which were predictable from those which were uncertain, and worked with uncertainties and how they influenced various scenarios. Nowadays, scenario planning then supports the notion that the world is inherently uncertain. Scenarios are used not so much as a tool for predicting the future, but rather as a process which challenges assumptions, values and mental models of various stakeholders about how uncertainties might affect their collective futures. By encouraging scenario planning processes at different levels of an organization or community, old paradigms are challenged, and innovation encouraged through surprising possible stories of the future. Scenarios therefore help develop new and valuable knowledge.

By bringing multiple perspectives into a conversation about the future, a rich and multidimensional variety of scenarios are created. Scenarios encourage storytelling and dialogue between people who would not necessarily share their perspectives with each other.

7.5. INDUSTRY ANALYSIS FOR STAKEHOLDERS

Identifying Stakeholders

The first step in stakeholder analysis is identifying major stakeholder groups. As you can imagine, the groups of stakeholders who will, either directly or indirectly, be affected by or have an effect on a firm's strategy and its execution can run the gamut from employees, to customers, to competitors, to the government. Ultimately, we will take these stakeholders and plot them on a chart, similar to that shown in the following table.

Table 7.1. Stakeholder's Analysis Map

	Power of the stakeholder over strategic decision			
Effect of strategy on the stakeholder	Unknown	Little or no power	Moderate degree of power	Significant Power
	Unknown			
	Little or no Effect			
	Moderate Effect			
	Significant Effect			

Let's pause for a moment to consider the important constituencies we will be charting on our stakeholder map. Before we start, however, we need to remind ourselves that stakeholders can be individuals or groups—communities, social or political organizations, and so forth. In addition, we can break groups down demographically, geographically, by level and branch of government, or according to other relevant criteria. In so doing, we're more likely to identify important groups that we might otherwise overlook. With these facts in mind, you can see that, externally, a map of stakeholders will include such diverse groups as governmental bodies, community-based organizations, social and political action groups, trade unions and guilds, and even journalists. National and regional governments and international regulatory bodies will probably be key stakeholders for global firms or those whose strategy calls for greater international presence. Internally, key stakeholders include shareholders, business units, employees, and managers.

7.6. STEPS IN IDENTIFYING STAKEHOLDERS

Identifying all of a firm's stakeholders can be a daunting task. In fact, as we will note again shortly, a list of stakeholders that is too long actually may reduce the effectiveness of this important tool by overwhelming decision makers with too much information. To simplify the process, we suggest that you start by identifying groups that fall into one of four categories: *organizational, capital market, product market, and social.* Let's take a closer look at this step.

Step 1: Determining Influences on Mission, Vision, and Strategy Formulation. One way to analyze the importance and roles of the individuals who compose a stakeholder group is to identify the people and teams who should be consulted as strategy is developed or who will play some part in its eventual implementation. These are organizational stakeholders, and they include both high-level managers and frontline workers. Capital-market stakeholders are groups that affect the availability or cost of capital—shareholders, venture capitalists, banks, and other financial intermediaries. Product-market stakeholders include parties with whom the firm shares its industry, including suppliers and customers. Social stakeholders consist broadly of external groups and organizations that may be affected by or exercise influence over firm strategy and performance, such as unions, governments, and activist groups. The next two steps are to determine how various stakeholders are affected by the firm's strategic decisions and the degree of power that various stakeholders wield over the firm's ability to choose a course of action.

Step 2: Determining the Effects of Key Decisions on the Stakeholder. Step 2 in stakeholder analysis is to determine the nature of the effect of the firm's strategic decisions on the list of relevant stakeholders. Not all stakeholders are affected equally by strategic decisions. Some effects may be rather mild, and any positive or negative effects may be secondary and of minimal impact. At the other end of the spectrum, some stakeholders bear the brunt of firm decisions, good or bad. In performing step 1, companies often develop overly broad and unwieldy lists of stakeholders. At this stage, it's critical to determine the stakeholders who are most important based on how the firm's strategy affects the stakeholders. You must determine which of the groups still on your list have direct or indirect material claims on firm performance or which are potentially adversely affected. For instance, it is easy to see how shareholders are affected by firm strategies—their wealth either increases or decreases in correspondence with the firm's actions. Other parties have economic interests in the firm as well, such as parties the firm interacts with in the marketplace, including suppliers and customers. The effects on other parties may be much more indirect. For instance, governments have an economic interest in firms doing well—they collect tax revenue from them. However, in cities that are well diversified with many employers, a single firm has minimal economic impact on what the government collects. Alternatively, in other areas, individual firms represent a significant contribution to local employment and tax revenue. In those situations, the effect of firm actions on the government would be much greater.

Step 3: Determining Stakeholders' Power and Influence over Decisions. The third step of a stakeholder analysis is to determine the degree to which a stakeholder group can exercise power and influence over the decisions the firm makes. Does the group have direct control over what is decided, veto power over decisions, nuisance influence, or no influence? Recognize that although the degree to which a stakeholder is affected by firm decisions (i.e., step 2) is sometimes highly correlated with their power and influence over the decision, this is often not the case. For instance, in some companies, frontline employees may be directly affected by firm decisions but have no say in what those decisions are. Power can take the form of formal voting power (boards of directors and owners), economic power (suppliers, financial institutions, and unions), or political power (dissident stockholders, political action groups, and governmental bodies). Sometimes the parties that exercise significant power over firm decisions don't register as having a significant stake in the firm (step 2). In recent years, for example, Wal-Mart has encountered significant resistance in some communities by well-organized groups who oppose the entry of the mega-retailer. Wal-Mart executives now have to anticipate whether a vocal and politically powerful community group will oppose its new stores or aim to reduce their size, which decreases Wal-Mart's per store profitability. Indeed, in many markets, such groups have been effective at blocking new stores, reducing their size, or changing building specifications. Once you've determined who has a stake in the outcomes of the firm's decisions as well as who has power over these decisions, you'll have a basis on which to allocate prominence in the strategy-formulation and strategy-implementation processes. The framework in the figure will also help you categorize stakeholders according to their influence in determining strategy versus their importance to strategy execution. For one thing, this distinction may help you identify major omissions in strategy formulation and implementation. Having identified stakeholder groups and differentiated them by how they are affected by firm decisions and the power they have to influence decisions, you'll want to ask yourself some additional questions:-

1. Have I identified any vulnerable points in either the strategy or its potential implementation?
2. Which groups are mobilized and active in promoting their interests?
3. Have I identified supporters and opponents of the strategy?
4. Which groups will benefit from successful execution of the strategy and which may be adversely affected?
5. Where are various groups located? Who belongs to them? Who represents them?

7.7. SOCIAL RESPONSIBILITY

Social responsibility is the duty and obligation of a business to other stakeholders.

Table 7.2.

Stakeholder	Example of responsibility to that stakeholder
Shareholder	Good return on investment
Employee	Fair pay and working conditions
Supplier	Regular business and prompt payment
Customer	Fair price and safe product
Local community	Jobs and minimum disruption
Government	Employment for local community
Environment	Less pollution

Social responsibility for one group can conflict with other groups, especially between shareholders and stakeholders.

7.8. ETHICS

Ethics refers to the **moral rights and wrongs of any decision a business makes**. It is a value judgment that may differ in importance and meaning between different individuals. Businesses may adopt ethical policies because they believe in them or they believe that by showing they are ethical, they improve their sales. Two good examples of businesses that have strong ethical policies are The Body Shop and Co-operatives. Some examples of ethical policies are

- Reduce pollution by using non-fossil fuels.
- Disposal of waste safely and in an environmentally friendly manner.
- Sponsoring local charity events.
- Trading fairly with developing countries

7.9. CORPORATE SOCIAL RESPONSIBILITY

Corporate social responsibility has become an integral part of corporate strategy. It means open and transparent business practice that are based on ethical values and respect for employees, community and the natural environment. It is designed to deliver sustainable value to society at large as well as to shareholders. Some of the benefits of being socially responsible is that they can attract good employees who prefer working for responsible firm.

Definitions

1. *CSR is a company's positive impact on society and the environment through its operations, products or services and through its interaction with key stakeholders such as employees, customers, investors, communities and suppliers"* **—Business in the Community.**
2. *"CSR means open and transparent business practices that are based on ethical values and respect for employees, communities and the environment"* **—CSR Forum.**
3. *"CSR is about how companies manage the business processes to produce an overall positive impact on society"* **—Mallen Baker.**
4. *"Corporate Social Responsibility is the continuing commitment by business to behave ethically and contribute to economic development while improving the quality of life of the workforce and their families as well as of the local community and society at large"* **—World Business Council for Sustainable Development.**

7.10. CORPORATE RESPONSIBILITY DRIVERS

The main driving forces for corporate responsibility are investor and consumer demands and governmental and public pressures as shown in the following diagram.

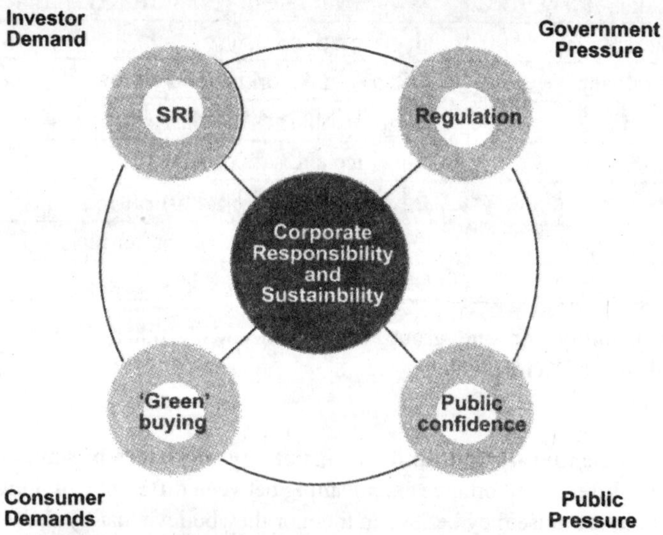

Figure 7.2. Corporate Responsibility Driving Forces.

7.11. THREE DIMENSIONS OF CORPORATE PERFORMANCE

Table 7.3. Carrol's Three Dimensional Conceptual Model of Corporate Performance

Economics	Legal	Ethical	Discretionary
Must Do	Have to Do	Should Do	Might Do

According to Archie Carroll business organizations have four responsibilities: - Economic, Legal, Ethical and Discretionary

1. The firms are expected to produce goods and services of value to society.
2. The firms should obey laws which are in force.
3. Ethical Behaviour includes the firm's responsibility to follow generally held beliefs about behaviour in a society.
4. Discretionary responsibilities are purely voluntary obligations, which a corporation undertakes such as training to agriculturists, rural development schemes etc.
5. Friedman believes that socially responsible actions hurt a firms' Efficiency whereas Carroll points out that absence of social responsibility results in government regulations resentment in the minds of various stakeholders.

Keith Davi's point of view provides another perspective to social responsibility. According to Davis, organizations draw resource from society as members of society. They have a responsibility to return to society the value of those resources as desired by the society. In his opinion-

1. Social responsibility arises from social power enjoyed by the firm
2. The firm should disclose its activities to the public through social audit
3. The social costs and benefits of social responsibility activities and services should be calculated for decision making.
4. The social costs should be included in the price.
5. The firms should solve societal problems by improving education.

7.12. AREAS OF SOCIAL RESPONSIBILITY

1. Pollution Control
2. Health and Hygiene
3. Training Self Help
4. Philanthropic Activities

Indian organizations like ICICI and Canara Bank have proved that socially responsible behaviour and world-class performance together

A few case studies of Indian IT companies are worth mentoring:-

- Tata consultancy services has developed computerized programmes to address the adult literacy problem in India. TCS has undertaken special adult literacy projects in Andra Pradesh and Tamilnadu.
- V. Moksha is educating young girls with necessary hardware training programs.
- Sundrop is a popular edible oil company which contribute to Rs.1 to Narayana Hrudayalay Heart Hospital for every one litre of Sundrop sold in order to treat children with cardiac disorders.
- India Today set up care today Foundation during the kargil conflict in1999. The Foundation works for rehabilitation of Kargil soldi*ers, Cyclone Victims, Drought Victims and earthquake* Victims with medical care

7.13. DIVERSITY AND HUMAN RIGHTS IN CSR

The following summaries of perspectives of different organizations serve to indicate the diversity of views on CSR that exist in Canada and around the world. They reflect the challenges and opportunities for both the public and private sectors to effectively operationally and align CSR between domestic, continental and international levels. They also indicate the challenges and opportunities to develop the most appropriate relationships between shareholders and other stakeholders as well as to use the optimal policy mix of legislative and voluntary instruments.

Canada

1. The Conference Board of Canada

Views CSR as helping "an organization to achieve a balance between economic, environmental and social imperatives, address stakeholder expectations and demands and sustain shareholder value. As such, CSR is perceived to "incorporate the three pillars of sustainability while placing an emphasis on the active engagement of stakeholders". The Conference Board is working in partnership with Imagine and Canadian companies on a project to develop a CSR self-assessment and benchmark framework which consists of the following five elements:

- corporate governance and management practices
- community involvement
- human resource management practices
- environment, health and safety
- human rights

2. Canadian Business for Social Responsibility

Canadian Business for Social Responsibility (CBSR) defines CSR as "a company's commitment to operating in an economically and environmentally sustainable manner while recognizing the interests of its stakeholders. Stakeholders include investors, customers, employees, business partners, local communities, the environment and society at large."

CBSR notes that "CSR goes beyond good works such as voluntarism and charity". CBSR specifies that companies practicing CSR develop policies and programs in such areas as:

- employee relations
- community development
- environmental stewardship
- international relationships
- marketplace practices
- fiscal responsibility and accountability

International

1. The World Business Council for Sustainable Development (recently renamed to Business Actions for Sustainable Development) Integrate and place CSR in the context of sustainable development. CSR is viewed as being one of three key corporate responsibilities that also include economic responsibility and environmental responsibility. CSR falls under the auspices of corporate responsibility. To this organization, CSR is "the continuing commitment by business to behave ethically and contribute to economic development while improving the quality of life of the workforce and their families as well as of the local community and society at large." The priority **CSR elements are identified as:**

- Human Rights
- Employee Rights
- Environmental Protection
- Supplier Relations
- Community Involvement
- Stakeholder Rights and
- CSR Performance Monitoring and Assessment

2. The Organization for Economic Cooperation and Development (OECD): Takes the view that CSR can mean different things to different groups, sectors and stakeholders and that it is evolving. The OECD believes that "there is general agreement that in a global economy, businesses are often playing a greater role beyond job and wealth creation and CSR is business's contribution to sustainable development" and that "corporate behavior must not only ensure returns to shareholders, wages to employees, and products and services to consumers, but they must respond to societal and environmental concerns and values." In 2000, the OECD revised the Guidelines for Multinational Enterprises and these were endorsed by OECD members including Canada. The Guidelines establish voluntary policies that promote corporate transparency and accountability, specifically addressing:

- disclosure of material information
- employment and industrial relations
- environmental management
- bribery
- competition
- consumer interests
- science and technology diffusion, and
- taxation

3. Business for Social Responsibility (BSR)

Defines CSR as business practices that "strengthen accountability, respecting ethical values in the interests of all stakeholders". BSR also proposes that "responsible business practices respect and preserve the natural environment" and that by "helping to improve the quality and opportunities of life, they empower people and invest in communities where a business operates. CSR addressed comprehensively, can deliver the greatest benefits to a company and its stakeholders when integrated with business strategy and operations." The key CSR issues challenging businesses, according to BSR include:

- Business Ethics
- Community Investment
- Environment
- Governance and Accountability
- Human Rights
- Marketplace
- Mission, Vision and Values
- Workplace

4. The Commission for European Communities: In its recent Green Paper views CSR as "essentially a concept whereby companies decide voluntarily to contribute to a better society and a cleaner environment." The Green Paper notes that for an organization to be socially responsible means not only that legal expectations be fulfilled, but it also means "going beyond compliance and investing more in human capital, the environment, and stakeholder relations". The Paper describes CSR in two categories: 1) the internal dimension, and 2) the external dimension. The former is interpreted to include human resources management, health and safety at work, adaptation to change, and management of environmental impacts and natural resources. The latter is projected to include local communities, business partners including suppliers and consumers, human rights, and global environmental concerns. A holistic approach to CSR is defined to include:

- social responsibility integrated management
- social responsibility reporting and auditing
- quality in work

- social and eco labels
- socially responsible investment

5. Globe Scan: Based in part upon their periodic surveys of consumers and citizens in a variety of countries, tend to see company social responsibilities falling into two general categories: a) operational responsibilities which are seen as the standards which companies should achieve in their normal course of business, and b) citizenship responsibilities that are not actions companies need to undertake in their normal business operations, and therefore allow a company to differentiate itself from competitors. The operational category is interpreted to include responsibilities such as the following:

- protecting health and safety of workers
- not engaging in bribery or corruption
- not using child labour
- protecting the environment
- making profit and paying taxes
- treating employees fairly
- providing quality products at lowest price
- providing secure jobs
- applying universal standards across the world

The citizenship responsibilities include:

- responding to public concerns and viewpoints
- reducing human rights abuses
- increasing economic stability
- reducing the gap between the rich and poor
- supporting charities and communities
- solving social problems
- supporting progressive government policies

6. The Global Reporting Initiative (GRI): Has developed a framework that differentiates between the economic and social and environmental performance of an organization. To GRI, the social dimension of sustainability "captures the impact of an organization's activity on society, including employees, customers, community, and supply chain and business partners." The activities cover four contexts:

- The workplace (health & safety, wages and benefits, non-discrimination, training, child labour, etc.)
- Human Rights
- Suppliers, and
- Products and Services.

7.14. CORPORATE GOVERNANCE

Introduction

Before delving further on the subject, it is important to define the concept of corporate governance. The vast amount of literature available on the subject ensures that there exist innumerable definitions of corporate governance. To get a fair view on the subject it would be prudent to give a narrow as well as a broad definition of corporate governance. In a narrow sense, corporate governance involves a set of relationships amongst the company's management, its board of directors, its shareholders, its auditors and other stakeholders. These relationships, which involve various rules and incentives, provide the structure through which the objectives of the company are set, and the means of attaining these objectives as well as monitoring performance are determined. Thus, the key aspects of good corporate governance include transparency of corporate structures and operations; the accountability of managers and the boards to shareholders; and corporate responsibility towards stakeholders. While corporate governance essentially lays down the framework for creating long term trust between companies and the external providers of capital, it would be wrong to think that the importance of corporate governance lies solely in better access of finance. Companies around the world are realizing that better corporate governance adds considerable value to their operational performance:

- It improves strategic thinking at the top by inducting independent directors who bring a wealth of experience, and a host of new ideas.
- It rationalizes the management and monitoring of risk that a firm faces globally.
- It limits the liability of top management and directors, by carefully articulating the decision making process.
- It assures the integrity of financial reports.
- It has long term reputation effects among key stakeholders, both internally and externally

In a broader sense, however, good corporate governance- the extents to which companies are run in an open and honest manner- is important for overall market confidence, the efficiency of capital allocation, the growth and development of countries' industrial bases, and ultimately the nations' overall wealth and welfare. It is important to note that in both the narrow as well as in the broad definitions, the concepts of disclosure and transparency occupy centre-stage. In the first instance, they create trust at the firm level among the suppliers of finance. In the second instance, they create overall confidence at the aggregate economy level. In both cases, they result in efficient allocation of capital. Having committed to the above definitions, it is important to note that ever since the first writings on the subject appeared in the academic domain, there have been many debates on the true scope and nature of corporate governance mechanisms around the world. More specifically on the question 'Who should corporate governance really represent?' This issue of whether a company should be run solely in the interest of the shareholders or whether it should take account the interest of all constituents1 has been widely discussed and debated for a long time now.

Definitions

1. *"Corporate governance is a field in economics that investigates how to secure/ motive efficient management of corporations by the use of incentives mechanisms such as contracts, organizational design and legislation. This often limited to the question of improving financial performance. For example, how the corporate owners can secure/ motivate that the corporate managers will deliver a competitive rate of return.-* ***Mathiesen (2002)***
2. *Corporate governance deals with the ways in which suppliers of finance to corporate assure themselves of getting a return on their investment -* ***Journal of Finnace Shleifer and Vishny(1997)***
3. *"Enhancement of long - term shareholder value while, at the same time, protecting the interests of other stakeholders.-* ***Kumar Mangalam Birla committee.***

Governance highlights the variation in the points of view

While companies are encouraged to foster long-term relationships with stakeholders by taking their interests into account, there is no concomitant pressure to build into corporate governance, structures and processes that would ensure company accountability towards stakeholder groups. It is frequently argued that attempts to mediate stakeholder claims may obscure performance evaluation and therefore facilitate discretionary behavior by management. The issue raised in the stakeholder theories is whether the recognition of a wider set of claims than those of shareholders alone is the legitimate concern of corporate governance. It is argued that the new high technology world has significantly reduced the opportunity, ability, and motivation of consumers to engage in rational decision making. Therefore, the development of loyal, inclusive stakeholder relationships, rather than the production of a better product at a lower price, will be the most important determinant of commercial viability and business success. The main intention of the stakeholder's concept as theory is to affirm and show that the company together with its executive board is responsible not only for shareholders but also for individuals or groups that have a stake in the actions and decisions of such organization. Concerning the concept of company, the theory implies understanding the company as a social institution that conforms a plural project in which distinct groups with rights and demands take part.

7.15. MODELS OF CORPORATE GOVERNANCE

Although the US model of corporate governance is the most notorious, there is a considerable variation in corporate governance models around the world. The intricated shareholding structures of keiretsus in Japan, the heavy presence of banks in the equity of German firms, the chaebols in South Korea and many others are examples of arrangements which try to respond to the same corporate governance challenges as in the US.

- Anglo-American Share Holder Wealth Maximization Model (SWM)
- Non Anglo-American Model / Corporate Wealth Maximization Model (CWM)

Anglo–American Share holder Wealth Maximization Model (SWM)

There are many different models of corporate governance around the world. These differ according to the variety of capitalism in which they are embedded. The liberal model that is common in Anglo-American countries tends to give priority to the interests of shareholders. The coordinated model that one finds in Continental Europe and Japan also recognizes the interests of workers, managers, suppliers, customers, and the community. Both models have distinct competitive advantages, but in different ways. The liberal model of corporate governance encourages radical innovation and cost competition, whereas the coordinated model of corporate governance facilitates incremental innovation and quality competition. However, there are important differences between the U.S. recent approach to governance issues and what has happened in the U.K..In the United States, a corporation is governed by a board of directors, which has the power to choose an executive officer, usually known as the chief executive officer. The CEO has broad power to manage the corporation on a daily basis, but needs to get board approval for certain major actions, such as hiring his/her immediate subordinates, raising money, acquiring another company, major capital expansions, or other expensive projects. Other duties of the board may include policy setting, decision making, monitoring management's performance, or corporate control. The board of directors is nominally selected by and responsible to the shareholders, but the bylaws of many companies make it difficult for all but the largest shareholders to have any influence over the makeup of the board; normally, individual shareholders are not offered a choice of board nominees among which to choose, but are merely asked to rubberstamp the nominees of the sitting board. Perverse incentives have pervaded many corporate boards in the developed world, with board members beholden to the chief executive whose actions they are intended to oversee. Frequently, members of the boards of directors are CEOs of other corporations, which some see as a conflict of interest. The U.K. has pioneered a flexible model of regulation of corporate governance, known as the "comply or explain" code of governance. This is a principle based code that lists a dozen of recommended practices, such as the separation of CEO and Chairman of the Board, the introduction of a time limit for CEOs' contracts, the introduction of a minimum number of non-executives Directors, of independent directors, the designation of a senior non executive director, the formation and composition of remuneration, audit and nomination committees. Publicly listed companies in the U.K. have to either apply those principles or, if they choose not to, to explain in a designated part of their annual reports why they decided not to do so. The monitoring of those explanations is left to shareholders themselves. The tenet of the Code is that one size does not fit all in matters of corporate governance and that instead of a statuary regime like the Sarbanes-Oxley Act in the U.S., it is best to leave some flexibility to companies so that they can make choices most adapted to their circumstances. If they have good reasons to deviate from the sound rule, they should be able to convincingly explain those to their shareholders.The code has been in place since 1993 and has had drastic effects on the way firms are governed in the U.K. A study by Arcot, Bruno and Faure-Grimaud from the Financial Markets Group at the London School of Economics shows that in 1993, about 10% of the UK companies member of the FTSE 350 were compliants on all dimensions while they were more than 60% in 2003. The same success was not achieved when looking at the explanation part for non compliant companies. Many deviations are simply not explained and a large majority of explanations fail to identify specific circumstances justifying those deviations. Still, the overall view is that the U.K.'s system works fairly well and in fact is often branded as a benchmark, followed by several countries.

- The suppliers of equity capital bear the entire risk of the enterprise and are the residual claimants of income
- The shareholders elect a board of directors for the corporation on a one share-equals-one-vote basis.

Non Anglo-American Model / Corporate Wealth Maximization Model (CWM)

In East Asian countries, family-owned companies dominate. A study by Claessens, Djankov and Lang (2000) investigated the top 15 families in East Asian countries and found that they dominated listed corporate assets. In countries such as Pakistan, Indonesia and the Philippines, the top 15 families controlled over 50% of publicly owned corporations through a system of family cross-holdings, thus dominating the capital markets. Family-owned companies also dominate the Latin model of corporate governance, that is companies in Mexico, Italy, Spain, France (to a certain extent), Brazil, Argentina, and other countries in South America. Europe and Asia exemplify the insider system: Shareholder and stakeholder

- A small number of listed companies, an illiquid capital market where ownership and control are not frequently traded
- High concentration of shareholding in the hands of corporations, institutions, families or government
- The insider model uses a system of interlocking networks and committees.
- At the same time that developing countries are undergoing a process of economic growth and transformation, they are also experiencing a revolution in the business and political relationships that characterize their private and public sectors. Establishing good corporate governance practices is essential to sustaining long-term development and growth as these countries move from closed, market-unfriendly, undemocratic systems towards open, market-friendly, democratic systems. Good corporate governance systems will allow organizations to realize their maximum productivity and efficiency minimize corruption and abuse of power, and provide a system of managerial accountability. These goals are equally important for both private corporations and government bodies. Because of the implicit relationship between private interests and the larger government, good corporate governance practices are essential to establishing good governance at the national level in developing countries. A number of ties the keep the public and private sectors closely linked. On one hand, judiciary and regulatory bodies as well as legislatures play a role in corporate management and oversight. At the same time cartels and large corporate interests use their size to exert not only economic, but also political power. These two sectors are so intertwined that a country cannot

significantly change one without simultaneously instituting changes in the other. According to Nicolas Meisel, there are four priorities which developing countries should concentrate on while experimenting with new forms of corporate and public governance. The first is to focus on improving the quality of information and increasing the speed at which it is created and distributed to the public. Good communication is important to the functioning of any organization. The second is to allow individual actors more autonomy while at the same time maintaining or increasing accountability. Thirdly, if a hierarchical organization used to orient private activities toward the general interest, new countervailing powers should be encouraged to fill this role. Finally, the part the state plays and how government officials are selected must be considered if a developing economy is to achieve sustainable growth. This may involve making it easier for newcomers with new ideas incumbents who may hold to older, possibly outdated, models.

- The board of directors chooses the management who are supposed to make decisions such as to maximize the value of the shares owned by the shareholders
- The value of shares is based upon the present value of expected future dividends
- Dividends are based upon after-tax profits

7.16. MECHANISMS AND CONTROLS OF CORPORATE GOVERNANCE

Corporate governance mechanisms and controls are designed to reduce the inefficiencies that arise from moral hazard and adverse selection. For example, to monitor managers' behaviour, an independent third party (the auditor) attests the accuracy of information provided by management to investors. An ideal control system should regulate both motivation and ability.

- Internal corporate governance controls
- External corporate governance controls

Internal Corporate Governance Controls

Internal corporate governance controls monitor activities and then take corrective action to accomplish organizational goals. Examples include:

- **Monitoring by the Board of Directors:** The board of directors, with its legal authority to hire, fire and compensate top management, safeguards invested capital. Regular board meetings allow potential problems to be identified, discussed and avoided. Whilst non-executive directors are thought to be more independent, they may not always result in more effective corporate governance and may not increase performance. Different board structures are optimal for different firms. Moreover, the ability of the board to monitor the firm's executives is a function of its access to information. Executive directors possess superior knowledge of the decision-making process and therefore evaluate top management on the basis of the quality of its decisions that lead to financial performance outcomes, ex ante. It could be argued, therefore, that executive directors look beyond the financial criteria.
- **Remuneration:** Performance-based remuneration is designed to relate some proportion of salary to individual performance. It may be in the form of cash or non-cash payments such as shares and share options, superannuation or other benefits. Such incentive schemes, however, are reactive in the sense that they provide no mechanism for preventing mistakes or opportunistic behaviour, and can elicit myopic behaviour.

External Corporate Governance Controls

External Corporate Governance controls encompass the controls external stakeholders exercise over the organization. Examples include:

- Competition
- Debt covenants

- Demand for and assessment of performance information (especially financial statements)
- Government regulations
- Managerial labour market
- Media pressure
- Takeovers

7.17. CODES/GUIDELINES/CHOICE OF GOVERNANCE MODELS

Corporate governance principles and codes have been developed in different countries and issued from stock exchanges, corporations, institutional investors, or associations (institutes) of directors and managers with the support of governments and international organizations. As a rule, compliance with these governance recommendations is not mandated by law, although the codes linked to stock exchange listing requirements may have a coercive effect.

For Example, companies quoted on the London and Toronto Stock Exchanges formally need not follow the recommendations of their respective national codes. However, they must disclose whether they follow the recommendations in those documents and, where not, they should provide explanations concerning divergent practices. Such disclosure requirements exert a significant pressure on listed companies for compliance.

In the United States, companies are primarily regulated by the state in which they incorporate though they are also regulated by the federal government and, if they are public, by their stock exchange. The highest number of companies are incorporated in Delaware, including more than half of the Fortune 500. This is due to Delaware's generally business-friendly corporate legal environment and the existence of a state court dedicated solely to business issues (Delaware Court of Chancery).

Most states' corporate law generally follow the American Bar Association's Model Business Corporation Act. While Delaware does not follow the Act, it still considers its provisions and several prominent Delaware justices, including former Delaware Supreme Court Chief Justice E. Norman Veasey, participate on ABA committees.

One issue that has been raised since the Disney decision in 2005 is the degree to which companies manage their governance responsibilities; in other words, do they merely try to supersede the legal threshold, or should they create governance guidelines that ascend to the level of best practice. For example, the guidelines issued by associations of directors (see Section 3 above), corporate managers and individual companies tend to be wholly voluntary. For example, The GM Board Guidelines reflect the company's efforts to improve its own governance capacity. Such documents, however, may have a wider multiplying effect prompting other companies to adopt similar documents and standards of best practice. One of the most influential guidelines has been the 1999 OECD Principles of Corporate Governance. This was revised in 2004. The OECD remains a proponent of corporate governance principles throughout the world. Building on the work of the OECD, other international organizations, private sector associations and more than 20 national corporate governance codes, the United Nations Intergovernmental Working Group of Experts on International Standards of Accounting and Reporting (ISAR) has produced voluntary Guidance on Good Practices in Corporate Governance Disclosure. This internationally agreed benchmark consists of more than fifty distinct disclosure items across five broad categories:

- Auditing
- Board and management structure and process
- Corporate responsibility and compliance
- Financial transparency and information disclosure
- Ownership structure and exercise of control rights

The World Business Council for Sustainable Development WBCSD has done work on corporate governance, particularly on accountability and reporting, and in 2004 created an frameworks. This document aims to provide general information, a "snap-shot" of the landscape and a perspective from a think-tank/professional association on a few key codes, standards and frameworks relevant to the sustainability agenda

7.18. GOVERNANCE ISSUES AND NATIONAL CULTURE

- Alterations in principles which are Universal
- Current problems
- Varied in national, regional, sector, institutional and organization
- Ethics norms
- Usage of international experience
- Remedies and reform system
- Humanities special commitment
- Public health
- Tourism and spirituality
- Economic & Habitual changes

7.19. INVESTOR PROTECTION

The Committee set up under the Chairmanship of Dr N. L. Mitra submitted the report on investor protection to the Government is as follows-

1. There is a need for a specific **Act for protecting investors' interest.** The Act should codify, amend and consolidate laws and practice for the purpose of protecting investors' interest in corporate investments.
2. A judicial forum is needed for the redressal of investors' grievance for the purpose of remedying the same with the award of compensation. The consumer forum should be the redressal forum only for the purpose of compensating the investors.
3. The provisions relating to investor education and protection fund should be **removed from the Companies Act, 1956 and included in the SEBI Act, 1992** *a*nd the fund should be administered by SEBI.
4. SEBI should be the only **regulator for the entire capital market**, both primary and secondary. It should have powers for investigation and to attach the public fund and all converted assets to prevent misappropriation. But it should not have powers to award compensation, which is the job of a justice delivery system.
5. The regulator may require **all IPOs to be insured on the principle of third party insurance** with differential premium based on the risk study by the insurance companies.
6. SEBI should have the power and function of an **on-and-off-the-field regulator.** The report has listed a number of additional powers to be conferred on SEBI. However, it cannot be an investigator, regulator and judge at the same time.
7. The SEBI Act, 1992 should be amended to provide for s**tatutory standing committees** on investors' protection, market operation and standard setting.
8. **The Securities Contract (Regulations) Act, 1956** should be amended to provide for corporatisation and principles of good governance for stock exchanges.
9. **Investor Education and Protection Fund (IEPF)** has been established under Section 205C of the Companies Act, 1956 by way Companies (Amendment) Act, 1999 for promotion of investors' awareness and protection of the interests of investors.

7.20. RECENT THEORETICAL DEVELOPMENT OF CORPORATE GOVERNANCE

1. **General Learning Outcomes**
   - Gain awareness of the theoretical underpinnings of corporate governance
   - Explain various models and mechanisms of corporate governance.
   - Recognize the shareholder/rights and responsibilities of stakeholder.
   - Elucidate the issues pertaining to the board of directors and management.
   - Analyze the best corporate practices of corporate around the world.
   - Summarize the legislations on corporate governance and responsibility.
   - To be acquainted with peculiarities of corporate governance in transition agrarian economy.
   - Understand current policy issues and how these may affect existing corporate law.
   - Comprehend and analyze relevant case law materials, statutory provisions, professional journal articles and Internet resources in relation to corporate governance.
2. **Shareholders and Stakeholders**
   - Shareholder Rights.
   - Responsibilities of Shareholders.
   - Minority Shareholders' Protection
   - Stakeholder Protection.
   - Influence of informal agrarian institutions on stakeholder protection.
3. **Board of Directors**
   - Structure and Independence of the Board.
   - Responsibilities and Duties of the Board.
   - Selection, Remuneration and Evaluation of the Board.
   - Board Committees.
   - The Board and the Management.
   - Legal issues.
4. **Financial Aspects of Corporate Governance**
   - Financial model of the corporation.
   - Financial goals and value of the company.
   - Company value, assessment of value.
   - Institutional investors on the capital market.
   - Financial Regulators and Corporate Governance.
5. **Corporate Governance Risks**
   - Board and risks.
   - Risk monitoring.
   - Shareholders risks.
   - Risk cycles.
6. **Capital Markets and Securities Regulations**
   - Design and operation of modern financial markets.
   - Modern stock, options, futures, debt, and currency markets. Concepts of arbitrage.
   - Legal definition of the term "security".
   - Security law.

7. **Models and Mechanisms of Corporate Governance**
   - Models of Corporate Governance.
   - Mechanisms of Corporate Governance.
   - Choice of governance models.
   - Governance issues and national cultures.
   - Features of Corporate Governance mechanisms in agricultural enterprises (peculiarities of formal and informal institutions).
8. **Codes of Corporate Governance**
   - Observation of codes.
   - New Russian Civil Code
   - Russian Code of Corporate Behavior.
9. **Corporate Governance Best Practices**
   - Best practices of corporate governance in the USA.
   - The Western context of governance. Best practices in West Europe.
   - Best practices of corporate governance in agribusiness.
   - Experience of corporate governance in transition economy.
10. **International Corporate Governance**
    - Role of international law and international organizations in corporate governance.
    - Comparative corporate governance as a new discipline of legal scholarship in the United States and in other countries.
    - Historical, political, cultural, and market approaches to corporate governance.
    - International capital market integration and international corporate governance rules.

7.21. GLOBALIZATION AND CORPORATE GOVERNANCE

1. **After the Second World War, people witnessed the rise of a global economy whose main hallmarks were, according to Gilpin (2000), the following ones:**
   - Open markets
   - Unrestricted capital flows
   - Pervasive activity and influence from multinational corporations.
   - In this perspective, multinational corporations carried out a decisive bearing in such broad issues as trade levels and location of economic activities. This understanding comes as an upside, because allows an easy embedding of globalization in the field of corporate governance. A downside of this approach consists of a constrained focus on economic development, leaving aside three distinctive features that have been shaping globalization ever since:
   - A market-led globalization that becomes intertwined with political nested interests
   - An interstate system plus a composite made up of crony capitalism, mafia partnerships and mega-terrorism setting up a world-system that depends on a capitalist world-economy and its security-structure
   - The growing role of some institutions aiming for a global governance target
2. **The market-led globalization and the political interests, as Friedman (2000) forcibly argues, are grounded on three wellsprings of conflicting interests:-**
   - The traditional balance between nation-states: at present, it encompasses the United States on the one hand, and the remaining nations on the other.

- Nation-states and global markets: the latter are led by the Electronic Herd (millions of investors and dealers wired by means of communication networks) that gathers in the most important financial centers in the world, places that Friedman called "the Supermarkets".
- Individuals and nation-states: Some individuals can influence markets and nation-states in more powerful ways than any time before, and that is why they are called "Super empowered Individuals".

3. **Within this standpoint, some corporate governance issues run smoothly, namely global accountability, tight budget constraints for private and government debtors, investment grade ratings, debt collaterals and securitization, short-term pressures, and global portfolio diversification. A more encompassing approach, however, Professor Escude has introduced it (1999, 2002a, 2002b), who stresses the sum and substance of the "Postmodern World-System":-**
   - A capitalist world-economy
   - A fragmented security-structure with weapons of mass destruction
4. **Escude points out the structure of the international system as built up by:**
   - An interstate composite that comprises those states that make the rules, those that takes rules, and "rogue" states that albeit they are not able to spell out rules for themselves, they are ready to reject those coming from the rule-makers.
   - A dominant newcomer: the mega terrorism.
5. **The advantages of this frame of reference for corporate governance seem manifold:**
   - The states which make the rules are also those that enjoy the best practices in governance of private or public organizations, while states that take the rules exhibit a wide range of achievers, from outstanding to substandard countries (transitional and emergent economies bearing witness to the latter group). However, the rogue states strike as counterexamples of what might be understood by good practices in corporate governance.
   - Criminal economic activities, first and foremost money laundering, drug dealing, smuggling of high-tech weaponry, and global terrorism, find out their way through special purpose entities allowed by the governance of global companies or the leniency of investment funds in offshore affiliates (Escude-Zavaleta, 2001).
6. **Finally, some scholars trailing behind the United Nations global have undertaken an institutional point of view governance targets (Scholte, 2000). They highlight the following matters of concern:**
   - Globalization conveys the emergence of a sort of post-sovereign governance, because States cannot be sovereign in the traditional sense.
   - The rise of supraterritoriality has promoted moves toward multilayered governance, where regulatory competences are more dispersed across manifold sub state, state, or suprastate arrangements and agencies.
7. **International Groups**

   The following is a partial listing of corporate governance guidelines from other international organizations:-
   - Centre for European Policy Studies (CEPS), Corporate Governance in Europe—Recommendations (June 1995).www.ecgn.org
   - Commonwealth Association for Corporate Governance (CACG), CACG Guidelines: Principles for Corporate Governance in the Commonwealth (November 1999). www.cbc.co

- European Association of Securities Dealers (EASD), Corporate Governance: Principles and Recommendations (April 2000). www.easd.com/recommendations
- European Bank for Reconstruction and Development (EBRD), Sound Business
- Standards and Corporate Practices: A Set of Guidelines (September 1997). www.ebrd.com
- Euro Shareholders, Euro Shareholders Corporate Governance Guidelines 2000 (February 2000). sss.dcgn.dk/publications/ 2000
- International Corporate Governance Network (ICGN), Global Share Voting Principles (July 1998). www.icgn .org
- ICGN, Statement on Global Corporate Governance Principles (July 1999).www.icgn.org

8. National Codes-for examples

- Australia
- Australian Institute of Company Directors (AICD)
- Investment and Financial Services Association (IFSA)
- France
- French business association, Association Française des Entreprises Privées (AFEP),
- Conseil National du Patronat Français (CNPF)
- India
- Securities and Exchange Board of India (SEBI)

7.22. GLOBAL LANDMARKS IN THE EMERGENCE OF CORPORATE GOVERNANCE

Capitalism which gave birth to the monopolies in the world, gave a real kick to start to the corporate governance. In most of the countries, way back in 19th century, capitalism stood as a system where a handful of immensely wealthy families controlled almost all of a country's great corporations, and often its government to boot. Competition was largely a mirage, for few firms are genuinely independent. Different countries economies are organized in very different ways and corporate governance- that is decisions about how capital is allocated and this is the very reason different countries have different paths to follow the corporate governance. Let us know the history of adapting the path to follow and implement corporate governance in different countries like, Canada, United States, and United Kingdom in detail.

1. Development in Canada

Canada, First as a French colony of resource extraction built around the fur trade, and then as first French and then a British colony of settlement. Their Theme is how the institutions built up during these colonial periods affected Canada's subsequent industrial development. This study has two key points. The first is that Canada was a remarkably corrupt country until a few generations ago. Canada inherited from her French colonial history a disposition to mercantilist policies that invite official abuse. Indeed, the country was a veritable laboratory for jean Baptiste Colbert, the father of French mercantilism. Subsequent British and Canadian elites preserved this disposition in the Canadian government, economy and culture. The second Key point is a remarkable pattern in Canadian corporate control. A full century ago, the large corporate sector looked much as it does now a slight predominance of family controlled pyramidal business groups supplemented by a large phalanx of freestanding widely firms. Canada looked much like the United States then, in the late 1960s and early 1970s pyramidal groups resurged, and regained their gilded age proportions by the century's end. This is because; in early 1960's institutional highlighted the necessity of entrepreneurial ideas. Thus, corporate governance was initiated.

2. Development in United States

Corporate Governance gained importance with the occurrence of the Watergate scandal in United States. Thereafter, as a result of subsequent investigations, US regulatory and legislative bodies were able to highlight control failures that had allowed several major corporations to make illegal political contributions and to bribe government officials. This led to the development of the Foreign and Corrupt Practices Act of 1977 that contained specific provisions regarding the establishment, maintenance and review of systems of internal control. This was followed in 1979 by Securities and Exchange Commission's proposals for mandatory reporting on internal financial controls. In 1985, following a series of high profile business failures in the US, the most notable one of which being the savings and loan collapse, the Trade way Commission was formed to identify the main cause of misrepresentation in financial reports and to recommend ways of reducing incidence thereof. The trade way Report published in 1987 highlighted the need for a proper control environment, independent audit committees and an objective internal audit function and called for published reports on the effectiveness of internal control The commission also requested the sponsoring organizations to develop an integrated set of internal control criteria to enable companies to improve their control.

3. Development in UK

In England, the seeds of modern corporate governance were sown by the Bank of Credit and Commerce International (BCCI) Scandal. The Barings Bank was another landmark. It heightened people's awareness and sensitivity on the issue and resolve that something ought to be done to stem the rot of corporate misdeeds. These couple of examples of corporate failures indicated absence of proper structure and objectives of top management. Corporate Governance assumed more importance in light of these corporate failures, which was affecting the shareholders and other interested parties. As a result of these corporate failures and lack of regulatory measurers from authorities as an adequate response to check them in future, the Committee of Sponsoring Organizations (COSO) was born. The report produced in 1992 suggested a control framework and was endorsed a refined in four subsequent UK reports: Cadbury, Ruthman, Hampel and Turbull. There were several other corporate failures in the companies like Polly Peck, British & Commonwealth and Robert Maxwell's Mirror Group News International were all victims of the boom-to-bust decade of the 1980s. Several companies, which saw explosive growth in earnings, ended the decade in a memorably disastrous manner. Such spectacular corporate failures arose primarily out of poorly managed business practices.

7.23. STRUCTURE OF CORPORATE GOVERNANCE

Corporate Governance is stakeholder's democracy. The stakeholders (mainly the shareholders or the stockholders) decide the directors in board of directors and one who has majority of the shares is appointed as a chairman of the company. The board of directors, analogous to the council of ministers (Cabinet) is the regulatory body, which is involved in decision-making. It is not the responsible for implementation of any decision taken by it. The board of directors decides the CEO (Chief Executive officer) of the corporate. The CEO or MD (Managing director) like prime minister is Executive authority responsible for executing the decisions taken by BOD. President along

Table 7.4.

Corporate Governance System
↓
Shareholder (Stockholder)
↓
Representatives (BOD)
↓
Executive Board
↓
CEO
↓
Chairman

with the parliament and assembly decides president. CEO may or may not be the part of BOD. Where chairman and managing director is the same, Separate CEO is appointed. The CEO selects or appoints the operative body (candidates at the level of general manager or GM).

7.24. 4 P's OF CORPORATE GOVERNANCE

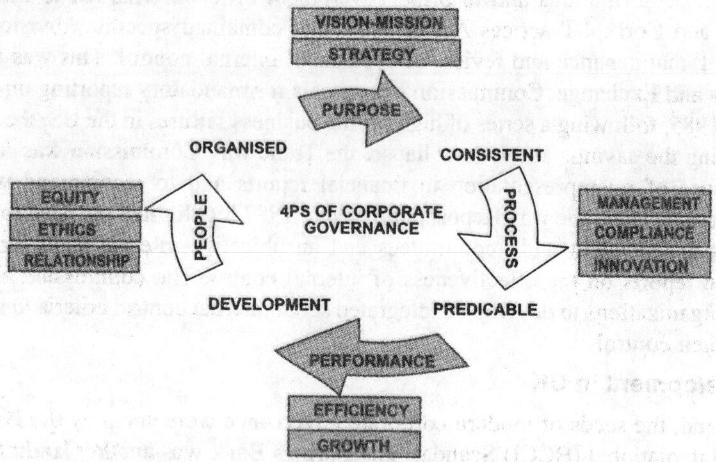

Figure 7.3. 4 P's of Corporate Governance.

Corporate Governance is an integrated framework whereby people formally organize themselves for a defined purpose, and they apply critical processes consistently to achieve predicted performance for sustainable development. Much debated principles of corporate governance like independent directors, audit committees, control on related party transactions and Investor protection cannot ensure corporate sustainability and hence corporate governance has remained a rhetoric only far from reality. Recognizing the criticality of the theme, Life Development Foundation (Life DF) has redefined corporate governance and developed a comprehensive Corporate Governance System Standard based on 4Ps (People, Purpose, Process and Performance) after an extensive research on world greatest organizations, large Indian corporate, statutory bodies, public sector undertakings, trusts, societies, partnership firms, sole proprietorships and associations.

7.25. PRINCIPLES OF CORPORATE GOVERNANCE

Contemporary discussions of corporate governance tend to refer to principles raised in three documents released since 1990: The Cadbury Report (UK, 1992), the Principles of Corporate Governance (OECD, 1998 and 2004), the Sarbanes-Oxley Act of 2002 (US, 2002). The Cadbury and OECD reports present general principals around which businesses are expected to operate to assure proper governance. The Sarbanes-Oxley Act, informally referred to as SARBOX or SOX, is an attempt by the federal government in the United States to legislate several of the principles recommended in the Cadbury and OECD reports.

1. **Rights and equitable treatment of shareholders:** Organizations should respect the rights of shareholders and help shareholders to exercise those rights. They can help shareholders exercise their rights by openly and effectively communicating information and by encouraging shareholders to participate in general meetings.
2. **Interests of other stakeholders:** Organizations should recognize that they have legal, contractual, social, and market driven obligations to non-shareholder stakeholders, including employees, investors, creditors, suppliers, local communities, customers, and policy makers.
3. **Role and responsibilities of the board:** The board needs sufficient relevant skills and understanding to review and challenge management performance. It also needs adequate size and appropriate levels of independence and commitment.

4. **Integrity and ethical behavior:** Integrity should be a fundamental requirement in choosing corporate officers and board members. Organizations should develop a code of conduct for their directors and executives that promotes ethical and responsible decision making.

5. **Disclosure and transparency:** Organizations should clarify and make publicly known the roles and responsibilities of board and management to provide stakeholders with a level of accountability. They should also implement procedures to independently verify and safeguard the integrity of the company's financial reporting. Disclosure of material matters concerning the organization should be timely and balanced to ensure that all investors have access to clear, factual information.

7.26. REASONS FOR THE GROWING DEMAND FOR CORPORATE GOVERNANCE

1. Inadequacies and failures of an existing system often bring to the force the need for norms and codes to remedy them. This is true of corporate governance too. In the UK, deficiencies in the accounting standards became more evident after many companies, in their eagerness to increase earnings and accelerate growth, exploited the weakness in the accounting standards to show inflated profits and understate liabilities. While companies grew phenomenally, accounting standards went haywire. The tendency to combine the role of chairman and chief executive in one person and board structures that was not conducive tended to make matters very undesirable.

2. The resultant failures of several companies raised serious concerns regarding corporate governance and this eventually led to the appointment of the sir Adrian Cadbury committee on corporate governance by the London stock exchange and the financial reporting council in Britain in 1991. Several other notable reports and codes in the subjects were also published internationally, like the report of the Greenbury committee, the combined code of the London stock exchange, the OECD code on corporate governance and The Blue ribbon committee on corporate governance in the US. In India, CII has published a code of corporate governance. The need for a system of corporate governance has been described by SEBI by pointing out the background of the appointment of the Kumar Mangalam Birla committee on corporate governance. There was increasing concern about standards of financial reporting and accountability, especially after losses suffered by investors and lenders which could have been avoided, with better and more transparent reporting practices.

3. Investors suffered on account of unscrupulous management of the companies which have raised capital from the market at high valuations and have performed much worse than the past reported figures, leave alone the future projections at the time of raising money. Another example of bad governance had been allotment of promoter's shares, on preferential basis at preferential prices, disproportionate to market valuation of shares, lending to further dilution of wealth of minority shareholders. This practice has however since been contained.

4. There were also many companies which are not playing adequate attention to the basic procedure for shareholders service; For example, many of these companies do not pay adequate attention to redress investor's grievances such as delay in transfer of shares, delay in dispatch of share certificates and dividend warrants and non-receipt of dividend warrants; companies also do not pay sufficient attention to timely dissemination of information to investors as also to the quality of such information. While enough laws existed to take care of many of these investor's grievances, the implementation and inadequacy of penal provisions left a lot to be desired.

5. Corporate Governance is considered an important instrument of investor protection, and it is therefore priority on SEBI's agenda. To further improve the level of corporate governance, need was felt for a comprehensive approach at this stage of development of the capital market, to accelerate the adoption of globally acceptable practices of corporate governance. This would ensure that the Indian investors are in no way less informed and protected as compared to their counterparts in the best-developed capital markets and economics of the world.

6. Securities market regulators in almost all developed and emerging markets have for sometime been concerned about the importance of the subject and of the need to raise the standards of corporate governance. The financial crisis in the Asian Markets in the recent past have highlighted the need for improved lev el of corporate governance and the lack of it in certain countries have been mentioned as one of the causes of the crisis. Indeed corporate Governance has been `widely discussed topic at the recent meetings of the international organization of security commission (IOSCO).

7. An important facilitating factor is that there is a growing awareness and enthusiasm in the corporate India to embrace good corporate governance. Many captains of industry, corporate leaders and top executive are keen to usher in good corporate governance. In fact, few years prior to the formation of the Birla committee, the path for good corporate governance was paved by the Draft Code on desirable corporate governance drawn up the confederation of Indian industries (CII).

7.27. IMPORTANCE OF CORPORATE GOVERNANCE

The need, significance or importance of corporate governance is listed below.

Table 7.5.

1. Changing Ownership Sturcture
2. Importance of Social Reponsibility
3. Growing Number of Scams
4. Indifference on the part of Shareholders
5. Globalisation
6. Takeovers and Mergers
7. SEBI

1. Changing Ownership Structure: In recent years, the ownership structure of companies has changed a lot. Public financial institutions, mutual funds, etc. are the single largest shareholder in most of the large companies. So, they have effective control on the management of the companies. They force the management to use corporate governance. That is, they put pressure on the management to become more efficient, transparent, accountable, etc. The also ask the management to make consumer-friendly policies, to protect all social groups and to protect the environment. So, the changing ownership structure has resulted in corporate governance.

2. Importance of Social Responsibility: Today, social responsibility is given a lot of importance. The Board of Directors has to protect the rights of the customers, employees, shareholders, suppliers, local communities, etc. This is possible only if they use corporate governance.

3. Growing Number of Scams: In recent years, many scams, frauds and corrupt practices have taken place. Misuse and misappropriation of public money are happening everyday in India and worldwide. It is happening in the stock market, banks, financial institutions, companies and government offices. In order to avoid these scams and financial irregularities, many companies have started corporate governance.

4. Indifference on the part of Shareholders: In general, shareholders are inactive in the management of their companies. They only attend the Annual general meeting. Postal ballot is still absent in India. Proxies are not allowed to speak in the meetings. Shareholders associations are not strong. Therefore, directors misuse their power for their own benefits. So, there is a need for corporate governance to protect all the stakeholders of the company.

5. Globalization: Today most big companies are selling their goods in the global market. So, they have to attract foreign investor and foreign customers. They also have to follow foreign rules and regulations. All this requires corporate governance. Without Corporate governance, it is impossible to enter, survive and succeed the global market.

6. Takeovers and Mergers: Today, there are many takeovers and mergers in the business world. Corporate governance is required to protect the interest of all the parties during takeovers and mergers.

7. SEBI: SEBI has made corporate governance compulsory for certain companies. This is done to protect the interest of the investors and other stakeholders.

7.28. PREREQUISITES OF CORPORATE GOVERNANCE

1. A proper system consisting of clearly defined and adequate structure of roles, authority and responsibility.
2. Vision, principles and norms which indicate development path, normative considerations and guidelines and norms for performance.
3. A proper system for guiding, monitoring, reporting and control.

7.29. CORPORATE GOVERNANCE COMMITTEES

The main committees, known by the names of the individuals who chaired them are discussed hereunder

1. Cadbury Committee on Corporate Governance –1992: The stated objectives of the Cadbury Committee was "To help raise the standards of corporate governance and the level of confidence in financial reporting and auditing by setting out clearly what it sees as the respective responsibilities of those involved and what it believes his expected of them. The committee investigated the accountability of the board of directors to shareholders and to society. It submitted its report and associated "Code of Best Practices" in 1992 wherein it spelt out the methods of governance needed to achieve a balance between the essential power of the board of directors and their proper accountability. Its recommendations were not mandatory. The Cadbury code of best practices had 19 recommendations. The recommendations are in the nature of guidelines relating to the board of directors, non-executive directors, executive directors and those on reporting and control. The stress in the Cadbury committee report is on the crucial role of the board and the need for it to observe the Code of Best Practices. Its important recommendations include the setting up of an audit committee with independent members.

2. The Paul Ruthman Committee: The committee was constituted later to deal with the said controversial point of Cadbury Report. It watered down the proposal on the grounds of practicality. It restricted the reporting requirement to internal financials controls only as against "the effectiveness of the company's system of internal control" as stipulated by the Code of Best Practices contained in the Cadbury Report. The final report submitted by the Committee chaired by Ron Hampel had some important and progressive elements, notably the extension of directors' responsibilities to "all relevant control objectives including business risk assessment and minimizing the risk of fraud"

3. The Greenbury Committee: This committee was setup in January 1995 to identify good practices by the Confederation of British Industry (CBI), in determining directors' remuneration and to prepare a code of such practices for use by public limited companies of United Kingdom. The committee aimed to provide an answer to the general concerns about the accountability by the proper allocation of responsibility for determining directors' remuneration, the proper reporting to shareholders and greater transparency in the process. The committee produced the Greenbury Code of Best Practice which was divided into the four sections: Remuneration Committee, Disclosures, Remuneration Policy and Service Contracts and Compensation. The Greenbury committee recommended that UK companies should implement the code as set out to the fullest extent practicable, that they should make annual compliance statements, and that investor institutions should use their power to ensure that the best practice is followed.

4. The Hampel Committee: The Hampel committee was setup in November 1995 to promote high standards on Corporate Governance both to protect investors and preserve and enhance the standing of companies listed on the London Stock Exchange. The committee developed further the Cadbury report. And it made the following recommendations. The auditors should report on internal control privately to the directors. The directors maintain and review all controls. Companies should time to time review their need for internal audit function and control.

5. The Turnbull Committee: The Turnbull Committee was set up by the Institute of Chartered Accountants in England and Wales (ICAEW) in 1999 to provide guidance to assist companies in implementing the requirements of the Combined Code relating to internal control. The committee provided guidance to assist companies in implementing the requirements of the Combined Code relating to internal control. It recommended that where companies do not have an internal audit function, the board should consider the need for carrying out an internal audit annually. The committee also recommended that board of directors confirm the existence of procedures for evaluation and managing key risks.

7.30. CORPORATE GOVERNANCE: HISTORY IN INDIA

There have been several major corporate governance initiatives launched in India since the mid-1990s. The first was by the Confederation of Indian Industry (CII), India's largest industry and business association, which came up with the first voluntary code of corporate governance in 1998. The second was by the SEBI, now enshrined as Clause 49 of the listing agreement. The third was the Naresh Chandra Committee, and the fourth was again by SEBI- The Narayana Murthy Committee.

7.31. RECOMMENDATIONS OF THE VARIOUS COMMITTEES

1. The CII Code: More than a year before the onset of the Asian crisis, CII set up a committee to examine corporate governance issues, and recommend a voluntary code of best practices. The committee was driven by the conviction that good corporate governance was essential for Indian companies to access domestic as well as global capital at competitive rates. The first draft of the code was prepared by April 1997, and the final document (Desirable Corporate Governance: A Code), was publicly released in April 1998. The code was voluntary, contained detailed provisions, and focused on listed companies.

2. Desirable Disclosure: "Listed companies should give data on high and low monthly averages of share prices in a major stock exchange where the company is listed; greater detail on business segments, up to 10% of turnover, giving share in sales revenue, review of operations, analysis of markets and future prospects." Major Indian stock exchanges should gradually insist upon a corporate governance compliance certificate, signed by the CEO and the CFO." If any company goes to more than one credit rating agency, then it must divulge in the prospectus and issue document the rating of all the agencies that did such an exercise. These must be given in a tabular format that shows where the company stands relative to higher and lower ranking." "Companies that default on fixed deposits should not be permitted to accept further deposits and make inter-corporate loans or investments or declare dividends until the default is made good"

3. Kumar Mangalam Birla committee report and Clause 49: While the CII code was well-received and some progressive companies adopted it, it was felt that under Indian conditions a statutory rather than a voluntary code would be more purposeful, and meaningful. Consequently, the second major corporate governance initiative in the country was undertaken by SEBI. In early 1999, it set up a committee under Kumar Mangalam Birla to promote and raise the standards of good corporate governance. In early 2000, the SEBI board had accepted and ratified key recommendations of this committee, and these were incorporated into Clause 49 of the Listing Agreement of the Stock Exchanges. This report pointed out that the issue of corporate governance involves besides shareholders, all other stakeholders. The committee's recommendations have looked at corporate governance from the point of view of the stakeholders and in particular that of shareholders and investors. The control and reporting functions of boards, the roles of the various committees of the board, the role of management, all assume special significance when viewed from this perspective. At the heart of committee's report is the set of recommendations, which distinguish the responsibilities, and obligations of the boards and the management in instituting the systems for good Corporate Governance. Many of them are mandatory. These recommendations are expected to be enforced on listed companies for initials disclosures. This enables shareholders to know, where the companies are in which they have involved. The committee recognized that India had in place a basic system of corporate governance and that SEBI has already taken a number of initiatives towards raising the existing standards. The committee also recognized that the Confederation of Indian Industries (CII) had published a code entitled "Desirable code of corporate of Governance and was encouraged to note that some of the forward looking companies have already reviewed their annual report through complied with the code. Now to protect investors especially shareholders from any malpractices and injustice the Securities and Exchange Board of India appointed committee on corporate governance on May 7, 1999 under chairmanship of Shri Kumar Managalam Birla, Member of SEBI Board to promote standard of Corporate Governance.

4. The constitutions of Committee: The committee has identified the three key constituents of corporate Governance as the share holders, the Board of Directors and the Management. Along with this the committee has identified major 3 aspects namely accountability, transparency and equality of treatment for all shareholders. Crucial to good corporate governance are the existence and enforceability of regulations relating to insider information and insider trading. These matters are currently being examined over here. The committee had received good comments from almost all experts institutions, chamber of commerce Adrian Cadbury – Cadbury Committee etc.

5. Corporate Governance Objectives: Corporate Governance has several claimants – shareholders, suppliers, customers, creditors, the bankers, employees of company and society. The committee for SEBI keeping view has prepared primarily the interests of a particular class of stakeholders namely the shareholders this report on corporate governance. It means enhancement of shareholder value keeping in view the interests of the other stack holders. Committee has recommended C.G. as company's principles rather than just act. The company should treat corporate governance as way of life rather than code.

6. Recommendations: Mandatory Non-Mandatory: The committee was of the firm view that mandatory compliance of the recommendations at least in respect of essential the essential would be most appropriate in the Indian context for the present. The committee felt that some of the recommendations are absolutely essential for the framework of corporate governance and virtually from its core while others could be considered desirable.

7. Applicability: The committee was of the opinion that the recommendations should be made applicable to the listed companies them directors, management, employees and professionals associated with such companies, in accordance with time table proposed in the schedule given later in this section.According to the committee, the recommendations were to be applied to all the listed private and public sector companies, in accordance with the schedule of implementation. As for listed entitles which are not companies, but body corporate e.g. private sector banks, financial institutions, insurance companies etc. incorporated under statutes, the recommendations will apply to the extent that they do not violate guidelines issued by prevalent authority.

7.32. MANDATORY RECOMMENDATIONS

1. Board of Directors

An effective corporate governance system is one, which allows the board to perform these dual functions efficiently. The board of directors of a company thus directs and controls the management of a company and is accountable to the shareholders. The board directs the company, by formulating and reviewing company's policies strategies, major plans of action, risk policy, annual budgets and business plans, setting performance objectives, monitoring implementation and corporate performance and over seeing major capital expenditures, appositions and change in financial control and compliance with applicable law taking into the account the interests of the stake holders.

2. Composition of the B.O.D

The composition of the Board is as important as it determines the ability of the board to collectively provide leadership and ensures that no one individual or a group is able to dominate the board. This has undergone a change and increasingly the boards comprise of following groups of directors. Promoters, director executives and non-executive directors, a part of who are independent.

3. Independent Direction

Independent directions are those directors who apart from receiving director's remuneration do not have any other material pecuniary relationship with company. Further, all pecuniary relationship or transactions of the non executive directors should be disclosed in the annual report. The committee recommended that the board of a company have an optimum combination of executive and non-executive directors with not less than fifty percent of the board comprising the non-executive directors. In case a company has a non-executive chairman, at least one third of board should comprise of independent directors and in case a company has an executive chairman at least half of board should be independent.

4. Nominee Directors

These directors are the nominees of the financial as investment institutions to safeguard their interest it may be present of retired employee of financial institution on outsider. The committee recommend that institutions should appoint nominees on the boards of companies only on a selective basis where such appointment is pursuant to a right under loan agreements as where such appointment in is considered necessary to protect like interest of the institutions.

5. Chairman of the Board

The committee recommended that a non-executive chairman should be entitled to maintain a chairman's office at the company's expense and also allowed reimbursement of expenses incurred in performance of his duties. This will enable him to discharge the responsibilities effectively.

6. Audit Committee (Non Mandatory)

The Committee is of the view that the need for having an audit committee grows from the recognition of the audit committees' position in the larger mosaic of governance process. The audit committee's job is one of oversight and monitoring and carrying out this job it relies on similar financial management and outside auditors. The committee believes that the progressive standards of governance applicable to the full board should also be applicable to the audit committee.The committee therefore recommended that the board of a company should set up a qualified and independent audit committee. The committee states that audit committee should have minimum three members, all being non-executive directors, with the majority being independent and with at least one director having financial and accounting knowledge.

7. Frequency of Meeting and Quorum (Mandatory Recommendation)

The committee recommends that to begun with the audit committee should meet at least thrice a year. One meeting must be held before finalization of annual accounts and one necessarily every six months. The quorum should be either two members or one third of members of audit committee, whichever is higher and there should be a minimum of two Independent directors.

8. Powers of Audit Committee (Mandatory)

(1) To investigate any activity within its terms of reference.

(2) To seek information from any employee.

(3) To obtain outside legal on other professional advice.

(4) To secure attendance of outsiders with relevant expertise, if it considers necessary.

9. Functions of Audit Committee (Mandatory)

(1) To ensure that the financial statement is correct, sufficient and creditable.

(2) Recommending the appointment and removal of external audit.

(3) Reviewing with management annual financial statement before submission to board related to changes in accounting policies and practices.

   (a) Major accounting entries.

   (b) Qualifications in draft audit report.

   (c) Significant adjustments arising out of audit.

   (d) Compliance with accounting standards.

   (e) Compliance with stock exchange and legal requirement concerning financial statements.

   (f) Any transaction that may have potential conflict with the interest of company at large.

(4) Reviewing with the management about adequacy of control.

(5) Discuss with internal auditors into the matter suspecting fraud on irregularity.

(6) Discuss with external auditors before the audit commences and also post-audit discussion to ascertain any area of concern.

10. Remuneration Committee (Mandatory)

The committee is of the view that a company must have a creditable and transparent policy in determining and accounting for the remuneration of the directors. For this purpose the committee recommends that the board should set up a remuneration committee to determine on their behalf and on behalf of the shareholders with agreed terms of references. The Remuneration Committee should comprise of at least three directors, all of them should be non-executive directors, the chairman being an independent one. The chairman of Remuneration Committee should present at AGM. It is important for the shareholders to be informed of the remuneration of the directors of the company, which is mandatory.

11. Naresh Chandra Committee Report

The Naresh Chandra committee was appointed in August 2002 by the Department of Company Affairs (DCA) under the Ministry of Finance and Company Affairs to examine various corporate governance issues. The Committee submitted its report in December 2002. It made recommendations in two key aspects of corporate governance: financial and non-financial disclosures: and independent auditing and board oversight of management. The committee submitted its report on various aspects concerning corporate governance such as role, remuneration, and training etc. of independent directors, audit committee, the auditors and then relationship with the company and how their roles can be regulated.

The committee stingily believes that "a good accounting system is a strong indication of the management commitment to governance. Good accounting means that it should ensure optimum disclosure and transparency, should be reliable and credible and should have comparability. According to the committee, the statutory auditor in a company is the "lead actor" in disclosure front and this has been amply recognized sections 209 to 223 of the companies act. The chief aspects concerning the auditors functioning as per the act are:

- Auditors are fiduciaries of the shareholders not of the management as they are appointed as the shareholders appoint them.
- Auditor's independence is guaranteed as rules for removing on replacing an auditor as more stringent than for reappointment.
- The statutory auditor of a company can, at all times, have the right of access to all books of accounts and vouchers of a company and his repeat can be quite exhaustive to specify whether, The auditor could obtain from management all information and explanations that were necessary for the purpose of audit.
- Proper books of accounts have been kept by the company
- Brained offices have been audited by him
- Company's accounts conform to accounting standards set by the institute of chartered Accountants of India.

12. Narayana Murthy Committee report on Corporate Governance:

The fourth initiative on corporate governance in India is in the form of the recommendations of the Narayana Murthy committee. The committee was set up by SEBI, under the chairmanship of Mr. N. R. Narayana Murthy, to review Clause 49, and suggest measures to improve corporate governance standards. Some of the major recommendations of the committee primarily related to audit committees, audit reports, independent directors, related party transactions, risk management, directorships and director compensation, codes of conduct and financial disclosures.

7.33. LEADER

What is Leadership?

"What makes a leader?" has been a key question asked throughout the organizations of this century. Although there is a tremendous research in the subject, however no clear blueprint of effective leadership has emerged that strongly relates to the success in variety of organizations.

General Electric Corporation defined, "A leader is considered to be someone with vision and ability to articulate that vision to the team, so vividly and powerfully that it becomes their vision".

Another text defined, "A leader is someone who brings to the situation a clear and compelling sense of the future as well as an understanding of the actions needed to get there successfully."

There are as many definitions of leadership as there are people who have attempted to define it. Thus defining leadership is perhaps a futile exercise since it remains open to multiple interpretations by different individuals. However, a more rational way to comprehend leadership is to focus on a particular framework, like an organization and try to define the expected role of a leader.

7.34. 3- DIMENSIONS OF LEADERSHIP TASKS

The most fundamental role of a leader is to define the organizational goal, formulate plans and organize people to achieve the goals through the execution of plans.

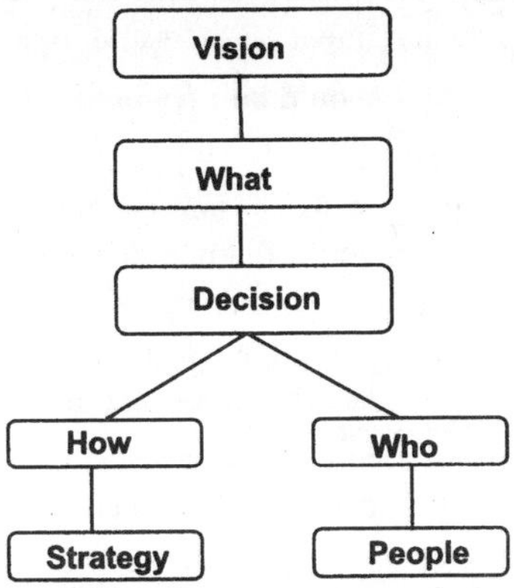

Figure 7.4. 3-Dimensions of Leadership Tasks.

1. Vision — It defines the purpose, or simply "What to do?" A vision includes determining the next product or feature, finding new markets for the product, adoption of new technology etc.
2. Strategy—*It* articulates the plans, "How to achieve the vision?" Plans or strategies demonstrate the job knowledge or the skills of a leader. It includes restructuring organization, product management, strategic management etc.
3. People—"Who should carry out the Strategy?" How to make people accomplish the strategy and hence the goal, the peop*le* skills include providing inspiration & motivation.

Minzberg has concluded in his research study that CEO does as many as ten roles such as—

1. Figure head role
2. Leader role
3. The Liason role
4. The Recipient role
5. The Disseminator role
6. The Spokesperson role
7. The Entrepreneur role
8. The Disturbance handler role
9. The Negotiator role
10. The resource allocator role CEO's responsibilities include executive leadership and strategic vision.

7.35. REQUISITES/TRAITS/CHARACTERISTICS TO BE A GOOD LEADER

1. **Physical Appearance:** A leader must have a pleasing appearance. Physique and health are very important for a good leader.
2. **Vision and Foresight:** A leader cannot maintain influence unless he exhibits that he is forward looking. He has to visualize situations and thereby has to frame logical programmes.
3. **Intelligence:** A leader should be intelligent enough to examine problems and difficult situations. He should be analytical who weighs pros and cons and then summarizes the situation. Therefore, a positive bent of mind and mature outlook is very important.

4. **Communicative Skills:** A leader must be able to communicate the policies and procedures clearly, precisely and effectively. This can be helpful in persuasion and stimulation.
5. **Objective:** A leader has to be having a fair outlook which is free from bias and which does not reflects his willingness towards a particular individual. He should develop his own opinion and should base his judgment on facts and logic.
6. **Knowledge of Work:** A leader should be very precisely knowing the nature of work of his subordinates because it is then he can win the trust and confidence of his subordinates.
7. **Sense of Responsibility:** Responsibility and accountability towards an individual's work is very important to bring a sense of influence. A leader must have a sense of responsibility towards organizational goals because only then he can get maximum of capabilities exploited in a real sense. For this, he has to motivate himself and arouse and urge to give best of his abilities. Only then he can motivate the subordinates to the best.
8. **Self-confidence and Will-power:** Confidence in him is important to earn the confidence of the subordinates. He should be trustworthy and should handle the situations with full will power).
9. **Humanist:** This trait to be present in a leader is essential because he deals with human beings and is in personal contact with them. He has to handle the personal problems of his subordinates with great care and attention. Therefore, treating the human beings on humanitarian grounds is essential for building a congenial environment.
10. **Empathy:** It is an old adage "Stepping into the shoes of others". This is very important because fair judgment and objectivity comes only then. A leader should understand the problems and complaints of employees and should also have a complete view of the needs and aspirations of the employees. This helps in improving human relations and personal contacts with the employees.

Chapter 8

STRATEGIC CHANGE, DECISION MAKING AND FORMULATION

Introduction, Meaning and Nature of Strategic Change - Creative Problem Analysis, Strategic Decision Making Process - Dimensions of Strategic Decisions, Characteristics of Decision Making, Types of Business Decisions, Decision Making Stages, Steps in Decision Making Process, Advantages, Constraints - Barriers to Change, Change Requirements, Implementation of Strategic Change, Types of Changes in Organization, Managing Strategic Change, A General Frame Work for Managing Change - Input Stage, the Matching Stage, Selection of Matrix and Decision Stage - Introduction, Meaning and Steps of Strategy Formulation.

8.1. INTRODUCTION

Strategic change management plays an important role in the development process of a company. Modern-day business goes through several change processes to cope with the changes taking place in the market. Introduction of these changes is done in a systematic manner in today's corporate world. The task of introducing a change in an existing system is a difficult job. Management of these changes is even more difficult. These changes may be of any kind, it may be a change in the project, change in the line of action, change in the production level, change in the mechanism or change in the ownership. If initiated properly, these changes can yield heavily for the company. However, if the process is not controlled, it can affect the entire business. The changes according to their nature can be termed as internal changes or external changes.

Strategic Internal Change Management

There are certain situations in which it becomes necessary for the companies to introduce several changes in the internal system of the company. This restructuring may be done in the production process, in the labor codes, in the machineries and so on. The changes may occur at any level and it is the proper management of the process that decides the future of the company. A company may consider that introduction of a particular piece of modern machinery would increase the level of production and decrease the cost of operation. Now, before the introduction of such a modern piece of machinery, it is essential to provide enough training to the workers of the company who are going to handle the particular machine. If it is done, the production level will rise but if it is not done properly, it will surely cause downfall in the production. The bottom line is that planning is very important to introduce something new in the process of production.

Strategic External Change Management

Strategic change management is crucial in the context of the introduction of external change in a company's product-line or in the marketing policy. If a company wants to introduce a new marketing policy, it is necessary to undertake the basic surveys and prepare a strategy to apply the new policy in the market. If the process is introduced all of a sudden, it may create confusion amongst the common people thereby resulting in a downfall in the sale of product. Again there are certain changes that influence internal as well as external factors. Such a change in the management of a company may be caused by mergers, acquisitions or something else. In order to introduce such changes, it is necessary to prepare the ground well before the plan is initiated. Otherwise, these can create confusions inside the company and at the same time, this confusion may also reach the share market that can bring down the stock prices of the particular company.

There are four key features of Change Management

- Change is the result of dissatisfaction with present strategies
- It is essential to develop a vision for a better alternative
- Management have to develop strategies to implement change
- There will be resistance to change

Many factors drive change in a business. Lewin identified four forces

In Lewin's Model there are forces driving change and forces restraining it. Where there is equilibrium between the two sets of forces there will be no change. In order for change to occur the driving force must exceed the restraining force.

Lewin's Analysis can be used to

- Investigate the balance of power involved in an issue
- Identify the key stakeholders on the issue
- Identify opponents and allies
- Identify how to influence the target groups

Forces for change include

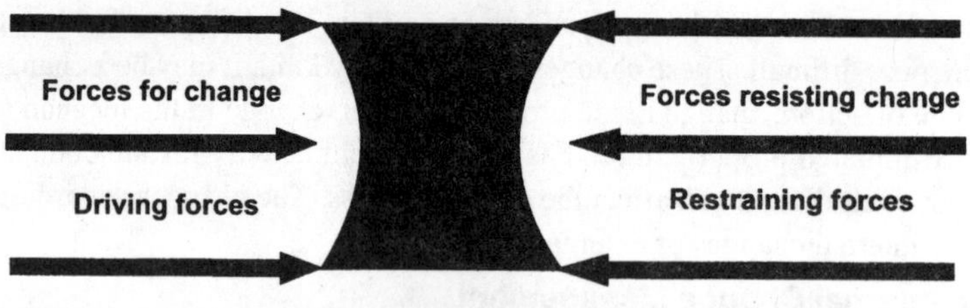

Figure 8.1.

Some examples of the forces that drive change include

Internal Forces

- Desire to increase profitability
- Re-organization to increase efficiency
- Conflict between departments
- To change organisational culture

External Forces

- Customer Demand
- Competition
- Cost of inputs
- Legislation & Taxes
- Political
- Ethics & Social Values
- Technological Change

8.2. MEANING AND DEFINITION OF STRATEGIC CHANGE

Strategic change means changing the organizational Vision, Mission, Objectives and of course the adopted strategy to achieve those objectives.

Strategic change is defined as "changes in the contez competitive advantages, and synergy"

—Hofer and Schendel 1978.

Strategic change is defined as a difference in the form, quality, or state over time in organization's alignment with its external environment ***—Rajagopalan & Spreitzer, 1997 Van de Ven & Pool, 1995.***

Considering the definition of strategic change, Strategic change could be affected by the states of firms and their external environments. Because the performance of firms might dependent on the fit between firms and their external environments, the appearances of novel opportunities and threats in the external environments, in other words, the change of external environments, require firms to adopt to the external environments again; as a result, firms would change their strategy in response to the environmental changes. The states of firms will also affect the occurrence of strategic change.

8.2.1 What Organization can Change?

What organizations can change fall into the following broad areas

1. **Mission, Vision, & Strategy:** Organizations should continually ask themselves, "What is our business and what should it be?" Answers to these questions can lead to changes in the organization's mission (the purpose of its business), its vision for the future (what the organization should look like), and its competitive strategy.
2. **Technology:** Organizations can change their technology (For example the way they produce whatever they sell) in order to increase efficiency and lower costs.
3. **Human-Behavioral Changes:** Training can be provided to managers and employees to provide new knowledge and skills, or people can be replaced or downsized. As result of the recent financial crisis, many organizations downsized creating massive unemployment that continues to this day.
4. **Task-Job Design:** The way work is performed in the organization can be changed with new procedures and methods for performing work.
5. **Organizational Structure:** Organizations can change the way they are structured in order to be more responsive to their external environment. Again to be more responsive to the marketplace, this also includes where decisions should be made in the organization (centralized or decentralized).
6. **Organizational Culture:** Entities can attempt to change their culture, including management and leadership styles, values and beliefs. Of all the things organizations can change, this is by far the most difficult to undertake.

These are the major elements that organizations can change. It is important to note that changes in one of these elements will usually have an impact on another element. As an example, changing technology may require changes in the human-behavioral area (new knowledge and skills on how to use the technology).

8.2.2 Why Organizations Change?

Organizations change for a number of different reasons, so they can either react to these reasons or be ahead of them. These reasons include:

1. **Crisis:** Obviously September 11 is the most dramatic example of a crisis which caused countless organizations, and even industries such as airlines and travel, to change. The recent financial crisis obviously created many changes in the financial services industry as organizations attempted to survive.

2. **Performance Gaps:** The organization's goals and objectives are not being met or other organizational needs are not being satisfied. Changes are required to close these gaps.
3. **New Technology:** Identification of new technology and more efficient and economical methods to perform work.
4. **Identification of Opportunities:** Opportunities are identified in the market place that the organization needs to pursue in order to increase its competitiveness.
5. **Reaction to Internal & External Pressure:** Management and Employees, particularly those in organized unions often exert pressure for change. External pressures come from many areas, including customers, competition, changing government regulations, shareholders, financial markets, and other factors in the organization's external environment.
6. **Mergers & Acquisitions:** Mergers and acquisitions create change in a number of areas often negatively impacting employees when two organizations are merged and employees in duel functions are made redundant.
7. **Change for the Sake of Change:** Often times an organization will appoint a new CEO. In order to prove to the board he is doing something, he will make changes just for their own sake.
8. **Sounds Good:** Another reason organization may institute certain changes is that other organizations are doing so (such as the old quality circles and re-engineering fads). It sounds good, so the organization tries it.
9. **Planned Abandonment:** Changes as a result of abandoning declining products, markets, or subsidiaries and allocating resources to innovation and new opportunities.

8.3. NATURE OF STRATEGIC CHANGE

- **Accountability**—responsibility is assigned for successful completion of initiatives.
- **Balance**—the plans guide not only financial decision-making, but also operational and human resources issues.
- **Flexibility**—a mechanism for changing and updating the plan is built into the process.
- **Manageability**—in-process measures are identified to ensure processes are working as intended, critical performance issues are addressed, resources required are projected, and methods of status reporting are in place.
- **Prioritization**—priorities are established whenever there are multiple interdependent action plans.
- **Realism**—the question of what the organization can do versus what it would like to do is addressed rationally, though the tone is optimistic.
- **Specificity**—expected results and milestones are clearly defined, along with the specific actions for implementation and the deliverables for each step.
- **Sustainability**—a sufficient time period is covered to close performance gaps.

8.4. CREATIVE PROBLEM ANALYSIS

The words "Creative Problem Solving" has almost become more like buzzwords tossed around the workplace and never really landing anywhere. Everyone knows intuitively that creative problem solving can work, and it's the "thing to do" in a participatory organization, but exactly what does it mean and what benefits can be obtained?

Creative problem solving is a method of approaching change within the organization. It usually involves a team approach, because people within the workplace are empowered to participate in the change process when looking for creative solutions. An effective organization recognizes that its own personnel often hold the keys to innovation within themselves and only need the right outlet to share their experience based ideas.

- **A Creative Change Agent**

In other words, creative problem solving is a method of finding innovative approaches for problem resolution. The problem may be any of a number of situations or needs. For example, the problem may be stated in terms of the need to resolve interdepartmental conflict which is reducing efficiency. On the other hand, the problem may be a need for a product innovation in order to improve the company's competitive standing within its industry.

No matter what the problem or need the business may be addressing, creative ideas and fresh approaches can often make the difference between a successful company and one that is unable to remain efficient and competitive. It also offers a way to introduce change into an organization that minimizes the normal fear that usually accompanies change. The creative problem solving process becomes a change agent that can turn resistance into action.

- **Seeing a Problem as an Opportunity**

One of the most important features of the creative problem solving process is the fact it turns a problem into an opportunity to improve the organization. Instead of just relying on traditional ideas or past practices to resolve a problem, the creative approach encourages people to participate in a dynamic setting which encourages new ideas and approaches.

The fact is that most organizations have the creative power within their own setting among the staff. The creative process brings together various people including managers, office personnel, line workers or supervisors, and many others. The people chosen to participate depend on the problem being solved.

The creative process follows a format which takes the group up to the moment when creativ thinking is unleashed. In the initial stages, the process first accomplishes the following:

- Identifies the problem in traditional terms.
- Establishes goals.
- Empowers participants.
- Develops criteria for choosing ideas.
- Focuses on how to "sell" the creative idea.

Popular creative problem solving strategies which have been developed include brainstorming, mind mapping, and even role or team game playing. In every situation, the goal is to empower people to feel comfortable enough to freely generate ideas without fear of criticism.

- **The Path of Creativity**

In both brainstorming and mind mapping, ideas are suggested which may or may not seem reasonable on the surface. But no idea is eliminated and all ideas are welcomed. One idea is mapped or associated with another idea and a path of ideas leads to one or more creative solutions to a problem. The solution chosen depends on the criteria established at the beginning of the process.

In creative problem solving, organizational members are encouraged to participate and the process provides recognition to the people who are major contributors to the success of the business to date. It promotes teamwork, unity, creative approaches, and positive energy. However, possibly the most important success factor in creative problem solving is ensuring that time is dedicated regularly to the creativity process.

8.5. STRATEGIC DECISION MAKING PROCESS

8.5.1 Meaning of Decision Making

Decision-making is an essential aspect of modern management. It is a primary function of management. A manager's major job is sound/rational decision-making. He takes hundreds of decisions consciously and subconsciously. Decision-making is the key part of manager's activities.

Decisions are important as they determine both managerial and organizational actions. A decision may be defined as "a course of action which is consciously chosen from among a set of alternatives to achieve a desired result." It represents a well-balanced judgment and a commitment to action.

It is rightly said that the first important function of management is to take decisions on problems and situations. Decision-making pervades all managerial actions. It is a continuous process. Decision-making is an indispensable component of the management process itself. Means and ends are linked together through decision-making. To decide means to come to some definite conclusion for follow-up action. Decision is a choice from among a set of alternatives. The word 'decision' is derived from the Latin words "deciso" which means 'a cutting away or a cutting off or in a practical sense' to come to a conclusion. Decisions are made to achieve goals through suitable follow-up actions. Decision-making is a process by which a decision (course of action) is taken. Decision-making lies embedded in the process of management.

According to Peter Drucker, "Whatever a manager does, he does through decision-making". A manager has to take a decision before acting or before preparing a plan for execution. Moreover, his ability is very often judged by the quality of decisions he takes. Thus, management is always a decision-making process. It is a part of every managerial function. This is because action is not possible unless a firm decision is taken about a business problem or situation.

This clearly suggests that decision-making is necessary in planning, organizing, directing, controlling and staffing. For example, in planning alternative plans are prepared to meet different possible situations. Out of such alternative plans, the best one (i.e., plan which most appropriate under the available business environment) is to be selected. Here, the planner has to take correct decision. This suggests that decision-making is the core of planning function. In the same way, decisions are required to be taken while performing other functions of management such as organizing, directing, staffing, etc. This suggests the importance of decision-making in the whole process of management.

The effectiveness of management depends on the quality of decision-making. In this sense, management is rightly described as decision-making process. According to R. C. Davis, "management is a decision-making process." Decision-making is an intellectual process which involves selection of one course of action out of many alternatives. Decision-making will be followed by second function of management called planning. The other elements which follow planning are many such as organizing, directing, coordinating, controlling and motivating.

Decision-making has priority over planning function. According to Peter Drucker, it is the top management which is responsible for all strategic decisions such as the objectives of the business, capital expenditure decisions as well as such operating decisions as training of manpower and so on. Without such decisions, no action can take place and naturally the resources would remain idle and unproductive. The managerial decisions should be correct to the maximum extent possible. For this, scientific decision-making is essential.

8.5.2 Definition of Decision Maikng

1. The Oxford Dictionary defines the term Decision-making as "the action of carrying out or carrying into effect".
2. According to Trewatha & Newport, "Decision-making involves the selection of a course of action from among two or more possible alternatives in order to arrive at a solution for a given problem".

8.5.3 Dimensions of Strategic Decisions

- **Top Management Involvement:** The CEO has to assess the impact of strategic decision various divisions, and allocate the resources effectively and oversee the implementation process carefully.

- **Allocation of large amount of resources:** Strategic decisions require allocation of large quantity of external and internal resources over an extended period of time.
- **Effect on long term prosperity of the firm:** Strategic decisions have long term effects in firms. Once a firm adopts a strategy its image and competitive advantages are invariably linked with the strategy. It gains recognition in certain market for certain products with certain technologies. The firm would seriously jeopardize all its previous gains if it shifts focus from these markets, products or technologies by adopting a radically different strategy.
- **Future Oriented:** Strategic decisions are built around forecast. The firm has to select a suitable course of action from available alternatives.
- **Multi functional:** Strategic decisions have complex implications on various areas of the firm. They impact various strategic business units.
- **Focus on External Groups:** In order to successfully position a firm in a competitive environment, strategists must look beyond its operations. They must keep in mind how the other stake holders (competitors, customers, government, suppliers, creditors and labour) are likely to react to the strategic decisions from time to time.

8.5.4 Characteristics of Decisions Making

1. **Decision Making implies Choice:** Decision making is choosing from among two or more alternative courses of action. Thus, it is the process of selection of one solution out of many available. For any business problem, alternative solutions are available. Managers have to consider these alternatives and select the best one for actual execution. Here, planners/ decision-makers have to consider the business environment available and select the promising alternative plan to deal with the business problem effectively. It is rightly said that "Decision-making is fundamentally choosing between the alternatives". In decision-making, various alternatives are to be considered critically and the best one is to be selected. Here, the available business environment also needs careful consideration. The alternative selected may be correct or may not be correct. This will be decided in the future, as per the results available from the decision already taken. In short, decision-making is fundamentally a process of choosing between the alternatives (two or more) available. Moreover, in the decision-making process, information is collected; alternative solutions are decided and considered critically in order to find out the best solution among the available. Every problem can be solved by different methods. These are the alternatives and a decision-maker has to select one alternative which he considers as most appropriate. This clearly suggests that decision-making is basically/fundamentally choosing between the alternatives. The alternatives may be two or more. Out of such alternatives, the most suitable is to be selected for actual use. The manager needs capacity to select the best alternative. The benefits of correct decision-making will be available only when the best alternative is selected for actual use.
2. **Continuous Activity/Process:** Decision-making is a continuous and dynamic process. It pervades all organizational activity. Managers have to take decisions on various policy and administrative matters. It is a never ending activity in business management.
3. **Mental/Intellectual Activity:** Decision-making is a mental as well as intellectual activity/ process and requires knowledge, skills, experience and maturity on the part of decision-maker. It is essentially a human activity.
4. **Based on Reliable Information/Feedback:** The quality of decision-making at all levels of the Organization can be improved with the support of an effective and efficient management information system (MIS).

5. **Goal Oriented Process:** Decision-making aims at providing a solution to a given problem/ difficulty before a business enterprise. It is a goal-oriented process and provides solutions to problems faced by a business unit.
6. **Means and Not the End:** Decision-making is a means for solving a problem or for achieving a target/objective and not the end in itself.
7. **Relates to Specific Problem:** Decision-making is not identical with problem solving but it has its roots in a problem itself.
8. **Time-Consuming Activity:** Decision-making is a time-consuming activity as various aspects need careful consideration before taking final decision. For decision makers, various steps are required to be completed. This makes decision-making a time consuming activity.
9. **Needs Effective Communication:** Decision-taken needs to be communicated to all concerned parties for suitable follow-up actions. Decisions taken will remain on paper if they are not communicated to concerned persons. Following actions will not be possible in the absence of effective communication.
10. **Pervasive Process:** Decision-making process is all pervasive. This means managers working at all levels have to take decisions on matters within their jurisdiction.
11. **Responsible Job:** Decision-making is a responsible job as wrong decisions prove to be too costly to the Organization. Decision-makers should be matured, experienced, knowledgeable and rational in their approach. Decision-making need not be treated as routing and casual activity. It is a delicate and responsible job.

8.5.5 The Differences Between Strategic, Administrative and Operational Decisions can be Summarized as Follows

Table 8.1.

Strategic Decisions	Administrative Decisions	Operational Decisions
Strategic decisions are long term decisions.	Administrative decisions are taken daily.	Operational decisions are not frequently taken.
These are considered where the future planning is concerned.	These are short-term based decisions.	These are medium-period based decisions.
Strategic decisions are taken in accordance with organizational mission and vision.	These are taken according to strategic and operational decisions.	These are taken in accordance with strategic and administrative decision.
These are related to overall counter planning of all organization.	These are related to working of employees in an organization.	These are related to production.
These deal with organizational growth.	These are in welfare of employees working in an organization.	These are related to production and factory growth.

8.5.6 Types of Business Decisions

1. **Programmed Decisions.** These are standard decisions which always follow the same routine. As such, they can be written down into a series of fixed steps which anyone can follow. They could even be written as computer program.
2. **Non-Programmed Decisions.** These are non-standard and non-routine. Each decision is not quite the same as any previous decision.

3. **Strategic Decisions.** These affect the long-term direction of the business. For Eg: whether to take over Company A or Company B.
4. **Tactical Decisions.** These are medium-term decisions about how to implement strategy. For Eg: what kind of marketing to have, or how many extra staff to recruit
5. **Operational Decisions.** These are short-term decisions (also called administrative decisions) about how to implement the tactics. For Eg: which firm to use to make deliveries.

8.5.7 Decision-Making Stages

Developed by B. Aubrey Fisher, there are four stages that should be involved in all group decision making. These stages, or sometimes called phases, are important for the decision-making process to begin

- Orientation stage: This phase is where members meet for the first time and start to get to know each other.
- Conflict stage: Once group members become familiar with each other, disputes, little fights and arguments occur. Group members eventually work it out.
- Emergence stage: The group begins to clear up vague in opinions is talked about.
- Reinforcement stage: Members finally make a decision, while justifying themselves that it was the right decision

8.5.8 Step Involved in Decision Making Process

Decision-making involves a number of steps which need to be taken in a logical manner. This is treated as a rational or scientific 'Decision-Making Process' which is lengthy and time consuming. Such lengthy process needs to be followed in order to take rational/scientific/result oriented decisions. Decision-making process prescribes some rules and guidelines as to how a decision should be taken / made. This involves many steps logically arranged. It was Peter Drucker who first strongly advocated the scientific method of decision-making in his world famous book 'The Practice of Management' published in 1955. Drucker recommended the scientific method of decision-making which, according to him, involves the following six steps

1. Defining / Identifying the Managerial Problem
2. Analyzing the Problem
3. Developing Alternative Solutions
4. Selecting the Best Solution out of the Available Alternatives
5. Converting the Decision into Action and
6. Ensuring Feedback for Follow-up

Figure 8.2 suggests the steps in the decision-making process.

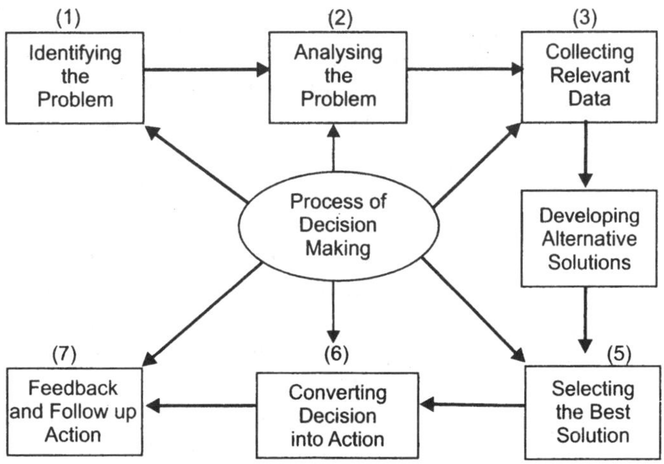

Figure 8.2. Decision-making Process.

1. Identifying the Problem: Identification of the real problem before a business enterprise is the first step in the process of decision-making. It is rightly said that a problem well-defined is a problem half-solved. Information relevant to the problem should be gathered so that critical analysis of the problem is possible. This is how the problem can be diagnosed. Clear distinction should be made between the problem and the symptoms which may cloud the real issue. In brief, the manager should search the 'critical factor' at work. It is the point at which the choice applies. Similarly, while diagnosing the real problem the manager should consider causes and find out whether they are controllable or uncontrollable.

2. Analyzing the Problem: After defining the problem, the next step in the decision-making process is to analyze the problem in depth. This is necessary to classify the problem in order to know who must take the decision and who must be informed about the decision taken. Here, the following four factors should be kept in mind.

a. Futurity of the decision,

b. The scope of its impact,

c. Number of qualitative considerations involved, and

d. Uniqueness of the decision.

3. Collecting Relevant Data: After defining the problem and analyzing its nature, the next step is to obtain the relevant information/ data about it. There is information flood in the business world due to new developments in the field of information technology. All available information should be utilized fully for analysis of the problem. This brings clarity to all aspects of the problem.

4. Developing Alternative Solutions: After the problem has been defined, diagnosed on the basis of relevant information, the manager has to determine available alternative courses of action that could be used to solve the problem at hand. Only realistic alternatives should be considered. It is equally important to take into account time and cost constraints and psychological barriers that will restrict that number of alternatives. If necessary, group participation techniques may be used while developing alternative solutions as depending on one solution is undesirable.

5. Selecting the Best Solution: After preparing alternative solutions, the next step in the decision-making process is to select an alternative that seems to be most rational for solving the problem. The alternative thus selected must be communicated to those who are likely to be affected by it. Acceptance of the decision by group members is always desirable and useful for its effective implementation.

6. Converting Decision into Action: After the selection of the best decision, the next step is to convert the selected decision into an effective action. Without such action, the decision will remain merely a declaration of good intentions. Here, the manager has to convert 'his decision into 'their decision' through his leadership. For this, the subordinates should be taken in confidence and they should be convinced about the correctness of the decision. Thereafter, the manager has to take follow-up steps for the execution of decision taken.

7. Ensuring Feedback: Feedback is the last step in the decision-making process. Here, the manager has to make built-in arrangements to ensure feedback for continuously testing actual developments against the expectations. It is like checking the effectiveness of follow-up measures. Feedback is possible in the form of organized information, reports and personal observations. Feed back is necessary to decide whether the decision already taken should be continued or be modified in the light of changed conditions.

Every step in the decision-making process is important and needs proper consideration by managers. This facilitates accurate decision-making. Even quantitative techniques such as CPM, PERT/OR, linear programming, etc. are useful for accurate decision-making. Decision-making is important as it facilitates entire management process. Management activities are just not possible without decision-making as it is an integral aspect of management process itself. However, the quality of decision-making should be always superior as faulty/irrational decisions are always dangerous.

For accurate/rational decision-making attention should be given to the following points:

1. Identification of a wide range of alternative courses of action i.e., decisions. This provides wide choice for the selection of suitable decision for follow-up actions.
2. A careful consideration of the costs and risks of both positive and negative consequences that could follow from each alternation.
3. Efforts should be made to search for new information relevant to further evaluation of the alternatives. This is necessary as the quality of decision depends on the quality of information used in the decision-making process.
4. Re-examination of the positive and negative effects of all known alternatives before making a final selection.
5. Arrangements should be made for implementing the chosen course of action including contingency plans in the event that various known risks were actually to occur.
6. Efforts should be made to introduce creativity and rationality in the final decision taken.

Why Rational and Right Decisions Are Not Possible: Rational decisions are the best decisions under the available circumstances. All decisions should be rational as such decisions facilitate expansion of business and give more profit, goodwill and prosperity to a business unit. Rationality and decision-making are closely related concepts. Rationality principle is applicable to all types of decisions. All decisions (business, economic, social etc.) should be fair and rational. They should serve as examples over a long period. For such decisions, rational/scientific/balanced approach is essential while making decisions. In the absence of such approach, decisions are likely to be faulty and dangerous to the Organization and also to all concerned parties. Rationality in decision-making is possible through human brain which has the ability to learn, think, analyze and relate complex facts and variables while arriving at a decision. A manager has to introduce rationality in his decision-making by using his skills, experience, knowledge and mental abilities. On some occasions, such rational and right decisions are not taken due to variety of possible reasons. It is also possible that the decision taken may be rational when taken but is treated as wrong/irrational/faulty because' the results available from the decision taken are not as expected/positive/encouraging. Rational decisions may not be possible when the approach of the decision-maker is casual and superficial. He may not be alert, careful and cautious while taking the decisions or he might not have followed the decision-making process in a scientific manner. In brief, all business decisions should be rational as far as possible as such rational decisions offer many benefits/advantages. However, rational decisions may not be taken on certain occasions. According to Herbert A. Simon, human beings are not always rational in the decisional process.

Reasons Why Rational and Right Decisions May Not Be Possible?

1. **Inadequate Information, Data and Knowledge:** For rational decision-making accurate, reliable and complete information about various aspects of the problem under investigation is necessary. The possible future trends can be estimated with the help of such information. This facilitates rational decision-making. However, adequate and reliable information may not be available at the time of decision-making. As a result, the decisions become defective or irrational. Such decision may prove to be faulty in the course of time. This is how the decisions become irrational to certain extent.
2. **Uncertain Environment:** Decisions are taken on the basis of information available about various environmental variables. However, the variables are many and complex in nature. They may be related to political, economic, social and other aspects. It is not possible to study all such variables in depth due to inadequate information/data. This leads to inaccurac in decision making and the decisions taken are not fully rational.

3. **Limited Capacity of Decision-Maker**. A decision-maker should be expert, knowledgeable, intelligent and matured. He needs vision and capacity to imagine possible future situation. In the absence of such qualities, the decision-maker may not be able to take rational decisions. Similarly, the decision taken may not be rational if the decision-maker fails to follow all necessary steps required for scientific decision-making. A hasty decision or decision taken without full use of all mental faculties may not be fully rational. Thus, decisions are likely to be less rational if the decision maker lacks capacity to take rational decisions.
4. **Personal Element In Decision-Making:** Decision-making should be always impartial and also favorable to the Organization. Decision against Organization but favorable to decision maker or other employees will be unfair. Such decision will not be rational. Similarly, every decision-maker has his own personal background in the form of personal beliefs, attributes, preferences, likes and dislikes and so on. A decision-maker is expected to keep these elements away while taking management decisions. This may not be possible in the case of all decision-makers and on all occasions. However, decisions are not fully rational when such personal element comes in the picture.
5. **A Decision Cannot Be Fully Independent:** Managerial decisions are interlinked and interdependent. A manager has to make adjustments or compromises while making decisions. For example, for reducing price, some compromise with the quality may be necessary. A manager gives more importance to one and less to the other. He takes one decision which is rational at the same time makes some compromise in the other decision. As a result, other decision is not likely to be fully rational. In short, business decisions are interlinked. This brings an element of irrationality in some decisions.

8.5.9 Advantages of Decision Making

1. **Decision Making is the Primary Function of Management:** The functions of management starts only when the top-level management takes strategic decisions. Without decisions, actions will not be possible and the resources will not be put to use. Thus decision-making is the primary function of management.
2. **Decision-Making Facilitates the Entire Management Process:** Decision-making creates proper background for the first management activity called planning. Planning gives concrete shape to broad decisions about business objectives taken by the top-level management. In addition, decision-making is necessary while conducting other management functions such as organizing, staffing, coordinating and communicating.
3. **Decision-Making is a Continuous Managerial Function:** Managers working at all levels will have to take decisions as regards the functions assigned to them. Continuous decision making is a must in the case of all managers/executives. Follow-up actions are not possible unless decisions are taken.
4. **Decision-Making is Essential to face New Problems and Challenges:** Decisions are required to be taken regularly as new problems, difficulties and challenges develop before a business enterprise. This may be due to changes in the external environment. New products may come in the market, new competitors may enter the market and government policies may change. All this leads to change in the environment around the business unit. Such change leads to new problems and new decisions are needed.
5. **Decision-Making is a Delicate and Responsible Job:** Managers have to take quick and correct decisions while discharging their duties. In fact, they are paid for their skill, maturity and capacity of decision-making. Management activities are possible only when suitable

decisions are taken. Correct decisions provide opportunities of growth while wrong decisions lead to loss and instability to a business unit.

8.5.10 Constraints on Decision-Making

I. Internal Constraints

These are constraints that come from within the business itself.

- **Availability of Finance:** Certain decisions will be rejected because they cost too much
- **Existing Business Policy:** It is not always practical to re-write business policy to accommodate one decision
- **People's Abilities and Feelings:** A decision cannot be taken if it assumes higher skills than employees actually have, or if the decision is so unpopular no-one will work properly on it.

II. External Constraints

These come from the business environment outside the business.

- **National & EU legislation**
- **Competitor's behavior,** and their likely response to decisions your business makes
- **Lack of technology**
- Economic climate

8.5.11 Decision Making at Hair Telecom

Decision-making increasingly happens at all levels of a business. The Board of Directors may make the grand strategic decisions about investment and direction of future growth, and managers may make the more tactical decisions about how their own department may contribute most effectively to the overall business objectives. But quite ordinary employees are increasingly expected to make decisions about the conduct of their own tasks, responses to customers and improvements to business practice. This needs careful recruitment and selection, good training, and enlightened management.

8.6. BARRIERS TO CHANGE

Change and the phenomenon of it, is fundamental to evolution; and yet it implies some sort of resistance.

Resistance to change can take various forms and the task of filtering out the cause of resistance can often be difficult. Examples include change in work processes where the Needs, Expectations, and concerns of individuals are ignored.

Change and resistance to it forms a knock-on-effect to both the construction and destruction of any organization. Fear is one of the major forms of resistance to change. Resistance to change can be categorized to the organizational level and the individual level. It is these two separate levels which shall discuss further exploring what steps may be taken to overcome resistance at both the organizational and individual level.

A. The Organisational Barriers to Change

There are a number of barriers to change at the organizational level that, need to be addressed to allow change to be implemented with the least amount of resistance. These include:

1. **Undefined Goals and Objectives:** An organization should clarify continually the goals and objectives, outlining roles and specifying performance standards.
2. **Financial and Environmental:** Lack of working capital in an organization can prevent it from introducing change that is necessary to stay ahead of competitors or merely survive as

a business. In these circumstances redundancies are almost inevitable. The lack of finance could be due to a variety of factors. These include: a fall in market demand, rise in competition or the degree of turbulence in the market place such as the September 11th World Trade Disaster; which caused a significant effect on businesses and investment worldwide.

3. **Lack of Resources and Bad Resource Allocation:** Lack of resources is an onset of financial and/or environmental issues as discussed in the above paragraph. Bad resource allocation, occur when managers make bad decisions in allocating resources such as money, time, machinery and staff. Managers should use their imagination to avoid causing conflict situations.
4. **Structural:** An organization that follows the traditional hierarchical structure tends to resist change more than that which has a more flat structure. Communication between head of departments and employees in traditional hierarchical structures are usually poor which causes a rift between Management and Employees.
5. **Insufficient Communication:** There are two branches of communication, which are communication Internally, within the organization between Employees and Management and Externally between the organization and suppliers and customers. Organizations that fail to communicate with their Customers and Suppliers, changes that are in effect can face disastrous consequences. For Example the Tiptree Company that had implemented a £1.5 million warehousing system to handle a larger number of books failed to notify, its customers that it had undergone a radical change without informing it's customers. Unfortunate for Tiptree, which encountered problems with their new systems for about six months; had tarnished its 1992 British Book Awards Distributor of the Year. (Judy Collins, CRASH 28 th October 2000)
6. **Lack of or Bad Leadership:** Strong leadership is required in order to direct the change management process in any organization. Bad leaders who merely provide are not doing enough to inspire the employees to march ahead. People want to be shown the way.
7. **Lack of preparation for New Roles:** Organizations may lack in their planning phase. Failing to Prepare and define the new roles that will need to be satisfied when change is implemented; shall give rise to resistance.
8. **Cultural Issues:** The culture of an organization is a set of "unwritten rules". Management may have a set of protocols for employees to adhere to perform business processes. The way a task is actually carried out depends namely on the culture. The culture of the organization can strongly resist changing as employees become too familiar with the current way of doing things.

B. Individuals Barriers to Change

There are a number of barriers to change at the individual level that, need to be addressed to allow change to be implemented with the least amount of resistance. These include:

1. **Fear:** News of change can invoke fear among employees. Employees may feel afraid of not being able to fulfil the new proposed changes to work practices that are being imposed. Employees may begin to question the future of their job, which shall cause much discomfort. People resist change due to anxiety, pessimism and different personal ambitions.
2. **Lack of Input into the Change**: Individuals tend to resist change where they play not part in change. The idea of not knowing the change can cause a rift between the employees and management.

8.6.1 Overcoming Barriers

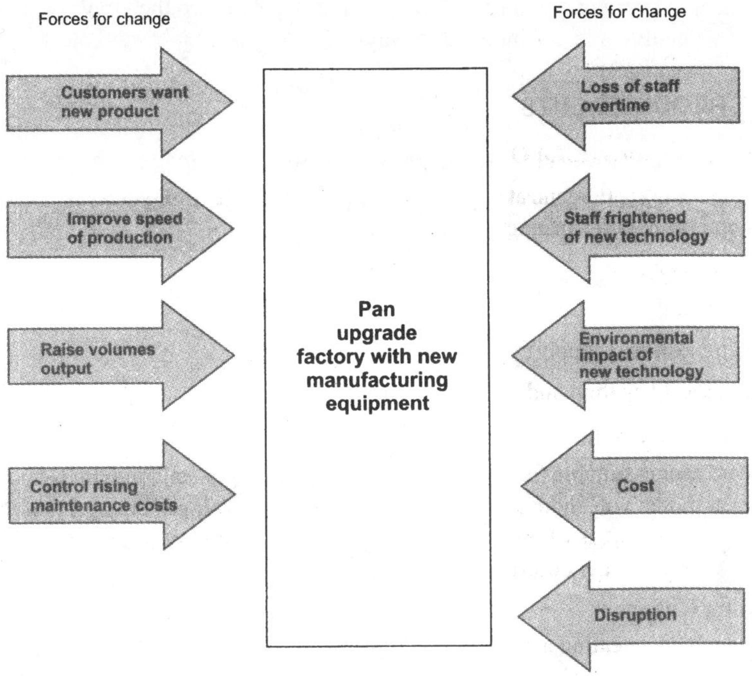

Figure 8.3.

1. **Overcoming Undefined Goals and Objectives:** Goals and objectives should be frequently redefined and relayed to all employees. This shall aid towards clearing up any misunderstanding and possible conflicts.
2. **Overcoming Financial and Environmental Issues:** Organizations should have a contingency fund to cater for changes in demand or develop a very good relationship with their bank manager in case you need to borrow money at hard times. At the other end of the scale if demand sores suppliers must be able to satisfy demand. Benchmarking suppliers shall help determine your best suppliers. A good supplier may be one that allows you to have a 30 day or more credit accounts, which leave you with more working capital. Essentially corporate business strategies should have a degree of flexibility to act as a defense to sudden changes.
3. **Overcoming Structural Problems and Insufficient Communication:** In a large organization employees may wish to elect a spokes person who can act as a collective voice to air potential barriers directly to management. Surveys can be conducted and results analyzed. In a small organization employees should be encouraged to speak up if they feel that change is causing a conflict.
4. **Overcoming Lack of or Bad Leadership:** It is a natural human instinct to follow leadership as children we look up to our parents and as adults we look up towards our superiors. Leaders must lead the way and be an example for others to follow. In leading and setting an example to others leaders must take an active role a "hands on approach" side by side with the employees in order to motivate and encourage.
5. **Overcoming Lack of Preparation for New Roles:** The importance of planning must be emphasized and reflected. The new roles should be concisely explained to the respective employees prior to implementing change, to stifle out any doubts, fears or resistance.

6. **Overcoming Cultural Issues:** The cultural characteristics once identified need to be overcome and evolved into a non-blame culture. By doing so the employees shall have the freedom to evolve and try innovative ways of doing their jobs without the fear of being penalized for mistakes.

8.7. CHANGE REQUIREMENTS

Requirements for Successful Organizational Change

Cummings and Worley (Organization Development and Change, 1995) describe a comprehensive, five-phase, general process for managing change, including

1) Motivating change,

2) Creating vision,

3) Developing Political support,

4) Managing the Transition and

5) Sustaining Momentum.

That process seems suitable for organizing and describing general guidelines about managing Change. Whatever model you choose to use when guiding organizational change, that model should include the priorities and areas of emphasis described in the following five phases of change. The collaborative consulting model described integrates highlights from all of the five phases.

1. Motivating Change

This phase includes creating a readiness for change in your client organization and developing approaches to overcome resistance to change. General guidelines for managing this phase include enlightening members of the organization about the need for change, expressing the current status of the organization and where it needs to be in the future, and developing realistic approaches about how change might be accomplished. Next, organization leaders need to recognize that people in the organization are likely to resist making major changes for a variety of reasons, including fear of the unknown, inadequacy to deal with the change and whether the change will result in an adverse effect on their jobs. People need to feel that their concerns are being heard. Leaders must widely communicate the need for the change and how the change can be accomplished successfully. Leaders must listen to the employees – People need to feel that the approach to change will include their strong input and ongoing involvement.

2. Creating Vision

Leaders in the organization must articulate a clear vision that describes what the change effort is striving to accomplish. Ideally, people in the organization have strong input to the creation of the vision and how it can be achieved. The vision should clearly depict how the achievement of the vision will improve the organization. It is critically important that people believe that the vision is relevant and realistic. Research indicates that cynicism is increasing in organizations in regard to change efforts. People do not want to hear the need for the latest "silver bullet" that will completely turn the organization around and make things better for everyone all the time. They want to feel respected enough by leaders to be involved and to work toward a vision that is realistic, yet promising in the long run. Often the vision is described in terms of overall outcomes (or changes) to be achieved by all or parts of the organization, including associated goals and objectives to achieve the outcomes. Sometimes, an overall purpose, or mission, is associated with the effort to achieve the vision, as well.

3. Developing Political Support

This phase of change management is often overlooked, yet it is the phase that often stops successful change from occurring. Politics in organizations is about power. Power is important among members of the organization when striving for the resources and influence necessary to successfully carry out their jobs. Power is also important when striving to maintain jobs and job security. Power usually comes from credibility, whether from strong expertise or integrity. Power also comes from the authority of one's position in the organization. Some people have a strong negative reaction when talking about power because power often is associated with negative applications, For example, manipulation, abuse or harassment. However, power, like conflict, exists in all human interactions and is not always bad. It is how power and conflict are used and managed that determine how power and conflict should be perceived. Matters of power and politics are critically important to recognize and manage during organizational change activities. Change often means shifts in power across management levels, functions and groups. To be successful, the change effort must recruit the support of all key power players, for example, senior management, subject matter experts and others who are recognized as having strong expertise and integrity. A strong mechanism for ensuring alignment of power with the change effort is to develop a network of power-players who interact and count on each other to support and guide the change effort. Means to manage power can include ensuring that all power-players are involved in recognizing the need for change, developing the vision and methods to achieve the vision, and organization-wide communication about the status of change. Any recommendations or concerns expressed by those in power must be promptly recognized and worked through.

4. Managing Transition

This phase occurs when the organization works to make the actual transition from the current state to the future state. In consultations, this phase usually is called implementation of the action plans. The plans can include a wide variety of "interventions," or activities designed to make a change in the organization, for example, creating and/or modifying major structures and processes in the organization. These changes might require ongoing coaching, training and enforcement of new policies and procedures. In addition, means of effective change management must continue, including strong, clear, ongoing communication about the need for the change, status of the change, and solicitation of organization members' continuing input to the change effort. Ideally, the various actions are integrated into one overall Change Management Plan that includes specific objectives, or milestones, that must be accomplished by various deadlines, along with responsibilities for achieving each objective. Rarely are these plans implemented exactly as planned. Thus, as important as developing the plan, is making the many ongoing adjustments to the plan with key members of the organization, while keeping other members up-to-date about the changes and the reasons for them.

5. Sustaining Momentum

Often, the most difficult phase in managing change is this phase when leaders work to sustain the momentum of the implementation and adjustment of plans. Change efforts can encounter a wide variety of obstacles, for example, strong resistance from members of the organization, sudden departure of a key leader in the organization, or a dramatic reduction in sales. Strong, visible, ongoing support from top leadership is critically important to show overall credibility and accountabilities in the change effort. Those participating in the change effort often require ongoing support, often in the form of provision of resources, along with training and coaching. The role of support cannot be minimized – despite its importance during organizational change; the role of support is often forgotten. At this point in a consulting project, it may be wise for you to ensure you have ongoing support (often from other consultants) that can provide you ongoing objectivity, affirmation, provision of resources and other forms of support. Employee performance management systems play a critical role in this phase of organizational change, including in setting goals, sharing feedback about accomplishment of goals, rewarding behaviors that successfully achieve goals and accomplish change, and addressing performance issues.

8.8. IMPLEMENTATION OF STRATEGIC CHANGE

Introduction

A key role of a CEO's is to communicate a vision and to guide strategic planning. Those who have successfully implemented strategic plans have often reported that involving teams at all levels in strategic planning helps to build a shared vision, and increases each individual's motivation to see plans succeed. Clarity and consistent communication, from mapping desired outcomes to designing performance measures, seem to be essential to success. Successful leaders have often engaged their teams by simply telling the story of their shared vision, and publicly celebrating large and small wins, such as the achievement of milestones. To ensure that the vision is shared, teams need to know that they can test the theory, voice opinions, challenge premises, and suggest alternatives without fear of reprimand.Implementing strategic plans may require leaders who lead through inspiration and coaching rather than command and control. Recognizing and rewarding success, inspiring, and modeling behaviors is more likely to result in true commitment than use of authority, which can lead to passive resistance and hidden rebellion.

Organizational Change is Systemic

The systemic model developed by Dr. Resnick has been tested and used successfully with many companies. It offers a comprehensive yet simple way of identifying and applying the leverage points that guide the change process.

The model starts with the organization's vision. A vision is not simply the sentence that gets mounted on the plaque in the lobby. The vision must be sufficiently comprehensive to provide guidance and direction to every employee in the company. The next basic component is a clear understanding of the markets the company serves and its desired customer profiles.

Once these two elements are defined, the elements in the middle of the diagram are the organizational system. This system exists for only one purpose—to deliver the power of the organization's vision to its customers. Every element needs to be examined and re-designed to *make* sure that it is "fit for purpose"—to deliver the vision to customers.

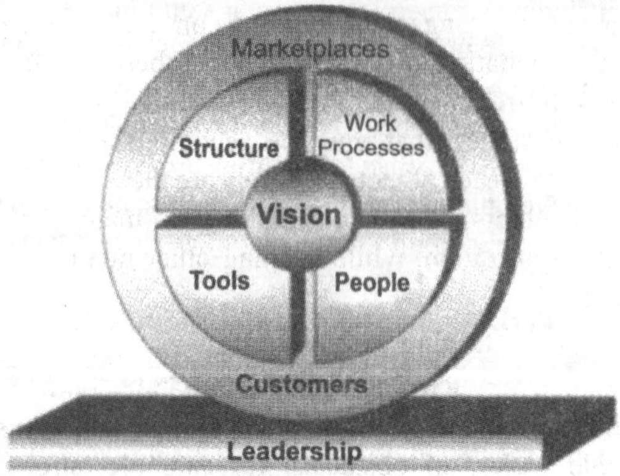

Figure 8.4.

The elements that comprise an organization are shown in the four quadrants: structure, work processes, people and tools. These are four key interdependent components.

1. **Structure** is the traditional view of an organization. It is the "faces and spaces" figure 8.4 that is shown as an organization chart. It defines the boundaries of authority and decision-making and identifies the key personnel responsible for the business.
2. **Work processes** describe how work gets done in an organization. They range from a few high-level cross-functional integrated core processes that drive the business down to detailed departmental processes and procedures.
3. **People** identifies the skill sets needed for the company and the numbers of people with various skills. The essence of this category is about getting the right people doing the right job in the right place.
4. **Tools** represents physical facilities and capital equipment - hardware and software systems, management and reporting systems, written documents such as policies, procedures

and manuals, and compensation tools. An organization undergoing major change should examine all of these quadrants and assess their alignment to its vision, its customers and each other. This will enable senior management to identify the leverage points that will create sustainable breakthrough change.

8.8.1 Steps in Implementation of Strategic Change

- **Step One – Confirming the Compelling need to Change:** It is not uncommon for the process to begin with significant discussion about whether broad-based systemic change is needed, or whether smaller incremental improvements will do the job. This often requires some external data (market share, competitive information, etc.) as well as objective internal data (how long does it take to complete projects vs. plan; are costs per unit increasing or decreasing; is our organization getting better at what it does; is competitive positioning weakening, etc.).
- **Step Two – Identifying the Boundary Conditions:** Boundary conditions define the limits (or playground) within which change might be considered. When senior teams begin their discussion some large topics usually emerge very quickly. *Issues s*uch as mergers, acquisitions, international or global initiatives, large capital investments, strategic alliance partners, equity situations, private vs. public ownership, etc. may be debated.
- **Step Three – Creating the Vision of the desired End State:** A group of people aligned around a common vision are a very powerful force. John Kennedy's vision of "put a man on the moon by the end of the decade" spurred NASA to unprecedented performance. Martin Luther King's vision in his "I have a dream" speech energized the civil rights movement. Jack Welch's vision for GE in which he said that "We will be number one or number two in every category or we won't be in it" drove incredible energy and focus through GE. The vision of Mercedes Benz to "always make the best engineered car in the world" has been the hallmark of its focus for decades.
- **Step Four – Developing the Core Work Processes:** The mention of work processes typically creates mixed reactions. Everyone agrees that some degree of process is required. Without defined processes a company would not be able to produce a consistent payroll. It would not be able to hire people. It would not have any consistent methodologies for its work. It could never assure any consistency or reliability.

  The problem for most cross-functional work processes is in the hand-offs. When processes cut across functions there are typically miscues and conflicting expectations or requirements between functional groups. Most companies have only a few core processes – about five – that drive their entire business. Everything else is an enabler. These core processes are virtually always cross-functional. Therefore, they must be developed by the entire senior management team – together. And that is the next step of the process of creating breakthrough change. Once these major cross-functional processes are developed – at a fairly high level – they can then be handed down to the next levels of the organization for more detailed implementation. One member of the senior management team must then be designated as the owner of the entire process – throughout the organization.

  This step typically surfaces the strongest points of contention in the entire breakthrough change process. If this step is addressed seriously, issues of organizational structure begin to resolve themselves. After all, the structure should be designed to support how the work gets done.
- **Step Five–Defining Key Roles and Responsibilities:** Every company has a relatively small number of key roles that are central to its business. There are usually a number of people who perform these roles, and they are the linking pins for one or several core processes. Some

examples of such key roles are: project director, lead engineer, national account manager, customer service representative, senior consultant, systems engineer, account executive, etc.

The next step is to identify the few key roles in the organization that are central to how the company's work gets done and then for the senior team collectively to define them.

- **Step Six–Modifying the Organizational Structure:** Most changes begin with a modification of the organizational structure. Unfortunately, most changes end there as well – which is precisely why most large scale change is unsuccessful. Step six represents the point where examining and possibly modifying the organizational structure is both appropriate and necessary. Structure should exist to support what an organization is trying to accomplish (vision and strategy); how it is trying to do it (core work processes) and the requirements people have for their work (key roles). Now that these have been identified, the structure should be reviewed and, if necessary, re-designed.

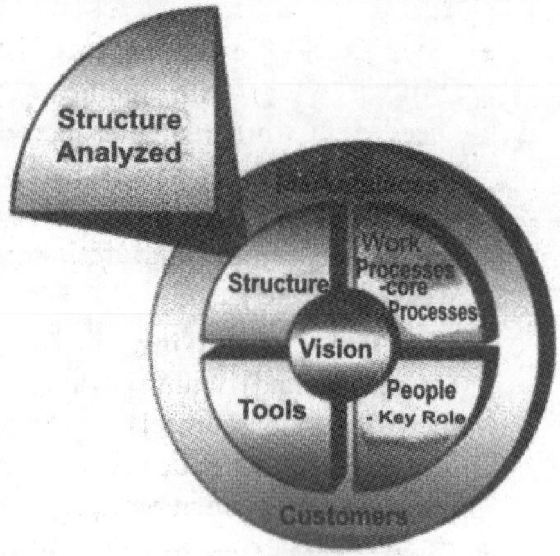

Figure 8.5

  The fundamental question is: Does the existing structure enhance or at least not interfere with how the work needs to get done? If the structure is helpful or neutral, the general guideline is to leave it alone. Structural changes are very disruptive. They should only be made if they are truly necessary.

  If the structure is a barrier to the work that needs to be done, then it should quickly be re-aligned to meet its new requirements. This analysis and re-design should be a collaborative effort by the senior team. If individual team members cannot "check their positions and their egos at the door" then it may be necessary for the President to impose the new organization. This step should be reviewed and implemented quickly, in its entirety, based on what best serves the needs of the whole organization. This is not the time to allow the "right of infinite refusal" to stall the change process.

- **Step Seven–Establishing the Key Performance Measures:** Every organization measures its performance. Unfortunately, most organizational measures have two fundamental flaws. First, there is a disproportional emphasis on financial measures. Financial measures are not direct performance measures. They are the consequences of company performance achieved or not achieved. By themselves, they indicate very little. Second, most performance measures cause the company to look through its rear view mirror. These measures indicate past performance and do little to help guide future performance or have a positive impact on organizational results.

  This next step calls for the creation of a balanced scoreboard – or dashboard – of the key internal and external measures that provide a comprehensive view of the organization's performance, with as much insight as possible regarding their implications for the future.

  At the completion of this process by the senior management team you should have a limited set of defined measures that provide a balanced understanding of current performance, guidelines for improving short-term results, and the ability to assess and improve long-term organizational performance.

- **Step Eight – Reviewing System-Wide Tools:** Tools are powerful forces in defining how an organization behaves. An enterprise-wide tool can be one of the most dramatic vehicles to create (or force) organizational change.

Enterprise software systems have become very powerful forces for driving organizational behavior, and potentially creating highly value increased productivity. Such tools require an organization to define how it conducts its business, and impose a discipline on all individuals and functional areas to conform to the standards and processes defined by the tools. However, if the tool is not sufficiently flexible or does not match how business is actually conducted, the effect will be disastrous. Tools that impose their way of working in conflict with established business norms or practices will be strongly resisted.

- **Step Nine – Develop Training that Enables Performance:** Training is an integral part of organizational design and behavior. It is essential to ensure that individuals have the knowledge and skills to perform in their current jobs and prepare for new ones. Training is also perceived by employees as a measure of the organization's commitment to them. In the current marketplace employees are encouraged to think of themselves as independent contractors selling their services for the best opportunity. Training (as a part of continuous learning) is an essential ingredient for retaining a nimble workforce.

  Training is one of the most powerful vehicles for a company to create breakthrough change. It can achieve three simultaneous results. First, it builds alignment to the desired change. Second, it provides individuals with the knowledge and skills to implement the change. Third, it creates the opportunity for cross-functional communication in the implementation of company-wide initiatives.

- **Step Ten – Aligning the Reward Systems:** Traditionally reward systems have been approached conservatively in the form of salaries for professional employees and hourly wages for non-exempt employees. In some companies annual bonuses or profit-sharing programs have been added, tied to organizational performance for that year.

  Companies have now started to use more sensitive vehicles to align reward systems to individual, team and organizational performance. Commissions for a sales force have long been in place. More recently, defined bonuses for the achievement of individual quarterly goals has become fairly widespread. Team rewards tied to specific project completion has also become common. Annual bonuses based on the achievement of specific performance goals are becoming the new norm.

  Though the techniques may differ, two dominant themes emerge. The first is the trend toward broad band job classification, providing much more flexibility in establishing individual compensation. The second is a much higher degree of at risk compensation tied to individual, team and organizational performance.

  If possible, reward systems should to be tied to the desired breakthrough change. Employees will pay great attention to adjustments in the reward system, especially if it is modified to focus on the desired behaviors and effects of the breakthrough changes.

8.8.2 Barriers and Challenges to Strategic Change Implementation

- **Planning :** Without step-by-step planning, change in an organization is likely to fall apart or cause more problems than benefits. You need to understand exactly what changes will take place and how those changes will occur. For example, if you're transitioning to a new content management system, you'll need to know if the new system is compatible with the old system, how you will transition the old information to the new system and if there will be limited access during the transition. You also need to assign roles to individuals who are responsible for the change so all duties are covered. The time line for the change is also a key component. You need to plan for downtime or difficulties in completing regular work tasks while the change occurs.

- **Lack of Consensus:** If you fail to get everyone on board with the corporate changes, you are likely to face barriers during the process. The decision to implement changes should come from the top level of the organization. All management level staff needs to be on board and able to deal with the changes or you may face dissension within the staff. You may not have everyone on board right from the beginning. Showing managers how the changes will affect the company and the steps for implementing the changes helps get them on board if they initially have reservations.
- **Communication:** Failing to communicate with all employees invites rumors and fear into the workplace, particularly if you're facing major changes, such as downsizing or a merger. Employees want to know what's going on, whether it is positive or negative news. The feeling of uncertainty when management doesn't communicate disrupts work and makes employees feel as if they aren't a part of the decision. Keep employees updated regularly about the plans and progress toward the change implementation. Involve all employees as much as possible through meetings or brainstorming sessions to help during the planning phase.
- **Employee Resistance:** In some cases, Employees resist change. They become comfortable with the way the business is run. They know the expectations and their role within the company. When a major change disrupts their familiarity, some Employees become upset. They don't want to relearn their jobs or change the way they do things. Supporting your employees and providing training for any new responsibilities can help ease the transition.

  Change affects every business at some point. They may range from minor staff restructuring to merging or acquiring another company. While the changes may be necessary for the future of the company, you are likely to face certain barriers and challenges. Anticipating these roadblocks helps you avoid them before they become major issues in the change implementation.

8.9. TYPES OF CHANGES IN ORGANIZATION

Organizational leaders must determine the type of change necessary in order to adapt to the needs of its internal or external environment. Consequently, organizational change can affect people, systems, processes, culture, business units, or the entire organization.

1. Changes Related to People

- **Personnel Change:** Sometimes people changes are a direct result of other organizational changes. At other times, companies simply seek to change worker's attitudes and behaviors in order to increase their effectiveness. Bateman and Zeithaml suggest that attempting a strategic change, introducing a new technology, and other changes in the work environment may affect people's attitudes (sometimes in a negative way). Frequently, management initiates programs with a conscious goal of directly and positively changing the people themselves. The science of organization development deals with changing people. This may be through on the job through techniques such as education and training, team building, and career planning.
- **Culture Change:** Culture change within an organization aims at changing the behavior patterns of the organization's employees. Some examples of culture change include reward-and-recognition programs, employee empowerment, and training. These programs attempt to improve motivation, improve decision-making skills, and increase sensitivity to diversity issues.
- **People-centered Change:** People-centered process changes attempt to alter the attitudes, behaviors, skills, or performance of employees within an organization. Communication, employee motivation, leadership, and group interaction are some primary focuses of people-

centered change. This type of change may affect the employees and their behaviors in many areas. Some examples are improved problem-solving skills, the way employees learn new skills, and how employees perceive themselves, their jobs, and the organization.

- **Social Change:** "Social change refers to the modification of established relationships in the organization. Social change encompasses the large set of goals that organizations establish around people. This includes an empowered workforce, collaborative work arrangements, and matching personal fulfillment to organizational needs."
- **Customer Relationship Management:** Customer relationship management intends to create processes that will build customer loyalty to the organization, which increases profits. Customer relationships can be increased through marketing, employee professional development, or and improved customer service.

2. Changes Related to Organizations

- **Leadership Change:** Leadership transitions are critical moments. Transitions in leadership offer an opportunity to make changes in many areas of the organization. The situation is fluid or, in Lewin's framework of organizational change, 'unfrozen.' "The transition is an occasion to rethink the commitment to the present agenda, to reflect on roads not taken in the past, and to review future choices. Many significant changes – in policy, people, organizational structure, procedures – are more easily introduced simultaneously with a leadership change."
- **Structural Change:** Changes within an organization's structure can occur due to external influences. Structural changes may involve structural characteristics, administrative procedures, or management systems. They may involve simple policy changes or be as complex as a complete restructuring of the management hierarchy.
- **Reengineering:** Change centered on reengineering focuses on making major structural change to the organization. Implementations of these changes typically focus on everyday tasks or procedures. The goal is to substantially improve productivity, efficiency, quality, or customer satisfaction.
- **Incremental Organizational Change:** "Incremental change is a step-by-step approach to re-designing an organization." Each small increment that is changed produces changes in other parts of the organization. By changing specific processes or details in portions, the entire organization changes over time.
- **Fundamental Organizational Change:** When major organizational changes are necessary and time constraints are a significant factor, a more radical transformation becomes essential. Fundamental organizational change focuses on changing major characteristics of the entire organization rather than specific parts.
- **Divestiture:** Business divestiture means that a firm disposes a significant part of its assets. This may result in the sell-off or dissolution of whole business units, or divisions. 'Tactical' divestors and 'distress' divestors appear to focus directly on the short-term. In contrast, the 'strategic' divestors appear to take a broader view triggering a reevaluation of the organizational strategy.
- **Acquisition:** Acquisition is the process through which one company takes over the controlling interest of another company. Acquisition includes obtaining supplies or services by contract or purchase order with appropriated or non-appropriated funds.
- **Merger:** Merger is the combining of two or more entities into one. This may occur through a purchase acquisition or a pooling of interests. Merger differs from a consolidation in that no new entity is created from a merger.

- **Consolidation:** Consolidation is the combining of separate companies, functional areas, or product lines, into a single organization. Consolidation differs from a merger in that a new entity is created in the consolidation. Another form of consolidation results from the process of maturation in some markets. The consequences of this process are that larger companies acquire smaller companies or run them out of business. This leaves only a few dominant players in the market.

3. Changes Related to System

"Systems change means making change that endures and changes at the heart of the organization. Such change is systematic, takes time, planning and patience. Such change is not done by just tweaking parts of the system in isolation. But, it means ultimately impacting change across all elements of the system."

- **Process-oriented Change:** The goal of process-oriented change is to improve productivity. Process-oriented change affects the way in which an organization delivers services, produces products, or handles current business practices. As the environmental factors of an organization change, the need for process-oriented change increases.
- **Technological Change:** This type of approach concerns the implementation or integration of technology into the processes of an organization. Primarily, technology includes large hardware or software systems.
- **Software Development and Installation:** The development and installation of software may include more change categories than this change effort would indicate. Other change types affected by development and installation of software may include systems, processes, technology, etc. Success is generally assessed in terms of project management criteria: on time, on budget, with the promised features and functionalities.

4. Changes Related to Transactional

Transactional change occurs in a situation in which the organization experiences some feature of change but the fundamental nature of the organization remains the same. This may include a company's organizational climate, which encompasses the perceptions and attitudes of people about the organization. Included in transactional change are structure, management practices, and systems.

- **TQM Driven Change:** "TQM efforts are aimed at the continuous improvement of the organization's operations. These efforts include the use of employee teams to generate and implement ideas for improving organizational performance. The theme is the gradual improvement of the organization, not radical or sudden range."
- **Re-engineering or process design:** "This term designates the design of a new business process or the radical redesign of an existing process. The goal here is to achieve levels of performance beyond the organization's current capability."
- **Business Expansion:** "This category includes approaches to Expanding a business. This change may come through product development, new lines of business, or selling to new markets."
- **Benchmarking:** "Benchmarking is the search for best practices. Benchmarking allows your organization to see what others are doing, what is working for them and what to avoid. The American Productivity & Quality Center defines benchmarking as: "the process of identifying, understanding, and adapting outstanding practices and processes from organizations anywhere in the world to help your organization improve its performance."
- **Business Process Reengineering:** Business process reengineering is the redesign of business processes and the associated systems and organizational structures. The goal of this type of change is to achieve a dramatic improvement in business performance.

5. Major types of change in general

- **Growth**: Organizational growth, while considered a positive change, can have a negative effect on the environment and employee attitude. The company's culture, current leadership styles, and business systems may no longer accommodate the organization in its new form.
- **"Growth needs to be managed on multiple levels:** having the right leaders leading the right people to do the right things at the right time."
- **Unplanned Change:** "Unplanned change usually occurs because of a major, sudden surprise to the organization. This causes its members to respond in a highly reactive and disorganized fashion."At times, organizational change happens when it becomes necessary to react to a sudden development. All kinds of emergency can force organizations to introduce new ways of doing things, or of structuring themselves."
- **Planned Change:** "Planned change occurs when leaders in the organization recognize the need for a major change and proactively organize a plan to accomplish the change. Planned change occurs with successful implementation of a Strategic Plan, Plan for reorganization, or other implementation of a change of this magnitude."
- **Radical Change:** "We view radical organizational change as a process by which firms regain competitive advantage after it has been lost or threatened significantly. We find that the type and extent of change undertaken depends upon the firm's resources and capabilities; its competitive environment; and its leadership. Radical change is divergent, meant to fundamentally change the firm's processes, systems, structures, strategies, and core values."
- **Radically Innovative Change:** Radically innovative change, the most intimidating type of change, consists of replacing an existing process, product, or technology with one that is new to the industry. Radically innovative change may produce a high degree of uncertainty. There is also a high potential for resistance to the change within the organization.
- **Developmental change:** Developmental change concentrates on improving an already successful environment. Development occurs through improving aspects of an organization such as increasing customer base or introducing a product expansion.
- **Transformational Change:** Transformational change occurs when organizations incur drastic changes and must essentially transform themselves. This can occur when an organization faces different technologies, significant changes in supply and demand, unexpected competition, lack of revenue or other major shifts in how they do business.
- **Evolutionary Change:** "Evolutionary change involves setting direction, allocating responsibilities, and establishing reasonable timelines for achieving objectives. It is rarely fast enough or comprehensive enough to move ahead of the curve in an evolving world where stakes are high, and the response time is short."
- **Revolutionary Change:** "When faced with market-driven urgency, abrupt and sometimes disruptive change, such as dramatic downsizing or reengineering, may be required to keep the company competitive. In situations when timing is critical to success, and companies must get more efficient and productive rapidly, revolutionary change is demanded."
- **Proactive Change:** "Proactive change involves actively attempting to make alterations to the work place and its practices. Companies that take a proactive approach to change are often trying to avoid a potential future threat or to capitalize on a potential future opportunity."
- **Reactive Change:** "Reactive change occurs when an organization makes changes in its practices after some threat or opportunity has already occurred."

8.10. MANAGING STRATEGIC CHANGE

Change management is a systematic approach to dealing with change, both from the perspective of an organization and on the individual level. A somewhat ambiguous term, change management has at least three different aspects, including: adapting to change, controlling change, and effecting change. A proactive approach to dealing with change is at the core of all three aspects. For an organization, change management means defining and implementing procedures and/or technologies to deal with changes in the business environment and to profit from changing opportunities. Successful adaptation to change is as crucial within an organization as it is in the natural world. Just like plants and animals, organizations and the individuals in them inevitably encounter changing conditions that they are powerless to control. The more effectively you deal with change, the more likely you are to thrive. Adaptation might involve establishing a structured methodology for responding to changes in the business environment (such as a fluctuation in the economy, or a threat from a competitor) or establishing coping mechanisms for responding to changes in the workplace (such as new policies, or technologies).

In a computer system environment, change management refers to a systematic approach to keeping track of the details of the system (For example, what operating system release is running on each computer and which fixes have been applied).

8.10.1 Definition

Terry Paulson, the author of Paulson on Change, quotes an uncle's advice: "It's easiest to ride a horse in the direction it is going." In other words, don't struggle against change; learn to use it to your advantage.

Why Need a Change Management Strategy?

A "one-size-fits-all" approach is not effective for change management. Think about these changes:

- Acquiring a company of near equal size
- Getting suppliers to use a new web-based form and process
- Relocating office spaces within an existing building
- Implementing an Enterprise Resource Planning solution
- Reorienting around processes instead of functions
- Releasing a new product

8.10.2 What Goes into the Change Management Strategy?

1. Situational Awareness

- **Change Characteristics:** Begin by understanding the change that is being introduced. Changes can be formalized projects, strategic initiatives or even small adjustments to how the organization operates. Understanding the characteristics of the change requires you to answer questions like: What is the scope of the change? How many people will be impacted? Who is being impacted? Are people being impacted the same or are they experiencing the change differently? What is being changed - processes, systems, job roles, etc? What is the timeframe for the change?
- **Organizational Attributes:** Next, work to understand the people and groups being impacted by the change. The organizational attributes are related to the history and culture in the organization and describe the backdrop against which this particular change is being introduced. What is the perceived need for this change among employees and managers? How have past changes been managed? Is there a shared vision for the organization? How much change is going on right now?

- **Impacted Groups**: The final step in building the situational awareness is developing a map of who in the organization is being impacted by the change and how they are being impacted. A single change - say the deployment of a web-based expense reporting program - will impact different groups very differently. Employees that do not have expenses to report will not be impacted at all. Staffs who travel once a quarter will be only slightly impacted. Associates who are on the road all the time will be more impacted, although filing expenses is only a portion of their day-to-day work. And for those in accounting who manage expense reporting, their jobs will be completely altered.

2. Supporting structure

- **Team Structure:** The change management team structure identifies who will be doing the change management work. It outlines the relationship between the project team and the change management team. The most frequent team structures include i) change management being a responsibility assigned to one of the project team members or ii) an external change management team supporting a project team. The key in developing the strategy is to be specific and make an informed decision when assigning the change management responsibility and resources.
- **Sponsor Coalition:**The sponsor coalition describes the leaders and managers that need to be on-board for the change to be successful. Starting with the primary sponsor (the person who authorized and funded the change), the sponsor model documents the leaders of the groups that are being impacted by the change. The change characteristics will determine who must be part of the coalition. Each member of the sponsor coalition has the responsibility to build support and communicate the change with their respective audiences.

3. Strategy analysis

- **Risk Assessment:** The risk of not managing the people side of change on a particular change is related to the dimensions described in the situational awareness section. Changes that are more 'dramatic' and father reaching in the organization have a higher change management risk. Likewise, organizations and groups with histories and cultures that resist change face higher change management risk. In developing the strategy, overall risk and specific risk factors are documented.
- **Anticipated Resistance:** Many times, after a project is introduced and meets resistance, members of the team reflect that "they saw that reaction coming." In creating the change management strategy, identify where resistance can be expected. Are particular regions or divisions impacted differently than others? Were certain groups advocating a different solution to the same problem? Are some groups heavily invested with how things are done today? Note particular anticipated resistance points depending on how each group is related to the change.
- **Special Tactics:** The final step of the change management strategy is the identification of any special tactics that will be required for this particular change initiative. The special tactics formalize many of the learning's from the strategy development related to the change and how it impacts different audiences in the organization. Throughout the change implementation, special tactics may need to be revisited and updated.

8.10.3 How to Manage the Strategic Change in Organization?

1. Decide on your Change Goal

- Start with the end in mind.
- What do you want to achieve?

- How will you know if it has been achieved? Who is affected and how will they react?
- How much can you do yourself and how much help do you need?
- You need to have a clear vision - people like to either see/hear or feel the change.

2. Consider Timing

Think about the best time to instigate change. The greater the degree of change needed, the more useful it is to "piggy back" the change on some actual or perceived crisis. For example, improvements in work practices may be more acceptable in times of recession when people are concerned about keeping their jobs.

You may find that there is a natural window of opportunity where the change makes sense to the majority of people. Realize that major change takes time and allow for that. If you attempt to rush through a change, attitudes may not have changed and the change effect may not last in the long term.

3. Be Aware of Culture

Most change initiatives fail because of a lack of recognition of the importance of culture. It is difficult to define, but if change is to work, you need to be aware of "the way we do things around here".

When planning strategies for managing change, aim to involve people in identifying the "cultural web" in your business.

4. Create Visible Short-Term Wins

Help people to see the benefits of change in the short term. For example, if you are changing how you interact with customers, publicize some of the positive feedback from them to encourage staff to continue with the new ways of working.

5. Communicate

Effective communication may be the single most important factor in overcoming resistance to change. Communicate your vision and strategic intent clearly. Be honest and encourage two way discussion. Use a variety of media (1 to 1, 1 to many, circulars, notice boards etc.) depending on nature and sensitivity of the change. And involve all levels in the business in communicating the change.

8.10.4 Why Change Management Programmes Fail?

Here are some common reasons why strategies for managing change do not work. Take note if you are the change agent, so that you don't make the same mistakes when planning your strategies for managing change:

- Unclear or incorrect goals or vision
- Insufficient communication and motivation
- Change seen as a senior management issue only
- Implementation strategy not thought through
- Initial problems throw project off course
- Too much focus on the technical side of change – rather than people issues
- Culture not changed

8.10.5 Strategies for Managing Change—Step By Step

If you are the change agent responsible for managing a change, follow these steps as well as the change management strategies outlined above to help the change happen smoothly:

- Hold Management Visioning and Planning workshops using change management tools (click here for suggestions)
- Agree a clear vision of what change will achieve
- Assemble a change management team
- Engage and involve all employees through workshops and other communication methods
- Amend vision and plan based on discussions with employees
- Communicate with imagination
- Manage change project
- Stay committed until change is established (refrozen)

8.10.6 Strategies for Managing Change in a Crisis

Different change management methodologies are called for when the business is in real danger. A turnaround strategy is needed, with the emphasis on speed of change, rapid cost reduction and/or revenue generation.

Managers need to be able to prioritize the things that give quick and significant improvements. Here are important steps that need to be taken in a crisis:

- Stabilize crisis
- Prioritize critical improvement areas
- Restructure finances
- Refocus on vision and goals
- Clarify target markets
- Win stakeholder support
- Change management team if necessary

8.11. A GENERAL FRAMEWORK FOR MANAGING CHANGE

Organizational Change Management (OCM) is a framework for managing the effect of new business processes, changes in organizational structure or cultural changes within an enterprise. Simply put, OCM addresses the people side of change management. A systematic approach to OCM is beneficial when change requires people throughout an organization to learn new behaviors and skills. By formally setting expectations, employing tools to improve communication and proactively seeking ways to reduce misinformation, stakeholders are more likely to buy into a change initially and remain committed to the change throughout any discomfort associated with it.

Successful organization change management strategies include

- Agreement on a common vision for change -- no competing initiatives.
- Strong executive leadership to communicate the vision and sell the business case for change.
- A strategy for educating employees about how their day-to-day work will change.
- A concrete plan for how to measure whether or not the change is a success - and follow-up plans for both successful and unsuccessful results.
- Rewards, both monetary and social, that encourage individuals and groups to take ownership for their new roles and responsibilities.

8.11.1 Framework for Managing Change

The extent of the change (both actual and perceived) and implications are significant. But how should they be addressed? The purpose of this section is to outline an approach and methodology to manage all the complex work streams and numerous stakeholders involved in successfully moving to a shared service/BPO operation.

The diagram below describes a framework for change management.

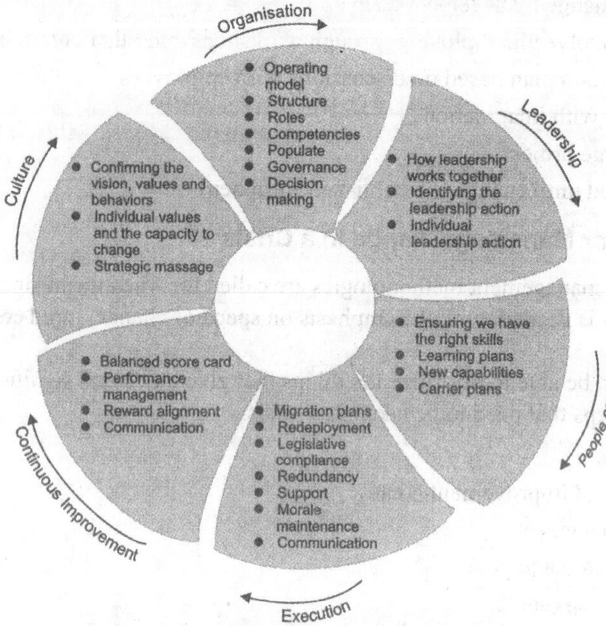

Figure 8.6. Framework for Change Management.

The segments in the wheel describe the various components that fit together in order to support and deliver the result (i.e. the SSC vision and the transformed function). It's important that all segments are addressed in order to ensure the success organization.

- **Culture**

This includes confirming the case for change and how the shared service initiative will contribute to realizing the organization's strategic goals, and assessing the capacity and readiness of both individuals and the organization to assimilate change. It's important to identify and articulate potential blockers and to agree on strategies and plans to deal with these so they don't derail the initiative.

- **Organization**

This covers design of the new world, including the operating model, organizational structures, role definitions, competency frameworks, and governance and decision-making frameworks. Care should be taken to design realistic and effective interfaces between the shared service capability and the retained organization.

- **Leadership**

This activity aims to clarify how the organization will be led, and to equip the leaders to carry out their leadership roles. Specific activities include defining the role of the leadership team, how the leadership team will work together both during implementation of shared services and subsequently, and the roles and responsibilities of individual leaders. This activity may identify the need for training and/or coaching of leaders and potential leaders.

- **People Capability**

This activity aims to establish the skills and competencies required for the new world, and how to meet those requirements, including skills audits, gap analysis, job and role definitions and career planning. Involvement of those who will lead the new organization is key to the success of this activity.

- **Execution**

This activity ensures delivery of the new model ("making it happen"). It includes both "hard" deliverables in the form of project plans, milestones, progress reports and budget analysis, and "soft" deliverables in the form of communications and stakeholder management.

- **Continuous Improvement**

This covers "life after the change" and includes frameworks and processes (E.g. performance management, balanced scorecards and reward alignment) to measure the effectiveness of the changes, and mechanisms to ensure that opportunities for further improvement are identified and acted upon in a timely manner. It's important to manage the expectations of all those impacted by the shared service initiative, so that they become accustomed to the idea that change will be a constant feature of the new model.

These various elements can be put together in a program change plan as shown below.

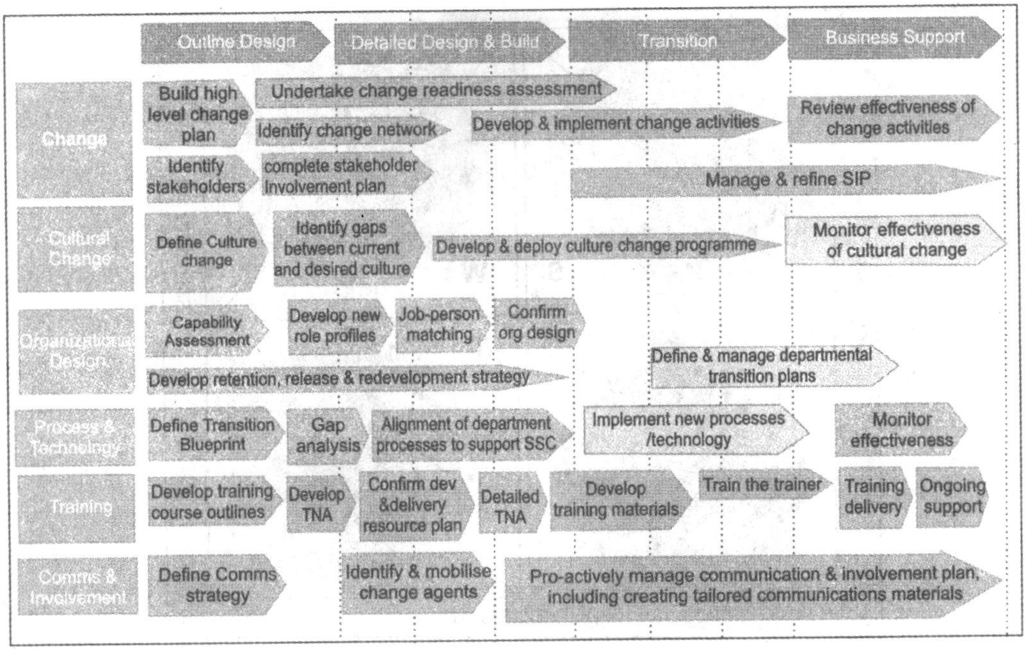

Figure 8.7. A Generic Business Unit Transition Plan.

This transition plan is an example of how the various dimensions of the change wheel fit together. Please note that in this example a Process and Technology stream is included for completeness, although this is not always included in a change management plan. The table below shows the types of activities that are undertaken at each stage in a program, for each stage in the change wheel

8.12. INPUT STAGE, MATCHING STAGE (SELECTION OF MATRIX) AND DECISION STAGE

STAGE-1 (INPUT STAGE)

Stage 1 of the formulation framework consists of the EFE Matrix, the IFE Matrix, and the Competitive Profile Matrix. Called the Input Stage, Stage 1 summarizes the basic input information needed to formulate strategies.

- External factor evaluation
- Competitive matrix profile
- Internal factor evaluation

STAGE-2 (MATCHING STAGE)

Stage 2, called the Matching Stage, focuses upon generating feasible alternative strategies by aligning key external and internal factors. Stage 2 techniques includes the following

i) **TOWS Matrix** (Threats-Opportunities-Weaknesses-Strengths)
ii) **SPACE Matrix** (Strategic Position and Action Evaluation)
iii) **BCG Matrix** (Boston Consulting Group)
iv) **IE Matrix** (Internal and external)
v) **GS Matrix** (Grand Strategy)

i) The Threats- Opportunities –Weakness-Strengths (TOWS) Matrix

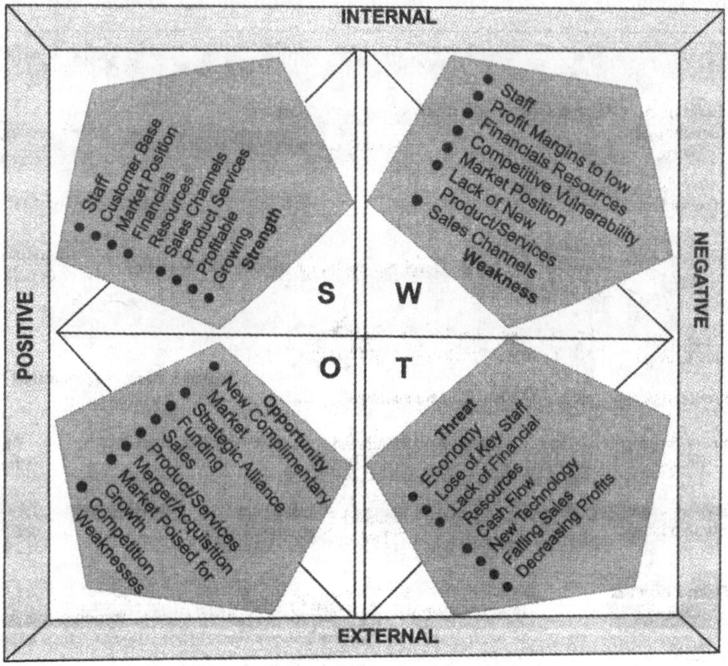

Figure 8.8.

The Threats-Opportunities-Weaknesses-Strengths (TOWS) is also named as SWOT analysis. A TOWS Analysis is a strategic planning tool used to evaluate the Threats, Opportunities and Strengths, Weaknesses, involved in a project or in a business venture or in any other situation requiring a decision. This is an important tool in order to formulate strategy. This Matrix is an important matching tool that helps managers develops four types of strategies: SO Strategies (strength-opportunities), WO Strategies (weakness- opportunities), ST Strategies (strength-threats), and WT Strategies (weakness-threats).The most difficult part of TOWS matrix is to match internal and external factor. Once the objective has been identified, TOWS are discovered and listed. TOWS are defined precisely as follows

- **Strengths** are attributes of the organization that are helpful to the achievement of the objective.

Table 8.2. Change Management Activities Across the Shared Service Lifecycle Stages of the Programme

Framework segment	Feasibility	Outline design	Detailed design and build	Transition/implementation
Organization 1. Operating model 2. Structure 3. Roles 4. Competencies 5. Populate 6. Governance decision-making	1. Agree high level blueprint for operating model 2. Outline governance 3. Stakeholder groups for engagement	1. Agree on service design model Agree on high-level 2. Agree on broad role outlines 3. Agree on and commence governance process 4. Complete initial impact assessment 5. Agree on and manage design sign-off 6. High-level briefings	1. Verify sizing assumptions 2. Complete detailed operating design 3. Complete detailed organization design 4. Complete final impact assesment 5. Brief impacted populations on change implication 6. Prepare organizational cutover plan	1. Manage the implementation 2. Recruit external hires 3. Manage the cutover of people to new roles
Leadership 1. How leadership works together 2. Identifying leadership actions 3. Individual leadership action	1. Agree on compel ling case for change 2. Agree on strategic reasons for shared services with leadership team 3. Agree on general scope and operating model 4. Agree on messages for all communications			
People capability 1. Ensuring we have the right skills 2. Learning plans 3. New capabilities 4. Career paths		1. Identify key skills needed for roles 2. Define high-level career paths 3. Identify capabilities 4. High-level training needs analysis	1. Identify skills/capabilities gaps 2. Confirm career/learning paths andbrief impacted audiences 3. Detailed training needs analy sis sign-off 4. Design development programs 5. Develop pilot programs 6. Role-based learning plan	1. Deliver training programs 2. Revise career/talent management programs to reflect new career paths

Execution 1. Migration plans 2. Redeployment 3. Legislative compliance 4. Redundancy 5. Support 6. Morale maintenance 7. Communication	Complete high-level transition plans	1. Prepare migration blueprint 2. Identify redeployment options/process 3. Check legislative compliance of design and blueprint 4. Development communications and engagement plan 5. Define business as usual 6. Define transition strategy (phased vs. big-bang) 7. Formal consultation planned initial communications activities	1. Launch formal consultation 2. Commence redeployment and Manage selection appointment to new roles 3. Detailed planning of business as usual 4. Continue communications	1. Implement cutover and migration plans 2. Complete redeployment and redundancy processes 3. Manage business as usual 4. Transition communication activities
Continuous Improvement 1. Balanced scorecard 2. Performance management 3. Reward Alignment 4. Communication			Plan continuous improvement approach and activities	1. Launch continuous improvement program 2. Track performance 3. Identify and agree upon priorities
Culture 1. Confirming the vision, values and behaviors 2. Individual values and capacity to change 3. Strategic message	Define high-level vision values and behaviors	1. Confirm required vision, values and behaviors gap from current 2. Develop key messages 3. Review implications for succession planning, reward and performance management processes to support cultural and behavioral goals	Communication cultural and behavioral expectation to scope audiences-	1. Implement new processes (succession planning, reward, etc.) 2. Review and manage as part of continuous improvement

- **Weaknesses** are attributes of the organization that are harmful to the achievement of the objective.
- **Opportunities** are external conditions that are helpful to the achievement of the objective.
- **Threats** are external conditions that are harmful to the achievement of the objective.

a) **Strengths and weaknesses are Internal Factors**. For example, strength could be your specialist marketing expertise. A weakness could be the lack of a new product.

b) **Change management activities across the shared services lifecycle stages of the program**

developing distribution channel such as the Internet, or changing consumer lifestyles that potentially increase demand for a company's products. A threat could be a new competitor in an important existing market or a technological change that makes existing products potentially obsolete. it is worth pointing out that SWOT analysis can be very subjective - two people rarely come-up with the same version of a SWOT analysis even when given the same information about the same business and its environment. Accordingly, SWOT analysis is best used as a guide and not a prescription. Adding and weighting criteria to each factor increases the validity of the analysis.

- **SO Strategies:** Every firm desires to obtain benefit form its resources such benefit can only be obtained if utilize its strength to take external opportunity. Resources (Assets) an important firm's strength to get opportunity for external resources. For example the firm enjoying a good financial position which is strength for a firm and externally opportunity to expand business. The strong financial position provides an opportunity to expand the business. The matched strategy is known as SO strategy.
- **WO Strategies:** WO Strategies developed to match weakness with opportunities of the firm. WO strategy is very useful if the firm take advantage to external resources in order to overcome the weakness. For example the firm is in the critical financial problems that is weakness and firm is availing merger with Multinational Corporation.
- **ST Strategies:** ST Strategies is an important strategy to overcome external threats. This does not mean that a strong organization should always meet threats in the external environment head-on. This strategy is adopted by various colleges by opening new branches in order to overcome competitive threat. These threats also explain by the Porter in its competitive model.
- **WT Strategies:** Every firm has a desire to overcome its weakness and reducing threats. This type of strategy helpful when weaknesses are removed to overcome external threats. It is difficult to target WT strategy. For example weak distribution network creating many problems for the firm if it strong many external threats can be removed.

Steps for Developing Strategies

There are eight steps involved in constructing a TOWS Matrix

- Rank external opportunities
- Rank external threats
- Rank internal strength
- Rank internal weaknesses.
- Match internal strengths with external opportunities and mention the result in the SO Strategies cell.
- Match internal weaknesses with external opportunities and mention the result in the WO Strategies cell.
- Match internal strengths with external threats and mention the result in the ST Strategies cell.

- Match internal weaknesses with external threats and mention the result in the WT strategies cell.

ii) The Strategic Position and Action Evaluation (Space) Matrix

The SPACE matrix is a management tool used to analyze a company. It is used to determine what type of a strategy a company should undertake.

The Strategic Position & Action Evaluation matrix or short a SPACE matrix is a strategic management tool that focuses on strategy formulation especially as related to the competitive position of an organization.

The SPACE matrix can be used as a basis for other analyses, such as the SWOT analysis, BCG matrix model, industry analysis, or assessing strategic alternatives (IE matrix).

What is the SPACE matrix strategic management method?

To explain how the SPACE matrix works, it is best to reverse-engineer it. First, let's take a look at what the outcome of a SPACE matrix analysis can be, take a look at the picture below. The SPACE matrix is broken down to four quadrants where each quadrant suggests a different type or a nature of a strategy:

- Aggressive
- Conservative
- Defensive
- Competitive

This is what a completed SPACE matrix looks like

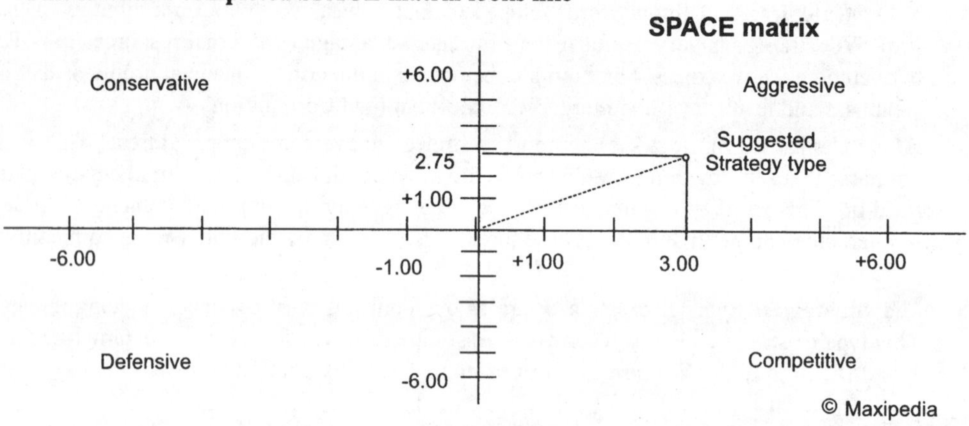

Figure 8.9.

- This particular SPACE matrix tells us that our company should pursue an aggressive strategy. Our company has a strong competitive position it the market with rapid growth. It needs to use its internal strengths to develop a market penetration and market development strategy. This can include product development, integration with other companies, acquisition of competitors, and so on.
- Now, how do we get to the possible outcomes shown in the SPACE matrix? The SPACE Matrix analysis functions upon two internal and two external strategic dimensions in order to determine the organization's strategic posture in the industry. The SPACE matrix is based on four areas of analysis.
- **Internal strategic dimensions**
  a) Financial strength (FS)
  b) Competitive advantage (CA)

- **External strategic dimensions**
  a) Environmental stability (ES)
  b) Industry strength (IS)

There are many SPACE matrix factors under the internal strategic dimension. These factors analyze a business internal strategic position. The financial strength factors often come from company accounting. These SPACE matrix factors can include for example return on investment, leverage, turnover, liquidity, working capital, cash flow, and others. Competitive advantage factors include for example the speed of innovation by the company, market niche position, customer loyalty, product quality, market share, product life cycle, and others.

Every business is also affected by the environment in which it operates. SPACE matrix factors related to business external strategic dimension are for example overall economic condition, GDP growth, inflation, price elasticity, technology, barriers to entry, competitive pressures, industry growth potential, and others. These factors can be well analyzed using the Michael Porter's Five Forces model.

The SPACE matrix calculates the importance of each of these dimensions and places them on a Cartesian graph with X and Y coordinates.

The following are a few model technical assumptions

- By definition, the CA and IS values in the SPACE matrix are plotted on the X axis.
- CA values can range from -1 to -6.- IS values can take +1 to +6.
- The FS and ES dimensions of the model are plotted on the Y axis.
- ES values can be between -1 and -6.
- FS values range from +1 to +6.

The steps required to develop a SPACE Matrix are listed below

- The SPACE matrix is constructed by plotting calculated values for the competitive advantage (CA) and industry strength (IS) dimensions on the X axis. The Y axis is based on the environmental stability (ES) and financial strength (FS) dimensions. The SPACE matrix can be created using the following seven steps
- **Step 1:** Choose a set of variables to be used to gauge the competitive advantage (CA), industry strength (IS), environmental stability (ES), and financial strength (FS).
- **Step 2:** Rate individual factors using rating system specific to each dimension. Rate competitive advantage (CA) and environmental stability (ES) using rating scale from -6 (worst) to -1 (best). Rate industry strength (IS) and financial strength (FS) using rating scale from +1 (worst) to +6 (best).
- **Step 3:** Find the average scores for competitive advantage (CA), industry strength (IS), environmental stability (ES), and financial strength (FS).
- **Step 4:** Plot values from step 3 for each dimension on the SPACE matrix on the appropriate axis.
- **Step 5**: Add the average score for the competitive advantage (CA) and industry strength (IS) dimensions. This will be your final point on axis X on the SPACE matrix.
- **Step 6:** Add the average score for the SPACE matrix environmental stability (ES) and financial strength (FS) dimensions to find your final point on the axis Y.
- **Step 7:** Find intersection of your X and Y points. Draw a line from the center of the SPACE matrix to your point. This line reveals the type of strategy the company should pursue.

SPACE Matrix Example

- The following table shows what values were used to create the SPACE matrix.

	Internal Strategic Position		External Strategic Position	
Axis X	Competitive (CA)		Industry (IS)	
	(-6 worst, -1 best)		(+1 worst, +6 best)	
	-1	Product quality	+6	Barriers to entry
	-1	Market share	+4	Growth potential
	-3	Brand & image	+4	Access to financing
	-2	Product life cycle	+5	Consolidation
	Average -1.75		Average +4.75	
	Total axis X score : 3.00			
Axis Y	Financial (FS)		Environmental (ES)	
	(+1 worst, +6 best)		(-6 worst, -1 best)	
	+5	ROA	-2	Inflation
	+4	Leverage	-1	Technology
	+6	Liquidity	-2	Demand elasticity
	+5	Cash Flow	-4	Taxation
	Average +5.00		Average -2.25	
	Total axis Y score: 2.75			

Each factor within each strategic dimension is rated using appropriate rating scale. Then averages are calculated. Adding individual strategic dimension averages provides values that are plotted on the axis X and Y.

iii) Boston Consulting Group (BCG)

The BCG Growth-Share Matrix is a portfolio planning model developed by Bruce Henderson of the Boston Consulting Group in the early 1970's. It is based on the observation that a company's business units can be classified into four categories based on combinations of market growth and market share relative to the largest competitor, hence the name "growth-share". Market growth serves as a proxy for industry attractiveness, and relative market share serves as a proxy for competitive advantage. The growth-share matrix thus maps the business unit positions within these two important determinants of profitability.

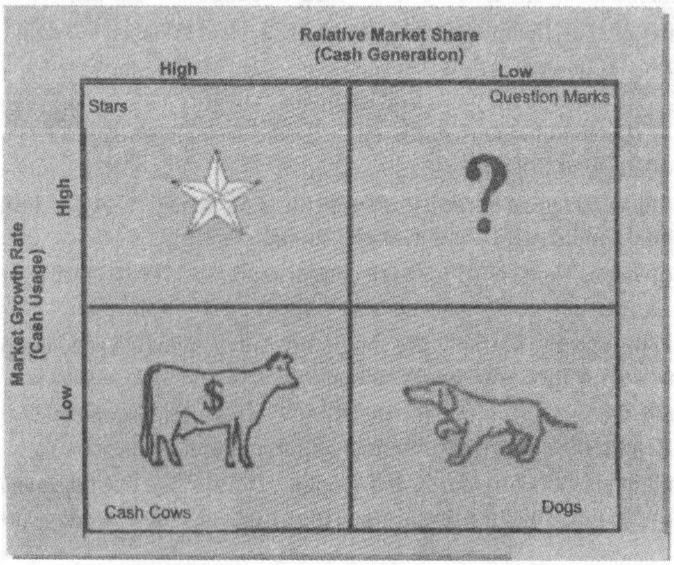

Figure 8.10. BCG Growth-Share Matrix.

This framework assumes that an increase in relative market share will result in an increase in the generation of cash. This assumption often is true because of the experience curve; increased relative market share implies that the firm is moving forward on the experience curve relative to its competitors, thus developing a cost advantage. A second assumption is that a growing market requires investment in assets to increase capacity and therefore results in the consumption of cash. Thus the position of a business on the growth-share matrix provides an indication of its cash generation and its cash consumption.

Henderson reasoned that the cash required by rapidly growing business units could be obtained from the firm's other business units that were at a more mature stage and generating significant cash. By investing to become the market share leader in a rapidly growing market, the business unit could move along the experience curve and develop a cost advantage. From this reasoning, the BCG Growth-Share Matrix was born.

The four categories are

- **Dogs:** Dogs have low market share and a low growth rate and thus neither generate nor consume a large amount of cash. However, dogs are cash traps because of the money tied up in a business that has little potential. Such businesses are candidates for divestiture.
- **Question Marks:** Question marks are growing rapidly and thus consume large amounts of cash, but because they have low market shares they do not generate much cash. The result is a large net cash consumption. A question mark (also known as a "problem child") has the potential to gain market share and become a star, and eventually a cash cow when the market growth slows. If the question mark does not succeed in becoming the market leader, then after perhaps years of cash consumption it will degenerate into a dog when the market growth declines. Question marks must be analyzed carefully in order to determine whether they are worth the investment required to grow market share.
- **Stars:** Stars generate large amounts of cash because of their strong relative market share, but also consume large amounts of cash because of their high growth rate; therefore the cash in each direction approximately nets out. If a star can maintain its large market share, it will become a cash cow when the market growth rate declines. The portfolio of a diversified company always should have stars that will become the next cash cows and ensure future cash generation.
- **Cash Cows:** As leaders in a mature market, cash cows exhibit a return on assets that is greater than the market growth rate, and thus generate more cash than they consume. Such business units should be "milked", extracting the profits and investing as little cash as possible. Cash cows provide the cash required to turn question marks into market leaders, to cover the administrative costs of the company, to fund research and development, to service the corporate debt, and to pay dividends to shareholders. Because the cash cow generates a relatively stable cash flow, its value can be determined with reasonable accuracy by calculating the present value of its cash stream using a discounted cash flow analysis.

Under the growth-share matrix model, as an industry matures and its growth rate declines, a business unit will become either a cash cow or a dog, determined soley by whether it had become the market leader during the period of high growth.

While originally developed as a model for resource allocation among the various business units in a corporation, the growth-share matrix also can be used for resource allocation among products within a single business unit. Its simplicity is its strength - the relative positions of the firm's entire business portfolio can be displayed in a single diagram.

Limitations

The growth-share matrix once was used widely, but has since faded from popularity as more comprehensive models have been developed. Some of its weaknesses are:

- Market growth rate is only one factor in industry attractiveness, and relative market share is only one factor in competitive advantage. The growth-share matrix overlooks many other factors in these two important determinants of profitability.
- The framework assumes that each business unit is independent of the others. In some cases, a business unit that is a "dog" may be helping other business units gain a competitive advantage.
- The matrix depends heavily upon the breadth of the definition of the market. A business unit may dominate its small niche, but have very low market share in the overall industry. In such a case, the definition of the market can make the difference between a dog and a cash cow.

While its importance has diminished, the BCG matrix still can serve as a simple tool for viewing a corporation's business portfolio at a glance, and may serve as a starting point for discussing resource allocation among strategic business units.

iv) The Internal-External (IE) Matrix

Introduction

The Internal-External (IE) matrix is another strategic management tool used to analyze working conditions and strategic position of a business. The Internal External Matrix or short IE matrix is based on an analysis of internal and external business factors which are combined into one suggestive model. The IE matrix is a continuation of the EFE matrix and IFE matrix models.

How does the Internal-External IE matrix work?

The IE matrix belongs to the group of strategic portfolio management tools. In a similar manner like the BCG matrix, the IE matrix positions an organization into a nine cell matrix.

The IE matrix is based on the following two criteria

1. Score from the EFE matrix -- this score is plotted on the y-axis
2. Score from the IFE matrix -- plotted on the x-axis

The IE matrix works in a way that you plot the total weighted score from the EFE matrix on the y axis and draw a horizontal line across the plane. Then you take the score calculated in the IFE matrix, plot it on the x axis, and draw a vertical line across the plane. The point where your horizontal line meets your vertical line is the determinant of your strategy. This point shows the strategy that your company should follow.

On the x axis of the IE Matrix, an IFE total weighted score of 1.0 to 1.99 represents a weak internal position. A score of 2.0 to 2.99 is considered average. A score of 3.0 to 4.0 is strong.

On the y axis, an EFE total weighted score of 1.0 to 1.99 is considered low. A score of 2.0 to 2.99 is medium. A score of 3.0 to 4.0 is high.

IE Matrix Example

Let us take a look at an example. We calculated IFE matrix for an anonymous company on the IFE matrix page. The total weighted score calculated on this page is 2.79 which points at a company with an above-average internal strength.

We also calculated the EFE matrix for the same company on the EFE matrix page. The total weighted score calculated for the EFE matrix is 2.46 which suggests a slightly less than average ability to respond to external factors.

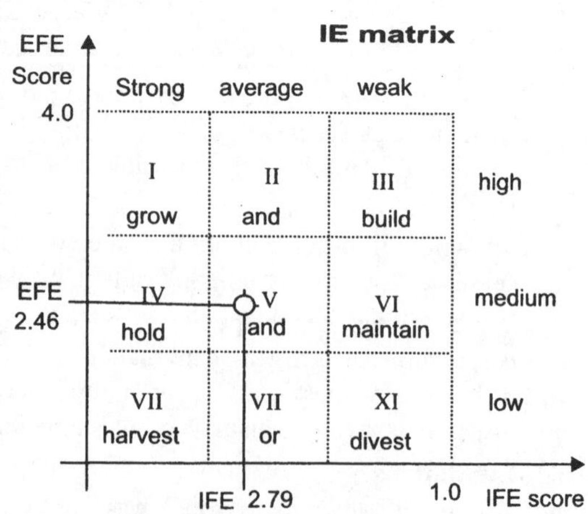

Figure 8.11.

Now we plot these values on axes in the IE matrix.

This IE matrix tells us that our company should hold and maintain its position. The company should pursue strategies focused on increasing market penetration and product development (more about this below).

Result of IE matrix

Your horizontal and vertical lines meet in one of the nine cells in the IE matrix. You should follow a strategy depending on in which cell those lines intersect.

The IE matrix can be divided into three major regions that have different strategy implications.

Cells I, II, and III suggest the grow and build strategy. This means intensive and aggressive tactical strategies. Your strategies should focus on market penetration, market development, and product development. From the operational perspective, a backward integration, forward integration, and horizontal integration should also be considered.

Cells IV, V, and VI suggest the hold and maintain strategy. In this case, your tactical strategies should focus on market penetration and product development.

Cells VII, VIII, and IX are characterized with the harvest or exit strategy. If costs for rejuvenating the business are low, then it should be attempted to revitalize the business. In other cases, aggressive cost management is a way to play the end game.

v) Grand Strategy Matrix (G S Matrix)

This is also an important matrix of strategy formulation frame work. Grand strategy matrix it is popular tool for formulating alternative strategies. In this matrix all organization divides into four quadrants. Any organization should be placed in any one of four quadrants. Appropriate strategies for an organization to consider are listed in sequential order of attractiveness in each quadrant of the matrix.

It is based two major dimensions

1. Market growth
2. Competitive position

All quadrant contain all possible strategies

Rapid Market Growth

Quadrant 2	**Quadrant 1**
Product Development Market development Market penetration Horizontal/vertial integration Liquidation/Divestiture	Product and Market Development Market Penectration Backward Integration Forward Integration Concentric Diversification
Quadrant 3	**Quadrant 4**
Retrenchment Related/unrelated diversification Conglomerate diversification Liquidation/Divestiture	Rlated/unrelated diversification Horizontal/vertical diversification Conglomerate diversification Joint ventures

Slow Market Growth

Figure 8.12.

Quardant-1 contains that company's strong having competitive situation and rapid market growth. Firms located in Quadrant I of the Grand Strategy Matrix are in an excellent strategic position. These firms must focus on current market and appropriate to follow market penetration, market development and products development are appropriate strategies.

Quardant-2 contains that company's having weak competitive situation and rapid market growth. Firms positioned in Quadrant II need to evaluate their present approach to the marketplace seriously. Although their industry is growing, they are unable to compete effectively, and they need to determine why the firm's current approach is ineffectual and how the company can best change to improve its competitiveness. Because Quadrant II firms are in a rapid-market-growth industry, an intensive strategy (as opposed to integrative or diversification) is usually the first option that should be considered.

Quardant-3 contains that company's weak competitive situation and slow market growth. The firms fall in this quadrant compete in slow-growth industries and have weak competitive positions. These firms must make some drastic changes quickly to avoid further demise and possible liquidation. Extensive cost and asset reduction (retrenchment) should be pursued first. An alternative strategy is to shift resources away from the current business into different areas. If all else fails, the final options for Quadrant III businesses are divestiture or liquidation.

Quardant-4 contains that company's strong competitive situation and slow market growth. Finally, Quadrant IV businesses have a strong competitive position but are in a slow-growth industry. These firms have the strength to launch diversified programs into more promising growth areas. Quadrant IV firms have characteristically high cash flow levels and limited internal growth needs and often can pursue concentric, horizontal, or conglomerate diversification successfully. Quadrant IV firms also may pursue joint ventures As above figure there are four quadrants in grand matrix that further contain various set strategies.

Conclusion

Every firm fall any one four quadrants and if the firm fall in quadrant-1 it must follow the list of strategies given in it. As further if the firm falls in quarrant-2 must adopt the strategies given in quadrant-2 and so on.

STAGE-3 (DECISION STAGE)

Stage 3 called the Decision Stage and involves a single technique, the Quantitative Strategic Planning Matrix (QSPM).

Quantitative Strategic Planning Matrix (QSPM) is a high-level strategic management approach for evaluating possible strategies. Quantitative Strategic Planning Matrix or a QSPM provides an analytical method for comparing feasible alternative actions. The QSPM method falls within so-called stage 3 of the strategy formulation analytical framework.

When company executives think about what to do, and which way to go, they usually have a prioritized list of strategies. If they like one strategy over another one, they move it up on the list. This process is very much intuitive and subjective. The QSPM method introduces some numbers into this approach making it a little more "expert" technique.

What is a Quantitative Strategic Planning Matrix or a QSPM?

The Quantitative Strategic Planning Matrix or a QSPM approach attempts to objectively select the best strategy using input from other management techniques and some easy computations. In other words, the QSPM method uses inputs from stage 1 analyses, matches them with results from stage 2 analyses, and then decides objectively among alternative strategies.

Stage 1 Strategic management tools

The first step in the overall strategic management analysis is used to identify key strategic factors. This can be done using, for example, the EFE matrix and IFE matrix.

Stage 2 Strategic management tools

After we identify and analyze key strategic factors as inputs for QSPM, we can formulate the type of the strategy we would like to pursue. This can be done using the stage 2 strategic management tools, for example the SWOT analysis (or TOWS), SPACE matrix analysis, BCG matrix model, or the IE matrix model.

Stage 3 Strategic management tools

The stage 1 strategic management methods provided us with key strategic factors. Based on their analysis, we formulated possible strategies in stage 2. Now, the task is to compare in QSPM alternative strategies and decide which one is the most suitable for our goals.

The stage 2 strategic tools provide the needed information for setting up the Quantitative Strategic Planning Matrix - QSPM. The QSPM method allows us to evaluate alternative strategies objectively.

Conceptually, the QSPM in stage 3 determines the relative attractiveness of various strategies based on the extent to which key external and internal critical success factors are capitalized upon or improved. The relative attractiveness of each strategy is computed by determining the cumulative impact of each external and internal critical success factor.

Result of QSPM

First, let us take a look at a sample Quantitative Strategic Planning Matrix QSPM, see the picture below. This QSPM compares two alternatives. Based on strategies in the stage 1 (IFE, EFE) and stage 2 (BCG, SPACE, IE), company executives determined that this company XYZ needs to pursue an aggressive strategy aimed at development of new products and further penetration of the market

They also identified that this strategy can be executed in two ways. One strategy is acquiring a competing company. The other strategy is to expand internally. They are now asking which option is the better one.

Table 8.3.

QSPM (Quantitative Strategic Planning Matrix) for XYZ Company

Key Factors	Alternative 1- *Acquire competitor*			Alternative 2- *Expand internally*		
	Weight	Attractiveness Score	Total Attractiveness Score	Weight	Attractiveness Score	Total Attractiveness Score
Strenghts						
Unique product	0.11	2	**0.22**	0.08	1	**0.08**
Location of your business	0.09	3	**0.27**	0.06	2	**0.12**
Worker's unique skill set	0.15	1	**0.15**	0.13	4	**0.52**
Quality of product	0.11	4	**0.44**	0.15	4	**0.60**
Increasing work productivity	0.09	0	**0.00**	0.12	3	**0.36**
Weaknesses						
Lack of quality and customer service	0.10	4	**0.40**	0.13	3	**0.39**
Poor marketing and sales	0.15	2	**0.30**	0.10	1	**0.10**
Undifferentiated product	0.08	3	**0.24**	0.17	0	**0.00**
Negatively sensitive to globalization	0.12	1	**0.12**	0.06	1	**0.06**
Sum Weight	*100 %*			*100 %*		
Opportunities						
A new emerging or developing market						
Possible acquisition of a sales	0.09	4	**0.36**	0.12	0	**0.00**
Undifferentiated product	0.14	4	**0.56**	0.08	2	**0.16**
Membership in trade alliance	0.16	0	**0.00**	0.10	1	**0.10**
Threats						
Increasing competition in the market	0.08	4	**0.32**	0.12	1	**0.12**
Price war	0.10	3	**0.30**	0.14	0	**0.00**
Competitor oligopoly	018	2	**0.36**	0.09	1	**0.09**
US dollar exchange rate	0.09	0	**0.00**	0.20	0	**0.00**
Infavorable taxes	0.16	0	**0.00**	0.15	0	**0.00**
Sum Weight	*100 %*			*100%*		
Sum Total Attractiveness Score			4.04	>		2.70

(Attractiveness Score: 1 = not acceptable; 2 = possibly acceptable; 3 = probably acceptable; 4 = most acceptable; 0 = not relevant)

Doing some easy calculations in the Quantitative Strategic Planning Matrix QSPM, we came to a conclusion that acquiring a competing company is a better option. This is given by the Sum Total Attractiveness Score figure. The acquisition strategy yields higher score than the internal expansion strategy. The acquisition strategy has a score of 4.04 in the QSPM shown above whereas the internal expansion strategy has a smaller score of 2.70.

Steps in constructing QSPMs

You can see a sample Quantitative Strategic Planning Matrix QSPM above. The left column of a QSPM consists of key external and internal factors (identified in stage 1). The left column of a QSPM lists factors obtained directly from the EFE matrix and IFE matrix. The top row consists of feasible alternative strategies (provided in stage 2) derived from the SWOT analysis, SPACE matrix, BCG matrix, and IE matrix. The first column with numbers includes weights assigned to factors. Now let us take a look at detailed steps needed to construct a QSPM.

Step 1: Provide a list of internal factors -- strengths and weaknesses. Then generate a list of the firm's key external factors -- opportunities and threats. These will be included in the left column of the QSPM. You can take these factors from the EFE matrix and the IFE matrix.

Step 2: Having the factors ready, identify strategy alternatives that will be further evaluated. These strategies are displayed at the top of the table. Strategies evaluated in the QSPM should be mutually exclusive if possible.

Step 3: Each key external and internal factor should have some weight in the overall scheme. You can take these weights from the IFE and EFE matrices again. You can find these numbers in our example in the column following the column with factors.

Step 4: Attractiveness Scores (AS) in the QSPM indicates how each factor is important or attractive to each alternative strategy. Attractiveness Scores are determined by examining each key external and internal factor separately, one at a time, and asking the following question:

Does this factor make a difference in our decision about which strategy to pursue?

If the answer to this question is yes, then the strategies should be compared relative to that key factor. The range for Attractiveness Scores is 1 = not attractive, 2 = somewhat attractive, 3 = reasonably attractive, and 4 = highly attractive. If the answer to the above question is no, then the respective key factor has no effect on our decision. If the key factor does not affect the choice being made at all, then the Attractiveness Score would be 0.

Step 5: Calculate the Total Attractiveness Scores (TAS) in the QSPM. Total Attractiveness Scores are defined as the product of multiplying the weights (step 3) by the Attractiveness Scores (step 4) in each row.

The Total Attractiveness Scores indicate the relative attractiveness of each key factor and related individual strategy. The higher the Total Attractiveness Score, the more attractive the strategic alternative or critical factor.

Step 6: Calculate the Sum Total Attractiveness Score by adding all Total Attractiveness Scores in each strategy column of the QSPM. The QSPM Sum Total Attractiveness Scores reveal which strategy is most attractive. Higher scores point at a more attractive strategy, considering all the relevant external and internal critical factors that could affect the strategic decision.

Advantages of QSPM

A QSPM provides a framework to prioritize the strategies; it can be used for comparing strategies at any level such as corporate, business and functional. The other positive feature of QSPM that it integrates external and internal factors into decision making process. A QSPM can be developed for small and large scale profit and non-profit organizations.

Limitations of QSPM

A limitation of the QSPM is that it can be only as good as the prerequisite information and matching analyses upon which it is based. Another limitation is that it requires good judgment in assigning attractiveness scores. Also, the sum total attractiveness scores can be really close such that a final decision is not clear. Like all analytical tools however, the QSPM should not dictate decisions but rather should be developed as input into the owner's final decision.

8.13. STRATEGY FORMULATION

Meaning and Steps of Stretegy Formulation

Strategy formulation refers to the process of choosing the most appropriate course of action for the realization of organizational goals and objectives and thereby achieving the organizational vision. The process of strategy formulation basically involves six main steps. Though these steps do not follow a rigid chronological order, however they are very rational and can be easily followed in this order.

1. **Setting Organizations' Objectives:** The key component of any strategy statement is to set the long-term objectives of the organization. It is known that strategy is generally a medium for realization of organizational objectives. Objectives stress the state of being there whereas Strategy stresses upon the process of reaching there. Strategy includes both the fixation of objectives as well the medium to be used to realize those objectives. Thus, strategy is a wider term which believes in the manner of deployment of resources so as to achieve the objectives.
2. **Evaluating the Organizational Environment:** The next step is to evaluate the general economic and industrial environment in which the organization operates. This includes a review of the organizations competitive position. It is essential to conduct a qualitative and quantitative review of an organizations existings product line. The purpose of such a review is to make sure that the factors important for competitive success in the market can be discovered so that the management can identify their own strengths and weaknesses as well as their competitors' strengths and weaknesses. After identifying its strengths and weaknesses, an organization must keep a track of competitors' moves and actions so as to discover probable opportunities of threats to its market or supply sources.
3. **Setting Quantitative Targets:** In this step, an organization must practically fix the quantitative target values for some of the organizational objectives. The idea behind this is to compare with long term customers, so as to evaluate the contribution that might be made by various product zones or operating departments.
4. **Aiming in Context with the Divisional Plans:** In this step, the contributions made by each department or division or product category within the organization is identified and accordingly strategic planning is done for each sub-unit. This requires a careful analysis of macroeconomic trends.
5. **Performance Analysis:** Performance analysis includes discovering and analyzing the gap between the planned or desired performance. A critical evaluation of the organizations past performance, present condition and the desired future conditions must be done by the organization. This critical evaluation identifies the degree of gap that persists between the actual reality and the long-term aspirations of the organization. An attempt is made by the organization to estimate its probable future condition if the current trends persist.
6. **Choice of Strategy:** This is the ultimate step in Strategy Formulation. The best course of action is actually chosen after considering organizational goals, organizational strengths, potential and limitations as well as the external opportunities.

Chapter 9

STRATEGY CONTROL AND EVALUATION

Introduction and Meaning of Strategy Control - Types - Characteristics of an Effective Control System - Guidelines for Effective Strategic Control System - Organization Structure and Strategy Control - Process of Strategic Evaluation and Control - Strategy Evaluation and Control - Types of Strategic Control Systems - Control Process (Feedback Model) - Designing Strategic Control Systems - Objectives of Strategy Evaluation and Control - Strategies and Tactics to Acquire Power - Managing Conflict - How to Resolve Conflict - Techniques of Strategic Evaluation and Control - Strategic Analysis - Tools and Techniques for Strategic Analysis (Corporate Portfolio Analysis, Corporate Parenting Analysis, Experience Curve Analysis, Life Cycle Analysis, Porter's Five Forces Model, DuPont Analysis) - Product Diversification - Product Classification - Market Penetration and Market Development - New Product Development.

9.1. INTRODUCTION AND MEANING OF STRATEGIC CONTROL SYSTEM

Strategic control precisely defined as the practice of assessing the direction of the organization, as evidenced by its implicit or explicit goals, objectives, strategies, and capacity to perform in the context of changing environmental and competitive actions.

Strategic control is concerned with tracking the strategy as it is being implemented, detecting any problems areas or potential problem areas, and making any necessary adjustments. Newman and Logan use the term control to highlight some important characteristics of strategic control ordinarily, a significant time span occurs between initial implementation of a strategy and achievement of its intended results. During that time, numerous projects are undertaken, investments are made, and actions are undertaken to implement the new strategy. Also the environmental situation and the firm internal situation are developing and evolving. Strategic controls are necessary to steer the firm through these events. They must provide some means of correcting the directions on the basis of intermediate performance and new information.

Strategic control involves the monitoring and evaluation of plans, activities and results with a view towards future action, providing a warning signal through diagnosis of data, and triggering appropriate interventions, be they either tactical adjustments or strategic reorientations. Towards this end, strategic control processes are focused on collecting data, making a determination as to its meaning through comparison to pre-existing standards or aspirations, and then facilitating appropriate interventions. It is important to discover sufficient amount of relevant information and to aid in interpretation of data through intelligent sense-making that gives meaning to complex data, for facilitating value-adding managerial interventions.

Strategic controls are largely subjective criteria intended to verify that the firm is using appropriate strategies for the conditions in the external environment and the company competitive advantages. Thus, strategic controls are concerned with examining the fit between what the firm might do (as suggested by opportunities in its external environment) and what it can do (as indicated by its competitive advantages). Effective strategic controls help the firm to understand what it takes to be successful. Strategic controls demand rich communications between managers responsible for using them to judge the firm performance and those with primary responsibility for implementing the firm strategies (such as middle- and first-level managers). These frequent exchanges are both formal and informal in nature.

Strategic controls are also used to evaluate the degree to which the firm focuses on the requirements to implement its strategies. For example, for a business-level strategy the strategic controls are used to study primary and support activities to verify that the critical activities are being emphasized and properly executed. With related corporate-level strategies, strategic controls are used by corporate strategic leaders to verify the sharing of appropriate strategic factors such as knowledge, markets, and technologies across businesses. To effectively use strategic controls when evaluating related diversification strategies, headquarter executives must have a deep understanding of each unit business-level strategy.

From the perspective of top executives, a strategic control system is a system to support managers in assessing the relevance of the organization strategy to its progress in the accomplishment of its goals and when discrepancies exist, to support areas needing attention. Many existing control systems are based almost exclusively on accounting measures such as Return on Investment (ROI). Since financial reporting requirements include figures for income, assets, and sales, managers can easily calculate ROI or related measures from existing data. In some organizations they are considered the only important measure of success.

9.2. TYPES OF CONTROL

A. Strategic Evaluation and Control Operates at Two Levels

1) Strategic Control: Strategic controls are early warning systems and differ from post action controls, which evaluate only after the implementations have been completed.

2) Operational Control: Operational control is aimed at the allocation and use of organizational resources through an evaluation of the performance of organization units, such as divisions, SBUs and so on, to assess their contribution to the achievement of organizational objectives. Operational control is concerned with action or performance, and this is probably the reason why it is used so extensively in organization.

Table 9.1. Difference between Strategic Control and Operational Control

Basis of Difference	Strategic Control	Operational Control
Basic Question	Are we moving in the right direction?	How are we performing?
Aim	Proactive, continuous questioning of the basic direction of strategy	Allocation and use of organizational resources
Main Concern	Steering the organization future direction	Action control
Focus	External environment	Internal organization
Time Horizon	Long-term	Short-term
Exercise of Control	Exclusively by top management, may be through lower-level support	Mainly by executive or middle-level management on the direction of the top management
Main Techniques	Environmental scanning, information gathering, questioning and review	Budgets, schedules, and MBO

B. The Other Types of Strategic Control

Four basic types of strategic controls are

1. **Premise Control:** Every strategy is based on certain assumptions about environmental and organizational factors. Some of these factors are highly significant and any change in them can affect the strategy to a large extent. Premise control is necessary to identify the key assumption and keep track of any change in them so as to assess their impact on strategy and its implementation. For example, a company may base its strategy on important assumption related to environmental factors (i.e., government policies), industrials factors (i.e., nature of competition) and organizational factors (i.e., breakthrough in R&D). Premise control serves the purpose of continually testing the assumptions to find out whether they are still valid or not. This enables the strategists to take corrective action at the right time rather than continuing with a strategy, which is base on erroneous assumptions.
2. **Implementation Control:** The implementation of strategy result in a series of plans, programmes, and projects. Resource allocation is done to implement these. Implementation control is aim at evaluation whether the plans, programs and projects are actually guiding the organization towards its predetermined objectives or not. If, at any time, it is felt that the commitment of resources to a plan, programme or project would not benefit the organization as envisage, they have to be revised. In this manner, implementation control may lead to strategic rethinking.
3. **Strategic Surveillance:** Strategic surveillance is designed to monitor a broad range of events inside and outside the company that are likely to threaten the course of the firm strategy. The premise and implementation types of strategic controls are specific in nature. Strategic surveillance, on the other hand, is aimed at a more generalized and overarching control to monitor a broad range of events inside and outside the company that are likely to threaten the course of firm strategy Strategic surveillance can be done through a broad-based, general monitoring on the basis of selected information sources to uncover events that are likely to affect the strategy of an organization. Strategic surveillance systems refer to the management systems with the purpose of making a corporation capable of reacting quickly and competently to changes in its environment.
4. **Special Alert Control:** The strategic control system is the special alert control which is based on a trigger mechanism for rapid response and immediate reassessment of strategy in the light of sudden and unexpected events. Special alert control can be exercised through the formulation of contingency strategies and assigning the responsibility of handling unforeseen events to crisis management teams. Example of such events can be the sudden fall of government at the central or state level, instant change in a competitor posture, an unfortunate industrial disaster, or a natural catastrophe.
5. **Financial Controls:** These controls are largely objective criteria used to measure the firm performance against previously established quantitative standards. Accounting- based measures such as Return on Investment (ROI) and Return on Assets (ROA) as well as market-based measures such as economic value-added are examples of financial controls. Partly because strategic controls are difficult to use with extensive diversification, financial controls are emphasized to evaluate the performance of the firm using the unrelated diversification strategy. The unrelated diversification strategy focus on financial outcomes, requires using standardized financial controls to compare performances between business units and associated managers.
6. **Output Control:** This is a system in which strategic manager estimate or forecast appropriate performance goals for each division, department, and employee and then measure actual

performance relative to these goals. Often company reward system is linked to performance on these goals, so output control also provides an incentive structure for motivation employees at all levels in the organization.

7. **Behavior Control:** Behavior control is control through the establishment of a comprehensive system of rules and procedures to direct the actions or behavior of divisions, functions, and individuals. The intention of using behavior controls is not to specify the goals but to standardize the way of reaching them. Rules standardize behavior and make outcomes predictable. If employees follow the rules, then actions are performed and decisions handled the same way time and time again. The result is predictability and accuracy, the aim of all control systems. The main kind of behavior controls is operation budgets. Standardization, rules and procedures.

9.3. CHARACTERISTICS OF AN EFFECTIVE STRATEGIC CONTROL SYSTEM

Effective control systems tend to have certain qualities in common

1. **Suitable:** The control system must be suitable to the needs of an organization. It must conform to the nature and needs of the job and the area to be controlled. For example, the control system used in production department will different from that used in sales department.
2. **Simple:** The control system should be easy to understand and operate. A complicated control system will cause unnecessary mistakes, confusion and frustration among employees. When the control system is understood properly, employees can interpret the same in a right way and ensure its implementation.
3. **Selective:** To be useful, the control system must focus attention on key, strategic and important factors which are critical to performance. Insignificant deviations need not be looked into. By concentrating attention on important aspects, managers can save their time and meet problems head on in an effective manner.
4. **Sound and Economical:** The system of control should be economical and easy to maintain. Any system of control has to justify the benefits that it gives in relation to the costs it incurs. To minimize costs, management should try to impose the least amount of control that is necessary to produce the desired results.
5. **Flexible:** Competitive, technological and other environmental changes force organizations to change their plans. As a result, control should be necessarily flexible. It must be flexible enough to adjust to adverse changes or to take advantage of new opportunities.
6. **Forward-Looking:** An effective control system should be forward-looking. It must provide timely information on deviations. Any departure from the standard should be caught as soon as possible. This helps managers to take remedial steps immediately before things go out of gear.
7. **Reasonable:** According to Robbins, controls must be reasonable. They must be attainable. If they are too high or unreasonable, they no longer motivate employees. On the other hand, when controls are set at low levels, they do not pose any challenge to employees. They do not stretch their talents. Therefore, control standards should be reasonable they should challenge and stretch people *to reach higher performance without being de-motivating.*
8. **Objective:** A control system would be effective only when it is objective and impersonal. It should not be subjective and arbitrary. When standards are set in clear terms, it is easy to evaluate performance. Vague standards are not easily understood and hence, not achieved in a right way. Controls should be accurate and unbiased. If they are unreliable and subjective. People will resent them.

9. **Responsibility for Failures:** An effective control system must indicate responsibility for failures. Detecting deviations would be meaningless, unless one knows where in the organization they are occurring and who is responsible for them. The control system should also point out what corrective actions are needed to keep actual performance in line with planned performance.
10. **Acceptable:** Control will not work unless people want them to. They should be acceptable to those whom they apply. Controls will be acceptable when they are:
    - Quantified
    - Objective
    - Attainable
    - Understood by one and all.

9.4. GUIDELINES FOR EFFECTIVE STRATEGIC CONTROL SYSTEM

In designing control system, top management should remember that controls should follow strategy. Unless controls ensure the use of the proper strategy to achieve objectives, there is a strong likelihood that dysfunctional side effects will completely undermine the implementation of the objectives. The following guidelines are recommended

1. **Involving Minimum Amount of Information:** Control should involve only the minimum amount of information needed to give a reliable picture of events. Too many controls create confusion. Focus on the strategic factors by following the 80/20 rule i.e., monitor those 20% of the factors that determine 80% of the results.
2. **Monitor Only Meaningful Activities and Results:** Controls should monitor only meaningful activities and results, regardless of measurement difficulty. If cooperation between divisions is important to corporate performance, some form of qualitative or quantitative measures should be established to monitor co-operation.
3. **Timely Control:** Controls should be timely so that corrective action can be taken before it is too late. Steering controls, controls that monitor or measure the factors influencing performance, should be stressed so that advance notice of problems is given.
4. **Both Long-term and Short-term Controls Should be Used:** If only short-term measures are emphasized, a short-term managerial orientation is likely.
5. **Pinpointing Exceptions:** Controls should aim at pinpointing exceptions; only those activities or results that fall outside a predetermined tolerance range should call for action.
6. **Emphasizing the Reward of Meeting of Exceeding Standards:** Emphasize the reward of meeting of exceeding standards rather than punishment for failing to meet standards. Heavy punishment of failure typically results in goal displacement. Managers will reports and lobby for lower standards.

9.5. ORGANIZATION STRUCTURE AND STRATEGIC CONTROL

The strategic control systems must be designed keeping in view the structure of the organization. Three elements of structure are of special concern

1. **Centralization:** The degree to which higher levels in the hierarchy perform target setting, monitoring, evaluation, and feedback activities to improve task performance.
2. **Formalization:** The degree of rationalization using standardized procedures and data sources such as market studies, published statistics, budgets, and audits, which provide management with information about whether the organization strategy and structure are meeting strategic intent.

3. **Specialization:** The division of labor and the span of control that would allow the subordinates to perform their activities efficiently and allow the managers to coordinate the performance of the subordinates.

In traditional environments, the structure of a firm tends to be bureaucratic in nature. The control systems tend to be specialized with a high degree of formalization and specialization. However, increasingly, a network-type structure is becoming popular. In these structures, the employees are given more influence on their jobs, informal approaches for control gain prominence, and teamwork is common that encourages the employees to become multi-skilled. In most real world situations, the structure is a mix of bureaucratic and network types. Here the strategic control should encourage both compliance and learning in the organization. This may be done through a combination of incentive-based reward systems and informal motivational processes, as illustrated by the case of Tata Steel.

9.6. PROCESS OF STRATEGIC EVALUATION AND CONTROL

1. **Setting the Standards**
   - Setting standards for every operation is an unavoidable task of management.
   - Before setting standards, an executive must study the characteristics of the work.
   - Executives must consider ordinarily flexible and generally acceptable levels of good performance in terms of work characteristics.
   - As nature of work differs with every operation (unit), the characteristics are different and so are the standards.
   - Standards are set, thus, depending on the characteristics of the task.

Requirements of Performance Standards.

- Set in precise quantitative terms.
- Flexible enough to modify whenever required.
- Acceptable range of deviations to be laid down.
- Clear and understandable to all.
- Workable and acceptable.
- Take care of all strategic points that cover the entire organization.
- Revise periodically and keep up-to-date.

2. **Evaluating/Measuring Performance:** The evaluation process operates at the performance level as action takes place, (actual performance is depicted within a dotted boundary as it is not a part of the evaluation process). Standards of performance act as the benchmark against which the actual performance is to be compared. It is important, however, to understand how the measurement of performance can take place. The information system is the key element in any measurement exercise. Operationally, measuring is done through the accounting, reporting, and communication systems. A variety of evaluation techniques are used for measurement. Apart from the methods of measuring performance, the other important aspects of measurement relate to the difficulties, timing, and periodicity in measuring.
3. **Problems in Measuring Performance:** The measurement of performance is a crucial part of evaluation and control. The lack of quantifiable objectives or performance standards and the inability of the information system to provide timely and valid information are two obvious control problems. Without objective and timely measurements, it would be extremely difficult to make operational, let alone strategic, decisions. Nevertheless, the use of timely, quantifiable standards does not guarantee good performance, The very act of monitoring and measuring performance can cause side effects that interfere with overall

corporate performance. Among the most frequent negative side effects are a short-term orientation and goal displacement.

4) **Analyzing Variances:** The measurement of actual performance and its comparison with standard or budgeted performance leads to an analysis of variances. Broadly, the following three situations may arise;

i) **Actual Performance Matches the Budgeted Performance:** The first situation is ideal but not realistic. In practice, the actual performance rarely matches the budgeted performance. Here, the strategists would have to specify a range of tolerance limits between which the results may be accepted satisfactorily. So, actual performance, which deviates from the budgeted performance within the established tolerance limits, can be acceptable and the variance is considered as not significant.

ii) **Actual Performance Deviates Positively over the Budgeted Performance:** This situation is welcome as it is an indication of superior performance. But exceeding the target continually should be considered as unusual and a check needs to be made to test the validity of standards and the efficacy of the measurement system.

iii) **Actual Performance Deviates Negatively from the Budgeted Performance:** The third type of situation is alarming as it indicates a shortfall in achievement. The strategists need to pinpoint the areas where performance is below standard and go into the causes of deviation. Corrective action is taken on the basis of the analysis of the causes of deviation.

5) **Taking Corrective Action:** There are three courses for corrective action- checking of performance, checking of standards, and reformulating strategies, plans, and objectives.

i) Initiating corrective action is not an insignificant part of the evaluation process. It involves a variety of managerial functions, which are preformed during strategy implementation. **For example, checking of performance** requires going into the details of organizational structure and systems as well as, behavioral implementation. Performance can be affected adversely due to a number of factors such as distortions in resource allocation inappropriateness of structure and systems, and wrong leadership and motivational styles. if the evaluation process shows that performance is consistently lower than expected, the strategists would have to undertake an in- depth analysis and diagnosis of the factors that might be responsible for bad performance. Taking corrective action for checking performance is, therefore, a significant part of the day-to-day activities of managers.

ii) **Checking of standards** is less frequent than a performance check but it has to be done as soon as it is felt that there is nothing significantly wrong with performance. A standards check may result in a lowering of standards if it is concluded that organizational capabilities do not match the performance requirements. It may also lead to an elevation of standards if the conditions have improved to allow better performance to take place. For example, better equipment, improved systems, and upgraded skills are sure to make existing standards partly irrelevant. Productivity frontiers too keep moving farther and competitive pressures compel companies to continually strive to improve their operational effectiveness. In such a situation, standards check would become necessary.

iii) A more radical and infrequent corrective action is to **reformulate strategies, plans, and objectives.** Strategic, rather than operational, control will lead to the conclusion whether strategies need reformulation, plans need to be remodeled, or objectives need to be redefined. Reformulation of strategy will take strategist back to the process of strategic management where a fresh strategic choice has to be made. A remodeling of plans will entail a new resource allocation pattern and subsequent changes in strategy implementation. Redefinition of objectives, however, takes strategist back full-circle to the start of the strategic management process.

9.7. STRATEGY EVALUATION AND CONTROL

The final stage in strategic management is strategy evaluation and control. All strategies are subject to future modification because internal and external factors are constantly changing. In the strategy evaluation and control process managers determine whether the chosen strategy is achieving the organization's objectives. The fundamental strategy evaluation and control activities are: reviewing internal and external factors that are the bases for current strategies, measuring performance, and taking corrective actions.

Strategic Evaluation generally operates at **two levels:**

- Stratagic level
- Operational level

At the strategic level managers try to examine the consistency of strategy with environment. At the **operational level,** the focus is on finding how a given strategy is effectively pursued by an organisation.

IMPORTANCE: Strategy Evaluation and Control (SEC) helps an organisation in several ways.

- **Feedback:** SEC offers valuable feedback on how well things are moving ahead. It also throws light on the relevance and validity of strategic choice. It helps to answer critical questions such as: Are we moving in the proper direction? Are our assumptions about major trends are correct? Should we adjust or abort strategy?
- **Reward:** SEC helps in identifying rewarding behaviours that are in tune with formulated strategies. It helps in pinpointing responsibilities for failure as well. Where people find it difficult to stick to a planned course of action due to circumstances beyond their control, managers can take note of such things and initiate suitable rectification steps immediately.
- **Future Planning:** SEC offers a considerable amount of information and experience to decision makers that can be quite valuable in the formulation of new strategic plans.

BARRIERS: There are three types of barriers in evaluation the limits of control, difficulties in measurement, and motivational problems.

- **The Limits of Control:** It is not easy for strategists to decide the limits of control. Too much control prevents mangers from taking initiative, experiment with their creative ideas and gain through calculated risk taking. On the other hand, when there is very little control people tend to go off the hook, waste resources without any fear of punishment and work at cross purposes – putting a big question mark on the very survival of the firm.
- **Difficulties in Measurement:** It is not easy to find measurement techniques that are valid and reliable. Validity is the extent to which an instrument measures what it intends to measure (for example measuring the speed and accuracy of a typist in a typing test). Reliability is the confidence that an indicator will measure the same thing every time. In the absence of reliability and validity, the control system gets distorted. It may fail to measure results uniformly or measure attributes that are not required to be measured. When people are not confident about the measures used for judgement, they resist the whole process vehemently.
- **Motivational Problems:** Having taken a position while formulating and implementing the strategy, strategists are often reluctant to admit their mistakes when things go off the track. They tend to shift the blame on others. This may also prevent them from hiving off unprofitable divisions, reversing wrong decisions and go in search of more viable alternations quickly.

EVALUATION CRITERIA: The critical factors that could help in evaluating a strategy may broadly be classified into two categories: quantitative factors and qualitative factors.

Quantitative Factors: Quantitative criteria commonly employed in evaluate strategies are financial ratios, which strategists use to make three important comparisons: (i) comparing the firm' s performance over different time periods (ii) comparing the firm's performance to competitors' and (iii) comparing the firm's performance to industry averages. Some key financial ratios those are particularly useful as criteria for strategy evaluation may be stated thus:

- Return on investment
- Return on equity
- Z score
- Employee turnover
- Employee satisfaction index
- Return on capital employed
- Profit margin
- Market share
- Debt to equity
- Earnings per share
- Sales growth
- Asset growth

Qualitative Factors: Many managers feel that qualitative organizational measurements are best arrived at simply by answering a series of important questions at revealing important facets of organizational operations. Some qualitative questions that are useful in evaluating strategies.

1. Is the strategy internally consistent?
2. Is the strategy consistent with the environment?
3. Is the strategy appropriate in view of available resource?
4. Does the strategy involve an acceptable degree of risk?
5. Does the strategy have an appropriate time framework?
6. Is the strategy workable?

9.8. STRATEGIC CONTROL SYSTEMS TYPES

Strategic control focuses on the dual questions of whether

(1) the strategy is being implemented as planned; and

(2) the results produced by the strategy are those intended."

Strategic control is "the critical evaluation of plans, activities, and results, thereby providing information for the future action". **There are four types of strategic control: premise control, implementation control, strategic surveillance and special alert control**

1. Premise Control: Planning premises/assumptions are established early on in the strategic planning process and act as a basis for formulating strategies. Premise control has been designed to check systematically and continuously whether or not the premises set during the planning and implementation processes are still valid. It involves the checking of environmental conditions. Premises are primarily concerned with two types of factors

- Environmental factors (for example, inflation, technology, interest rates, regulation, and demographic/social changes).
- Industry factors (for example, competitors, suppliers, substitutes, and barriers to entry).

All premises may not require the same amount of control. Therefore, managers must select those premises and variables that (a) are likely to change and (b) would a major impact on the company and its strategy if the did.

2. Implementation Control: Strategic implantation control provides an additional source of feed forward information. "Implementation control is designed to assess whether the overall strategy should be changed in light of unfolding events and results associated with incremental steps and actions that implement the overall strategy." The two basis types of implementation control are

i) Monitoring strategic thrusts (new or key strategic programs). Two approaches are useful in enacting implementation controls focused on monitoring strategic thrusts:

(a) one way is to agree early in the planning process on which thrusts are critical factors in the success of the strategy or of that thrust;

(b) the second approach is to use stop/go assessments linked to a series of meaningful thresholds (time, costs, research and development, success, etc.) associated with particular thrusts.

ii) Milestone Reviews. Milestones are significant points in the development of a programme, such as points where large commitments of resources must be made. A milestone review usually involves a full-scale reassessment of the strategy and the advisability of continuing or refocusing the direction of the company. In order to control the current strategy, must be provided in strategic plans.

3. Strategic Surveillance. It is designed to monitor a broad range of events inside and outside the company that are likely to threaten the course of the firm's strategy. The basic idea behind strategic surveillance is that some form of general monitoring of multiple information sources should be encouraged, with the specific intent being the opportunity to uncover important yet unanticipated information.

Strategic surveillance appears to be similar in some way to "environmental scanning." The rationale, however, is different. Environmental, scanning usually is seen as part of the chronological planning cycle devoted to generating information for the new plan. By way of contrast, strategic surveillance is designed to safeguard the established strategy on a continuous basis.

4. Special Alert Control: Special alert controls are the need to thoroughly, and often rapidly, reconsider the firm's basis strategy based on a sudden, unexpected event. (i.e., natural disasters, chemical spills, plane crashes, product defects, hostile takeovers etc.). Special alert controls should be conducted throughout the entire strategic management process.

9.9. THE CONTROL PROCESS-FEEDBACK MODEL

Regardless of the type or levels of control systems an organization needs, control may be depicted as a six-step feedback model:

1. Determine What to Control: The first step in the control process is determining the major areas to control. Managers usually base their major controls on the organizational mission, goals and objectives developed during the planning process.

Managers must make choices because it is expensive and virtually impossible to control every aspect of the organization's .

2. Set Control Standards: The second step in the control process is establishing standards. A control standard is a target against which subsequent performance will be compared. Standards are the criteria that enable managers to evaluate future, current, or past actions. They are measured in a variety of ways, including physical, quantitative, and qualitative terms. Five aspects of the performance can be managed and controlled: **quantity, quality, time cost, and behavior.**

Standards reflect specific activities or behaviors that are necessary to achieve organizational goals. Goals are translated into performance standards by making them measurable. An organizational goal to increase market share, for example, may be translated into a top-management performance standard to increase market share by 10 percent within a twelve-month period. Helpful measures of strategic performance include: sales (total, and by division, product category, and region), sales growth, net profits, return on sales, assets, equity, and investment cost of sales, cash flow, market share, product quality, valued added, and employees productivity.

Quantification of the objective standard is sometimes difficult. For example, consider the goal of product leadership. An organization compares its product with those of competitors and determines the extent to which it pioneers in the introduction of basis product and product improvements. Such standards may exist even though they are not formally and explicitly stated.

Setting the timing associated with the standards is also a problem for many organizations. It is not unusual for short-term objectives to be met at the expense of long-term objectives. Management must develop standards in all performance areas touched on by established organizational goals. The various forms standards are depend on what is being measured and on the managerial level responsible for taking corrective action.

3. Measure Performance: Once standards are determined, the next step is measuring performance. The actual performance must be compared to the standards. Many types of measurements taken for control purposes are based on some form of historical standard. These standards can be based on data derived from the **PIMS (Profit Impact of Market Strategy)** program, published information that is publicly available, ratings of product / service quality, innovation rates, and relative market shares standings.

Strategic control standards are based on the practice of **competitive benchmarking** - the process of measuring a firm's performance against that of the top performance in its industry. The proliferation of computers tied into networks has made it possible for managers to obtain up-to-minute status reports on a variety of quantitative performance measures. Managers should be careful to observe and measure in accurately before taking corrective action.

4. Compare Performance to Standards: The comparing step determines the degree of variation between actual performance and standard. If the first two phases have been done well, the third phase of the controlling process - comparing performance with standards - should be straightforward. However, sometimes it is difficult to make the required comparisons (e.g., behavioral standards). Some deviations from the standard may be justified because of changes in environmental conditions, or other reasons.

5. Determine the Reasons for the Deviations: The fifth step of the control process involves finding out: "why performance has deviated from the standards?" Causes of deviation can range from selected achieve organizational objectives. Particularly, the organization needs to ask if the deviations are due to internal shortcomings or external changes beyond the control of the organization. A general checklist such as following can be helpful:

- Are the standards appropriate for the stated objective and strategies?
- Are the objectives and corresponding still appropriate in light of the current environmental situation?
- Are the strategies for achieving the objectives still appropriate in light of the current environmental situation?
- Are the firm's organizational structure, systems (e.g., information), and resource support adequate for successfully implementing the strategies and therefore achieving the objectives?
- Are the activities being executed appropriate for achieving standard?

6. Take Corrective Action: The final step in the control process is determining the need for corrective action. Managers can choose among three courses of action: (1) they can do nothing (2) they can correct the actual performance (3) they can revise the standard.

When standards are not met, managers must carefully assess the reasons why and take corrective action. Moreover, the need to check standards periodically to ensure that the standards and the associated performance measures are still relevant for the future.

The final phase of controlling process occurs when managers must decide action to take to correct performance when deviations occur. Corrective action depends on the discovery of deviations and the ability to take necessary action. Often the real cause of deviation must be found before corrective action can be taken. Causes of deviations can range from unrealistic objectives to the wrong strategy being selected achieve organizational objectives. Each cause requires a different corrective action. Not all deviations from external environmental threats or opportunities have progressed to the point a particular outcome is likely, corrective action may be necessary.

9.10. DESIGNING STRATEGIC CONTROL SYSTEMS

Introduction

Strategic control systems provide managers with required information to find out whether strategy and structure move in the same direction. It includes target setting, monitoring, evaluation and feedback system.

Evaluation and Control in Strategic Management

Evaluation & control information consists of performance data and activity reports (gather in step –3), operational Managers must know about any undesired performance caused by the inappropriate use of SMP in order to correct the employee activity. Top management need not be involved. It, however, the processes themselves cause the undesired performance, both top managers and operational managers must know about it so that they can develop new implementation programme or procedures. Evaluation and Control information must be relevant to what is being monitored. Evaluation and Control are not easy activities; one of the obstacles to effective control is the difficulty in developing appropriate measures of important activities and outputs. This process provides the feedback necessary for management to evaluate the results and take corrective action, as needed. The process could be as follows

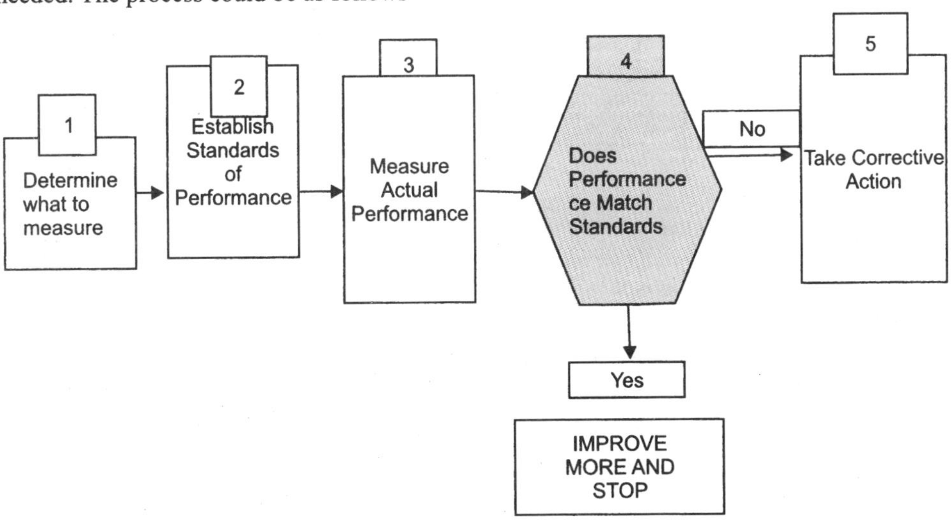

Figure 9.1.

1. **Determine what to measure:** Top managers and operational managers must specify implementation process and results to be monitored and evaluated. The processes and results

must be measurable in a reasonably objective and consistent manner. The focus should be on the most significant elements in a process – the ones that account for the highest proportion of exposure or the greatest no. of problems.

2. **Establish standards of performance:** Standards used to measure performance are detailed expressions of strategic objectives. They are measures of acceptable performance results. Each standard can be usually includes a tolerance range, which defines any acceptable deviations. Standards can be set not only for final output, but also for intermediate stages of production output.
3. **Measure actual performance**: Measurements must be made at predetermined times.
4. **Compare actual performance with the standard:** If the actual performance results are within the desired tolerance range, the measurement process stops here
5. **Take corrective action:** If the actual results fall outside the desired tolerance range, action must be taken to correct the deviation. The action must not only correct the deviation but also prevent its recurrence. The following issues must be resolved:
   - Is the deviation only a chance fluctuation?
   - Are the processes being carried out in correctly?
   - Are the processes appropriate for achieving the desired standards?

9.11. OBJECTIVES OF STRATEGY EVALUATION AND CONTROL

- Organizations are most vulnerable when they are at the peak of their success
- Erroneous strategic decisions can inflict severe penalties and can be exceedingly difficult, if not impossible, to reverse.
- Strategy evaluation is vital to an organization's well-being; timely evaluations can alert management to problems or potential problems before a situation becomes critical.

Through evaluation and control process, corporate activities and performance results are monitored so that actual performance can be compared with desired performance.

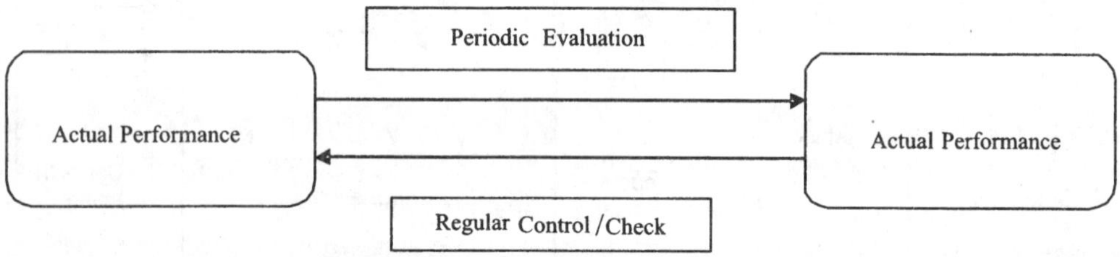

Figure 9.2.

Steps in Strategic Control Process

- Establish standards and Targets
- Create Measuring and monitoring systems
- Compare Actual with targets
- Evaluate and take corrective actions

Levels of Control

- Corporate level managers
- Divisional level managers
- Functional level managers
- First level managers

Types of Control System

- Personal control
- Output control
- Behavior contro

9.12. STRATEGIES AND TACTICS TO ACQUIRE POWER

Various political strategies are pursued by individuals with a view to enhance their image and gain respect from others. Successful political behaviour involves keeping people happy, cultivating contacts and wheeling and dealing. Some commonly employed political strategies are given below (Dubrin):

- **Forming Alliances:** Maintain alliances with powerful people, especially those who are close to the most powerful person in the organisation.
- **Selective use of Information:** Control the flow of important pieces of information to suit personal ends. Includes withholding unfavourable information from superiors, keeping useful information from competitors, interpreting information in a way that is favourable to oneself.
- **Scapegoating:** Ensuring that someone else is blamed for a failure. Skilled politicians make sure that they never blamed when something goes wrong and are given get credit when something goes right.
- **Image Building:** Skilled politicians know the importance of being viewed positively and go out of their way to create positive images of themselves. Includes dressing appropriately, highlighting one's successes, being enthusiastic about the organisation, adhering to group norms etc. Also they always try to present a conservative image of themselves. It can be disadvantageous to be seen as too radical an agent of change.
- **Networking:** Insuring that one has many friends in positions of influence. Skilful politicians extend favours to cultivate rewarding relationships with others. They praise people and avoid critical, negative remarks about others. They are generally very cordial in their interpersonal dealings.
- **Compromise:** Giving in on an important issue in order to gain an ally who will be on your side when an issue of importance to you arises at a later date.
- **Rule Manipulation:** Refusing an opponent's request on the grounds that it is against company policy but granting an identical request from an ally on grounds that it is a 'special occasion.'
- **Fabianism:** Avoiding decisive engagement. This means going slow and easy — an evolutionary rather than a revolutionary approach to change. By not 'ruffling feathers', the power seeker can slowly but steadily become entrenched and gain the cooperation and trust of others.
- **One Step at a Time:** Skilful politicians take one step at a time instead of pushing the whole project or reorganisation attempt at a time. One small step can be a foothold that the power seeker can use as a basis to get other, more major .things accomplished.
- **Persuasion:** Another tactic is persuasion which relies on both emotion and logic. An operations manager wanting to construct a new plant on a certain site might persuade others to support his goal on grounds that are objective and logical (land is cheap, tax concessions are great) as well as subjective and personal.

Managing Political Behaviour while Implementing Strategies

Political behaviour, by its very nature, defies logical thinking and systematic handling. But managers can prevent excessive damage to organisational performance by initiating certain *steps.*

- **Define Job Duties Clearly:** It is better to define job duties to recognise individual contributions. This helps employees know what they are expected to do and provides a criterion for evaluation. As a result, they are less prone to use politics as a means to gain recognition.
- **Design Jobs Properly:** For another thing, design jobs to stimulate excitement and enthusiasm. If employees are busy and focus attention on getting things done, they may not have time for gossip and office politics.
- **Demonstrate Proper Behaviours:** The leader should set an example by not condoning or encouraging gossip. Better not to rely on reports from 'Yes-men' alone and act hurriedly on inaccurate and one-sided information. Managers should avoid covert activities. Behind the scene activities give the impression of political intent even if none really exists.
- **Promote Understanding:** Discuss issues clearly, encourage divergent views, clarify doubts and present various options before the subordinates — every time an assignment is made. There is no use pitting units and managers against each other thus compelling people to engage in a permanent game of mutual recrimination and shifting of blame. The leader must encourage informal meets as well so as to gain a clear insight into what people feel about organisational activities. He should get disagreements out in the open so that subordinates will have less opportunity for political behaviour using conflict for their own purposes.
- **Allocate Resources Judiciously:** Set a justifiable criteria for allocation of scarce inputs, giving no room for political battles later on. 'Firmly established policies and guidelines are mandatory, but managers must be careful to apply them consistently.' Competitive approaches always encourage empire-building tendencies at the sub-unit level, leading to street battles if things go out of hand. In such a scenario, teamwork and cooperation among units will not develop. For example, 'manufacturing might be acquiring resources that could be better utilised to enhance a firm's marketing network. Ultimately, the overall effectiveness of the firm is likely to suffer.'

9.13. MANAGING CONFLICT

Conflict is a process in which an effort is purposefully made by one person or unit to block another that results in frustrating the attainment of the other's goals or the furthering of his interests.

Features of Conflict

- Two parties pursuing exclusive goals, values or events.
- A tries to prevent B from attaining his (B's) goals deliberately.
- Conflict must be perceived by the parties to it. It arises out of two perceptions. If A perceives his goals to be incompatible with those of B and A has no opportunity to frustrate the goals attainment of B, there is no conflict.
- Conflict is related to overt acts only.

Conflict is a basic fact of life in groups and organisations. The very nature of organization guarantees the emergence of conflict. First, organisations contain people with divergent personalities, perceptions and values. Second, these people are put on jobs that have different requirements at different levels. Finally, people in organisations have to compete for scarce resources in order to realise goals. Conflicts, thus, can develop from several sources in an organisation. A manager must understand the nature of conflict clearly before trying to manage the same through various strategies.

Conflicts occur routinely because of personality differences, scarce resources whicl need to be distributed to various subunits, incompatible goals of different functional heads (e.g. the production man may perceive his goals to be potentially incompatible with that of the marketing man. The production manager may feel — why don't we have accurate sales forecasts? The marketing manager may retort: why don't we have enough capacity? Why don't we ever have the right merchandise in inventory), task interdependence of people working at various levels (for information, resources etc).

9.13.1 How To Resolve Conflict?

Conflict, which is somewhat dysfunctional, may be dealt with in the following ways:

1. **Separate the warring factions**: Use your authority and disallow the warring groups to interact with each other.
2. **Create a procedure of appeal:** Make people follow a procedure obviously created by you, for getting their grievances resolved.
3. **Appoint an integrator:** Appoint an integrator, who knows the language of both parties, to resolve the dispute. However, much depends on the experience, expertise and persuasive skill of the integrator to get the parties to agree to one thing.
4. **Rotate members:** Force people to move out of their departments. 'When placed in another department, people will see the big picture. Break the departmental boundaries. Allow them to step into the shoes of another. Role reversal helps people to come out of their 'shell' and look at things in a broad way.
5. **Reduce interdependence:** Make the people and departments fully equipped, to the extent possible. The feeling of scarcity and competition for a bigger share, often, makes people insensitive to other's needs. When they stand on their own, the scope for conflicting situations gets reduced.
6. **Emphasise overall goals:** Make people realise that they are working for the firm not for the department where they are placed. Politicians often speak about external threats from neighboring countries so that internal groups do not fight beyond a point. Putting emphasis on goals such as market share, service with a smile, profitability makes people to be on the target instead of working toward mutually conflicting departmental goals.
7. **Ignore the conflict:** At times this may also work. Allow the fire to take its own course for some time, especially when the issue is trivial.
8. **Bargain with both groups:** Bring both groups to the negotiating table. Allow them to make their respective demands. Make them realise the importance of 'give and take'. When concessions are agreed upon by both parties, agreements are bound to come.
9. **Practice integrative problem solving:** When there is a minimum level of trust between both parties and there is no time pressure for a quick solution, the best way is to follow integrative problem solving. Here, parties are made to define the problem, develop as many alternative solutions as possible and pick up the one which is best suited. Supply information, facts, etc., and force the parties to deliberate the issues fully and develop the solution (s) in a dispassionate way.

9.14. TECHNIQUES OF STRATEGIC EVALUATION AND CONTROL

Value chain analysis: Firms employ value chain analysis to identify and evaluate the competitive potential of resources and capabilities. By studying their skills relative to those associated with primary and support activities, firms are able to understand their cost structure, and identify their activities through which they can create value.

Quantitative performance measurements: Most firms prepare formal reports of quantitative performance measurements (such as sales growth, profit growth, economic value added, ration analysis etc.) that manager's review at regular intervals. These measurements are generally linked to the standards set in the first step of the control process. For example if sales growth is a target, the firm should have a means of gathering and exporting sales data. If the firm has identified appropriate measurements, regular review of these reports helps managers stay aware of whether the firm is doing what it should do. In addition to there, certain qualitative bases based on intuition, judgement, opinions, or surveys could be used to judge whether the firm's performance is on the right track or not.

Benchmarking: It is a process of learning how other firms do exceptionally high-quality things. Some approaches to bench marking are simple and straightforward. For example Xerox Corporation routinely buys copiers made by other firms and takes them apart to see how they work. This helps the firms to stay abreast of its competitors' improvements and changes.

Key Factor Rating: It is based on a close examination of key factors affecting performance (financial, marketing, operations and human resource capabilities) and assessing overall organisational capability based on the collected information.

9.15. STRATEGIC ANALYSIS

Strategic analysis is the investigation of the objective factors being considered in the process of strategic choice. Questions such as which industries to enter and which industries to leave, which businesses to create/ acquire/divest, which products and markets to retain/grow/divest face the strategists of organisations during strategic analysis. Strategic analysis is meant to help answer these questions.

Tools and Techniques for Strategic Analysis

Strategic analysis isa dynamic area of strategic management where new tools and techniques are conni4 being developed, often replacing some of the older techniques. The following Exhibit peeps into the exciting world management tools and techniques. With internationalization and digitalization, the availability and usage novel tools and techniques is likely to spread and increase.

Exhibit the Exciting World of Management Tools and Techniques

The onslaught of globalisation, increasing competitiveness, rising complexity of doing business and access to a wide variety of sources of information are factors that prod managers to embark on a continual search management tools and techniques that might have the potential for implementation and helping them in developing competitive advantage, increasing shareholders' wealth and enhancing profitability for their organisations. Among these techniques, many turn out to be mere fads in passing. Some of them remain as solid ideas worth considering and applying widely and consistently.

There are surprisingly, a large number of management tools and techniques available. In one of the earlier studies by Hussey (1992), 57 techniques were listed. Clark's 1997 study considered 80'strategic management tools and techniques. In fact, the proliferation of tools and techniques has posed a problem of classification and creating taxonomies and categories.

The usage of management tools and techniques has attracted the attention of researchers. There have been studies on the usage of such tools and techniques by organisations globally, as well as in specific countries. There have also been context-specific studies such as the usage of management tools and techniques in small and medium enterprises or agricultural cooperatives.

Bain and Company, a management consultancy organisation, have been performing an annual survey a management tools and trends. Every year, they focus on 25 most popular techniques that managers around the world find to be relevant, topical and measurable. The 2007 survey finds the most popular technique to be of strategic planning. Customer relationship management, customer segmentation, benchmarking and vision and mission statements are among the top techniques. Among other popular techniques are scenario and contingency planning, strategic alliances, balanced scorecard and growth strategy tools. Some of the less popular techniques are mergers and acquisitions, six sigma, offshoring, consumer ethnography and corporate blogs. As you will notice, many of these management techniques are relevant for strategic management and strategic planning.

Unfortunately, we do not find such systematic empirical studies in the Indian context as yet. What we can know about the usage of management tools and techniques in India is only through what is reported occasionally in the business press and media and in journal articles arid oblique references in studies related to other management topics.

Sources: D. Rigby & B. Bilodeau, Management Tools and Trends 2007, Gain & Company,(This report along with its executive guide is available at http://www.tooIsandtrends.com/management_tooIs/home.asp Retrieved July 1, 2007; D.E. Hussey 1992), "Glossary of management techniques", International Review of Strategic Management, 3, pp. 47-75; Clark DN. 1997, "Strategic management tool usage: a comparative study", Strategic Change, Volume 6, Issue 7, pp. 417-427.

Information technology has provided the benefit of having ready-made strategic planning software that provides spreadsheets and templates for data, various types of reports and plan formats. The popular technique of SWOT analysis, for instance, can be used with the help of software that provides templates for listing the strengths, weaknesses, opportunities and threats and evaluating them.

There are myriad tools and techniques available to perform strategic analysis. Environmental appraisal, for instance, uses the techniques of forecasting, SWOT analysis and Scenario-writing. Organisational appraisal is done by internal, comparative and comprehensive analyses using techniques such as financial and non-financial analysis, value chain analysis, benchmarking and balanced scorecard.

Strategic analysis can be done at two levels: the corporate and the business levels. Corporate-level strategic analysis focuses on techniques for analysing businesses under the same corporate umbrella. Business level strategic analysis focuses on individual businesses under the corporate umbrella from the perspective of the industry to which each of those businesses belong and on the unique competitive situations they face in respective industries.

Corporate level strategic analysis treats a corporate entity as constituting a portfolio of businesses under a corporate umbrella. The analysis focuses on the question of what a corporate entity should do regarding the several businesses in its portfolio. The strategic alternatives here are basically the corporate strategies of stability, expansion, retrenchment and combination strategies. It is to be noted that the corporate-level strategic analysis is relevant to the case of a diversified corporation having several businesses. For companies that are single-business entities, a business-level strategic analysis is sufficient.

The central theme in business-level strategic analysis is competition. The arena for analysis is therefore, the markets and industries where the organisations compete. The analysis here *focuses on* the question of what means should the organisation adopt with regard to the business that it does. These means are the strategic alternatives of cost leadership, differentiation and focus. We provide further, a description of the major corporate-level and business-level strategic analysis techniques.

1. Corporate Portfolio Analysis

Cooperate portfolio analysis (or simply, portfolio analysis) could be defined as a set of techniques that help strategists in taking strategic decisions with regard to individual products or businesses in a firm's portfolio. It is primarily used for competitive analysis and strategic planning in multi-product and multi business firms. If may also be used in less diversified firms, if these consist of a main business and other minor complementary interests. The main advantages in adopting a portfolio approach in a multi-product, multi business firm is that resources could be targeted at the corporate level to those businesses that possess the greatest potential for creating competitive advantage. For instance, a diversified company may decide to divert resources from its cash-rich businesses to more prospective ones that hold promise of a faster growth, so that the company achieves its corporate level objectives in an optimal manner.

Corporate portfolio techniques evolved during the mid-1960s and several of these soon became quite popular. During the 1970s, there arose a tendency to discredit the techniques when it was realized that the assumptions underlying them did not always hold good. Currently, however, it is accepted that these techniques are useful, not as being purely prescriptive, but as an important and decisive part of a set of criteria—normative as well as descriptive—that assist strategists in exercising a strategic choice.

There are a number of techniques that could be considered as corporate portfolio analysis techniques. Among them we have the Boston Consulting Group (BCG) or product portfolio, General Electric's nine cells, Hofer's Product-Market Evolution, Directional Policy and the Strategic Position and Action Evaluation juices. Not all of these techniques have retained their popularity and importance though. We will describe General Electric's Nine-cell matrix as an illustration of the corporate portfolio matrices.

2. Corporate Parenting Analysis

Campbell, Goold and Alexander suggest that two issues must be addressed by the diversified corporation: (a) What businesses should a diversified corporation own and why and (b) What organisational structure, management processes and philosophy will foster superior performance from the corporation's individual business units? They proposed the concept of corporate parenting to consider the role of the corporate headquarters in managing a set of businesses in a portfolio. A diversified corporation or a multi-business company is often viewed as consisting of a corporate headquarter or center with SBUs acting as satellites. The manner in which the center manages and nurtures the individual businesses is termed as corporate parenting. The total corporation is viewed in terms of resources and capabilities that can be used to build individual businesses as well as create synergies across these businesses. In this manner, corporate parenting attempts to do away with one major drawback of the corporate portfolio techniques. While portfolio techniques consider the industry attractiveness of various industries and focuses on the cash contributions that each business could make to the overall portfolio of businesses, corporate parenting views the organisation in its totality as a diversified corporation and focuses on the value created from the relationship between the parent and its businesses.

3. SWOT Analysis - refer chapter 6.

4. Experience Curve - refer chapter 6.

5. Life Cycle Analysis - refer chapter 6.

6. M.Porter's Five Forces Model - refer chapter 6.

7. Dupont Analysis

DuPont analysis (also known as the Dupont identity, DuPont equation, DuPont Model or the DuPont method) is an expression which breaks ROE (Return on Equity) into three parts. The name comes from the DuPont Corporation that started using this formula in the 1920s.

Dupont Model

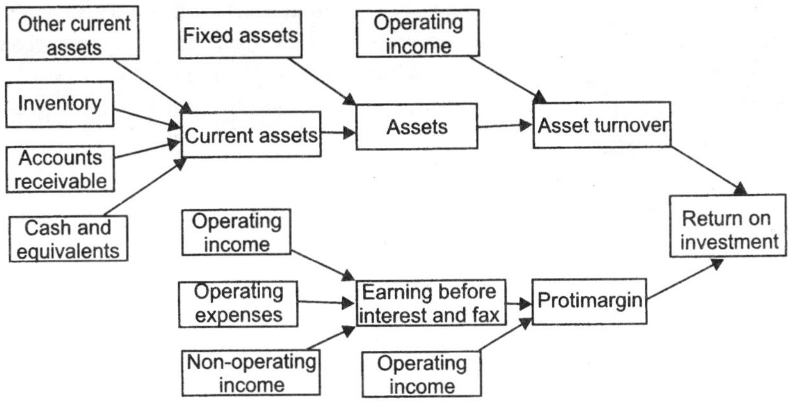

Figure 9.3.

Basic formula

ROE = (Profit margin)*(Asset turnover)*(Equity multiplier) = (Net profit/Sales)*(Sales/Assets)*(Assets/Equity) = (Net Profit/Equity)

- Profitability (measured by profit margin)
- Operating efficiency (measured by asset turnover)
- Financial leverage (measured by equity multiplier)

ROE Analysis

The Du Pont identity breaks down Return on Equity (that is, the returns that investors receive from the firm) into three distinct elements. This analysis enables the analyst to understand the source of superior (or inferior) return by comparison with companies in similar industries (or between industries).

The Du Pont identity, however, is less useful for some industries, such as investment banking, that do not use certain concepts or for which the concepts are less meaningful. Variations may be used in certain industries, as long as they also respect the underlying structure of the Du Pont identity.

Du Pont analysis relies upon the accounting identity, that is, a statement (formula) that is by definition true.

Examples

- **High Turnover Industries**

Certain types of retail operations, particularly stores, may have very low profit margins on sales, and relatively moderate leverage. In contrast, though, groceries may have very high turnover, selling a significant multiple of their assets per year. The ROE of such firms may be particularly dependent on performance of this metric, and hence asset turnover may be studied extremely carefully for signs of under-, or, over-performance. For example, same store sales of many retailers is considered important as an indication that the firm is deriving greater profits from existing stores (rather than showing improved performance by continually opening stores).

- **High margin industries**

Other industries, such as fashion, may derive a substantial portion of their competitive advantage from selling at a higher margin, rather than higher sales. For high-end fashion brands, increasing sales without sacrificing margin may be critical. The Du Pont identity allows analysts to determine which of the elements is dominant in any change of ROE.

- **High leverage industries**

Some sectors, such as the financial sector, rely on high leverage to generate acceptable ROE. In contrast, however, many other industries would see high levels of leverage as unacceptably risky. Du Pont analysis enables the third party (relying primarily on the financial statements) to compare leverage with other financial elements that determine ROE among similar companies.

- **ROA and ROE ratio**

The return on assets (ROA) ratio developed by DuPont for its own use is now used by many firms to evaluate how effectively assets are used. It measures the combined effects of profit margins and asset turnover.[1]

$$\text{ROA} = \frac{\text{Net income}}{\text{Sales}} \times \frac{\text{Sales}}{\text{Total assets}} = \frac{\text{Net income}}{\text{Tottal assets}}$$

The **return on equity (ROE) ratio** is a measure of the rate of return to stockholders.[2] Decomposing the ROE into various factors influencing company performance is often called the **Du Pont System**

$$\text{ROE} = \frac{\text{Net income}}{\text{Equity}} = \frac{\text{Net income}}{\text{Pretax income}} \times \frac{\text{Pretax income}}{\text{EBIT}} \times \frac{\text{EBIT}}{\text{Sales}} \times \frac{\text{Sales}}{\text{Accets}} \times \frac{\text{Assets}}{\text{Equity}}$$

Where

- Net income = net income after taxes
- Equity = shareholders equty
- EBIT = Earning before interest and taxes

This decomposition presents various ratios used in fundamental analysis.

- The company's tax burden is (Net income ÷ Pretax profit). This is the proportion of the company's profits retained after paying income taxes. [NI/EBT]
- The company's interest burden is (Pretax income ÷ EBIT). This will be 1.00 for a firm with no debt or financial leverage. [EBT/EBIT]
- The company's operating income margin or return on sales (ROS) is (EBIT ÷ Sales). This is the operating income per dollar of sales. [EBIT/Sales]
- The company's asset turnover (ATO) is (Sales ÷ Assets).
- The company's leverage ratio is (Assets ÷ Equity), which is equal to the firm's debt to equity ratio + 1. This is a measure of financial leverage.
- The company's return on assets (ROA) is (Return on sales × Asset turnover).
- The company's compound leverage factor is (Interest burden × Leverage).

ROE can also be stated as:

ROE = Tax burden × Interest burden × Margin × Turnover × Leverage

ROE = Tax burden × ROA × Compound leverage factor

Profit margin is (Net income ÷ Sales), so the ROE equation can be restated:

$$\text{ROE} = \frac{\text{Net income}}{\text{sales}} \times \frac{\text{Sales}}{\text{Assets}} \times \frac{\text{Assets}}{\text{Equity}}$$

9.16. PRODUCT DIVERSIFICATION

Definition

The process of expanding business opportunities through additional market potential of an existing product. Diversification may be achieved by entering into additional markets and/or pricing strategies. Often the product may be improved, altered or changed, or new marketing activities are developed. The planning process includes market research, product adaptation analysis and legal review.

Any modification of a current product that serves to expand the potential market implies that the company is following a strategy of product diversification.

The product diversification strategy is different from product development in that it involves creating a new customer base, which by definition expands the market potential of the original product. This is almost always done through brand extensions or new brands, but in some cases the product modification may "create" a new market by creating new uses for the product.

Teen People was an example of product diversification since it was a new product that expanded the market potential of the original product, People magazine. While some teenagers undoubtedly bought People magazine, they were not People's target market. Eventually, however, the product and Web site were merged into the People brand. Courtyard by Marriott and Fairfield Inn are other examples of product diversification since before Marriott offered those new brands they had little potential to expand sales in the business and budget categories. Marriott had business and budget guests, but they were not specifically targeted, so by concentrating on these two markets they were able to add to their market potential. It should be apparent why Marriott could not expand into such different categories with their original brand name.

When Heinz realized that children play with food and it would be more fun to play with ketchup if it were green or purple rather than red, they also were following a product diversification strategy since the market potential for ketchup increased from food to food plus play. Notice in this case that the brand name was unchanged.

Sometimes product diversification takes the form of a product extension with the same brand name. Heinz's introduction of "black label" ketchup, Heinz Tomato Ketchup Blended with Balsamic Vinegar, targets the upscale buyer who might not consider Heinz's regular ketchup, thus expanding market potential.

The dangers of product diversification

The main dangers facing a company following a product diversification strategy for a brand are that it could fail to adequately understand the new customer base and that any new brand name may result in loss of meaning for the original brand and/or cannibalization of the original brand, particularly if it is a brand extension.

The risk of not understanding the new customer base is present as it is with market development. And the risks of loss of meaning and/or cannibalization are just as significant as with product development.

For while Teen People had limited success, all of the women's sports magazines failed. The new market (women) was not interested in the new product (new magazines with various titles) since—unlike men—women did not want to read a magazine about sports without some link to fitness. And the few who did buy the new magazines simply switched from the men's versions.

The special case of retailers

Just as with product development, retailers present a special case. Thus, Subway's conversion from a ordinary sub shop to a healthy food outlet not only changed the brand's positioning substantially but also added new potential customers since, before the change, many of them would have never considered a Subway.

9.17. PRODUCT CLASSIFICATION

Product classification or **product taxonomy** organizes products for a variety of purposes. Some standard product classifications include:

- **CPC — Central Product Classification:** The **Central Product Classification** (CPC) is a product classification for goods and services promulgated by the United Nations Statistical Commission. It is intended to be an international standard for organizing and analyzing data on industrial production, national accounts, trade, prices and so on.
- **HS—Harmonized Commodity Description and Coding System: The Harmonized Commodity Description and Coding System (HS)** of tariff nomenclature is an internationally standardized system of names and numbers for classifying traded products developed and maintained by the World Customs Organization (WCO) (formerly the Customs Co-operation Council), an independent intergovernmental organization with over 170 member countries based in Brussels, Belgium.
- **CPA — Classification of Products by Activity**
- **SITC — Standard International Trade Classification: Standard International Trade Classification (SITC)** is a classification of goods used to classify the exports and imports of a country to enable comparing different countries and years. The classification system is maintained by the United Nations. The SITC classification, is currently at revision four, which was promulgated in 2006. The SITC is recommended only for analytical purposes - trade statistics are recommended to be collected and compiled in the Harmonized System instead. The following excerpt was taken from the United Nations Statistics Division, international trade statistics branch: "For compiling international trade statistics on all merchandise entering international trade, and to promote international comparability of international trade statistics. The commodity groupings of SITC reflect (a) the materials used in production, (b) the processing stage, (c) market practices and uses of the products, (d) the importance of the commodities in terms of world trade, and (e) technological changes
- **Trade in Services: Trade in Services** refers to the sale and delivery of an intangible product, called a service, between a producer and consumer. Trade in services takes place between a producer and consumer that are, in legal terms, based in different countries, or economies, this is called International Trade in Services.

  International trade in services is defined by the Four Modes of Supply of the General Agreement on Trade in Services (GATS).

  - **(Mode 1) Cross border trade,** which is defined as delivery of a service from the territory of one country into the territory of other country;
  - **(Mode 2) Consumption abroad** - this mode covers supply of a service of one country to the service consumer of any other country;
  - **(Mode 3) Commercial presence** - which covers services provided by a service supplier of one country in the territory of any other country, and
  - **(Mode 4) Presence of natural persons** - which covers services provided by a service supplier of one country through the presence of natural persons in the territory of any other country.

A "Natural person" is a human being, as distinct from legal persons such as companies or organisations. Countries can freely decide where to liberalize on a sector-by-sector basis, including which specific mode of supply they want to cover for a given sector.

The tourism sector, the financial services sector and the telecommunications services sector are examples of services sectors.

During the Uruguay Round of the General Agreement on Tariffs and Trade (GATT), the General Agreement on Trade in Services was drafted, and became enshrined as one of the four pillars of the international treaty comprising the World Trade Organization Agreement in 1995.

Regional trade in services agreements are also negotiated and signed between regional economic groupings such as CARICOM, North American Free Trade Agreement (NAFTA) and ASEAN.

- **Global Classification and Harmonized Schedule Numbers for Customs Classification**

Global classification is the process of classifying products for the purpose of complying with customs authorities, qualifying for free trade agreements and filing entries to customs during the importation or exportation of those products. A slight difference in classification can mean a huge difference in the duties that are paid.

Classification Data includes:

- Harmonized Schedule Numbers
- Special tariff preference programs
- Product descriptions and pictures
- Schematics
- Material Safety Data Sheets (MSDS)
- Toxic Substance Control Act (TSCA) documentation
- Country of Origin credentials
- Value Information

With the growing complexity of supply chains as well as the increasing number of government regulations around importing and exporting, companies are realizing the need to proactively manage trade compliance data in order to minimize risk, such as the inaccurate classification of data. Providing classification data on imported and exported products is required, regardless of an organization's global location and classifying products is typically a manual and time consuming process. Companies need to establish data management standards to help reduce inaccurate classification, strengthen the exchange of data between trading partners, and provide version control in order to track all changes that take place.

UNSPSC, the United Nations Standard Products and Services Code: The United Nations Standard Products and Services Code (UNSPSC) is a taxonomy of products and services for use in E-Commerce. It is a five-level hierarchy coded as an 8-digit number.

9.18. MARKET PENETRATION

Market Penetration is one of the four growth strategies of the Product-Market Growth Matrix as defined by Ansoff. Market penetration occurs when a company penetrates a market in which current or similar products already exist. The best way[citation needed] to achieve this is by gaining competitors' customers (part of their market share). Other ways include attracting non-users of your product or convincing current clients to use more of your product/service (by advertising etc.). Ansoff developed the Product-Market Growth Matrix to help firms recognize if there was any advantage of entering a market. The other three growth strategies in the Product-Market Growth Matrix are:

- **Product development (existing markets, new products):** McDonalds is always within the fast-food industry, but frequently markets new burgers.
- **Market development (new markets, existing products):** Lucozade was first marketed for sick children and then rebranded to target athletes.
- **Diversification (new markets, new products):** Mohen A.S, Bion Products, Selectron Ltd, bk

"Penetration is a measure of brand or category popularity. It is defined as the number of people who buy a specific brand or a category of goods at least once in a given period, divided by the size of the relevant market population.

Market Penetration and Market Development

When assessing intent to participate, it can be useful to group respondents by their current participation levels. Using the baseline data gathered on target audiences, it is possible to disaggregate "market penetration" effects from "market development" effects. In other words, does an event simply act as a catalyst for increasing engagement by a predisposed population, or does it genuinely enthuse new audiences?

Ansoff Matrix

To portray alternative corporate growth strategies, Igor Ansoff presented a matrix that focused on the firm's present and potential products and markets (customers). By considering ways to grow via existing products and new products, and in existing markets and new markets, there are four possible product-market combinations. Ansoff's matrix is shown below:

	Existing Products	New Products
Existing Markets	Market Penetration	Product Development
New Markets	Market Development	Diversification

Ansoff's matrix provides four different growth strategies:

- Market Penetration—the firm seeks to achieve growth with existing products in their current market segments, aiming to increase its market share.
- Market Developmen—the firm seeks growth by targeting its existing products to new market segments.
- Product Development—the firms develops new products targeted to its existing market segments.
- Diversification—the firm grows by diversifying into new businesses by developing new products for new markets.

Selecting a Product-Market Growth Strategy:

Market Penetration: The market penetration strategy is the least risky since it leverages many of the firm's existing resources and capabilities. In a growing market, simply maintaining market share will result in growth, and there may exist opportunities to increase market share if competitors reach capacity limits. However, market penetration has limits, and once the market approaches saturation another strategy must be pursued if the firm is to continue to grow.

Market development options include the pursuit of additional market segments or geographical regions. The development of new markets for the product may be a good strategy if the firm's core competencies are related more to the specific product than to its experience with a specific market segment. Because the firm is expanding into a new market, a market development strategy typically has more risk than a market penetration strategy.

A product development strategy may be appropriate if the firm's strengths are related to its specific customers rather than to the specific product itself. In this situation, it can leverage its strengths by developing a new product targeted to its existing customers. Similar to the case of new market development, new product development carries more risk than simply attempting to increase market share.

Diversification is the most risky of the four growth strategies since it requires both product and market development and may be outside the core competencies of the firm. In fact, this quadrant of the matrix has been referred to by some as the "suicide cell". However, diversification may be a reasonable choice if the high risk is compensated by the chance of a high rate of return. Other advantages of diversification include the potential to gain a foothold in an attractive industry and the reduction of overall business portfolio risk.

9.19. NEW PRODUCT DEVELOPMENT

In business and engineering, **New Product Development** (NPD) is the complete process of bringing a new product to market. A product is a set of benefits offered for exchange and can be tangible (that is, something physical you can touch) or intangible (like a service, experience, or belief). There are two parallel paths involved in the NPD process: one involves the idea generation, product design and detail engineering; the other involves market research and marketing analysis. Companies typically see new product development as the first stage in generating and commercializing new product within the overall strategic process of product life cycle management used to maintain or grow their market share.

The stages

1. Idea Generation is often called the "fuzzy front end" of the NPD process.

- Ideas for new products can be obtained from basic research using a SWOT analysis (Strengths, Weaknesses, Opportunities & Threats). Market and consumer trends, company's R&D department, competitors, focus groups, employees, salespeople, corporate spies, trade shows, or ethnographic discovery methods (searching for user patterns and habits) may also be used to get an insight into new product lines or product features.
- Lots of ideas are generated about the new product. Out of these ideas many are implemented. The ideas are generated in many forms. Many reasons are responsible for generation of an idea.
- Idea Generation or Brainstorming of new product, service, or store concepts - idea generation techniques can begin when you have done your OPPORTUNITY ANALYSIS to support your ideas in the Idea Screening Phase (shown in the next development step).

2. Idea Screening

The object is to eliminate unsound concepts prior to devoting resources to them.

The screeners should ask several questions:

- Will the customer in the target market benefit from the product?
- What is the size and growth forecasts of the market segment / target market?
- What is the current or expected competitive pressure for the product idea?
- What are the industry sales and market trends the product idea is based on?
- Is it technically feasible to manufacture the product?
- Will the product be profitable when manufactured and delivered to the customer at the target price?

3. Concept Development and Testing

Develop the marketing and engineering details

- Investigate intellectual property issues and search patent databases
- Who is the target market and who is the decision maker in the purchasing process?
- What product features must the product incorporate?
- What benefits will the product provide?

- How will consumers react to the product?
- How will the product be produced most cost effectively?
- Prove feasibility through virtual computer aided rendering and rapid prototyping
- What will it cost to produce it?
- Testing the Concept by asking a number of prospective customers what they think of the idea - usually via Choice Modeling.

4. **Business Analysis**
   - Estimate likely selling price based upon competition and customer feedback
   - Estimate sales volume based upon size of market and such tools as the Fourt-Woodlock equation
   - Estimate profitability and break-even point
5. **Beta Testing and Market Testing**
   - Produce a physical prototype or mock-up
   - Test the product (and its packaging) in typical usage situations
   - Conduct focus group customer interviews or introduce at trade show
   - Make adjustments where necessary
   - Produce an initial run of the product and sell it in a test market area to determine customer acceptance
6. **Technical Implementation**
   - New program initiation
   - Finalize Quality management system
   - Resource estimation
   - Requirement publication
   - Publish technical communications such as data sheets
   - Engineering operations planning
   - Department scheduling
   - Supplier collaboration
   - Logistics plan
   - Resource plan publication
   - Program review and monitoring
   - Contingencies - what-if planning
7. **Commercialization** (often considered post-NPD)
   - Launch the product
   - Produce and place advertisements and other promotions
   - Fill the distribution pipeline with product
   - Critical path analysis is most useful at this stage
8. **New Product Pricing**
   - Impact of new product on the entire product portfolio
   - Value Analysis (internal & external)
   - Competition and alternative competitive technologies
   - Differing value segments (price, value and need)

- Product Costs (fixed & variable)
- Forecast of unit volumes, revenue, and profit

These steps may be iterated as needed. Some steps may be eliminated. To reduce the time that the NPD process takes, many companies are completing several steps at the same time (referred to as concurrent engineering or time to market). Most industry leaders see new product development as a proactive process where resources are allocated to identify market changes and seize upon new product opportunities before they occur (in contrast to a reactive strategy in which nothing is done until problems occur or the competitor introduces an innovation). Many industry leaders see new product development as an ongoing process (referred to as continuous development) in which the entire organization is always looking for opportunities.

For the more innovative products indicated the great amounts of uncertainty and change may exist which makes it difficult or impossible to plan the complete project before starting it. In this case, a more flexible approach may be advisable.

Chapter **10**

STRATEGY IMPLEMENTATION

Introduction and Meaning of Strategic Implementation - S's in the 7-S Framework - A General Framework of Strategic Implementation - Various Approaches and Issues in Strategy Implementation - Regulatory Framework Governing Business Activity - Corporate Parenting - Cost of Equity Capital - Capital Budgeting - Business Valuation - Divestiture Decision - Strategic Implementation of All Functional Areas - Resource Allocation - Importance - Approaches - Techniques - Factors Affecting Resource Allocation - Difficulties - Caution - Organisation Structure - Organisational Design - Building the Organisation Structure - External Environment and Internal Organization Contribution - Implementation of Strategy Designing Organisational Structure - Checklist for Determining Appropriateness of Organisational Structure - Behavioural Issues - Strategic Leadership - Guidelines to Create Cultured Organization - Strategy Capital - Organizational Culture - Strategy and Staffing Decisions.

10.1. INTRODUCTION

Strategy Implementation is a crucial issue because any strategy is as good as the effort behind it to move it forward. Successful strategy implementation requires support, discipline, motivation work from all managers and employees. More importantly, it requires a suitable organisation structure to translate ideas into concrete action plans. Inspite of having all these elements, strategy implementation, on most occasions prove to be a tricky job. Creating a 'fit' between a firm's goals and its other activities proves to be a tough exercise. Multifarious reasons could be cited in support of this statement. Strategy is dependent on many variables internal as well as external and to compound the problem further there are countless, interrelated change factors that could upset managerial calculations overnight. Because change factors interrelate, changing only one or two things seldom brings any significant overall organisational change. There are certainly no magic bullets to assist about organisational change either automatically or slowly. Given the complexities inherent in organisational change and strategy implementation, it is easy to find why often fail. The Mckinsey Company, a well known management consultancy States, towards the end of 1970s was asked to find a solution to this knotty issue. The researchers Peters and Waterman found after examining America's best run companies that the problem in strategy lay in its implementation and structure was only one lever in the hands of management. The other levers were systems, staff, style, skills and super ordinate goals.

10.2. A STRATEGY IS USUALLY SUCCESSFUL WHEN THE OTHER S'S IN THE 7-S FRAMEWORK FIT INTO OR SUPPORTS THE STRATEGY

- **Strategy:** *A set of decisions and actions aimed at gaining a sustainable competitive advantage.*
- **Structure:** The organisation chart and associated information that shows who reports to whom and how tasks are both divided and integrated.

- **Systems:** The flow of activities involved in the daily operation of a business, including its core processes and its support systems.
- **Style:** How managers collectively spend their time and attention and how they use symbolic behaviour. How management acts is more important than what management says.
- **Staff:** How companies develop employees and shape basic values.
- **Shared Values:** Commonly held beliefs, mindsets and assumptions organisation behaves—its corporate culture.
- **Skills:** An organisation's dominant capabilities and competencies.

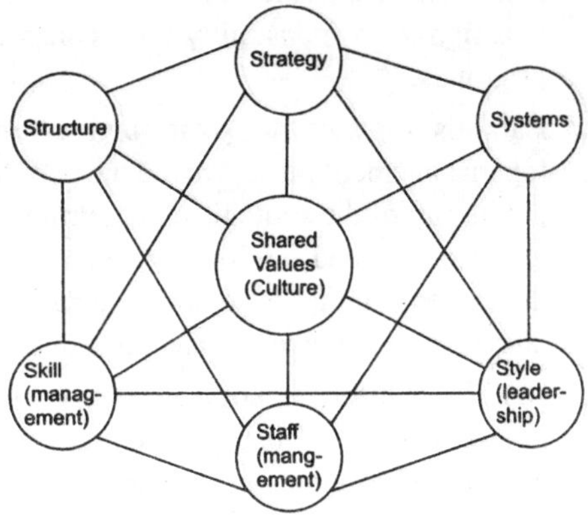

Figure 10.1. The 7-S Framework.

The 7-S framework highlights the importance of some interrelated and interconnected factors within the organisation and their role in successful implementation of strategy. The successful implementation of a strategy depends on the right alignment of all the seven-Ss. "When the seven-Ss are in good alignment, an organisation is poised and energized to excuse strategy to the best of its ability". Of course there is no starting point or implied order of preference in the shape of the diagram. It is also not very obvious which of the seven factors would be the driving force in changing an organisation at a point of time. The principal job of strategists then is to achieve a good fit among the Seven Ss by making alterations from time to time.

What is Strategic Implementation?/Meaning and Definition

- ***Striner, Miner and Gray,*** "Implementation of strategies is concerned with the design and management of systems to achieve the best integration of people, structures, processes, and resources in reaching organisational purposes."
- ***Glueck,*** "Strategic implementation is the assignment or reassignment of corporate and SBU leaders to match the strategy. The leaders will communicate the strategy to the employees. Implementation also involves the development of functional policies about the organisation structure and climate to support the strategy and help to achieve organisational objectives."
- ***Harvey,*** "Implementation involves actually executing the strategic game plan. This includes setting policies, designing the organisation structure, and. developing a corporate culture to enable the attainment of organisational objectives."

10.3. A GENERAL FRAMEWORK OF STRATEGIC IMPLEMENTATION

The first step in implementation is identifying the activities, decisions, and relationships critical to accomplishing the activities.

There are six principal administrative tasks that shape a manager's action agenda for implementing strategy. In general, every unit of an organization has to ask, "What is required for us to implement our part of the overall strategic plan and how can we best get it done?"

The specific components of each of the six strategy-implementation tasks:

1. **Building an organization capable of executing the strategy.** The organization must have the structure necessary to turn the strategy into reality. Furthermore, the firm's personnel

must possess the skill needed to execute the strategy successfully. Related to this is the need to assign the responsibility for accomplish key implementation tasks to the right individuals or groups.

2. **Establishing a strategy-supportive budget.** If the firm is to accomplish strategic objectives, top management must provide the people, equipment, facilities, and other resources to carry out its part of the strategic plan. Further, once the strategy has been decided on, the key tasks to performed and kinds of decision required must be identified, formal plans must also be developed. The tasks should be arranged in a sequence comprising a plan of action within targets to be achieved at specific dates.
3. **Installing internal administrative support systems**. Internal systems are policies and procedures to establish desired types of behavior, information systems to provide strategy-critical information on a timely basis, and whatever inventory, materials management, customer service, cost accounting, and other administrative systems are needed to give the organization important strategy-executing capability. These internal systems must support the management process, the way the managers in an organization work together, as well as monitor strategic progress.
4. **Devising rewards and incentives that are tightly linked to objectives and strategy.** People and departments of the firm must be influenced, through incentives, constraints, control, standards, and rewards, to accomplish the strategy.
5. **Shaping the corporate culture to fit the strategy.** A strategy-supportive corporate culture causes the organization to work hard (and intelligently) toward the accomplishment of the strategy.
6. **Exercising strategic leadership**. Strategic leadership consists of obtaining commitment to the strategy and its accomplishment. It also involves the constructive use of power and politics, and politics in building a consensus to support the strategy.

10.4. APPROACHES OF STRATEGIC IMPLEMENTATION

1. The Commander Approach

The strategic leader concentrates on formulating the strategy, applying rigorous logic and analysis. The leader either develops the strategy himself or supervises a team of planners charged with determining the optimal course of action for the organization. He typically employs such tools as experience curves, growth/share matrices and industry and competitive analysis.

This approach addresses the traditional strategic management question of **"How can I, as a general manager, develop a strategy for my business which will guide day-today decisions in support of my longer-term objectives?"** Once the "best" strategy is determined, the leader passes it along to subordinates who are instructed to executive the strategy. The leader does not take an active role in implementing the strategy. The strategic leader is primarily a thinker/planner rather than a doer. The Commander Approach helps the executive make difficult day-to-day decision from a strategic perspective. However, three conditions must exist for the approach to succeed

- The leader must wield enough power to command implementation; or, the strategy must pose little threat to the current management, otherwise implementation will be resisted.
- Accurate and timely information must be available and the environment must be reasonably stable to allow it to be assimilated.
- The strategist (if he is not the leader) should be insulated from personal biases and political influences that might affect the content of the plan.

A drawback of this approach is that it can reduce employee motivation. If the leader creates the belief that the only acceptable strategies are those developed at the top, he may find himself an extremely unmotivated, un-innovative group of employees. However, several factors account for the Commander popularity.

First, it offers a valuable perspective to the chief executive.

Second, by dividing the strategic management task into two stages -"thinking" and "doing" -the leader reduces the number of factors that have to be considered simultaneously.

Third, young managers in particular seem to prefer this approach because it allows them to focus on the quantitative, objective elements of a situation, rather than with more subjective and behavioral considerations.

Finally, such an approach may make some managers feel as an all-powerful hero, shaping the destiny of thousands with his decisions.

2. The Organisational Change Approach

This approach starts where the Commander Approach ends: with implementation. The organizational Change Approach addresses the question **"I have a strategy -now how do I get my organization to implement it?"** The strategic leader again decides major changes of strategy and considers the appropriate changes in structure, personnel, and information and reward systems if the strategy is to be implemented effectively. The most obvious tool for strategy implementation is to reorganize or to shift personnel in order to lead the firm in the desired direction. The role of the strategic leader is that of an architect, designing administrative systems for effective strategy implementation. The Change Approach is often more effective than the Commander Approach and can be used to implement more difficult strategies because of used the several behavioral science techniques. This technique for introducing change in an organization include such fundamentals as: using demonstrations rather than words to communicate the desired new activities; focusing early efforts on the needs that are already recognized as important by most of the organization; and having solutions presented by persons who have high credibility in the organization. However, the Change Approach doesn't help managers stay abreast of rapid changes in the environment. It can backfire in uncertain or rapidly changing conditions. Finally, this approach calls for imposing the strategy in "top-down" fashion; it is subject to the same motivational problems as the Commander Approach.

3. Collaborative Approach

This approach extends strategic decision-making to the organization's top management team in answer to the question **"How can I get my top management team to help develop and commit to a good set of goals and strategies?"**

The strategic leader and his senior manager (divisional heads, business unit general managers or senior functional managers) meet for lengthy discussion with a view to formulating proposed strategic changes. In this approach, the leader employs group dynamics and "brainstorming" techniques to get managers with differing points of view to contribute to the strategic planning process. The Collaborative Approach overcomes two key limitations inherent in the previous two. By capturing information contributed by managers closer to operations, and by offering a forum for the expression of managers closer to operations, and by offering a forum for the expression of many viewpoints, it can increase the quality and timeliness of the information incorporated in the strategy. And to the degree than participation enhances commitment to the strategy, it improves the chances of efficient implementation. However, the Collaborative Approach may gain more commitment that the foregoing approaches, it may also result in a poorer strategy. The negotiated aspect of the process brings with several risks -that the strategy will be more conservative and less visionary than one developed by a single person or staff team. And the negotiation process can take so much time that an organization misses opportunities and fails to react enough to changing environments. A more fundamental criticism of the Collaborative Approach is that it is not really collective decisions making from an organizational viewpoint because upper-level managers often retain centralized control. In effect, this approach preserves the artificial distinction between thinkers and doers and fails to draw on the full human potential throughout the organization.

4. The Cultural Approach

This approach extends the Collaborative Approach to lower levels in the organization as an answer to the strategic management question **"How can I get my whole organization committed to our goals and strategies?"** The strategic leader concentrates on establishing and communicating a clear mission and purpose for the organization and the allowing employees to design their own work activities with this mission. He plays the role of coach in giving general direction, but encourages individual decision-making to determine the operating details of executive the plan. The implementation tools used in building a strong corporate culture range from such simple notions as publishing a company creed and singing a company song to much complex techniques. These techniques involve implementing strategy by employing the concept of *"third-order control."* **First-order control** is direct supervision; **second - order control** involves using rules, procedures, and organizational structure to guide behavior. **Third - order control** is more subtle - and potentially more powerful. It consists of influencing behavior through shaping the norms, values, symbols, and beliefs that managers and employees use in making day-to-day decisions. This approach begins to break down the barriers between *"thinkers" and "doers."* The Cultural Approach has a number of advantages which establish an organization-wide unity of purpose. It appears that the cultural approach works best where the organization has sufficient resources to absorb the cost of building and maintaining the value system. However, this approach also has several limitations. *First*, it only works with informed and intelligent people. *Second,* it consumes enormous amounts of time to install. *Third*, it can foster such a strong sense of organizational identity among employees that it becomes a handicap; For example, bringing outsider in a top management levels can be difficult because they aren't accepted by other executives. The strongest criticism of this approach is that it has such an overwhelming doctrinal air about it, and foster homogeneity and inbreeding.

5. The Crescive Approach

This approach addresses the question **"How can I encourage my managers to develop, champion, and implement sound strategies?" (Crescive** means "increasing" or "growing"). The strategic leader is not interested in strategizing alone, or even in leading others through a protracted planning process. He encourage subordinates to develop, champion, and implement sound strategies on their own. The crescive approach differs from the others in several ways.

- First, instead of strategy being delivered downward by top management or a planning department, it moves upward from the "doers" (salespeople, engineers, production workers) and lower middle-level managers.
- Second, "strategy" becomes the sum of all the individual proposals that surface throughout the year.
- Third, the top management team shapes the employees' premises -that is, their notions of what would constitute supportable strategic projects.
- Fourth, the chief executive functions more as a judge, evaluating the proposals that reach his desk, than as a master strategist. Brodwin and Bourgeois suggest use of the Crescive Approach primarily for managers of large, complex, diversified organizations. In these organizations the strategic leader cannot know and understand all the strategic and operating situations, facing each division.

If strategies are to be formulated and implemented effectively, the leader must give up some control to spur opportunism and achievement. Therefore, the Crescive Approach for strategic management suggests some generalizations concerning how the chief executive of the large divisionalized firm should help the organization generate and implement sound strategies. The recommendation consists of the following four elements:

- Maintain the openness of the organization to new and discrepant information.
- Articulate a general strategy to guide the firm's growth.
- Manipulate systems and structures to encourage bottom-up strategy formulation.
- Use the "the logical incrementalist" manner described by James Brian Quinn, to select from among the strategies which emerge.

The Crescive approach has several advantages. For example, it encourages middle-level managers to formulate effective strategies and gives them opportunity to carry out the implementation of their own plans. Moreover, strategies developed, as these are, by employees and managers closer to the strategic opportunity are likely to be operationally sound and readily implemented. However, this approach requires that funds be available for individuals to develop good ideas unencumbered by bureaucratic approval cycles and that tolerance be extended in the inevitable cases where failure occurs despite a worthy effort having been made.

One of the most important and potentially elusive of these methods is the process of shaping managers' decision-making premises. The strategic leader can emphasize a particular theme or strategic thrust to direct strategic thinking. Second, the planning methodology endorsed by the leader can be communicated to affect the way managers view the business. Third, the organizational structure can indicate the dimensions on which strategies should focus. The choice of approach should depend on the size of the company, the degree of diversification, the degree of geographical dispersion, the stability of the business environment, and, finally, the managerial style currently embodied in the company's culture.

Brodwin and *Bourgeois*'s research suggests that the Commander, Change, and Collaborative Approaches can be effective for smaller companies and firms in stable industries. The Cultural and Crescive alternatives are used by more complex corporations.

10.5. ISSUES IN STRATEGY IMPLEMENTATION

The successful implementation of strategy requires an effective organization. People working within a firm should know how their actions interrelate with the actions of others to support and execute the firm's strategy. Without a structural framework, the roles of management and employees can't be drawn-up clearly—leading to confusion, duplication of efforts and chaos at various levels. Apart from a sound organisation structure, the services of talented and capable leaders are also required to translate corporate vision into a concrete reality. The principal task of leaders then would be to see that the various elements of an organisation fit together and make logical sense. In the race to get ahead, of course, they should not sacrifice ethical and social values

Functional plans and policies need to be formulated carefully and implemented with active support from employees at various levels. These should help employees find solutions to several operational issues that need to be resolved on a day-to-day basis. The political factors than come in the way of effective implementation of strategies should also be understood properly. Every attempt should be made to remove the irritants first before minor problems turn into major emergencies at a later date.

Activating Strategy

There is no guarantee that a well designed strategy is likely to be approved and implemented automatically. The strategic leader must, therefore, defend the strategy from every angle, communicate how the strategy when implemented would benefit the whole organisation and secure the wholehearted support of employees working at various levels. To keep things on track, he can list out priorities, programme implementation process, budgets, etc. on paper so that nothing is left to chance. While giving a concrete shape to the strategy, he should also take note of regulatory mechanisms that govern business activity and see that everything is in order. Some of the important things to be kept in mind are listed below:

10.6. REGULATORY FRAMEWORK GOVERNING BUSINESS ACTIVITY

- ***Formation of a company:*** This must be in line with provisions of the Companies Act, 1956, covering issues such as formation of a company, its registration, obtaining suitable licenses before commencing operations, raising funds from various sources in accordance with the provisions of SEBI Act, 1992.
- ***Operations of a company:*** The company must compete in a fair way andearn the profits through legally blessed routes only observing the (a) provisions of competition law; (b) Import/export restrictions, (c) FERA regulations (FEMA regulations, 2000); (d) Patent, trademark, copyright (Indian Patents Act 1995, The Trade and Merchandise Marks Act 1958, The Copyrights Act 1957 etc.) stipulations; (e) Labour Laws (regarding employment of women, children, payment ofwages, providing welfare amenities, keeping healthy industrial relations etc.); (f) environmental protection (The Environment Protection Act 1986), (g) pollution control requirements; (h) consumer protection measures, etc.
- ***'Winding up operations:*** Even when the company decides to get out of a venture/ business, the rules of the game need to be followed scrupulously (whether in offering golden handshake to employees or asking all the employees to quit in one go). After the institutionalization of strategy in the above manner, action plans could be formulated. These are basically functional level strategies undertaken at the departmental level and usually deal with operational aspects of a strategy.

The action plans, however, must try to translate the overall strategic plan in letter and spirit without any deviations. Issues like who will do what, what kind of support is required at various stages, what kind of privities have to be fixed while implementing active plans, how does a particular active plan contribute to the broad objectives of the strategy etc. must also be carefully looked into. Once the action plans are ready, the strategist must resolve issues relating to allocation of scarce resources over the entire organisation.

10.7. CORPORATE PARENTING

In corporate parenting, the corporate headquarters tries to get synergy among business units by allocating resources, transferring critical skills and capabilities among various units and coordinating the activities of shared units in order to attain economies of scope. In portfolio analysis, attractiveness of industries and cash flow of mature units that could be diverted to new product lines, investment opportunities and financial aspects are studied. The scope of corporate parenting is much more than that of portfolio analysis. According to Campbell, Good and Alexander, strategists should answer two critical issues.

- Which business the company should own and run?
- Which organization structure, management process and philosophy will bring in better performance across various units?

In multi business companies' corporate parenting enables the headquarters to focus on core competencies and tries to create value among various business units by establishing relationship and a good fit between needs and opportunities of units and resources and capabilities within the firm.

Developing a corporate parenting strategy involves three analytical steps.

1. Each business unit should be examined for critical success factors, which are the basis of its competitive advantage.
2. Each business unit should be examined in order to identify for areas of performance improvement. Such parenting opportunities result in combining sales forces of different units to achieve economies of scope or transfer of skills among units, which require capabilities.
3. The parenting opportunities in each business unit should be studied in terms of fit between the parent's characteristics and the strategic factors of each business unit.

Portfolio fit matrix has been recommended by Campbell, Goold and Alexander in order to judge whether the individual business unit fits with the whole corporate business. This matrix is drawn on two dimensions, such as positive contribution of parent and parents negative effects. It gives rise to five different positions like

i. Heartland

ii. Edge of heartland

iii. Ballast

iv. Alien territory and

v. Value trap.

Parenting Fix Matrix

1. **Heartland businesses,** which lie at the top right corner of the matrix, present opportunities for improvement by the parent. Their critical success factors are well understood by the parent and should have priority for all corporate activities.
2. **For business in the edge of the heartland,** the parent may not understand the unit's critical success factors. The parent should know when to interfere and not to interfere in the business unit's activities and decision-making process.
3. **Ballast business units are successful units,** which are with the parent for a very long time. It fits well with the corporation but there is a possibility of moving to alien territory in times of environmental change. At appropriate stage divesting those units are undertaken by the management.
4. **Businesses in alien territory do not have opportunities for growth.** There exists misfit between parenting characteristics and unit's critical success factors.
5. **Units in the value trap businesses** fit with parental opportunity but parent's understanding of critical success factors of the individual business shows a misfit. Hence the possibility of parent's committing a mistake is always there.

Evolving of directional strategy which is otherwise known as corporate strategy requires portfolio analysis and corporate parenting in order to provide overall direction to the organization. A horizontal strategy means a corporate strategy that cuts across the boundaries of business units to build synergy to gain competitive position in a few business units. In multipoint competition, big business firms compete with diversified groups in a number of markets in number of business. Eg., HLL, P&G, Nirma and Colgate.

10.8. COST OF EQUITY CAPITAL

The management has always to look to the interest of the existing equity shareholder, i.e., at least their present position should not be adversely affected. This would e so only if the funds obtained by the issue of new equity shares, when invested, earn at least so much that the new earnings per share (EPS) of the company do not fall below the existing EPS.

In other words, the cost of equity capital is an imputed cost which is measured by current earnings per share relative to the current market price per share. This is the Earning / Price ratio (E/P ratio). The formula can be stated as follows:

$$C_e = \frac{EPS}{NP} \times 100$$

Where, EPS = the minimum earnings that a new share must earn, and

NP = Net proceeds per share

10.9. CAPITAL BUDGETING

Capital Budgeting techniques can be used for long-term commitment of resources, such as capital investments in mergers, acquisitions, joint ventures, and setting up of new plants etc. Various techniques like payback period, net present value, internal rate of return, etc. can be used to find which investments would earn maximum returns.

Operating Budgets

Operating budgets are necessary for more routine resource allocation for conducting operations. There are two types of systems:

a. **Fixed budgeting system:** This system commits resources based on activity levels. In this type of budgeting, there may be a tendency to retain the committed resources even if the activity levels are not being achieved, thus depriving other divisions of the resources, which have a better potential.

b. **Flexible budgeting system:** This system provides for transfer of funds from one unit to another if a fall is expected in actual activity level in a particular unit, thus ensuring better resource utilization. But this system has the disadvantage of encouraging non-seriousness about budgetary allocations. The different types of routine budgets are:

- Operating budget specifies materials, labour, overheads and other costs.
- Financial budget projects cash receipts and disbursements.
- Sales budget specifies sales revenues and selling, distribution and marketing costs.
- Expenses budget projects expenses not carried out in other budgets.

10.10. BUSINESS VALUATION IN REFERENCE WITH PROFITABILITY

Business valuation is a process and a set of procedures used to estimate the economic value of an owner's interest in a business. Valuation is used by financial market participants to determine the price they are willing to pay or receive to perfect a sale of a business. In addition to estimating the selling price of a business, the same valuation tools are often used by business appraisers to resolve disputes related to estate and gift taxation, divorce litigation, allocate business purchase price among business assets, establish a formula for estimating the value of partners' ownership interest for buy-sell agreements, and many other business and legal purposes.

Elements of Business Valuation

- **Economic Conditions:** A business valuation report generally begins with a description of national, regional and local economic conditions existing as of the valuation date, as well as the conditions of the industry in which the subject business operates. A common source of economic information for the first section of the business valuation report is the Federal Reserve Board's Beige Book, published eight times a year by the Federal Reserve Bank. State governments and industry associations also publish useful statistics describing regional and industry conditions.

- **Financial analysis:** The financial statement analysis generally involves common size analysis, ratio analysis (liquidity, turnover, profitability, etc.), trend analysis and industry comparative analysis. This permits the valuation analyst to compare the subject company to other businesses in the same or similar industry, and to discover trends affecting the company and/or the industry over time. By comparing a company's financial statements in different time periods, the valuation expert can view growth or decline in revenues or expenses, changes in capital structure, or other financial trends. How the subject company compares to the industry will help with the risk assessment and ultimately help determine the discount rate and the selection of market multiples.
- **Normalization of Financial Statements:** The most common normalization adjustments fall into the following four categories:
  a. **Comparability Adjustments.** The values may adjust the subject company's financial statements to facilitate a comparison between the subject company and other businesses in the same industry or geographic location. These adjustments are intended to eliminate differences between the way that published industry data is presented and the way that the subject company's data is presented in its financial statements.
  b. **Non-operating Adjustments.** It is reasonable to assume that if a business were sold in a hypothetical sales transaction (which is the underlying premise of the fair market value standard), the seller would retain any assets which were not related to the production of earnings or price those non-operating assets separately. For this reason, non-operating assets (such as excess cash) are usually eliminated from the balance sheet.
  c. **Non-recurring Adjustments**. The subject company's financial statements may be affected by events that are not expected to recur, such as the purchase or sale of assets, a lawsuit, or an unusually large revenue or expense. These non-recurring items are adjusted so that the financial statements will better reflect the management's expectations of future performance.
  d. **Discretionary Adjustments**. The owners of private companies may be paid at variance from the market level of compensation that similar executives in the industry might command. In order to determine fair market value, the owner's compensation, benefits, perquisites and distributions must be adjusted to industry standards. Similarly, the rent paid by the subject business for the use of property owned by the company's owners individually may be scrutinized.
- **Income, Asset and Market Approaches:** Three different approaches are commonly used in business valuation: the Income Approach, the Asset-based Approach, and the Market Approach. Within each of these approaches, there are various techniques for determining the value of a business using the definition of value appropriate for the appraisal assignment. Generally, the income approaches determine value by calculating the net present value of the benefit stream generated by the business (Discounted cash flow); the Asset-Based approaches determine value by adding the sum of the parts of the business (Net asset value); and the market approaches determine value by comparing the subject company to other companies in the same industry, of the same size, and/or within the same region. A number of business valuation models can be constructed that utilize various methods under the three business valuation approaches. Venture Capitalists and Private Equity professionals have long used the first chicago method which essentially combines the income approach with the Market approach. In certain cases equity may also be valued by applying the techniques and frameworks developed for financial options, via a real options framework. In determining

which of these approaches to use, the valuation professional must exercise discretion. Each technique has advantages and drawbacks, which must be considered when applying those techniques to a particular subject company. Most treatises and court decisions encourage the valuator to consider more than one technique, which must be reconciled with each other to arrive at a value conclusion. A measure of common sense and a good grasp of mathematics is helpful.

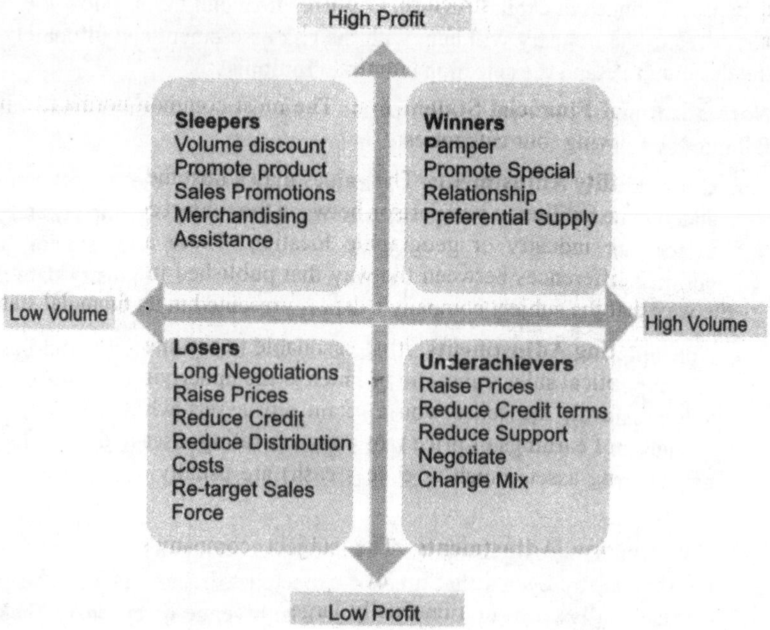

Figure 10.2. Profitability Matrix.

10.11. DIVESTITURE DECISION

It is defined as a sale of segment of a company to a third party, Sale for cash or securities or some combination thereof and Assets revalued for purpose of future depreciation by the buyer.

Diverse Motives for Divestitures

- Dismantling segments of conglomerates which had higher values as independent operations or better fit with other firms.
- Sale of original business due to changing opportunities or circumstances.
- Change in strategic focus which may reflect realignment with firm's changing environments
- Adding value by selling into a better fit.
- Firm is unable or unwilling to make additional investments to remain in a business.
- Harvesting past successes to make resources available for developing other opportunities.
- Discarding unwanted businesses from prior acquisitions to value-increasing buyer.
- Divestiture to finance major acquisitions or LBOs.
- Divestiture used as a takeover defense by selling off "Crown jewel" .
- Divestiture to obtain government approval of a combination of segments with competing products.
- Corporate sale of divisions or business units to operating managements.

- Divestiture of unrelated divisions to focus on core businesses.
- Divestiture of low margin product lines to improve margins and profitability.
- Divestiture to finance another firm.
- Divestiture to reverse prior mistakes.
- Divestiture of businesses after learning more about them.

10.12. STRATEGIC IMPLEMENTATION OF ALL FUNCTIONAL AREAS

Introduction

Once corporate level and business level strategies are developed, management must turn its attention to formulating strategies for each functional area of the business unit. For effective implementation of strategies, functional strategies provide direction to functional managers regarding the plans and policies to be adopted in each functional area.

What is functional strategy?

Functional Strategy is the approach taken by a functional area to achieve corporate and business unit objectives and strategies by maximizing resource productivity. It is concerned with developing and nurturing a distinctive competence to provide a company or business unit with a competitive advantage. Just as a multi-divisional corporation has several business units, each with its own business strategy; each business unit has its own set of departments, each with its own functional strategy'. Within the general framework created by the corporate and business strategies, each business function needs to identify and undertake activities unique to the function. The functional strategies delineate the activities to be undertaken in each part of the business and usually include them as a core part of their action plan. Functional strategies are, thus, detailed statements of the "means" or activities that will be used to achieve short-term objectives and establish competitive advantage. A functional strategy is also defined as a short-term 'game plane" for a key functional area.

Even through functional strategies are formulated after developing the corporate and business strategies, the capabilities of various functional areas need to be considered even while considering various corporate and business strategic options. For example, an airline considering expansion, should consider factors such as the need for additional manpower and the organization's ability to finance additional airplanes before settling the expansion plan as the preferred strategic option.

Nature of Functional Strategy

Functional strategies are essential to implement business strategy. In fact, the effectiveness of a corporate or business strategy execution depends critically on the manner in which strategies are implemented at the functional level. The corporate strategy provides the long-term direction and scope of a firm. The business strategy outlines the competitive posture of its operations in an industry. The functional strategy clarifies the business strategy, giving specific, short-term guidance to operating managers in the areas of operations, marketing, finance, HR, R&D etc., and increases the likelihood of their success.

Orientation of the functional strategy, therefore, depends on the business strategy. For example, if a business unit follows a differentiation strategy through high quality products, its production strategy emphasizes expensive quality assurance processes over cheaper, high-volume production; a human resource functional strategy that emphasizes hiring and training of a highly skilled, but costly, workforce; and a marketing functional strategy that emphasizes extensive advertising to increase demand rather than using marketing incentives to retailers. Similarly, if the business unit follows a low-cost competitive strategy, a different set of functional strategies emphasizing cost-cutting measures would be needed to support the business strategy.

Need For Functional Strategies

Functional managers need guidance from the corporate and business strategies in order to make decisions. In simple terms, functional strategies tell the functional manager what to do in his area to achieve business objectives. Glueck and Jauch have suggested five reasons to show why functional strategies are needed. Functional strategies are developed to ensure that

- The strategic decisions are implemented by all the parts of an organization.
- There is a basis available for controlling activities in different functional areas of a business.
- The time spent by functional managers on decision-making may be reduced.
- Similar situations occurring in different functional areas are handled by the functional managers in a consistent manner.
- Coordination across different functions takes place where necessary.

Difference between Functional Strategy and Business Strategy

Functional strategies are different from business or corporate strategies in three fundamental ways:

1. Time horizon 2. Specificity 3. Participants who develop them

Just as a competitive strategy may need to vary from one region of the world to another, functional strategies may need to vary from region to region. For example, when Maggi Noodles expanded into India, it had to market noodles not as a main course meal, but as a snack food because Indians prefer to eat noodles in the evening. Thus Maggi Noodles was marketed as a fast to cook and ready to serve evening meal, especially to children.

Table 10.1

	Functional Strategy	Business Strategy
Time Horizon	Functional strategies focus on short-term goals (one year) short term horizon of functional strategies is critical to the successful implementation of a business strategy for two reasons: It focuses the attention of functional managers on what needs to be done now. It allows functional managers to adjust to changing current conditions.	Business strategies focus on the firm's long term competitive posture (3 to 5 years).
Specificity	Functional strategies provide more specific direction to functional managers by: Helping them to know what needs to be done and focus on results. Clarifying for top management how they intend to accomplish the business strategy. This increases top management's confidence and sense of control. Facilitating co-ordination among functional units by clarifying areas of interdependence and potential conflict.	Business strategies provide general direction.
Participants	Functional strategy is the responsibility of the operating managers of the functional area. Functional strategies are approved through negotiation between business unit managers and operating managers of the functional area.	Business strategy is the responsibility of the head of the business unit. Business strategies are approved through negotiation between corporate managers and business unit managers.

Involving operating mangers in the development of functional strategies improves their understanding of long-term objectives, and, this contributes to their successful implementation. It also helps ensure that functional strategies reflect the reality of the day-to-day operating situation most important of all, it increases the commitment and ownership of operating mangers to the strategies developed.

Functional strategies will:

1. Specify more precisely how corporate and business strategies are to be implemented.
2. Establish a mechanism to make sure that strategies are implemented.
3. Lead to new strengths which can be used for strategy in the future.

Development of Functional Strategies

The process of developing functional strategies is quite similar to that of strategy formulation, with the difference that functional heads are responsible for their formulation and implementation. Environmental factors relevant to each functional area will have an impact on the choice of strategies. Finally, the actual process of choice involves a negotiation between functional managers and business unit managers. Thus, functional strategies are generally formulated in all key functional areas.

For each of the functional strategies, a set of policies will have to establish for appropriate areas of the business. The policies will ensure that the strategies are carried out as intended and that the different functional areas are working towards the same ends. Companies have plans and policies that cover nearly every major aspect of the firm. The firm should have strategies in every major aspect of business, at least in key functional areas. We will highlight some of the more important issues for each functional area that need to be addressed in their respective functional strategies.

The functional strategies should be comprehensive; but at the same time, they should not leave so much choice to operating mangers that they work sub-optimally or at cross purposes. At the same time, the functional strategies should be flexible enough to leave room to managers for responding quickly to situations and make exceptions for good reasons. The functional strategies required in key functional areas are outlined below:

i) Financial Strategy

In the financial management area, the major concern of the strategy relates to the acquisition and utilization of funds. Major issues involved are the sources from where the funds will come, from equity or by borrowing. How much of the borrowing will be short-term and how much long-term. In terms of usage of funds, the policy decisions would relate to whether and to what extent funds have to be deployed in fixed assets and current assets. The long-term or capital investment decisions relate to buying or leasing the fixed assets. A retrenchment strategy or paucity of funds may compel the organization to lease rather than buy. In case of an organization where capital investment decisions are decentralized, a "hurdle rate" may be fixed so as to avoid investment in weaker projects by one division and non-investment by another division.

Cash Flow

Apart from capital budgeting, another consideration in financial strategy which influences other functional areas is the cash flow A company may frame bonus and dividend policies based on availability of cash. In case a company proposes expansion through internally generated funds, it may reduce bonus and dividend. This is particularly so when it has formulated ambitious growth strategies which require large cash. Similarly, if the firm has high risk business, it should have a conservative debt/equity ratio to guard against heavy interest burden. The funds position and optimization orientation of top management also determines the accounts receivable and payable policies. Financial strategies and policies may even determine the accounting policies as these affect the profitability, balance-sheet and hence cash flow through taxes, dividend, bonus etc.

ii) Marketing Strategy

Functional strategies in marketing area are required for marketing — mix decisions, i.e. the four Ps of marketing, viz. Product design, Product distribution, Pricing and Promotion aspects of marketing. In terms of specifics, the product decisions relate to such issues as the variety of product (shape, size, model etc.), quality requirements, introduction/withdrawal of products, nature of customers etc. Specific policies are also required regarding distribution channels i.e. through retailers or direct selling? What would be the spread of distribution network? Whether new dealers will be established or old ones developed? The promotion strategies will relate to mode of promotion, coverage and nature (corporate, product or brand promotion). Again, very clear and specific strategies will have to be made about pricing, etc., full cost or standard cost based pricing. Offensive vs. defensive postures also influence pricing policies.

iii) HR Strategy

HR strategy deals with matters like HR planning, recruitment and selection, training and development, compensation management, performance management, rewards and incentives etc. What compensation/reward system will be able to attract people of the desired type to join the organization so as to meet the task requirements demanded by the strategy? What strategy is necessary to groom internal people for new positions? The problem becomes acute in the context of turnaround strategies. On the one hand, the most competent people leave and the firm finds it difficult to attract suitable replacements. On the other hand, it faces the problem of surplus staff. HR strategies for retrenchment, though painful, are quite necessary but difficult to develop.

iv) Production Strategy

The functions relating to production need strategies relating to quality assurance, machine utilization, location of facilities, balancing the line, scheduling of production, and materials management. The strategy for entering into export market will dictate a different policy regarding quality of products and maintenance. Location of facilities may be determined by closeness to market or input supply points. Decisions must be made to determine whether and how much to make or buy, on the basis of cost differential, availability, criticality of the item, capacity if expansion becomes necessary. In case of bought out items, policies regarding number of suppliers and the criteria for selecting them are necessary.

v) R&D Strategy

In the area of research and development, functional strategies regarding the nature of research are necessary. In case of expansion through new product development, heavy emphasis has to be laid on basic and applied research. On the contrary, for expansion in the same line, research emphasis has to be on product/process improvement to cut cost and to add value. It may be noted that in case of basic research the firm should be prepared to commit resources and wait for outcome for several years. It cannot have basic research unless it is prepared to commit resources on long-term basis. The functional strategies have a lot of inter linkages between themselves and therefore, cannot be developed independent of each other. If there is no consistency among them for whatever reason, that may lead to chaos and serious mismatches resulting in failure of the organizational strategies.

10.13. RESOURCE ALLOCATION

While implementing strategies, the scarce resources of a firm (Financial, Physical, Human, Technological) need to be allocated carefully, according to a plan. In this regard, one can follow a top-down or a bottom-up approach. In a top-down approach resources are allocated through a process of segregation down to the operating levels. The Board of Directors, Managing Directors and other members of Top management typically decide the requirements of each subunit and distribute resources accordingly. In the bottom-up approach, resources are distributed after a process of aggregation from the operating level. A mix of these two may also find favour in fairly large, multi-plant organisations.

10.13.1 Means/Sources/Mode of Resource Allocation

There are several ways of allocating resources in a systematic way, namely

- ***Strategic budget:*** Keeping the assumptions made before the formulation of a budget, divisional heads (SBUs and functional managers focus their efforts on allocating funds, through an interactive exercise—taking the opinions of all those who matter most. The external influences and their likely impact and the internal capabilities of a firm are also kept mind in this joint budgeting effort (hence, the name strategic budget).
- ***Capital budget:*** The primary purpose of a capital budget is to maximise the long term profitability of a firm while deploying resources. Various techniques like internal rate of return, payback period, net present value are used to find where a rupee invested would earn maximum returns.
- ***Performance budget:*** Here the basic purpose is to focus attention on the work to be carried out, services to be rendered rather than things to be spent for or acquired. It concentrates attention on physical aspects of achievement. Here, there is not only a work plan but also a work plan in terms of work done. It takes a systems view of activities trying to associate the inputs of the expenditure with the output of accomplishment in terms of services, benefits etc.
- ***Zero based budget*:** The key element of ZBB is future-objective orientation of past objectives. Instead of taking the last year's budgets and adjusting them for finding out the future level of activity and preparation of budget there from, ZBB forces managers to review the current, ongoing objectives and operations. ZBB is, therefore, a type of budgets that requires managers to rejustify the past objectives, projects, and budget and to set prioritiesfor the future. The essential idea budget that differentiates ZBB from traditional budgetis that it requires managers to justify their budget request in detail from scratch, without any reference to the level of previous appropriations. It tantamount to recalculation of all organisational activities to see which should be eliminated, funded at a reduced level, funded at the current level or increased finances must be provided.

  ZBB process runs into the following cardinal sequence of steps

i) ***Decision package:*** Each discrete department activity and programme is broken down into a decision package. Decision package summaries the scope of work, requirements, anticipated benefits, time schedule, and expected consequences if the element is not performed, etc. Thus decision package provides a running commentary of all the activities in a particular project.

ii) ***Ranking:*** Each decision package is ranked against packages for other proposed projects or activities, and the projects that are running (operating) currently. Decision packages are ranked according to their benefits to the total organisation during the budget period.

iii) ***Resource allocation:*** The above ranking leads to 'organisation-wide' list of prioritised and priced out decision packages built from zero-base or ground up. Resources are then allocated to the packages according to the preferential rank in the organisation. When properly executed, the zero-base budgeting provides an opportunity for the managers to carefully examine, evaluate and prioritize each organisational activity and see whether modification, continuance or termination is feasible.

10.13.2 Importance of Resource Allocation

A company ability to acquire sufficient resources needed to support new strategic initiatives and steer them to the appropriate organizational units has a major impact on the strategy implementation process. Too little funding arising from constrained financial resources or from sluggish management action slows progress and impedes the efforts of organizational units to execute their part of the strategic plan effectively.

At the same time, too much funding wastes organizational resources and reduces financial performance. Both these extremes emphasize the need for managers to be careful about resource allocation. Resource allocation becomes a critically important exercise when there are major shifts from the past strategies in terms of product/market scope. For example, if the firm strategy is expansion in one line, withdrawal from another and stability in the rest of the products, then greater resources will have to flow to the first and lesser to the second and the third. Similarly, if the strategy is to develop competitive edge through product development, greater resources will have to be committed to R&D.

Resource allocation is a powerful means of communicating the strategy in the organization as it gives the signals to all concerned. It will demonstrate what strategy is really in operation. Resource allocation decisions should be taken judiciously because using a formula approach (i.e. allocating funds as a percentage of sales or profits), may be inappropriate and counter-productive. Care should be taken to see that the resources are not allocated or withdrawn because of easy availability or paucity. For example, cutting down R&D budget in view of sudden fall of profitability should be avoided as such expenditure may be most critical for developing future competitive advantage.

The resource allocation decisions are generally linked to the objectives. For example, decision about dividend payment is linked to the ability of the company to attract capital. How to distribute the expected profits among investors, employees and the company own needs is an important resource allocation decision from the viewpoint of long-term implications of the strategy.

10.13.3 Approaches to Resource Allocation

Broadly, there are three approaches to resource allocation:

1. Top-Down approach
2. Bottom-up approach
3. Strategic Budgeting

1. Top-down approach: In this approach, resources are allocated through a process of segregation down to the operating levels. The Board of Directors, the Managing Director or members of top management typically decide the requirements of each subunit and distribute resources accordingly.

2. Bottom-up approach: In this approach, resources are distributed through a process of aggregation from the operating level. The operating levels work out the requirements of each subunit and the resources are allocated accordingly.

3. Strategic budgeting: This approach is a mix of the above two approaches, and involves an interactive form of decision-making between different levels of management.

10.13.4 Techniques for Resource Allocation

The common approach to resource allocation is through budgetary system. There are however, many other tools, which can be used for this purpose. Some of the important tools used for resource allocation are discussed below:

i) BCG Matrix

The BCG matrix, which is generally used for portfolio analysis, can also be used as a guideline for resource allocation. The surplus resources from cows can be reallocated to or marks In so far as businesses categorized as are concerned, with low growth and low market share, they may not need any thrust, and resources can be gradually withdrawn from such businesses and invested in other promising businesses. The BCG matrix is a useful tool because it impresses upon a portfolio approach to resource allocation. It helps in averting over-investment in any particular type of business and under-investment in promising businesses from the long-term perspective. Despite the utility of the BCG matrix, however, it should be used with care and only as a guideline. It does not provide a concrete measure for making a finer choice, particularly among the businesses of the same nature.

ii) PLC-based Budgeting

Resource allocation can also be linked to different stages of a Product Life Cycle (PLC). A product in introductory and growth stages may require more resources than a product in mature and decline stages.

iii) Zero-based Budgeting (ZBB)

The key differences between ZBB and traditional budgeting are that ZBB requires managers to justify their budget requests in detail from the scratch, without relying on the previous budget allocations. Therefore, instead of taking the last year budget as the base for projecting the future allocations, ZBB forces the managers to review the objectives and operations afresh and justify the budget requests. ZBB is, therefore, a type of budget that requires managers to re-justify the past objectives, projects and budgets and set priorities for the future. It amounts to recalculation of all organizational activities to see which should be eliminated or funded at a reduced or increased level.

10.13.5 Criteria for Resource Allocation Process

In large, diversified companies, the corporate office pıays a major role in allocating resources among various strategies proposed by its operating units or divisions. In many cases, product groups, business units or functional areas may bid for funds to support their strategic proposals.

There are two criterias which can be used when allocating resources.

1. Contribution towards fulfillment of organizational objectives: At the centre of the organization, the resource allocation task is to steer resources away from areas that are poor at delivering the organization objectives and towards those that are good at delivering the organization objectives.

2. Support of key strategies: In many cases, the problem with resource allocation is that the requests for funds usually exceed the funds normally available. Thus, there needs to be some further selection mechanism beyond the delivery of the organisation mission and objectives. This second criterion relates to three aspects of resource analysis:

a. **Support of core competencies:** Resources should develop and enhance core competencies which, in turn, help achieve competitive advantage.
b. **Enhancement of value chain activities:** Resources should assist particularly those activities of the value chain which help the organization to achieve low cost or differentiation and thereby enhance and sustain competitive advantage of the firm.
c. **Risk-acceptance level of the organisation:** Clearly if the risk is higher, there is a lower likelihood that the strategy will be successful. Some organizations will be more comfortable with accepting higher levels of risk than others. So, the criterion in this case needs to be considered in relation to the risk-acceptance level of the organization.

Special Circumstances Surrounding Allocation of Resources

Sometimes, special circumstances may cause an organization to amend the criteria for allocation of resources, those considerations are: -

- **When major strategic changes are unlikely:** In this situation, resources may be allocated on the basis of a formula, e.g. marketing funds might be allocated as a percentage of sales based on past history and experience. The major difficulty with such an approach is its arbitrary nature. It may, however, be a useful shortcut
- **When the major strategic changes are predicted:** In this situation, additional resources may be required to respond to an expected competitive initiative. In this case, special negotiation with the corporate office is required for resourcing rather than the adherence to dogmatic criteria.
- **When resources are shared between divisions:** In this situation, the corporate office may seek to enhance its role beyond that of resource allocator. It may need to establish the degree of collaboration and, where the areas disagree, impose a solution.

10.13.6 Factors Affecting Resource Allocation

Resource allocation may not necessarily be a purely decision-making process. It is also a behavioral and political process involving people who may be motivated by different objectives. Some of the major factors affecting resource allocation are discussed below:

1. **Objectives of the organization**: People motivated by different objectives exercise their influence over the funding of projects. There are two types of objectives. Official (explicit) objectives and operative (implicit) objectives. Allocations of resources are more guided by implicit objectives than explicit objectives. The formal and informal organizations also influence the perception of which projects should be chosen for funding.
2. **Powerful units**: Sometimes, powerful SBU heads secure larger allocation of funds than their share.
3. **Dominant strategists:** The preferences of dominant strategists like the CEO, Directors, SBU heads, etc. are reflected in the way resources are allocated. The divisional and departmental heads know that such preferences matter and try to present their demands in line with them.
4. **Internal politics:** Resources are often construed as power, and those units, which manage to secure substantial resources, are perceived as more powerful than others. Internal politics within the organization to secure more and more resources, affect the process of resource allocation.
5. **External influences:** Apart from internal politics, external influences like government policy, demands of shareholders, financial institutions, community and others, also affect resource allocation. For example, legal requirements may require additional finances in labour welfare and social security, pollution control, safety equipment's and energy conservation. The shareholders may expect higher dividends, and resources have to be directed to them. Financial institutions may impose restrictions or require companies to invest in technology up-gradation and R&D. Similarly, the discharge of social responsibilities by the firm requires allocation of sufficient funds. Thus, external influences affect the process of resource allocation.

   To sum up, we can say that the and considerations are inevitable in a typical organization, but one must ensure that they do not dominate the considerations in allocation of resources. Otherwise, irrational allocation of funds may jeopardize effective implementation of the strategy and lead to problems in achieving the desired strategic change.

10.13.7 Difficulties in Resource Allocation

The resource allocation process can sometimes become fairly complex, and may even create several difficulties to the strategists. Some of the difficulties that can create problems are

1. **Scarcity of Resources:** Resources are hard to find. Even if finance is available, the cost of capital could be a constraint. Non-availability of highly skilled people could be another problem.
2. **Restrictions on Generating Resources:** Within organizations, the new units which have greater potential for growth in the future, may not be able to generate resources in the short run. Allocation of resources on par with existing SBUs, divisions and departments through the usual budgeting process, will put them at a disadvantage.
3. **Bloated demands:** Unit managers may sometimes submit inflated or overstated demands for funds to guard against any budget-cuts. This subverts the decision process.
4. **Negative attitude:** Units, which do not get the desired allocations, may develop a negative attitude towards the corporate managers. They may work at cross purposes, which may obstruct the implementation of the intended strategy.
5. **Budget Battles:** The actual allocation of funds to any unit has a major effect on the work environment of the unit and the career of the manager concerned. If a manager loses the battle his subordinates feel that the manager has failed them, and may not cooperate with him.
6. **Budgetary process:** The budgetary process itself can lead to problems if it is not tied to the strategic plans of the firm. If top management fails to communicate the shifts in the strategic plans and the lower levels are unaware of the shifts, any intended strategy is unlikely to succeed.
7. **New SBUs:** The budgetary process is tied to the way units and divisions are arranged organizationally. New SBUs can be at a disadvantage if they are unaware of the intricacies of the budget procedures used in their organizations.

   To avoid the above difficulties, strategists should pay maximum attention to resource allocation, and prioritize budget allocations in the initial stages taking overall objectives into account. Many battles can be avoided if targets, resource sharing, prioritization, midway revisions etc. are decided in an atmosphere of cooperation and participation, especially at departmental and divisional levels. Allocating resources to specific divisions and departments alone does not mean successful implementation of the strategy. If major strategic shifts are occurring, the organization structure is likely to change along with the way resources are allocated.

10.13.8 Caution Regarding the Resource Allocation Process

Hamel and Prahalad have reservations about the whole process of resource allocation itself. They view it as offering the wrong mental approach to the strategy task, arguing that it is more concerned with dividing up the existing resources than with using the resources more effectively and strategically. They make an important cautionary point

"If top management devotes more to assessing the strategic feasibility of projects in its resource allocation role than it does to the task of multiplying resource effectiveness, its value added will be modest indeed".

Problems in Resource Allocation

Resource allocation, in actual practice, is not an easy job. Strategists should prioritise tasks that require maximum attention initially taking political relations, overall objections, external influences etc., into account. Each department may fight for garnering a maximum share of the scarce resources that are available-leading to destructive conflict and bitter personality clashes. External influences such as government regulations, shareholder preferences for higher dividends, credit restrictions imposed by financial institutions also affect the process of resource allocation considerably. To avoid trouble at a later stage, strategists need to prioritise everything and decide budgetary allocations in the initial stages. Many 'budget battles' could be avoided if targets, resource sharing, prioritisation and midway revisions etc., are decided in an atmosphere. Of close cooperation and participation, especially at departmental and divisional levels. Allocating resources to specific divisions and departments alone does not mean successful strategy nip1ementation. There are other troublesome issues to be looked into more closely. After resolving the knotty issues concerning resource allocation, the strategists should look for a suitable organisation structure for implementing strategies.

Strategy- Structure Relationship

A suitable organisation structure is essential to implement strategies and achieve stated goals. According to Classical Organisation Theorists (Fayol, Taylor, Webber), the manager generally determines the work activities to get the job done, writes job descriptions, puts people into groups and assigns them to superiors. He then fixes goals and deadlines and establishes standards of performance. Operations are then controlled through a reporting system. The whole structure takes the shape of a pyramid. Thus the term 'organisation structure' describes the framework of an organisation in which individual effort is coordinated. It is nothing but a chart of relationships. Generally speaking, organizations perform more effectively when they implement strategy with the most appropriate structure, while evaluating whether an organisation is properly structured and stuffed to meet the requirements of the strategy, the following questions need a careful analysis:

10.14. ORGANIZATIONAL STRUCTURE

Introduction

To implement its strategy successfully a firm must have an appropriate organizational structure. An organizational structure is a set of formal tasks and reporting relationships which provide a framework for control and coordination within the organization. The visual representation of an organizational structure is called organisational chart. The purpose of an organizational structure is to coordinate and integrate the efforts of employees at all levels corporate, business and functional levels so that they work together to achieve the specific set of strategies.

Importance of Organizational Structure

Organizational structure is a tool that managers use to harness resources for getting things done. It is defined as (1) the set of formal tasks assigned to individuals and departments. (2) Formal reporting relationships, including lines of authority, responsibility, number of hierarchical levels and span of manager control and (3) the design of systems to ensure effective coordination of employees across departments. The set of formal tasks and formal relationships provides a framework for vertical control of the organization. There are two different aspects of the organizational structure:

- Superstructure
- Infrastructure

- **Superstructure:** This is the highly visible part of the organizational structure. This depicts how people are grouped into different divisions, departments and sections and how they are related to each other. The superstructure also indicates the principal ways in which the organizational operations are integrated and coordinated. By showing their levels, it indicates which groups have relatively more strategic importance.
- **Infrastructure:** This is comparatively less visible part of the organizational structure. It is concerned with issues like delegation of authority, specialization, communication,

information systems and procedures. The infrastructure enables the organization to engage in a number of disparate activities and still keep them coordinated. The design of organizational structure is a critical task of the top management of an organization. It is the skeleton of the whole organization. It provides relatively more durable organizational arrangements and relationships. Thus an organizational structure fulfills two fundamental and opposing requirements:

a) Division of labour into various tasks

b) Coordination of these tasks to accomplish effective control of an organization.

However, as an organization grows and becomes more complex, it needs appropriate changes in its design.

Basic Principles of Organizational Structure

There are several important principles of organization, which need to be understood before building an organization structure. They are

1. **Hierarchy:** Hierarchy defines who reports to whom and the span of control. Span of control is the number of people reporting to a supervisor. It determines how closely a supervisor can monitor subordinates. Tall structures have many levels in the hierarchy and a narrow span. Communication up and down the hierarchy becomes difficult. Flat structures are horizontally dispersed having fewer levels in the hierarchy. The trend in recent years has been towards flat structures allowing for wider spans of control as a way to facilitate better communication and co-ordination.
2. **Chain of Command:** The chain of command is an unbroken line of authority that links all persons in an organization and shows who reports to whom. It has two underlying principles. Unity of command means that each employee is held accountable to only one supervisor. The scalar principle means a clearly defined line of authority in the organization. Authority and responsibility for different tasks should be distinct. All persons in the organization should know to whom they report as well as the successive management levels all the way to the top.
3. **Specialization:** Specialization, sometimes called division of labour, is the degree to which organizational tasks are subdivided into separate jobs. Work can be performed more efficiently if employees are allowed to specialize. This is because an employee in each department performs only the tasks relevant to his specialized function. Despite the apparent advantages of specialization, many organizations are moving away from this principle. With too much specialization, employees are isolated performing only a single, boring job. Many companies are, therefore, enlarging jobs to provide greater challenges or assigning tasks to teams so that employees can rotate among several jobs performed by the team.
4. **Authority, Responsibility and Delegation:** Authority is the formal and legitimate right of a manager to make decisions, issue orders, allocate resources and command obedience. Responsibility is the duty to perform the task or activity an employee has been assigned. Accountability means that the people with authority and responsibility are subject to reporting and justifying task outcomes to those above them in the chain of command. Delegation is the process managers use to transfer authority and responsibility to positions below them in the hierarchy. The principle is that there must be parity between authority and responsibility. It means managers can be made accountable for results only when they are delegated with sufficient authority commensurate with the responsibility.
5. **Centralization and Decentralization:** Centralization and decentralization refer to the level at which decisions are made. Centralization means that decision-making is done at the top levels of the organization. Decentralization means that decision making is pushed

down to the lower levels in the organization. Centralization helps in better coordination, but too much centralization results in slow response and demotivates people at lower levels. Decentralization relieves the burden on top managers, makes greater use of worker skills, ensures decision making by well-informed people and permits rapid response to external changes. But it does not mean that every organization should decentralize. Managers should diagnose the organizational situation and select the decision-making level.

6. **Formalization:** Formalization is the extent to which written documentation is used to direct and control employees. Written documentation includes rules, regulations, policies, procedures, job descriptions etc. They are inexpensive ways to coordinate activities. These documents complement the organizational structure by providing descriptions of tasks, responsibilities and authority. The use of rules and regulations is a part of bureaucratic model of organization. Although written documentation is intended to be rational and helpful to the organization, it often creates tape that causes more problems than it solves. Narrowly defined job descriptions, For example, tend to limit the creativity, flexibility and rapid responses needed in today knowledge-based organizations. Many organizations today are reducing formalization and bureaucracy.
7. **Departmentalization:** Another fundamental characteristic of organizational structure is departmentalization, which means grouping positions into departments and departments into the total organization.

10.15. ORGANISATIONAL DESIGN

Introduction

Organizational design is the design of the organizational structure. It entails decisions about structure and culture. In design, we use the term structure in the widest sense. Organizational structure is the design of the pattern of positions and functions in the organization. Organizational design includes organizational structure as well as the design of the organizational process of work, in particular the decision making process. Through organizational are different from each other in their respective fields and types, but there are certain basic features which are to be taken into consideration while designing the organizational structure or while changing it.

Features of Organizational Design

- It examines the link between the goals of the corporation and how managers and staff are working to achieve those objectives.
- It is a formal, guided process for integrating the people, information, technology of an organization.
- It is a process of improving the profitability that an organization will be successful by assessing and re-shaping structure and positions to better meet the goals.
- It deals with allocation of tasks, and achieving full organizational alignment between the "people " aspects and the "function".

10.15.1 Importance of Organizational Design

1. **Dealing with contingencies**

   A contingency is an event that might occur and must be planned for, such as a changing environment. The design of an organization determines how effectively an Organization controls various factors in its environment and obtain scare resources.

2. **Gaining competitive advantage**
   Competitive advantage springs from a firm's competences, manager's skills and abilities in value creation activities such as manufacturing, research and development.

3. **Employee satisfaction**
   Effective Organization design create a culture of accountability. Employees are well managed and understand their accountabilities and authorities and the goals of the corporation.

4. **Improved customer satisfaction**
   Employees are better able to deliver high quality services and products, and to meet customer expectations.

5. **Improves financial performance**
   When a corporation's employees, productivity, and goals are properly aligned, there is greater productivity and less waste.

6. **Significant return on investment**
   Investing in improving organization design can lead to significant returns for any corporation in any sector.

10.15.2 Dimensions of Organization Design

1. **Structural Dimensions:** It describes the internal characteristics of an organization.
2. **Formalization:** It is amount of written documentation, including procedures, job descriptions, regulations and policy manuals.
3. **Specialization:** It is the degree to which Organization tasks are sub-divided into separate jobs.
4. **Hierarchy:** Hierarchy of authority describes who reports to whom and the span of control for each manager. Span of control is the number of subordinates reporting to superior.
5. **Centralization:** It is extent to which decision making is done by the top management. Decentralization is the extent to which authority to make decision is delegated to lower levels of management.
6. **Professionalism:** It is the level of formal education and training of employees.
7. **Contextual Dimensions** – (Environment, Goals and Strategy, Culture, Technology)

The process of designing an organization structure to match with its situation is called organizational design. The best design for an organization is determined by many aspects of its situation, viz. the size, technology, environment and strategy. Managers make choices about how to use the chain of command to group people together to perform their work. The functional, divisional and matrix structures are traditional approaches that rely on the chain of command to define departmental groupings and reporting relationships along the hierarchy. Newer approaches such as teams, networks and virtual organizations have emerged to meet changing organizational needs in an increasingly global, knowledge-based business environment. We discuss below some of the important organizational structures adopted by different organizations.

Types of Organizational Structures

There are seven basic types of organizational structures:

1. Simple structure
2. Functional structure
3. Divisional structure

(*a*) SBU structure (*b*) Holding company structure

4. Matrix structure
5. Network structure
6. Virtual structure

1. Simple Structure

In this structure, the owner-manager controls all activities and makes all the decisions. This structure may be appropriate for small and young organizations. Coordination of tasks is done through direct supervision. There is little specialization of tasks, few rules and regulations and communication is informal.

Advantages

1. Quick decision-making
2. Flexible
3. Efficient
4. Ability to respond quickly

Disadvantage

1. Not suitable for big organizations functional structure.

2. Functional Structure

Functional structures are grouped based on major functions performed. Each function is led by a functional specialist. Functional structures are formed in organizations in which there are a single or closely related products or services.

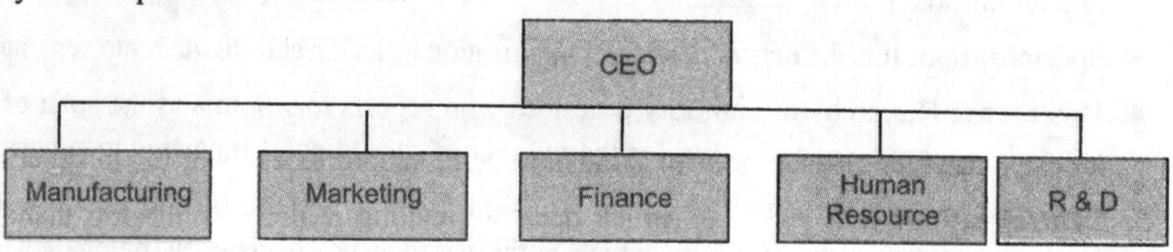

Figure 10.3

Advantages

1. Allows for functional specialization
2. Allows for career paths and professional development
3. Centralized decision-making
4. More efficient use of managerial and technical talent

Disadvantages

1. Tends to create functional silos that hinder communication and coordination
2. Overburdens the top management, as functional conflicts are pushed up.
3. Line-staff conflicts
4. Difficult to establish uniform standards across the organization.

3. Divisional Structure

Divisional structures are used by diversified organizations. In a divisional structure, divisions are created as self-contained units with separate functional departments for each division. A division may be organized around geographic area, products, customers etc. The head office determines corporate strategy, allocates resources among divisions and appoints and rewards the heads of these divisions. Each division is responsible for product, market and financial objectives for the division as well as their division contribution to overall corporate performance.

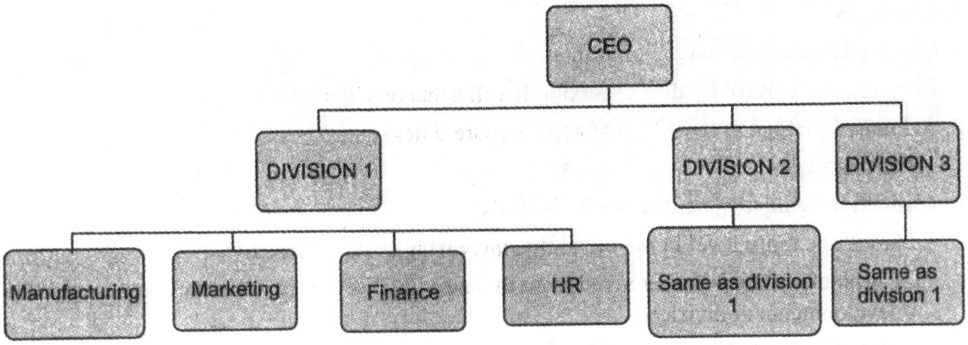

Figure 10.4

Advantages

1. Separation of strategic and operational control
2. Quick response to changes in external environment
3. Conflicts across functional areas are minimized
4. Development of general management talent is enhanced
5. Increasing accountability and focus

Disadvantages

1. Increased costs due to duplication of functions and personnel
2. Dysfunctional competition among divisions for resources
3. Differences in image and quality may occur across divisions
4. Divisions may focus on short-term performance (i.e. short-term focus to meet financial targets)
5. Divisional perspective may dominate the organization-wide perspective.

There are two variations of divisional structure:

a) **SBU structure:** Corporations that are highly diversified may consist of numerous divisions. It will be difficult for corporate office to coordinate their activities. Hence, the diverse businesses are grouped into SBUs (Strategic Business Units). Generally, divisions with similar products, markets or technologies are grouped into an SBU, as a distinct profit centre.

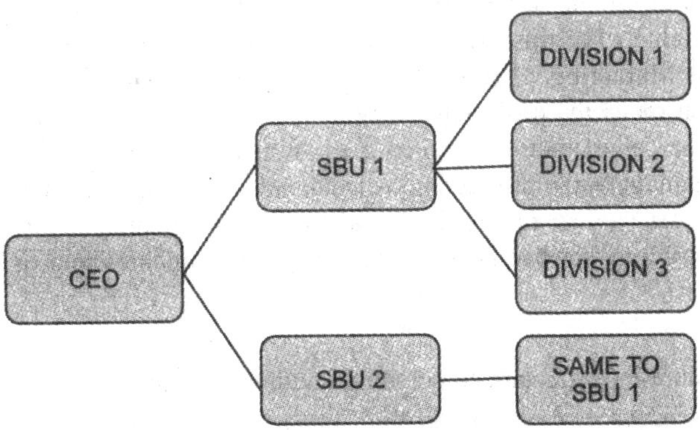

Figure 10.5

Advantages

1. Greater decentralization of authority
2. Planning and control by the corporate office becomes more manageable
3. Individual SBUs can react to changes more quickly.

Disadvantages

1. Difficult to achieve synergies across SBUs
2. Adds one more level in the hierarchy, increasing costs and overheads
3. Corporate office is far removed from the individual divisions and may be unaware of key developments in divisions.

b) **Holding Company Structure:** In this structure, individual businesses operate as autonomous subsidiaries, and the corporate office acts as the holding company. Such a structure is appropriate for companies that follow conglomerate diversification. The corporate office provides a great deal of autonomy to operating units and relies on financial controls and incentives to obtain high levels of performance from the individual businesses. The holding company structure is used successfully by companies likeJohnson and Johnson.

Advantages

1. There is no need to have a large corporate office
2. Autonomy increases motivational levels of divisional executives
3. Can respond quickly to marketing opportunities

Disadvantages

1. Inherent lack of corporate control over divisional executives
2. Major problems arise if key divisional executives leave the firm, as corporate office does not have additional managerial talent
3. Turnaround strategies are difficult to implement because of limited staff support from the corporate office.

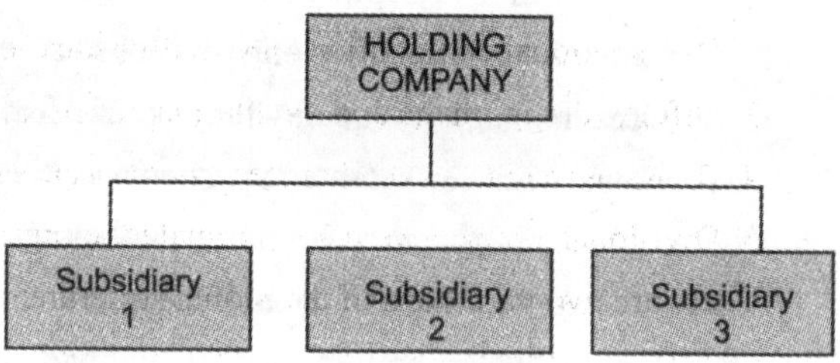

Figure 10.6

4. Matrix Structure

The matrix structure is, in effect, a combination of functional and divisional structures. In this structure, there are functional managers and product or project managers. Employees report to one functional manager and to one or more project managers. For example, a product group wants to develop a new product. For this project it obtains personnel from functional departments like Finance, Production, Marketing, HR. Engineering etc. These personnel work under the product manager for the duration of the project. Thus, they are responsible for two managers the product manager and the manager of their functional area. While functional heads have vertical control over the functional managers, the product or project heads have horizontal control over them. Thus, matrix structure provides a dual reporting. The dual line of authority makes the matrix structure unique. The matrix structure has been used successfully by companies such as IBM, Unilever, Ford Motor Company, etc.

Advantages

1. It facilitates the use of specialized personnel without duplication
2. Firms can use resources more efficiently
3. Experienced managers can divide their time among multiple products/projects
4. It is flexible and permits innovation
5. It provides professionals with broader range of responsibilities.

Matrix Structure

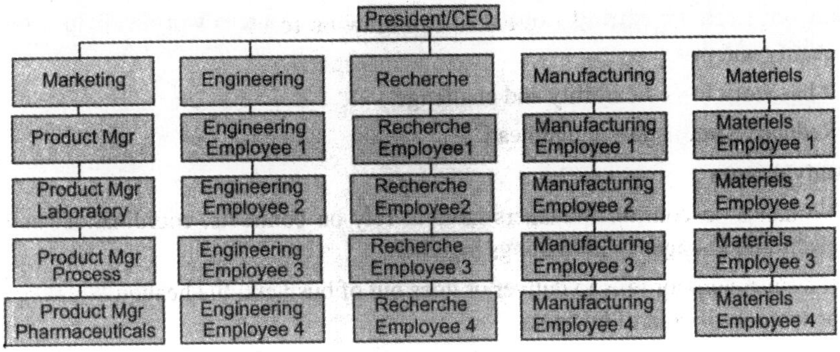

Figure 10.7

Disadvantages

1. Dual reporting may lead to politics, power play and conflicts
2. Working relationships may become complicated
3. Excessive reliance on group processes and teamwork
4. Diffusion of accountability
5. May erode timely decision-making

5. Network Structure

A network organization outsources or subcontracts many of its major functions to separate companies and coordinates their activities from a small headquarters. Rather than being housed under one roof activities like design, manufacturing, marketing, distribution etc. are outsourced to separate organizations that are connected electronically to the central office. For example, athletic shoe companies like Nike and Reebok have outsourced manufacturing of their shoes to countries such as China and Indonesia, where labour costs are low. What Nike or Reebok does is the design and marketing of shoes. Networked computer systems and the Internet enable the organization to exchange data and information. The organization may be viewed as a hub surrounded by a network of outside specialists, as shown in the Exhibit. As may be seen from the above, the core organization is only a shell with a small headquarters acting as a broker connected to supplier, design, manufacturing etc. organizations.

Global Organization

Figure 10.8

Advantages

1. Network structure is truly global. It can draw on resources worldwide to achieve the best quality and price
2. It has work force flexibility and challenge
3. Reduced administrative overhead.

Disadvantages

1. No hands-on control. Managers have to rely on contracts, coordination, negotiation, and electronic linkages to hold things together
2. If a subcontractor fails to deliver or goes out of business, the headquarters organization will be temporarily out of business
3. Employee loyalty can weaken, because they may feel they can be replaced by contract services.

6. Virtual Organization

This is an extension of the network structure. In this approach, independent organizations form temporary alliances to exploit specific opportunities, and then disband when their objectives are met. The term virtual means in effect but not actually so The virtual organizations consist of a network of independent companies suppliers, customers or even competitors linked together to share skills, costs, markets and rewards. The members of a virtual organization pool and share the knowledge and expertise of each other. The virtual organization will have few full-time employees or may temporarily hire outside specialists to complete a specific project, such as a new software application. These people do not become a part of the organization, but join together as a separate entity for a specific purpose. Sometimes companies use a virtual approach to harness the talents and energies of the best people for a particular job, rather than trying to develop those capabilities in house. When an organization uses a virtual approach, the virtual group typically has full authority to make decisions and take actions within certain predetermined boundaries and goals. Most virtual organizations use electronic media for sharing of information and data. Some organizations have redesigned offices to provide temporary space for virtual workers to meet or work on-site.

Advantages

1. It can draw on expertise worldwide
2. It is highly flexible and responsive
3. It reduces overhead costs.

Disadvantages

1. Lack of control because the boundaries of a virtual organization are weak and ambiguous.
2. Virtual teams place new demands on managers, who have to work with new people, new ideas and new problems.
3. Virtual organization poses communication difficulties, and managers may lose motivation.

Which Structure is the Best

Unfortunately, there is no best structure that can serve as a model for all organizations. The best structure for an organization is determined by many aspects of its situation the technology size, environment and strategy. Frequently, structures evolve as the organization moves from one stage of growth to the next. The external and internal environments affect structural design in different ways. For example, an organization which faces a stable environment may use functional structure. On the other hand, a volatile environment demands a rapid- response capability, flexibility and quick decision-making. Such demands can be better met by the creation of a divisional or a matrix type of structure. The internal environment may also affect the structure in a similar way. A bureaucratic, slow-moving organization may work better with a functional structure while a dynamic and innovative organization may have to use a divisional or network structure1. In sum, it can be said that there is no one best way to structure an organization and the organizational design has to be based on the particular needs of the organization at a given time. This aspect is dealt with in detail in the later sections.

Relation between Strategy and Structure

Strategic management posits that the strategy and the organization structure of the firm must match. In a classic study of large U.S. corporations such as DuPont, General Motors, Sears, and Standard Oil, Alfred Chandler concluded that structure follows strategy. This means that changes in corporate strategy lead to changes in organizational structure. He also concluded that organizations follow a pattern of development from one kind of structural arrangement to another as they expand. According to Chandler, these structural changes occur because the old structure was not suitable. Chandler therefore proposed the following as the sequence of what occurs: -

1. New strategy is created
2. New administrative problems emerge
3. Economic performance declines
4. New appropriate structure is invented
5. Profit returns to its previous level

Chandler found that in their early years, corporations such as Du Pont and General Motors had a centralized functional structure, which was suitable for a limited range of products. As they added new product lines and created their own distribution networks, the old structure became too complex. Therefore, they shifted to a decentralized structure with several autonomous divisions.

Strategy before Structure

A major debate has been taking place over the last 30 years regarding the relationship between the strategy and the structure of the organization. In the past, following Chandler conclusion, it was considered that the strategy was decided first and the organization structure then followed, Recent research has questioned this approach and taken the view that strategy and structure are interrelated. In this section, we examine the reasons why the views have changed: strategy no longer comes before structure.

Strategy before Structure: Chandler Contribution

To understand the logic behind this approach to the development of organizational structures, it is helpful to look at the historical background. As already mentioned, prior to the early 1960s, the US strategist Alfred Chandler studied how some leading US corporations had developed their strategies in the first half of the twentieth century. He then drew some major conclusions from this empirical evidence, the foremost one being that the organization first needed to develop its strategy and, after this, to devise the organization structure that delivered that strategy. Chandler drew a clear distinction between devising a strategy and implementing it. He defined strategy as:

"The determination of the basic long-term goals and objective of an enterprise, and the adoption of courses of action and the allocation of resources necessary for carrying out these goals ".

The task of developing the strategy took place at the corporate and business levels of the organization. The job of implementing it then fell to the various functional areas. Chandler research suggested that, once a strategy had been developed, it was necessary to consider the structure needed to carry it out. A new strategy might require extra resources, or new personnel or equipment which would alter the work of the enterprise.

Changes in Business Environment and Social Values

To understand why it is no longer appropriate to develop an organization structure after deciding a strategy, the earlier theory needs to be placed in its historic strategic context. Since Chandler research in the early twentieth century, the environment has changed substantially. The workplace itself the relationship between workers and managers, and the skills of employees have all altered substantially. Old organizational structures embedded in past understandings may therefore be suspect. Table 10.2 summarises how the environment has changed from the early twentieth century to early twenty-first century.

Table 10.2

Early twentieth century	Early twenty- first century
Uneducated workers, typically just moved from agricultural work into the cities	Better educated, computer- literate, skilled
Knowledge of simple engineering and technology	Complex, computer-driven, large-scale
The new science of management recognized simple cause-and-effect relationship	Multifaceted and complex nature of management now partially understood
Growing, newly industrializing markets and suppliers	Mix of some mature, cyclical markets and some high-growth, new-technology markets and suppliers
Sharp distinctions between management and workers	Greater overlap between management and workers in some industrialized countries

Strategy and Structure are interlinked

According to modern strategists, strategy and structure are interlinked. It may not be optimal for an organization to develop its structure after it has developed its strategy. The relationship is more complex in two respects

1. Strategy and the structure associated with it may need to develop at the same time in an experimental way. As the strategy develops, so does the structure. The organization learns to adapt to its changing environment and to its changing resources, especially if such change is radical.
2. If the strategy process is emergent, then learning and experimentation involved major need a more open and less formal organization structure.

Managing the Complexity of Strategic Change

Quinn suggests that strategic change may need to proceed incrementally, i.e. in small stages. He called the process instrumentalism . The clear implication is that it may not be possible to define the final organization structure, which may also need to evolve as the strategy moves forward incrementally. He recognizes the importance of informal organization structures in achieving agreement to strategy shifts. If the argument is correct, it will be evident that any idea of a single, final organization structure after deciding on a defined strategy is dubious.

Criticism of the Strategy First, Structure- Afterwards Process.

1. Structures may be too rigid, hierarchical and bureaucratic to cope with the newer social values and rapidly changing environment.
2. The type of structure is just as important as the business area in developing the organization strategy. It is the structure that will restrict, guide and form the strategy.

3. Value chain configurations that favour cost cutting or, alternatively, new market opportunities may also alter the organization required.
4. The complexity of strategic change needs to be managed, implying that more complex organizational considerations will be involved. Simple configurations such as a move from a functional to a divisional structure are only a starting point in the process.
5. The role of top and middle management in the formulation of strategy may also need to be reassessed: Chandler view that strategy is decided by the top leadership alone has been challenged. Particularly for new, innovative strategies, middle management and the organisation culture and structure may be important. The work of the leader in empowering middle management may require a new approach the organic style of leadership.

The Concept of Strategic Fit

Although it may not be possible to define which comes first, there is a need to ensure that strategy and structure are consistent with each other. For example, Pepsi Co reorganized its North American business to ensure that its strengths in the growing non-carbonated drinks market could be exploited across its full range of drinks. For an organization to be economically effective, there needs to be a matching process between the organization strategy and its structure. This is the concept of strategic fit. In essence, organizations need to adopt an internally consistent set of practices in order to undertake the proposed strategy effectively. It should be said that such practices will involve more than the organisation structure. They will also cover such areas as reward systems, information systems and processes, culture, leadership styles, etc. There is strong empirical evidence, both from **Chandler and Senge,** that there does need to be a degree of strategic fit between the strategy and the organization structure.

Although the environment is changing all the time, organizations may only change slowly and not keep pace with external change, which can often be much faster for example, the introduction of digital technology. It follows that it is unlikely that there will be a perfect fit between the organisation strategy and its structure. There is some evidence that a minimal degree of fit is needed for an organization to survive. It has also been suggested that, if the fit is ensured early during the strategic development process, then higher economic performance may result. However, as the environment changes, the strategic fit will also need to change.

10.16. BUILDING THE ORGANISATION STRUCTURE

Basic Principles or Steps to Build the Organisations Structure

Every organization is to some extent unique the result of its past, its resources and its situation. In addition, the key factors for success and the major strategies chosen by whatever process will depend on the situation at that time. It is difficult to specify clear and unambiguous rules to translate strategy into organisational structures and people processes. Thompson and Strickland recommend five useful steps that will assist this process but they caution against certainty:

1. Identity the tasks and people that are crucial to the strategy implementation.
2. Consider how such tasks and people relate to the existing activities and routines of the organization.
3. Use key factors for success to identify the chief areas around which the organization needs to be built.
4. Assess the levels of authority needed to implement the identified strategies.
5. Agree the levels of co-ordination between the units in the organization necessary to achieve the strategy.

The above steps are all rather generalized but this is inevitable in view of the unique nature of each organization.

Main Elements of Organisation Design

It is important to remember that many organizations have existing structures and that the primary task of organization design is usually not to invent totally new organization but to adapt the existing one. These matters are reflected in the nine primary determinants of organization design given below:

1. ***Age:*** Older organizations tend to be more formal.
2. ***Site:*** As organizations grow in size, there is usually an increasing need for formal methods of communication and greater co-ordination, suggesting that more formal structures are required.
3. ***Environment:*** Rapid changes in any of the environmental forces acting on the organisation will need a structure that is capable of responding quickly. If the work undertaken by the organization is complex, then this will make its ability to respond to the environment more difficult to organize and co-ordinate.
4. ***Centralization/decentralization decisions:*** To some extent, most organizations have a choice over how much they wish to control from the Centre. In summary, there are four main areas that need to be explored.
   a. The nature of the business, e.g., economies of scale will probably need to be centralized.
   b. The style of the chief executive: a dominant leader will probably centralize the need for local responsiveness.
   c. The need for local service.
5. ***Overall work to be undertaken:*** Value chain linkages across the organisation will clearly need to be coordinated and controlled. They may be especially important where an organization has grown and become more diverse. Divisional or matrix structure may be needed, with the precise details depending on the specific requirements and strategies of the organization.
6. ***Technical content of the work:*** In standardized mass production, the work to be undertaken controls the workers and their actions. However, Japanese production methods have recently shown that flexibility may be highly desirable in mass-production.
7. ***Different tasks in different parts of the organization:*** It is clear that the tasks of operations (production) are not the same as those of the sales and marketing areas. Different organizations have different balances of such functions for example, the strong role of research in a major pharmaceutical company versus the dominance of creative people in some media companies. The different tasks need to be reflected in the way the organization structure is designed.
8. ***Culture:*** The degree to which the organization accepts change, the ambitions of the organization and its desire for experimentation are all elements to be considered.
9. ***Leadership:*** The style, background and beliefs of the leader may have an impact on organization design. This will be particularly true in innovative and missionary organizations. In bringing all the above elements together, there is a danger of overcomplicating the considerations and arguments. Simplicity in design should guide the proposals because the structure needs to be understood and operated after it has been agreed. It is usual in undertaking such an analysis to consider the responsibilities and powers of the main individuals and groups involved, even if they are deliberately left vague in some structures. Responsibility and power need to be controlled and monitored and this needs to be built into the organizational structure. However, the control systems of the organization can usually be considered after the proposed structure has been resolved.

10.17. EXTERNAL ENVIRONMENT AND INTERNAL ORGANISATION CONTRIBUTION

According to Mintzberg, there are four main characteristics of the environment that influence structure (see the following Exhibit).

- **Rate of Change**

When the organization operates in a more dynamic environment, it needs to be able to respond quickly to the rapid changes that occur. In static environments, change is slow and predictable and does not require great sensitivity on the part of the organization. In dynamic environments, the organization structure and its people need to be flexible, well co-ordinated and able to respond quickly to outside influences. The dynamic environment implies a more flexible, organic structure.

Table 10.3

Type of environment	Range	Consequences for organizational structure
Rate of change	Static ←→ Dynamic	As rate of change increases, the organization needs to be kept more flexible
Degree of complexity	Simple ←→ Complex	Greater complexity needs more formal co-ordination
Market complexity	Involved in single market ←→ involved in diversified markets	As markets become more diversified, divisionalisation becomes advisable
Competitive situation	Passive ←→ Hostile	Greater hostility probably needs the protection of greater centralization

- **Degree of Complexity**

Some environments can be easily monitored from a few key data movements. Others are highly complex, with many influences that interact in complex ways. One method of simplifying the complexity is to decentralize decisions in that particular area. The complex environment will usually benefit from a decentralized structure.

- **Market Complexity**

Some organizations sell a single product or variations on one product. Others sell ranges of products that are essentially diverse. As markets become more diverse, there is usually a need to decentralize the organization as long as synergy or economies of scale are unaffected.

- **Competitive Situations**

With friendly rivals, there is no great need to seek the protection of the Centre. In deeply hostile environments, however, extra resources and even legal protection may be needed; these are usually more readily provided by central headquarters. As markets become more hostile, the organization usually needs to be more centralized. Two examples will make the point clear:

1. *The machine organizations* typified by work standardization. Such an organization may not wish to seek higher value-added work in small market segments because this would not be consistent with its current resources and work methods.
2. *The innovative organization* is typified by mutual adjustments between members of the organisation rather than standardization of work, skills or output. An organization structured in this way changes radically, invests in totally new resources and learns new skills. It should be noted that most organizations will rarely match Mintzberg six configurations precisely.

However, they do provide guidelines that link the earlier characteristics with their strategy and structure implications. Moreover, they could be used to show the implications of what might happen as the organization changes for example, becoming larger, with a more complex product range.

Conclusion

Thus, organizational structure plays a critical role in implementation of strategies. When organizations diversify, functional structures are no longer appropriate to implement a strategy Most diversified organizations use divisional structure. When they become more complex they switch over to matrix structure. A number of modern structures like circular structure, honeycomb structure, latticed structure etc, are emerging. So the top management should pay adequate attention in designing an appropriate structure to suit the requirements of the strategy.

10.18. IMPLEMENTATION OF STRATEGY DESIGNING ORGANISATIONAL STRUCTURE

Strategy implementation is an essential part of strategic management process. Bad implementation often results in strategic failures. A survey among 93, Fortune 500 U.S. firms indicates that business organizations face the following 10 problems while implementing strategy:

1. Implementation takes longer time than required.
2. Unanticipated major problems crop up.
3. Ineffective coordination of activities.
4. Crisis management took lot of time.
5. Employees have less than required capabilities.
6. Inadequate training of lower level employees.
7. Problems arising from uncontrollable external environment.
8. Inadequate leadership on the part of departmental environment.
9. Lack of precise definition of implementation of tasks and activities.
10. Inadequate monitoring of activities through information system.

Arvind Mills experienced all these problems and could not come out of them. Strategy implementation process requires development of programmes, budgets and procedures. All managers down to supervisors are involved in strategy implementation. Strategy implementation deals with the way in which a firm creates the organizational arrangements that allow it to pursue its strategy. Strategy is mainly implemented through appropriate structure and control. Selecting the right combination of organizational structure and control system is known as organizational design. The purpose of organization structure and control is to coordinate employees' activities and to motivate them for better performance. The organization structure has got definite bearing qn the behavior of employees in organizational setting. Good structure allows the organization to improve its ability, to create value and develop competitive advantage. Organizational structure and control shape the way people behave and determine how they will act in the organizational set up.

The structure also provides a mechanism through which managers coordinate the activities of various functions and divisions to fully exploit their skills and capabilities. Right kind of organization structure facilitates the management of resources and capabilities between departments and divisions. Chandler conducted a research study among DuPont, General Motors, Sears and Standard Oil and argued in his book 'Strategy and Structure' that structure follows strategy. According to him, changes in corporate strategy would lead to changes in organisation structure. The sequences of activities are as follows:

1. Creation of new strategy.
2. Emergence of administrative problems.
3. Economic performance declines.
4. Invention of new appropriate structure.
5. Profits return to its previous level.

Chandler argues that Dupont during its early period dealt with limited range of products and used centralized structure successfully. With increasing number of products, it created complex decentralized structure with semi autonomous divisions. General Motors adopted centralized policy determination with decentralized operating management. General Motors realized that decentralized multidivisional structure provided adequate freedom for product development and return on investment. Chandler concluded that changes in the environment get reflected in strategy and it leads to changes in structure. Organization's performance will suffer if structure, strategy and environment are not aligned. However, there is no consensus about optimal structure. GMs divisional concept and P&Gs brand management concept were emulated by firms in those industries.

Basics of Designing structure

Two basic aspects, which require a strategists' attention while designing structure, are:

- Differentiation and
- Integration

Differentiation

Differentiation means the way in which a company allocates people and resources to organizational tasks in order to create value. Differentiation is of two types.

- Vertical differentiation and
- Horizontal differentiation.

Integration

In order to promote coordination between functions and divisions, integration and control systems are established. Integration is the means by which a firm tries to coordinate people and functions to accomplish organizational tasks.

Bureaucratic Cost: The costs of operating a structure and control system are known as bureaucratic costs. Depending upon the complexity of the structure, differentiation and integration tend to be complex and bureaucratic costs will vary. If the firm is differentiated, more managers and resources will be required and the bureaucratic costs will increase which will erode the company's profits. Good design that economies on bureaucratic costs will give a company, a low cost advantage and enhances profits. Poor organizational design with many levels and badly thought out pattern of work relationship raises cost and reduces profits.

Vertical differentiation

Vertical differentiation involves establishment of reporting relationship, which connects people, tasks and functions at all, levels of the firm. The managers have to choose appropriate number of hierarchical levels, which is the outcome of their decisions regarding span of control. Span of control means the number of subordinate's manager controls effectively.

Two types of structure emanates from span of control

- Flat structure
- Tall structure

Flat structure involves few hierarchical levels and tall structure involves too many levels. Flat structure results in wide span of control and tall structure results in narrow span of control. Managers have to make a choice between flat structure and tall structure.

i) Problems with Tall Structure

As organizations grow in size, the number of levels in the hierarchy increases. However tall structure is often associated with slow communication and slow decision-making, information distortion, high bureaucratic costs, information overload, lesser authority and less motivation on the part of middle managers. So strategic managers tend to lose control over the hierarchy, which means that they lose control over strategies.

ii) Coordination: A lengthy chain of command takes longer time to communicate between the top and the bottom of the hierarchy. Communication between rank and file is slow and co-ordination among functions is difficult which will raise bureaucratic costs. It also results in inflexibility. Keeping pace with technological developments and commercialization of new product development becomes slow.

iii) Information Distortion: The information passed on between ranks and file, is often distorted. Any information may be interpreted differently at different levels deliberately. Manipulation of information to suit individual needs and omission of information by chance are possible and information never reaches the destination intact. Information passed on from subordinates may be distorted when the subordinates suppress relevant information and pass on information which will improve their prospects in the organization. The more the number of hierarchical levels, the more the distortion. Similarly when supervision is not very close, managers tend to hoard information to promote their self-interests at the expense of organization's interests.

iv) Motivational Problems: The authority given to mangers is a function of the hierarchy. More the levels less will be the authority possessed by them and with few levels, the performance of managers will be visible. Managers in flat structure have more authority and it increases their motivation to perform effectively. In tall structure they do not get enough authority and responsibility and hence the motivation level is not remarkable. Thus the structure and span affects the motivation level.

v) Number of Middle Managers: In tall structure, more number of middle managers is needed to be employed which involves additional salary and perks on the part of the organization, which involves bureaucratic costs. During times of prosperity, companies do not bother about too many middle managers but, the positions are revamped in times of adversity.

vi) Centralization/Decentralization: Another aspect of vertical differentiation is centralization and decentralization. The extent to which decision making authority is kept at the top decides centralization. When decision making authority is delegated to divisions, functional departments and lower levels, it is said to have decentralization of authority. The dispersal of authority to lower levels for operational performance helps strategic managers to have time for strategic decision making. Decentralization facilitates managers to respond to local conditions and enhances their motivation and accountability levels. It also promotes organizational flexibility. However, centralization has its own advantages

- Centralization enables coordination of various activities required to implement a strategy.
- It enhances fit Lietween organizational objectives and strategic decisions.
- Centralization permits authority being focused in one single person in times of crisis to take speedy and strategic decision.

Horizontal Differentiation

Horizontal differentiation involves decision to group organizational activities and tasks in order to create value and to fulfill organizational objectives. Alfred Chandler pointed out that 'structure follows strategy. A company's structure changes as its strategy changes in a predictable way'.

i) Simple Structure

Simple structure is suitable when a small entrepreneurial company is involved in producing one or more related products for a specific market segment. There is no formal organization structure existing and employees do multiple roles and duties and entrepreneur assumes responsibilityfor all managerial tasks. There is flexibility, dynamism and planning is for short term. Mr.Ranganathan, Promoter of Cavin Care introduced Velvet Shampoo in sachets. He is a pioneer in marketing and positioning a product and created waves in rural India.

ii) Functional Structure

The needs for specialists arise when the small enterprise grows and the tasks performed increase in number. Employees cannot perform multiple tasks. The need for professional accountant, marketing expert and production specialists arise. The functional structure groups employees on the basis of their common expertise and experience as they use the same resources. Each department concentrates on one specialized activity such as production, marketing, finance, engineering and human resources. Functional structure follows the principle of occupational specialization. It facilitates tight control at the top. The work process is efficient, reduces manufacturing costs and increases operational efficiency.

However, functional structure will not be suitable if the organization goes for diversification and spreads to different geographical areas. Functional structure makes it difficult to adapt quickly to environmental changes. Communication and coordination across functions is difficult due to functional orientation.

Once, more number of products are added, the measurement of contribution of profitable/ unprofitable products to overall productivity is difficult to be assessed with functional structure. In case of companies having operations spread in different locations, functional structure does not cope up with regional diversity. Functional orientation gives rise to communication problem and focuses on short-term performance and short-term goals. Resource allocation for profitable products may not be possible as the difficulty involved in identifying and differentiating profitable product from unprofitable products. Coordination and control will be slow down if the activities are carried out in various locations. Too much of obsession with coordination and communication may prevent the managers from attending to strategic problems. Oracle Corporation is a typical example for this stage of development.

The following guidelines could be kept in mind while trying to motivate people to peak performance.

- ***Recognise individual differences:*** Employees are not homogeneous. They have different needs. They also differ in term of attitudes, personalities and other important variables. So, recognise these differences and handle the motivational issues carefully.
- ***Match people to jobs:*** People with high growth needs perform better on challenging jobs. Achievers will do best when the job provides opportunities to participatively set goals and when there is autonomy and feedback. At the same time, keep in mind that not everybody is motivated in jobs with increased autonomy, variety and responsibility When the right job is given to the right person, the organisation benefits in innumerable ways.

- ***Use goals:*** Provide specific goals so that the employee knows what he is doing. Also, let people know what you expect of them. Make people understand that they can achieve the goals in a smooth way. If you expect resistance to goals, invite people to participate in the goal-setting process.
- ***Individualise rewards:*** Use rewards selectively, keeping the individual requirements in mind. Some employees have different needs — what acts as a motivator for one may not for another. So, rewards such as pay, promotion, autonomy, challenging jobs, participative management must be used keeping in mind the mental make-up of the employees in question.
- ***Link rewards to performance:*** Make rewards contingent on performance. The reward factors other than performance (favouritism, nepotism, regionalism, apple-polishing, yes-sir culture etc.) will only act to reinforce (strengthen) those other factors. The employee should be rewarded immediately after attaining the goals. At the same time, managers should look for ways to increase the visibility of rewards. Publicise the award of performance bonus, lumpsum payments for showing excellence, discuss reward structure with people openly — these will go a long way in increasing the awareness of people regarding the reward-performance linkage.
- ***Check the system for equity:*** The inputs for each job in the form of experience, abilities, effort, special skills, must be weighed carefully before arriving at the compensation package for employees. Employees must see equity between rewards obtained from the organisation and the efforts put in by them.
- ***Don't ignore money:*** Money is a major reason why most people work. Money is not only a means of satisfying the economic needs but also a measure of one's power, prestige, independence, happiness and so on. Money can buy many things. It can satisfy biological needs (food, shelter, sex, recreation etc.) as well as security, social and esteem needs. The following guidelines could be kept in mind while trying to motivate people to peak performance.

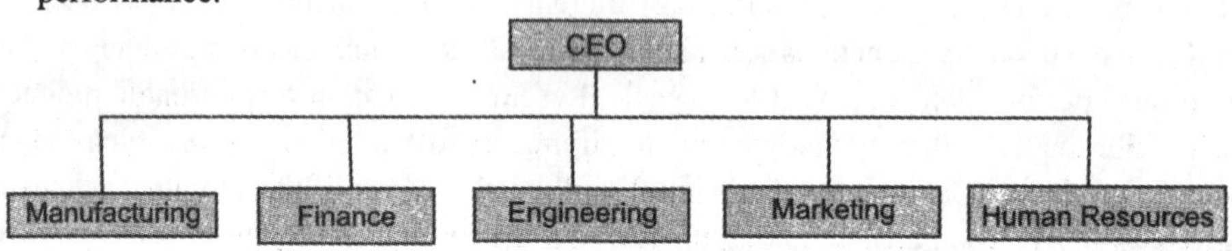

Figure 10.9

iii) Multidivisional Structure

As the organization grows and diversifies, divisional structure comes into existence. Divisions are self-contained business units with all support functions such as sales, accounts and human resource departments. In divisional structure corporate headquarters exercise financial control and monitor divisions. High level of horizontal differentiation is noticed in divisional structure. Compared to functional structure, one more level is found in this structure and thereby a higher level of vertical integration is embedded in it. However, the bureaucratic costs associated with divisional structure are high compared to functional structure. Each division works like a profit center, making it easier to monitor and evaluate each division's activities. In divisional structure, divisions carry out the day-to-day operations. Divisions have operating responsibility whereas head quarters have strategic responsibility for supervising long term strategic plan and guidance for interdivisional projects. General Motors, DuPont and General Electric are examples for this stage of development.

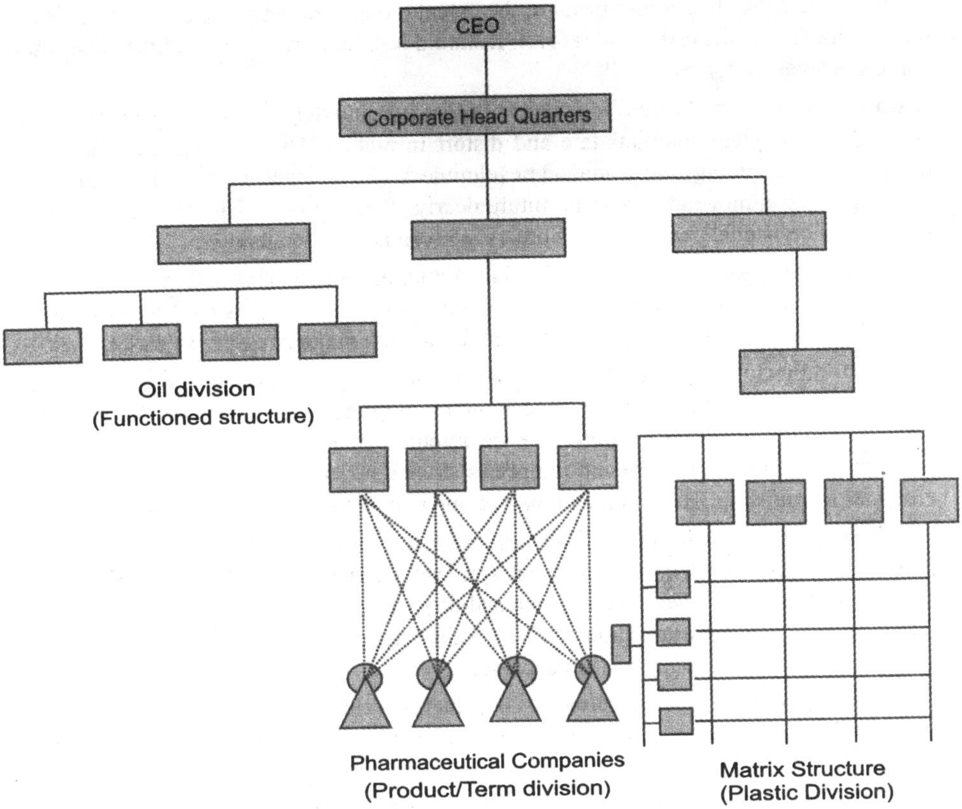

Figure 10.10

Advantages

1. **Financial control:** Since each division is a profit center, the head quarters set targets and monitor performance on regular basis, which ensures long-term returns and better performance.
2. **Strategic control:** Strategic control includes quick response to environmental changes which is exercised by head quarters whereas the divisions perform the operational functions. Application of portfolio technique is one such measure undertaken for strategic control by the headquarters.
3. **Growth:** For corporate headquarters, divisional structure reduces information overload. Communication problems are taken care by applying accounting and financial control techniques and 'Management by Exception' technique. So opportunities for growth and diversification are immense.
4. **Internal Efficiency:** Divisional structure ensures autonomy for divisions operations. Divisions are responsible for their own performance and their efficiency is measurable in terms of profit, which leads to better performance.

Disadvantages

1. **Divisional Corporate Authority Relationship:** The authority relationship between head office and division is a critical issue. Strategist should oversee how much authority to be given to the head quarters and how much to the operating division so that there is no friction and efficiency is ensured. If corporate office retains more power the division lacks autonomy. If divisions are delegated with more power, the possibility of losing sight of corporate goal

is always there. So the success lies in the extent of centralization at the corporate office and decentralization at the divisional level. It should be decided on the basis of the business and corporate level strategies.

2. **Distortion of information:** Whenever corporate headquarters exercises stringent financial control, the divisions manipulate and distort information. Divisions develop short- term orientation by avoiding new product development, and new investments and take to window dressing. Such a move affects the future dearly. Delicate power issues are involved when powerful divisional managers hide others' performance deliberately.
3. **Competition for Resources:** Divisions always compete among themselves to demand more resources. Hence synergy does not flow between divisions. Inter divisional coordination gets reduced. Strong divisions become stronger by getting major share of the profit.
4. **Transfer Pricing:** In related diversification and vertical integration, competition among divisions over transfer pricing is quite common. Supplying divisions always set high prices for their outputs in order to increase their return on investment. Intense rivalry creates problem of fixing reasonable and fair prices. The culture turns out to be unfriendly and non-cordial relationship. The organizations become a battlefield consequently.
5. **Research and Development:** The corporate headquarters usually set high targets for divisions. Hence the divisions cut down R & D expenditures in order to improve ROI on the short run. This will reduce the division's ability to innovate new products and affect long-term profits. Headquarters should have continuous interactions with divisions so that the long term and short-term goals are achieved.
6. **Bureaucratic Costs:** Each division has its own finance, marketing, production and R & D, which give room for duplication of specialist services. In times of crisis and recession, it may not be justified and centralization of advisory services and planning functions and R × D may be resorted to as viable alternative.

iv) Matrix Structure

The essence of matrix structure is that it is a combination of functional, product or project patterns of departmentation. This structure is widely used in construction (building dams, bridges), aerospace (satellite building), marketing (advertising campaign for a new product) and high technology industries. Two forms of horizontal differentiation rather than one as in functional structure characterize a matrix structure. In a product matrix structure, activities are grouped by function such as production, research and development and engineering. Another horizontal differentiation based on product or project is super imposed on this vertical pattern. A complex network of reporting relationship emanates among projects and functions. There will be a functional boss and a project boss.

10.19. CHECKLIST FOR DETERMINING APPROPRIATENESS OF ORGANISATIONAL STRUCTURE

Is the structure compatible with the corporate profile and the corporate strategy?

1. At the corporate level, is the structure compatible with the outputs of the firm's business units?
2. Are there too few or too many hierarchical levels at either the corporate or business unit level of analysis?
3. Does the structure promote coordination among its parts?
4. Does the structure allow for appropriate centralization or decentralization of authority?
5. Does the structure permit the appropriate grouping of activities?

It is, more or less, agreed now that changes in strategy lead to changes in organizational structure. Structure should be designed to facilitate the strategic pursuit of a firm and, therefore, follows strategy. Without a strategy or reasons for being (mission), structure is not important (David). Institutionalizing a strategy definitely requires a strategy-structure fit. Functional structure is useful when the firm begins operations at a single site. The emphasis here is on increasing volumes. As business expands, the firm begins to perform the same function in different locations. Such geographical dispersal of activity calls for inter-unit coordination. Vertical integration is the next growth strategy. Firms operate within the same industry but carry out additional functions. In the final phase, according to Alfred Chandler, firms indulge in product diversification - resulting in a large, multi-divisional structure. Current research indicates that the greater the diversity among the businesses in multi business firms, the greater is the necessary degree of decentralisation and self containment. Four important guidelines can be advanced in this regard: (Pearce and Robinson).

- A single product firm or single dominant business firm (where one business accounts 70-95% of sales) should employ a functional structure.
- A firm in several lines of business that are somehow related should employ a multi divisional structure.
- A firm in several unrelated lines of business should be organised into strategic business units (SBUs).
- Early achievement of a strategy-structure fit can be a competitive advantage.

While trying to relate the structure to strategy; managers have a wide choice based on how authority relationships are prescribed, how departments are created etc. The design choices basically revolve around the following types: the functional structure, the divisional structure, and matrix forms, the emerging structures like teams, virtual teams and boundary less organizations, etc.

1. Functional Structure

In the functional structure, activities are grouped together by common function. Each functional unit has a dissimilar set of duties and responsibilities. In a university; functional structure would mean a set of departments like marketing, management, business economics, finance, similar and related occupational specialties are grouped together. Functional structure tries to incorporate the positive aspects of specialization.

Features of Functional Structure

Functional structures are characterised by the following:

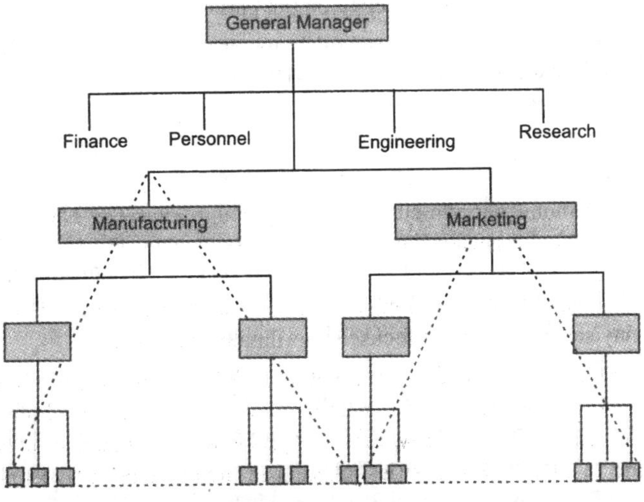

Figure 10.11

Advantages of Functional Structure

1. ***Carity:*** Functional design has the great advantage of clarity. Everybody has a 'home'. Everybody understands his own task. As a result, functional structures bring order and clarity to organisational activities.
2. ***Economies of scale within function:*** It provides economy of scale within functions. It reduces duplication and waste. For example, the total floor space shared by several products in functional organisation leading to economy of ɔperations.
3. ***Specialisation:*** Each departmental manager is concerned with only one kind of work and can concentrate all his energies upon it with minimum diversion. Specialisation being built into the organisation brings about competitive advantage for the firm. By putting its limited resources into one specialised activity, 'Even the small company can compete with the giant corporation on quantity, delivery and price'.
4. ***Coordination:*** Coordination within functions is easy. Centralised decision-making ensures unity of performance.
5. ***In-depth skill development:*** The functional structure also promotes skill development of employees. Employees are exposed to a range of functional activities within their departments allowing them to embody their outstanding skills in every activity of the company.
6. ***Suitability:*** The functional type of organisation is best for small to medium sized organisation producing one or a few products where the dominant competitive issue and goals of the organisation emphasise functional specialisation, efficiency and quality. In fact, Fayol's model for functional structure was a coal-mining company where there was only one product, demanding simple, mechanical operations. The operations were more or less standardised.

Limitations of Functional Structures

The weaknesses of the functional structure, unfortunately, are legendary as the following li. indicates.

1. ***Effort focus:*** Every functional manager considers his function the most important one and develops a narrow dimension of the organisation. He becomes so enamoured with his own specialty that he forgets the organisation's overall goals. In his anxiety to achieve departmental goals he may try to subordinate the welfare of the other functions. 'The lust for aggrandisement on the part of each function is the price paid for the laudable desire of each manager to do a good job.' Again, functional specialisation may lead to extremely narrow, dull and boring jobs in the organisation with routine technologies. Functional structure also contributes to a short term perspective on the part of specialists.
2. ***Poor decision-making:*** No one except the man at the top sees the entire picture of business. Consequently, decisions are easily misunderstood and poorly executed. Questions like 'who is right?', who has scored better?' force organisational participants into a tug-of-war.
3. ***Sub-unit conflicts:*** As the functional organisation balloons to a reasonable size, boundaries are erected between departments. The structure turns out to be a 'Berlin Wall Building. Coordination among departments becomes a tough exercise. No one functional group is totally responsible for performance. As a result, tendencies like buckpassing, sidetracking of issues, etc., develop. Overlapping authority and divided responsibility adds to the confusion and chaos prevailing. Accountability suffers. If functional structure is employed, important projects may suffer for lack of focused coordinated attention.
4. ***Managerial vacuum:*** Emphasis on functional skill makes a man unfit for top management post requiring a broad perspective on the organisation's activities. Functional structure does not prepare people for tomorrow, for it has no position in which a functional head can learn and prepare to handle complexities inherent in the chief executive's position. In course of time, a chronic shortage of top management generalists may be felt.

The weaknesses of the functional structure are legendary. As the functional organisation grows in size, it rapidly becomes an organisation of misunderstandings, feuds, empires and Berlin Wall Building.' It soon requires elaborate, expensive clumsy management crutches, coordinators, committees, meetings, trouble shooters, special dispatchers which waste everybody's time without, as a rule, solving much! The problem of coordination between functions becomes more difficult. The administrative distance between top management and functional department grows. Divisionalisation or product organisation structure helps in relieving this position.

Divisionalisation: Product and Geographic Forms

Divisionalisation is the process of dividing the large functional pyramids into smaller, flexible administrative units. It is essentially designed to foster independent and self-contained units. It creates a set of essentially autonomous 'little companies' in terms of product or geography. It is particularly adaptable to the large and complex modern organisation.

2. Product Departmentation

Product or commodity departmentation is particularly adaptable to tremendously large, complex and multiproduct organisations. Product departmentation calls for division of organisation work on product basis. The large functional units in the organisation are divided into smaller units, each grouped in terms of product manufactured and sold. Product departmentation increases emphasis on product development, it helps in orderly and even development of products. Those products which need to be carefully nursed and skillfully developed will receive prompt and improved attention. Other products whose life is over may be discontinued. In response to changing conditions, products can be developed, added or dropped.

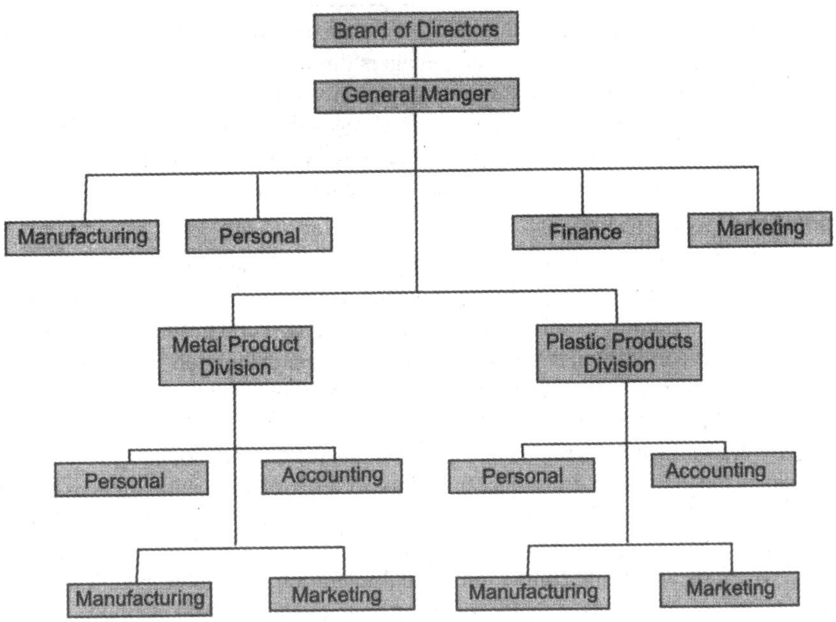

Figure 10.12

Features of Product Structure

Product departmentation is characterised by the following:

(a) Product departmentation focuses on results and performance than on means. The product structure is organised, basically, according to organisational outputs.

(b) Product structures involve dismemberment of the monolithic functional organisation into autonomous units. Within each of these units lies another organisational form and it's almost always of the functional type.

(c) The divisional head is responsible for performance and holds complete strategic and operating decision-making authority.

(d) The organisation is split into product divisions, each of which is responsible for its own profit or loss.

(e) In addition to providing for a central headquarters, divisionalisation helps in promoting decentralisation in a fruitful way. It facilitates a wide span of control at the top leading to a flat organisation structure. It frees the top management for the top management tasks.

(f) It is usually adopted by a multiproduct enterprise whose basic aim is to expand and diversify its products having distinct manufacturing and marketing features.

Advantages

The resources of one complete administrative unit are deployed on the product. All the activities for a single project or purpose are brought under one manager. It is easy to fix accountability. Procedures and systems can be standardised, leading to better integration across different specialities. The different units like marketing, sales, engineering, finance and personnel are dedicated to the interests of one or a few related products. All this increases emphasis on product development, market exploitation, etc. Further, autonomous units enable a manager to acquire a broad range of experience, the individual responsibility and independence forces him to face challenges and run an entire company with its frustrations and satisfactions. Thus, divisionalised form serves as an excellent vehicle for training and development of general managers. Managers know what they are doing and can direct themselves toward the performance of the whole, instead of becoming prisoners of their own work, effort and skill. Divisionalised form, further, allows for a wide span of control. It focuses the vision and efforts of managers directly on business performance and results. The divisions have the responsiveness, the accountability and the benefits of specialisation and are able to process information as if they were organisations unto themselves. Unprofitable lines are not allowed to be carried on the backs of the profitable ones. Whenever necessary the autonomous units can be lopped off with minimal effect on the entire organisation.

Limitations

Divisionalisation tends to create additional departments and divisions leading to duplication of effort. The overhead costs of the product division multiply. There is little incentive to promote cooperation among divisions. Conflicts are created as divisions and headquarters argue about where to locate support services. Often, it is difficult to draw a clear distinction between different units and settle the priorities. A tremendous amount of managerial time and energy is wasted on adjudicating disputes between them with reference to scarce inputs, etc. The smallest adjustment between departments becomes a trial of strength or a matter of prestige and honour. The rivalry and territorial protectionism by the individual divisions can make coordination by headquarters extremely difficult. Further, the autonomy of divisional manager is exercised within limits and this breeds resentment as divisional heads feel that authority is inadequate to meet the challenges. Divisionalisation makes high human demands on self discipline, on mutual toleration, on subordinating one's self interest. High-quality managers possessing these exceptional qualities are rarely available.

3. Geographic Divisionalisation

Geographic divisionalisation sets up separate regional units, each self-sufficient in manufacturing, marketing, etc., to cater to the needs of local markets. As organisations grow, they divide their activities among branches, regional offices or other facilities from the main centre of their operations. To develop an appropriate sales campaign, to exploit the latent advantages available in a region or a good customer service programme, organisations draw a territorial fence around their operations. Sometimes, the nature of the product also demands geographical fencing, for example, dairy products, candies, drinks, etc. In such cases, territorial allotment leads to intensive exploitation of markets. These days geographic departmentation is also adopted to avoid the congestion of large urban centres, as well as the problems of recruiting and utilising labour.

4. Strategic Business Units (SBUs)

The SBU structure is an extension of the divisional structure. In its most extreme form, the SBU operates as a separate autonomous organisation and may periodically send profits to the corporate parent. Each unit will have a clearly defined strategy, based on its capabilities and overall organisational needs. The SBU's autonomy will decrease if profits are lower than the parent expects. The parent may impose controls at various levels to ward off risks arising out of independent operations at a different location.

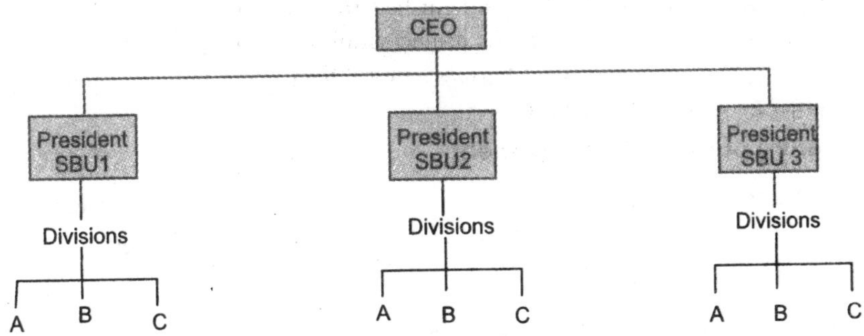

Figure 10.13

Advantages

- Improves coordination between divisions with similar strategic concerns and product market environments.
- Tightens the strategic management and control of large, diverse business enterprises.
- Facilitates distinct and in-depth business planning at the corporate and business levels.
- Channels accountability to distinct business units.

Disadvantages

- Places another layer of management between the divisions and the corporate management.
- Unhealthy completion for corporate resources.
- The role of the group vice president can be difficult to define.
- Defining the degree of autonomy for the group vice presidents and division managers can be difficult.

5. Project Organisation

The project structure is an effective way of focusing all of the necessary talent and organization resources for a given period on a specific project goal. The best talent is pooled to achieve a specific and complex undertaking within time, cost and or quality parameters. It permits large doses of information and activity to be managed without overloading the hierarchical structure. The organisation can continue to focus on its routine activities without interruption. It allows the main organisation to proceed normally while providing concentrated attention to a new project.

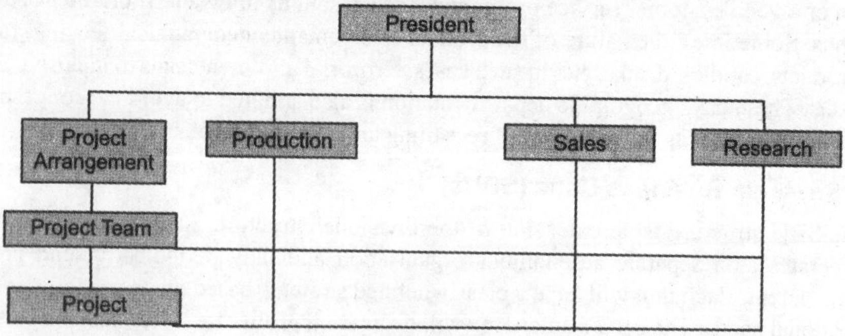

Figure 10.14

The project structure is quite similar to product organisation. Project structures usually have limited life whereas product structures are created to deal with profitable products having a long life. The project structure can also be distinguished from the matrix organisation (the Terms are interchangeably employed these days). The project employees' in the matrix structure are only lent to the project managers for a specific purpose, rather than being purely responsible only to the project manager for some period of time.'

The Nature of Project Management

Project Manager: Project management calls for the appointment of a project manager who is responsible for the completion of the project. The project manager makes sure that the project does not get lost in the shuffle of organisational activities. He specifies what is to be done, when is to be completed, and how much of the resources are required. In turn, the functional managers decide who in their units will perform the task and how it will be done. The project manager is a unifying agent and a focal point for the project activities.

Team Members: The project involves members from various functional departments or from outside. Team members report directly to the project manager. Membership is temporary. The size of the group may change with the different phases of the work. As soon as the project is completed, team members go to another project.

Project Authority: A project possesses a vertical as well as a horizontal dimension. It cuts across the normal organisation structure. A project manager is expected to work with various functional managers by seeking their support through persuasive bargaining. He must convince them that they should help the project by lending its manager the support needed to finish the undertaking within the time. In reality; the project managers face an 'Authority gap'. They do not have authority to promote or reward their personnel. They lack complete authority over the team and possess what is known as 'Project Authority'. Further, in a project structure, the role perceptions are unclear and lack specificity. The relationship of project manager with functional heads is quite ambiguous. His authority is more fluid than in a stable organisation composed of line and staff relationships only. The project manager is expected to accomplish goals by working not only with the functional groups of the company but also with outside organizations. 'The total project organisation has no discrete boundaries; it is a complex structure that facilitates the coordination and integration of many project activities.

Advantages

1. Project management allows maximum use of specialised knowledge which is available to all projects on an equal basis. Knowledge and experience can be transferred from one project to another.
2. Project people have a functional home when they are no longer required on a given project. In between they are provided with stimulating opportunities to participate in the decision process.

3. The project structure reduces environmental complexity. It facilitates rapid collection and processing of new information.
4. Project structures are one way of promoting and maintaining organisational flexibility. Through projects, specialisation required to achieve a goal is brought together for as long as necessary, but no longer.

Problems

1. Project structure creates feelings of insecurity and uncertainty among members. Their relationship with functional members is unclear. Dual loyalty creates anxiety and tension.
2. The project structure is an ad hoc arrangement, having a limited life. Once the project is completed, the project team is disbanded. In other words, the project manager and project staff work themselves out of a job. Some people feel lost without a permanent department with which they can identify. Security for such people is threatened when it appears that the organisation's only commitment to them is a temporary project. They fear that completion of the project will mean the end of their job. This can encourage project slowdowns.
3. The project management violates the principle of unity of command. Role prescriptions are unclear. The relationship between functional managers and the project manager is not defined properly leading to ambiguity and conflict.
4. The project structure creates insecurity and fear of unemployment as the project completion. Members may even create work to avoid dangers of being laid off
5. Contacts with the mainstream of organisational life are severed. Members may be bypassed when opportunities arise in their fields leading to career advancement
6. Project manager has to perform a tightrope walk: he must build the team straightaway obtain cooperation from other departments, battle to meet the schedule, grapple with cost figures and decide things quickly. Decisions to sacrifice time for cost, cost for quality or quality for time are common in most projects and the project manager must be able to make them without panicking.
7. The project organisation creates an authority gap for project managers where responsibility outweighs authority. Most projects are not self-sufficient. They need support from various quarters. Top management can easily jeopardise the projects' success by lack of awareness. Functional cooperation may be difficult to obtain. All such factors seriously hamper the project performance.

6. Matrix Organisation Structure

In the matrix structure, project managers are assigned to a variety of projects—rather than a single one—whose activities cut across traditional departments. Matrix structure is simply an extension of the project management concept. The matrix breaks the unity of command concept. The classical principle 'one man one boss' is violated. The normal vertical hierarchy is 'overplayed' by a form of lateral influence. The matrix legitimates lateral chains of influence.

At any given time, a number of project managers direct the activities of a number of projects, while the functional heads allocate their resources to meet the requirements of these various projects. Project managers have authority over project employees relative to the projects' goals. Decisions such as promotion, salary increases, employee performance appraisal typically remain a part of the functional manager's responsibility. In the matrix structure, the authority of the project manager is generally greater than that given under the more traditional project management concept. There is usually a more equal division of authority between project managers and functional line managers. Figure 13.6 shows key matrix participants: top leadership, matrix bosses and the two-boss managers.

Key Matrix Roles

Top leadership: The top leader holds the balance of power. He must be willing to delegate decisions. He must emphasise direct contact and group problem solving at lower levels so as to promote effective communication throughout the organisation. He must also see that the power balance is maintained properly.

Matrix bosses: Matrix bosses have authority over project employees relative to projects' goals. They share subordinates in common with other bosses. They do not have full control over subordinates. The functional head's responsibilities pertain to functional rules and standards. The project manager acts as an integrator. He is required to achieve the specific project by balancing time, cost and performance. Matrix bosses must also be willing to face one another on disagreements. Managing highly competent professional employees demands a great deal of time, patience, and skill from project heads.

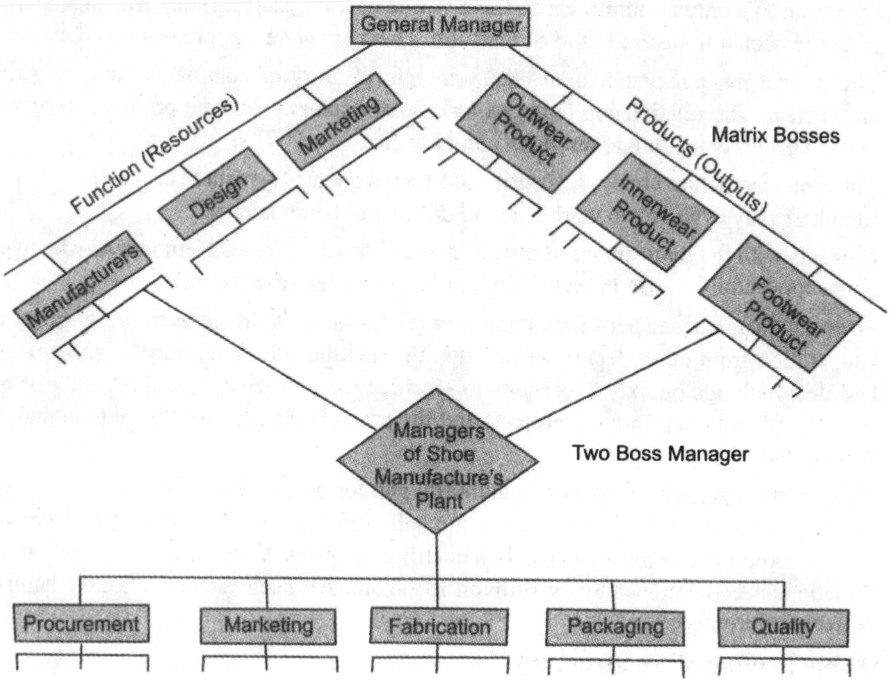

Figure 10.15

10.20. BEHAVIOURAL ISSUES

Successful strategy formulation does not at all guarantee successful strategy implementation. It is always more difficult to actually carry out something than to say you are going to do it. Strategy implementation requires support, discipline, motivation and hard work from all managers and employees. Managers should pay careful attention to a number of key issues while executing the strategies. Chief among them are how the organisation should be structured to put its strategy into effect and how such variables as leadership, power and organisational culture should be managed to enable employees to work together while inplementing the firm's strategic plans. Organisations in stable, predictable environments often become relatively tall, with many hierarchical levels and narrow spans of control. On the other hand, companies in dynamic, rapidly changing environments usually adopt flat structures with few hierarchical levels and wide spans of control:

An organisation is said to have a 'functional structure' when it forms departments along functional lines such as finance, manufacturing, marketing, personnel, R&D etc. This helps employees to carry out assigned tasks within certain set boundaries. But as the organisation begins to grow, 'a product divisional structure' offers several advantages such as focus on each product, easy coordination, development of general managers, fixing responsibility for profits or losses etc. In case of multi-product and multi-plant firms, 'a geographic divisional structure' helps in responding to the unique requirements of customers in different locations in a better way. As the firm adds more product lines, a multi-divisional structure is generally preferred, offering operational freedom and autonomy to divisional heads. Further, growth may lead an organisation to adopt the 'strategic business unit structure' especially in the case of very large, diversified firms where divisions with similar missions, products, markets or technologies are combined under a strategic business unit.

Generally speaking, organisations perform more effectively when they implement strategy with the most appropriate structure. While evaluating whether an organisation is properly structured and stuffed to meet the requirements of the strategy, the following questions need a careful analysis.

10.21. STRATEGIC LEADERSHIP

Introduction

Leadership is the art and process of influencing people so that they will strive willingly and enthusiastically towards achievement of the organization purpose. Specific styles of leadership are often associated with specific approaches to the crafting and execution of strategies. The organization purpose and strategy do not just drop out of a process of discussion, but are actively directed by an individual with strategic vision, whom we call leader.

It may be noted that announcing a new strategy does not automatically inspire those responsible for implementing the change. The top management has to encourage managers and employees to implement the strategy, through proper leadership. The CEO is recognized as the organisation principal leader, one who sets the tone for its activities. Leadership is thus a vital ingredient in the implementation of strategy.

10.21.1 Importance of Strategic Leadership

Strategic leadership establishes the firm direction by developing and communicating a vision of the future and inspiring organization members to move in that direction. Unlike managerial leadership which is generally concerned with the short-term day-to-day activities, strategic leadership is concerned with determining the firm strategy, direction, aligning the firm strategy with its culture, modeling and communicating high ethical standards, and initiating changes in the firm strategy when necessary. The most successful leadership is not just to define the vision and mission of an organization in a cold, abstract manner but to communicate trust, enthusiasm and commitment to strategy. Bill Gates of Microsoft, Akio Morita of Sony, Jack Welch of General Electric, Gianni Agnelli of Fiat, Narayana Murthy of Infosys, are all examples of strategic leaders who have guided and shaped the direction of their companies. It is rightly said:

"Visionary leadership inspires the impossible:fiction becomes truth".

Strategic leadership thus enhances prospects for the organisation long-term success, while at the same time maintaining its short-term financial stability. Strategic leadership is vital in ensuring that strategies are formulated and implemented in an effective manner.

Strategic leadership involves action on two fronts. The first is in guiding the organization to deal with constant change, the second is in providing the management skill to cope with the change.

Change has become an integral part of what leaders and managers deal with daily. The leadership challenge is to galvanize commitment among people within an organization, as well as stakeholders outside the organization, to embrace change and implement strategies.

10.21.2 Analysing Leadership

In order to understand the link between strategic implementation and leadership, it is useful to analyse the leadership role. There are three main approaches:

1. **Trait Theories** argue that individuals with certain characteristics (traits) can be identified who will provide leadership in virtually any situation.
2. **Behavioral theories** suggest that individuals with certain behaviorscan be identified who will provide leadership appropriate to the organization.
3. **Contingency theories** suggest that leaders emerge according to the needs of the organization at a particular point in time. The choice is contingent on the strategic issues facing the organization at that time and leaders need to be changed as the situation itself changes. From a strategic perspective, the contingency theory approach holds good.
4. **Best-fit approach:** Within the context of contingency theory, the best-fit approach can be useful in strategy because it allows each situation to be treated differently. Leadership style can vary from shared vision to dominance. The style needs to be modified to set the strategic situation. With regard to implementation of strategies, leaders need to generate trust in the strategic process.

   They need to draw upon the intellectual capital of the organization and to demonstrate passion and determination. In some circumstances, leadership may be better served by allowing the solutions to emerge from the group working on a strategic task, rather than be imposed by the leader from the centre. There is no agreement on how to analyse leadership. Contingency theories are probably the most useful approach. They state that the choice and style of leadership are contingent on the strategic issues facing the organization at that time.

10.21.3 Role of a Strategic Leader

Leaders play a central role in performing six critical and interdependent activities in implementation of strategies

1. Clarifying strategic intent
2. Setting the direction
3. Building an organization
4. Shaping organization culture
5. Creating a learning organization
6. Instilling ethical behaviour

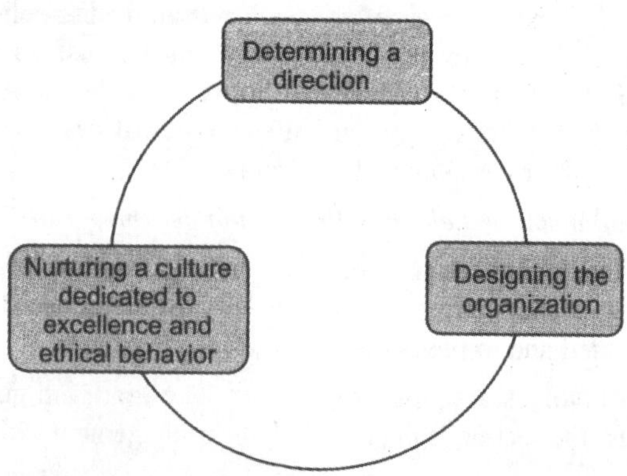

Figure 10.16. Three interdependent activities of leadership.

1. **Clarifying strategic intent:** Leaders motivate employees to embrace change by setting forth a clear vision of where the business strategy needs to take the organization.
2. **Setting the direction:** Leaders set the direction and scope of the organization through formulating appropriate corporate and business strategies.
3. **Building the organization:** Since leaders are attempting to embrace change, they are often required to rebuild their organization to align it with the ever changing environment and needs of the strategy. And such an effort often involves overcoming resistance to change and addressing problems like the following:
    - Ensuring a common understanding about organizational priorities
    - Clarifying responsibilities among managers and organizational units
    - Empowering managers and pushing authority lower in the organization
    - Uncovering and remedying problems in coordination and communication across the organization
    - Gaining personal commitment from managers to a shared vision
    - Keeping closelyconnected with going on in the organization
4. **Shaping organizational culture:** Leaders play a key role in developing and sustaining a strategy supportive culture. Leaders know well that the values and beliefs shared throughout their organization will shape how the work of the organization is done. And when attempting to embrace accelerated change, reshaping their organization culture is an activity that occupies considerable time for most leaders.
5. **Creating a learning organization:** Leaders must also play a central role in creating a learning organization. Learning organization is one that quickly adapts to change. The five elements central to a learning organization are
    - Inspiring and motivating people with a mission or purpose
    - Empowering people at all levels throughout the organization
    - Accumulating and sharing internal knowledge
    - Gathering external information
    - Challenging the status quo to stimulate creativity
6. **Instilling ethical behaviour:** Ethics may be defined as a system of right and wrong. Business ethics is the application of general ethical standards to commercial enterprises. A leader plays a central role in instilling ethical behaviour in the organization.

    The ethical orientation of a leader is generally considered to be a key factor in promoting ethical behaviour among employees. Leaders who exhibit high ethical standards become role models for others in the organization and raise its overall level of ethical behaviour. In essence, ethical behaviour must start with the leader before the employees can be expected to perform accordingly.

10.21.4 Leader Tasks

Successful leaders have to do many things in leading the drive for good strategy execution and operating excellence. (Thompson and Strickland)

1. ***Leaders stay on top of things.*** They keep a finger on the organization pulse by spending considerable time outside their offices, listening and talking to organization members, coaching, cheer-leading and picking up important information. This technique is often labelled by walking around (MBWA).
2. ***They are active and visible*** in putting constructive pressure on the organization to achieve good results. Generally, this is best accomplished by promoting team spirit that mobilizes and energizes organizational members to execute strategy in a competent fashion and deliver the targeted results.

3. ***They keep the organization focused on operating excellence*** by championing innovative ideas for improvement and promoting the use of best practices and benchmarking to measure value chain activities in first rate fashion.
4. ***They not on/y strengthen existing competencies and capabilities, but also build new ones*** that offer a competitive edge over rivals. Core competencies and competitive capabilities typically reside in the combined efforts of different work groups, departments and strategic allies. Leaders enforce the necessary networking and cooperation among individuals, groups, departments and integrate them to forge competitively advantageous competencies and capabilities.
5. ***Leaders serve as a role mode*** lin displaying high ethical standards, and insist that company personnel conduct the business ethically and in a socially responsible manner.
6. ***It is the leader responsibility*** to step forward and push corrective action when a company strategy execution effort is not delivering good results and the organization is not making measurable progress toward operating excellence.

10.21.5 Leadership Approaches

Research has found that some leadership approaches are more effective than others for bringing about change in organization. Three types of leadership that can have a substantial impact are transactional, transformational and charismatic leadership. These types of leadership are briefly explained below:

1. **Transactional Leadership:** Transactional leaders clarify the role and task requirements of subordinates, initiate structure, provide appropriate rewards, and try to be considerate to and meet the social needs of subordinates. The transactional leader ability to satisfy subordinates may improve productivity. Transactional leaders excel at management functions. They are hardworking, tolerant and fair minded. They take pride in keeping things running smoothly and efficiently. Transactional leaders often stress the impersonal aspects of performance, such as plans, schedules and budgets. They have a sense of commitment to the organization and conform to organizational norms and values. In short, transactional leaders use the authority of their office to exchange rewards such as pay and status for employees and generally seek to enhance an organization performance steadily, but not dramatically. In other words, transactional leadership is important to all organizations, but leading change requires a different approach, viz, transformational leadership.
2. **Transformational Leadership:** Transformational leaders have a special ability to bring about innovation and change. They encourage the followers to question the status quo. They have the ability to lead change in the organization mission, strategy, structure and culture as well as promote innovation in products and technologies. Transformational leaders do not rely solely on tangible rules and incentives to control specific transactions with followers. They focus on intangible qualities such as vision, shared values, and ideas to build relationships and find common ground to enlist in the change process.
3. **Charismatic and Visionary Leadership:** Charismatic leadership goes beyond transactional and transformational leadership. Charisma is a that ignites followers energy and commitment, producing results above and beyond the call of duty The charismatic leader has the ability to inspire and motivate people to do more than what they would normally do, despite obstacles and personal sacrifice. Followers transcend their own self-interests for the sake of the leader. Charismatic leaders are often skilled in the art of visionary leadership. A vision is an attractive, ideal future that is credible yet not readily attainable. Visionary leaders see beyond current realities and help followers believe in a brighter future. They speak to the hearts of their followers, letting them be part of something bigger than themselves. Thus, visionary leaders have a strong vision for the future and can motivate others to help realize it. They

have an emotional impact on subordinates because they strongly believe in the vision and can communicate itto others in a way that makes the vision real, personal and meaningful to others. When charismatic and visionary leaders respond to organizational problems, they can have a powerful, positive influence on organizational performance.

10.21.6 Leadership Style

Every leader has a distinctive leadership style. Leadership style means a consistent pattern of behaviour that a leader exhibits in the process of governing and making decisions. Some leaders are flamboyant, whereas others are reserved and contemplative. Some seek broad- based participation when making decisions, whereas others arrive at decisions primarily on their own with little input from others. Specific styles of leadership are often associated with specific approaches to strategy.

The path-goal theory suggests a fourfold classification of leader styles they are:

1. **Supportive leadership** involves leader behaviour that shows concern for subordinates well-being and personal needs. Leadership style is open, friendly, and approachable, and the leader creates a team climate and treats subordinates as equals.
2. **Directive leadership** occurs when the leader tells subordinates exactly what they are supposed to do. Leader behaviour includes planning, making schedules, setting performance goals and behaviour in an authoritative style.
3. **Participative leadership** means that the leader consults with his or her subordinates about decisions. Leader behaviour includes asking for opinions and suggestions, encouraging participation in decision-making and meeting with subordinates in their workplace. The participative leader encourages group discussion and written suggestions.
4. **Achievement-oriented leadership** occurs when the leader sets clear and challenging goals for subordinates. Leader behaviour stresses high-quality performance and improvement over current performance. Achievement leaders also show confidence in subordinates and assist them in learning how to achieve high goals.

   The four types of leader behaviour mentioned above are not considered ingrained personality traits. They reflect types of behaviour that every leader is able to adopt, depending on the situation.

   In fact, the style of the leader will have an impact on strategy implementation because there is a need to have a degree of between the strategy and the style. There is little agreement on what might constitute a best leadership style Hart4 however, has suggested a range of styles from which the choice can be made. They vary from imperial style to organic s and are summarized below:

Table 10.4

Descriptors	Command	Symbolic	Rational	Tansactive	Generative
Style	**Imperial Strategy** driven by leader or small top team	**Cultural Strategy** driven by mission and a vision of the future d	**Analytical Strategy** driven by formal structure and planning systems	**Procedural Strategy** driven by internal process and mutual adjustment	**Organic Strategy** driven by the initiatives of those empowered in the organization
Role of top management	**Commander** Provide direction	Coach Motivate and inspire	Boss Evaluate and control	Facilitator Empower and enable	Sponsor Endorse and sponsor
Role of organizational members	**Soldier** Obey orders	**Player** Respond to challenge	**Subordinate.** Follow the system	Participant Learn and improve	Entrepreneur Experiment and take risks

The work of a leader is crucial in the development and implementation of strategy. The imperial leader will continue to decide strategy and then define the organization to achieve this. But this type of leadership is no longer suitable for strategy. The leader should have organic style, which has the following characteristics:

1. **Creative tension:** The tension that exists as a new leader moves to close the gap between his/her vision of the future and the current position of the organization.
2. **New leadership role:** The former role of the imperial decision-maker may be too simplistic for the new millennium. The new organic role will involve:
   - Building the core values and purpose of the organization.
   - Allowing strategy to emerge.
   - Putting in place processes that allow an organization to develop and renew itself.
   - Motivating, inspiring and coaching others in the organization.
   - Adopting the role of custodian or steward of the organization people and its purpose.
   - New Skills: None of the above will be achieved unless new skills are developed and employed, both by the leader and others in the organization. The four main skill areas are:
   - Building a shared vision.
   - Challenging deeply held assumptions.
   - Identifying the key interrelationships and the factors critical to the success of the organization.
   - Distinguishing the complex but unimportant details from the dynamic and important events that really shape strategy in the organization.

Although every organization is the result of its history, products and people, it periodically has the chance to renew itself. In other words, it is able to change its style of management. To some extent, an organization will evolve in response to its continually changing environment. Furthermore, the leadership and top management at any point in time will clearly influence the organization style. Nevertheless, organizations can also make the deliberate choice to change their style as part of a major shift in strategy. The issues are therefore:

- Should the organization change its style?
- If so, in what way should the company change this?

It should be noted that this is not just an issue of implementation after the strategy has been chosen, but a fundamental choice available as part of the process. Most of the writers and researchers argue that a shift in style is essential if a fundamental change in strategy is proposed. They would support this view for three reasons:

Fundamental strategic change needs to impact on people in the organization as well as on decision making. People issues are essentially summarized in culture and style.

Leadership is usually important for major changes in strategy.

Such a shift in style is a powerful symbol of the related change in strategy.

Conclusion

Every organization has the choice of changing its style when it changes its strategy. In many cases, a change of style is essential when a fundamental change of strategy is proposed. The content of the style depends on the strategies proposed. There needs to be a degree of strategic fit between the two areas. Importantly, culture and style take time to change and may move more slowly than the proposed strategy.

Leadership Style and Culture Change

To bring about change and to implement strategies successfully, organisations are now pinning hopes on the unique capabilities of transformational leaders. Le lacocca is often used as an example of a successful transformational leader because of his successful efforts in transforming Chrysler Corporation from a floundering company into a much more successful company that could avoid bankruptcy. The word, 'transformational leadership' is used to signify leadership that goes beyond ordinary expectations by transmitting a sense of mission, stimulating learning experiences and inspiring new ways of thinking. In 1914 Henry Ford, for example, offered unusually high wages for workers @$5 a day in exchange for their accepting tight controls to be imposed on them (strict discipline, no idle time etc.).

10.21.7 Who are Transformational Leaders?

Transformational leaders are distinguished (from charismatic leaders) by their unique ability to bring about innovation and change. They create significant change in both followers and the organisation. They have the special capabilities required to lead changes in the organisation's mission, strategy, structure and culture, as well as to promote innovation in products and technologies. They generally do not put emphasis on tangible rules and incentives alone while motivating followers. They focus on intangible qualities such as vision, shared values and ideas to build relationships, give larger meaning to diverse activities and find common ground to enlist followers in the change process. (R L Daft and R H Lengel, Fusion leadership, Barrett-Koehler San Francisco, 1998.)

Henry Ford wanted a simple, inexpensive car, Model T, to be within the reach of ordinary citizens. Standardised production, focus on a single model, massive scale, reduced prices enabled Ford to realise his dream sooner than expected. By 1913, the selling price dropped to $ 500; it fell to $ 390 by 1915 and sold for only $260 by 1925. The time to produce the car had declined from 12 ½ worker-hours in 1912 to 1½ worker-hours in 1914 (B M Bass). To bring about change within an organisation, leaders must benchmark their performance against their competitors (not just against last year's quarter's performance) and try to switch gears when the organisation is successful (certainly not when it is in trouble as stated by Drucker) by focussing attention on measures such as new product innovations, customer satisfaction, product quality as compared with competitors. Once the need for change is recognised, the leader must inspire organisational members with a 'vision' of what the organisation can become — by inviting followers to extend a helping hand, stretching their abilities fully (A E Pearson). He must lead from the front, setting a glorious example of dedication, sacrifice and single-minded devotion to the vision mapped out by him. It is also important that this vision be repeated over and over and not be allowed to fade away (Bennis & Nanus). He must also try to ensure that the changes occur as desired and suitable feedback mechanisms be incorporated to see that the desired changes in organisational culture actually take place.

The culture of an organisation is the set of values, beliefs, behaviours that helps its members understand what the organisation stands for, how it does things and what it considers important. Culture is a kind of social glue that binds people together through shared symbols, language, stories, and practices.

Elements of Strong Corporate Cultures

- ***A widely shared philosophy.*** This philosophy is not an abstract notion of the future but a real understanding of what the firm stands for, often embodied in slogans.
- ***A concern for individuals.*** This concern often places individual concerns overrules, policies, procedures and adherence to job duties.
- ***Recognition of heroes.*** Heroes are individuals whose actions illustrate- the shared philosophy and concerns of the company
- ***A belief in ritual and ceremony.*** Management understands that rituals and ceremonies are real and important to members and to building a common identity.

- ***A well-understood sense of the in formal rules and expectations.*** Employees understand what is expected of them.
- ***A belief that what employees do is important to others.*** Networking, to share information and ideas, is encouraged. –

To be successful, the firm's culture must be appropriate to and supportive of that firm. The culture must invariably have certain values that can help the firm adapt to environmental change. Changes in strategy should be accompanied by corresponding alterations in the firm's culture. For example, mere formation of new goals and plans do not transform conservative organisations instantaneously unless there are significant changes in the thinking of members and organisational practices. Leaders play a great role in maintaining or changing the culture and setting a new road map for the firm. Leaders, generally, use several mechanisms to help develop and reinforce a desired corporate culture.

10.22. GUIDELINES TO CREATE CULTURED ORGANISATION STRATEGY

Research evidence indicates that new strategies are often market driven and dictated by competitive forces. Therefore, changing a firm's culture to a new strategy is usually more effective than changing a strategy to fit an existing culture. While linking culture to a new strategy, the following guidelines are quite helpful (Schein):

- Formal statements of organisational philosophy, charters, creeds, materials used for recruitment and selection and socialisation,
- Designing of physical space, facades, buildings.
- Deliberate role modeling, teaching and coaching by leaders.
- Explicit reward and status system, promotion criteria.
- Stories, legends, myths and parables about key people and events.
- What leaders pay attention to, measure and control.
- Leader reactions ro critical incidents and organisarional crises.
- How the organisation is designed and structured.
- Organisational systems and procedures.
- Criteria used for recruitment selection, promotion, leveling off, retirement, and "ex-communication" of people.

1. Values and Culture

A value is something that has worth and importance to an individual. As such values help shape human behaviour. Parents, friends, teachers and external reference groups can all influence individual values. Indeed, a person's values develop as a product of learning and experience in the cultural setting in which he or she lives. As learning and experiences vary from one person to the next, value differences are the inevitable result. As a system of shared values, the corporate 'Culture reflects a climate within which people value the same things and apply these to benefit the corporation as a whole. One example is the dominant value of customer service at TELCO. This value helps keep everyone — from top management down to persons on the factory floor — pulling in the same direction. Other examples are found in corporate slogans or creeds such as General Electric: "Progress is our most important product'; Delta Airlines, "The Family Feeling"; Sears, "Quality at a good price"; Bata India Ltd. "Customer is the king". The strength of such slogans in communicating value lies in the basic premise that values can influence behaviour. To the extent that employees understand and share values such as those reflected in the slogans, their behaviour should be more uniform and consistent. Performance of individuals, groups and the organisation as a whole should benefit as a result. Research shows that managers who sense a compatibility and experience feelings of success in their lives show high regard for organisational objectives and significant stakeholders and have a healthy assessment of the values and ethics of their colleagues, subordinates and bosses.

The concept of "corporate culture" and its companion notion of shared values is important in the field of strategic management. Researchers recognize that organizations develop different cultures, that these cultures have different performance implications and that they can be changed. Strong cultures that fit the needs and challenges of the situation are "in", whereas weak or poorly matched cultures are "out". The case of AT&T, the telecommunications giant, is a good example. For many years the company operated as a regulated monopoly and created what many observers felt was the best phone system in the world. All this was achieved in a highly structured corporate culture where "universal service at reasonable cost" was the predominant value. Things are different for AT&T today. The culture is changing, albeit slowly, as the company tries to instill in itself the new sense of innovation and competition that is necessary to prosper in a deregulated environment (like what is happening in public sector banks, insurance firms and oil companies after deregulation).

2. Values and Behaviour Formation

People are not born with values; rather they acquire and develop them early in life. Parents, teachers, relatives, friends and others influence an individuals' values. Values such as — stealing is bad, 'honestly is the best policy' respect your elders and teachers', 'be kind to people' are taught and reinforced in schools, religious institutions and social groups. Over the years these values become relatively stable and enduring. As we grow in years, we often seek environments that are compatible with the values we learned as children. For example, values help find out what companies we are attracted to and how long we stay therein. They also influence how motivated we are at work; people who share same values as the organisation are more committed to the organisation than those who do not.

Impact

Whenever people make decisions or talk about what constitutes appropriate behaviour at work, we can easily see the impact of values or even conflicts between different values. For example, consider the question of laying off employees. Managers with dominant economic values would be less hesitant to lay them off quickly than would managers with high social values.

3. Criterion for Behaviour

Once a particular value is internalised, it becomes a standard for guiding action, for devloping and maintaining attitudes towards relevant objects and situations, for justifying ones own and other actions and attitudes, for morally defining self and others and for comparing self with others.

4. Cloud Objectivity and Rationality

When individuals enter an organisation with certain pre-set values of what is right or wrong, they tend to look at the world through coloured glasses. For example if you think that the organisation should promote people on the basis of merit and not on seniority and the organization does the opposite thing, you feel greatly disappointed and totally out of place. Your attitude and behaviour toward the organisation, perhaps, would be very optimistic if your values match with the organization's promotion policies. Values, thus, overpower objectivity and rationality. Achieving the desired 'fit' between the person and the job is not always easy. It requires special attention and consistent effort on the part of mangers. While formulating and implementing strategies, managers must pay attention to individual differences in employees. To develop strong and desired values among employees, the following things need to be looked into carefully.

- ***Clarify and communicate:*** Managers must state, and clarify, values respected by their organisation. This can be achieved through formal orientation programmes. Every attempt should be made to expose new employees to the correct values and expectations and to teach them the way things are done in the organisation.

- ***Train and develop:*** To improve skills of employees, managers must focus on training and development programmes continually. Values can and should be emphasised along with other important individual attitudes.
- ***Reward and reinforce:*** Rewards can reinforce individual values and maintain enthusiasm in support of key organisational values. Creative managers can find many ways to reward people for displaying the values that are considered essential to organisational success.

10.23. ORGANIZATIONAL CULTURE–MEANING AND DEFINITION

Meaning

Organizational culture is another element which affects strategy implementation as it provides a framework within, which the behavior of the members takes place. Through there are differing views on what constitute an organizational culture, generally it is defined as a set of assumptions the members of an organization share in common.

Definition: According to O' Reilly, "organizational culture is the set of assumptions, beliefs, values, and norms that are shared by organization's members"

10.23.1 Characteristics of Organizational Culture

a. **Individual initiative:** The degree of responsibility, freedom, and independence that individuals have.

b. **Risk tolerance:** The degree to which employees are encouraged to be aggressive, innovative and risk-seeking.

c. **Direction**: The degree to which the organization creates clear objectives and performance expectations.

d. **Management support:** The degree to which managers provide clear communication, assistance and support to their subordinates

e. **Control:** The number of rules and regulations, and the amount of direct supervision that is used to oversee and control employee behavior.

10.23.2 Functions of Organizational Culture

- The organization is recognized by its culture. Wherever people name an organization, the culture is attached to the organization is immediately remembered. One organizations is distinctively different from other organization by its culture.
- Organizational culture provides the facilities for self-satisfaction. Employees get internal satisfaction with an esteemed culture. People are more satisfied this way than when their individuals interests are fulfilled.
- The culture of organization provides its stability. People prefer to continue with the organization.
- The social recognition of the organizational culture makes the organization grow and develop in all dimensions.
- Organizational culture acts as a motivator that guides and control the employees. Satisfied employee get more spirit and enthusiasm for performing their respective jobs.
- Culture gives rises to a positive attitude and behavior which are again an addition to culture. It refers to the various cycles of a positive behaviour i.e culture leads to good behaviour and good behaviour makes a culture which is instrumental for better behaviuor. This cycle goes on. Both the employees and theb organization enjoy the culture.

10.23.3 Relating Organizational Culture and Strategy

In relating strategy and culture, strategists have four alternatives, each of these alternative has different implications for the total strategic management

1. **Ignore the corporate culture:** Strategies can simply ignore the corporate culture while implementing a strategy especially when it is not possible to change corporate culture. In fact, corporate culture is build over a period of time and therefore can not be changed overnight; cultural change is a slow process and is time-consuming. Ignoring culture in strategic management is not better alternative because it may be dysfunctional.
2. **Adapt the strategy implementation to suit the corporate culture:** Strategies may have flexibility in organizational design, organizational systems and processes for strategy implementation. These variables can be manipulated to serve the interests of organizational culture.
3. **Change the strategy to fit the corporate culture:** The third alternative is to change the strategy itself if it does not fit with corporate culture. However changing strategy mid-way is-not a very desirable proposition. Therefore the corporate culture should be considered as a determinant for strategic choice.
4. **Change corporate culture to suit strategic requirements:** The last alternative in relating strategy is to change corporate culture to suit strategic requirements. This is the optimum choice in the present prevailing Indian business environment, which is becoming more and more competitive day-by-day necessitating change in old methods.

10.24. STRATEGY AND STAFFING DECISIONS

Introduction

Staffing is that part of the process of management which is concerned with obtaining, utilizing, and maintaining a satisfactory and satisfied workforce. It is the process of identifying, assessing, placing, evaluating and developing individuals at work.

Staffing is very important function of management. No organization is successful unless it can fill and keep filled the various positions with the right type of employees.

Definition

According to Mc Farland, "Staffing is the function by which mangers build an organization through recruitment, selection and development of individuals as capable employees".

10.24.1 Need for Staffing

1. **Increasing the size of organizations:** In a large organization there are several positions. Systematic programs for the selection, training ad appraisal of employees are required for efficient functioning of enterprise.
2. **Advancement of technology:**Significant improvements have taken place in technology. In order to make use of the latest technology, the appointment of right type of persons is necessary. Right personnel can be procured, developed and maintained for new jobs only if the management performs its staffing function effectively.
3. **Long range need for manpower:** In order to execute the long-term plans, management must determine the manpower requirements well in advance. It is also necessary to develop mangers for succession in future. The need for staffing has increased due to shortage of good managerial talent, and high rate of labor turnover.
4. **High wage bill:** Personnel cost accounts for a major portion of operating costs today. Efficient performance of the staffing function is essential to make the best use of personnel.

For Eg: If the right type of people are selected and trained, management can obtain optimum results from the expenses incurred on recruitment, selection and training.

5. **Human relation movement:** Managers use the knowledge of behavioral sciences in molding the behavior of employees in right direction. By performing the staffing function well, management can show the significance it attaches to the human resources in the organization.

10.24.2 Steps in Staffing Process

Step 1: Human resource planning: The purpose of human resource planning is to ensure that the personnel need of the organization will be met. Three elements of human resource planning are:

- Forecasting the personnel requirements
- Comparing the requirements to the inventory of potential candidates within the organizations.
- Developing specific plans for how many people to recruit or whom to train.

Step 2: Recruitment: The actual recruitment of potential employees is traditionally done through newspaper and professional journal advertisement.

Step 3: Selection: Following recruitment, those candidates who have applied for the position advertised must be evaluated and one chosen whose qualifications match job requirements. The steps in selection process include completing an application form, interview, and physical examinations.

Step 4: Induction and Orientation: Once selected, the employee must be integrated into the organization. The induction and orientation process includes introduction of new employee to the work-group.

Step 5: Training and development: Through training and development the organization tries to improve the employee's ability to contribute to the organization's effectiveness. Training is concerned with improvement of the employee's skill.

Step 6: Performance Appraisal: A system designed to measure the actual job performance of an employee compared tom designated performance standards.

10.24.3 Firm's Strategic Staffing Decisions

1. **Flexible workforce:** An organization's core workforce consists of people who are perceived by the organization to be regular employees who are central to what the organization does or produces. These workers are considered to be important, longer-term contributors to the company. Therefore, the company tries to retain them for longer periods.
2. **Internal or external talent focus:** An internal talent requires hiring people with the capability to perform well in currently open positions, who having the capability to perform well in the organizational; training and development programs, and who have the potential to assume leadership positions in the organization. An external talent focus on often requires paying a premium to acquire talent with the existing skills and experience to perform well in the organizations currently open positions.
3. **Hiring people with the skills or Training them to develop those skills:** Another strategic staffing decision is whether the organization prefers to hire people who already possess the desired skills and competence or whether it is willing to hire people without those skills and train them instead.
4. **Job Focused:** Another aspect of successful talent strategy involves identifying key jobs on which to focus additional attention and resources because of their importance to the company's performance and execution of its business strategy.